P O W E R Learning

Strategies for Success in College and Life

EIGHTH EDITION

Robert S. Feldman
University of Massachusetts Amherst

Mc Graw Hill Education

P.O.W.E.R. LEARNING: STRATEGIES FOR SUCCESS IN COLLEGE AND LIFE, EIGHTH EDITION

Published by McGraw-Hill Education, 2 Penn Plaza, New York, NY 10121.

This book is printed on acid-free paper.

2 3 4 5 6 7 8 9 LKV 21 20 19

ISBN 978-1-260-07057-6 (student edition)
MHID 1-260-07057-3 (student edition)
ISBN 978-1-260-70971-1 (loose-leaf edition)
MHID 1-260-70971-X (loose-leaf edition)
ISBN 978-1-260-70966-7 (annotated instructor's edition)
MHID 1-260-70966-3 (annotated instructor's edition)

Associate Portfolio Manager: *Kevin White*
Product Developer: *David Ploskonka*
Marketing Manager: *Lisa Granger*
Content Project Managers: *Melissa M. Leick; Bruce Gin; Karen Jozefowicz*
Buyer: *Sandy Ludovissy*
Design: *Jessica Cuevas*
Content Licensing Specialist: *Carrie Burger*
Cover Image: *©Roman Samborskyi/Shutterstock*
Compositor: *SPi Global*

All credits appearing on page or at the end of the book are considered to be an extension of the copyright page.

Library of Congress Cataloging-in-Publication Data

Names: Feldman, Robert S. (Robert Stephen), 1947-
Title: P.O.W.E.R. learning : strategies for success in college and life /
Robert S. Feldman, University of Massachusetts, Amherst.
Other titles: POWER learning
Description: Eighth edition. | New York, NY : McGraw-Hill, [2019]
Identifiers: LCCN 2018044379 | ISBN 9781260070576 (alk. paper)
Subjects: LCSH: College student orientation. | Study skills. | Life skills. | Success.
Classification: LCC LB2343.3 .F44 2019 | DDC 378.1/98–dc23
LC record available at https://lccn.loc.gov/2018044379

mheducation.com/highered

Dedication

To my students, who make teaching a joy.

About the Author

ROBERT S. FELDMAN

Courtesy Bob Feldman

Bob Feldman still remembers those moments of being overwhelmed when he started college at Wesleyan University. "I wondered whether I was up to the challenges that faced me," he recalls, "and—although I never would have admitted it at the time—I really had no idea what it took to be successful at college."

That experience, along with his encounters with many students during his own teaching career, led to a life-long interest in helping students navigate the critical transition that they face at the start of their own college careers. Professor Feldman, who went on to receive a doctorate in psychology from the University of Wisconsin-Madison, is now Senior Advisor to the Chancellor and Professor of Psychological and Brain Sciences at the University of Massachusetts Amherst. He is founding director of *POWER Up for Student Success,* the first-year experience course that has introduced thousands of incoming students to UMass.

Professor Feldman's proudest professional accomplishment is winning the College Outstanding Teaching Award at UMass. He also has been named a Hewlett Teaching Fellow and was Senior Online Instruction Fellow. He has taught courses at Mount Holyoke College, Wesleyan University, and Virginia Commonwealth University.

Professor Feldman is a Fellow of the American Psychological Association, the Association for Psychological Science, and the American Association for the Advancement of Science. He is a winner of a Fulbright Senior Research Scholar and Lecturer award and has written over 200 scientific articles, book chapters, and books. His books, some of which have been translated into Spanish, French, Portuguese, Dutch, Japanese, and Chinese, include *Improving the First Year of College: Research and Practice; The First Year of College: Research, Theory, and Practice on Improving the Student Experience and Increasing Retention; Understanding Psychology,* 14/e; and *Development Across the Life Span,* 8/e. His research interests encompass the study of honesty and truthfulness in everyday life, development of nonverbal behavior in children, and the social psychology of education. His research has been supported by grants from the National Institute of Mental Health and the National Institute on Disabilities and Rehabilitation Research.

With the last of his three children completing college, Professor Feldman occupies his spare time with pretty decent cooking and earnest, but admittedly unpolished, piano playing. He also loves to travel. He lives with his wife, who is an educational psychologist, in a home overlooking the Holyoke mountain range in western Massachusetts.

Brief Table of Contents

Table of Contents

PART 1 Getting Started

3 Discovering Your Learning Styles, Self-Concept, and Values 57

PART 2 Using P.O.W.E.R. for Academic Success

6 Reading and Remembering 148

7 Writing and Speaking 177

8 Choosing Your Courses and Major 210

PART 3 Life Beyond the Classroom

Preface

In the first edition of ***P.O.W.E.R. Learning,*** I wrote about Mark Johnson, a student whom I encountered early in my teaching career. Smart, articulate, and likable, he certainly wanted to succeed in college, and he seemed every bit as capable as those students who were doing quite well. Yet Mark was a marginal student, someone who allowed multiple opportunities to succeed to pass him by. Although he clearly had the talent necessary to be successful in college—and ultimately in life—he lacked the skills to make use of his talents.

Over the years, I encountered other students like Mark. I began to wonder: Was there a way to teach *every* student how to succeed, both academically and beyond the classroom? ***P.O.W.E.R. Learning*** embodies the answer to this question.

Based on the conviction that *good students are made, not born,* the central message of ***P.O.W.E.R. Learning*** is that students can be successful in college if they follow the basic principles and strategies presented in this book. Once mastered, these principles and strategies can help students to maximize their accomplishments, both in and out of the classroom.

This text is designed to be used by students in first-year experience courses. For many students, the first-year experience course is a literal lifeline. It provides the means to learn what it takes to achieve academic success and to make a positive social adjustment to the campus community. If students learn how to do well in their first term of college, they are building a foundation that will last a lifetime.

I wrote ***P.O.W.E.R. Learning*** because no existing text provided a systematic framework that could be applied in a variety of topical areas and that would help students to develop learning and problem-solving strategies that would work effectively both in and out of the classroom. The book is an outgrowth of my experience as a college instructor, most of it involving first-year students, combined with my research on the factors that influence learning.

Judging from the response to the prior editions—now in use at hundreds of colleges and universities around the world, and translated into Chinese, Spanish, and other languages—the approach embodied in the book resonates with the philosophy and experience of many educators. Specifically, ***P.O.W.E.R. Learning*** provides a framework that students can begin to use immediately to become more effective students. That framework is designed to be

- Clear, easy to grasp, logical, and compelling, so that students can readily see its merits.
- Effective for a variety of student learning styles—as well as a variety of teaching styles.
- Workable within a variety of course formats and for supplemental instruction.
- Valuable for use in learning communities.
- Transferable to settings ranging from the classroom to the dorm room to the board room.
- Effective in addressing both the mind *and* the spirit, presenting cognitive strategies and skills, while engaging the natural enthusiasm, motivation, and inclination to succeed that students carry within them.

Based on comprehensive, detailed feedback obtained from both instructors and students, ***P.O.W.E.R. Learning*** meets these aims. The book will help students confront and master the numerous challenges of the college experience through use of the P.O.W.E.R. Learning approach, embodied in the five steps of the acronym *P.O.W.E.R.* (*P*repare, *O*rganize, *W*ork, *E*valuate, and *R*ethink). Using simple—yet effective—principles, *P.O.W.E.R. Learning* teaches the skills needed to succeed in college and careers beyond.

The Goals of *P.O.W.E.R. Learning*, 8/e

P.O.W.E.R. Learning addresses five major goals:

- **To provide a systematic framework for organizing the strategies that lead to success:** First and foremost, the book provides a systematic, balanced presentation of the skills required to achieve student success. Using the *P.O.W.E.R.* framework and relying on proven strategies, ***P.O.W.E.R. Learning*** provides specific, hands-on techniques for achieving success as a student.
- **To offer a wide range of skill-building opportunities: *P.O.W.E.R. Learning*** provides a wealth of specific exercises, diagnostic questionnaires, case studies, and journal writing activities to help students to develop and master the skills and techniques they need to become effective learners and problem solvers. *Readers learn by doing.*
- **To demonstrate the connection between academic success and success beyond the classroom:** Stressing the importance of *self-reliance* and *self-accountability,* the book demonstrates that the skills required to be a successful student are tied to career and personal success as well.
- **To develop critical thinking skills:** Whether to evaluate the quality of information found on the Internet or in other types of media, or to judge the merits of a position taken by a friend, colleague, or politician, the ability to think critically is more important than ever in this age of information. Through frequent questionnaires, exercises, journal activities, and guided group work, ***P.O.W.E.R. Learning*** helps students to develop their capacity to think critically.
- **To provide an engaging, accessible, and meaningful presentation:** The fifth goal of this book underlies the first four: to write a student-friendly book that is relevant to the needs and interests of its readers and that will promote enthusiasm and interest in the process of becoming a successful student. Learning the strategies needed to become a more effective student should be a stimulating and fulfilling experience. Realizing that these strategies are valuable outside the classroom as well will provide students with an added incentive to master them.

In short, ***P.O.W.E.R. Learning: Strategies for Success in College and Life*** is designed to give students a sense of mastery and success as they read the book and work through its exercises. It is meant to engage and nurture students' minds and spirits, stimulating their intellectual curiosity about the world and planting a seed that will grow throughout their lifetime.

Changes That Make a Difference: New to the Eighth Edition

The valuable input we have received from **P.O.W.E.R. Learning**'s reviewers, along with the feedback from the tens of thousands of students, the hundreds of instructors who used the prior editions, and classroom testing, have resulted in the addition of new and updated information, reflecting advances in our understanding of what makes students successful and changes in college instruction. The following sample of new and revised topics provides a good indication of the book's currency:

CHAPTER 1—P.O.W.E.R. LEARNING: BECOMING A SUCCESSFUL STUDENT

- Refined description of economic value of college
- New statistics on lifetime monetary value of a college education
- New statistics on annual gap between high-school and college-educated earners
- Rephrased how service learning is defined
- Brain wave passwords
- Self-driving cars
- Refined definition of service learning
- Defined acronym
- Internet access as part of preparation
- Redefined growth mindset
- Introduced concept of grit
- Introduced definition of fixed mindset
- Cultivating grit
- Clarified importance of reading material assigned, but not discussed, by instructors

CHAPTER 2—MAKING THE MOST OF YOUR TIME

- Clarified the goals of time management
- Clarified directions for completing time log
- Added strategies for scheduling homework and study time
- Changed section on "study time" to "homework and study time"
- Monitor children's screen time
- Clarified the value of doing less
- Revised description of to-do list
- Smartphone apps to time study sessions
- Revised *Resources* section
- New Animations In Connect

CHAPTER 3—DISCOVERING YOUR LEARNING STYLES, SELF-CONCEPT, AND VALUES

- Rephrased definition of receptive learning style
- Clarified separate intelligences in multiple intelligences theory
- Refined definition of spatial intelligence
- Clarified Myers-Briggs four-dimension approach
- Refined explanation of intuitors versus sensors in Myers-Briggs approach
- Clarified left versus right brain processing
- Relationship of learning styles to success
- Clarified definition of learning theories
- Refined explanation of reinforcer
- Refined description of consequences of exposure to negative messages
- Expanded explanation of values
- Clarified need to revise personal mission statements

CHAPTER 4—TAKING NOTES

- Refined explanation of why less can be more in taking notes
- Refined section on instructor limitations
- Research on off-task laptop use during class
- Clarified significance of instructor nonverbal cues
- Revised concept map key term
- Clarified taking study notes on material that can't be written on or annotated
- Use of note-taking apps to take notes in class
- Importance of using critical thinking skills to evaluate information
- Fake news and social media
- Revised *Resources* section
- New Animations in Connect on Note Taking

CHAPTER 5—TAKING TESTS

- Refined explanation on importance of learning about tests before taking them
- Clarified different types of test questions
- Clarified description of essay questions
- Refined description of short-answer and fill-in questions
- Provide examples of apps for taking study notes (Evernote and OneNote)
- Refined description of value of test anxiety
- Cultivation of growth mindset to deal with math anxiety
- Added more strategies to deal with math anxiety and testing
- Use of scanners to grade tests
- Importance of bringing photo ID to tests
- Identification verification at testing centers
- Taking tests at testing centers
- Self-talk prior to starting tests
- Visualization of success before starting tests

- Clarified strategies for starting essay exams
- Clarified short answer and fill-in questions
- Refined description of absolute words in testing items
- Clarified educated guessing strategy
- Refined discussion of end-of-test strategies
- Politely consulting with instructor after poor test performance

CHAPTER 6—READING AND REMEMBERING

- Clarified concept of advance organizers
- Clarified creation of advance organizers
- Refined description of identifying length of chapters before starting to study
- Clarified rationale for purchasing new vs. used textbooks
- Clarified use of online dictionaries
- Clarified SQ4R study system
- Refined memorization technique availability
- Clarified discussion of multiple memory strategies
- Clarified ways of rehearsing material
- Refined description of acrostics
- Clarified how retention can be hindered by mnemonics that don't focus on meaning
- Clarified example of overlearning
- Explanation of memory consolidation process
- Refined importance of rethinking for comprehension

CHAPTER 7—WRITING AND SPEAKING

- Clarified explanation of writing as a process
- Refined description of liberating value of starting a blank page
- Refined description of goal of writing assignments
- Clarified rationale for brainstorming
- Clarified the value of virtual or hard-copy information folders
- Updated citation examples
- Refined description of common knowledge
- Clarified the use of scaffolding
- Added argument as a key term
- Added background as a key term
- Refined description of writing in short chunks
- Clarified value of putting aside first drafts for a time
- Clarified need for multiple drafts
- Clarified need to cut extraneous information
- Refined the description of the process of rethinking
- Importance of noting source material
- Reiterated importance of the first few minutes of a talk
- Clarified importance of notes
- Described importance of using reliable sources and avoiding fake news

CHAPTER 8—CHOOSING YOUR COURSES AND MAJOR

- Clarified requirements for majors and other academic unit requirements
- Redefined articulation agreement
- Clarified definition of registrar
- Refined description of personal schedule choices
- Refined definition of registering
- Strengthened description of importance of meeting with an advisor
- Verification of enrollment in courses
- Importance of taking stock of your choices
- Refined description of education as a lifelong activity
- Statistics on what graduates with particular majors earn over a lifetime
- Highlighted the shortsightedness of choosing a major based on primarily on salary

CHAPTER 9—TECHNOLOGY AND INFORMATION COMPETENCY

- Clarified concept of digital divide
- Role of course websites
- Removed reference to wikis
- Clarified and updated individual response technology
- Clarified importance of keeping e-mails short
- Avoiding use of postscripts in e-mail
- Expanded online netiquette
- Avoiding use of sarcasm
- Expanded phishing material
- Safety issues on social media
- Revised statistics on Facebook and Twitter use
- New character limit on tweets
- Free online courses such as edX and Coursera
- Necessity of good Internet service for distance learning courses
- Asking for help in online courses
- Making the most of online feedback
- Redefined online database
- Expanded explanation of encyclopedias to include handbooks
- Clarified reserve collections
- Clarified online catalog content
- Clarified description of interlibrary loan
- Avoiding fake news websites
- Updated web search statistics
- Refined description of use of search engine results

CHAPTER 10—MAKING GOOD DECISIONS

- Criteria for making optimal decisions based on critical thinking
- Clarified assessing the alternatives

- Clarified working through the steps of assessing alternatives
- Refined description of tossing a coin
- Clarified going with a gut feeling
- Clarified the necessity of generating appropriate solutions in problem solving
- Refined description of importance of defining problems to be solved
- Clarified need to use different strategies to solve life's more complex problems
- Rephrased strategy of temporary stopping efforts at problem solving
- Clarified need for clear and unbiased critical thinking
- Clarified how naming something is not explaining it
- Refined description of how generalities can be made to seem definitive
- Clarified fallacy of common sense
- New principle of conflict resolution
- Strategy of blocking a person from social media after the end of a relationship

CHAPTER 11—DIVERSITY AND YOUR RELATIONSHIPS WITH OTHERS

- Added gender diversity to learning objective
- Intersectionality and diversity
- Race as a social construction
- Increase in foreign students and implications for diversity
- Controversies regarding appropriate labels for members of racial and ethnic groups
- Redefined prejudice
- Refined description of considering people as individuals rather than in the aggregate
- Clarified how the groups to which we belong affects how others view us
- Gender identity
- Transgender identity
- Sexual orientation

CHAPTER 12—MONEY MATTERS

- Refined description of importance of budgeting
- Clarified necessity for identifying short- and long-terms goals
- Refined ways of keeping track of past expenditures
- Updated examples of daily expenditures
- Refined necessity of taking action if there's a lack of funds
- Redefined variable interest rate
- Added credit score definition
- Clarified description of establishing a credit history
- Clarified how lenders make profit from the interest they charge
- Clarified how interest rate, principal, and term of the loan work together to determine repayment amount
- PLUS loan payback period of 10 to 25 years
- Revised amount of student indebtedness statistics

- Added maximum amounts for Pell Grants and FSEOG grants
- Eliminated HOPE credit
- Added American Opportunity Tax Credit
- Clarified use of FAFSA and CSS Profile
- Advisability of writing a letter of explanation of special circumstances with financial aid applications
- New Animation in Connect on Budgeting

CHAPTER 13—STRESS, HEALTH, AND WELLNESS

- Clarified the physiological responses to stress
- Clarified the negative consequences of long-term physiological responses to stress
- HHS federal helpline website
- Clarified relaxation techniques to reduce stress
- Refined importance of keeping commitments
- National suicide telephone number
- Online chat and texting for suicide help
- Clarified importance of seeking help for suicide problems
- E-cigarettes increase likelihood of using traditional tobacco products
- Opioid addiction epidemic
- Refined description of difficulty of overcoming addiction without professional help
- Updated material on STIs, including addition of human papilloma virus (HPV)

McGraw Hill Education **connect**®

Students—study more efficiently, retain more and achieve better outcomes. Instructors—focus on what you love—teaching.

SUCCESSFUL SEMESTERS INCLUDE CONNECT

FOR INSTRUCTORS

You're in the driver's seat.

Want to build your own course? No problem. Prefer to use our turnkey, prebuilt course? Easy. Want to make changes throughout the semester? Sure. And you'll save time with Connect's auto-grading too.

65%

Less Time Grading

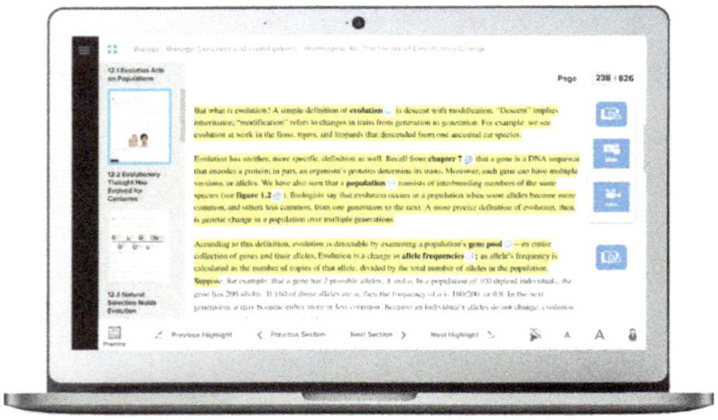

They'll thank you for it.

Adaptive study resources like SmartBook® help your students be better prepared in less time. You can transform your class time from dull definitions to dynamic debates. Hear from your peers about the benefits of Connect at **www.mheducation.com/highered/connect**.

Make it simple, make it affordable.

Connect makes it easy with seamless integration with any of the major Learning Management Systems—Blackboard®, Canvas, and D2L, among others—to let you organize your course in one convenient location. Give your students access to digital materials at a discount with our inclusive access program. Ask your McGraw-Hill representative for more information.

Solutions for your challenges.

A product isn't a solution. Real solutions are affordable, reliable, and come with training and ongoing support when you need it and how you want it. Our Customer Experience Group can also help you troubleshoot tech problems—although Connect's 99% uptime means you might not need to call them. See for yourself at **status.mheducation.com**

For Students

Effective, efficient studying.

Connect helps you be more productive with your study time and get better grades using tools like SmartBook, which highlights key concepts and creates a personalized study plan. Connect sets you up for success, so you walk into class with confidence and walk out with better grades.

©Shutterstock/wavebreakmedia

"I really liked this app—it made it easy to study when you don't have your text-book in front of you."

- Jordan Cunningham,
Eastern Washington University

Study anytime, anywhere.

Download the free ReadAnywhere app and access your online eBook when it's convenient, even if you're offline. And since the app automatically syncs with your eBook in Connect, all of your notes are available every time you open it. Find out more at **www.mheducation.com/readanywhere**

No surprises.

The Connect Calendar and Reports tools keep you on track with the work you need to get done and your assignment scores. Life gets busy; Connect tools help you keep learning through it all.

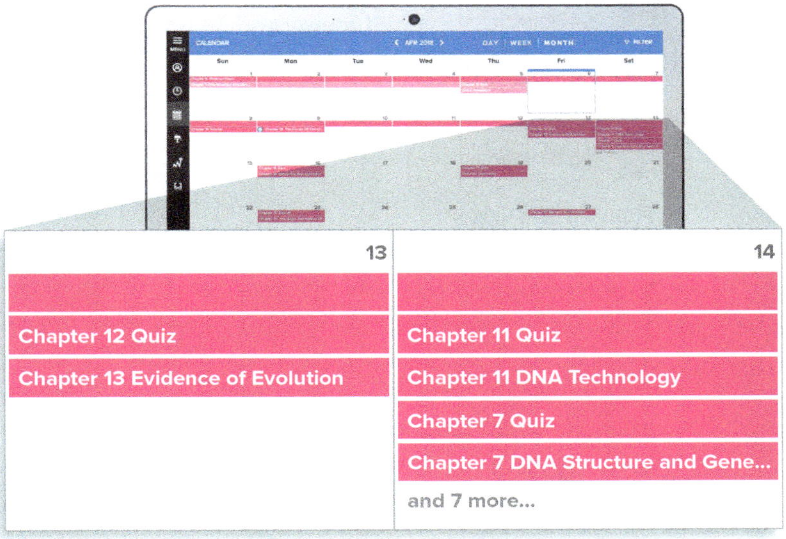

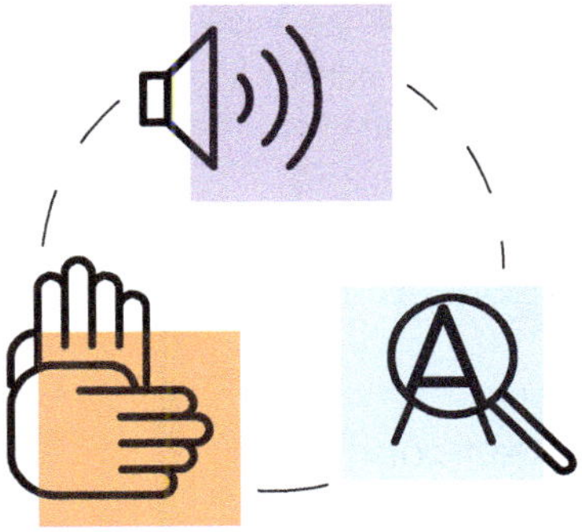

Learning for everyone.

McGraw-Hill works directly with Accessibility Services Departments and faculty to meet the learning needs of all students. Please contact your Accessibility Services office and ask them to e-mail accessibility@mheducation.com, or visit **www.mheducation.com/accessibility** for more information.

Text Features: Achieving P O W E R the Goals of Learning

P.O.W.E.R. Learning provides a systematic framework for organizing the strategies that lead to success

P.O.W.E.R. Plan

Each chapter utilizes the principles of the **P.O.W.E.R. system (Prepare, Organize, Work, Evaluate, and Rethink),** so students can clearly see how easy it is to incorporate this effective process into their everyday routine. The P.O.W.E.R. plan illustration highlights the key steps for the corresponding chapter material.

The goals of *P.O.W.E.R. Learning: Strategies for Success in College and Life* are achieved through a consistent, carefully devised set of features common to every chapter. Students and faculty endorsed each of these elements.

Handy, updated **reference charts** appear throughout the text for quickly accessing and organizing important material.

table 7.1 Major Types of College Writing

Research paper	A paper requiring abstract, critical thinking supported through the collection of existing information. Often requires analysis and synthesis of the material to develop a conclusion.
Essay	A paper written from an author's personal point of view and arguing a particular point. It may take the form of a review, criticism, or personal recollection, or it may argue a political viewpoint.
Critical review	Criticism of an argument, article, musical piece, or other work.
Journal	Personal reflections on class readings or assignments.

P.O.W.E.R. Learning offers a wide range of skill-building opportunities

Every chapter offers numerous updated **Try It!** activities for gaining hands-on experience with the material covered in the chapter. These include questionnaires, self-assessments, and group exercises to do with classmates. The **Try It!** activities, along with other assessment opportunities, are also available on the POWER Learning Connect Library.

1 **Try It!** P O W E R

Get to Know Your College Advisor

It is helpful to get a feel for who your advisor is, so schedule a 15- to 30-minute appointment with him or her. Before you meet with your advisor, do some background research by looking at your college requirements. You can also usually find information on the background of faculty and staff, listing their titles, where they went to college and graduate school, what departments they teach in, and what their areas of academic interest are. In addition, many instructors have their own home pages that describe their background.

To learn more about your advisor, cover some of these topics when you meet:

- Philosophy of college advising
- Words of advice
- Things to try at the college
- Things to avoid at the college

After you have met with your advisor, answer the following questions:

1. How would you describe your advisor as a person?
2. What things did you learn that can help you?
3. How can you use your advisor's responses to take better advantage of what your college has to offer?

Every chapter includes an updated list of the three types of **resources** that are useful in finding and utilizing information relevant to the chapter: a list of on-campus resources, books, and websites. This material helps students study and retain important concepts presented in the chapter, as well as guide their future inquiry.

[RESOURCES]

ON CAMPUS

If you are interested in learning more about your pattern of learning styles, visit your campus counseling center or career center, where you may be able to take special assessment tests that can pinpoint your learning preferences and offer study strategies based on those preferences.

When dealing with the uncertainties of life and establishing your own sense of direction, it may help to speak to someone who has perspective and experience with college students. Here, too, a good place to start on campus is either a general counseling center or one that is designed to help students choose career paths. Mental health offices can also be helpful in putting you in touch with a therapist with whom you can explore issues revolving around your self-concept and self-esteem. Don't hesitate to get help. You are doing it for yourself.

IN PRINT

Thomas Armstrong and Sue Teele's *Rainbows of Intelligence: Exploring How Students Learn* (2015) provides an introduction to learning styles, offering tips and suggestions for making use of the ways that people learn.

Writing in Class: Strategies for Getting It Right

Your instructor pauses halfway through her lecture and says that for the next 5 minutes you are to complete a short written assignment. Whether she calls it an in-class essay, a reaction paper, or a "pop paper," it calls for somewhat different strategies than an out-of-class writing assignment. Unlike traditional paper assignments—in which you have the luxury of time—an in-class writing assignment requires that you react immediately.

Here are some tips for completing in-class writing assignments:

- *Be prepared.* You should always come to class with pen and pencil, as well as knowing your student ID number (at least in big classes). Just as important, make sure you're up to date in the reading assignments.
- *Think first.* Before you start writing, spend a minute thinking about the assignment. What is its goal? How can you best approach it? What is it that you want to get across?
- *Make a quick outline.* Creating an outline—even a short one—will help you collect your thoughts and prepare for what you're going to say.
- *Timing is everything.* Assuming your instructor lets you know how much time you'll have (and ask how much, if he or she doesn't mention it), plan ahead appropriately. You don't want to run out of time before completing your assignment.
- *Be sure to answer every part of the question.* If your instructor asks for your opinion, be sure to give it, but if he or she also wants to know *why* you feel the way you do, don't forget that part.
- *Neatness counts.* Be sure your answer is legible. If your handwriting is terrible, then print. The most brilliant of responses does you no good if your instructor can't read it.

Course Connections

Every chapter includes a **Course Connections** box that shows students how to use the chapter's content to maximize their success in particular classes.

P.O.W.E.R. Learning demonstrates the connection between academic success and success beyond the classroom

The **Career Connections** feature links the material in the chapter to the world of work, demonstrating how the strategies discussed in the chapter are related to career choices and success in the workplace.

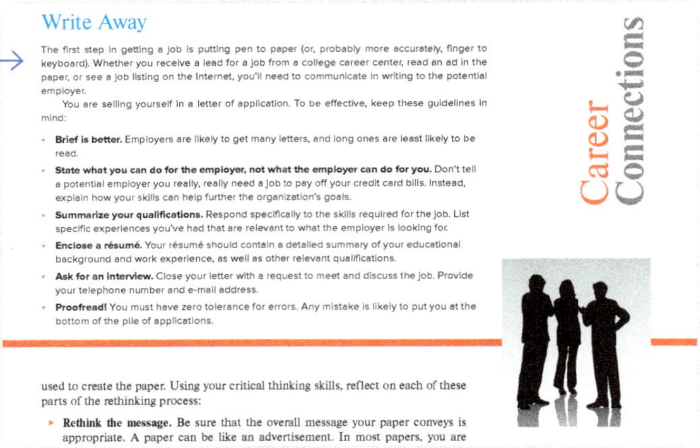

Write Away

Career Connections

The first step in getting a job is putting pen to paper (or, probably more accurately, finger to keyboard). Whether you receive a lead for a job from a college career center, read an ad in the paper, or see a job listing on the Internet, you'll need to communicate in writing to the potential employer.

You are selling yourself in a letter of application. To be effective, keep these guidelines in mind:

- **Brief is better.** Employers are likely to get many letters, and long ones are least likely to be read.
- **State what you can do for the employer, not what the employer can do for you.** Don't tell a potential employer you really, really need a job to pay off your credit card bills. Instead, explain how your skills can help further the organization's goals.
- **Summarize your qualifications.** Respond specifically to the skills required for the job. List specific experiences you've had that are relevant to what the employer is looking for.
- **Enclose a résumé.** Your résumé should contain a detailed summary of your educational background and work experience, as well as other relevant qualifications.
- **Ask for an interview.** Close your letter with a request to meet and discuss the job. Provide your telephone number and e-mail address.
- **Proofread!** You must have zero tolerance for errors. Any mistake is likely to put you at the bottom of the pile of applications.

used to create the paper. Using your critical thinking skills, reflect on each of these parts of the rethinking process:

- **Rethink the message.** Be sure that the overall message your paper conveys is appropriate. A paper can be like an advertisement. In most papers, you are

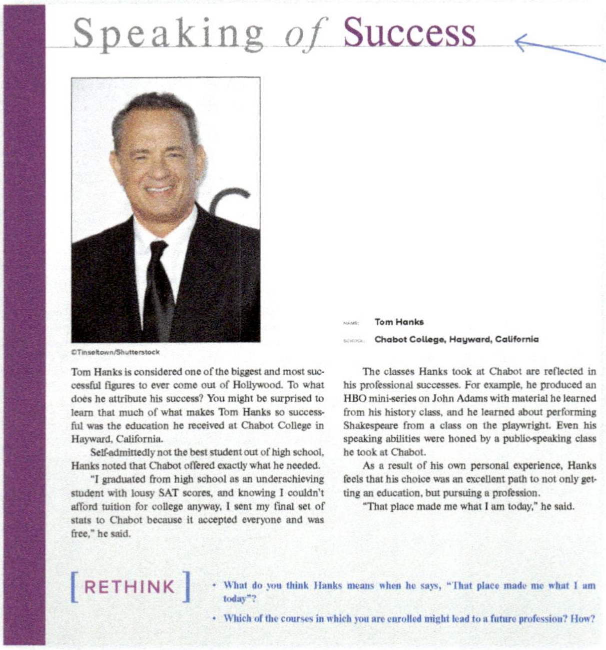

Speaking *of* Success

©Tinseltown/Shutterstock

NAME: **Tom Hanks**

SCHOOL: **Chabot College, Hayward, California**

Tom Hanks is considered one of the biggest and most successful figures to ever come out of Hollywood. To what does he attribute his success? You might be surprised to learn that much of what makes Tom Hanks so successful was the education he received at Chabot College in Hayward, California.

Self-admittedly not the best student out of high school, Hanks noted that Chabot offered exactly what he needed.

"I graduated from high school as an underachieving student with lousy SAT scores, and knowing I couldn't afford tuition for college anyway, I sent my final set of stats to Chabot because it accepted everyone and was free," he said.

The classes Hanks took at Chabot are reflected in his professional successes. For example, he produced an HBO mini-series on John Adams with material he learned from his history class, and he learned about performing Shakespeare from a class on the playwright. Even his speaking abilities were honed by a public-speaking class he took at Chabot.

As a result of his own personal experience, Hanks feels that his choice was an excellent path to not only getting an education, but pursuing a profession.

"That place made me what I am today," he said.

[RETHINK]

- What do you think Hanks means when he says, "That place made me what I am today"?
- Which of the courses in which you are enrolled might lead to a future profession? How?

Many new **Speaking of Success** articles have been added that profile real-life success stories. Some of these people are well-known individuals, whereas others are current students or recent graduates who have overcome academic difficulties to achieve success. In addition, **critical thinking questions** end each **Speaking of Success** profile.

P.O.W.E.R. Learning helps you develop critical thinking skills

Chapter 1 features a **P.O.W.E.R. Profile Assessment tool** that gives students a sense of where they stand—both numerically and graphically—in relation to the key topics addressed in the book. The "P.O.W.E.R. Profile" helps students identify their strengths and weaknesses and determine how they want to improve. Students can return to the P.O.W.E.R. Profile at the end of the course to assess and chart their progress.

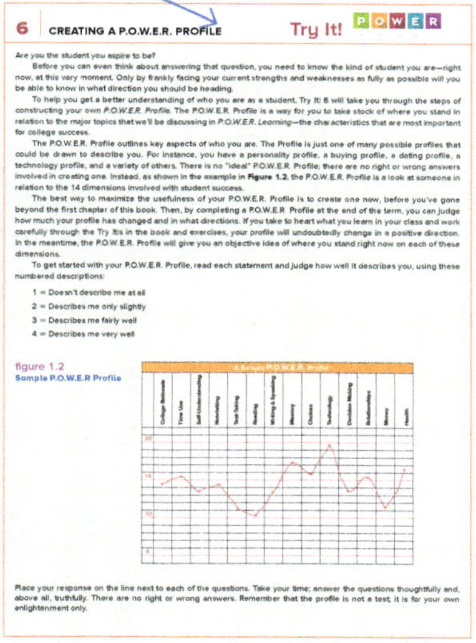

6 | CREATING A P.O.W.E.R. PROFILE — Try It! P O W E R

Are you the student you aspire to be?

Before you can even think about answering that question, you need to know the kind of student you are—right now, at this very moment. Only by frankly facing your current strengths and weaknesses as fully as possible will you be able to know in what direction you should be heading.

To help you get a better understanding of who you are as a student, Try It! 6 will take you through the steps of constructing your own *P.O.W.E.R. Profile*. The P.O.W.E.R. Profile is a way for you to take stock of where you stand in relation to the major topics that we'll be discussing in *P.O.W.E.R. Learning*—the characteristics that are most important for college success.

The P.O.W.E.R. Profile outlines key aspects of who you are. The Profile is just one of many possible profiles that could be drawn to describe you. For instance, you have a personality profile, a buying profile, a dating profile, a technology profile, and a variety of others. There is no "ideal" P.O.W.E.R. Profile; there are no right or wrong answers involved in creating one. Instead, as shown in the example in **Figure 1.2**, the P.O.W.E.R. Profile is a look at someone in relation to the 14 dimensions involved with student success.

The best way to maximize the usefulness of your P.O.W.E.R. Profile is to create one now, before you've gone beyond the first chapter of this book. Then, by completing a P.O.W.E.R. Profile at the end of the term, you can judge how much your profile has changed and in what directions. If you take to heart what you learn in your class and work carefully through the Try It's in the book and exercises, your profile will undoubtedly change in a positive direction. In the meantime, the P.O.W.E.R. Profile will give you an objective idea of where you stand right now on each of these dimensions.

To get started with your P.O.W.E.R. Profile, read each statement and judge how well it describes you, using these numbered descriptions:

1 = Doesn't describe me at all
2 = Describes me only slightly
3 = Describes me fairly well
4 = Describes me very well

figure 1.2
Sample P.O.W.E.R Profile

Place your response on the line next to each of the questions. Take your time; answer the questions thoughtfully and, above all, truthfully. There are no right or wrong answers. Remember that the profile is not a test; it is for your own enlightenment only.

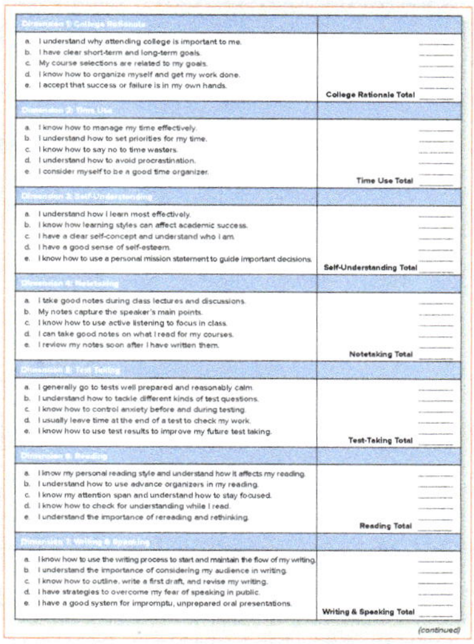

Dimension 1: College Rationale	
a. I understand why attending college is important to me.	____
b. I have clear short-term and long-term goals.	____
c. My course selections are related to my goals.	____
d. I know how to organize myself and get my work done.	____
e. I accept that success or failure is in my own hands.	____
	College Rationale Total ____
Dimension 2: Time Use	
a. I know how to manage my time effectively.	____
b. I understand how to set priorities for my time.	____
c. I know how to say no to time wasters.	____
d. I understand how to avoid procrastination.	____
e. I consider myself to be a good time organizer.	____
	Time Use Total ____
Dimension 3: Self-Understanding	
a. I understand how I learn most effectively.	____
b. I know how learning styles can affect academic success.	____
c. I have a clear self-concept and understand who I am.	____
d. I have a good sense of self-esteem.	____
e. I know how to use a personal mission statement to guide important decisions.	____
	Self-Understanding Total ____
Dimension 4: Notetaking	
a. I take good notes during class lectures and discussions.	____
b. My notes capture the speaker's main points.	____
c. I know how to use active listening to focus in class.	____
d. I can take good notes on what I read for my courses.	____
e. I review my notes soon after I have written them.	____
	Notetaking Total ____
Dimension 5: Test Taking	
a. I generally go to tests well prepared and reasonably calm.	____
b. I understand how to tackle different kinds of test questions.	____
c. I know how to control anxiety before and during testing.	____
d. I usually leave time at the end of a test to check my work.	____
e. I know how to use test results to improve my future test taking.	____
	Test-Taking Total ____
Dimension 6: Reading	
a. I know my personal reading style and understand how it affects my reading.	____
b. I understand how to use advance organizers in my reading.	____
c. I know my attention span and understand how to stay focused.	____
d. I know how to check for understanding while I read.	____
e. I understand the importance of rereading and rethinking.	____
	Reading Total ____
Dimension 7: Writing & Speaking	
a. I know how to use the writing process to start and maintain the flow of my writing.	____
b. I understand the importance of considering my audience in writing.	____
c. I know how to outline, write a first draft, and revise my writing.	____
d. I have strategies to overcome my fear of speaking in public.	____
e. I have a good system for impromptu, unprepared oral presentations.	____
	Writing & Speaking Total ____

(continued)

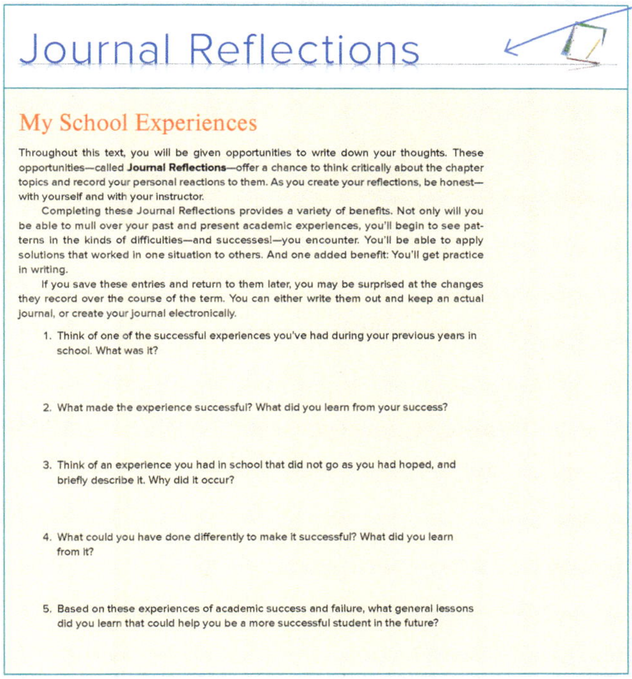

Journal Reflections

My School Experiences

Throughout this text, you will be given opportunities to write down your thoughts. These opportunities—called **Journal Reflections**—offer a chance to think critically about the chapter topics and record your personal reactions to them. As you create your reflections, be honest—with yourself and with your instructor.

Completing these Journal Reflections provides a variety of benefits. Not only will you be able to mull over your past and present academic experiences, you'll begin to see patterns in the kinds of difficulties—and successes!—you encounter. You'll be able to apply solutions that worked in one situation to others. And one added benefit: You'll get practice in writing.

If you save these entries and return to them later, you may be surprised at the changes they record over the course of the term. You can either write them out and keep an actual journal, or create your journal electronically.

1. Think of one of the successful experiences you've had during your previous years in school. What was it?

2. What made the experience successful? What did you learn from your success?

3. Think of an experience you had in school that did not go as you had hoped, and briefly describe it. Why did it occur?

4. What could you have done differently to make it successful? What did you learn from it?

5. Based on these experiences of academic success and failure, what general lessons did you learn that could help you be a more successful student in the future?

The **Journal Reflections** feature provides students with the opportunity to keep an ongoing journal, making entries relevant to the chapter content. Students are asked to reflect and think critically about related prior experiences. These conclude with questions designed to elicit critical thinking and exploration.

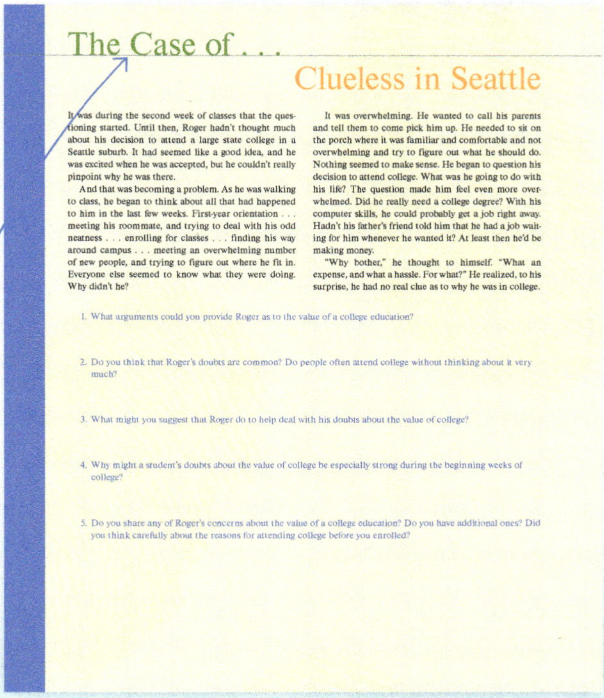

The Case of . . . Clueless in Seattle

It was during the second week of classes that the questioning started. Until then, Roger hadn't thought much about his decision to attend a large state college in a Seattle suburb. It had seemed like a good idea, and he was excited when he was accepted, but he couldn't really pinpoint why he was there.

And that was becoming a problem. As he was walking to class, he began to think about all that had happened to him in the last few weeks. First-year orientation . . . meeting his roommate, and trying to deal with his odd neatness . . . enrolling for classes . . . finding his way around campus . . . meeting an overwhelming number of new people, and trying to figure out where he fit in. Everyone else seemed to know what they were doing. Why didn't he?

It was overwhelming. He wanted to call his parents and tell them to come pick him up. He needed to sit on the porch where it was familiar and comfortable and not overwhelming and try to figure out what he should do. Nothing seemed to make sense. He began to question his decision to attend college. What was he going to do with his life? The question made him feel even more overwhelmed. Did he really need a college degree? With his computer skills, he could probably get a job right away. Hadn't his father's friend told him that he had a job waiting for him whenever he wanted it? At least then he'd be making money.

"Why bother," he thought to himself. "What an expense, and what a hassle. For what?" He realized, to his surprise, he had no real clue as to why he was in college.

1. What arguments could you provide Roger as to the value of a college education?

2. Do you think that Roger's doubts are common? Do people often attend college without thinking about it very much?

3. What might you suggest that Roger do to help deal with his doubts about the value of college?

4. Why might a student's doubts about the value of college be especially strong during the beginning weeks of college?

5. Do you share any of Roger's concerns about the value of a college education? Do you have additional ones? Did you think carefully about the reasons for attending college before you enrolled?

Each chapter ends with a **case study (The Case of . . .)** to which the principles described in the chapter can be applied. Case studies are based on situations that students might themselves encounter. Each case provides a series of questions that encourage students to consider what they've learned and to use critical thinking skills in responding to these questions.

P.O.W.E.R. Learning provides an engaging, accessible, and meaningful presentation

An appealing design and visual presentation highlight large, clear photos carefully selected to show the diversity of students as well as the latest in technological aids and devices.

Chapter-opening scenarios describe an individual grappling with a situation that is relevant to the subject matter of the chapter. Readers will be able to relate to these vignettes, which feature students running behind schedule, figuring out a way to keep up with reading assignments, or facing a long list of vocabulary words to memorize.

Learning Outcomes

By the time you finish this chapter you will be able to

- » LO8-1 Create a plan to prepare for the academic choices that college demands.
- » LO8-2 Outline a strategy for choosing courses that ensures you are getting the most out of your studies.
- » LO8-3 Explain the criteria for choosing a major.

"Physics for Poets." The course title jumped out at Gwen Izell. She had never liked science much, but she was intrigued by this title. Here was a class that seemed designed with her in mind. "Physics for Poets," the description began, "is designed for nonscience majors. It presents the links between physics and the arts." Gwen decided to take a chance and enroll in the class.

It turned out to be one of the best decisions she ever made. She loved the course. The instructor was terrific, making physics fascinating. Not only did she begin to like the subject matter, but she was also good at it.

Gwen was hooked. She took several other science courses over the next semesters. And during her senior year she found herself in an interview with a middle school principal, telling him—a bit to her surprise—that she'd be glad to teach seventh-grade physical science.

Looking Ahead

Our academic and professional careers are propelled by many forces, not the least of which is chance. Gwen Izell, like many other students, found a new direction while leafing through her course list. Although she never would have predicted at the start of college that she would end up taking a variety of science courses and teaching physics, her willingness to take a chance in selecting a course led to a new passion and to a career opportunity.

In this chapter we focus on choosing an academic course of study, one of the central challenges of college life. Not only do the choices we make color our entire college experience, but they also may determine the path we follow once we graduate.

This chapter begins by considering the many choices that you'll have to make as a routine part of attending college, including the choice of courses, instructors, and especially majors—each of which has long-term implications. You'll learn ways to select courses each term that meet your personal needs and maximize your chances of getting the courses you want.

Ultimately, the degree to which your college education benefits you is in your hands. By learning various strategies, you can act decisively to get the most out of your college experience.

» LO8-1 Making Academic Choices

It's a moment filled with promise.

A list of courses for the upcoming term pops up on the computer screen in front of you. Many of the courses sound interesting. Each offers the possibilities of new knowledge and therefore has the potential to change your life in significant ways.

As you scroll through the listing of courses and begin to make your decisions, you may be feeling a range of emotions: anticipation over what you'll learn; hope that the course can bring you closer to your dreams; fear that you won't be able to do well; and excitement that you're proceeding with your college career, taking another of the many small steps that will eventually add up to a complete journey through college.

Key terms appear in boldface in the text and are linked to a glossary definition. In addition, they are listed alphabetically in a **Key Terms and Concepts** section at the end of the chapter, which is also linked to the glossary definition.

[KEY TERMS AND CONCEPTS]

College advisor (p. 213)	Major (p. 212)	Service learning (p. 225)
Distance learning (p. 223)	Minor (p. 230)	Transcript (p. 217)
Double major (p. 229)	Prerequisites (p. 213)	Unique major (p. 230)
Electives (p. 218)	Register (p. 218)	
Grade point average (GPA) (p. 212)	Registrar (p. 217)	

All of these reviewed and tested features are designed not only to help students understand, practice, and master the core concepts presented in this text, but also to collectively support the main goals and vision of this text, as demonstrated here.

The P.O.W.E.R. Resources

The same philosophy and goals that guided the writing of *P.O.W.E.R. Learning: Strategies for Success in College and Life* led to the development of a comprehensive teaching package. Through a series of focus groups, questionnaires, and surveys, we asked instructors what they needed to optimize their courses. We also analyzed what other publishers provided to make sure that the ancillary materials accompanying *P.O.W.E.R. Learning* would surpass the level of support to which instructors are accustomed. As a result of the extensive research that went into devising the teaching resources, we are confident that whether you are an instructor with years of experience or are teaching the course for the first time, this book's instructional package will enhance classroom instruction and provide guidance as you prepare for and teach the course.

Print Resources

ANNOTATED INSTRUCTOR'S EDITION

The Annotated Instructor's Edition (AIE), prepared by Joni Webb Petschauer and Cindy Wallace of Appalachian State University, contains the full text of the student edition of the book with the addition of notes that provide a rich variety of teaching strategies, discussion prompts, and helpful cross-references to the Instructor's Resource Manual. The AIE has been completely redesigned in an effort to provide more frontline teaching assistance.

INSTRUCTOR'S RESOURCE MANUAL

Written by Joni Webb Petschauer and Cindy Wallace of Appalachian State University with additional contributions from experienced instructors across the country, this manual provides specific suggestions for teaching each topic, tips on implementing a first-year experience program, handouts to generate creative classroom activities, audiovisual resources, sample syllabi, and tips on incorporating the Internet into the course.

CUSTOMIZE YOUR TEXT

P.O.W.E.R. Learning can be customized to suit your needs. The text can be abbreviated for shorter courses and can be expanded to include semester schedules, campus maps, additional essays, activities, or exercises, along with other materials specific to your curriculum or situation. Chapters designed for student athletes, career preparation, and transferring students are also available.

Human Resources

WORKSHOPS WITH AUTHOR AND AUTHOR TEAM

Are you faced with the challenge of launching a first-year experience course on your campus? Would you like to invigorate your college success program, incorporating the most recent pedagogical and technological innovations? Is faculty recruitment an obstacle to the success of your program? Are you interested in learning more about the P.O.W.E.R. system?

Workshops are available on these and many other subjects for anyone conducting or even just considering a first-year experience program. Led by author Robert Feldman, *P.O.W.E.R. Learning* Instructor's Resource Manual authors Joni Webb Petschauer and Cindy Wallace, or one of the McGraw-Hill *P.O.W.E.R. Learning* consultants, each workshop is tailored to the needs of individual campuses or programs. For more information, contact your local representative, or e-mail us at student.success@mheducation.com.

Digital Resources

LASSI: LEARNING AND STUDY STRATEGIES INVENTORY

The LASSI is a 10-scale, 80-item assessment of students' awareness about and use of learning and study strategies related to skill, will, and self-regulation components of strategic learning. The focus is on both covert and overt thoughts, behaviors, attitudes, and beliefs that relate to successful learning and that can be altered through educational interventions. Research has repeatedly demonstrated that these factors contribute significantly to success in college and that they can be learned or enhanced through educational interventions such as learning and study skills courses.

The LASSI provides standardized scores and national norms for 10 different scales. The LASSI is both diagnostic and prescriptive. It provides students with a diagnosis of their strengths and weaknesses compared to other college students in the areas covered by the 10 scales, and it is prescriptive in that it provides feedback about areas where students may be weak and need to improve their knowledge, attitudes, beliefs, and skills.

The LASSI is available in print or online at **www.hhpublishing.com**. Ask your McGraw-Hill sales representative for more details.

IMPLEMENTING A STUDENT SUCCESS COURSE

This innovative web content assists you in developing and sustaining your Student Success course. Features include a "how to" guide for designing and proposing a new course, with easy-to-use templates for determining budget needs and resources. Examples of model programs are provided from two-year, four-year, and career schools. The site explores course goals, such as orientation and retention, and provides research data to support your proposal. Also included are materials to help sustain your course, such as faculty development programs and online resources.

MCGRAW-HILL *CONNECT*®

Connect® is proven to deliver better results for students and instructors. Proven content integrates seamlessly with enhanced digital tools to create a personalized learning experience that provides students with precisely what they need, when they need it. With Connect, the educational possibilities are limitless.

LEARNSMART

LearnSmart is an adaptive study tool proven to strengthen memory recall, increase class retention, and boost grades. Students are able to study more efficiently because they are made aware of what they know and don't know. Real-time reports quickly identify the concepts that require more attention from individual students–or the entire class.

SMARTBOOK

SmartBook is the first and only adaptive reading experience designed to change the way students read and learn. It creates a personalized reading experience by highlighting the most impactful concepts a student needs to learn at that moment in time. As a student engages with SmartBook, the reading experience continuously adapts by highlighting content based on what the student knows and doesn't know. This ensures that the focus is on the content he or she needs to learn, while simultaneously promoting long-term retention of material. Use SmartBook's real-time reports to quickly identify the concepts that require more attention from individual students–or the entire class. The end result? Students are more engaged with course content, can better prioritize their time, and come to class ready to participate.

MCGRAW-HILL CAMPUS™

McGraw-Hill Campus™ is a new one-stop teaching and learning experience available to users of any learning management system. This institutional service allows faculty and students to enjoy single-sign-on (SSO) access to all McGraw-Hill Higher Education materials, including the award-winning McGraw-Hill *Connect* platform, from directly within the institution's website. McGraw-Hill Campus provides faculty with instant access to teaching materials (e.g., eTextbooks, test banks, PowerPoint slides, animations, and learning objectives), allowing them to browse, search, and use any ancillary content in our vast library. Students enjoy SSO access to a variety of free products (e.g., quizzes, flash cards, narrated presentations) and subscription-based products (e.g., McGraw-Hill *Connect*). With McGraw-Hill Campus, faculty and students will never need to create another account to access McGraw-Hill products.

The POWER to Succeed!

The Power of Support!

Let the McGraw-Hill Student Success Team support your course with our workshop program.

- Planning to develop a first-year experience course from scratch?
- Reenergizing your first-year experience course?
- Trying to integrate technology in your class?
- Exploring the concept of learning communities?

We offer a range of author- and consultant-led workshops that can be tailored to meet the needs of your institution.

Our team of experts, led by *P.O.W.E.R. Learning* author Robert Feldman, can address issues of course management, assessment, organization, and implementation. How do you get students to commit to your program? How do you achieve support from your institution? How can you evaluate and demonstrate the effectiveness of your First-Year Experience course? These are questions that every program faces. Let us help you to find an answer that works for you.

Other workshop topics may include

- Classroom Strategies for Enhancing Cultural Competence: The P.O.W.E.R. of Diversity
- Using Learning Styles in the Classroom
- Creating Student Success Courses Online
- Motivating Your Students

To schedule a workshop, please contact your local McGraw-Hill representative. Alternately, contact us directly at student.success@mheducation.com to begin the process of bringing a P.O.W.E.R. Learning workshop to you.

The POWER to Create Your Own Text!

Do you want to

- Only cover select chapters?
- Personalize your book with campus information (maps, schedules, registration materials, etc.)?
- Add your own materials, including exercises or assignments?
- Address specific student populations, such as student athletes and transferring students?

P.O.W.E.R. Learning can be customized to suit your needs.

WHY CUSTOMIZE?

Perhaps your course focuses on study skills and you prefer that your text not cover life issues such as money matters, health and wellness, or information on choosing a major. Whatever the reason, we can make it happen, easily. McGraw-Hill Custom Publishing can deliver a book that perfectly meets your needs.

WHAT WILL MY CUSTOM BOOK LOOK LIKE?

Any chapters from the *P.O.W.E.R. Learning* book that you include will be in full color. Additional materials can be added between chapters or at the beginning or end of the book in black and white. Binding (paperback, three-hole punch, you name it) is up to you. You can even add your own custom cover to reflect your school image.

WHAT CAN I ADD?

Anything! Here are some ideas to get you started:

- **Campus map** or anything specific to your school: academic regulations or requirements, syllabi, important phone numbers or dates, library hours.
- **Calendars** for the school year, for local theater groups, for a concert series.
- **Interviews** with local businesspeople or your school's graduates in which they describe their own challenges and successes.
- **Your course syllabus or homework assignments** so your students have everything they need for your course under one cover and you don't have to make copies to hand out.

SPECIAL CHAPTERS DESIGNED FOR THE UNIQUE NEEDS OF YOUR STUDENTS!

Three additional chapters are available for your customized text and have been designed to address the needs of specific student populations.

- *Strategies for Success for Student Athletes.* This chapter discusses the unique challenges of student athletes, such as managing school and team pressures, using resources and understanding eligibility, and knowing when and how to ask for help. It also addresses special concerns such as burnout, dealing with injury, and hazing.
- *Taking Charge of Your Career.* This chapter helps students determine the best career choices that fit personal goals. It provides important tips on how to develop a career portfolio, prepare a résumé and cover letters, and have a successful interview, including follow-up strategies.
- *Transfer Strategies: Making the Leap from Community College to a Four-Year School.* Designed for the potential transfer student, this chapter looks at the pros and cons of moving beyond a two-year degree and what personal decisions to make. It guides students through the transfer process, including applications, credit transfer, financial assistance, and transfer shock.

HOW DO I CREATE A CUSTOM BOOK?

The secret to custom publishing is this: *Custom Publishing Is Simple!*

Here are the basic steps:

- You select the chapters you would like to use from *P.O.W.E.R. Learning* with your McGraw-Hill sales representative.
- Together, we discuss your preferences for the binding, the cover, etc., and provide you with information on costs.
- We assign your customized text an ISBN and your project goes into production. A custom text will typically publish within 6–8 weeks of the order.

- Your book is manufactured and it is put into inventory in the McGraw-Hill distribution center.
- You are sent a free desk copy of your custom publication.
- Your bookstore calls McGraw-Hill's customer service department and orders the text.

You select what you want–we handle the details!
Contact us:

Canada: 1-905-430-5034
United States: 1-800-446-8979
E-mail: student.success@mheducation.com

Acknowledgments

I am indebted to the many reviewers of *P.O.W.E.R. Learning* who provided input at every step of development of the book and the ancillary package. These dedicated instructors and administrators provided thoughtful, detailed advice, and I am very grateful for their help and insight. They include the following:

Judith Lynch, Kansas State University; Dr. G. Warlock Vance, Randolph Community College; Leah Graham, Broward College; Sara Henson, Central Oregon Community College; Jamie Jensen, Boise State University; Barbara West, Central Georgia Technical College; Pauline Nugent, Missouri State University; Rob Bertram, Bradley University; Anne Knop, Manor College; Ashley Stark, Dickinson State University; Christie Carr, Austin Community College; Andrea Smith, Florida Gateway College; Dale S. Haralson, Hinds Community College; Donna Burton, NC State University; Norman Smith, Eckerd College; Sam Mulberry, Bethel University; Diane Fox, Saint Mary's College; Amy Hassenpflug, Liberty University; Mary Beth Willett, University of Maine; Jennifer Clevenger, Virginia Tech; Heidi Zenie, Three Rivers Community College; Jeffrey Hall, Ashford University; Jennifer Scalzi-Pesola, American River College, Sierra; Jarlene DeCay, Cedar Valley College; Beverly Dile, Elizabethtown Community and Technical College; Linda Girouard, Brescia University; Malinda Mansfield, Ivy Tech Community College; Karline Prophete, Palm Beach State College; Kelley Butler Heartfield, Ivy Tech Community College; Stephen Coates-White, South Seattle College; Erin Wood, Catawba College; Cari Kenner, St. Cloud State University; Amanda Bond, Georgia Military College-Columbus; Alex E. Collins, Miami Dade College; Erik Christensen, South Florida State College; J. Andrew Monahan, Suffolk County Community College; Chad Brooks, Austin Peay State University; Cindy Stewart, Blue Ridge CTC; Sherri Stepp, Marshall University; Amy Colon, SUNY Sullivan; Darla Rocha, San Jacinto College; Suzanne F. Pearl, Miami Dade College, Wolfson Campus; Kalpana Swamy, Santa Fe College; Rebecca Samberg, Housatonic Community College; Jeannette McClendon, Napa Valley College; Jeri O'Bryan-Losee, Morrisville State College; Donna Ragauckas, Santa Fe College; Professor Terry Rae Gamble, Palm Beach State College; Barbara Putman, Southwestern Community College; Nikita Anderson, University of Baltimore; Maria Christian, Oklahoma State University Institute of Technology; Alexandra Lis, Miami Dade College, Kendall Campus; Kim Cobb, West Virginia State University; Kim Thomas, Polk State College; Michael Turner, Northern Virginia Community College; Candace Weddle, The South Carolina School of the Arts at Anderson University; Elizabeth Kennedy, Florida Atlantic University; Ronda Jacobs, College of Southern Maryland; Kim Crockett, West Georgia Technical College; Melissa Woods, Hinds Community College; Joe French, Columbia Southern University and Waldorf College; Faye Hamrac, Reid State Technical College; Jyrece McClendon, Palm Beach State College; Aubrey Moncrieffe, Jr., Housatonic Community College; Karen Jones, Zane State College; Peggy Whaley, Murray State University; Marilyn Olson, Chicago State U; Joyce McMahon, Kansas City, Kansas Community College; Kaye Young, Jamestown Community College; Diana Ivankovic, Anderson University; Joseph, Ivy Tech Community College; Matt Kelly, Murray State University; Ronda Dively, Southern Illinois University-Carbondale; Dr. Julia Cote,

Houston Community College; Beverly Russell, College of Southern Maryland; Donna Hanley, Kentucky Wesleyan College; Shane Williamson, Lindenwood University; Cheyanne Lewis, Blue Ridge Community and Technical College; Linda Randall, Georgia Southwestern State University; Linda Gannon, College of Southern Nevada (CSN); Ronnie Peacock, Edgecombe Community College; Deborah Vance, Ivy Tech Community College; Melinda Berry, Trinity Valley Community College; Sandy Lory-Snyder, Farmingdale State College; Melody Hays, South College-Asheville; Dwedor Ford, Central State University; Kim Smokowski, Bergen Community College; Dr. Brenda Tuberville, Rogers State University; Professor Jeannie Gonzalez, Miami Dade College, Kendall Campus; Joyce Kevetos, Palm Beach State College; Kelly S. Moor, Idaho State University; Brad Broschinsky, Idaho State University; Debbie Gilmore, Temple College; Miriam Chiza, North Hennepin Community College; Paul Hibbitts, Jr., Central Georgia Technical College; Mark Hendrix, Palm Beach State College; Laurie Sherman, Community College of Rhode Island; Pamela Moss, Midwestern State University; Alison Collman, Palm Beach State College; Julie Hernandez, Rock Valley College; Nina M. Scaringello, Suffolk County Community College-Grant Campus; Dr. J. Brown, Temple College, Temple, Texas; Stephen Phelps, Temple College; Yvonne Mitkos, Southern Illinois University Edwardsville; Annette Fields, University of Arkansas at Pine Bluff; Christopher L. Lau, Hutchinson Community College; Mary Davis, Angelina College; Pat Wall, Isothermal Community College; Winifred Ferguson Adams, Angelina College; Barbara A. Sherry, Northeastern Illinois University; Jose L. Saldivar, The University of Texas-Pan American; Dr. Michael J. Alicea, Miami Dade College; Karen Nelson, Craven Community College; Jennifer Boyle, Davidson County Community College; Dianna Stankiewicz, Anderson University; Brent Via, Virginia Western Community College; Brent Jackson, Central Carolina Technical College; Professor Lottie T. McMillan, Miami Dade College, North Campus; John Pigg, Tennessee Technical University; Andrea Serna, National American University; Mirjana M. Brockett, Georgia Institute of Technology; Linda McCuen, Anderson University; Charlene Latimer, Daytona State College; Eleanor Paterson, Erie Community College; Keri Keckley, Crowder College; June DeBoer, Calvin College; Chareane Wimbley-Gouveia, Linn-Benton Community College; Ross Bandics, Northampton Community College; Gloria Alexander, Bowie State University; Bickerstaff, Holmes; Scott H. O'Daniel, Ivy Tech Community College; Lourdes Delgado, Miami Dade College; Julie Bennett, Central Methodist University; Miriam McMullen-Pastrick, Penn State Erie; Kay Flowers, Idaho State University; Joseph Kornoski, Montgomery County Community College; Jacqui Slinger, Bluffton University; Mark A. Dowell, Randolph Community College; Eva Menefee, Lansing Community College; Shari Waldrop, Navarro College; Liese A. Hull, University of Michigan; Jenny Beaver, Rowan-Cabarrus Community College; Kenneth Christensen, University of Southern Mississippi; Susan Bossa, Quincy College; Daniel Thompson, CSU Long Beach; Betty Stack, Rowan Cabarrrus Community College; Kristin Asinger, University of Pittsburgh-Bradford; Carmalita M. Kemayo, EdD, University of Illinois Springfield; MaryJo Slater, Community College of Beaver County; Jeannette Sullivan, Palm Beach State College; Michael Corriston, Southeast Kentucky Community and Technical College.

The students in my own First-Year Experience courses (some of whom are shown in the photo) provided thoughtful and wise advice. I thank them for their enthusiasm and eager willingness to provide constructive feedback.

Professors Cindy Wallace and Joni Webb Petschauer of Appalachian State University wrote the Instructor's Resource Manual and provided notes and tips for the Annotated Instructor's Edition. I thank both of them for their enthusiasm, good ideas, dedication, and friendship.

Edward Murphy, Ed.D., an educational testing expert, helped develop the exercises in the book, and I'm grateful for his excellent work.

John Graiff was a great help on every level in putting this book together, and I thank him for his willingness to go the extra mile.

I am proud to be part of an extraordinary McGraw-Hill editorial, marketing, and sales team. My portfolio manager, Brian Sylvester, has brought enthusiasm, savvy, and intelligence to the project, and I welcome his good work, support, and friendship. I am also extremely grateful to David Ploskonka, senior product developer who does much of the heavy lifting on the project. David has a keen editorial eye, creativity, and wealth of good ideas that have improved this title significantly. Many thanks also go to Douglas Ruby, director of digital content. He continues to offer suggestions on navigating the publishing world, and the esteem he holds for authors is remarkable. I would also like to thank team members Melissa Leick and Karen Jozefowicz, senior content project managers; and Jessica Cuevas, designer who helped modify and create the P.O.W.E.R. series digital content. Finally, thanks go to Deepa Chungi, who brought intelligence and thoughtfulness to all the P.O.W.E.R. titles.

Courtesy Bob Feldman

P.O.W.E.R. Learning author Bob Feldman and some of his First-Year Experience program participants.

There are several folks who, while no longer officially working on the project, still patiently answer my queries and offer their advice, for which I am extremely grateful. Andy Watts made superb contributions in extending the reach of *P.O.W.E.R. Learning,* and I'm very grateful for his work and even more for his friendship. Phil Butcher, Thalia Dorwick, David Patterson, Allison McNamara, and Alexis Walker were part of the team that developed the book, and I'm ever thankful for their efforts. Above all, I'm grateful to Rhona Robbin, the first development editor on the project, and sponsoring editor Sarah Touborg, who provided the impetus for the book. Certainly, the pages of *P.O.W.E.R. Learning* continue to reflect their many contributions.

Without a doubt, there is no better publishing group in the business than the one that worked on *P.O.W.E.R. Learning.* I count myself extremely lucky not only to have found myself a part of this world-class team, but to count each of them as friends.

In the end, I am eternally indebted to my family, both extended and immediate. Sarah, Jeff, and Lilia; Josh, Julie, and Naomi; Jon, Leigh, Alex, and Miles; and of course Kathy, thank you for everything.

Robert S. Feldman

Dear Student

Congratulations! You are at the beginning of an academic journey that will impact your future in ways you can only imagine. This text and this course are designed to help make that journey as meaningful and enriching as possible. As you begin this chapter of your life, remember that you are not alone.

Every first-year student (as well as many returning students) encounters challenges. Whether it be juggling family, work, and school or preparing for a test, the challenges you face are daunting.

This is where ***P.O.W.E.R. Learning: Strategies for Success in College and Life*** comes in. It is designed to help you to master the challenges you'll face in school as well as in life after graduation. The P.O.W.E.R. Learning system—which is based on five key steps embodied in the word P.O.W.E.R. (Prepare, Organize, Work, Evaluate, and Rethink)—teaches strategies that will help you become a more successful student and that will give you an edge in attaining what you want to accomplish in life.

But it's up to you to make use of the book. Familiarize yourself with the features of the book (described above) and use the built-in learning aids within the book, on the accompanying website, and in Connect. By doing so, you'll maximize the book's usefulness and get the most out of it.

Finally, I welcome your comments and suggestions about ***P.O.W.E.R. Learning P.O.W.E.R. Learning: Strategies for Success in College and Life,*** as well as the website that accompanies the book. You can write me at the Chancellor's Office at the University of Massachusetts, Amherst, Massachusetts 01003. Even easier, send me an e-mail message at feldman@chancellor.umass.edu. I will write back!

P.O.W.E.R. Learning: Strategies for Success in College and Life presents the tools that can maximize your chances for academic and life success. But remember that they're only tools, and their effectiveness depends on the way in which they are used. Ultimately, you are the one who is in charge of your future. Make the journey a rewarding, exciting, and enlightening one!

Robert S. Feldman

CHAPTER 1

P.O.W.E.R. Learning: Becoming a Successful Student

©Tyler Olson/123RF

Learning Outcomes

By the time you finish this chapter you will be able to

» LO 1-1 Explain the benefits of a college education.

» LO 1-2 Identify the basic principles of P.O.W.E.R. Learning.

» LO 1-3 Discuss how expert students use P.O.W.E.R. Learning to achieve college success.

The day has started off with a bang. Literally. As Jessie Trevant struggles sleepily to turn off her smartphone's pulsing ringing, she knocks it off the desk next to her bed. The thud as it hits the floor not only wakes her fully but also rouses her roommate, who grumbles resentfully.

Struggling out of bed, Jessie reflects on the day ahead. It's one of her most intense class days–four different classes, scattered across the campus. She also must put in several hours of work in the college bookstore, where she has a 15-hour-a-week job, and she knows she'd better get started on her history paper, due next week. And then there's that biology test that she must take this morning.

After a quick shower, Jessie joins the flood of students making their way to classes. She glances at her biology textbook and feels a wave of anxiety flood over her: Will I do well enough? How will I manage to hold down a job and have enough time to study? Will I make friends here? Will it ever feel like home? Will I make my family proud? . . . *And underlying them all is a single challenge: Will I be successful in college?*

©Leszek Glasner/Shutterstock

Looking Ahead

Whether academic pursuits are a struggle or come easily to you . . . whether you live on campus or commute . . . whether you are fresh out of high school or are returning to school many years after high school graduation—college is a challenge. Every one of us has concerns about our capabilities and motivation, and new situations—like starting college—make us wonder how well we'll succeed.

That's where this book comes in. It is designed to help you learn the most effective ways to approach the challenges you encounter, not just in college, but outside the classroom too. It will teach you practical strategies, hints, and tips that can lead you to success, all centered around an approach to achieving college success: P.O.W.E.R. Learning.

This book is designed to be useful in a way that is different from other college texts. It presents information in a hands-on format. It's meant to be used—not just read. Write on it, underline words and sentences, use a highlighter, circle key points, and complete the questionnaires right in the book. The more exercises you do, the more you'll get from the book. Remember, this is a book to help you with your coursework throughout college, so it's a good idea to invest your time here and now. If the learning techniques you master here become second nature, the payoff will be enormous.

» LO 1-1 Why Go to College?

Congratulations. You're in college.

But *why*? Although it seems as if it should be easy to answer why you're continuing your education, for most students it's not so simple. The reasons that people go to college vary from the practical ("I want to get a good job"), to the lofty ("I want to learn about people and the world"), to the unreflective ("Why not?–I don't have anything better to do"). Consider your own reasons for attending college as you complete **Try It! 1**.

1 WHY AM I GOING TO COLLEGE?

Try It! P O W E R

Place 1, 2, and 3 by the three most important reasons that you have for attending college:

____ I want to get a good job when I graduate.

____ My parents want me to go.

____ I couldn't find a job.

____ I want to get away from home.

____ I want to get a better job.

____ I want to try something different.

____ I want to gain a general education and appreciation of ideas.

____ I want to improve my reading and study skills.

____ I want to become a more cultured person.

____ I want to make more money.

____ I want to learn more about things that interest me.

____ A mentor or role model encouraged me to go.

____ I want to prove to others that I can succeed.

Now consider the following:

- What do your answers tell you about yourself?
- What reasons besides these did you think about when you were applying to college?
- How do you think your reasons compare to those of other first-year students who are starting college with you?

Surveys of first-year college students show that the vast majority say they want to learn about things that interest them, get training for a specific career, land a better job, and make more money (see **Figure 1.1**). And, in fact, it's not wrong to expect that a college education will help people find better jobs. The income gap between high school and college graduates averages around $17,500 a year. That difference adds up: Over the course of their working lifetimes, college graduates are likely to earn a million dollars more than those with only a high school degree. Furthermore, as jobs become increasingly complex and technologically sophisticated, college will become more and more of a necessity.

But the importance of a college degree is far greater than its economic value. Consider these added reasons for pursuing a college education:

- **You'll learn to think critically and communicate better.** Here's what one student said about his college experience after he graduated: "It's not about what you major in or which classes you take. . . . It's really about learning to think and to communicate. Wherever you end up, you'll need to be able to analyze and solve problems–to figure out what needs to be done and do it."[1]

  Education improves your ability to understand the world–to understand it as it is now, and to prepare to understand it as it will be.

- **You'll be able to better deal with advances in knowledge and technology that are changing the world.** Genetic engineering . . . drugs to reduce forgetfulness . . .

figure 1.1

Choosing College

These are the most frequently cited reasons that first-year college students gave for why they enrolled in college when asked in a national survey.

Source: Eagan, M. K., Stolzenberg, E. B., Zimmerman, H. B., Aragon, M. C., Whang Sayson, H., & Rios-Aguilar, C. (2017). *The American Freshman: National Norms Fall 2016*. Los Angeles: Higher Education Research Institute, UCLA.

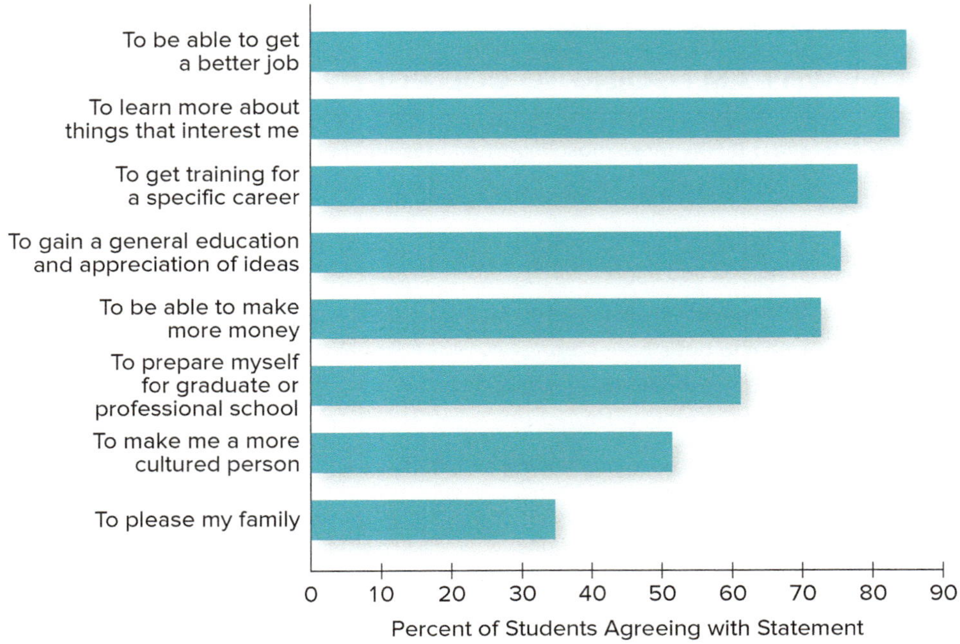

> "Education is not the filling of a pail, but the lighting of a fire."
>
> **William Butler Yeats, quoted in *"Congressional Record, V. 150, PT. 6, April 20, 2004 to May 4, 2004"* U.S. Congress, Government Printing Office, 2009.**

brain wave passwords. . . self-driving cars and trucks. No one knows for sure what the future will hold, but you can prepare for it through a college education. Education can provide you with intellectual tools that you can apply regardless of the specific situation in which you find yourself.

- **You'll acquire skills and perspectives that will shape how you deal with new situations and challenges.** The only certainty about how your life will unfold is that you will be surprised at what is in store for you. College prepares you to deal with the unexpected that characterizes all our lives.
- **You'll be better prepared to live in a world of diversity.** The racial and ethnic composition of the United States is changing rapidly. Whatever your ethnicity, chances are you'll be working and living with people whose backgrounds, lifestyles, and ways of thinking are entirely different from your own. You cannot be prepared for the future unless you understand others and their cultural backgrounds–as well as how your own cultural background affects you.
- **You'll learn to lead a life of community service.** In its broadest sense, **community service** involves making contributions to the society and community in which you live. College provides you with the opportunity to become involved in community service activities. Furthermore, **service learning** courses, which allow students to engage in community service activities while getting course credit, may be part of your college experience.
- **You'll make learning a lifelong habit.** Higher education isn't the end of your education. There's no job you'll have that won't change over time, and you'll be required to learn new skills. College starts you down the path to lifelong learning.
- **You'll understand the meaning of your own contributions to the world.** No matter who you are, you are poised to make your own contributions to society and the

community service
Making contributions to the society and community in which you live.

service learning
Courses that allow a student to engage in community service activities while getting course credit for the experience.

Journal Reflections

My School Experiences

Throughout this text, you will be given opportunities to write down your thoughts. These opportunities—called **Journal Reflections**—offer a chance to think critically about the chapter topics and record your personal reactions to them. As you create your reflections, be honest—with yourself and with your instructor.

Completing these Journal Reflections provides a variety of benefits. Not only will you be able to mull over your past and present academic experiences, you'll begin to see patterns in the kinds of difficulties—and successes!—you encounter. You'll be able to apply solutions that worked in one situation to others. And one added benefit: You'll get practice in writing.

If you save these entries and return to them later, you may be surprised at the changes they record over the course of the term. You can either write them out and keep an actual journal, or create your journal electronically.

1. Think of one of the successful experiences you've had during your previous years in school. What was it?

2. What made the experience successful? What did you learn from your success?

3. Think of an experience you had in school that did not go as you had hoped, and briefly describe it. Why did it occur?

4. What could you have done differently to make it successful? What did you learn from it?

5. Based on these experiences of academic success and failure, what general lessons did you learn that could help you be a more successful student in the future?

world. Higher education provides you with a window to the past, present, and future, and it allows you to understand the significance of your own contributions. Your college education provides you with a compass to discover who you are, where you've been, and where you're going.

In short, there are numerous benefits for attending college. To help you attain these benefits, it's time to introduce you to a process that will help you achieve success, both in college and in life beyond: P.O.W.E.R. Learning.

» LO 1-2 P.O.W.E.R. Learning: The Five Key Steps to Achieving Success

P.O.W.E.R. Learning
A system designed to help people achieve their goals, based on five steps: Prepare, Organize, Work, Evaluate, and Rethink.

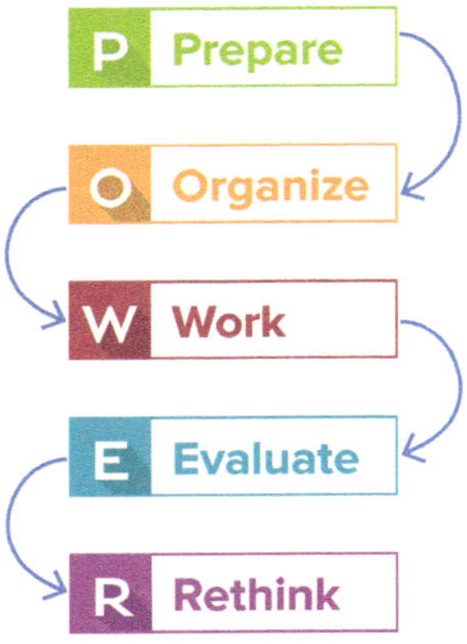

P.O.W.E.R. Plan

P.O.W.E.R. Learning is an *acronym*—a word formed from the first letters of a series of steps—that will help you take in, process, and make use of the information you'll acquire in college. It will help you to achieve your goals, both while you are in college and later, after you graduate.

Prepare, **O**rganize, **W**ork, **E**valuate, and **R**ethink. That's it. It's a simple framework but an effective one. Using the systematic framework that P.O.W.E.R. Learning provides (which is illustrated in the *P.O.W.E.R. Plan* diagram) will increase your chances of success at any task, from writing a college paper to purchasing your weekly groceries.

Keep this in mind: P.O.W.E.R. Learning isn't a product that you can simply pull off a bookshelf and use without thinking. P.O.W.E.R. Learning is a process, and you are the only one who can make it succeed. Without your personal investment in the process, P.O.W.E.R. Learning consists of just words on paper.

Relax, though. You already know each of the elements of P.O.W.E.R. Learning, and you may discover that you are already putting this process, or parts of it, to work for you. You've graduated from high school and been accepted into college. You may have also held down a job, had a first date, and registered to vote. Each of these accomplishments required that you use strategies of P.O.W.E.R. Learning. What you'll be doing throughout this book is becoming more aware of these strategies and how they can be used to help you in situations you will encounter in college and beyond.

P Prepare

Chinese philosopher Lao Tzu said that travelers taking a long journey must begin with a single step.

But before they even take that first step, travelers need to know several things: what their destination is, how they're going to get there, how they'll know when they reach the destination, and what they'll do if they have trouble along the way. In the same way, you need to know where you're headed as you embark on the intellectual journeys involved in college. Whether it be a major, long-term task, such as college attendance, or a more limited activity, such as getting ready to complete a paper due in the near future, you'll need to prepare for the journey.

Setting Goals

Before we seek to accomplish any task, all of us do some form of planning. The trouble is that most of the time such planning is done without conscious thinking, as if we are on autopilot. However, the key to success is to make sure that planning is systematic.

The best way to plan systematically is to use goal-setting strategies. In many cases, goals are clear and direct. It's obvious that our goal in washing dishes is to have the dishes end up clean. We know that our goal at the gas station is to fill the car's tank with gas. We go to the post office to buy stamps and mail letters.

Other goals are not so clear-cut. In fact, larger and more complicated tasks (such as going to college) may involve a variety of different kinds of goals.

What's the best way to set appropriate goals? Here are some guidelines:

- **Set both long-term and short-term goals. Long-term goals** are aims relating to major accomplishments that take some time to achieve. **Short-term goals** are relatively limited steps you would take on the road to accomplishing your long-term goals. For example, one of the primary reasons you're in college is to achieve the long-term goal of getting a degree. But to reach that goal, you have to accomplish a series of short-term goals, such as completing a set of required courses, taking a series of elective courses, and choosing a major. Even these short-term goals can be broken down into shorter-term goals. In order to complete a required course, for instance, you have to accomplish short-term goals, such as completing a paper, taking several tests, and so on. For practice in setting long- and short-term goals, complete **Try It! 2**.

long-term goals
Aims relating to major accomplishments that take some time to achieve.

short-term goals
Relatively limited steps toward the accomplishment of long-term goals.

- **Recognize that who you are determines your goals.** Goal setting starts with knowing yourself. As you'll see later when we focus on understanding yourself and your values—those qualities that you hold most desirable—it is self-knowledge that tells you what is and is not important to you. This understanding of yourself will help you keep your goals in focus and your motivation up when things get tough.

> "Goal setting, as far as I can see it, is simply a state of mind, a way of thinking about things. A goal setter makes sure he accomplishes what he needs to accomplish."
>
> Gottesman, G. (1994). *College Survival.* NY: Macmillan. P. 70.

- **Make sure goals are realistic and reasonably attained.** We'd all like to win Olympic gold medals or be multimillionaires or write best-selling novels. Few of us are likely to achieve such goals. Be honest with yourself. There is nothing wrong with having big dreams. But it is important to be realistically aware of all that it takes to achieve them. If our long-term goals are unrealistic and we don't achieve them, the big danger is that we may wrongly reason that we are inept and lack ability and use this as an excuse for giving up. If goals are realistic, we can develop a plan to attain them, spurring us on to attain more.
- **State goals in terms of behavior that can be measured against current accomplishments.** Goals should represent some measurable change from a current set of circumstances. We want our behavior to change in some way that can usually be expressed in terms of quantities—to show an increase ("raise my grade point average 10 percent") or a decrease ("reduce wasted time by two hours each week") or to be maintained ("keep in touch with my out-of-town friends by sending four text messages each month"), developed ("participate in one workshop on critical thinking"), or restricted ("reduce my phone expenses 10 percent by speaking and texting less").
- **Choose goals that involve behavior over which you have control.** We all want world peace and an end to poverty. Few of us have the resources or capabilities to bring either about. On the other hand, it is realistic to want to work in small ways to help others, such as by becoming a Big Brother or Big Sister or by volunteering at a local food bank.
- **Take ownership of your goals.** Make sure that the goals you choose are your goals, and not the goals of your parents, teachers, brothers and sisters, or friends. If you're

College is not an end-point, but part of a lifelong journey.

2 WHAT ARE YOUR GOALS?

Try It! P O W E R

Before you begin any journey, you need to know where you are going. To plan your academic journey—and your later career—you first need to set goals. *Short-term goals* are relatively limited objectives that bring you closer to your ultimate goal. *Long-term goals* are aims relating to major accomplishments that take more time to achieve.

In this *Try It*, think about your short- and long-term academic goals for a few minutes, and then list them. Because short-term goals are based on what you want to accomplish in the long term, first identify your long-term goals. Then list the short-term goals that will help you reach your long-term goals. An example is provided for each kind of goal:

Long-Term Goal #1: Get a college degree

Related Short-Term Goals:

- Complete four courses with a grade of B or above each term.
- ________________
- ________________
- ________________
- ________________

Long-Term Goal #2: ________________

Related Short-Term Goals:

- ________________
- ________________
- ________________
- ________________
- ________________
- ________________

Long-Term Goal #3: ________________

Related Short-Term Goals:

- ________________
- ________________
- ________________
- ________________
- ________________

Long-Term Goal #4: ________________

Related Short-Term Goals:

- ________________
- ________________
- ________________
- ________________
- ________________

Long-Term Goal #5: ________________

Related Short-Term Goals:

- ________________
- ________________
- ________________
- ________________
- ________________

After you complete the chart, consider how easy or difficult it was to identify your long-term goals. How many of your long-term goals relate to college, and how many to your future career? Do any of your short-term goals relate to more than one long-term goal?

attending college only because others have told you to, and you have no commitment of your own, you'll find it hard to maintain the enthusiasm—not to mention the hard work—required to succeed.

- **Identify how your short-term goals fit with your long-term goals.** Your goals should not be independent of one another. Instead, they should fit together into a larger dream of who you want to be. Every once in a while, step back and consider how what you're doing today relates to the kind of person you would ultimately like to be.

To get more practice in using these goal-setting principles, consider the goals that underlie taking a particular college class in which you are currently enrolled. You probably have several goals for each course you are taking this term. Completing **Try It! 3** will give you a chance to evaluate them.

O Organize

By determining where you want to go and expressing your goals in terms that can be measured, you have already made a lot of progress. But there's another step you must take on the road to success.

The second step in P.O.W.E.R. Learning is to organize the tools you'll need to accomplish your goals. Building upon the goal-setting work you've undertaken in the preparation stage, it's time to determine the best way to accomplish the goals you've identified.

How do you do this? Suppose you've decided to build a set of bookshelves for one room in your house. Let's say that you've already determined the kind of bookshelves you like and figured out the basic characteristics of the ones you will build (the preparation step in P.O.W.E.R. Learning). The next stage involves gathering the necessary tools, buying the wood and other building materials, sorting the construction supplies, and preparing the room for the shelving project—all aspects of organizing for the task.

Similarly, your academic success will hinge to a large degree on the thoroughness of your organization for each academic task that you face. In fact, one of the biggest mistakes that students make in college is plunging into an academic project—studying for a test, writing a paper, completing an in-class assignment—without being organized.

The Two Kinds of Organization: Physical and Mental

On a basic level is *physical organization* involving the mechanical aspects of task completion. For instance, you need to ask yourself if you have the appropriate tools, such as pens, paper, and a calculator. If you're using a computer, do you have access to the Internet and will you need to use a printer? Do you have a way to back up your files? Do you have the books and other materials you'll need to complete the assignment? Will the campus bookstore be open if you need anything else? Will the library be open when you need it? Do you have a comfortable place to work?

Mental organization is even more critical. Mental organization is accomplished by considering and reviewing the academic skills that you'll need to successfully complete the task at hand. You are an academic general in command of

3 COURSE GOALS

Try It! P O W E R

Think about one of the classes that you are taking this term. List your goals for the class in the first column below:

Goals for Class	Goals in Order of Importance
____	__________
____	__________
____	__________
____	__________
____	__________
____	__________
____	__________
____	__________

The goals you've listed most likely range from the specific ("passing the class with a good grade") to the more general and vague ("becoming educated in the subject matter of the class").

Now, rank order them to determine which are the most important to you. Note that some of these goals may be short-term goals ("get a decent grade") and some represent longer-term goals ("complete all college requirements"). In addition, your goals may be specific ("get an A in the course") or relatively vague ("do well in the class").

Now consider the following:

- What is the difference between those goals that are most important to you and those that are least important to you?
- Are your goals mostly short-term or long-term?
- How specific are your goals?
- What implications might your different goals have for your future success in the course?

WORKING IN A GROUP

Compare your goals for the course with those of other students and consider the similarities and differences.

considerable forces; you will need to make sure your forces—the basic skills you have at your command—are at their peak of readiness.

For example, if you're working on a math assignment, you'll want to consider the basic math skills that you'll need and brush up on them. Just actively thinking about this will help you organize mentally. Similarly, you'd want to mentally review your understanding of the causes of the American Civil War before beginning an assignment on the Reconstruction period that followed the war.

Why does producing mental organization matter? Because it provides a context for when you actually begin to work. Organizing paves the way for better subsequent learning of new material.

Too often students are in a hurry to meet a deadline and figure they'd better just dive in and get it done. Organizing can actually *save* you time, because you're less likely to be anxious and end up losing your way as you work to complete your task.

Much of this book is devoted to strategies for determining—*before* you begin work on a task—how to develop the mental tools for completing an assignment.

Looking at the Big Picture

It's natural to view a college course as a series of small tasks—classes to attend, a certain number of pages to read each week, a few papers due during the term, three quizzes and a final exam to study for, and so on.

But such a perspective may lead you to miss what the course, as a whole, is all about. Using the P.O.W.E.R. framework can help you take the long view of a course, considering how the class helps you achieve your long- and short-term goals (the *Prepare* step) and what you'll need to do to maximize your success in it (the *Organize* step). By preparing and organizing even before you step foot in the classroom for the first time, you'll be able to consider what it is that you want to get out of the course and how it fits into your education as a whole.

However, as you'll see, all of these strategies share a common theme: that success comes not from a trial-and-error approach but from following a systematic plan for achievement. Of course, this does not mean that there will be no surprises along the way, nor that simple luck is never a factor in great accomplishments. But it does mean that we often can make our own luck through careful preparation and organization.

W Work

You're ready. The preliminaries are out of the way. You've prepared and you've organized. Now it's time to get started actually doing the work.

In some ways work is the easy part, because–if you conscientiously carried out the preparation and organization stages–you should know exactly where you're headed and what you need to do to get there.

It's not quite so easy, of course. How effectively you'll get down to the business at hand depends on many factors. Some may be out of your control. There may be a power outage that closes down the library or a massive traffic jam that delays your getting to campus. But most factors are–or should be–under your control. Instead of getting down to work, you may find yourself thinking up "useful" things to do–like finally hanging that poster that's been rolled up in a corner for three months–or simply sitting captive in front of the TV. This kind of obstacle to work relates to motivation.

Finding the Motivation to Work

"If only I could get more motivated, I'd do so much better with my ________" (fill in the blank: *schoolwork, diet, exercising,* or something similar).

All of us have said something like this at one time or another. We use the concept of **motivation**–or its lack–to explain why we just don't work hard at a task. But when we do that, we're fooling ourselves. We all have some motivation, that inner power and psychological energy that directs and fuels our behavior. Without any motivation, we'd never get out of bed in the morning.

motivation
The inner power and psychological energy that directs and fuels behavior.

We've also seen evidence of how strong our motivation can be. Perhaps you love to work out at the gym. Or maybe your love of music helped you learn to play the guitar, making practicing for hours a pleasure rather than a chore. Or perhaps you're a single mother, juggling work, school, and family, and you get up early every morning to make breakfast for your kids before they go off to school.

All of us are motivated. The key to success in and out of the classroom is to tap into, harness, and direct that motivation.

In one sense, then, everything you'll encounter in this book can help you improve your use of the motivation that you already have. But there's a key concept that underlies the control of motivation—viewing success as a consequence of effort:

Effort ⟶ Success

Suppose, for example, you've gotten a good grade on your midterm. The instructor beams at you as she hands back your test. How do you feel?

You will undoubtedly be pleased, of course. But at the same time you might think to yourself, "Don't get too cocky. It was just luck. If she'd asked other questions, I would have been in trouble." Or perhaps you explain your success by thinking, "Pretty easy test."

If you often think this way—and you can find out if you do by completing **Try It! 4**—you're cheating yourself. Using this kind of reasoning when you succeed, instead of patting yourself on the back and thinking with satisfaction, "All my hard work really paid off," is sure to undermine your future success.

A great deal of psychological research has shown that thinking you have no control over what happens to you sends a powerful and damaging message to your self-esteem—that you are powerless to change things. Just think of how different it feels to say to yourself, "Wow, I worked at it and did it," as compared with "I lucked out" or "It was so easy that anybody could have done well."

In the same way, we can delude ourselves when we try to explain our failures. People who see themselves as the victims of circumstance may tell themselves, "I'm just not smart enough" when they don't do well on an academic task. Or they might say, "Those other students don't have to work five hours a day."

The way in which we view the causes of success and failure is, in fact, directly related to our success. Students who generally see effort and hard work as the reason behind their performance usually do better in college. It's not hard to see why: When they are working on an assignment, they feel that the greater the effort they put forth, the greater their chances of success. So they work harder. They believe that they have control over their success, and if they fail, they believe they can do better in the future.

> "The function of the university is not simply to teach bread-winning, or to furnish teachers for the public schools or to be a center of polite society; it is, above all, to be the organ of that fine adjustment between real life and the growing knowledge of life, an adjustment which forms the secret of civilization."
>
> **W.E.B. DuBois, author, *The Souls of Black Folk*, 1903.**

Developing a Growth Mindset and Grit

Do you think some people are born smart and are destined to be high achievers, while others—maybe even yourself—don't have enough intelligence to ever do really well in school?

If you believe this, you need to think again. Intelligence is something that is not fixed. Instead, it is fluid and flexible, and through hard work and effort, people can

4 PERSONAL STYLES **Try It!** P.O.W.E.R

Who's in Charge?

To get a sense of your ideas of why things happen to you, check the statement from each of the pairs below that best describes your views:[2]

- ☐ 1a. In the long run, people get the respect they deserve in this world.
- ☐ 1b. Unfortunately, an individual's worth often passes unrecognized no matter how hard he or she tries.

- ☐ 2a. The idea that teachers are unfair to students is nonsense.
- ☐ 2b. Most students don't realize the extent to which their exam results are influenced by accidental happenings.

- ☐ 3a. I have often found that what is going to happen will happen.
- ☐ 3b. Trusting fate has never turned out as well for me as making a decision to take a definite course of action.

- ☐ 4a. In the case of the well-prepared student, there is rarely if ever such a thing as an unfair exam.
- ☐ 4b. Many times exam questions tend to be so unrelated to course work that studying is really useless.

- ☐ 5a. Becoming a success is a matter of hard work; luck has little or nothing to do with it.
- ☐ 5b. Getting a good job depends mainly on being in the right place at the right time.

- ☐ 6a. It is not always wise to plan too far ahead because many things turn out to be a matter of good or bad fortune anyhow.
- ☐ 6b. When I make plans, I am almost certain that I can make them work.

- ☐ 7a. In my case, getting what I want has little or nothing to do with luck.
- ☐ 7b. Many times I might just as well decide what to do by flipping a coin.

- ☐ 8a. Many times I feel that I have little influence over the things that happen to me.
- ☐ 8b. It is impossible for me to believe that chance or luck plays an important role in my life.

- ☐ 9a. What happens to me is my own doing.
- ☐ 9b. Sometimes I feel that I don't have enough control over the direction my life is taking.

- ☐ 10a. Sometimes I can't understand how teachers arrive at the marks they give.
- ☐ 10b. There is a direct connection between how hard a person studies and the grades he or she gets.

Scoring: Give yourself one point for each of the following answers and then add up your score:

1. a. 2. a. 3. b. 4. a. 5. a. 6. b. 7. a. 8. b. 9. a. 10 b.

Your total score can range from 0 to 10. The higher your score, the more you believe that you have a strong influence over what happens to you and are in control of your life and your own behavior. The lower your score, the more you believe that your life is outside of your control and what happens to you is caused by luck or fate.

If you score below 5 on this questionnaire, consider how rethinking your views of the causes of behavior might lead to greater success. In addition, consider how your values might influence your success.

do better than they ever thought possible. In fact, the brain is like any muscle: The more you use it, the stronger it becomes.

Students who hold a **growth mindset** believe that individual characteristics, such as intelligence, talent, and motivation, can improve through hard work. They challenge themselves to try to increase their success, even if at first they fail. They are more persistent in the face of obstacles, and they try harder.

growth mindset
The belief that individual characteristics, such as intelligence, talent, and motivation, can improve through hard work.

©Shutterstock/Air Images

grit
Perseverance and passion for long-term goals.

fixed mindset
The erroneous belief that individual characteristics, such as intelligence, talent, and motivation, are set at birth and vary little throughout the life span.

Students holding a growth mindset have **grit**, perseverance and passion for long-term goals. They think about the goals they want to accomplish, and they are passionate about achieving those goals.

In contrast, those with a **fixed mindset** erroneously believe that individual characteristics, such as intelligence, talent, and motivation, are set at birth and vary little throughout the life span. Students with fixed mindsets may label themselves as "not smart" or "incompetent," rather than believing that with effort they can do better.

Can you develop a growth mindset and avoid a fixed mindset? The answer is yes. By telling yourself that success is the result of effort, not of how smart you are, you are more likely to do better on tasks in the future. Remember, success is about analyzing the causes of your performance, and thinking about how you might do things differently to bring about a better outcome. It's a matter of motivation.

Energizing Your Motivation and Grit

Here are some tips for keeping your motivation alive, so you can work with your full energy behind you:

- **Take responsibility for your failures–and successes.** When you do poorly on a test, don't blame the teacher, the textbook, or a job that kept you from studying. Don't say you're not smart enough. Instead, analyze the situation, and see how you could have changed what you did to be more successful in the future. At the same time, when you're successful, think of the things you did to bring about that success.
- **Think positively.** Assume that the strengths that you have will allow you to succeed and that, if you have difficulty, you can figure out what to do, or get the help you need to eventually succeed.
- **Accept that you can't control everything.** Seek to understand which things can be changed and which cannot. You might be able to get an extension on a paper due date, but you are probably not going to be excused from a college-wide requirement.
- **Develop a growth mindset and cultivate your grit.** Keep in mind that you aren't born with a fixed level of intelligence and talent that determine your future success. Instead, we all are capable of growth and improvement, which comes from effort, determination, and working hard. Cultivate your grit, thinking about the passion you have for your goals and why it is necessary to persevere to accomplish those goals.

To further explore the causes of academic success, consider the questions in **Try It! 5**, and then discuss them with your classmates.

E Evaluate

"Great, I'm done with the work. Now I can move on."

It's natural to feel relief when you've finished the work necessary to fulfill the basic requirements of an assignment. After all, if you've written the five

5  WORKING IN A GROUP

Try It! P O W E R

Examining the Causes of Success and Failure

Complete this Try It while working in a group. First, consider the following situations:

1. Although he studied for a few hours the night before his biology test, Jack gets a D on a midterm. When he finds out his grade, he is disgusted and says to himself, "I'm just not smart enough, and I'll probably never do any better in this course. I might as well just blow it off for the rest of the term and put my energies into my other classes."
2. Anne gets an A– on her history exam. She is happy, but when her instructor tells the class that they did well as a group and that the average grade was B+, she decides that she did well only because the test was so easy.
3. Chen gets a C on his first math quiz. Because he didn't do as well as he expected, he vows to perform better the next time. He doubles the amount of time he studies for the next quiz, but still his grade is only slightly higher. Distressed, he considers dropping the class because he thinks that he'll never be successful in math.

Now consider the following questions about each of the situations:

1. What did each student conclude was the main cause of his or her performance?
2. What effect does this conclusion seem to have on the student?
3. Taking an outsider's point of view, what would *you* think was the main cause of the student's performance?
4. What advice would you give each student?

Now consider these broader questions:

1. What are the most important reasons some students are more academically successful in college than others?
2. How much does ability determine success? How much does luck determine success? How much do circumstances determine success?
3. If someone performs poorly on an exam, what are the possible reasons for his or her performance? If someone performs well on an exam, what are the possible reasons for his or her performance? Is it harder to find reasons for good compared with poor performance? Why?

double-spaced pages required for an assignment, why shouldn't you heave a sigh of relief and just hand your paper in to the instructor?

The answer is that if you stop at this point, you'll almost be guaranteed a mediocre grade. Do you think Shakespeare dashed off the first draft of *Hamlet* and, without another glance, sent it off to the Globe Theater for production? Do professional athletes just put in the bare minimum of practice to get ready for a big game? Think of one of your favorite songs. Do you think the composer wrote it in one sitting and then performed it in a concert?

In every case, the answer is no. Even the greatest creation does not emerge in perfect form, immediately meeting all the goals of its producer. Consequently, the fourth step in the P.O.W.E.R. process is **evaluation**, which consists of determining how well the product or activity we have created matches our goals for it. Let's consider some steps to follow in evaluating what you've accomplished:

evaluation
An assessment of the match between a product or activity and the goals it was intended to meet.

- **Take a moment to congratulate yourself and feel some satisfaction.** Whether it's been studying for a test, writing a paper, preparing a review sheet, or reading an assignment, you've done something important. You've moved from ground zero to a spot that's closer to your goal.

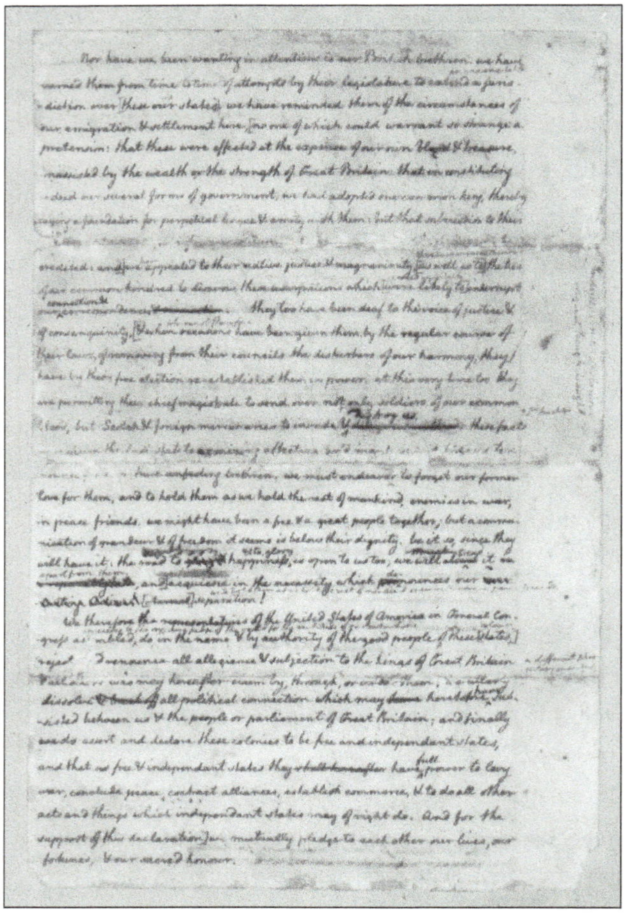

Even the Declaration of Independence underwent revisions before the final version was signed.

- **Compare what you've accomplished with the goals you're seeking to achieve.** Think back to the goals, both short-term and long-term, that you're seeking to achieve. How closely does what you've done match what you're aiming to do? For instance, if your short-term goal is to complete a statistics problem set with no errors, you'll need to check over the paper carefully to make sure you've made no mistakes.
- **Have an out-of-body experience: Evaluate your accomplishments as if you were a respected teacher from your past.** If you've written a paper, reread it from the perspective of that teacher. If you've completed a worksheet, think about what comments you'd write across the top if you were that teacher.
- **Evaluate what you've done as if you were your current instructor.** Now exchange bodies and minds again. This time, consider what you're doing from the perspective of the instructor who gave you the assignment. How would he or she react to what you've done? Have you followed the assignment to the letter? Is there anything you've missed?
- **Be fair to yourself.** The guidelines for evaluation will help you determine just how much further work is necessary and, even more important, what work is necessary. Don't go too far, though: It's as counterproductive to be too hard on yourself as it is to be too easy. Stick to a middle ground, always keeping your final goal in mind.
- **Based on your evaluation, revise your work.** If you're honest with yourself, it's unlikely that your first work will satisfy you. So go back to *Work* and revise what you've done. But don't think of it as a step back: Revisions you make as a consequence of your evaluation bring you closer to your final goal. This is a case where going back moves you forward.

R Rethink

They thought they had it perfect. But they were wrong.

In fact, it was a $1.5 billion mistake—a blunder on a grand scale. The finely ground mirror of the Hubble space telescope, designed to provide an unprecedented glimpse into the vast reaches of the universe, was not so finely ground after all.

Despite an elaborate system of evaluation designed to catch any flaws, there was a tiny blemish in the mirror that was not detected until the telescope had been launched into space and started to send back blurry photographs. By then, it seemed too late to fix the mirror.

Or was it? NASA engineers rethought the problem for months, devising, and then discarding, one potential fix after another. Finally, after bringing a fresh eye to the situation, they formulated a daring solution that involved sending a team of astronauts into space. Once there, a space-walking Mr. Goodwrench would install several new mirrors in the telescope, which could refocus the light and compensate for the original flawed mirror.

Although the engineers could not be certain that the $629 million plan would work, it seemed like a good solution, at least on paper. It was not until the first photos were beamed back to Earth, though, that NASA knew their solution was A-OK. These photos were spectacular.

It took months of reconsideration before NASA scientists could figure out what went wrong and devise a solution to the problem they faced. Their approach exemplifies—on a grand scale—the final step in P.O.W.E.R. Learning: rethinking.

To *rethink* what you've accomplished earlier means bringing a fresh—and clear—eye to what you've done. It involves using **critical thinking**, thinking that involves reanalyzing, questioning, and challenging our underlying assumptions.

Whereas evaluation means considering how well what you have done matches your initial goals, rethinking means reconsidering not only the outcome of your efforts but also your goals and the ideas and the process you've used to reach them. Critically rethinking what you've done involves analyzing and synthesizing ideas and seeing the connections between different concepts.

Rethinking involves considering whether your initial goals are practical and realistic or if they require modification. It also entails asking yourself what you would do differently if you could do it over again.

We'll be considering critical thinking throughout this book, examining specific strategies in every chapter. For the moment, the following steps provide a general framework for using critical thinking to rethink what you've accomplished:

- **Review how you've accomplished the task.** Consider the approach and strategies you've used. What seemed to work best? Do they suggest any alternatives that might work better the next time?
- **Question the outcome.** Take a "big picture" look at what you have accomplished. Are you pleased and satisfied? Is there something you've somehow missed?
- **Identify your underlying assumptions, then challenge them.** Consider the assumptions you made in initially approaching the task. Are these underlying assumptions reasonable? If you had used different assumptions, would the result have been similar or different?
- **Consider alternatives rejected earlier.** You've likely discarded possible strategies and approaches prior to completing your task. Now's the time to think about those approaches once more and determine if they might have been more appropriate than the road you've followed.
- **Ask yourself: What would I do differently if I had the opportunity to try things again?** It's not too late to change course.
- **Finally, reconsider your initial goals.** Are they achievable and realistic? Do your goals, and the strategies you used to attain them, need to be modified? Critically rethinking the objectives and goals that underlie your efforts is often the most effective route to success.

The daring mission to repair the Hubble space telescope was the culmination of months of rethinking how to fix a flaw in the telescope. It worked: A new time-lapse movie of images taken by the telescope showed the seasonal changes on Uranus, as well as other celestial wonders.
Source: NASA

critical thinking
A process involving reanalysis, questioning, and challenge of underlying assumptions.

Completing the P.O.W.E.R. Process

The rethinking step of P.O.W.E.R. Learning is meant to help you understand your process of work and to improve the final product if necessary. But mostly it is meant to help you grow, to become better at whatever it is you've been doing. Like a painter looking at his or her finished work, you may see a spot here or there to touch up, but don't destroy the canvas. Perfectionism can be as paralyzing as laziness. Keep in mind these key points:

- **Know that there's always another day.** Your future success does not depend on any single assignment, paper, or test. Don't fall victim to self-defeating thoughts such as "If I don't do well on this test, I'll never graduate" or "Everything is riding on this one assignment." Nonsense. There is almost always an opportunity to recover from a failure.
- **Realize that deciding when to stop work is often as hard as getting started.** Knowing when you have put in enough time studying for a test, or have revised a paper sufficiently, or have reviewed your answers adequately on a math problem set is as much a key to success as properly preparing. If you've carefully evaluated what you've done and seen that there's a close fit between your goals and your work, it's time to stop work and move on.
- **Use the strategies that already work for you.** Although the P.O.W.E.R. framework provides a proven approach to attaining success, employing it does not mean that you should abandon strategies that have brought you success in the past. Using multiple approaches, and personalizing them, is the surest road to success.

» LO 1-3 Are You Ready for College Success?

Maybe you're asking yourself why you should bother with P.O.W.E.R. Learning and the techniques that will be described in this book. You may believe that because you did OK in high school, you'll be just fine in college without changing the way you did things there.

But college isn't high school.

In high school, you were probably told what you needed to learn from assignments; in college, it will be up to you to read and understand assignments on your own. You'll be tested on material in college that your instructor may never have mentioned in class, but that appeared in the materials you were told to read.

High school teachers monitored your class attendance and graded all homework; in college, professors may not take attendance and may not look at every bit of homework—although they expect you to be in class and do all homework. And while you may be used to frequent tests in high school, in college you may have only a few exams, covering large chunks of material.

In high school, your time was mostly structured by others; in college, you have to manage it yourself. In a broader sense, in high school, you were told what your responsibilities were, while in college you're viewed as an adult who needs to figure out on your own what your responsibilities are.

In addition to differences in the style of instruction between high school and college, you're different, too. Whether you finished high school a few months ago or you deferred college and are returning after a lapse of many years, you are not the same person you were in high school. College offers a fresh start, with instructors who have no predetermined expectations about who you are.

Career Connections

P.O.W.E.R. Learning Meets the World of Work

Although the focus of the P.O.W.E.R. Learning system is on developing school success, its applications extend well beyond the classroom. In particular, the principles of P.O.W.E.R. Learning are useful in the world of work, and your ability to use them will provide you with keys to success in the workplace.

Skeptical? In **Career Connections** boxes in future chapters we'll explore how the principles we're discussing can help you choose an appropriate career and excel in the workplace. For now, though, take a look at these "help wanted" advertisements and online postings. They illustrate the importance of the components of P.O.W.E.R. Learning in the workplace.

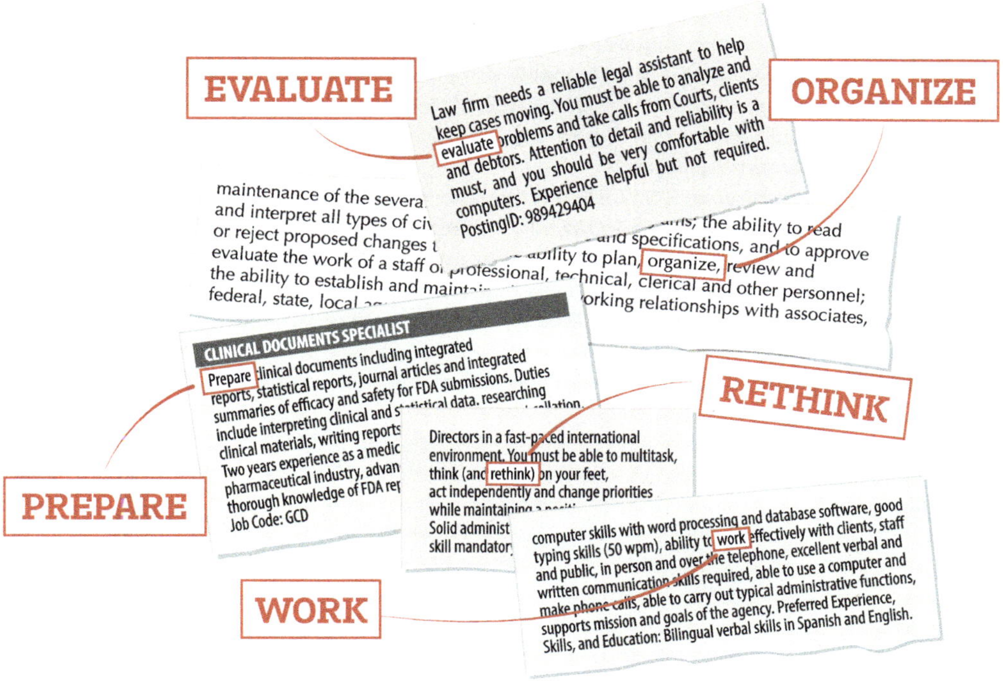

But in order to get that fresh start, you need to have a clear sense of your own strengths and weaknesses. Accurately knowing who you are, and your own competencies, can help you focus on those strategies presented in future chapters that will be most beneficial to you. To get a more objective sense of your own strong and weak points, complete **Try It! 6**.

Ultimately, to become an accomplished student, you must be open to change in yourself and must embrace success. The techniques for doing this are in this book, but only you can implement them. The road to success may not be simple or direct (see the **Speaking of Success** interview with Lev Sviridov later in the chapter for a glimpse of one student's real-life journey), but there are few goals that are more important than attaining a college education.

6 CREATING A P.O.W.E.R. PROFILE

Try It! P O W E R

Are you the student you aspire to be?

Before you can even think about answering that question, you need to know the kind of student you are—right now, at this very moment. Only by frankly facing your current strengths and weaknesses as fully as possible will you be able to know in what direction you should be heading.

To help you get a better understanding of who you are as a student, Try It! 6 will take you through the steps of constructing your own *P.O.W.E.R. Profile.* The P.O.W.E.R. Profile is a way for you to take stock of where you stand in relation to the major topics that we'll be discussing in *P.O.W.E.R. Learning*—the characteristics that are most important for college success.

The P.O.W.E.R. Profile outlines key aspects of who you are. The Profile is just one of many possible profiles that could be drawn to describe you. For instance, you have a personality profile, a buying profile, a dating profile, a technology profile, and a variety of others. There is no "ideal" P.O.W.E.R. Profile; there are no right or wrong answers involved in creating one. Instead, as shown in the example in **Figure 1.2**, the P.O.W.E.R. Profile is a look at someone in relation to the 14 dimensions involved with student success.

The best way to maximize the usefulness of your P.O.W.E.R. Profile is to create one now, before you've gone beyond the first chapter of this book. Then, by completing a P.O.W.E.R. Profile at the end of the term, you can judge how much your profile has changed and in what directions. If you take to heart what you learn in your class and work carefully through the Try It!s in the book and exercises, your profile will undoubtedly change in a positive direction. In the meantime, the P.O.W.E.R. Profile will give you an objective idea of where you stand right now on each of these dimensions.

To get started with your P.O.W.E.R. Profile, read each statement and judge how well it describes you, using these numbered descriptions:

1 = Doesn't describe me at all

2 = Describes me only slightly

3 = Describes me fairly well

4 = Describes me very well

figure 1.2
Sample P.O.W.E.R Profile

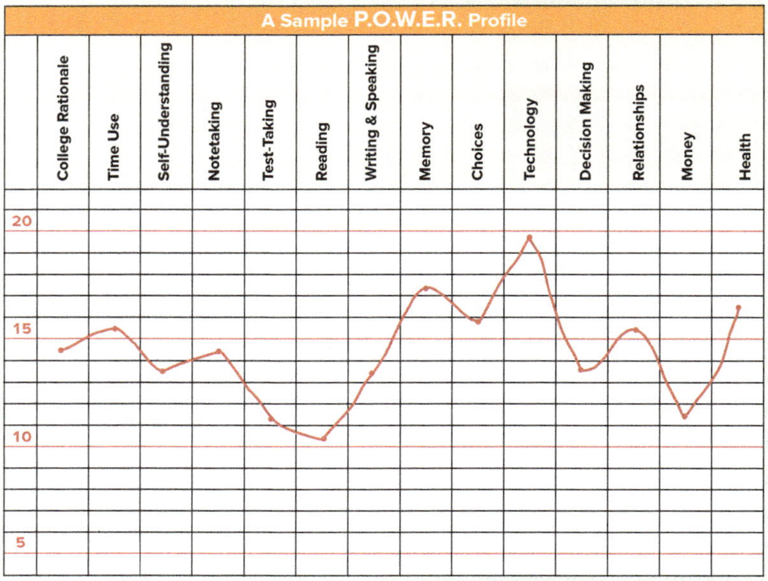

Place your response on the line next to each of the questions. Take your time; answer the questions thoughtfully and, above all, truthfully. There are no right or wrong answers. Remember that the profile is not a test; it is for your own enlightenment only.

Dimension 1: College Rationale	
a. I understand why attending college is important to me. b. I have clear short-term and long-term goals. c. My course selections are related to my goals. d. I know how to organize myself and get my work done. e. I accept that success or failure is in my own hands.	________ ________ ________ ________ ________ **College Rationale Total** ________
Dimension 2: Time Use	
a. I know how to manage my time effectively. b. I understand how to set priorities for my time. c. I know how to say no to time wasters. d. I understand how to avoid procrastination. e. I consider myself to be a good time organizer.	________ ________ ________ ________ ________ **Time Use Total** ________
Dimension 3: Self-Understanding	
a. I understand how I learn most effectively. b. I know how learning styles can affect academic success. c. I have a clear self-concept and understand who I am. d. I have a good sense of self-esteem. e. I know how to use a personal mission statement to guide important decisions.	________ ________ ________ ________ ________ **Self-Understanding Total** ________
Dimension 4: Notetaking	
a. I take good notes during class lectures and discussions. b. My notes capture the speaker's main points. c. I know how to use active listening to focus in class. d. I can take good notes on what I read for my courses. e. I review my notes soon after I have written them.	________ ________ ________ ________ ________ **Notetaking Total** ________
Dimension 5: Test Taking	
a. I generally go to tests well prepared and reasonably calm. b. I understand how to tackle different kinds of test questions. c. I know how to control anxiety before and during testing. d. I usually leave time at the end of a test to check my work. e. I know how to use test results to improve my future test taking.	________ ________ ________ ________ ________ **Test-Taking Total** ________
Dimension 6: Reading	
a. I know my personal reading style and understand how it affects my reading. b. I understand how to use advance organizers in my reading. c. I know my attention span and understand how to stay focused. d. I know how to check for understanding while I read. e. I understand the importance of rereading and rethinking.	________ ________ ________ ________ ________ **Reading Total** ________
Dimension 7: Writing & Speaking	
a. I know how to use the writing process to start and maintain the flow of my writing. b. I understand the importance of considering my audience in writing. c. I know how to outline, write a first draft, and revise my writing. d. I have strategies to overcome my fear of speaking in public. e. I have a good system for impromptu, unprepared oral presentations.	________ ________ ________ ________ ________ **Writing & Speaking Total** ________

(continued)

Try It! POWER

Dimension 8: Memory	
a. I know my preferred memory style and use it to help me study.	______
b. I know about rehearsal and overlearning and use them in my studies.	______
c. I know how to link new information to information that I already possess.	______
d. I am familiar with several memorization techniques.	______
e. I know how to consolidate my memories to improve test performance.	______
	Memory Total ______
Dimension 9: Choices	
a. I understand the options and choices available to me at my college.	______
b. I know where I stand in terms of completing my course requirements.	______
c. I know exactly what to do if there's a problem with my course selections or records.	______
d. I am satisfied that my course choices are moving me in the right direction.	______
e. I am confident that I will choose a major that makes sense in terms of my life goals.	______
	Choices Total ______
Dimension 10: Technology	
a. I understand how to use computer applications effectively for my college work.	______
b. I know how to use the Internet for communication, staying up to date, and research.	______
c. I understand distance learning and know whether or not it's right for me.	______
d. I know how to use library resources and the World Wide Web to gather information.	______
e. I know how to evaluate the accuracy and reliability of information I have found.	______
	Technology Total ______
Dimension 11: Decision Making	
a. I use a structured process for making important decisions.	______
b. I know how to identify my goals and generate alternatives.	______
c. I am good at assessing alternatives and making decisions I am happy with.	______
d. I use an array of strategies for solving problems.	______
e. I understand the most common obstacles to effective critical thinking.	______
	Decision Making Total ______
Dimension 12: Relationships	
a. I understand the importance of diversity on campus and in the broader society.	______
b. I have good relationships with people of many different backgrounds.	______
c. I understand cultural competence and consider myself culturally competent.	______
d. I know what it takes to build good relationships.	______
e. I know how to handle conflict in my relationships.	______
	Relationships Total ______
Dimension 13: Money	
a. I know my short- and long-term financial goals.	______
b. I understand where my money comes from and where it goes.	______
c. I know how to prepare a realistic budget and stick to it.	______
d. I am realistic about the advantages and disadvantages of credit cards.	______
e. I know where to go if I need financial aid for college.	______
	Money Total ______

Dimension 14: Health	
a. I understand stress and know how to cope with it.	_______
b. I understand the importance of a good diet, exercise, and rest.	_______
c. I have strategies for avoiding the abuse of alcohol and other drugs.	_______
d. I am responsible about my sexuality and know how to stay sexually healthy.	_______
e. I know where to go to get help with all aspects of my health.	**Health Total** _______

Now you're ready to construct your P.O.W.E.R. Profile. Add up the numbers on each line to derive a total for each dimension. This total will range from 5 to 20. Finally, place a dot in each appropriate box on the chart in **Figure 1.3** corresponding to your score, and connect the dots to form your P.O.W.E.R. Profile.

There—it's done. But it's really just a start. Your P.O.W.E.R. Profile is an objective way to mark the beginning of your journey through college. Its shape will continue to change and evolve the more years of school you have under your belt.

After taking some time to study your P.O.W.E.R. Profile and to maximize its usefulness, consider the following:

- Does your profile seem like an accurate reflection of your strengths and weaknesses as a student? Were there any surprises?
- To be a successful student, what do you think the "ideal" profile would look like?
- Most important, how can you use the results of the P.O.W.E.R. Profile to help you in the future? What are the most important areas for improvement? What strategies might you use to bring about those improvements?

figure 1.3
P.O.W.E.R. Profile

Your P.O.W.E.R. Profile

	College Rationale	Time Use	Self-Understanding	Notetaking	Test-Taking	Reading	Writing & Speaking	Memory	Choices	Technology	Decision Making	Relationships	Money	Health
20														
15														
10														
5														

Speaking *of* Success

Courtesy of Lev Sviridov

NAME: **Lev Sviridov**

SCHOOL: **City College of New York, New York**

MAJOR: **Science**

For Lev Sviridov, a senior at the City College of New York, the road to success was a roundabout one. In one sense it began after the Chernobyl nuclear power plant exploded when he was a young boy in the former Soviet Union. The accident triggered a deep interest in science and research.

Sviridov and his mother fled the Soviet Union in the mid-1990s, fearful of arrest because his mother, a journalist, had exposed some government officials as KGB agents. Coming to the United States with no money, Sviridov needed not only to learn a new language, but to help support himself. In the early years, he picked through garbage cans to find bottles and cans, and he was homeless for a time. But he credits his poverty with creating motivation to succeed.

"The fact that I was broke and working at so many jobs—gardening, moving furniture, tutoring, working in the laboratory—paved the way for having great credentials,"[3] said Sviridov.

Sviridov not only became successful academically in college, earning extraordinary grades, but he was involved in a variety of activities. He served as president of his college student government and was a member of a Russian human rights organization. He also conducted research in computational biophysical chemistry. His academic credentials were so strong that he won one of the highest of academic awards: a Rhodes Scholarship that supported graduate school study.

But even for an excellent student like Sviridov, studying presents challenges. For example, he says, "I consider myself to be a slow reader, so I have to compensate for that." In addition, it is easier for him to absorb information through the spoken word. "I feel that study groups are important," he said. "The only time you really know something is when you can explain it to somebody else. I'm always putting together study groups for this purpose."

How does he maintain his busy schedule and remain successful academically? Sviridov follows a basic strategy. "My approach is that if you do the work that is required of you at a steady pace through the semester, you will be fine," he said. "I just pace myself, go slowly, and make sure I understand the material."

[RETHINK]

- **What were the study skills that were most important in helping Lev Sviridov maintain his success in college?**
- **What do you think Sviridov means when he says that poverty provided the motivation to succeed? Do you think he would have been just as academically successfully if he hadn't been so poor?**

Looking Back

LO 1-1 Explain the benefits of a college education.

- The reason first-year college students most often cite for attending college is to get a better job, and college graduates do earn more on average than nongraduates.
- College also provides many other benefits. These include becoming well educated, learning to think critically and communicate effectively, understanding the interconnections between different areas of knowledge and our place in history and the world, practicing community service, and understanding diversity.

LO 1-2 Identify the basic principles of P.O.W.E.R. Learning.

- P.O.W.E.R. Learning is a systematic approach people can easily learn, using abilities they already possess, to acquire successful habits for learning and achieving personal goals.
- P.O.W.E.R. Learning involves **P**reparation, **O**rganization, **W**ork, **E**valuation, and **R**ethinking.

LO 1-3 Discuss how expert students use P.O.W.E.R. Learning to achieve college success.

- To *prepare,* learners set both long-term and short-term goals, making sure that their goals are realistic, measurable, and under their control—and will lead to their final destination.
- They *organize* the tools they will need to accomplish those goals.
- They get down to *work* on the task at hand. Using their goals as motivation, expert learners also understand that success depends on effort.
- They *evaluate* the work they've done, considering what they have accomplished in comparison with the goals they set for themselves during the preparation stage.
- Finally, they *rethink,* reflecting on the process they've used, taking a fresh look at what they have done, and critically rethinking their goals.

[KEY TERMS AND CONCEPTS]

Community service (p. 4)
Critical thinking (p. 17)
Evaluation (p. 15)
Fixed mindset (p. 14)
Grit (p. 14)
Growth mindset (p. 13)
Long-term goals (p. 7)
Motivation (p. 11)
P.O.W.E.R. Learning (p. 6)
Service learning (p. 4)
Short-term goals (p. 7)

[RESOURCES]

ON CAMPUS

Every college provides a significant number of resources to help its students succeed and thrive, ranging from the activities coordination office to a multicultural center to writing labs. You can check them out on your college's website, in the catalog, or in the phone directory.

For example, here's a list of some typical campus resources, many of which we'll be discussing in future chapters:

- Adult and reentry center
- Advising center
- Alumni office
- Bookstore
- Career center
- Chaplain/religious services
- Childcare center
- Computer labs
- Continuing education
- Disability center (learning or physical disabilities)
- Diversity, inclusion, and cultural support organizations
- Financial aid office
- Fitness center/ gymnasium
- Gender and sexuality resource or support center
- Health center
- Honors program
- Information center
- Intramural sports
- Language lab
- Learning center
- Lost and found
- Math lab
- Multicultural center
- Museum
- Online Education (distance learning) office
- Off-campus housing and services
- Ombudsperson/conflict resolution office
- Police/campus security
- Post office
- Printing center
- Registrar's office
- Residential Life (Housing) office
- School newspaper
- Student Government office
- Student Affairs office
- Student employment center
- Study abroad/ exchange programs
- Testing center
- Veterans Affairs office
- Volunteer services
- Writing lab

If you are commuting to school, your first "official" encounters on campus are likely to be with representatives of the college's Student Affairs office or its equivalent. The Student Affairs office has the goal of maintaining the quality of student life and ensuring that students receive the help they need. Student Affairs personnel often are in charge of student orientation programs that help new students familiarize themselves with their new institution.

If you are living on campus, your first encounter may be with representatives of the residence halls, often called the Residential Life office. Their job is to help you settle in and orient you to campus. Your residence hall also probably has student residential advisors living on every floor; they can give you an insider's view of college life.

Whatever college representatives you deal with during your first days of college, remember that their job is to help you. Don't be shy about asking questions about what you may expect, how to find things, and what you should be doing.

Above all, if you are experiencing any difficulties, be certain to make use of your college's resources. Starting college is one of the biggest transitions that you'll ever experience in life, and it's a time when you should make use of whatever support your college offers.

IN PRINT

For a variety of views of what it takes to be a successful college student, read *How to Survive Your Freshman Year: By Hundreds of College Sophomores, Juniors, and Seniors Who Did,* 5th edition, published by Hundreds of Heads Books (2013).

The Naked Roommate: And 107 Other Issues You Might Run Into in College, 7th edition (Sourcebooks, 2017), offers a wealth of information on college life from a student's vantage point.

Finally, to learn more about who your first-year classmates are across the United States, take a look at Kevin Eagan and colleagues' *The American Freshman: National Norms for Fall 2016* (Higher Education Research Institute, 2017). The book provides a comprehensive look at the attitudes and opinions of first-year college students, based on the results of a national survey.

ON THE WEB

- Here's a useful online guide (**http://scholars.in.gov/wp-content/uploads/2017/10/171025_Scholar_CSG.pdf**) to adjusting to campus life.
- The Learn More Resource Center (**www.learnmoreindiana.org**) provides information on a variety of useful topics regarding adjustment to college life, including comments by students on their experiences. It covers such topics as where to live, how to select classes, how to study and learn, and much more.

The Case of . . .

Clueless in Seattle

It was during the second week of classes that the questioning started. Until then, Roger hadn't thought much about his decision to attend a large state college in a Seattle suburb. It had seemed like a good idea, and he was excited when he was accepted, but he couldn't really pinpoint why he was there.

And that was becoming a problem. As he was walking to class, he began to think about all that had happened to him in the last few weeks. First-year orientation . . . meeting his roommate, and trying to deal with his odd neatness . . . enrolling for classes . . . finding his way around campus . . . meeting an overwhelming number of new people, and trying to figure out where he fit in. Everyone else seemed to know what they were doing. Why didn't he?

It was overwhelming. He wanted to call his parents and tell them to come pick him up. He needed to sit on the porch where it was familiar and comfortable and not overwhelming and try to figure out what he should do. Nothing seemed to make sense. He began to question his decision to attend college. What was he going to do with his life? The question made him feel even more overwhelmed. Did he really need a college degree? With his computer skills, he could probably get a job right away. Hadn't his father's friend told him that he had a job waiting for him whenever he wanted it? At least then he'd be making money.

"Why bother," he thought to himself. "What an expense, and what a hassle. For what?" He realized, to his surprise, he had no real clue as to why he was in college.

1. What arguments could you provide Roger as to the value of a college education?

2. Do you think that Roger's doubts are common? Do people often attend college without thinking about it very much?

3. What might you suggest that Roger do to help deal with his doubts about the value of college?

4. Why might a student's doubts about the value of college be especially strong during the beginning weeks of college?

5. Do you share any of Roger's concerns about the value of a college education? Do you have additional ones? Did you think carefully about the reasons for attending college before you enrolled?

CHAPTER 2

Making the Most of Your Time

Learning Outcomes

By the time you finish this chapter you will be able to

- » LO 2-1 Discuss strategies to manage your time effectively.
- » LO 2-2 Explain ways to balance competing priorities.
- » LO 2-3 Identify ways to deal with surprises and distractions.

As Meadow Baresi stands in the long line at the cafeteria, she mentally goes over the things she needs to get done during the day: *Review notes for the 8:30 a.m. management quiz . . . work on philosophy paper . . . computer sci class at 11:15 a.m . . . pick up ticket receipts from last night's game . . . work at Student Affairs office from 1:00 to 4:00 . . . go to library to research philosophy paper.* She has the nagging feeling that there's something else she needs to do, but she can't put her finger on it.

She finally gets to the head of the line to pay for her bagel, which she's already half devoured. Glancing at a clock as she leaves the Commons, she gives up the thought of getting in some last-minute studying for her management quiz. It will be a minor miracle if she even makes it to class on time.

She's been up less than an hour, and already Meadow is running behind schedule.

©Doreen Kennedy/Alamy

Looking Ahead

Are your days like Meadow's? Are you constantly trying to cram more activities into less time? Do you feel as if you never have enough time?

You're not alone: Most of us wish we had more time to accomplish the things we need to do. However, some people are a lot better at juggling their time than others. What's their secret?

There is no secret. No one has more than 24 hours a day and 168 hours a week. The key to success lies in figuring out our priorities and better using the time we do have.

Time management is like juggling a bunch of tennis balls: For most of us, juggling doesn't come naturally, but it is a skill that can be learned. Not all of us will end up perfect jugglers (whether we are juggling tennis balls or time), but with practice, we can become a lot better at it.

This chapter will give you strategies for improving your time management skills. After first helping you learn to account for the ways you currently use—and misuse—time, it gives you strategies for planning your time, including some ways to deal with the inevitable interruptions and counterproductive personal habits that can sabotage your best intentions. It will provide you with skills that are important not only for success in college but for your future life as well.

We also consider techniques for dealing with competing goals. There are special challenges involved in juggling the priorities of college work with other aspects of life, such as child rearing or holding a job.

» LO 2-1 Time for Success

Without looking up from the screen or page, answer this question: What time is it?

Most people are pretty accurate in their answer. And if you don't know for sure, it's very likely that you can find out. Your cellphone may display the time; there may be a clock on the wall, desk, or computer screen; or maybe you're riding in a car that shows the time in the instrument panel.

Even if you don't have a clock of some sort nearby, your body keeps its own beat. Humans have an internal clock that regulates the beating of our heart, the pace of our breathing, the discharge of chemicals within our bloodstream, and myriad other bodily functions.

Journal Reflections

Where Does My Time Go?

1. On the typical weekday, what time do you wake up? When would you prefer to wake up if you did not have the obligations and responsibilities you currently have?

2. When do you typically go to bed on a typical weekday night? When would you prefer to go to bed if you did not have the obligations and responsibilities you currently have?

3. Would you characterize yourself as a "morning person," who accomplishes the most in the early morning, or more as a "night person," who is most comfortable doing work in the evenings? What implications does this have for your scheduling of classes and when you do the most work?

4. If a day suddenly contained more than 24 hours, how would it change your life? What would you do with the extra time? Do you think you would accomplish more?

5. Generally speaking, how would you characterize your time management skills? What would be the benefit to you personally if you could manage time more effectively? What goals might you accomplish if you had more time at your disposal?

Time is something from which we can't escape. Even if we ignore it, it's still going by, ticking away, second by second, minute by minute, hour by hour. So the main issue in using your time well is, "Who's in charge?" We can allow time to slip by and let it be our enemy. Or we can take control of it and make it our ally.

By taking control of how you spend your time, you'll increase your chances of becoming a more successful student. Perhaps more important, the better you are at managing the time you devote to your studies, the more time you will have to spend on your outside interests. (You can get a sense of your own personal time style by completing **Try It! 1**.)

The goal of time management is *not* to schedule every moment so we become pawns of a timetable that governs our lives. Instead, the goal of time management is to permit us to make informed choices as to how we use our time.

Consequently, instead of letting the day slip by, largely without our awareness, the time management procedures we'll be discussing can make us better able to harness time for our own ends. In short, time management doesn't confine us. On the contrary, it frees us to do the things we want and need to do.

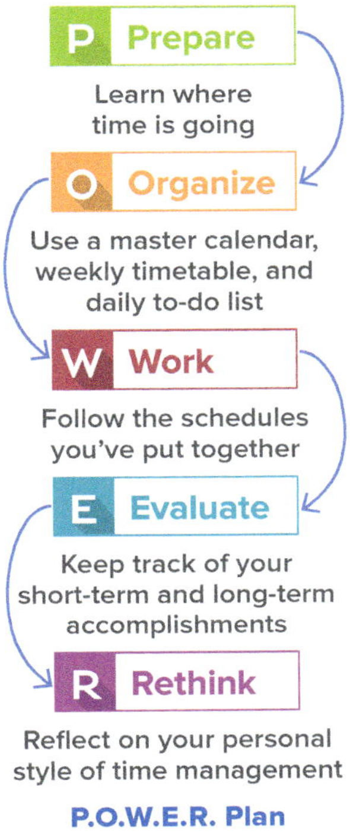

1 PERSONAL STYLES

Try It! POWER

Find Your Time Style

Rate how well each of the statements below describes you. Use this rating scale:

1 = Doesn't describe me at all

2 = Describes me only slightly

3 = Describes me fairly well

4 = Describes me very well

	1	2	3	4
1. I often wake up later than I should.				
2. I am usually late for classes and appointments.				
3. I am always in a rush getting places.				
4. I put off big tasks and assignments until the last minute.				
5. My friends often comment on my lateness.				
6. I am easily interrupted, putting aside what I'm doing for something new.				
7. When I look at a clock, I'm often surprised at how late it is.				
8. I often forget appointments and have to reschedule them.				
9. When faced with a big task, I feel overwhelmed and turn my mind away from it until later.				
10. At the end of the day, I have no idea where the time went.				

Rate yourself by adding up the points you assigned. Use this scale to assess your time style:

10–15 = Very efficient time user

16–20 = Efficient time user

21–30 = Time use needs work

31–40 = Victim of time

P Prepare

Learning Where Time Is Going—and Where It Should Go

Before you get somewhere, you need to know where you're starting from and where you want to go. So the first step in improving your time management skills is figuring out how you're managing your time now.

Create a Time Log

"Where did the day go?" If you've ever said this to yourself, one way of figuring out where you've spent your time is to create a time log. A time log is the most essential tool for improving your use of time.

2 **Try It!** P O W E R

Create a Time Log

Keep track of the way you spend your time across seven days on time logs. Insert the amount of time you spend on each activity during each one-hour period for a single day. Do the same thing for every day of the week on separate time logs. **Be sure to make copies of this log before you fill it in for the first day.**

Analyze your log. After you complete your log for a week, analyze how you spend your time according to the major categories on the log. Add up the amount of time you spend on each category. You can also create other broad categories that eat up significant amounts of time.

Now consider the following:

1. What do you spend most of your time on?

2. Are you satisfied with the way that you are using your time? Are there any areas that seem to use up excessive amounts of time?

3. Do you see some simple fixes that will allow you to use time more effectively?

WORKING IN A GROUP

Compare your use of time during an average week with that of your classmates. What are the major differences and similarities in the use of time?

(continued)

A **time log** is simply a record of how you actually have spent your time–including interruptions. It doesn't have to be a second-by-second record of every waking moment. But it should account for blocks of time in increments as short as 15 minutes.

time log A record of how one spends one's time.

Complete the blank time log in **Try It! 2**. As you fill out the time log, try to be as specific as you can. Indicate not only what you were doing at a given time (for example, "read history assignment") but also the interruptions or off-task behavior that occurred (such as "answered three texts" or "surfed web for 10 minutes").

By examining how much time you spend doing various activities, you now know where your time goes. How does it match with your perceptions of how you spend your time? Be prepared to be surprised, because most people find that they're spending time on a lot of activities that just don't matter very much.

Try It! POWER

Weekly Timetable

Week of:__________ Week #_____

	Mon	Tues	Wed	Thurs	Fri	Sat	Sun
6–7 a.m.							
7–8 a.m.							
8–9 a.m.							
9–10 a.m.							
10–11 a.m.							
11–12 (noon)							
12 (noon)–1 p.m.							
1–2 p.m.							
2–3 p.m.							
3–4 p.m.							
4–5 p.m.							
5–6 p.m.							
6–7 p.m.							
7–8 p.m.							
8–9 p.m.							
9–10 p.m.							
10–11 p.m.							
11 p.m.–12 (midnight)							
12 (midnight)–1 a.m.							
1–2 a.m.							
2–3 a.m.							
3–4 a.m.							
4–5 a.m.							
5–6 a.m.							

Identify the "Black Holes" That Eat Up Your Time

Do you feel like your time often is sucked into a black hole, disappearing without a trace?

We all waste time, spending it on unimportant activities that keep us from doing the things that we should be doing or really want to do. For example, suppose when

3 **Try It!** POWER

Identify the Black Holes of Time Management

The first 20 items on this list are common problems that prevent us from getting things done. Check off the ones that are problems for you, and indicate whether you have control over them (controllable problems) or they are out of your control (uncontrollable problems).

	Big Problem for Me	Often a Problem	Seldom a Problem	Controllable (C) or Uncontrollable (U)?
1. Phone interruptions				
2. Drop-in visitors				
3. Texting				
4. Facebook and other social networking sites				
5. E-mail				
6. Inability to say no				
7. Socializing				
8. Snacking				
9. Errands and shopping				
10. Meals				
11. Children's interruptions				
12. Perfectionism				
13. Family appointments				

(continued)

you're studying, your cell phone rings, and you end up speaking with a friend for a half hour. You could have (a) let the phone ring and not answered it; (b) answered, but told your friend you were studying and promised to call him or her back; or (c) spoken to him or her, but only for a short while. If you had done any of these things, you would have taken control of the interruption, and kept time from sinking into a black hole.

To get a sense of how your time is sucked into black holes, complete **Try It! 3**.

» LO 2-2 Set Your Priorities

By this point you should have a good idea of what's taking up your time. But you may not know what you should be doing instead.

To figure out the best use of your time, you need to determine your priorities. **Priorities** are the tasks and activities you need and want to do, rank-ordered from

priorities The tasks and activities that one needs and wants to do, rank-ordered from most important to least important.

3 *continued*

Try It! P O W E R

	Big Problem for Me	Often a Problem	Seldom a Problem	Controllable (C) or Uncontrollable (U)?
14. Looking for lost items				
15. Redoing mistakes				
16. Jumping from task to task				
17. Surfing the web				
18. Reading newspapers, magazines, recreational books				
19. Car trouble				
20. Waiting for public transportation				
21. Other				
22. Other				
23. Other				
24. Other				
25. Other				

WORKING IN A GROUP

Examine the problems that affect each group member and then discuss these questions: Do time management problems fall into any patterns? Are there problems that at first seem uncontrollable that can actually be controlled? What strategies for dealing with such problems have you used in the past?

most important to least important. There are no right or wrong priorities; you have to decide for yourself what you wish to accomplish. Maybe spending time on your studies is most important to you, or maybe your top priority is spending time with your family. Only you can decide. Furthermore, what's important to you at this moment may be less of a priority to you next month, next year, or five years from now.

For the purpose of effective time management in college, the best procedure is to start off by identifying priorities for an entire term. What do you need to accomplish? Don't just choose obvious, general goals, such as "passing all my classes." Instead, think about your priorities in terms of specific, measurable activities, such as "studying six hours before each chemistry exam"—*not* "studying harder," which is too vague. (Look at the example of a priority list in **Figure 2.1**and also at the **Course Connections** feature.)

Priority	Ranking
Study for each class at least 30 minutes/day	1
Start each major paper 2 weeks in advance of due date	2
Hand in each paper on time	1
Review for test starting a week before test date	2
Be on time for job	1
Check in with Mom once a week	3
Work out 3x/week	3

figure 2.1
Sample List of Priorities

Write your priorities on the chart in **Try It! 4**. After you've filled out the chart, organize it by giving each priority a ranking from 1 to 3. A "1" represents a priority that absolutely must be done; without it you'll suffer a major setback. For instance, a paper with a fixed due date should receive a "1" for a priority ranking; carving out time to take those guitar lessons you always wanted to take might be ranked a "3" in terms of priority. The important point is to rank-order your priorities to reveal what is and is not important to accomplish during the term.

Setting priorities will help you to determine how to make best use of your time. No one has enough time to complete everything; prioritizing will help you make informed decisions about what you can do to maximize your success.

Identify Your Prime Time

Take a look inward. Do you enthusiastically bound out of bed in the morning, ready to start the day and take on the world? Or is the alarm clock a hated and unwelcome sound that jars you out of pleasant slumber? Are you the kind of person who is zombie-like by 10:00 at night, or a person who is just beginning to rev up at midnight?

Each of us has our own style based on some inborn body clock. Some of us are at our best in the morning, while others do considerably better at night. Being aware of the time or times of day when you can accomplish your best work will help you plan and schedule your time most effectively. If you're at your worst in the morning, try to schedule easier, less-involving activities for those earlier hours. On the other hand, if morning is the best time for you, schedule activities that require the greatest concentration at that time.

Each of us has an internal body clock that helps govern when we feel most alert. Becoming aware of your own body clock can help you schedule study sessions at times when you're able to work at peak efficiency.
©Kristy-Anne Glubish/Design Pics

Course **Connections**

Homework and Study Time: How Much Is Enough?

What would you guess is the average number of hours instructors think you should be doing homework and studying outside of class each week? In the view of instructors queried in surveys, students should spend, on average, 6 hours per week preparing for *each* class in which they're enrolled. And if they're taking courses in the sciences and engineering, instructors expect their students to put in even more hours.

Keep in mind that study time does not include actual class time. If you add that in, someone taking four classes would need 24 hours of outside class preparation and would be in class for 16 hours—for a total of 40 hours, or the equivalent of full-time employment.

How can you manage out-of-class study and homework time? One strategy is to schedule it as a repeating appointment in your calendar. By scheduling a time period each day that you devote to reading, homework, and studying, you're more likely to find the time to get your homework and studying done.

If you've underestimated the amount of time instructors believe is necessary to devote to class preparation, you may need to rethink the amount of time you'll need to allocate to studying. You might also speak to your individual instructors to see what they believe is an appropriate amount of preparation. Although they may not be able to give exact figures, their estimates will help you to prioritize what you need to do to be a successful student.

> "Time moves slowly, but passes quickly."
>
> Alice Walker. (1982). *The Color Purple: A Novel.* New York: Harcourt Brace Jovanovich.

But don't be a slave to your internal time clock. Even night people can function effectively in the morning, just as morning people can accomplish quite a bit in the evening. On the other hand, listen hard to your internal time clock if you're tired much of the time. If you frequently feel sleepy, your body is giving you a simple, yet important, message: Get more sleep.

Organize Mastering the Moment

Because you now know where you've lost time in the past and your priority list is telling you where you need to head in the future, you now can organize yourself to take control of your time. Here's what you'll need:

Master Calendars

master calendar A schedule showing the weeks of a longer time period, such as a college term, with all assignments and important activities noted on it.

Your first requirement is a **master calendar** that shows all the weeks of the term on one page. You don't need to buy one; you can make it easily enough yourself. It need not be great art; a rough version will do. The important point is that it must include every week of the term and seven days per week. (See the example of a master calendar in **Figure 2.2**.)

Weekly Timetables

weekly timetable A schedule showing all regular, prescheduled activities due to occur in the week, together with one-time events and commitments.

The **weekly timetable** is a master grid with the days of the week across the top and the hours, from 6:00 a.m. to midnight, along the side. This will permit you to write in all your regularly scheduled activities, as well as one-time appointments when they arise. (A blank weekly timetable is provided in **Figure 2.3**.)

4 Try It! POWER

Set Priorities

Set your priorities for the term. They may include getting to class on time, finishing papers and assignments by their due dates, finding a part-time job that fits your schedule, and reading every assignment before the class for which it is due. To get started, list priorities in any order. Be sure to consider priorities relating to your schoolwork, other work, family, social obligations, and health. After you list them, assign a number to each one indicating its level—giving a "1" to the highest-priority items, a "2" to medium-priority items, and a "3" to the items with the lowest priority.

List of Priorities	
Priority	**Priority Index**

Now redo your list, putting your number 1s first, followed by at least some of your number 2s and 3s–the ones to which you feel you can reasonably commit.

(continued)

Make a single copy of this blank timetable or use the online version. Then fill in your regular, predictable time commitments.

Next, make as many copies as you need to cover each week of the term. Then, for each week, fill in the date on the left and the number of the week in the term on the right, and add in your irregular commitments.

Daily To-Do Lists

Finally, you'll need a **daily to-do list.** You can enter your daily to-do list into a smartphone or tablet. Or you could write it on a small, portable calendar that includes a separate page for each day of the week. Whatever format you use for your daily to-do list, make sure you have access to it all the time.

daily to-do list
A schedule showing the tasks, activities, and appointments due to occur during the day.

4 *continued* **Try It!** POWER

Final List of Priorities
Priority
1.
2.
3.
4.
5.
6.
7.
8.
9.
10.
11.
12.

Now consider the following:

- What does this list tell you about your greatest priorities? Are they centered around school, friends and family, jobs, or some other aspect of your life?
- Do you have so many "1" priorities that they will be difficult or impossible to accomplish successfully? How could you go back to your list and trim it down even more?
- What does this listing of priorities suggest about how successful you'll be during the upcoming term?

The basic organizational task you face is filling in these three schedules. You'll need at least an hour to do this, so set the time aside. In addition, there will be some repetition across the three schedules, and the task may seem a bit tedious. *But every minute you invest now in organizing your time will pay off in hours that you will save in the future.*

Follow these steps in completing your schedule:

- **Start with the master calendar, which shows all the weeks of the term on one page.** In most classes, you'll receive a syllabus, a course outline that explains what the course is all about. Traditionally, a syllabus includes course assignments and their due dates and the schedule for tests that will be given during the term. Write on the master calendar every assignment you have, noting it on the date that it is due. If the instructor hasn't included due dates, ask; he or she probably

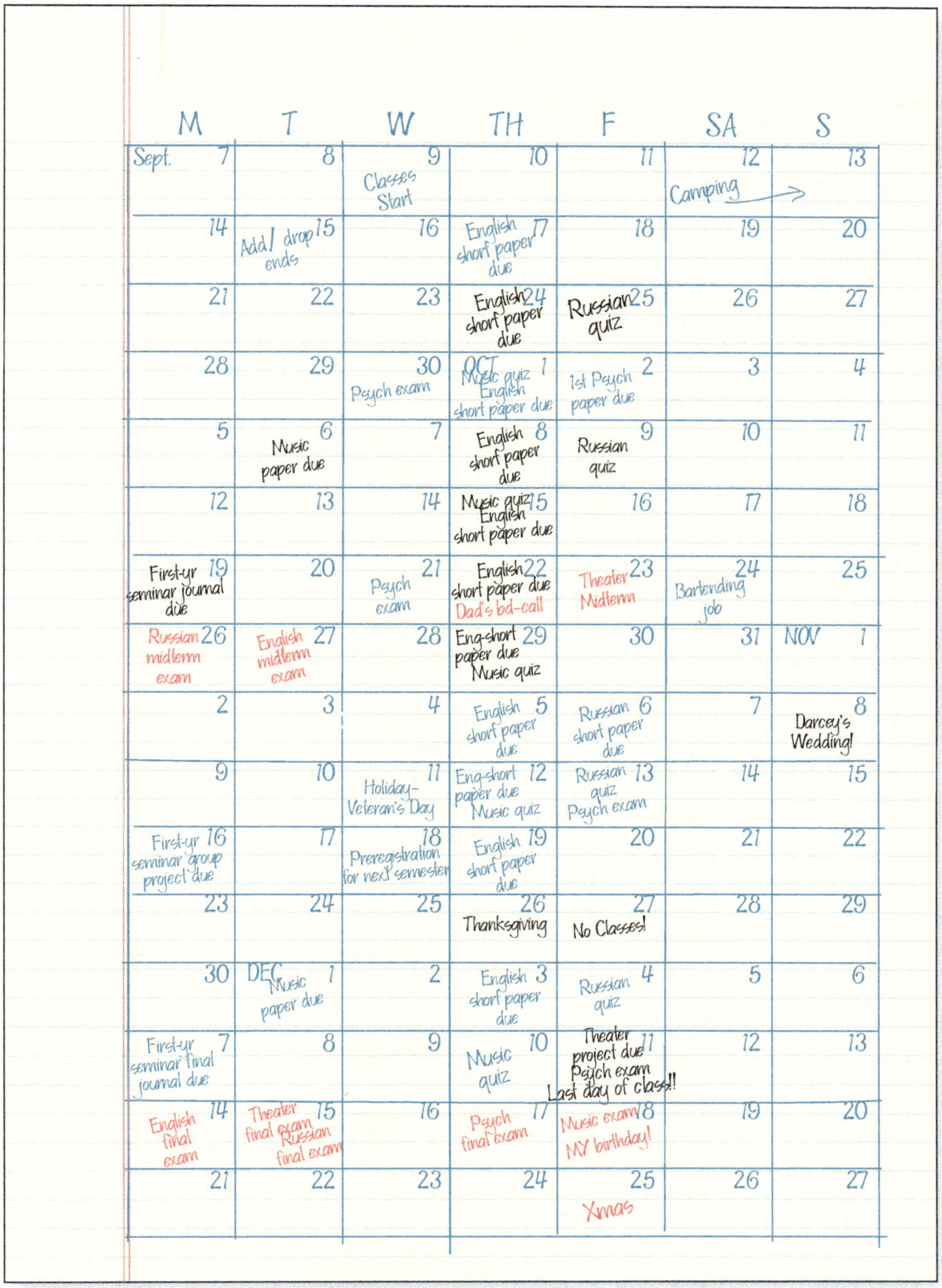

figure 2.2
Master Calendar Sample

already knows, or at least has a general idea, of the week that various assignments will be due. Pencil in tentative assignments on the appropriate date.

Don't put only assignments on the master calendar. Also include important activities from your personal life, drawn from your list of priorities. For instance, if you're involved in a club that is bringing a guest speaker to campus, mark down the date of the event.

Finally, schedule some free time—time when you promise yourself you will do something that is just plain fun. Consider these days to be written in stone, and promise yourself that you won't use them for anything other than something enjoyable. Just knowing that you have some downtime planned will help you to throw yourself into more demanding tasks. In addition, getting into the

figure 2.3
Weekly Timetable

Weekly Timetable

Week of:__________ Week #_____

	Mon	Tues	Wed	Thurs	Fri	Sat	Sun
6–7 a.m.							
7–8 a.m.							
8–9 a.m.							
9–10 a.m.							
10–11 a.m.							
11–12 (noon)							
12 (noon)–1 p.m.							
1–2 p.m.							
2–3 p.m.							
3–4 p.m.							
4–5 p.m.							
5–6 p.m.							
6–7 p.m.							
7–8 p.m.							
8–9 p.m.							
9–10 p.m.							
10–11 p.m.							
11 p.m.–12 (midnight)							
12 (midnight)–1 a.m.							
1–2 a.m.							
2–3 a.m.							
3–4 a.m.							
4–5 a.m.							
5–6 a.m.							

habit of allowing yourself time to relax and reflect on your life is as important as any other time management skill you may learn.

You now have a good idea of what the term has in store for you. In most cases, the first few weeks have few assignments or tests. But as the term rolls on—particularly around the middle and end of the term—things will get more demanding. The message you should take from this: *Use the off-peak periods to get a head start on future assignments.*

Completing a master schedule also may help you head off disaster before it occurs. Suppose, for instance, you find that six weeks in the future you have two papers due and three tests—all in the same week!

After cursing your bad luck, it's time to take action. Begin to think of strategies for managing the situation, such as working on the papers or studying in advance. You might also try to change some due dates. Instructors are far more receptive to requests for extensions on papers if the requests are made well in advance. Similarly, it might be possible to take a test later—or earlier—if you make prior arrangements.

▸ **Now move to the weekly timetable provided in Figure 2.3**. Fill in the times of all your fixed, prescheduled activities—the times that your classes meet, when you have to be at work, the times you have to pick up your child at day care, and any other recurring appointments.

Once you've filled in the weekly timetable, as in the one on this page, you get a bare-bones picture of the average week. You will still need to take into account the specific activities that are required to complete the assignments on the master calendar.

To move from your "average" week to specific weeks, make photocopies of the weekly timetable that now contains your fixed appointments. Make enough copies for every week of the term. On each copy, write the week number of the term and the specific dates it covers.

Using your master calendar, add assignment due dates, tests, and any other activities on the appropriate days of the week. Then pencil in blocks of time necessary to prepare for those events. (See a sample in **Figure 2.4**.)

How much time should you allocate for schoolwork? One very rough rule of thumb holds that every one hour that you spend in class requires, on average, two hours of study outside of class to earn a B and three hours of study outside of class to earn an A. Do the arithmetic: If you are taking 15 credits (with each credit equivalent to an hour of class per week), you'll need to plan for 30 hours of studying each week to earn a B average—an intimidating amount of time. Of course, the amount of time you must allocate to a specific class will vary from week to week, depending on what is happening in the class.

For example, if you estimate that you'll need five hours of study for a midterm exam in a certain class, pencil in those hours. Don't set up a single block of five hours. People learn and remember best when their studying is spread out over shorter periods, rather than in one long block of time. (There are some smartphone apps, like *PomoDone,* that will help you space out studying.)

Similarly, if you need to write a paper that's due on a certain date, you can block out the different stages of the writing process, such as deciding on a topic, developing an outline, writing a rough draft, and so on. You'll need to estimate how much time each stage will take, but you probably have a pretty good idea from previous papers you've written.

Some classes may need only a few hours of study in a given week. With good luck, heavy weeks in one class will be compensated for by lighter weeks in others.

Keep in mind that estimates are just that: estimates. Don't think of them as set in stone. Mark them on your weekly calendar in pencil, not pen, so you can adjust them if necessary.

But remember: It's also crucial not to overschedule yourself. You'll still need time to eat, to talk with your friends, to spend time with your family, and to enjoy yourself in general. If you find that your life is completely filled with things that you feel you must do in order to survive and that there is no room for fun, then take a step back and cut out something to make some time for yourself in your daily schedule. Finding time for yourself is as important as carving out time for what others want you to do. Besides, if you are overworked, you're likely to "find" the time by guiltily goofing off without really setting aside the time and enjoying it.

figure 2.4

A Sample Weekly Timetable

Weekly Timetable

Week of: 9/28 **Week #** 3

	Mon	Tues	Wed	Thurs	Fri	Sat	Sun
6–7 a.m.							
7–8 a.m.							
8–9 a.m.							
9–10 a.m.	9:05 Psych	9:05 Music	9:05 Psych	9:05 Music	9:05 Psych		
10–11 a.m.		↓		↓			
11–12 (noon)		11:15 English		11:15 English			
12 (noon)–1 p.m.	12:20 Theater	↓	12:20 Theater	↓	12:20 Theater		
1–2 p.m.	↓		↓				
2–3 p.m.							
3–4 p.m.	3:00 Russian		3:00 Russian		3:00 Russian		
4–5 p.m.	First-year seminar	Work		Work			
5–6 p.m.	↓	↓		↓			
6–7 p.m.		↓		↓			
7–8 p.m.							
8–9 p.m.							
9–10 p.m.							
10–11 p.m.							
11 p.m.–12 (midnight)							
12 (midnight)–1 a.m.							
1–2 a.m.							
2–3 a.m.							
3–4 a.m.							
4–5 a.m.							
5–6 a.m.							

- **If you've taken each of the previous steps, you're now in a position to work on the final step of organization for successful time management: completing your daily to-do list.**

Unlike the master calendar and weekly timetable—both of which you develop at the beginning of the term—complete your daily to-do list just one day ahead of time, preferably at the end of the day.

List all the things that you intend to do during the next day and their priority. Start with the things that you know you *must* do and that have fixed times, such as classes, work schedules, and appointments. These are your first-priority items. Then add in the other things that you *should* accomplish, such as an hour of study for an upcoming test, working on research for an upcoming paper, or finishing up a lab report. Finally, list things that are lower priority but enjoyable, setting aside time for a run or a walk, for example.

To-Do List

for________________

(date)

Item Item	Priority	✓ Completed
Call Chris to get English notes	1	✓
Meet with Prof. Hernandez	1	✓
Review Russian	1	✓
Work on outline for psych paper	2	✓
Return books to library	2	
Call Nettie	2	✓
Set up meeting with music group	2	
Meet Deena	2	
Do laundry	3	

figure 2.5
Sample Daily To-Do List

Don't schedule every single minute of the day. That would be counterproductive, and you'd end up feeling like you'd failed if you deviated from your schedule. Instead, think of your daily to-do list as a path through a forest. If you were hiking, you would allow yourself to deviate from the path, occasionally venturing onto side tracks when they looked interesting. But you'd also be keeping tabs on your direction so you ended up where you needed to be at the end and not miles away from your car or home.

As in the sample daily to-do list in **Figure 2.5**, include a column to check or cross off after you've completed an activity. There's something very satisfying in acknowledging what you have accomplished.

LO 2-3 W Work Controlling Time

You're in luck: There is no work to time management—or at least not much more than you've already done. The work of time management is to follow the schedules that you've prepared and organized. But that doesn't mean it will be easy. Our lives are filled with surprises: Things take longer than we've planned. A friend we haven't spoken to in a while calls to chat, and it seems rude to say that we don't have time to talk. A crisis occurs; buses are late; computers break down; kids get sick.

The difference between effective time management and time management that doesn't work lies in how well you deal with the inevitable surprises.

There are several ways to take control of your days and permit yourself to follow your intended schedule:

- **Just say no.** You don't have to agree to every request and every favor that others ask of you. You're not a bad person if you refuse to do something that will eat up your time and prevent you from accomplishing your goals.

  Suppose, for example, a friend sees you in the library and asks to borrow the notes from a class that she missed yesterday and that you attended. It's not an unreasonable request. Here's the problem, though: You don't have your notebook with you, and you'd have to stop by your house to pick it up.

Think through what the request entails. *It may be only 10 minutes to your house, but it's another 10 minutes back. That's 20 minutes. And then there's the time that you'll spend meeting her to give her the notes. And then the time it takes to meet her again, once she's copied the notes. Or suppose you decide to wait while she copies them. Overall, you may end up losing an hour.*

The solution? You should probably say no to the immediate request. It's not unreasonable to tell your friend that you don't have the time today to get your notebook. You don't have to refuse her completely. She could stop by your house in the evening to pick up the notes, or you could bring them with you the next day. In short, there are ways to accomplish the goal of helping out your friend without wasting time and sabotaging your schedule.

- **Get away from it all.** Go to the library. Lock yourself into your bedroom. Find an out-of-the-way, unused classroom.

  Any of these places can serve to isolate you from everyday distractions and thereby permit you to work on the tasks that you wish to complete. Try to adopt a particular spot as your own, such as a corner desk in a secluded nook in the library. If you use it enough, your body and mind will automatically get into study mode as soon as you seat yourself at it.

- **Enjoy the sounds of silence.** Although many students insist they accomplish most while a television, radio, or CD is playing, scientific studies suggest otherwise: We are able to concentrate most when our environment is silent. So even if you're sure you work best with a soundtrack playing, experiment and work in silence for a few days. You may find that you get more done in less time than you would in a more distracting environment.

- **Take an e-break.** Text messages, phone calls, Facebook status updates, instant messages, e-mail. Who doesn't love to hear from others?

  We may not control when communications arrive, but we can make the message wait until we are ready to receive it. Take an e-break and shut down your communication sources for a period of time. Phone calls will be stored in voicemail, and text messages, Facebook updates, and e-mail will be saved on your phone. They'll wait.

- **Use technology to save time.** Many things–from shopping for clothing to ordering groceries–can be accomplished quickly via the web or phone rather than in person.

- **Expect the unexpected.** Interruptions and crises, minor and major, can't be eliminated. However, they can be prepared for.

  How is it possible to plan for surprises? Although it may still be too early in the term to get a clear picture of what sorts of unanticipated events you'll encounter, you should keep an eye out for patterns. Perhaps one instructor routinely makes surprise assignments that aren't listed on the syllabus. Maybe you're asked to work extra hours on the weekends because someone doesn't show up and you have to work overtime.

  You'll never be able to escape from unexpected interruptions and surprises that require your attention. But by trying to anticipate them in advance, and thinking about how you'll react to them, you'll be positioning yourself to react more effectively when they do occur.

Procrastination

procrastination
The habit of putting off and delaying tasks that need to be accomplished.

Procrastination, the habit of putting off and delaying tasks that need to be accomplished, is like a microscopic parasite. It is invisible to the naked eye, but it eats up your time nonetheless.

It's 10:30 a.m. You've just come out of your Spanish class. You know that there's going to be a test next week, and you've planned to go over the flash cards you made up last night. It's right there in your schedule: "10:30 a.m.–study Spanish vocabulary." But you're thirsty after sitting in class, so you decide to go and buy yourself something to drink.

As you head into the snack bar, you pass by the campus store, and you think about how you need to buy a couple of pens. After finding the kind of pen you like, you go to the checkout line. You pass by a rack of magazines, and, after leafing through a few, decide to purchase one. You can read it while you have your drink. You make your way to the snack bar, buy your soda, and sip it as you read the magazine.

Suddenly, a half hour has gone by. Because so much time has passed, you decide that it won't be worth it to start studying your Spanish vocabulary. So you spend a little more time reading the magazine and then head off to your next class, which is at 11:00 a.m.

You can't control interruptions and crises that are imposed upon you by others. But even when no one else is throwing interruptions at us, we make up our own. Procrastination is a problem that almost all of us face. To identify whether you are a procrastinator, find your "Procrastination Quotient" (see **Try It! 5**).

If you find yourself procrastinating, several steps can help you:

- *Break large tasks into small ones.* People often procrastinate because a task they're seeking to accomplish appears overwhelming. If writing a 15-page paper seems nearly impossible, think about writing a series of five 3-page papers. If reading a 600-page book seems impossible, think of it as reading three 200-page books.
- *Start with the easiest and simplest part of a task, and then do the harder parts.* Succeeding initially on the easy parts can make the harder parts of a task less daunting–and make you less apt to procrastinate in completing the task.
- *Get the hard parts of a task out of the way first.* In contrast to the previous strategy for avoiding procrastination, it sometimes helps to tackle the hardest part of a task first. Getting the hard parts out of the way will make it a lot easier to complete the remaining parts of what you are trying to accomplish.
- *Substitute something easier for a more difficult task.* If you have to write a letter, can you write a postcard instead? Sometimes it's possible to figure out an easier way to accomplish a task that works just as well.
- *Just begin!* Sometimes the hardest part of an activity is simply getting started. So take the leap and begin the task, and the rest may follow more easily.
- *Work with others.* Just being in the same physical location with others can motivate you sufficiently to accomplish tasks that you consider unpleasant and on which you might be tempted to procrastinate. For instance, studying vocabulary words can be made easier if you plan a study session with several of your classmates. Beware, though–if you spend too much time socializing, you lower the likelihood of success.
- *Understand that false starts are part of the learning process.* Accept that sometimes you will go in the wrong direction when working on a project. Don't let the fear of making mistakes hold you back. Such false starts are part of how we learn.

One antidote to procrastination is working in a study group. You'll be motivated by the presence of others who face the same challenges and assignments that you do.

Try It! POWER

Find Your Procrastination Quotient

Do you procrastinate? To find out, circle the number that best applies for each question using the following scale:

Strongly agree 4 3 2 1 **Strongly disagree**

1. I invent reasons and look for excuses for not acting on a problem.

Strongly agree 4 3 2 1 **Strongly disagree**

2. It takes pressure to get me to work on difficult assignments.

Strongly agree 4 3 2 1 **Strongly disagree**

3. I take half measures that will avoid or delay unpleasant or difficult tasks.

Strongly agree 4 3 2 1 **Strongly disagree**

4. I face too many interruptions and crises that interfere with accomplishing my major goals.

Strongly agree 4 3 2 1 **Strongly disagree**

5. I sometimes neglect to carry out important tasks.

Strongly agree 4 3 2 1 **Strongly disagree**

6. I schedule big assignments too late to get them done as well as I know I could.

Strongly agree 4 3 2 1 **Strongly disagree**

7. I'm sometimes too tired to do the work I need to do.

Strongly agree 4 3 2 1 **Strongly disagree**

8. I start new tasks before I finish old ones.

Strongly agree 4 3 2 1 **Strongly disagree**

9. When I work in groups, I try to get other people to finish what I don't.

Strongly agree 4 3 2 1 **Strongly disagree**

10. I put off tasks that I really don't want to do but know that I must do.

Strongly agree 4 3 2 1 **Strongly disagree**

Scoring: Total the numbers you have circled. If the score is below 15, you are not a chronic procrastinator and you probably have only an occasional problem. If your score is 16–25, you have a minor problem with procrastination. If your score is above 25, you procrastinate quite often and should work on breaking the habit.

Now, consider the following:

- If you do procrastinate often, why do you think you do it?
- Are there particular subjects or classes or kinds of assignments that you are more likely to procrastinate on?
- Is there something that you are putting off doing right now? How might you get started on it?

Source: Adapted from J. D. Ferner, Successful Time Management (New York: Wiley, 1980), p 33.

WORKING IN A GROUP

Think about the last time you procrastinated. Describe it as completely as you can. What was the task? What did you do rather than doing what needed to be done? What could you have done to avoid procrastinating in this situation? Ask others what strategy they might suggest for avoiding procrastinating.

- *Keep the costs of procrastination in mind.* Procrastination doesn't just result in delay; it may also make the task harder than it would have been if you hadn't procrastinated. Not only will you ultimately have less time to complete the task, but you may have to do it so quickly that its quality may be diminished. In the worst scenario, you won't even be able to finish it at all.

Balancing College and Life

Time management is especially challenging if you have caregiver responsibilities for children or other family members such as aging parents. Not only does your family demand—and deserve—substantial amounts of time, but juggling college and family (and often work) obligations is often more than a full-time job. However, there are some specific strategies that can help.

Dealing with Childcare Demands

- *Provide activities for your children.* Kids enjoy doing things on their own for part of the day. Plan activities that will keep them happily occupied while you're doing schoolwork.
- *Make spending time with your children a priority.* Carve out "free play" time for your kids. Even 20 minutes of good time devoted to your children will give all of you—you and them—a lift. No matter how busy you are, you owe it to your children—and yourself—to spend time as a family.
- *Enlist your child's help.* Children love to play adult and, if they're old enough, help you study. Maybe they can help you clear a space to study. Perhaps you can give them "assignments" that they can work on while you're working on your assignments.
- *Encourage your child to invite friends over to play.* Some children can remain occupied for hours if they have a playmate.
- *Use screen time appropriately.* Age-appropriate shows like Sesame Street, Netflix downloads, and even video games can be not only engaging, but educational. The trick is to monitor what your children watch.
- *Find the best childcare providers that are available.* The better the care your children are getting, the better you'll be able to concentrate on your schoolwork. You may still feel guilty that you're not with your children as much as you'd like, but accept that guilt. Remember, your attendance in college builds a better future for your children.
- *Use your children's "downtime" effectively.* If your children are young, use their nap time as a chance to catch up on schoolwork. Or consider getting up early, before your children wake up, for a period in which you will have fewer interruptions than later in the day.
- *Accept that studying will be harder with kids around.* It may take you longer to study, and your concentration may suffer from the noise that kids make. But remind yourself what that noise represents: the growth and development of someone that you love. One day your children will be grown, and without a doubt there will be times that you'll miss their high level of energy and activity.

> "I had a friend who was concentrating in pre-med. He put off studying for his chem midterm until 10 p.m. the night before, spending his time instead at the movies and the campus hangout. After bombing the exam, he told us he did not have enough time to study. Basically, he gave himself an excuse to fail."
>
> Gottesman, G. **(1994)**. *College Survival. NY: Macmillan. P. 70.*

Dealing with Eldercare Demands

- *Encourage as much independence as possible on the part of older adults for whom you are responsible.* Not only will it take some of the pressure off you, but it will be helpful to adults.
- *Ask for support from your siblings and other family members.* Caring for an ill or aging parent should be a family affair, not a burden that falls on any one individual.
- *Determine what community resources are available.* Local centers for aging may provide assistance not only to the elderly but also to their caregivers.
- *Respect your own needs.* Remember that your own priorities are important. Elders for whom you are responsible will understand that you will sometimes need to put yourself first.

Balancing College and Work Demands

Juggling college and a job can be exhausting. Not only must you manage your time to complete your schoolwork, but in many cases you'll also face time management demands while you are on the job. Here are some tips to help you keep everything in balance:

- *Make to-do lists for work, just as you would for your schoolwork.* In fact, all the time management strategies that we've discussed can be applied to on-the-job tasks.
- *If you have slack time on the job, get some studying done.* Try to keep at least some of your textbooks, class notes, or notecards always with you so you can refer to them. Of course, you should never do schoolwork without your employer's prior agreement. If you don't get permission, you may jeopardize your job.
- *Use your lunch or dinner hour effectively.* Although it's important to eat a nutritious lunch and not to wolf your food down, you may be able to use some of the time allotted to you for lunch to fit in some studying.
- *Ask your employer about flextime.* If your job allows it, you may be able to set your own hours, within reason, as long as the work gets done. If this is an option for you, use it. Although it may create more time management challenges for you than would a job with set hours, it also provides you with more flexibility.
- *Always keep in mind why you're working.* If you're working because it's your sole means of support, you're in a very different position from someone who is working to earn a bit of extra money for luxuries. Remember what your priorities are. In some cases, school should always come first; in others, your job may have to come first, at least some of the time. Whatever you decide, make sure it's a thoughtful decision, based on consideration of your long-term priorities.

E Evaluate Checking Your Time

Evaluating how you use your time is pretty straightforward: Either you accomplished what you intended to do in a given period, or you didn't. Did you check off all the items on your daily to-do list? If you go over your list at the end of every day, not only will you know how successful your time management efforts have been, but you will be able to incorporate any activities you missed into the next day's to-do list.

The check-off is important because it provides an objective record of what you have accomplished on a given day. Just as important, it provides you with concrete

Career Connections

On-the-Job Time Management

Think you're busy now? Just wait: Once you are building your career and working at a full-time job, you may look back on your college years as a period of relative leisure.

For employees with a demanding boss who may, without warning, give them an urgent assignment due the next morning, time is always at a premium. This means that time management is an essential survival skill when developing your career. In fact, time management may be a talent that you'll need in the working world even more than you did while you were getting your college education.

When you are in school, most assignments are scheduled far in advance—usually at the start of the term. Most often, requirements are set forth plainly on a syllabus, and typically there are no new assignments added as the term moves forward. That means you can carefully map out your use of time over the term.

In the business world, things are often different. Crises occur, perhaps due to manufacturing problems or client demands, that require sudden flurries of work. In some jobs, you may be forced to drop everything you normally work on and pitch in on a sudden new task. As a result, your plans to complete your everyday work may be disrupted completely.

You'll also need to learn new time-management strategies on the job. For instance, if you supervise other employees, it may be possible to delegate some work to them, allowing them to help you complete assignments. Or sometimes it may be possible to deflect assignments brought to you by a boss to some other unit or department.

In short, time management is a skill that will help you build a successful career. Learning the basic principles of time management now will help you well beyond your years in college.

reinforcement for completing the task. As we have noted, there are few things more satisfying than gazing at a to-do list with a significant number of check marks.

Of course, you won't always accomplish every item on your to-do list. That's not surprising, nor even particularly bad, especially if you've included some second- and third-level priorities that you don't absolutely have to accomplish and that you may not really have expected you'd have time for anyway.

Give yourself a virtual pat on the back for completing the things that you've accomplished. Successful time management is not easy, and if you've improved at all, you deserve to feel some personal satisfaction.

R Rethink

Reflecting on Your Personal Style of Time Management

At the end of the day, after you've evaluated how well you've followed your time management plan and how much you've accomplished, it's time to rethink where you are. Maybe you've accomplished everything you set out to do, and every task for the day is completed, and every item on your to-do list has a check mark next to it.

Or maybe you have the opposite result. Your day has been a shambles, and you feel as if nothing has been accomplished. Because of a constant series of interruptions and chance events, you've been unable to make headway on your list.

Or—most likely—you find yourself somewhere in between these two extremes. Some tasks got done, while others are still hanging over you. Now is the time to rethink in a broad sense how you manage your time by doing the following:

- **Reassess Your Priorities.** Are you expecting too much of yourself, given the constraints in your life? Sometimes it makes sense to reassess your priorities to be sure you're attempting to do what is most important to you. You need

Managing your time effectively will allow you to make the most of every moment, helping you accomplish the things that are most important to you.
©JGI/JamieGill/Getty Images

to take into account your strengths, weaknesses, and values. You also need to try to answer the question "Who am I?" in order to ensure that your priorities are optimal for *you.*

- **Reconsider Your Personal Style of Time Management.** We've outlined one method of time management. Although it works well for most people, it isn't for everyone. Some people just can't bring themselves to be so structured and scheduled. They feel hemmed in by to-do lists.

  If you're one of those people, fine. You don't need to follow the suggestions presented in this chapter exactly. In fact, there are lots of other aids to manage your time. Software companies produce time management apps, and you can keep your calendar in Microsoft's *Outlook* or Apple's *Calendar.* In addition, publishing companies produce elaborate hard-copy planners, such as Day-Timers.

  However you choose to manage your time, the important thing is to do so consistently. And remember that whatever approach to time management you take, it will work best if it is compatible with your own personal values and strengths. Keep experimenting until you find an approach that works for you.

- **Consider Doing Less.** If you keep falling behind, do less. There are only 24 hours in the day, and we need to sleep for about one-third of the time. In the remaining hours, it simply may be impossible to carry a full load of classes and work full-time and care for a child and still have some time left to have a normal life.

  Consequently, if you consistently fall behind in your work, it may be that you are doing too much. Reassess your goals and your priorities, and make choices. Determine what is most important to you. It's better to accomplish less, if it is accomplished well, than to accomplish more, but poorly.

> "Our costliest expenditure is time."
>
> **Theophrastus, quoted in *Diogenes Laertius's Lives and Opinions of Eminent Philosophers*, tr. R.D. Hicks, (1925). Loeb Classical Library.**

- **Do More.** Although it is a problem that many of us would envy, some people have too much time on their hands. Their classes may not be too demanding, or work demands may suddenly slacken off. If this happens to you, take advantage of your time. For example, you might use the extra time to simply relax and enjoy your more unhurried existence. There is a good bit to be said for having time to let your thoughts wander. We need to take time out to enjoy our friends, admire the flowers in the park, exercise, consider the spiritual side of our lives, and the like.

  On the other hand, if you consistently have more time than you know what to do with, reflect on what you want to accomplish and add some activities that help you reach your goals. For example, consider becoming involved in a service-learning activity. Volunteer your time to the community. Talk to your academic advisor about taking an extra course during the next term.

  But whatever you decide to do, make a real decision. Don't let the time slip away. Once it's gone, it's gone forever.

Speaking *of* Success

Source: Courtesy of Rebecka Clark

NAME: **Rebecka Marie Clark**

SCHOOL: **Pima Medical Institute**

When Rebecka Marie Clark entered college, she found quickly that different students learn in different ways. "Academics have never been my strong suit as I am a very strong kinesthetic learner," she says. "You can have me read all day and test me, but it's not until I apply and practice [what I've heard] do I understand concepts."

Because of this, a hands-on program like dental assisting seemed to be a perfect fit for Clark. She worked hard to get into a dental assisting program, taking and retaking courses to bring up her GPA, and after completing the program, eventually she landed an assistant job. But after a period of time, she decided that she wanted to further her education, and Rebecka began a dental hygiene program.

Though she was pleased to be in the program, balancing school, work, and life was difficult. "I was a single mom," she recalls. "I moved back in with my mom when I got into hygiene school to help with my daughter and alleviate debt accumulation. However, this also meant spending 4-6 hours in the car or bus every day." Trying to take advantage of a difficult situation, Clark learned to use her downtime on her commute to study, listen to lectures, work on homework and memorize notecards.

She also learned to study better. "I was that student that used to write down everything and anything," she says. "I didn't know what I needed to know so I tried to memorize the whole book." As she learned better study habits, she realized how to prioritize the important concepts and to take better notes. "I learned to get into a rhythm and apply what I read to real world situations," she recalls.

Clark encourages new students to eliminate "hard" from their vocabulary. "Nothing is ever hard, but it can be challenging," she says. "Looking at things as a challenge gives me reason and motivation to overcome that challenge." She hopes that when others look at situations as challenging instead of hard, they, too, can be motivated to succeed.

[RETHINK]

- **What do you think Clark means when she says students should eliminate "hard" from their vocabulary?**
- **As a single mother, how can technology make her academic pursuits easier?**

Looking Back

LO 2-1 Discuss strategies to manage your time effectively.

- Decide to take control of your time.
- Become aware of the way you use your time now.
- Find your time style and create a time log.

LO 2-2 Explain ways to balance competing priorities.

- Set clear priorities.
- Consider how your competing priorities relate to one another.
- Identify your prime time for working, and estimate needed study time.
- Use time management tools such as a master calendar, a weekly timetable, and a daily to-do list.

LO 2-3 Identify ways to deal with surprises and distractions.

- Deal with surprises by saying no, getting away from it all, working in silence, taking control of communications, using the phone to conduct transactions, and leaving slack in your schedule to accommodate the unexpected.
- Avoid procrastination by breaking large tasks into smaller ones; starting with the easiest parts of a task first; working with other people; and calculating the true costs of procrastination.
- Learn strategies for balancing school and other life responsibilities.
- Manage work time carefully, use slack time on the job to perform school assignments, use flextime, accept new responsibilities thoughtfully, and assign the proper priority to work.

[KEY TERMS AND CONCEPTS]

Daily to-do list (p. 39)
Master calendar (p. 38)
Priorities (p. 35)
Procrastination (p. 46)
Time log (p. 33)
Weekly timetable (p. 38)

[RESOURCES]

ON CAMPUS

The college official that determines when classes meet is known as the registrar. If you are having difficulty in scheduling your classes, the registrar's office may be helpful. In addition, your academic advisor can help you work out problems enrolling in the classes you want.

For help with issues such as planning a study schedule for the upcoming term, dealing with multiple assignments due on the same date, or finding tips on dealing with competing academic and work demands, consult with your campus learning center. The staff can help you sort out the various options you may have.

IN PRINT

Stephen Covey's *The Seven Habits of Highly Successful People* (Simon & Schuster, 2013, plus a 2017 infographics edition), David Allen's *Getting Things Done: The Art of Stress-Free Productivity* (Penguin Books, 2015), and Laura Vandenberg's *I Know How She Does It: How Successful Women Make the Most of Their Time* (Portfolio, 2017) offer practical, hands-on guides to time management.

Microsoft Outlook 2016 Step by Step (Microsoft Press), by Joan Lambert, provides a quick, hands-on introduction to Microsoft's Outlook software, a popular time management program that is part of the Microsoft Office Suite.

Finally, Andrew Smart's *Autopilot: The Art and Science of Doing Nothing* (Fingerprint Publishing, 2017) is an antidote to the impulse to schedule every minute of our days. The book celebrates taking time out and devoting it to oneself, using scientific findings to explain the importance of doing nothing.

ON THE WEB

The *P.O.W.E.R. Learning* Connect Library provides online versions of all the time management forms presented in this chapter. You can complete the forms online or download them and print out as many copies as you need.

- Penn State University offers helpful advice on time management at **http://pennstatelearning.psu.edu/time-management**.
- Useful tips for managing your time and prioritizing tasks can be found at the University of Nebraska website at **https://ianrhr.unl.edu/time-management**.

The Case of . . .

The Time of His Life

Will Linz couldn't believe it. On the same day he had completed his term paper and handed it in, his instructor announced a test for the following week. When the class protested that the test hadn't been listed in the syllabus, the instructor murmured that she'd made a mistake and was sorry about the short notice.

Will panicked when he remembered that next week he also had to complete two lab reports he had put off because he had been working on his term paper. Even worse, next weekend was lost. He had promised—promised!—his girlfriend, who wasn't in college and worked full-time, that he would go with her to her annual company picnic. Although he dreaded the thought of being with a bunch of people he barely knew, he'd finally agreed to go just last week.

As he was driving home thinking about all this, his car started to sputter and then stalled. He was unable to get it started. That was it. He sat there on the side of the road, feeling like his life had completely fallen apart and wondering how he'd ever get it back together again.

1. What might you tell Will that could help solve his predicament?

2. Is there anything Will could have done to prevent the situation he now faces from occurring in the first place?

3. What specific time management techniques might Will have employed in the past to avoid these problems?

4. What strategies might Will use now to take control over his limited time during the coming week?

5. What advice could you give Will to try to prevent problems in time management for his next term?

CHAPTER 3

©Wavebreak Media Ltd/Alamy

Discovering Your Learning Styles, Self-Concept, and Values

Learning Outcomes

By the time you finish this chapter you will be able to

» **LO 3-1** Identify your learning styles and how they affect your academic success.

» **LO 3-2** Explain how self-concept and self-esteem affect academic performance.

» **LO 3-3** Create a personal mission statement.

©James Woodson/Digital Vision/Getty Images

The transformation began when Shaniqua Turner got her first paper back from her English literature instructor. It wasn't the grade—which was good—that mattered so much, but what her instructor uttered, almost as an afterthought, as she handed the paper back to Shaniqua: "Nice job. Your insights were good, and you have great potential as a writer."

Shaniqua was thrilled. She had always thought of herself as having only modest talent in English, and though at one point she had harbored the fantasy of being a newspaper reporter, she had never felt she was good enough to make it.

But now something clicked: Maybe she did have the ability to succeed in a career involving writing.

Looking Ahead

Through the experiences we have in life, we build up a sense of our strengths and weaknesses, what we like and dislike about ourselves. In the process, the sense of who we are also affects the choices we make and the things that we do.

In this chapter you will be asked to consider various aspects of yourself. First you'll look at the ways in which you learn and how you can use your personal learning style to study more effectively.

You'll then explore who you are more broadly, considering the various aspects of your personality. You'll see how your self-esteem—the way you perceive your strengths and weaknesses—can lead to success or failure.

Finally, this chapter helps you investigate where you are headed. By creating your own personal mission statement, you'll begin to solidify the knowledge of who you are and where you would be happiest and most productive in the future.

» LO 3-1 Discovering Your Learning Styles

Members of the Trukese people, a small group of islanders in the South Pacific, often sail hundreds of miles on the open sea. They manage this feat with none of the navigational equipment used by Western sailors. No compass. No chronometer. No sextant. They don't even sail in a straight line. Instead, they zigzag back and forth. Yet they almost always reach their destination with precision.

Trukese sailors can't really explain how they learned to navigate nor explain the processes that they use, but clearly they are successful sailors.

The case of Trukese sailors vividly illustrates that there are different ways to learn and achieve our goals.

Each of us has preferred ways of learning, approaches that work best for us. Our success depends not just on how well we learn but also on *how* we learn.

Learning styles reflect our preferred manner of acquiring, using, and thinking about knowledge. We have not just one learning style, but a variety of styles. Even though our ability may be identical to someone else's, our learning styles might be quite different.

Some South Pacific islanders are able to navigate with great accuracy across open seas without the use of standard navigation tools used by sailors in Western cultures. Their abilities illustrate that there are multiple ways to attain our goals and that there is no single route to success.
©9 Peter Essick/Getty Images

You probably already know quite a lot about your learning styles. Maybe you do particularly well in your biology classes while struggling with English literature. Or it may be the other way around. Because biology tends to be about natural processes, teachers present the subject as a series of related facts. English literature, however, requires you to think more abstractly, analyzing and synthesizing ideas.

Although we may have general preferences for fact-based learning or for learning that requires more abstract thinking, we all use a variety of learning styles. Some involve our preferences regarding the way information is presented to us, some relate to how we think and learn most readily, and some relate to how our personality traits affect our performance. We'll start by considering the preferences we have for how we initially perceive information.

learning style
One's preferred manner of acquiring, using, and thinking about knowledge.

What Is Your Preferred Receptive Learning Style?

One of the most basic aspects of our learning styles concerns the way in which we first encounter information. Our **receptive learning style** pertains to how we initially receive information from our sense organs. People have different strengths in terms of how they most effectively process information and which of their senses they prefer to use in learning. Specifically, there are four different types of receptive learning styles:

receptive learning style
Learning style related to the way in which we initially receive information from our sense organs.

- **Read/write learning style.** If you have a **read/write learning style,** you prefer information that is presented visually in a written format. You feel most comfortable reading, and you may recall the spelling of a word by thinking of how the word looks. You probably learn best when you have the opportunity to read about a concept rather than listening to a teacher explain it.
- **Visual/graphic learning style.** Students with a **visual/graphic learning style** learn most effectively when material is presented visually in a diagram or picture. You might recall the structure of a chemical compound by reviewing a picture in your mind, and you benefit from instructors who make frequent use of visual aids such as videos, maps, and models. Students with visual learning styles find it easier to see things in their mind's eye—to visualize a task or concept—than to be lectured about them.
- **Auditory/verbal learning style.** Have you ever asked a friend to help you put something together by having her read the directions to you while you worked? If you did, you may have an auditory/verbal learning style. People with **auditory/verbal learning styles** prefer listening to explanations rather than reading them.

read/write learning style
A style that involves a preference for written material, favoring reading over hearing and touching.

visual/graphic learning style
A style that favors material presented visually in a diagram or picture.

auditory/verbal learning style
A style that favors listening as the best approach to learning.

Journal Reflections

How I Learn

How would you respond to the following learning situations?

1. Would you rather read a newspaper, listen to the news on the radio, watch it on TV, or click your way through it on a website? Why do you think you have this preference?
2. When you get a new piece of software or a new tool, do you like to read the instructions or just "play with it" until you get the hang of it?
3. Suppose a friend is teaching you a new and complex procedure (such as a new game or the way to use a piece of computer software). Do you prefer to get the "big picture" first or the details?
4. When you're in class, what do you do during lectures? Try to write down the instructor's exact words, draw diagrams and make tables, or jot down a few big ideas?
5. What do your answers to the previous questions reveal about the way you prefer to learn new information?

They love class lectures and discussions, because they can easily take in the information that is being talked about.

tactile/kinesthetic learning style
A style that involves learning by touching, manipulating objects, and doing things.

- **Tactile/kinesthetic learning style.** Students with a **tactile/kinesthetic learning style** prefer to learn by doing–touching, manipulating objects, and doing things. For instance, some people enjoy the act of writing because of the feel of a pencil or a computer keyboard–the tactile equivalent of thinking out loud. Or they may find that it helps them to make a three-dimensional model to understand a new idea.

To get a sense of your own receptive learning style, complete **Try It! 1**. But remember, having a particular receptive learning style simply means that it will be easier to learn material that is presented in that style. It does not mean you cannot learn any other way!

Receptive learning styles have implications for effective studying:

If you have a read/write style, consider writing out summaries of information, highlighting and underlining written material, and using flash cards. Transform diagrams and math formulas into words.

Try It! POWER

What's Your Receptive Learning Style?

Read each of the following statements and rank them in terms of their usefulness to you as learning approaches. Base your ratings on your personal experiences and preferences, using the following scale:

1 = Not at all useful

2 = Not very useful

3 = Neutral

4 = Somewhat useful

5 = Very useful

	1	2	3	4	5
1. Studying alone					
2. Studying pictures and diagrams to understand complex ideas					
3. Listening to class lectures					
4. Performing a process myself rather than reading or hearing about it					
5. Learning a complex procedure by reading written directions					
6. Watching and listening to film, computer, or video presentations					
7. Listening to a book or lecture on tape					
8. Doing lab work					
9. Studying teachers' handouts and lecture notes					
10. Studying in a quiet room					
11. Taking part in group discussions					
12. Taking part in hands-on classroom demonstrations					
13. Taking notes and studying them later					
14. Creating flash cards and using them as a study and review tool					
15. Memorizing and recalling how words are spelled by spelling them "out loud" in my head					
16. Writing down key facts and important points as a tool for remembering them					

(continued)

1 | *continued*

Try It! POWER

	1	2	3	4	5
17. Recalling how to spell a word by seeing it in my head					
18. Underlining or highlighting important facts or passages in my reading					
19. Saying things out loud when I'm studying					
20. Recalling how to spell a word by "writing" it invisibly in the air or on a surface					
21. Learning new information by reading about it in a textbook					
22. Using a map to find an unknown place					
23. Working in a study group					
24. Finding a place I've been to once by just going there without directions					

SCORING:

The statements cycle through the four receptive learning styles in this order: (1) read/write; (2) visual/graphic; (3) auditory/verbal; and (4) tactile/kinesthetic.

To find your primary learning style, disregard your 1, 2, and 3 ratings. Add up your 4 and 5 ratings for each learning style (i.e., a "4" equals 4 points and a "5" equals 5 points). Use the following chart to link the statements to the learning styles and to write down your summed ratings:

Learning Style	Statements	Total (Sum) of Rating Points
Read/write	1, 5, 9, 13, 17, and 21	
Visual/graphic	2, 6, 10, 14, 18, and 22	
Auditory/verbal	3, 7, 11, 15, 19, and 23	
Tactile/kinesthetic	4, 8, 12, 16, 20, and 24	

The total of your rating points for any given style will range from a low of 0 to a high of 30. The highest total indicates your main receptive learning style. Don't be surprised if you have a mixed style, in which two or more styles receive similar ratings.

If you have a visual/graphic style, devise diagrams and charts. Translate words into symbols and figures.

If you have an auditory/verbal style, recite material out loud when studying. Work with others in a group, talking through the material, and consider tape-recording lectures.

If you have a tactile/kinesthetic style, incorporate movement into your study. Trace diagrams, build models, arrange flash cards, and move them around. Keep yourself active during class, taking notes, drawing charts, and jotting down key concepts.

What type of learning style do you think this student is demonstrating?
©Huntstock/Getty Images

Multiple Intelligences: Showing Strength in Different Domains

Do you feel much more comfortable walking through the woods than navigating city streets? Are you an especially talented musician? Is reading and using a complicated map second nature to you?

If so, in each case you may be demonstrating a special and specific kind of intelligence. According to psychologist Howard Gardner, rather than asking "How smart are you?" we should be asking a different question: "How are you smart?" To answer the latter question, Gardner has developed a *theory of multiple intelligences* that offers a unique approach to understanding learning styles and preferences.

The multiple intelligences theory says that we have eight different forms of intelligence, each relatively independent of the others. Each of the separate intelligences is linked to a specific kind of information processing in our brains:

"To be fond of learning is to be near to knowledge."

Attributed to Confucius, in "The Doctrine of the the Mean" [Zhong Yong Chung Yung], trans. In Wing-Tsit Chan, *A Sourcebook in Chinese Philosophy.* Princeton, NJ: Princeton University Press, 1963, 95–115.

- *Logical-mathematical intelligence* involves skills in problem solving and scientific thinking.
- *Linguistic intelligence* is linked to the production and use of language.
- *Spatial intelligence* relates to skills involving spatial shapes, contours, and structures, such as those used by artists and architects.
- *Interpersonal intelligence* is found in learners with particularly strong skills involving interacting with others, such as sensitivity to the moods, temperaments, motivations, and intentions of others.
- *Intrapersonal intelligence* relates to a particularly strong understanding of the internal aspects of oneself and having access to one's own feelings and emotions.
- *Musical intelligence* involves skills relating to music.
- *Bodily kinesthetic intelligence* relates to skills in using the whole body or portions of it in the solution of problems or in the construction of products or displays, exemplified by dancers, athletes, actors, and surgeons.
- *Naturalist intelligence* involves exceptional abilities in identifying and classifying patterns in nature.

All of us have the same eight kinds of intelligence, though in different degrees, and they form the core of our learning styles and preferences. These separate intelligences do not operate in isolation. Instead, any activity involves several kinds of intelligence working together. And, as Gardner points out, these eight intelligences may be only scratching the surface of what our capabilities are. For example, he suggests there may be even more intelligences that shape how we interact with the world. For example, there may be an "existential intelligence," which involves identifying and thinking about the fundamental questions of human existence.

To get a sense of which of the basic eight intelligences best characterize you, complete **Try It! 2**.

Personality Styles

Our learning styles are also influenced by our personality. Are you likely to try out for school productions? Or is the idea of getting on a stage totally lacking in appeal (if not completely terrifying)? Do you relate to the world around you primarily through careful planning or by spontaneously reacting?

According to the rationale of the *Myers-Briggs Type Indicator* (MBTI), a questionnaire frequently used in business and organizational settings to place people in one of 16 categories, personality type plays a key role in determining how we react to different situations. Specifically, we work best in situations in which others—both students and instructors—share our preferences and in which our personality is most suited to the particular task on which we are working.

The Myers-Briggs approach suggests that four major personality dimensions are critical to understanding personality styles. Although we'll describe the extremes of each dimension, keep in mind that most of us fall somewhere between the end points of each dimension.

- **Introverts versus extraverts.** A key difference between introverts and extraverts is whether they enjoy working with others. Independence is a key characteristic of introverted learners. They enjoy working alone, and they are less affected by how others think and behave. In contrast, extraverts are outgoing and more affected by the behavior and thinking of others. They enjoy working with others, and they are energized by having other people around.
- **Intuitors versus sensors.** Intuitors enjoy being creative and solving problems that require leaps of judgment. They get impatient with details, and they enjoy the challenge of solving problems and taking a big-picture approach. People categorized as sensors, on the other hand, prefer a concrete, logical approach in which they can carefully analyze the facts of the situation and come to a reasoned conclusion. Although they are good with details, they sometimes miss the big picture.
- **Thinkers versus feelers.** Thinkers prefer logic over emotion. They reach decisions and solve problems by systematically analyzing a situation. In contrast, feeling types rely more on their emotional responses. They are aware of others and their feelings, and they are influenced by their personal values and attachments to others.
- **Perceivers and judgers.** Before drawing a conclusion, perceivers attempt to gather as much information as they can. Because they are open to multiple perspectives and appreciate all sides of an issue, they sometimes have difficulty completing a task. Judgers, in comparison, are quick and decisive. They like to set goals, accomplish them, and then move on to the next task.

The Origins of Our Learning Styles

For many of us, our learning style preferences result from the kind of processing the two halves of our brain "specialize" in. Although the two halves of the brain are interdependent, certain kinds of tasks are more likely to be controlled by a particular half of the brain.

Your Sense of Intelligence

In this Try It!, you will be able to get a sense of your own pattern of multiple intelligences. To start, place a check beside each statement that applies to you.

_____ 1. Sometimes people say that I am a born leader.
_____ 2. I am good at solving mazes and other visual puzzles.
_____ 3. My life would be much less meaningful without music.
_____ 4. I figure out how things work, and I can usually fix things when they break.
_____ 5. Conserving resources and sustainable growth are two of the biggest issues of our times.
_____ 6. I think about my life goals pretty often.
_____ 7. I love word games like Scrabble, anagrams, and crossword puzzles.
_____ 8. I keep track of advances in science.
_____ 9. I listen to music on a daily basis.
_____ 10. I am able to learn about things by touching them.
_____ 11. People often look to me to help resolve disputes.
_____ 12. I make lists of things that I want to accomplish.
_____ 13. I cherish my collection of books.
_____ 14. I enjoy thinking about big philosophical questions.
_____ 15. I can recognize and name many different types of trees, flowers, and plants.
_____ 16. I am usually sensitive to color.
_____ 17. I keep a diary.
_____ 18. I have a good sense of rhythm. I can usually keep time to a piece of music.
_____ 19. Sometimes I can think without words, using just abstract ideas.
_____ 20. I seldom get lost, even in new places.
_____ 21. I am open to attending counseling sessions to learn more about myself.
_____ 22. Math and science are harder for me than English, social studies, and history.
_____ 23. People sometimes tell me that my mind works like a computer.
_____ 24. I am in good contact with my personal feelings.
_____ 25. When I am outside, I notice things like tracks, nests, and wildlife.
_____ 26. I am great at reading maps. I am usually the navigator.
_____ 27. When I talk with people, I often bring up things that I have read.
_____ 28. I like to garden and make things grow.
_____ 29. I can play one or more musical instruments.
_____ 30. I read whenever I have a free minute.
_____ 31. I am very systematic when I have to solve a problem.
_____ 32. I am pretty well coordinated.
_____ 33. I have pets, or at least I want to have them.
_____ 34. I have a good idea of my own strengths and weaknesses.
_____ 35. I have an appreciation for the arts.
_____ 36. I have three or more close friends.
_____ 37. I often tap out rhythms or sing melodies during the day.
_____ 38. I am a pretty good "do-it-yourselfer."
_____ 39. I am physically active at least three times a week.
_____ 40. I like to teach people what I know.

Using the scoring keys that follow, give yourself one point for each question that corresponds to the sentence you checked.

2 *continued*

Try It! P O W E R

KEY: Types of Intelligence

Linguistic
Questions: 7, 13, 22, 27, 30
Number of these statements checked: ______

Musical
Questions: 3, 9, 18, 29, 37
Number of these statements checked: ______

Naturalist
Questions: 5, 15, 25, 28, 33
Number of these statements checked: ______

Logical-mathematical
Questions: 8, 14, 19, 23, 31
Number of these statements checked: ______

Bodily kinesthetic
Questions: 4, 10, 32, 38, 39
Number of these statements checked: ______

Interpersonal
Questions: 1, 11, 17, 36, 40
Number of these statements checked: ______

Intrapersonal
Questions: 6, 12, 21, 24, 34
Number of these statements checked: ______

Spatial
Questions: 2, 16, 20, 26, 35
Number of these statements checked: ______

Now fill in the summary chart below to identify your pattern of different kinds of intelligence.

Type of Intelligence	Score
Linguistic	
Musical	
Naturalist	
Logical-mathematical	
Bodily kinesthetic	
Interpersonal	
Intrapersonal	
Spatial	

Are you surprised by the pattern of strengths in the different kinds of intelligence described by Gardner? Why or why not? How do you think your profile affects the way you learn and your learning styles and preferences?

WORKING IN A GROUP

Compare your patterns of strengths in the different types of intelligence. Ask others how their pattern affects their studying. How might working in a study group with students with different patterns from yours affect the success of the study group?

Specifically, **left-brain processing** concentrates more on tasks requiring verbal competence. For example, speaking, reading, thinking, and reasoning are more apt to occur in the left half of the brain. Information is processed in small, sequential units in left-brain processing.

In contrast, **right-brain processing** concentrates more on the processing of information in nonverbal domains, such as the understanding of spatial relationships, recognizing patterns and drawings, music, and emotional expression. Furthermore, the right hemisphere tends to process information globally, considering it as a whole. Consequently, people who naturally tend toward right-brain processing might prefer visual/graphic learning styles.

Here are some key facts to remember about learning, personality, and processing styles:

- **You have a variety of styles.** As you can see in the summary of different categories of styles in **Table 3.1**, there are several types of styles. For any given task or challenge, some types of styles may be more relevant than others. Furthermore, success is possible even when there is a mismatch between what you need to accomplish and your own pattern of preferred styles. It may take more work, but learning to deal with situations that require you to use less-preferred styles is important practice for life after college.
- **Your style reflects your preferences regarding which abilities you like to use—not the abilities themselves.** Styles are related to our preferences and the mental approaches we like to use. However, you may do quite well in areas that relate to learning styles that you don't prefer. Furthermore, you may struggle in situations in which you are using your preferred learning styles. Learning styles don't dictate success; hard work does.
- **Your style will change over the course of your life.** You can learn new styles and expand the range of learning experiences in which you feel perfectly comfortable. In fact, you can conceive of this book as one long lesson in learning styles, because it provides you with strategies for learning more effectively in a variety of ways.
- **You should work on improving your less-preferred styles.** Although it may be tempting, don't consistently make choices that increase your exposure to preferred styles and decrease your practice with less-preferred styles. The more you use approaches for which you have less of a preference, the better you'll be at developing the skills associated with those styles.
- **Work with others who have different styles.** If your instructor asks you to work in groups, seek out classmates who have styles that are different from yours. Not only will your classmates' differing styles help you to achieve collective success, but you can also learn from observing others' approaches to tackling the assignment.

left-brain processing
Information processing primarily performed by the left hemisphere of the brain, focusing on tasks requiring verbal competence, such as speaking, reading, thinking, and reasoning; information is processed sequentially, one bit at a time.

right-brain processing
Information processing primarily performed by the right hemisphere of the brain, focusing on information in nonverbal domains, such as the understanding of spatial relationships and recognition of patterns and drawings, music, and emotional expression.

Learning about Learning: The Theories That Explain How You Learn

Learning styles reflect how each of us prefers to study and approach new information that we encounter in our classes. But all of us are affected by some basic processes that underlie learning.

Researchers have developed a number of theories to explain learning. **Learning theories** are broad explanations about how we learn. Each of these theories takes a different approach and looks at somewhat different factors that help us to learn. Understanding the theories behind learning will help you study, remember information, and ultimately be a better learner.

We'll consider the three main learning theories.

learning theory
A broad explanation about how one learns.

table 3.1 Learning, Personality, and Processing Styles

All of us have particular learning, personality, and processing styles that we tend to rely on. At the same time, we have capabilities in less-preferred styles. So for example, though you may be primarily a read/write learner, you have the capacity to use auditory/verbal and tactile/kinesthetic approaches. Note in particular that the four categories of personality styles are considered independent of one another. For instance, you may be an extravert and at the same time a sensor, a feeler, and a judger. Furthermore, though the "Using the Style" column suggests ways that students with a particular style can make the most of that style, you should also try strategies that work for styles different from your own.

Category	Type	Description	Using the Style
Receptive Learning Styles	Read/write	A style that involves a preference for material in a written format, favoring reading over hearing and touching.	Read and rewrite material, take notes and rewrite them; organize material into tables; transform diagrams and math formulas into words.
	Visual/graphic	A style that favors material presented visually in a diagram or picture.	Use figures and drawings; replay classes and discussions in your mind's eye; visualize material; translate words into symbols and figures.
	Auditory/verbal	A style in which the learner favors listening as the best approach.	Recite material out loud when studying; consider how words sound; study different languages; tape-record lectures; work with others, talk through the material.
	Tactile/ kinesthetic	A style that involves learning by touching, manipulating objects, and doing things.	Incorporate movement into studying; trace figures and drawings with your finger; create models; make flash cards and move them around; keep active during class, taking notes, drawing charts, jotting down key concepts.
Multiple-Intelligences	Logical-mathematical	Strengths in problem solving and scientific thinking.	Express information mathematically or in formulas.
	Linguistic	Strengths in the production and use of language.	Write out notes and summarize information in words; construct stories about material.
	Spatial	Strengths involving spatial configurations, such as those used by artists and architects.	Build charts, graphs, and flowcharts.
	Interpersonal	Strengths found in learners with particularly strong skills involving interacting with others, such as sensitivity to the moods, temperaments, motivations, and intentions of others.	Work with others in groups.
	Intrapersonal	Strengths in understanding the internal aspects of oneself and having access to one's own feelings and emotions.	Build on your prior experiences and feelings about the world; use your originality.

	Musical	Strengths relating to music.	Write a song or lyrics to help remember material.
	Bodily kinesthetic	Strengths in using the whole body or portions of it in the solution of problems or in the construction of products or displays, exemplified by dancers, athletes, actors, and surgeons.	Use movement in studying; build models.
	Naturalist	Exceptional strengths in identifying and classifying patterns in nature.	Use analogies based on nature.
Personality Styles	Introvert versus extravert	Independence is a key characteristic of introverted learners, who enjoy working alone and are less affected by how others think and behave. In contrast, extraverts are outgoing and more affected by the behavior and thinking of others. They enjoy working with others.	Experiment with studying in groups compared with working alone; consider your performance in class discussions compared with working on your own.
	Intuitor versus sensor	Intuitive people enjoy solving problems and being creative, often taking a big-picture approach. Sensors, on the other hand, prefer a concrete, logical approach in which they can carefully analyze the facts of the situation.	For intuitors, reflect on the personal meaning of material and seek out tasks that involve creativity. For sensors, seek out concrete tasks that involve the application of logical principles.
	Thinker versus feeler	Thinkers prefer logic over emotion, reaching decisions through rational analysis. In contrast, feelers rely more on their emotions and are influenced by their personal values and attachments to others.	Thinkers should seek to systematically analyze situations, attempting to identify patterns. For feelers, use emotional responses to reflect on material.
	Perceiver versus judger	Before drawing a conclusion, perceivers attempt to gather as much information as they can and are open to multiple perspectives. Judgers, in comparison, are quick and decisive, enjoying setting goals and accomplishing them.	Perceivers organize material sequentially and into component parts; for judgers, using goal-setting preferences facilitates learning.
Brain Processing Styles	Left-brain processing	Information processing that focuses on tasks requiring verbal competence, such as speaking, reading, thinking, and reasoning; information is processed sequentially, one bit at a time.	Organize material logically; identify patterns; make tables of key information; break material into component parts.
	Right-brain processing	Information processing that focuses on information in nonverbal domains, such as the understanding of spatial relationships, recognition of patterns and drawings, music, and emotional expression.	Identify patterns; use graphs and drawings; read aloud; create models.

Source: Adapted from Lazear, D. (1999). The intelligent curriculum: Using MI to develop your students' full potential. Tucson, AZ: Zephyr Press.

Operant Conditioning Learning Theory: The Reinforcement Behind Learning

Very good . . . What a clever idea . . . Fantastic . . . I agree . . . Excellent . . . Super . . . Great point . . . This is the best paper you've ever written . . . You are really getting the hang of it . . . I'm impressed . . . A+

Did you ever wonder why we love to be praised? It turns out that positive affirmations of this sort underlie a type of learning known as operant conditioning, which is the basis for many of the most important kinds of learning.

operant conditioning Learning in which a behavior is modified by the presence of a reinforcer.

reinforcer Action or consequence that increases the probability that a behavior will occur again.

Operant conditioning is learning in which a behavior is made more or less likely to recur regularly because of the presence of a reinforcer. **Reinforcers** are things that increase the probability that a behavior will occur again. If you study hard for a test and are rewarded with a high grade, the high grade serves as a reinforcer. Operant conditioning theory tells us that you are more like to study hard in the future because of the rewards you received from studying in the past.

Cognitive Learning Theory: The Thoughts Behind Learning

Some learning theorists focus on the thought processes that underlie learning. According to cognitive approaches to learning, our cognitions (or thoughts) shape the way we learn. In particular, they look at the importance of observational learning, in which we learn by watching, and imitating, the behavior of other people.

Observational learning takes place in four steps:

1. Paying attention and perceiving the most critical features of another person's behavior
2. Remembering the behavior
3. Reproducing the action
4. Being motivated to learn and carry out the behavior

Not all behavior that we witness is learned or carried out. Whether we later imitate someone else depends, in part, on what eventually happens to that person as a result of the behavior.

If we observe a friend who studies more frequently than we do and notice that she receives higher grades, we are more apt to model her behavior than if her studying leads to nothing more than a sharp decline in her social life and an increase in fatigue. Models who are seen receiving reinforcement for their actions are more likely to be mimicked than those who are observed receiving punishment.

Classical Conditioning Learning Theory: Does the Name Pavlov Ring a Bell?

Ivan Pavlov was a Russian scientist who discovered, quite accidentally, one of the basic kinds of learning, called classical conditioning. In studying salivation in dogs, he found that sometimes the mere sight of the person who normally brought the dog's food, or even the sound of that person's footsteps, was enough to produce salivation in the dogs.

Pavlov's genius lay in his ability to recognize the implications of this discovery. He saw that the dogs were responding not only on the basis of a biological need (hunger) but also as a result of learning–or, as it came to be called, classical conditioning. **Classical conditioning** is a type of learning in which a neutral stimulus (such as someone's footsteps) comes to elicit a response after being paired with a different stimulus (such as food) that naturally brings about that response.

classical conditioning A type of learning in which a neutral stimulus elicits a response after being paired with a natural stimulus.

To demonstrate classical conditioning, Pavlov (1927) attached a tube to the salivary gland of a dog, allowing him to measure precisely the dog's salivation. He then rang a bell and, just a few seconds later, presented the dog with meat. This pairing occurred repeatedly and was carefully planned so that each time exactly the same amount of time elapsed between the presentation of the bell and the meat. At first the dog would salivate only when the meat was presented, but soon it began to salivate at the sound of the bell. In fact, even when Pavlov stopped presenting the meat, the dog still salivated after hearing the sound. The dog had been classically conditioned to salivate to the bell.

But what about humans? In fact, Pavlov's discovery of classical conditioning has some very practical implications for how we come to associate various stimuli with responses. For example, you may not go to a dentist as often as you should because of previous associations of dentists with pain. Similarly, we may come to associate academic tests with negative emotions and anxiety, which can hinder our performance.

Why Learning Theories Matter

Although the basics of the three main learning theories are somewhat abstract, each has important practical implications for helping you to learn better. For example, operant conditioning suggests that rewarding yourself with periodic breaks while you study will make your study sessions more productive, because the breaks act as a reinforcer.

Similarly, using cognitive approaches to learning, you might watch the behavior of other students who have been successful. By observing the behavior of successful students, you can attempt to imitate their study habits.

Finally, classical conditioning, which focuses on learning through associations, suggests that studying in the room where you'll later be taking a test will help you to perform better on the test. Being in the same room will help trigger memories of the material you studied earlier—an idea that research has proven correct.

If you are wondering which of the theories is "best," you're asking the wrong question. Each of the theories takes a different approach and focuses on different aspects of learning, in much the same way that we can take multiple routes on a map to the same location. Understanding each of the learning theories, along with knowledge of your preferred learning styles, will help you develop your own personal learning system that can help you become a more successful student.

Using Your Instructors' Teaching Styles

In the same way that each of us has preferred learning styles, instructors have their own styles of teaching, often based on their own personal learning styles. They may not even be aware of them, but their learning styles have an important impact on the way they teach—and that, in turn, will help determine how well you do in their classes.

3  WORKING IN A GROUP **Try It!** POWER

Instructor Styles

Working as a group with your classmates, try to determine your course instructor's learning style by answering the following questions:

1. What clues does the language your instructor uses give you about his or her learning style?

2. What assignments has the instructor scheduled, and what do they tell you about the instructor's learning style?

3. Are there constraints (such as class size, scheduling factors, school traditions) that also influence the instructor's teaching style, apart from his or her underlying learning style?

Instructors who make frequent requests to "draw" or "diagram" may favor a more visual-graphic learning style. In contrast, if their tendency is to ask you to "list," or "discuss," or "analyze," they may be more in tune with a verbal/reading style.

Similarly, instructors who assign frequent projects that involve oral presentations and demonstrations might be indicating that their learning style is somewhat auditory. On the other hand, instructors whose assignments consist of frequent written work may have a more visual style. Work on "Instructor Styles" (**Try It! 3**) to get a sense of your instructor's learning style, and look at the **Course Connections** feature for strategies for dealing with what you find.

Learning styles are only one example of how the kind of person you are—your strengths and weaknesses, your likes and dislikes, your overall personality—affects your academic success. In fact, the totality of who you are is central in determining the path you follow in achieving success. Let's turn now to how an understanding of the totality of who you are influences your college performance by considering self-concept.

Course **Connections**

How Your Instructor's Teaching Style Can Guide Your Studying Strategies

Having a sense of your instructor's teaching style can help maximize your success in a course. It can give you insight into the kinds of test questions your instructor may favor and help you strategize about what to pay particular attention to when you're reading and studying course material.

If your instructor focuses on broad, conceptual views of material

- Be prepared for essay questions that ask you to pull different pieces of information together.
- Expect assignments in which you must synthesize different points of view into a coherent whole.
- As you read material, consider how different facts fit together into a broader picture.

If your instructor focuses on facts and details

- Prepare for tests by learning individual facts, which may be tested using multiple-choice or fill-in test questions.
- Expect assignments that are very specific and detailed.
- Study by focusing on specific facts. For instance, consider creating note cards on which you write individual bits of information.

What if your preferred learning style doesn't match up with your instructor's teaching style? Don't fall into the trap of assuming that you're at a disadvantage in the class. Keep in mind that there are benefits to the discomfort that you may experience when your instructor emphasizes activities that don't match your own learning styles. Remember that real learning is often difficult and uncomfortable, and the practice you get with less-preferred learning styles in the end will make you a more accomplished student.

It's also important to avoid using a mismatch of class requirements and your own learning style preferences as an excuse for not doing well in a class. You're going to be asked to carry out tasks throughout your academic and professional career that don't speak to your personal strengths and preferences. You need to overcome your own hesitance and throw yourself into tasks that don't speak to your strengths. That's how real learning and growth will occur.

» LO 3-2 Self-Concept and Self-Esteem

Of course you know who you are. You know your first and last name. You know where and when you were born, and you have no trouble identifying your ethnic background. You can probably recite your Social Security number with ease.

But if this is all that comes to mind when you think about who you are, you're missing a lot of the picture. There's a lot more to you than name, rank, and serial number. What makes you unique and special are your thoughts, your beliefs, your dreams. You have a unique history, and this set of experiences together with your genetic makeup–the combination of genes you inherited from your parents–is unlike anyone else's.

Our view of ourselves–our **self-concept**–has three parts:

self-concept
One's view of oneself that forms over time, comprising three components: the physical self, the social self, and the personal self.

1. Our physical self is both who we are physically–the color of our eyes or the curliness of our hair–and how we feel about our physical form. We all have our blemishes, protruding stomachs, long noses, or other physical quirks, but we don't all feel the same way about them.

2. Our social self is made up of the roles we play in our social interactions with others. As you're reading these words, you're not only a student but also a son or daughter, a friend, a citizen, and possibly an employee, a spouse, a lover, and/or a parent. Each of these roles plays an important part in defining your self-concept. Each also helps determine how you behave while acting in that particular role.

> "When I discover who I am, I'll be free."
> **Tze-Sze**, philosopher

3. Finally, our self-concept also contains a personal self—our inner core, which is that private part of ourselves that no one knows about except us. It consists of the innermost thoughts and experiences that we may or may not choose to share with others.

Self-Concept and Self-Fulfilling Prophecies

The way we view ourselves determines how we interact with others, what challenges we feel ready to take on, and our expectations for future success. If you look at yourself as a successful student, you are likely to expect that you'll be a successful student in the future. On the other hand, if you see yourself as an incapable, inept student, your chances for future success are diminished.

In short, our self-concept can act as a self-fulfilling prophecy. A **self-fulfilling prophecy** occurs when we hold a belief or expectation that affects our behavior, thereby increasing the likelihood that our beliefs or expectations will come true. For instance, a person who views herself as a poor student may find herself thinking: "Why bother working hard? I'm no good as a student; that's just the way I am." It's easy to see how such a view could lead to a self-fulfilling prophecy: By not working hard, the student guarantees that the prophecy of poor performance comes true.

self-fulfilling prophecy
A phenomenon that occurs when we hold a belief or expectation that affects our behavior, thereby increasing the likelihood that our beliefs or expectations will come true.

On the other hand, self-fulfilling prophecies can have positive effects. A person who sees herself as a good student will probably be motivated to study and complete assignments enthusiastically. Her view of herself can therefore bring about the expected behavior—in this case, success.

To get a clearer picture of your own self-concept:

- **Examine the roles you play.** To understand who we are, we need to understand the different roles that we play in life. Consider which of these roles are central to who you are—and who you want to be. Consider how an outsider might look at your actions, beliefs, and interests. How would that person characterize you?
- **Identify your strengths and weaknesses.** Look at yourself with a clear and objective eye, and consider what you do particularly well and what you don't do particularly well. If you're honest, you'll come up with several areas in which you need work—and many other areas in which you're already quite strong. Use **Table 3.2** to help you organize your thoughts and build an initial inventory of your strengths and weaknesses.

  As you consider your strengths and weaknesses, don't place a value on them. The fact that you procrastinate and put off tasks doesn't make you a bad person, just as the fact that you're a good student doesn't necessarily make you a good person. The point in seeking to identify who you are is to determine your self-concept with accuracy, not to determine how good (or bad) a human being you are.

table 3.2 Inventory Your Strengths and Weaknesses

To get a clearer picture of your self-concept, complete an honest inventory of your strengths and weaknesses. To help you organize your thoughts, use the following table, adding brief examples.

Aspects of Self	**Strengths**	**Weaknesses**
Physical self		
Health and fitness		
Sports		
Nutrition and diet		
Appearance		
Other		
Social self		
Friend		
Son/daughter		
Lover/spouse		
Citizen/community member		
Employee		
Student		
Roommate		
Classmate		
Team or group member (e.g., sports, band, club)		
Other		
Personal self		
Personal experiences		
Unique traits		
Personality		
Spiritual self		
Habits		
Attitudes/opinions		
Ideas/thoughts		
Other		

- **Construct your own definition of who you are.** Don't let what you believe others think about you determine what you think you're good at and bad at. See yourself through your own eyes, not someone else's.
- **Accept your entire self-concept.** If you're being honest with yourself, you'll find that there are parts of yourself that you like more than others. That's OK. Don't disown the parts you don't like; they're also part of who you are. Instead, accept that some parts of yourself need work, while others are the source of justifiable pride.

Make Sure Your Self-Concept Is Yours

Our self-concept is not only influenced by our own views of ourselves. In addition, we sometimes permit our behavior to be influenced by others' views of who we are and their expectations about us.

For example, if we think an instructor views us as a particularly hard worker, we may not want to disappoint him by slacking off. If we believe that our boss admires our persistence, we may be motivated to show her our persistence when we're working on a difficult problem on the job.

Responding to others' positive perceptions can be fine, for the results are good. But what happens if someone holds a negative view of who we are? What if we're constantly told that we're not working hard enough . . . or that we're not as smart as our older brother . . . or that we are the hard worker, but not the creative one?

"Respect yourself if you would have others respect you."

Baltasar Gracian, author

The results can be devastating. If we consistently hear such messages about who we are, we can come to believe them. Even worse, our behavior can start to mirror the negative messages we're hearing. If we're consistently told that we don't work hard enough, we may begin to slack off. If we're told we're not as smart as someone else, we may begin to think of ourselves as not very bright, and not try very hard on academic tasks. Or if someone tells us we're not creative, we may not try very hard to be creative.

In short, the negative messages that we hear from others can come to act as a prison, placing us in bondage to others' negative beliefs about who we are and what our capabilities are. It's crucial, then, not to buy into others' negative views of who we are. Our biggest help, and sometimes handicap, in this effort is self-esteem.

Self-Concept and the Returning Student

For students who return to college after a significant break in their education, answering the question "Who am I?" is complicated. Some returning students have held jobs with significant responsibilities. Or they may have been supervisors who made key decisions. Now they must follow the direction of multiple instructors who make assignments that affect their lives on a daily basis. In some ways, it's like having many bosses.

In other cases, returning students feel out of touch with their fellow students who may be younger than they are. It may feel strange to suddenly be placed in the role of "student," and it may make them wonder what they've gotten themselves into. Because they may not have taken classes or studied for years, they may lack self-confidence. Furthermore, if spouses or other family members are not supportive of those who return to college, students might feel threatened.

If you're a returning student, remember that you're still the same person you were before you came back to college. The competencies that you had prior to college, that helped you navigate the world, are still part of who you are. In fact, other students may look up to you or seek your advice because of pre-college experience.

Returning to College After Military Service: The Special Case of Veterans

Starting or returning to college can be particularly difficult for returning military veterans. Soldiers may have faced life-and-death decisions on a daily basis, and they may find the issues they face in college trivial in comparison. Furthermore, soldiers live in highly structured situations in which most decisions are made by others.

In contrast, college is unstructured in a way that can be unsettling. Furthermore, some veterans simply are bored with college, compared with the high levels of stimulation that accompanied their lives in combat zones.

If you are a returning veteran, how can you adjust to the new reality you face in college? Several strategies may be effective:

- **Go out of your way to establish relationships with other students and college faculty and staff.** Becoming involved in organized activities can help break down the barriers you may feel with other students.
- **Don't be afraid to show your feelings.** Although you may have learned to hide your emotions in a combat situation, you need to be able to express your emotions. You may be surprised to see how much non-veterans are interested in and accepting of how you react to situations.
- **Lead a balanced life.** Combat may have made you more pessimistic and cynical. Focus on people and institutions (such as a religion) that can produce more positive feelings.
- **Talk to other veterans on campus.** They have shared similar experiences and can understand the feelings that you may be having.
- **Seek out special services for veterans.** Many colleges have offices devoted to supporting returning veterans. Talk with counselors or other support staff. They will provide a sympathetic ear and can make a real difference in your well-being and ultimately your success in college.

Self-Esteem: Building a Positive View of Yourself

When you think about yourself as a student, you probably don't stop there. Instead, you may see yourself as a "good" student or maybe a "just OK" student. Similarly, when you consider yourself in the role of friend, you may view yourself as a "loyal-to-the-end" friend or maybe, in the opposite case, a "fair-weather" friend. In short, when we look inward at who we are, we don't just stop with a characterization of the different roles that we play in the world. Instead, we place a value on them. We see the various facets of our self-concept not in neutral terms, but as either positive or negative.

Self-esteem is the overall evaluation we give ourselves as individuals. It reflects the degree to which we see ourselves as individuals of worth and determines our general acceptance of ourselves. If we have high self-esteem, we generally feel respect for and acceptance of ourselves. On the other hand, if we have low self-esteem, we may lack respect for ourselves, reject parts of who we are, and judge ourselves negatively.

self-esteem
The overall evaluation we give ourselves as individuals.

To get a sense of your own general level of self-esteem, complete the self-assessment in **Try It! 4**.

4 **Try It!** POWER

Measuring Your Self-Esteem

To get an informal estimate of your self-esteem, complete the following scale..

Statement	Strongly Agree	Agree	Disagree	Strongly Disagree
1. On the whole, I am satisfied with myself.				
2. At times I think I am no good at all.				
3. I feel that I have a number of good qualities.				
4. I am able to do things as well as most other people.				
5. I feel I do not have much to be proud of.				
6. I certainly feel useless at times.				
7. I feel that I am a person of worth, at least the equal of others.				
8. I wish I could have more respect for myself.				
9. All in all, I am inclined to feel that I am a failure.				
10. I take a positive attitude toward myself.				

Scoring: For statements 1, 3, 4, 7, and 10, score as follows:

1. Strongly agree = 4 points
2. Agree = 3 points
3. Disagree = 2 points
4. Strongly disagree = 1 point

For statements 2, 5, 6, 8, and 9, score as follows:

1. Strongly agree = 1 point
2. Agree = 2 points
3. Disagree = 3 points
4. Strongly disagree = 4 points

Add your points together, and interpret the total as follows:

The highest possible score (i.e., an apparently very high level of self-esteem) is 40 points, and the minimum score (i.e., an apparently very low level of self-esteem) is 10. Most people score in the 30- to 40-point range. A much smaller number of people score in the 20s. A score of 10 to 20 is often found in people who suffer from chronic depression; those who score at this level should consider consulting a health care provider or call a 24-hour hotline such as 800-448-3000. Keep in mind that this is a very rough gauge of self-esteem and that scores will vary depending on a number of factors, including your mood when you complete the questionnaire.

Now consider the following:

- Do the results of the questionnaire match your own gut feelings about yourself?
- Do you think your self-esteem has changed? Do you have any ideas as to why?

Source: Rosenberg, Morris. 1989. *Society and the Adolescent Self-Image.* Revised edition. Middletown, CT: Wesleyan University Press.

Why Self-Esteem Matters

People with high self-esteem are generally happier and better able to cope with adversity. High self-esteem provides a sense of security, because people with high self-esteem feel they are able to deal with problems that may arise. They also have a sense of **self-efficacy**, the expectation that they are capable of achieving their goals in many different kinds of situations. High self-esteem can also give people a sense of purpose and the belief that they are productive members of society.

self-efficacy
The expectation that one is capable of achieving one's goals in many different kinds of situations.

In contrast, individuals lacking in self-esteem are more insecure, and their belief in their ability to reach their goals is weak. They feel less tied to others, and their sense of purpose is not firm. And when others are successful, people with low self-esteem may feel jealousy and envy.

Low self-esteem can produce a cycle of failure in which low self-esteem leads to low expectations, reduced effort, elevated anxiety, poor performance, and, finally, an affirmation of the low self-esteem that began the cycle in the first place. Such a cycle can be difficult to break (see **Figure 3.1**).

If a student with low self-esteem begins studying for a test believing that he is likely to do badly, he may put forth relatively little effort. Moreover, because he is virtually sure he is going to do poorly on the test, he may experience extremes of anxiety, feeling that (another) failure is lurking just ahead.

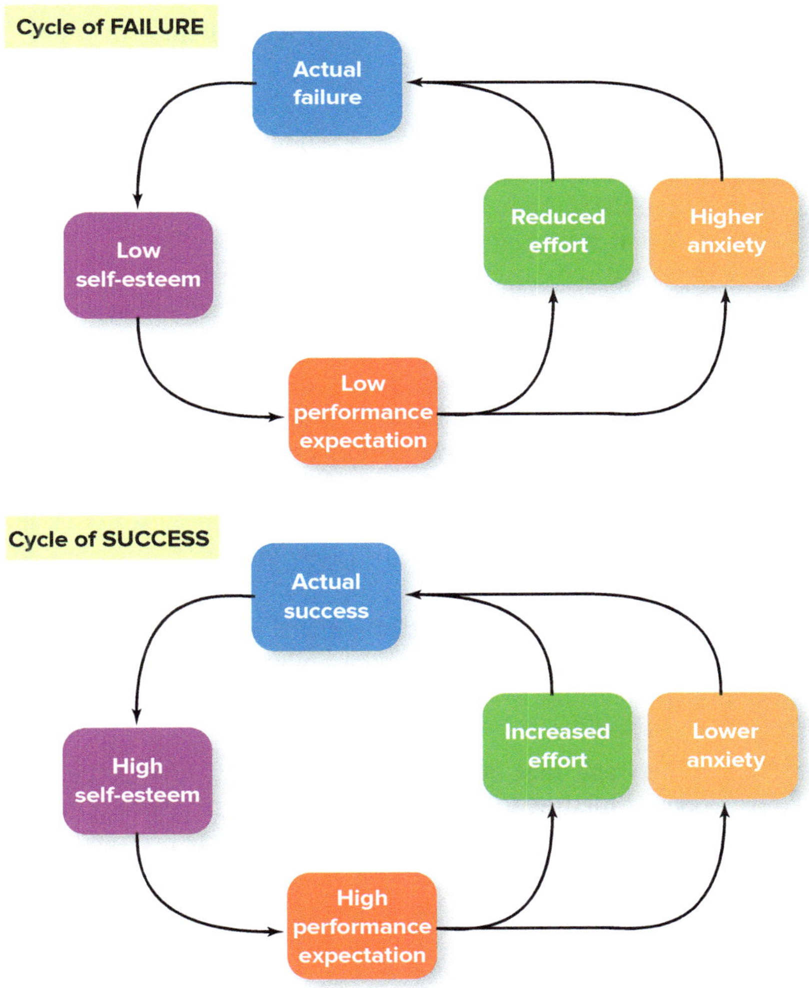

figure 3.1
The Cycle of Failure and the Cycle of Success
Low self-esteem can lead to low performance expectations. In turn, low performance expectations can produce reduced effort and high anxiety, both of which can lead to failure—and ultimately reinforce the low self-esteem that started the cycle. In contrast, those with high self-esteem expect success, and that expectation leads to greater effort and lower anxiety, thereby increasing the likelihood of actual success. Ultimately, this success boosts self-esteem.

Ultimately, the combination of lack of effort and anxiety produced by his low self-esteem does him in, and he actually does do poorly on the test. But the cycle of failure is not yet complete: Rather than telling himself that low effort and elevated anxiety caused his poor test performance, he views it as an affirmation of his inferior ability. In turn, this misperception serves to reinforce his low self-esteem.

On the other hand, people with higher self-esteem find themselves in a cycle of success shown in **Figure 3.1**. Their higher expectations lead to increased effort and lower anxiety, making the probability of success greater. In turn, this helps affirm their higher sense of self-esteem that started the cycle.

Breaking the Self-Esteem Cycle of Failure

"OK," you may be saying to yourself, "I understand that self-esteem is important. But how am I supposed to ignore a lifetime of learning and improve my self-esteem?"

It's not a simple matter to shed a less-than-ideal view of ourselves and adopt a more positive one. And you certainly won't be able to change your basic conception of yourself in the course of a few days. But there are steps you can take to bring yourself closer to an ideal level of self-esteem. They include the following:

- **Accept yourself, warts and all.** No one is perfect, and becoming a perfect person should not be your goal in life. If it were, you'd be doomed to failure, because you'd never measure up.

  Accept the fact that there are certain aspects of yourself and your life that you're not pleased with. In fact, embrace your awareness of your displeasure: If you didn't realize that there were some things about yourself that needed improvement, you'd be out of touch with who you are.
- **Understand that everyone has value and self-worth.** Every individual has value and self-worth, some unique spark that sets him or her apart from everyone else. Examine yourself and your life, and get a picture of the particulars that make *you* you.

  Low self-esteem can lead to low performance expectations. In turn, low performance can produce reduced effort and high anxiety, both of which can lead to failure—and ultimately reinforce the low self-esteem that started the cycle.
- **Distinguish the different parts of who you are.** No one is all bad, just as no one is all good. Understanding that you have failings in one arena of life doesn't mean that you can't be successful in others. It makes no sense to base your self-esteem on what you do worst in life, so don't make the mistake of focusing solely on your failings and minimizing your successes.
- **Don't just rely on—or wait for—others' praise.** Your self-esteem should not be solely dependent on the praise you get from others. Use your own judgment to evaluate the level of success you've achieved on a given task.
- **Understand that building self-esteem is a lifelong undertaking.** It's taken a lifetime to develop whatever level of self-esteem you currently have. Your self-esteem is not going to change overnight.

Rebuilding self-esteem isn't easy. It's particularly hard to do at a time when you face a major life transition, such as the beginning of your college experience; your oldest friends and family may not be

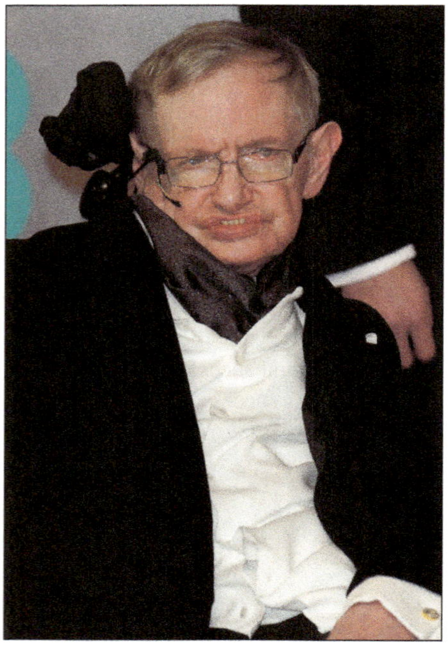

Physicist Stephen Hawking overcame significant challenges in the physical realm to make ground-breaking intellectual contributions.

nearby, and the level of academic work you encounter presents new challenges. In fact, starting college presents a special opportunity to grow and develop. It's a new environment, giving you the opportunity to unlearn old patterns of behavior that have held you back and master new ones that will permit you to have a more positive view of yourself. Don't let low self-esteem keep you from becoming what you can be.

» LO 3-3 Preparing a Personal Mission Statement

Twenty-five hundred years later, Plato's words are still true. If you never consider what you want out of life, what your dreams and aspirations are, and where you're heading, you're in danger of missing out on the most fundamental and meaningful parts of life. The day-to-day details of life will use up all your time, and you won't know exactly where it has gone.

> "The life that is unexamined is not worth living."
>
> **Plato, in Plato & Jowett, B. (1913).** ***Dialogues of Plato.*** **United Holdings Group.**

One way to get a clearer picture of our life is to create a formal document—called a **personal mission statement**—of what we actually hope to achieve during our lifetime. The P.O.W.E.R. framework provides a systematic series of steps (described below, and summarized in the P.O.W.E.R. Plan graphic) that can help us look inward and determine the way we wish to carry out our lives.

personal Mission Statement
A formal statement regarding what a person hopes to achieve during his or her lifetime.

P Prepare — Identifying Your Values

The first step toward understanding ourselves is to assess our underlying values. **Values** are the qualities we see as most desirable and important. They are the attributes that are most important to us, the ones that we use to guide our lives.

values
The qualities we see as desirable and most important.

To assess your values, work through the following steps:

1. Choose the five values that you hold most dear. Here are some examples, but don't necessarily restrict yourself to these: a comfortable life, an exciting life, a sense of accomplishment, world peace, beauty, equality, security, freedom, happiness, inner harmony, love, national security, pleasure, religion, self-respect, fame, friendship, wisdom, work, financial security, risk taking, being challenged.
2. For each value, answer each of these questions below: Why is it important to you, who taught it to you, how has it affected your behavior in the past, and in what ways can you affirm it through your future behavior?

Value # 1 ____________

Why it is important:

Who taught it to you:

How it has affected your past behavior:

In what ways you can affirm it through future behavior:

Value # 2 ____________

Why it is important:

Who taught it to you:

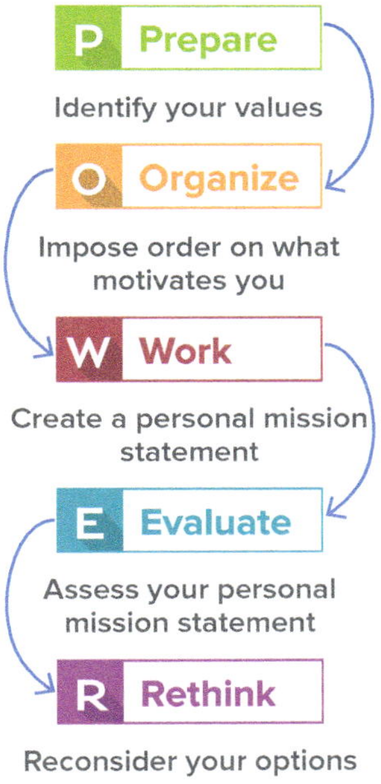

P.O.W.E.R. Plan

How it has affected your past behavior:

In what ways you can affirm it through future behavior:

Value # 3 ___________

Why it is important:

Who taught it to you:

How it has affected your past behavior:

In what ways you can affirm it through future behavior:

Value # 4 ___________

Why it is important:

Who taught it to you:

How it has affected your past behavior:

In what ways you can affirm it through future behavior:

Value # 5 ___________

Why it is important:

Who taught it to you:

How it has affected your past behavior:

In what ways you can affirm it through future behavior:

After you've identified your most important values, you'll be ready to move to the "organize" step in developing a mission statement: determining what motivates you.

O Organize

Imposing Order on What Motivates You

> "Authentic values are those by which a life can be lived."
>
> **Tze-Sze, philosopher**

Abraham Lincoln. Albert Einstein. Eleanor Roosevelt.

What is the common link among these three people? According to psychologist Abraham Maslow, each of them achieved self-actualization. **Self-actualization** is a state of self-fulfillment in which people realize their highest potential in their own unique way.

self-actualization
A state of self-fulfillment in which people realize their highest potential in their own unique way.

Maslow says that self-actualization is the highest of the various needs that motivate our behavior. As you can see in the illustration in **Figure 3.2**, our underlying needs form a pyramid. At the bottom of the pyramid are our most basic needs, such as the biological needs that drive our behavior, including food, water, sleep, and sex. The basic needs are not much different from those that drive the behavior of nonhuman animals. The needs on the next higher level of the pyramid are safety needs; we need a safe, secure environment to function effectively.

But as humans are able to meet their more basic survival needs, they have a chance to become acquainted with levels of need that relate to more advanced qualities, such as the need for love. As the pyramid indicates, our love and belongingness needs come next: our needs to form relationships with others and to look outside ourselves. We seek to give affection and to be contributing members of groups within society.

After these needs are fulfilled, we strive for the esteem of others. Esteem relates to the desire to develop a sense of self-worth. We want others to be aware of our competence and worth and to acknowledge our value in the world.

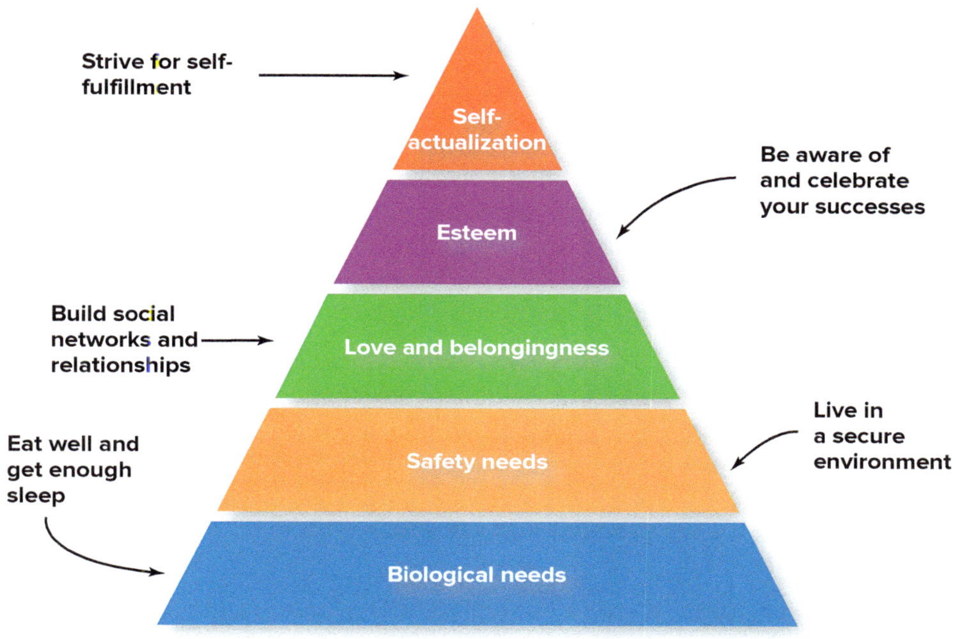

figure 3.2
Pyramid of Motivational Needs and Their Relationship to Student Behavior

Only after we meet these physiological, safety, love and belongingness, and esteem needs can we strive for self-actualization. Although early views of self-actualization restricted this quality to a few well-known individuals, self-actualization is now generally regarded as a need that can apply to any of us.

For instance, a parent with excellent nurturing skills who raises a family, a teacher who year after year creates an environment that maximizes students' opportunities for success, and an artist who realizes her creative potential might all be self-actualized individuals. The crucial characteristic of self-actualization is that we feel at ease with ourselves and satisfied that we are using our talents to the fullest.

W Work

Creating a Personal Mission Statement

- *To make, distribute, & sell the finest quality all natural ice cream & euphoric concoctions with a continued commitment to incorporating wholesome, natural ingredients and promoting business practices that respect the earth and the environment.*
- *To operate the Company on a sustainable financial basis of profitable growth, increasing value for our stakeholders & expanding opportunities for development and career growth for our employees.*
- *To operate the Company in a way that actively recognizes the central role that business plays in society by initiating innovative ways to improve the quality of life locally, nationally & internationally.*[1]

You may have already guessed the name of the business that would make the statements reproduced above: Ben & Jerry's ice cream company. Like almost every other major organization, Ben & Jerry's has a mission statement, a series of statements about what the organization does and the principles that guide its corporate life.

What's good for Ben & Jerry's is good for you. Each of us should set out a personal mission statement, a description encompassing our own personal objectives, long-term goals, and guiding philosophy. It's a kind of personal constitution that sets out broad principles of how we wish to conduct our lives. It is a guideline that allows us to adapt our behavior to changes in our lives without straying from our overall direction and purpose.

A personal mission statement also helps us move from our abstract values and motivational needs to something concrete by providing the foundation for developing specific goals to guide our behavior. By making our values explicit, we are better able to formulate short- and long-term goals that reflect what is important to us.

For example, consider the following mission statement created by one student:

> *My mission is to use my personal abilities fully to become an engineer who will work on projects that will help others improve the quality of their lives. In addition, I hope to form meaningful relationships with others and to marry and raise children who will make their own contributions to society. Finally, I wish to participate in bettering the world by volunteering in organizations that will enhance the quality of my own community.*

This mission statement reflects several underlying values and needs: the desire to use work to improve others' lives, the wish to form relationships with others, and the desire to make the world a better place. In some respects it is fairly specific (such as the desire to become an engineer and to marry and have children), while in others it is fairly vague (such as the wish to participate in organizations that can improve community life). The key point is that it provides a general framework, a way of evaluating whether any particular choice fits into this individual's overall personal mission.

To create your own personal mission statement, follow these three preliminary steps:

- **Summarize your most important values and motivational needs.** You've already assessed your values and motivational needs. Try to distill them into several key principles that will guide your life.
- **Consider what you want your major product to be.** Ben & Jerry's makes ice cream. What do you want to be known and remembered for? Your work? Your family? Your good deeds? Your relationships with others? Something you've created–art, photos, writings?
- **Reflect on the kind of person you want to be.** Do you wish to be kind, friendly, helpful, assertive, powerful, wealthy, altruistic?

Once you've completed these three steps, you're in a position to create your own mission statement. Write it in **Try It! 5**.

E Evaluate

Assessing Your Personal Mission Statement

After you've written a personal mission statement, consider whether it accurately captures what you are looking for out of life. Would a friend who knows you well see it as a valid reflection of who you are? Does the mission statement take a long-term view, reflecting not just where you are now, but where you wish to be in the future? Is it general enough to fit the many different circumstances in which you will find yourself?

Career Connections

Identifying Your Interests

Creating a personal mission statement can help you think more productively about one of the most important decisions of your college career: identifying your profession. One way to jump-start this process is to systematically identify your current interests, a critical step in determining what kind of work will be most fulfilling and satisfying for you.

However, few of us are fully aware of the complete range of our interests, primarily because we don't take the time to systematically inventory them. Consequently, career advisor Richard Bolles suggests answering the following questions in order to identify the scope of your interests:

- What are your favorite subjects and hobbies?
- What do you like to talk about most?
- When you go to a newsstand, what are the subjects of magazines that you are attracted to?
- When you read a newspaper, what section do you read first?
- If you're wandering around a bookstore, what kinds of books do you spend the most time looking at?
- When you surf the World Wide Web, what sites do you find yourself returning to regularly?
- When you watch TV game shows, what categories would you choose?
- If you were to write a book, what would you write about?
- When you get so engrossed in thought that you lose track of time, what is it you are thinking about?

Once you've got a better grip on your interests after answering each of these questions, the next step is to prioritize them, rank-ordering them from most interesting to least interesting. You can then use this rank-ordered list to investigate careers, seeking out work involving interests similar to your own. For example, if you have strong interests in the visual arts, you might explore careers involving graphic design, computer-assisted graphics, or architecture. If you avidly keep up with the news of the day, you might consider journalism or television news production. The critical point is to try to match what you like to do (as well as your learning and personality style strengths) with what you'll be doing when you're on the job. The closer the match, the happier and more successful you'll be.

Only you can determine the ability of your personal mission statement to capture what is important to you. If you feel it doesn't, rewrite it. Eventually you'll come up with a statement that illustrates what you feel makes you special.

R Rethink Reconsidering Your Options

Personal mission statements should not be seen as set in stone. Instead, they should be considered living documents that you can change periodically as you become clearer about what you want for yourself.

That's why it's important to periodically revisit your personal mission statement, the final step in the P.O.W.E.R. Plan for creating a personal mission statement. When you do rethink your statement, ask yourself if it's still representative of your values and motivational needs. Consider whether it should be amended to reflect changes that have occurred in your life.

Even if you don't modify it, periodically reading your personal mission statement is important. It will remind you of who you are and what you are trying to get out of the one life you have.

5 **Try It!** POWER

Write a Mission Statement

1. What are your most important values (e.g., comfort, environmental awareness, kindness to others, inner harmony, challenge, etc.)?

2. What are your motivational needs (e.g., love and belonging, esteem, self-actualization)?

3. In what general area or career do you wish to work?

4. What will be the most important "product" for which you want to be known and remembered (e.g., good deeds, wealth, power, prestige, artistic creations, business acumen, etc.)?

5. What kind of person do you want to be (helpful, kind, solitary, powerful, wealthy, etc.)?

6. In what sort of community do you want to live (large city, small city, small town, suburbs, country, woods, farm, etc.)?

7. With whom do you want to live (e.g., spouse, friends, children, etc.)?

8. What words describe your ideal lifestyle (e.g., sophisticated, woodsy, agricultural, down-home, laid-back, ambitious, etc.)?

Now write your mission statement. You might, for example, state how you plan to achieve your motivational needs and realize your values through your chosen career. Next you might describe the sort of person you want to be and the "product" you plan to contribute to the world. Finally, you might describe your intended lifestyle, including the type of community you would like to live in and the nature of your ideal family.

PERSONAL MISSION STATEMENT

Prepared by:____________

Date:____________

To Thine Own Self Be True: No One Is Responsible for Your Life but You

"Don't take many English courses; they won't help you get a decent job." "How about pre-med? You'd make a great doctor." "Sign up for management classes so you'll be ready to join the family business when you graduate."

Sound familiar? Many of us have heard suggestions like these proposed by parents or others close to us. Such comments often sound quite reasonable.

However, suggestions like these should be taken with great caution. The reason is that they relate to decisions that you, and only you, should make. You are the one who must live with their consequences. You are the one who must live with yourself.

One of the most questionable reasons to follow a particular path in life is that other people want you to do something. Decisions that affect your life should be your decisions—decisions you make after you've considered various alternatives and chosen the path that suits you best.

Making your own decisions does not mean that you should ignore the suggestions of others. For instance, family members have their own unique experiences that may make their advice helpful. Furthermore, having participated in a great deal of your personal history, they may have a clear view of your strengths and weaknesses.

Still, the views of family members are not necessarily accurate. They may still see you as a child, in need of care and protection. Or they may see only your strengths. Or, in some unfortunate cases, they may focus only on your flaws and shortcomings.

People will always be giving you advice. Ultimately, though, you have to make your own judgments about what's right for you, following your head—and your heart.

Speaking *of* Success

©stocklight/Shutterstock

NAME: **Colin Powell**

SCHOOL: **B.A., The City College of New York; M.S., George Washington University**

Few who knew Colin Powell when he was growing up would have guessed that he would become the highest-ranking military commander in the United States and later the country's Secretary of State.

The son of Jamaican immigrants, Powell characterizes himself as lacking drive while growing up in a poor South Bronx neighborhood in New York City. He describes himself as aimless.[2]

Although his parents, who had high educational expectations, urged him to transfer from his neighborhood high school to a more demanding school, his guidance counselor advised against it, citing his previous undistinguished academic performance. Powell ended up maintaining a C average in his neighborhood school, where simply showing up was largely what it took to pass.

But Powell's parents encouraged him to continue his education and apply to college. Bowing to their pressure, he entered The City College of New York, starting as an engineering major, and later switching to geology. Most important, though, Powell found a passion: participation in the college ROTC program, which provided training that allowed students to become officers in the military upon graduation. ROTC training provided him with a sense that he had found what he was looking for in life.

When Powell graduated, he immediately entered the Army, distinguishing himself early on as a military leader. But he also came to feel he needed more education. He enrolled in a master's degree program in Government and Business Administration at George Washington University, earning nearly straight A's.

Returning to the Army after receiving his master's degree, Powell moved up rapidly through the ranks, ultimately moving into the highest military post in the country. After retiring from the military, Powell became the U.S. Secretary of State, serving four years in that position.

As a highly visible and successful black American, Powell understands that he is seen as a role model, particularly by young blacks. In his own words, "Do not let the fact that you're a minority or that you come from a different background or that you are trapped structurally somewhere serve as an anchor to keep you down."[3] He certainly took his own advice.

[RETHINK]

- **How did Colin Powell's self-concept change over time, and why?**
- **How important a role did self-esteem play in Colin Powell's many successes?**

Looking Back

LO 3-1 Identify your learning styles and how they affect your academic success.

- People have patterns of diverse learning styles—characteristic ways of acquiring and using knowledge.
- Learning styles include read/write, visual/graphic, auditory/verbal, and tactile/kinesthetic styles (the receptive learning styles).
- The multiple intelligences view says that we have eight different forms of intelligence, each relatively independent of the others.
- Personality styles that influence learning are classified along dimensions of introversion/extraversion, intuition/sensing, thinking/feeling, and perceiving/judging.

LO 3-2 Explain how self-concept and self-esteem affect academic performance.

- Self-concept is the understanding of the self that a person forms over time. Its major components are the physical, social, and personal selves.
- Self-concept is important because of the effects it has on people's attitudes and behavior. Self-concept can act as a self-fulfilling prophecy, in that people act in accordance with their self-concepts.
- Self-esteem is the overall evaluation we give ourselves as individuals.
- High self-esteem can lead to greater happiness, an enhanced ability to cope with adversity, a sense of security and confidence, and a sense of self-efficacy.
- Low self-esteem can lead to insecurity, low self-efficacy, and a cycle of failure.

LO 3-3 Create a personal mission statement.

- A personal mission statement can be used to determine important values and to state the principles by which we intend to lead our lives.
- People's needs can be organized into a hierarchy in which the most basic and fundamental needs form the base of a pyramid and higher-order needs sit atop the basic needs.
- Although we should consider the ideas and opinions of others, we need to make our own decisions and choose our own path.

[KEY TERMS AND CONCEPTS]

Auditory/verbal learning style (p. 59)
Classical conditioning (p. 71)
Learning style (p. 59)
Learning theory (p. 67)
Left-brain processing (p. 67)
Operant conditioning (p. 70)
Personal mission statement (p. 81)
Read/write learning style (p. 59)
Receptive learning style (p. 59)
Reinforcer (p. 70)
Right-brain processing (p. 67)
Self-actualization (p. 82)
Self-concept (p. 73)
Self-efficacy (p. 79)
Self-esteem (p. 77)
Self-fulfilling prophecy (p. 74)
Tactile/kinesthetic learning style (p. 60)
Values (p. 81)
Visual/graphic learning style (p. 59)

[RESOURCES]

ON CAMPUS

If you are interested in learning more about your pattern of learning styles, visit your campus counseling center or career center, where you may be able to take special assessment tests that can pinpoint your learning preferences and offer study strategies based on those preferences.

When dealing with the uncertainties of life and establishing your own sense of direction, it may help to speak to someone who has perspective and experience with college students. Here, too, a good place to start on campus is either a general counseling center or one that is designed to help students choose career paths. Mental health offices can also be helpful in putting you in touch with a therapist with whom you can explore issues revolving around your self-concept and self-esteem. Don't hesitate to get help. You are doing it for yourself.

IN PRINT

Thomas Armstrong and Sue Teele's *Rainbows of Intelligence: Exploring How Students Learn* (2015) provides an introduction to learning styles, offering tips and suggestions for making use of the ways that people learn.

In addition, Bradley Staats' *Never Stop Learning* (Harvard Business Review Press, 2018), Ken Bain's *What the Best College Students Do* (Belknap Press, 2012) and Linda Beren's *Understanding Yourself and Others* (Telos, 2010) offer insight into learning strategies and personality types.

Don't Sweat the Small Stuff . . . and It's All Small Stuff (Hyperion, 2007), written by Richard Carlson, is a down-to-earth guide that is meant to help you sort out what is—and is not—important in your life.

ON THE WEB

- Greg Kearsley, an instructional designer and online course developer at Walden Institute, has developed a useful site called "Explorations in Learning & Instruction: The Theory into Practice Database" (**www.instructionaldesign.org/about.html**). This database contains short summaries of 50 major theories of learning and instruction.
- **EducationPlanner.org**, a public service unit of the Pennsylvania Higher Education Assistance Agency, offers an interactive set of questions that can help you find out what kind of student you are, what your learning style is, and which study habits you can improve. **http://www.educationplanner.org/students/self-assessments/kind-of-student.shtml**
- An excellent set of guidelines on setting up a personal mission statement can be found at Kent State University's Ohio Literacy Resource Center site (**http://literacy.kent.edu/Oasis/Leadership/mission.htm**).

Design Elements: *Pencil/Notebook: ©Squared Studios/Photodisc/Getty Images; Group/Laptop: ©Jacob Lund/Shutterstock; Apples: ©I. Rozenbaum/PhotoAlto; People/Silhouette: ©Ingram Publishing; Colorful Notebooks: ©Dragan Nikolic/Alamy; Group/Occupations: ©Rawpixel.com/Shutterstock; Woman/Laptop: ©JGI/Jamie Grill/Getty Images; Man/Laptop: ©Westend61/Getty Images.*

The Case of . . .

The Instructor Who Spoke Too Much

Lana Carlson, a 26-year-old woman living in Carlsbad, Missouri, was at her wits' end. The instructor in her introductory psychology class spent each 50-minute lecture talking nonstop. He barely paused to acknowledge students' questions, and his only goal seemed to be to present as much material as possible. He even gave assignments in the same fast, nasal tone that he used throughout class.

If it weren't for her friend Darren Rubbell, who was in the same class, Lana would never have managed to figure out how to complete the assignments, which the professor never bothered to write down. The strange thing was that Darren didn't seem to have much trouble with the professor's endless talking. In fact, he claimed to enjoy the class a lot. He had no trouble following the lectures and understanding the assignments, seeming to absorb like a sponge the information the instructor was spouting.

1. Based on what you know about learning styles, what might be the source of Lana's difficulties?

2. What learning style does the instructor apparently assume all students have? Do you think this is one of Lana's learning styles? Why or why not?

3. How might the instructor change his presentation to accommodate diverse learning styles?

4. Why does Lana's friend Darren have so little trouble with the instructor's lectures?

5. Why do you think Lana has less trouble understanding Darren after class than she has understanding her instructor?

6. If you were Lana, what might you do to improve your situation?

CHAPTER

4 Taking Notes

Learning Outcomes

By the time you finish this chapter you will be able to

- » LO **4-1** Describe techniques for taking notes in class.
- » LO **4-2** Apply techniques for taking notes from written materials.
- » LO **4-3** Explain methods for effective notetaking.

©Hero Images/Getty Images

When he sat himself down in the front row of his biology class at the start of his second semester in college, Hill Taylor realized that something fundamental had changed.

In the past, Hill would have sat as far back in the classroom as he could. That's what he had done all through high school and the beginning of his first semester.

But then he received C grades on three midterms.

In a notetaking workshop Hill enrolled in afterward, he learned the importance of active listening and taking good notes in class. He also learned that one way to become more engaged in class is to sit close to the instructor.

Trying out the strategies he was taught in the workshop, Hill found—a bit to his surprise—that they helped. By the end of the semester, he'd pulled his grades way up.

Looking Ahead

Hill Taylor's move from the back to the front of the classroom was both a source and a symbol of his academic success. Hill's ability to take good notes is also likely to pay off beyond the classroom, because notetaking skills not only help produce academic success in college but also contribute to career success.

In this chapter we discuss effective strategies for taking notes during class lectures, during other kinds of oral presentations, and from written sources such as textbooks. There's a lot more to good notetaking than you probably think—and a lot less if you view notetaking as essentially "getting everything down on paper." As we explore the ins and outs of notetaking, we'll pause along the way to discuss the tools of the notetaking trade, how to be an active learner, how to think your way to good notes, and how to deal with disorganized instructors.

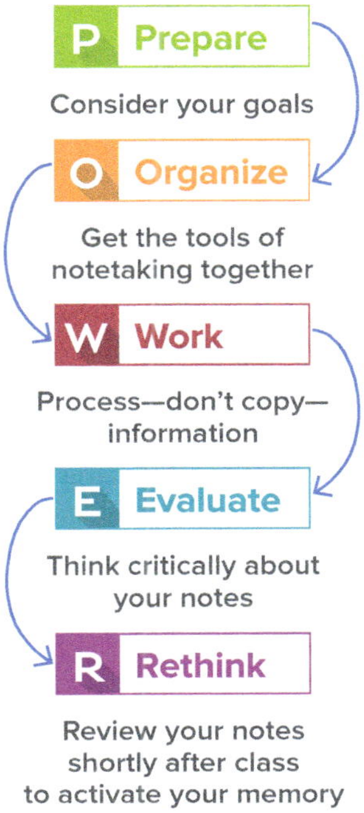

P.O.W.E.R. Plan

» LO 4-1 Taking Notes in Class

Perhaps you know a student who desperately tries to write down everything the instructor says, resulting in a set of notes that are virtually a transcript of everything spoken in class. And maybe you believe that if only you took such comprehensive notes, you'd be a much better student.

However, good notetaking does not mean writing down every word that an instructor utters. With notetaking, less is often more, meaning that strategically taking fewer notes can be more effective than taking more notes. We'll see why as we consider the basic steps in P.O.W.E.R. notetaking.

P Prepare — Considering Your Goals

As with other academic activities, preparation is a critical component of notetaking. The following steps will prepare you for action:

- **Identify the instructor's—and your—goals for the course.** On the first day of class, most instructors talk about their objectives, what they hope you'll get out of the class, and what you'll know when it's over. Most restate the information on the class syllabus, the written document that explains the assignments for the semester. For example, they may say that they want you to "develop an appreciation for the ways that statistics are used in everyday life."

The information you get during that first session and through the syllabus is critical. If the instructor's goals aren't stated explicitly, you should attempt to figure them out. In addition to those "external" goals, you should have your own goals. What is it you want to learn from the course? How will the information from the course help you to enhance your knowledge, achieve your dreams, improve yourself as a person?

- **Complete assignments before coming to class.** Your instructor enthusiastically describes the structure of the neuron, recounting excitedly how neurons don't physically touch one another and how electrons flow across neurons, changing their electrical charge. One problem: You have only the vaguest idea what a neuron is. And the reason you don't know is that you haven't read the assignment.

  Chances are you have found yourself in this situation at least a few times, so you know firsthand that sinking feeling as you become more and more confused. Because you can't follow the discussion, you can't get interested either, so the class seems boring, and you end up thinking about what you'll have for lunch or the movie you saw last night.

  The moral: Always go to class prepared. Complete all of your reading and other assignments beforehand. Instructors assume that their students have done what they've assigned, and their lectures are based on that assumption. It's virtually impossible to catch on to the gist of a lecture if you haven't completed the assignments.

"The highest result of education is tolerance."
Helen Keller, author

- **Accept the instructor, despite his or her limitations.** Not every instructor is a superb lecturer. You already know that, just as there are differences in skills among students, some instructors are better at lecturing than others. However, it's your responsibility to overcome a lecturer's flaws. A challenging lecturer is not an excuse to not try your hardest or to give up. Don't let a poor lecture style—or the fact that the instructor has a terrible haircut or a mouth that droops to one side or rumpled clothing—get in the way of your education. You're going to notice these things, but don't let them interfere with your goals. Good notetaking requires being prepared to listen to the material.

An engaging lecturer can make even the most complex material come alive in the classroom, whereas an instructor who is unorganized or dull can make coming to class sheer drudgery. No matter what the lecturer's style, however, you need to be prepared to take effective notes.
©sirtravelalot/Shutterstock

- **Perform a preclass warm-up.** No, this doesn't mean stretching just before each class. As you head to class or settle into your seat, skim your notes from the previous lecture, looking over what the instructor said and where that lecture left off. You should also briefly review the main headings or summary section of any reading you've been assigned.

  The warm-up doesn't have to be long. The goal is simply to refresh yourself, to get yourself into the right frame of mind for the class.

- **Choose a seat that will promote good notetaking.** You should certainly choose a seat that permits

Journal Reflections

How Do I Take Notes?

1. Describe your typical notetaking techniques in a few sentences. Do you try to write down as much of what the instructor says as possible? Do you tend to take only a few notes? Do you often find you need more time to get things down?

2. Overall, how effective would you say your notetaking techniques are?

3. In which classes do your techniques work best? Worst? Why?

4. Do your notes ever have "holes" in them—due to lapses of attention or times when you couldn't get down everything you wanted to? When do you usually discover them? What do you do about them?

5. How might the process of taking notes help develop a deeper understanding of the material being discussed?

you to see and hear clearly, but there's more to your choice than that. Picking the right seat in a classroom can make a big difference.

Where is the best place to sit? Usually it's front and center. Instructors make more eye contact with the people near them, and they sometimes believe that the best, most engaged students sit closest.

Furthermore, sitting in the back of the class may make you feel disengaged and out of touch with what is happening at the front of the room. In turn, this may make it easier for your mind to wander.

O Organize

Getting the Tools of Notetaking Together

Do you like to take notes in class using a favorite kind of pen? Or is your preference to take notes on a laptop computer?

By the time we reach college, most of us have developed distinct tastes when it comes to what we use to take notes. Although taking your favorite kind of pen to class or having access to your laptop will not make you a better notetaker, not having them certainly will interfere with your getting the most out of class.

There are several things to consider as you prepare for class:

- **If you are taking notes by hand, choose the appropriate writing utensil.** Generally, using a pen is better than using a pencil. Ink is less likely to smudge, and what you produce with ink is usually brighter and clearer–and therefore easier to use when studying. On the other hand, for math and science classes, where you may be copying down or even working through formulas in class, a pencil might be better, because it's easier to erase if you make a mistake when copying detailed, complex information.

  Sometimes you may want to use a combination of pen and pencil. And in some cases you might use several different colors. One color–such as red–might signify important information that the instructor mentions will be on the test. Another color might be reserved for definitions or material that is copied from the board. And a third might be used for general notes on the lecture.

- **Choose a notebook that assists in notetaking.** Loose-leaf notebooks are particularly good for taking notes because they permit you to go back later and change the order of the pages or add additional material in the appropriate spot. But whatever kind of notebook you use, *use only one side of the page for writing; keep one side free of notes.* There may be times when you're studying that you'll want to spread out your notes in front of you, and it's much easier if no material is written on the back of the pages.

- **Consider using the Cornell Method of Notetaking.** According to educator Walter Pauk,[1] who devised the *Cornell Method of Notetaking,* the best way to take notes is to divide each notebook page into three sections. First, draw a line across the bottom of the page, an inch or two from the bottom. Second, draw a line down the left side of the page, about 2½ inches from the left-hand margin (illustrated in **Figure 4.1**).

  To use the Cornell system, keep the notes you write in class within the largest area on the right-hand side of the page. Indent major supporting details beneath each main idea, trying to use no more than one line for each item, and leave space between topics to add information. Later, when you review your notes, you'll be able to jot down a keyword, catch phrase, or major idea on the left side of the page. Finally, you can use the area at the bottom of the page to summarize the key points covered on the page.

- **Consider the benefits of taking your textbook to class.** It's often a good idea to take your textbook to class, unless your instructor advises you otherwise. Sometimes instructors will refer to information contained in it, and sometimes it's useful to have it handy to clarify information that is being discussed. You can also use it to look up key terms that may momentarily escape you. But don't, under any circumstances, use class time as an opportunity to read the textbook!

- **Consider using a laptop computer to take notes in class.** There are several advantages: Legibility problems are avoided, and it's easy to go back and revise or add material after you've taken the notes.

  Furthermore, there are several terrific notetaking apps that can help you take notes efficiently. Among the best are Evernote, Microsoft OneNote, and Google Keep. They can help you organize your notes, scan images from instructor whiteboard notes or handouts, draw on and highlight your notes, and share notes with other students. On the other hand, there are potential pitfalls to using a computer to take notes. You may end up keyboarding more and thinking less. Or you may succumb to the temptation to check your e-mail or text your friends, rather than listening to your instructor. In fact, research shows that students spend as much of a third of their class time on online activities unrelated to class.

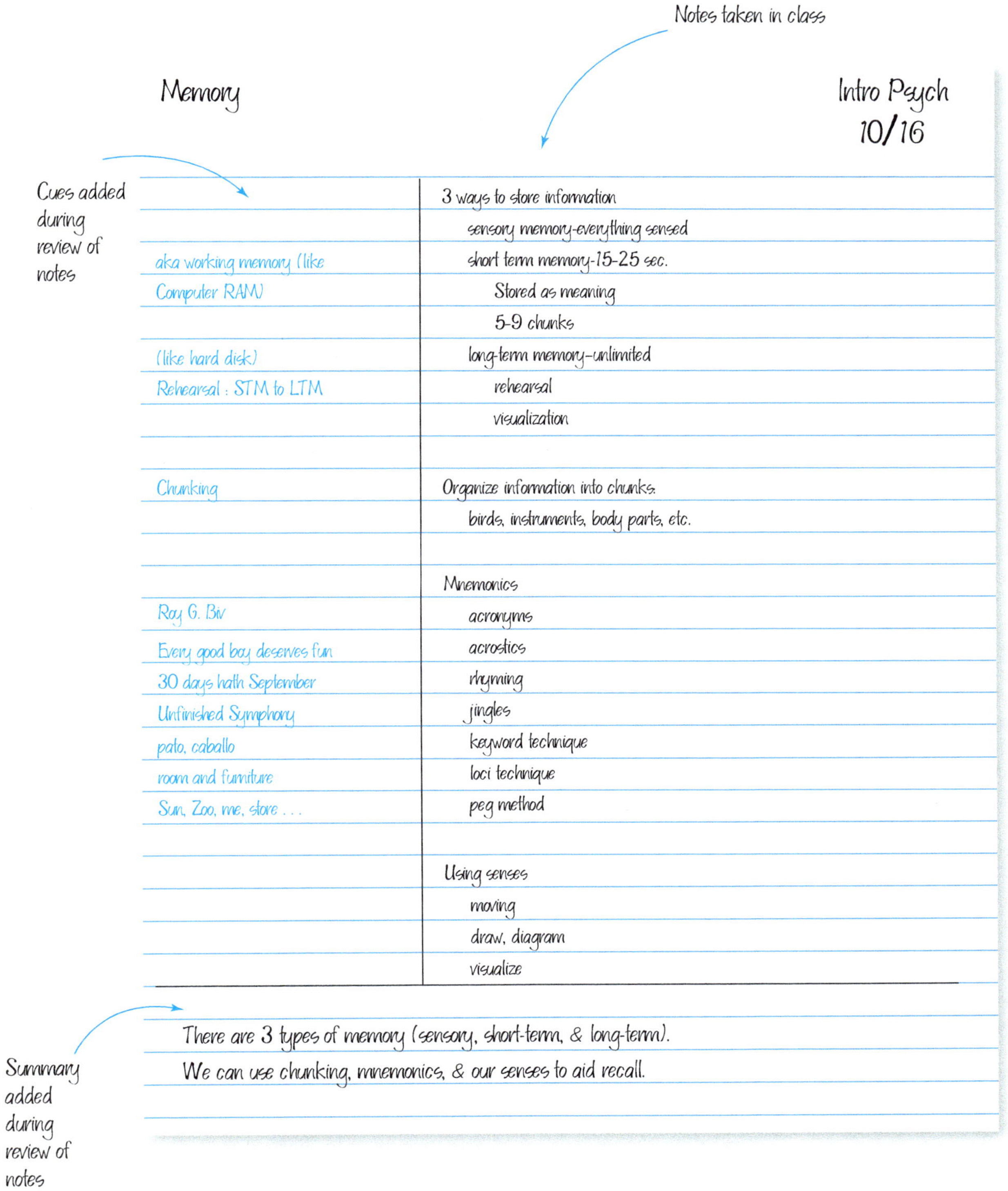

figure 4.1

A Notetaking Sample

In this example of a student's notes on a lecture about memory, she has used the Cornell Method of Notetaking; she has written the material in the right-hand column during class. Later, when reviewing her notes, she wrote down key pieces of information in the left-hand column and summarized the key points at the bottom.

Using a laptop to take class notes ensures that they will be legible and that it will be easy to revise them after class. However, it's difficult to input graphical material, such as complex formulas, and there's also a danger that you'll be tempted to take too many notes.
©Purestock/SuperStock

Because of their drawbacks, some instructors have strong feelings about the use of laptops in their class. Consequently, be sure to ask for permission before using your laptop to take notes.

Use these guidelines to make the most effective use of your laptop to take notes:

1. Make sure your computer is fully charged.
2. Use a computer that has a quiet keyboard so you don't annoy your fellow students, and make sure the built-in speaker is turned off. A tablet device, which allows you to write on the screen in the same way you write with paper and pencil, may be the best choice.
3. Stay focused on your instructor. Avoid the temptation to play computer games, surf the web, or respond to texts.
4. Finally, have an alternative, low-tech notetaking backup. Sometimes instructors present graphical material or formulas that are hard to input into a computer via a keyboard. And sometimes your computer may fail.

W Work

Processing—Not Copying—Information

With pen poised, you're ready to begin the work of notetaking. The instructor begins to speak, and you start to write as quickly as you can, taking down as many of the instructor's words as possible.

Stop! You've made your first mistake. The central act in taking notes is not writing; listening and thinking are far more important. The key to effective notetaking is to write down the right amount of information—not too much and not too little.

hearing
The involuntary act of sensing sounds.

active listening
The voluntary act of focusing on what is being said, making sense of it, and thinking about it in a way that permits it to be recalled accurately.

Successful notetaking involves not just *hearing* what the instructor says, but *listening actively.* **Hearing** is the involuntary act of sensing sounds. The annoying drip of a faucet or the grating sound of a roommate's voice speaking on the phone in the next room are two examples of how hearing is both involuntary and often meaningless. In contrast, **active listening** is the voluntary act of focusing on what is being said, making sense of it, and thinking about it in a way that permits it to be recalled accurately. Listening involves concentration. And it requires shutting out competing thoughts, such as what we need to pick up at the grocery store or why our date last night went so badly wrong. (To get a sense of your own listening skills, complete **Try It! 1**.)

Keeping the importance of active listening in mind, consider the following recommendations for taking notes:

- **Listen for the key ideas.** Not every sentence in a lecture is equally important, and one of the most useful skills you can develop is separating the key ideas from supporting information. Good lecturers strive to make just a few main points. The rest of what they say consists of explanation, examples, and other supportive material that expands on the key ideas.

1 PERSONAL STYLES

Try It! P O W E R

Determine Your Listening Style

Consider the following pairs of statements. Place a check next to the statement in each pair that more closely describes your style.

- ☐ 1a. When I'm listening in class, I lean back and get as comfortable as possible.
- ☐ 1b. When I'm listening in class, I sit upright and even lean forward a little.
- ☐ 2a. I let the instructor's words wash over me, generally going with the flow of the lecture.
- ☐ 2b. I try to guess in advance what the instructor is going to say and what direction the lecture is taking.
- ☐ 3a. I regard each lecture as a separate event, not necessarily related to what the instructor has said before or will say the next time.
- ☐ 3b. As I listen, I regularly ask myself how this relates to what was said in previous classes.
- ☐ 4a. When I take notes, I try to reproduce the instructor's words as closely as possible.
- ☐ 4b. When I take notes, I try to interpret and summarize the ideas behind the instructor's words.
- ☐ 5a. I don't usually question the importance of what the instructor is saying or why it's the topic of a lecture or discussion.
- ☐ 5b. I often ask why the content of the lecture is important enough for the instructor to be speaking about it.
- ☐ 6a. I rarely question the accuracy or logic of a presentation, assuming that the instructor knows the topic better than I do.
- ☐ 6b. I often ask myself how the instructor knows something and find myself wondering how it could be proved.
- ☐ 7a. I just about never make eye contact with the instructor.
- ☐ 7b. I often make eye contact with the instructor.

If you tended to prefer the "a" statements in most pairs, you have a more passive listening style. If you preferred the "b" statements, you have a more active listening style. Based on your responses, consider ways that you can become a more active listener.

Your job, then, is to distinguish the key ideas from their support. To do this, you need to be alert and always searching for your instructor's **meta-message**—that is, the underlying main ideas that a speaker is seeking to convey, or the meaning behind the overt message you hear.

meta-message
The underlying main ideas that a speaker is seeking to convey; the meaning behind the overt message.

How can you discern the meta-message? One way is to *listen for keywords.* Instructors know what's important in their lecture; your job is to figure it out, not just from what they say but from how they say it.

For instance, listen for clues about the importance of material. Phrases like "don't forget . . . ," "be sure to remember that . . . ," "you need to know . . . ," "the most important thing that must be considered . . . ," "there are four problems with this approach . . . ," and—a big one—"this will be on the test . . ." should cause you to sit up and take notice. Another good sign of importance is repetition. If an instructor says the same thing in several ways, it's a clear sign that the material being discussed is important.

> "I had tons of notes—I copied *every word* the professor said. Actually, I was so busy writing that I didn't understand a thing."
>
> **Student, Saint Joseph's University, in Tyler, S. (1997). *Been There, Should've Done That.* Haslett, MI: Front Porch Press. P. 117.**

Be on the lookout for nonverbal signals indicating the importance of a topic. Does an instructor get excited about a particular subject area? Or does he or she seem unenthusiastic when talking about something? Use nonverbal cues to gauge the significance of a particular topic.

Finally, listen for what is *not* being said. Sometimes silence is not only golden but informative as well. By noting what topics are not being covered in class, or are presented only minimally, you can gauge the relative importance of ideas in comparison with one another.

This is where preliminary preparation and organization come in. The only way to know what's left out of a lecture is to have done the assigned readings in advance. Also, don't be fooled into thinking that if a topic is not covered in class, it's unimportant: Most instructors believe students are responsible for all material that is assigned, whether or not it's explicitly covered in class.

- **Use short, abbreviated phrases—not full sentences—when taking notes.** Forget everything you've ever heard about always writing in full sentences. If you try to write notes in complete sentences, you'll soon become bogged down, paying more attention to your notes than to your instructor. In fact, if you use full sentences, you'll be tempted to try transcribing every word the instructor utters, which, as you now know, is not a good idea at all.

  Instead, write in phrases, using only key words or terms. Save full sentences for definitions or quotes that your instructor clearly wants you to know word for word. For example, consider the following excerpt from a lecture:

  > *There are two kinds of job analyses used by human resource experts: First, there are job- or task-oriented analyses, and second, there are worker- or employee-oriented analyses. Job analyses jus?t describe the tasks that need to be accomplished by a worker. For example, heart surgeons need to be able to operate on patients in order to carry out their jobs. In contrast, employee-oriented job descriptions need to describe knowledge, skills, and abilities the employee must have to get the job done. For example, surgeons need to understand the different types of blood vessels in the heart in order to be successful. Most job analyses include elements of both job-oriented and employee-oriented types.*

  If you were taking notes, you might produce the following:

  2 kinds job analyses:

  1. Job-oriented (=task-oriented): tasks needed to get job done. Ex: heart surgeon operates
  2. Worker-oriented (=employee-oriented): knowledge, skills, abilities, etc. necessary to do job.

     Ex: surgeon knows blood vessels

     Most j.a. a combination

  Note how the lecturer used almost 120 words, while the notes used only around 35 words—less than one-third of the lecture.

- **Use abbreviations.** One way to speed up the notetaking process is through the use of abbreviations. Among the most common:

and	& or +	with	w/	without	w/o
care of	c/o	leads to; resulting in	→	as a result of	←
percent	%	change	Δ	number	#
that is	i.e.	for example	e.g.	and so forth	etc.
no good	n.g.	question	?	compared with	c/w
page	p.	important!	!!	less than	<
more than	>	equals, same as	=	versus	vs.

I. Difficulties faced by college students seeking affordable housing
  A. Students subjected to high rents close to campus
    1. Forced to share apartments
    2. Sometimes must live far from campus
  B. Made to sign harsh leases
II. Possible solutions
  A. College offers subsidized housing
    1. Advantage: Housing costs can be lowered
    2. Potential problems
      a. College becomes students' landlord
      b. College uses funds for housing instead of investing in education
  B. Rent control
    1. Advantage: Can provide fixed, reasonably priced rents
    2. Disadvantages
      a. Creates permanent expensive rent-control bureaucracy
      b. Landlords may neglect rent-control property
      c. Little incentive for owners to increase the number of rental units
      d. Strong competition for rent-fixed units
III. Summary
  A. Advantages and disadvantages to both solutions
  B. May need new, creative solutions

figure 4.2
A Sample Outline

- **Take notes in outline form.** It's often useful to take notes in the form of an outline. An outline summarizes ideas in short phrases and indicates the relationship among concepts through the use of indentations.

  When outlining, it's best to be formal about it, using roman numerals, regular numbers, and capital and small letters (see the example in **Figure 4.2**).

  Or, if you prefer, you can also simply use outlining indentations without assigning numbers and letters.

  Outlining serves a number of functions. It forces you to try to determine the structure of the lecture. Organizing the key points and noting the connections among them helps you remember the material better because you have processed it more. The effort involved in outlining also keeps your mind from drifting away from the lecture.

  Use **Try It! 2**, "Outline a Lecture," to practice your outlining skills.

- **Copy key information instructors display on PowerPoint slides, overheads, whiteboards, or chalkboards.** If your instructor provides a definition, quotation, or formula, you probably should add it to your notes. In fact, such prominently displayed material has "test item" written all over it. You might want to highlight such material in some way in your notes.

- **Take advantage of PowerPoint slides provided online by your instructor.** Some instructors will post their PowerPoint slides before class. If they do, print them out and bring them to class. (To save paper, you can usually print them as an outline, rather than each slide on a separate page.)

2 **WORKING IN A GROUP** **Try It!** P O W E R

Outline a Lecture

Working with others in a group, take turns slowly reading sections of the following lecture to one another. As the paragraph is being read, outline the main arguments in the space provided.

In 1985 Joseph Farman, a British earth scientist working in Antarctica, made an alarming discovery. Scanning the Antarctic sky, he found less ozone than should be there—not a slight depletion but a 30% drop from a reading recorded 5 years earlier in the Antarctic!

At first the scientist thought that this "ozone hole" was an as-yet-unexplained weather phenomenon. Evidence soon mounted, however, pointing to synthetic chemicals as the culprit. Detailed analysis of chemicals in the Antarctic atmosphere revealed a surprisingly high concentration of chlorine, a chemical known to destroy ozone. The source of the chlorine was a class of chemicals called chlorofluorocarbons (CFCs). CFCs have been manufactured in large amounts since they were invented in the 1920s, largely for use as coolants in air conditioners, propellants in aerosols, and foaming agents in making styrofoam. CFCs were widely regarded as harmless because they were chemically unreactive under normal conditions. But in the thin atmosphere over Antarctica, CFCs condense into tiny ice crystals; warmed by the sun in the spring, they attack and destroy ozone without being used up.

The thinning of the ozone layer in the upper atmosphere 25 to 40 kilometers above the surface of the earth is a serious matter. The ozone layer protects life from the harmful ultraviolet (UV) rays from the sun that bombard the earth continuously. Like invisible sunglasses, the ozone layer filters out these dangerous rays. When UV rays damage the DNA in skin cells, it can lead to skin cancer. Every 1% drop in the atmospheric ozone concentration is estimated to lead to a 6% increase in skin cancers. The drop of approximately 3% that has already occurred worldwide, therefore, is estimated to have led to as much as a 20% increase in skin cancers.

The world currently produces about 1 million tons of CFCs annually, three-fourths of it in the United States and Europe. As scientific observations have become widely known, governments have rushed to correct the situation. By 1990, worldwide agreements to phase out production of CFCs by the end of the century had been signed. Nonetheless, most of the CFCs manufactured since they were invented are still in use in air conditioners and aerosols and have not yet reached the atmosphere. As these CFCs, as well as CFCs still being manufactured, move slowly upward through the atmosphere, the problem can be expected to grow worse. Ozone depletion has now been reported over the North Pole as well, and there is serious concern that the Arctic ozone hole will soon extend over densely populated Europe and the northeastern United States.

Write your outline here.

WORKING IN A GROUP

After you have outlined the passage, compare your outline with those of others who took notes on the same passage.

- Did you all agree on the main ideas of each passage?
- How do your notes differ from others', and what are the similarities?
- How might you improve your notes to better capture the main points?
- Would a different topic produce greater or fewer difficulties?

Collectively, produce what you believe is the ideal outline, and compare it with that produced by other groups.

You can use the printout of the slides as the basis for your notes, filling in the details provided during the lecture on the printout. Even if your instructor doesn't post the slides until after class, it's still a good idea to print them out and keep them with the notes you create in class. The combination of your notes and the PowerPoints will be invaluable when reviewing and studying the material.

Asking questions in class does more than just provide you with the opportunity to clarify points you don't understand. It often will make you feel more a part of the class, and it will encourage other students to participate.

- **Use different notetaking techniques for class discussions.** Not every course is structured as a lecture. Classes that are based less on lectures and more on class discussion pose greater challenges for notetaking.

  For example, a discussion of the use of tax support of private schools in a sociology class may raise a variety of issues. As students in the class offer their ideas, how much—and what—should you place in your notes?

  In such situations, the best approach is to take your cue from the course instructor. Often the instructor will pose some questions to get the discussion rolling. Note those questions—they're an important indicator of what the instructor is interested in. The instructor's reaction to particular comments is another clue. Listen to his or her responses. If the instructor responds enthusiastically to a particular point, you'll want to highlight it in your notes. (To practice taking notes during a discussion, go to **Try It! 3**.)

- **Pay particular attention to the points raised by instructors at the end of discussion and lecture classes.** Instructors often provide a summary of the discussion, which is worthy of inclusion in your notes.

- **Ask questions.** One of the most important things you can do during a class is to ask questions. Raising questions will help you evaluate, clarify, and ultimately better understand what your instructor is saying. Even beyond these critical goals, questions serve several other purposes.

  For one thing, raising questions will help you personalize the material being covered, permitting you to draw it more closely into your own framework and perspective. Furthermore, when you ask a question and it is answered, you become personally engaged in what the instructor is saying. In very large classes, asking questions may be the only way that an instructor can get a sense of you as an individual.

  Questioning also increases your involvement in the class as a whole. If you sit back and never raise questions in class, you are much less likely to feel a real part of the class. Becoming an active questioner will rightly make you feel like you have contributed something to the class. Remember, if you are unclear about some point, it is likely that others share your lack of clarity.

  Finally, by asking questions in class, you serve as a role model for other students. Your questions may help break the ice in a class, making it easier

3 **Try It!**

Take Notes during Discussions

Take notes on the following class discussion about the growth of English as a global language. Use cues from the instructor about the importance and accuracy of each point, and record in your notes only the key points that shed light on the topic.

Instructor: OK, so why is English so important globally, not just in English-speaking countries?

Alicia: Um, well, English is spoken by a lot of people. When I was in Denmark last summer, everyone spoke it. It just seems to be everywhere.

Instructor: OK. It's certainly a very widely used language. But we're trying to figure out why. We're looking for causes, not just symptoms, right? Anyone else? Bart?

Bart: Yeah, English is becoming, like, everyone's second language simply because it has established a good base. Not only did the *English* English people—you know, the British—spread the language all over through colonizing the world—you know, the sun never sets on the British Empire and all—but now America is everywhere, too. I mean, we're cool—our culture is cool and very influencing.

Instructor: Good, good. Yes, you've given two good reasons why English is widespread. The British Empire spread the language through parts of Asia, Africa, and the Caribbean in the 18th and 19th centuries, and modern U.S. culture is highly influential, which causes many people worldwide to welcome English. What else?

Catherine: Well, the way in which the American culture is spreading is very much language-centered. It's American movies and music that are everywhere, and these involve the language, not just the style. I mean, people know a lot more than how to say Coca-Cola and Nike, don't they? They listen to American CDs and movies, and they even produce songs and movies in English. So it's not just culture we're spreading, it's our language too.

Instructor: Exactly! The language is perhaps the most important aspect of the culture that we're distributing. Damon?

Damon: Yeah, I was just going to say, another thing that's caused the language to spread is global communications, which are just about always in English. Look at the language of aviation—pilots talk to each other in English, don't they? And the Internet. The universal language of the Internet is English. So if you want to communicate globally, and now everyone does because for the first time everyone *can*, you've got to pick up some English.

Rosario: Right. It's the universal second language. And it will only get more universal as American culture spreads further and other cultures develop to the point of being able to join the party—communicating and buying stuff and listening to our music and so on. I mean, it's the biggest game in town, and it's spoken by the people with the biggest wallets. Money talks, you know. And now it talks American English.

Instructor: You've really hit it now. Language has always gone where the resources are. If someone has what you want, you'd better speak their language. Money speaks American English. Very well put, Rosario! Excellent discussion, folks.

Write your notes here:

Were you able to identify the information that was most important? How would actually seeing the instructor's nonverbal reactions to the students' comments be helpful?

WORKING IN A GROUP

Compare your notes on the discussion with those of your classmates. As a group, try to create an optimal set of notes, reflecting the most important points.

Asking Questions in Class

Course Connections

Even in a small class, raising your hand and asking a question can be intimidating. You may be afraid that you'll say something dumb, making it clear to the whole class just how out of it you are. Or maybe you're afraid that everyone will be staring at you. Or perhaps your concern is that your instructor and fellow classmates will resent your wasting valuable class time with your own trivial questions.

Although it may not be possible to fully banish such self-defeating thoughts, there are several strategies that you can follow to make it easier to raise the questions you have.

1. Sit in the front of the room. Sitting close to the instructor will make it easier to ask questions. Moreover, if you sit in the back of the room and ask a question, the students in front of you will likely swivel around and look at you. In that case, if you already feel intimidated, your feelings of anxiety may soar off the charts.
2. Write down your question before you ask it. If you anticipate that you'll stumble or forget what you want to say, write down your question before raising your hand. The idea is not to read it word for word, or even refer to it at all when you actually ask your question. But writing it will help you quickly organize your thoughts, and provide a safety net in case you freeze momentarily.
3. Ask a question early in the term. By starting to ask questions early on in the term, you'll establish yourself as a student who participates in class. In fact, try asking a question on the first day of class, which will make it considerably easier for you to ask questions later in the term.
4. Be one of the first students to ask a question after a class has started. One reason people give for avoiding asking a question is that others have already asked so many questions that there's no time, or that others have already addressed the issue.

Using these strategies will help you overcome the stage fright of asking your questions and permit you to participate fully in class discussions.

for others to raise issues that they have about the material. And ultimately the answers that the instructor provides to others' questions may help you better understand and/or evaluate your understanding of the material. (For tips on asking questions in class, see the **Course Connections**.)

» LO 4-2 Strategies for Using Your Notes

Keep a Balance between Too Many Notes and Too Few Notes

The key to effective notetaking is to keep a balance between too many and too few notes.

The best way to achieve this balance is by paying close attention in class. By being engaged and involved in class, you'll be able to make the most of the techniques we've discussed. The result: notes that capture the most important points raised in class. Good notes will optimize your recall and mastery of the course subject matter (see a sample of two students' notes in **Figure 4.3**).

figure 4.3
Notes on a Lecture

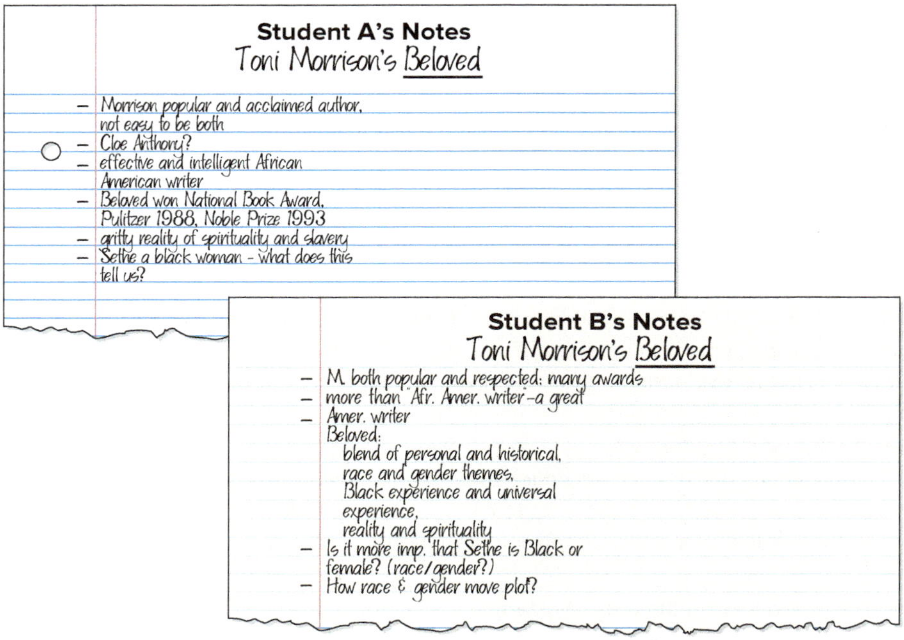

Use Special Techniques for "Problem Instructors"

He talks too fast . . . she mumbles . . . he puts down people when they ask a question . . . she rambles and goes off on boring tangents . . . she explains things in a way that doesn't make much sense.

In the real world of the college classroom, not every instructor comes to class with a clear, compelling lecture and then presents it beautifully. All of us have suffered through lectures that are deficient in one or more ways. What should you do when you find yourself in such a situation?

1. *Ask questions about the material.* Even if you have no idea what is going on in class—or especially if you have no idea—ask questions. You are probably not the only one struggling with the instructor's shortcomings. You will be doing everyone in the class a favor if you admit you're not following what an instructor is saying and respectfully ask for clarification.
2. *Ask—privately and politely—for the instructor to alter the way material is presented.* It is not bad classroom etiquette to ask an instructor to speak a little more slowly. Instructors sometimes get carried away with enthusiasm and begin speaking faster and faster without even being aware of it. Very often a reality check from a student will be welcome. But don't couch your comment in a way that makes the instructor feel inept ("Could you slow down; you're going too fast and losing me"). Instead, keep the comment neutral, without placing blame. For instance, you might simply say, "I'm having trouble keeping up with you; would it be possible for you to speak a little more slowly?"
3. *Pool your resources.* Get together with other students in the class and work out a strategy for dealing with the situation. If an instructor speaks too fast and you just can't keep up with the flow of information, meet with your fellow students and compare what you've gleaned from the class. They may have understood or

noted material that you missed, and vice versa. Together, you may be able to put the pieces of the puzzle together and get a fuller understanding of the material.

4. *Listen to the lecture again.* You might bring a digital recorder to class (but request the instructor's permission first!). Then, after class, you can play back the recording at your leisure. If you record it in a digital format, you could store it on your computer for a review before a test. In fact, in some cases instructors may use "lecture capture" software that uploads what they say in class to a website. Such software allows you to review the lecture, sometimes with the PowerPoint slides that were projected while the instructor was teaching.

   There's another option: Many instructors teach multiple sections of the same course. If this is the case, you might, schedule permitting, sit in on an additional section of the course. The second time around the information may become much clearer.

If you've ever been totally lost following a lecture, you may have discovered that speaking with your instructor immediately after class was helpful. Most instructors are very happy to go over and clarify key points that they've covered during class. They'll also appreciate your initiative and interest.

5. *Talk with the instructor after class.* If you feel totally lost after a lecture, or even if you've missed only a few points, speak with the instructor after class. Ask for clarification and get him or her to re-explain points that you missed. Such a dialogue will help you to understand the material better. But it will also do something more: help build your relationship with your instructor.

   In the very rare case in which an instructor oversteps the bounds of decency, by harshly putting students down; making discriminatory racial, ethnic, or religious remarks; or acting in a sexually harrassing manner, immediately report the matter to someone in the college administration. The appropriate person might be a department chair or dean of students. Such behavior is not only offensive but in many cases illegal.

6. *Remember that this too shall pass.* Finally, keep in mind that this is a temporary condition; your experience usually won't last more than one term. Most instructors are conscientious and well prepared, and unless you have enormously bad luck, the unpleasant experience you're having now will not be routine.

E Evaluate

Thinking Critically about Your Notes

Toward the end of class, take a moment to look over your notes. Now's the time—before the class has ended—to evaluate what you've written.

After being sure you can answer "yes" to the most basic question—can I read what I've written?—ask yourself these questions:

- Do my notes do a good job of representing what was covered in class?
- Do they reflect the emphases of the instructor?
- Are there any key points that are not entirely clear?
- Do I need help clarifying any of the points my instructor made?

4 | **Try It!** POWER

Evaluate Your Class Notes

Take a set of notes you made recently during one of your classes and evaluate it on the following criteria.

Statement	Not Even Slightly	Slightly	Moderately	Pretty Well	Very Well
1. I can read my notes (i.e., they are legible)					
2. Someone else can read my notes.					
3. My notes are complete; I missed nothing important.					
4. My notes represent the key points that were covered in class.					
5. My notes reflect the instructor's emphases.					
6. The instructor's key points are clear and understandable.					
7. The notes contain only important points, with no extraneous material.					
8. I understand not only the notes but also the class content they reflect.					
9. Using only the notes, I will be able to reconstruct the essential content of the class in 3 months.					

WORKING IN A GROUP

What do your answers tell you about the effectiveness of your notetaking skills? What might you do differently the next time you take notes?

Evaluate and compare the notes you've taken during the past 20 minutes of the class you are in now. How do your notes compare with those of the other members of your group?

Evaluating your notes is a critical part of the notetaking process. You can get a sense of how effective your notetaking has been while you still have a chance to ask your instructor to clarify anything that is still not clear.

Perhaps, for example, you've left out a key word in a definition. Maybe you don't understand a concept fully, even though you've written about it in your notes. Possibly you've left out the third step in a list of six steps necessary to accomplish something.

If you look over your notes while you're still in class, you'll have the opportunity to ask your instructor for clarification. Or you can wait until the end of class and raise your question privately. Most instructors will be happy to answer questions from students who have obviously been actively listening. Just make sure that you add what they tell you to your notes so you'll be able to refer to them later. (To practice evaluating your notes, complete **Try It! 4**.)

R Rethink Activating Your Memory

The lecture has ended and class is over. You put the top on your pen, close your notebook, stash everything in your backpack, and head out for a cup of coffee before your next class or before going to work.

Wait! Before you close up your notebook, finish the P.O.W.E.R. process. Rethink what you've heard. Spending 5 minutes reconsidering what you've written right now can save you *hours* of work later. The reason: Rethinking promotes the transfer of information into long-term memory (something discussed more in Chapter 6). Linking the new information you've recorded to what you already know integrates it into your memory in a more meaningful way. And that means you can remember it better and more easily.

> "I'd think to myself 'I don't need to write that down, I'll remember it.' A few days later, it was like, 'what did he say . . .?'"
>
> Student, Duke University, in Tyler, S. (1997). *Been There, Should've Done That.* Haslett, MI: Front Porch Press. P. 114.

If you looked over your notes to clarify and evaluate the information in them in class, you've already begun the process. But once class is over, you need to review the material more formally. Here's how to do it:

- **Rethink as soon as possible.** Time is of the essence! The rethinking phase of notetaking doesn't have to take long; 5 to 10 minutes are usually sufficient. The more critical issue is *when* you do it. The longer you wait before reviewing your notes, the less effective the process will be.

  There's no doubt that the best approach is to review the material just after the class has ended. As everyone else is leaving, just stay seated and go over your notes. This works fine for classes late in the day, when no other class is scheduled in the room. But what if you must vacate the room immediately after class? The next best thing is to find a quiet space somewhere nearby and do your rethinking there.

  In any case, don't let the day end without examining your notes. In fact, reconsidering material just before you go to sleep can be particularly effective.

- **Make rethinking an active process.** Some people feel the notes they take in class are akin to historical documents in a museum, with Do Not Touch! signs hanging on them. On the contrary, think of your notes as a construction project and of yourself as the person in charge of the project.

  When you review your notes, do so with an eye to improving them. If any information is not entirely clear, change the wording in your notes, adding to or amending what's there. If certain words are hard to read, fix them; it won't be any easier to read them the night before a test–in fact, chances are you'll have even more trouble.

  If, on rethinking the material, you don't understand something, ask your instructor or a friend to clarify it. And when you receive an explanation, add it to your notes so you won't forget it. (You might want to use a different colored pen for additions to your notes, so you'll know they came later.)

- **Use critical thinking to review the the material in your notes.** As you review the information, use your critical thinking skills to evaluate the material. Remember that all information is not equal: We live in a world where what appears to be legitimate information is sometimes fictional (think of "fake news," information that is intentionally misleading and often spread through social media). Consequently, you need to carefully evaluate the source and content of material you have collected. Just because something appears on Facebook doesn't mean it is accurate.

  In addition, as you rethink your notes, don't think of them only in terms of a single lecture or a single class. Instead, take a longer view. Ask yourself how they fit into the broader themes of the class and the goals that you and the instructor have for the semester. How will the information be useful to you? Why did the instructor emphasize a particular point?

  If you've configured your notes by leaving a 2½-inch column on the left-hand side of the page, now is the time to make use of that blank column. Write down keywords, significant points, major concepts, controversies, and questions. The process of adding this information will not only help you rethink the material now, but also provide guideposts when you study before a test.
- Go beyond the facts and pieces of information, integrating and evaluating the material.

concept map
A graphical representation that structures written material by grouping and connecting key ideas and themes.

- **Create concept maps.** A **concept map** is a graphical representation that structures written material by grouping and connecting key ideas and themes. In contrast to an outline, a concept map visually illustrates how related ideas fit together. The pictorial summary gives you another handle to store the information in memory, and it focuses your thinking on the key ideas from the lecture.

  In a concept map, each key idea is placed in a different part of the map, and related ideas are placed near it—above, below, or beside it. What emerges does not have the rigid structure of an outline. Instead, a "finished" concept map looks something like a map of the solar system, with the largest and most central idea in the center (the "sun" position), and related ideas surrounding it at various distances. It has also been compared to a large tree, with numerous branches and subbranches radiating out from a central trunk. (**Figure 4.4** presents a sample concept map.)

  Building a concept map has several advantages. It forces you to rethink the material in your notes in a new style—particularly important if you used traditional outlining while taking the notes. In addition, it helps you tie together the material for a given class session. Finally, it will help you to build a master concept map later, when you're studying the material for a final exam. (To practice in the techniques we've been discussing, see **Try It! 5**, "Practice Your Notetaking Skills.")

» LO 4-3 Taking Notes as You Study

Weighing as much as five pounds, bulky and awkward, and filled with more information than you think anyone could ever need to know, course textbooks have been a standard part of college life for generations. Although they are increasingly being replaced by digital versions, you still will likely encounter them as you proceed through college.

You might feel intimidated by the size of your textbooks; you might be annoyed at their cost; you might think you'll never be able to read them, let alone understand, learn, and recall the material in them. How will you manage?

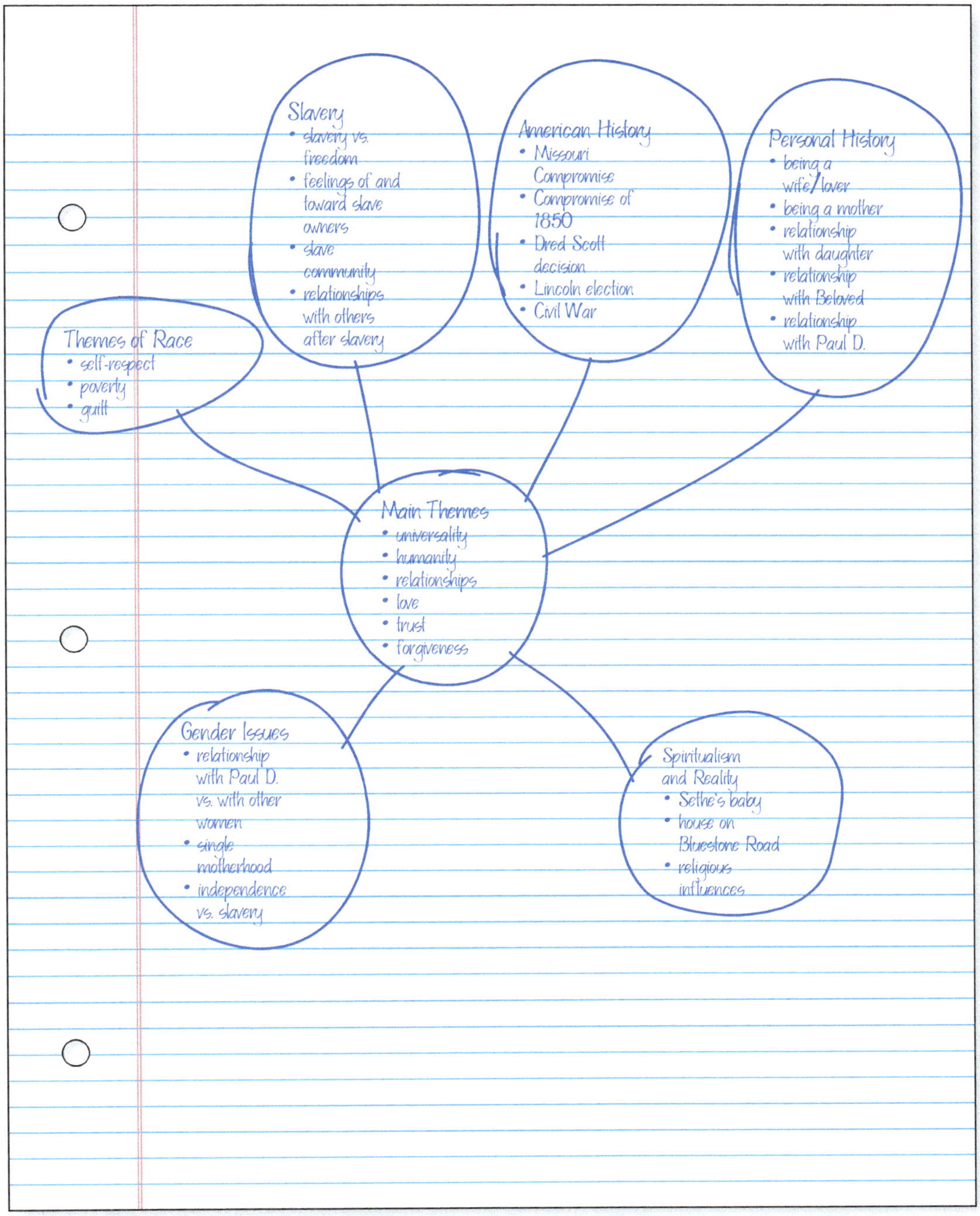

figure 4.4

A Concept Map of Toni Morrison's *Beloved*

The answer involves taking **study notes**, notes taken for the purpose of reviewing material. They are the kind of notes that you take now to study from later.

study notes
Notes taken for the purpose of reviewing material.

Several strategies are useful for taking study notes from written material such as magazines, books, journals, and websites. Which approach works best depends on whether you're able to write on the material you wish to take notes on.

5 **Try It!** POWER

Practice Your Notetaking Skills

Practice your notetaking skills, using any techniques you find helpful, in one of the classes in which you are enrolled this term. Use these notes to answer these questions:

1. Which specific techniques did I use in taking notes?

2. Which of the notetaking techniques detailed in this chapter was I unable to use, and why?

3. Could I take the notes I made in class and redo them, using one of the techniques in this chapter, such as creating a concept map?

After you have taken notes, use the techniques discussed in this chapter to evaluate and rethink them. Creating a concept map on a separate sheet of paper may be particularly helpful.

Taking Notes on Material You Can Write On or Annotate Digitally

Some forms of digital materials, such as the typical online textbook, have built-in software systems that allow you to create notes or to highlight the text. For such virtual material, as well as hard-copy materials that you own, here are some suggestions for creating study notes:

- **Use the annotation software capabilities on virtual material.** Most online textbooks or e-books allow you to highlight particular passages and insert, and save, notes about the material. Some devices, such as certain tablets, permit you to use a stylus to physically write (and save) notes on the material in the e-book. Furthermore, in some cases, you can even share your notes with other students, or view their notes. Be sure you understand the capabilities of the e-textbook software to get the most out of what it has to offer.
- **Integrate your text notes into your study notes.** Start by annotating the pages, using the techniques that work best for you: highlighting, underlining, circling, making marginal notes. Keep in mind that writing on the text, by itself, is not sufficient to promote learning–it's what you do next that counts.

  Specifically, after you've finished reading and annotating the material, create study notes. The study notes should provide a summary of the key points, in outline form or in the form of concept maps. Either form of summary should supplement the annotations you've made on the printed page.

Career Connections

Taking Notes on the Job: Meetings of the Minds

For many people, meetings take up a good part of their professional workdays, and being able to take effective notes can provide a significant career advantage.

Meetings are similar to class discussions. During a meeting you will want to look for key topics and make note of the ideas that receive the most emphasis or enthusiastic response. Note these areas and keep them in mind as likely priorities.

During meetings, tasks are often assigned. Not only do you want to clearly note what you are to do and when you are supposed to do it, but keeping track of what others are doing will also be helpful, because you may need to get information from them or otherwise coordinate efforts. For instance, if you are assigned the task of managing the development of your company's website, you'll want to clarify in your notes who has agreed to do what portion of the task.

Taking notes when others are speaking also shows that you are paying attention to what the speaker is saying. It's a kind of compliment that suggests you find what the speaker is saying to be so important that you will want to refer to it later.

Finally, notetaking plays another role: It can make seemingly interminable meetings appear to proceed faster by providing something for you to do that's more active than simply listening. In short, not only can notetaking provide you with a clear record of what occurred in a meeting, but it can also keep you engaged in what is going on.

Furthermore, any notes you take should stand on their own. For instance, they should include enough information to be useful whether or not you have the book or article on hand.

- **Use flash cards.** You also might consider taking notes on flash cards. **Flash cards** are simply index cards that contain key pieces of information that you need to remember. You can also use digital flash cards; a variety of apps, such as Anki or Cerego, allow you to create virtual versions of physical flash cards.

  Flash cards are particularly useful in subjects that present many small bits of information to remember, such as foreign language vocabulary words or math formulas. When you need to learn a list of foreign words, for instance, you can write a foreign word on one side of a card and its English meaning on the other side.

  One of the greatest virtues of both physical and virtual flash cards is their portability. You can review them at odd times when you have a spare moment.

flash cards
Index cards that contain key pieces of information to be remembered.

Taking Notes on Material You Are Unable to Write On

Taking study notes on material that can't be written on or annotated digitally is a different story. Some digital textbooks and other online materials don't offer the opportunity of making online annotations. Or you may be using a rental textbook that needs to be returned at the end of the term. Finally, you may be using a library book, magazine, journal article, or material on library reserve that is shared with others.

If you want to take notes on material that you can't write on or annotate digitally, consider these approaches:

- **Approach the written material as you would a class lecture.** The techniques we discussed earlier for taking notes in class can all be adapted for taking notes from written material. In fact, the task is often easier, because, as is not the case with the spoken word, you'll be able to refer back to what was said earlier—it's in black and white in front of you.

- **Laptops can be especially helpful in creating study notes.** If you're a good key-boarder, it's often easier and quicker to take notes using a word-processing program. However, don't be lured into typing too much. You need to be just as selective in what you input into your computer as you would be in taking notes during a class lecture.
- **Use the tricks of the trade we discussed earlier for taking notes from a class lecture.** Look for key ideas, definitions, quotations, and formulas, and include them in your notes. Use the headings that are included in the text, such as chapter and section titles. Bold or italic type is also a clue that an important point is being made. Graphs and charts often provide critical information.
- **Use the same form of notetaking that you use in class lectures.** If you take notes in class using the two-column method (in which you reserve a 2½-inch column on the left-hand side of your paper for adding comments during later review of the notes), use that technique here as well. If you write your notes in outline form, create an outline based on the written material. If you often create graphics such as concept maps, create them now. The point is to produce notes that are consistent with those you take during class lectures.

Speaking *of* Success

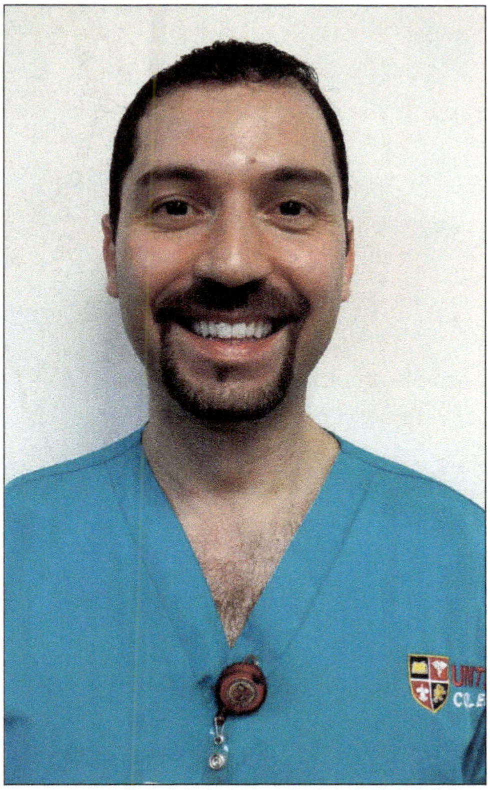

Courtesy of Luciano Virgilio

NAME: **Luciano Virgilio**

SCHOOL: **Unitek College**

HOME: **Freemont, California**

Sometimes the path to achieving your goals takes a longer and more twisted route than you ever imagined. This was certainly true in the case of Luciano Virgilio.

From a young age, Virgilio had a keen interest in biology and medicine. But a serious car accident left him with an even greater appreciation of the role nurses play in the process of healing.

"There, I was touched by the dedication and professionalism of the nurses who caringly watched after me," he recalled. "It was then I knew I wanted to become a nurse."

But rather than follow his dream, he followed the guidance of academic and family advisers and pursued careers ranging from land surveying to financial services.

"After years of working in jobs that left me feeling unfulfilled, and with the support of my spouse, I finally began the journey to achieving my dream of a nursing degree," said Virgilio.

Returning to school at a later point in life proved to be a challenge for Virgilio.

"Going back to school after so many years was challenging from a psychological standpoint, wondering, as I did, if I would be able to learn as I used to," he said. "But I was able to plan ahead financially, making sure that I could be a full-time student. Additionally, I had the moral and financial support of my wonderful partner who facilitated my complete transition to the role of a student."

Following his graduation from Unitek College's Vocational Nursing program, Virgilio was offered a job as a lab technician assistant at the college. This gave him the opportunity to practice his new skills and continue his studies by enrolling in the Registered Nursing program.

"It's hard to say exactly which area of specialization I most prefer, at this point in my journey," he explains. "But I know for certain that I want to provide high quality patient care and that I want to be part of a team that is likewise dedicated to excellence in the profession."

[RETHINK]

- What are some of the reasons it is so challenging to return to school later in life?
- What advice would you give Virgilio in terms of juggling the multiple demands on his time?

Looking Back

LO 4-1 Describe techniques for taking notes in class.

- The central feature of good notetaking is listening and distilling important information—not writing down everything that is said.
- Prepare for taking notes by identifying the instructor's and your own goals for the course, completing all assignments before arriving in class, and "warming up" for class by reviewing the notes and assignments from the previous class.
- Before writing notes, listen and think, processing the information that the instructor is attempting to deliver.
- Notes should be brief phrases rather than full sentences and, if possible, in outline form to reveal the structure of the lecture. Material written on the board should usually be copied word for word.

LO 4-2 Apply techniques for taking notes from written materials.

- Before leaving class, evaluate your notes, verifying that they are complete and understandable while there is still time to correct them.
- As soon as possible after class, actively rethink your notes.

LO 4-3 Explain methods for effective notetaking.

- Taking good study notes from written materials involves many of the principles that apply to taking good notes from oral presentations, although the source material can be consulted repeatedly, making it easier to get the information down accurately.
- Concept maps and flash cards can be helpful tools for notetaking from textbooks.

[KEY TERMS AND CONCEPTS]

Active listening (p. 98)
Concept map (p. 110)
Flash cards (p. 113)
Hearing (p. 98)
Meta-message (p. 99)
Study notes (p. 111)

[RESOURCES]

ON CAMPUS

If you are having difficulty taking class notes effectively, talk with your course instructor. Bring your notes with you soon after a class has ended, and let the instructor assess what you are doing correctly and what could stand improvement.

If your problems persist, and you have great difficulty translating the spoken word into notes, then there's a small possibility that you suffer from an auditory learning disability. Be tested by your college learning disabilities office or counseling office to rule this out.

IN PRINT

Fiona McPherson's *Effective Notetaking* (Wayz Press, 2012) and Angelos Georgakis's *How To Take Good Notes: The Science Behind Note-Taking* (CreateSpace Independent Publishing Platform, 2017) provide guides and frameworks for how to take good notes in class.

In addition, Deana Hippie's *Note Taking Made Easy!* (Scholastic, 2010) and Bobbi DePorter and Mike Hernacki's *Quantum Notes* (Learning Forum, 2000) provide strategies for increasing your listening and notetaking expertise.

ON THE WEB

- Brigham Young University's Career and Counseling Center offers this page (**https://casc.byu.edu/note-taking**) on the Cornell Notetaking System. This notetaking system can help you improve the organization of your notes, while allowing you to make use of your existing strengths as a notetaker.
- A learning style model formulated by Richard M. Felder and Linda K. Silverman from North Carolina State University, The Index of Learning Styles is an online instrument used to assess preferences on four dimensions (active/reflective, sensing/intuitive, visual/verbal, and sequential/global) (**www.ncsu.edu/felder-public/ILSpage.html**).

The Case of . . .
The Human Dictation Machine

Everyone wanted to borrow Lila Bauman's notes.

If they missed a class, or even if they had been there but had just spaced out, other students in Lila's classes knew that they could find out what had happened in class by borrowing her notes. It was all there in black and white. The woman was virtually a human dictation machine. She spent her time in class in a whirlwind of notetaking, writing down seemingly every word her instructor uttered in a clear, meticulous script. By the end of a term, her notebooks were so lengthy that they approached the size of telephone books from a small city.

The strange thing, though, was that—despite her copious notes—Lila was only a mediocre student. Before tests she studied her notes thoroughly, but she never seemed to get grades higher than a C+. She didn't know why, especially in light of what she saw as her notetaking expertise.

1. How do you think Lila defines "good notetaking"?

2. Why does Lila's method of notetaking produce such poor results? What is she missing?

3. If you asked Lila to summarize the instructor's main ideas after a class lecture, how successful do you think she would be? Why?

4. Do you think it would be easy or hard to study for a final exam using Lila's notes? Why?

5. Do you think Lila evaluates her notes during or after class? Do you think she ever rethinks them? What questions would you ask to help her perform these steps?

6. In general, what advice would you give Lila on notetaking?

CHAPTER 5

Taking Tests

Learning Outcomes

By the time you finish this chapter you will be able to

- » LO **5-1** Identify the kinds of tests you will encounter in college.
- » LO **5-2** Explain the best ways to prepare for and take various kinds of tests.
- » LO **5-3** Analyze the best strategies for answering specific kinds of test questions.

So it all comes down to a test. That was the thought that ran through Imani Brown's mind as he got ready to start the most important test he had ever faced. Yes, he had taken tests all through his high school career, and yes, he had suffered through the SAT to get into college.

But now, on the verge of starting his career as a high school teacher, he had one more hurdle to jump over. The state legislature had recently decided that all new graduates of teacher training programs had to pass a competency test before starting to teach. Imani had wanted to be a teacher as long as he could remember; he simply had to pass.

Although he was fairly confident—he had studied hard—he couldn't relax altogether. He told himself that he had always done well on tests in the past; he wasn't going to fail now. But still . . .

©Keith Bell/Alamy

Looking Ahead

Although many tests are not as critical as Imani Brown's teacher competency exam, tests do play a significant role in everyone's academic life. Students typically experience more anxiety over tests than over anything else in their college careers.

But tests don't have to be so anxiety producing. There are strategies and techniques you can learn to reduce your fear of test taking. In fact, learning how to take tests is in some ways as important as learning the content that they cover. Taking tests effectively does not just involve mastering information; it also requires mastering specific test-taking skills.

One of the most important goals of this chapter is to take the mystery out of the whole process of taking tests. To do that, you'll learn about the different types of tests and strategies you can start using even before you take a test. You'll gain insight into how different kinds of tests work and how best to approach them, and you'll learn about the various types of test questions and strategies for responding most effectively to each type.

This chapter also explores two aspects of test taking that may affect your performance: test anxiety and cramming. You will learn ways to deal with your anxiety and keep cramming to a minimum—but you will also learn how to make the most of cramming, if you do have to resort to it.

The chapter ends with suggestions for evaluating your performance toward the end of a test and for using what you learn to improve your performance the next time around.

» LO 5-1 Getting Ready

Tests may be the most unpopular part of academic life. Students hate them because they produce fear, anxiety, apprehension about being evaluated, and a focus on grades instead of learning for learning's sake. Instructors often don't like them very much either, because they produce fear, anxiety, apprehension about being evaluated, and a focus on grades instead of learning for learning's sake. That's right: Students and instructors dislike tests for the very same reasons.

But tests are also valuable. A well-constructed test identifies what you know and what you still need to learn. Tests help you see how your performance compares

Journal Reflections

How I Feel about Tests

1. How do you feel about tests in general?
2. What are your first memories of being in a testing situation? What were your feelings, and why?
3. What makes a test "good" and "bad" from your perspective?
4. What factors contribute to your success or failure on a particular exam? Which of these factors are under your control?
5. What strategies do you use when taking tests to maximize your performance? Which have been particularly effective, and why?

with that of others. And knowing that you'll be tested on a body of material is likely to motivate you to learn material more thoroughly.

However, there's another reason you might dislike tests: You may assume that tests have the power to define your worth as a person. If you do badly on a test, you may be tempted to believe that you've received some fundamental information about yourself from the professor and the college, information that says you're a failure in some significant way.

This is a dangerous–and completely wrong–assumption. If you do badly on a test, it doesn't mean you're a bad person. Or stupid. Or that you'll never do better again, or that your life is ruined. If you don't do well on a test, you're the same person you were before you took the test–no better, no worse. You just did badly on a test. Period.

In short, tests are not a measure of your value as an individual. They are only a measure of how well (and how much) you studied, and your test-taking skills. Tests are tools; they are indirect and imperfect measures of what we know. Someone with a great deal of knowledge can do poorly on a test; tension or going at too slow a pace can lead to unwelcome results in some cases. Another person may know considerably less and still do better on the test simply because he or she may have learned some test-taking skills along the way.

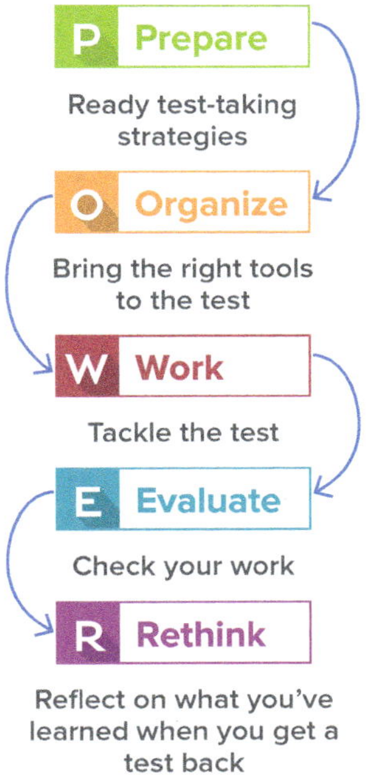

P.O.W.E.R. Plan

How we do on a test depends on a number of considerations: the kind of test it is, the subject matter involved, our understanding of test-taking strategies, and, above all, how well we prepare for it. Let's turn, then, to the first step in test-taking: preparation. (The five steps are summarized in the P.O.W.E.R. Plan on this page.)

P Prepare Readying Your Test-Taking Strategies

Preparation for tests requires a number of strategies. Among the most important are the following:

Remember: Everything You Do in a Course Is Preparation for a Test

All the things you do during a course help to prepare you for a test. There is no surer way to get good grades on tests than to attend class faithfully and to complete all class assignments seriously and on time.

Preparing for tests is a long-term proposition. It's not a matter of "giving your all" the night before the test. Instead, it's a matter of giving your all to every aspect of the course.

Know What You Are Preparing For

Learn as much as you can about the test before you begin to study for it. The more you know about a test beforehand, the more effective your studying will be.

To find out about an upcoming test, ask these questions:

- Is the test called a "test," "exam," "quiz," or something else? As you can see in **Table 5.1**, the names imply different things. For simplicity's sake, we'll use the term "test" throughout this chapter, but know that these distinctions exist, and they should affect the way you prepare.
- What material will the test cover?
- How many questions will be on it?

table 5.1 Quizzes, Tests, Exams . . . What's in a Name?
Although they may vary from one instructor to another, the following definitions are most commonly used:
Quizzes. A quiz is a brief assessment, usually covering a relatively small amount of material. Some quizzes cover as little as one class's worth of reading. Although a single quiz usually doesn't count very much, instructors often add quiz scores together, and collectively they can become a significant part of your final course grade.
Tests. A test is a more extensive, more heavily weighted assessment than a quiz, covering more material. A test may come every few weeks of the term, often after each third or quarter of the term has passed, but this varies with the instructor and the course.
Exams. An exam is the most substantial kind of assessment. In many classes, just one exam is given—a final exam at the end of the term. Sometimes there are two exams, one at the midpoint of the term (called, of course, a midterm) and the second at the end. Exams are usually weighted quite heavily because they are meant to assess your knowledge of all the course material covered up to that point.

- How much time is it expected to take? A full class period? Only part of a period?
- What kinds of questions will be on the test?
- How will it be graded?
- Will sample questions be provided?
- Will the instructor hand out a study guide?
- Are tests from previous terms available?
- How much does the test contribute to my final course grade?

Match Test Preparation to Question Types

There are different types of test questions (see **Table 5.2**), and each type of question requires a somewhat different style of preparation.

- **Essay questions.** Essay questions focus on the big picture. Their aim is for you to show how various pieces of information fit together. You'll need to know not only a series of isolated facts, but also the connections between them, and you will have to be able to discuss these ideas in an organized and logical way.

  The best approach to studying for an essay test involves four steps:

1. Carefully reread your class notes and any notes you've made on assigned readings that will be covered on the upcoming exam. Also go through the readings themselves, reviewing underlined or highlighted material and marginal notes.
2. Play professor: Think of likely exam questions. To do this, you can use the key words, phrases, concepts, and questions that come up in your class notes or in your text. Some instructors give out lists of possible essay topics; if yours does, focus on this list, but don't ignore other possibilities.

> "High school is memorization and regurgitation. Here you have to think."
>
> Junior, engineering student, Notre Dame University, in Tyler, S. (1997). *Been There, Should've Done That.* Haslett, MI: Front Porch Press. P. 126.

table 5.2 Types of Test Questions

Essay	Requires a fairly extended, on-the-spot composition about some topic. Examples include questions that call on you to describe a person, process, or event, or those that ask you to compare or contrast two separate sets of material.
Multiple-choice	Usually contains a question or statement, followed by a number of possible answers (usually four or five of them). You are supposed to choose the best response from the choices offered.
True–false	Presents statements about a topic that are either accurate or inaccurate. You are to indicate whether each statement is accurate (true) or inaccurate (false).
Matching	Presents two lists of related information, arranged in column form. Typically, you are asked to pair up the items that go together (e.g., a scientific term and its definition, a writer and the title of a book she or he wrote).
Short-answer	Requires brief responses (usually a few sentences at most) in a kind of mini-essay.
Fill-in	Requires you to add one or more missing words to a sentence or series of sentences.

3. Without looking at your notes or your readings, answer each potential essay question—aloud. Don't feel embarrassed about doing this. Talking aloud is often more useful than answering the question in your head.

   You can also write down the main points that any answer should cover. (Don't write out *complete* answers to the questions unless your instructor tells you in advance exactly what is going to be on the test. Your time is probably better spent learning the material than rehearsing precisely formulated responses.)

4. After you've answered the questions, check yourself by looking at the notes and readings once again. If you feel confident that you've answered particular questions adequately, check them off. You can go back later for a quick review.

   But if there are questions that you had trouble with, review that material immediately. Then repeat the third step above, answering the questions again.

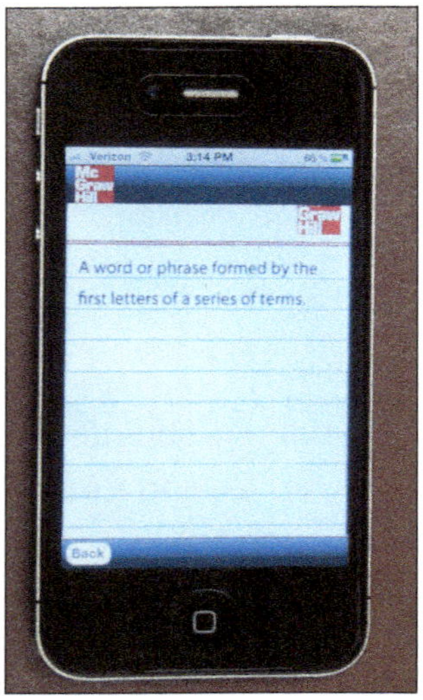

©McGraw-Hill Education. Mark Dierker, photographer

- **Short-answer and fill-in questions.** Short-answer and fill-in questions require similar skills as essays, in that they require you to recall key pieces of information rather than finding it on the page in front of you. However, short-answer and fill-in questions—unlike essay questions—typically don't demand that you integrate or compare different types of information. Consequently, the focus of your study should be on the recall of specific, detailed information.
- **Multiple-choice, true-false, and matching questions.** While the focus of review for essay questions should be on major issues and controversies, studying for multiple-choice, true-false, and matching questions requires more attention to the details.

  Almost anything is fair game for multiple-choice, true-false, and matching questions, so you can't afford to overlook anything when studying. True, these kinds of questions put the material right there on the page for you to react to—Did Columbus land in 1492, or not?—rather than asking you to provide the names and dates yourself (as in the case of the essay question). Nevertheless, to do well on these tests you must put your memory into high gear and master a great many facts.

It's a particularly good idea to record important facts on index cards like those in **Figure 5.1**. Either write them out by hand, or use one of the smartphone apps that are available to help you create them, such as Microsoft OneNote or Evernote. In addition, if you are using an e-textbook, the software may make it easy for you to create index cards automatically. They can be reviewed on your smartphone or computer, or you can print them out.

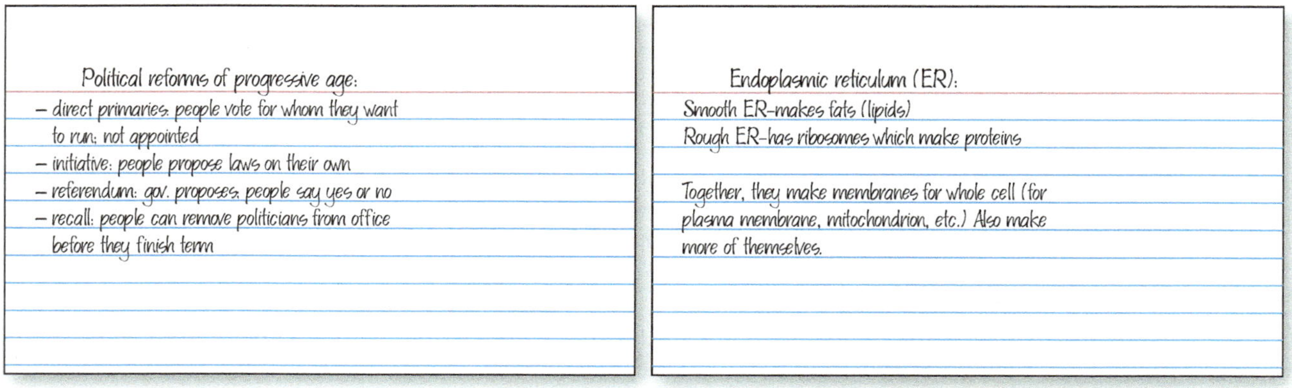

figure 5.1
Using Index Cards

1 | PERSONAL STYLES — Try It! POWER

Measure Your Test-Taking Style

Do you feel anxious at the very thought of a test, or are you cool and calm in the face of testing situations? Get a sense of your test-taking style by checking off every statement below that applies to you.

- ☐ 1. The closer a test date approaches, the more nervous I get.
- ☐ 2. I am sometimes unable to sleep on the night before a test.
- ☐ 3. I have "frozen up" during a test, finding myself unable to think or respond.
- ☐ 4. I can feel my hands shaking as I pick up my pencil to begin a test.
- ☐ 5. The minute I read a tough test question, all the facts I ever knew about the subject abandon me and I can't get them back no matter how hard I try.
- ☐ 6. I have become physically ill before or during a test.
- ☐ 7. Nervousness prevents me from studying immediately before a test.
- ☐ 8. I often dream about an upcoming test.
- ☐ 9. Even if I successfully answer a number of questions, my anxiety stays with me throughout the test.
- ☐ 10. I'm reluctant to turn in my test paper for fear that I can do better if I continue to work on it.

If you checked off more than four statements, you have experienced fairly serious test anxiety. If you checked off more than six statements, your anxiety is probably interfering with your test performance. In particular, statements 3, 5, 6, 7, and 10 may indicate serious test anxiety.

If, based on your responses to this questionnaire and your previous experience, your level of test anxiety is high, what are some of the steps described in this chapter that might be helpful to you?

Remember the advantages of these cards: They're portable and available all the time, and the act of creating them helps drive the material into your memory. Furthermore, you can shuffle them and test yourself repeatedly until you've mastered the material.

It also can be helpful to write the name of a particular concept or theory on one side of a note card, and then generate and write an example of it on the other side. Studying the cards will help ensure that you fully understand the concepts and theories and can generalize them to different situations.

Deal with Test Anxiety

What does the anticipation of a test do to you? Do you feel shaky? Frantic, like there's not enough time to get it all done? Do you feel as if there's a knot in your stomach? Do you grit your teeth?

Test anxiety is a temporary condition characterized by fears and concerns about test taking. It's a sign of a very real physical reaction: Your body is producing stress hormones as a reaction to your mental state of concern.

test anxiety A temporary condition characterized by fears and concerns about test taking.

Almost everyone experiences test anxiety to some degree, though for some people it's more of a problem than for others. The real danger with test anxiety is that it can become so overwhelming that it can hurt test performance. (To assess your own test-taking style and the degree of anxiety around tests that you experience, see **Try It! 1**.)

You'll never eliminate test anxiety completely, nor do you want to. A moderate degree of test anxiety can energize us, making us more attentive and vigilant. Consequently, as with any competitive event, anxiety can motivate us to do our best. You might think of moderate test anxiety as a sign of your desire to perform at your peak—a useful quality at test time.

On the other hand, for some students, anxiety can spiral into the kind of paralyzing fear that makes their minds go blank. There are several ways to keep this from happening to you:

1. *Prepare thoroughly.* The more you prepare, the less test anxiety you'll feel. Good preparation can give you a sense of control and mastery, and it will prevent test anxiety from overwhelming you.
2. *Take a realistic view of the test.* Remember that your future success does not hinge on your performance on any single exam. Think of the big picture: Put the task ahead in context, and remind yourself of all the hurdles you've passed so far.
3. *Eat right and get enough sleep.* Good mental preparation can't occur without your body being well prepared.
4. *Learn relaxation techniques.* You can learn to reduce or even eliminate the jittery physical symptoms of test anxiety by using relaxation techniques. These techniques are covered in Chapter 13, but the basic process is straightforward: Breathe evenly, gently inhaling and exhaling. Focus your mind on a pleasant, relaxing scene such as a beautiful forest or a peaceful farm, or on a restful sound such as that of ocean waves breaking on the beach.
5. *Visualize success.* Think of an image of your instructor handing back your test marked with a big fat "A." Or imagine your instructor congratulating you on your fine performance the day after the test. Positive visualizations that highlight your potential success can help replace images of failure that may fuel test anxiety.
6. Just before you take a test, spend 10 minutes writing about your feelings regarding the upcoming exam. It's a way to help free yourself of negative emotions, allowing you to concentrate better on the exam.

What if these strategies don't work? If your test anxiety is so great that it's getting in the way of your success, consider consulting a professional counselor or therapist. Many colleges provide a learning resource center or a counseling center that can provide you with personalized help. (To focus on dealing with math test anxiety, see the **Course Connections** feature.)

» LO 5-2 Studying for the Test

A key part of preparing for a test is a trial run-through. Like running practice trials before you participate in an actual race, it makes sense to ready yourself for the real event by taking a practice test.

Test Yourself

Once you feel you've mastered the material, test yourself on it. There are several ways to do this. Often textbooks are accompanied by websites that offer automatically scored practice tests and quizzes. (*P.O.W.E.R. Learning* does: Go to Connect to try one!)

You can also create a test for yourself. Make its form as close as possible to what you expect the actual test to be. For instance, if your instructor has told you the classroom test will be primarily made up of short-answer questions, your test should reflect that.

Course Connections

Special Techniques for Dealing with Math Anxiety

For many students, the greatest test anxiety comes when they're taking a math test. Math seems to bring out the worst fears in some people, perhaps because it's seen as a discipline in which answers are either totally right or totally wrong, or because they feel they've "hit the wall" and they'll never be able to understand a concept, no matter how hard they try.

Such feelings about math can be devastating, because they can prevent you from doing well even if you know the material. If you suffer from math anxiety, keep these things in mind:

- Math is like any other subject: The greatest component of success is the effort you put in, not whether you have a "math gene" that makes you naturally good at math. It's not true that you either are born "good at math" or not. It's a cultural myth that "math is hard" and that somehow it's fine if you're not good at it. So try to cultivate a growth mindset (as we discussed in Chapter 1): the belief that individual characteristics, such as intelligence, talent, and motivation, can improve through hard work.
- It's also not true that there's only one way to solve a math problem. Sometimes there are a variety of routes to coming up with a solution. And keep in mind that the solution to math problems often calls for creativity, not just sheer logic.
- It's a false stereotype that women are not as good at math as men, but it's a stereotype that many women buy into. Research has shown that when men do badly on a math test, they're most likely to think that they haven't put in enough effort. But when women don't do well on a math test, they're three times more likely than men to feel that they don't have enough ability to be successful.[1] That's an erroneous view of the world. Don't become a prisoner of stereotypes.
- Remember that math has practical uses. Some people are afraid of math because they view it as theoretical, with no practical value. But if you want to figure out the size of a room, how to calculate a tip in a restaurant, or how much interest you'll pay on a loan, you'll need to make use of geometry, arithmetic, and algebra.
- Finally, use these special strategies to deal with math problems on exams:

BEFORE TESTS:

1. Math is cumulative, building on prior concepts and knowledge. Make sure you review math fundamentals before moving on to more advanced topics.
2. Ask questions in class. Don't be afraid that you'll ask the wrong question in the wrong way. Math instructors love their subject, and they want others to understand it.
3. Make use of review sessions and other study resources.
4. Practice, practice, practice. The more experience you have completing math problems under pressure, the better you'll do. Practice math problems using a timer to simulate an actual test. Be sure to complete any chapter reviews in your textbook, without looking back at the chapter or your notes.
5. Get rid of negative self-talk ("I'm a born math loser" or "This stuff is so hard I'm bound to fail") by identifying such negative thoughts and understanding the lack of logic behind them. Try to replace them with more positive thoughts ("I learned the basics of math, and this new material is just a logical extension of the fundamentals" and "If I'm confident and proceed methodically, I can succeed").
6. The day of the test, warm up by doing a few practice problems before you get to class. Then get to the classroom early enough so you won't feel rushed.

DURING TESTS:

1. Read through all the problems first, and then tackle the easiest ones.
2. Analyze the math problems carefully. What are the known quantities or constants, and what pieces of information are missing? What formula(s) or theorem(s) apply?
3. For word problems, consider if they are similar to word problems that you've studied and mastered.
4. Consider drawing a diagram, graph, or probability tree.
5. Break down calculations into their component parts.
6. Check your math carefully.
7. Be neat and logical in your presentation, and show every step as you solve problems. Your instructor may give you partial credit if you lay out every step you're going through. In addition, some instructors require you to show your work.

You might also construct a test and administer it to a classmate or a member of your study group. In turn, you could take a test that someone else has constructed. Constructing and taking practice tests are excellent ways of studying the material and cementing it into memory. (To be sure you're fully prepared for your next test, complete **Try It! 2**.)

Form a Study Group

study group
A small, informal group of students whose purpose is to help members work together and study for a test.

Study groups are small, informal groups of students who work together to learn course material and study for a test. Forming such a group can be an excellent way to prepare for any kind of test. Some study groups are formed for particular tests, while others meet consistently throughout the term.

The typical study group meets a week or two before a test and plans a strategy for studying. Members share their understanding of what will be on the test, based on what an instructor has said in class and on their review of notes and text material. Together, they develop a list of review questions to guide their individual study. The group then breaks up, and the members study on their own.

A few days before the test, members of the study group meet again. They discuss answers to the review questions, go over the material, and share any new insights they may have about the upcoming test. They may also quiz one another about the material to identify any weaknesses or gaps in their knowledge.

Taking an online class? You can still form a study group by using Skype, Facetime, or other applications that allow you to communicate face-to-face virtually. It may seem a bit awkward at first, but the benefits of a virtual study group are very real.

Study groups can be extremely powerful tools because they help accomplish several things:

- They help members organize and structure the material to approach their studying in a systematic and logical way.
- They allow students to share different perspectives on the material.
- They make it more likely that students will not overlook any potentially important information.
- They force members to rethink the course material, explaining it in words that other group members will understand. This step enhances both understanding and recall of the information when it is needed on the test.
- Finally, they help motivate members to do their best. When you're part of a study group, you're no longer working just for yourself; your studying also benefits the other study group members. Not wanting to let down your classmates in a study group may encourage you to put in your best effort.

Study groups, made up of a few students who study together for a test, can help organize material, provide new perspectives, and motivate members to do their best.
©Moxie Productions/Blend Images

There are some potential drawbacks to keep in mind. Study groups don't always work well for students with learning styles that favor working independently. In addition, "problem" members–those who don't pull their weight–may cause difficulties for the group. In general, though, the advantages of study groups far outweigh their disadvantages.

2 **Try It!** POWER

Complete a Test Preparation Checklist

It takes more than simply learning the material to prepare for a test. You also need a strategy that will help you understand what it is you are studying for. To do that, learn as much as you can about what the test will be like. The more you understand about the kind of test and what it will cover, the better you'll be able to target your studying.

To focus your studying, complete the following test preparation checklist before your next test.

TEST PREPARATION CHECKLIST

- ☐ I know whether it's a quiz, test, or exam.
- ☐ I know what kinds of questions will be on the test.
- ☐ I understand what material will be covered.
- ☐ I know how many questions will be on the test.
- ☐ I know how long I will have to complete the test.
- ☐ I know how it will be graded and how the grade contributes to my final course grade.
- ☐ I obtained sample questions and/or previous tests, if available.
- ☐ I formed or participated in a study group.
- ☐ I used different and appropriate preparation strategies for different types of questions.
- ☐ I read and studied my class notes.
- ☐ I composed some questions of the kind that will be on the exam.
- ☐ I answered essay questions aloud.
- ☐ I actively memorized facts and details.
- ☐ I made and used index cards.
- ☐ I created and used a test like the real test.

After completing the checklist, ask yourself these questions: How can I use this checklist to study more effectively for tests? How might completing the checklist change the way I previously have studied for tests? What new strategies might I follow in order to prepare for tests more effectively in the future?

How do you form a study group? Follow these steps:

1. Identify motivated, enthusiastic classmates. Unenergetic classmates with negative attitudes do not make good study group members.
2. Include a variety of people. Involve classmates with different strengths to maximize what you can learn from them.
3. Choose a purpose for your study group. It might be to review class material and notes throughout the semester, meeting weekly. Or it might form to focus on test preparation and meet only prior to exams. Be clear on the focus when you form the group.
4. Don't make your study group too large. Groups larger than four or five people tend to get off task easily.

Regroup if necessary. If, after establishing your group, you find that the members don't function effectively, change membership or even disband your group. You want to make the most of a study group, and if it is not working well, think about starting over with a new group of classmates. (To set up your own study group, see **Try It! 3**.)

3  WORKING IN A GROUP

Try It! POWER

Form a Study Group

The next time you have to prepare for a test, form a study group with three to five classmates. They may have a variety of study habits and skills, but all must be willing to take the group seriously.

The first time you meet, compare notes about what is likely to be on the test and brainstorm to come up with possible test questions. If the instructor hasn't given you detailed information about the test (e.g., number and types of questions, weighting), one of you should be delegated to ask for it. Plan to meet once more closer to the test date to discuss answers to the questions you've come up with, share any new insights, and quiz one another on the material.

After you've taken the test and gotten your results, meet again and evaluate the experience by answering the following questions:

1. Did you and the other members of the group find the experience useful?
2. Did participating in the study group make the members feel more confident prior to the test?
3. What aspects of the study group were most effective?
4. What aspects of the study group didn't work effectively?
5. What would you do differently the next time you use a study group?

Use Your Campus Learning or Tutorial Center Resources

Many colleges have a learning center, tutorial center, or other office that can help you study for a test. Often they are staffed by advanced students who have already taken courses that you're studying for. Take advantage of any opportunities you have to get the advice of such "expert" students. Not only can they provide you with general study strategies, but they can give you tips on a particular instructor's tests.

Don't wait until after you do badly on a test to visit your campus learning or tutorial center. A visit prior to your first test is a good use of your time, even if you feel it's not essential. Just knowing what resources are available can boost your confidence.

Cramming: You Shouldn't, But . . .

cramming
Hurried, last-minute studying.

You know, of course, that **cramming**—hurried, last-minute studying—is not the way to go. You know that you're likely to forget the material the moment the test is over because long-term retention is nearly impossible without thoughtful study. But . . .

- . . . it's been one of those weeks where everything went wrong.
- . . . the instructor sprang the test on you at the last minute.
- . . . you forgot about the test until the night before it was scheduled.

Whatever the reason, there may be times when you can't study properly. What do you do if you have to cram for an exam?

Don't spend a lot of time on what you're unable to do. Beating yourself up about your occasional failings as a student will only hinder your efforts. Instead, admit you're human and imperfect like everyone else. Then spend a few minutes developing a plan about what you can accomplish in the limited time you've got.

The first thing to do is choose what you really need to study. You won't be able to learn everything, so you have to make choices. Figure out the main focus of the course, and concentrate on it.

Once you have a strategy, prepare a one-page summary sheet with hard-to-remember information. Just writing the material down will help you remember it, and you can refer to the summary sheet frequently over the limited time you do have to study.

Have you ever crammed for a test? If so, you know how exhausting it can be, and how easy it is to overlook crucial material. On the other hand, time pressures sometimes make cramming your only option. When that happens, there are strategies you can use to help you make the best use of limited time.

©AmmentorpDK/Getty Images

Next, read through your class notes, concentrating on the material you've underlined and the key concepts and ideas that you've already noted. Forget about reading all the material in the books and articles you're being tested on. Instead, read only the passages that you've underlined and the notes you've taken on the readings. Finally, maximize your study time. Using your notes, index cards, and concept maps, go over the information. Read it. Say it aloud. Think about it and the way it relates to other information. In short, use all the techniques we've talked about for learning and recalling information.

Just remember: When the exam is over, material that you have crammed into your head is destined to leave your mind as quickly as it entered. If you've crammed for a midterm, don't assume that the information will still be there when you study for the final. In the end, cramming often ends up taking more time for worse results than does studying with appropriate techniques.

O Organize Facing the Day of the Test

You've studied a lot, and you're happy with your level of mastery. Or perhaps you have the nagging feeling that there's something you haven't quite completed. Or maybe you know you haven't had enough time to study as much as you'd like, and you're expecting a disaster.

Whatever your frame of mind, it will help to organize your plan of attack on the day of the test. What's included on the test is out of your hands, but you can control what you bring to it.

For starters, bring the right tools to the test. Have several pens and pencils (with erasers) with you. It's usually best to write in pen because, in general, writing tends to be easier to read in pen than in pencil. But you also may need to have pencils on hand. Sometimes instructors will use a computer scanner to grade the test, and you may have to fill out an answer sheet in pencil. Or there may be test questions that involve computations, and solving them may entail frequent reworking of calculations.

You should also bring an identification card with a photo to the test. In large classes, instructors sometimes check ID's to make sure you are who you say you are.

You should also bring a watch to the test in case there is no clock on the wall of the classroom. You will want to be able to pace yourself properly during the test. If you usually use a cell phone to determine the time, remember that some instructors may not allow you to look at them during the test.

Sometimes instructors permit you to use notes and books during the test. If you haven't brought them with you, they're not going to be of much help. So make sure you bring them if they're permitted. (Even for closed-book tests, having such material available before the test actually starts allows you a few minutes of review after you arrive in the classroom.) And don't be lulled into thinking an open-book test is going to be easy. Instructors who allow you to use your notes and books during a test may not give you much time to look things up, so you still need to study.

On the day of a test, avoid the temptation to compare notes with your friends about how much they've studied. Yes, you might end up feeling good because many of your fellow classmates studied less than you did. But chances are you'll find others who seem to have spent significantly more time studying than you, and this will do little to encourage you.

In addition, you might want to plan in advance on panicking and think about how you'll react. Although it sounds like the worst possible approach, permitting yourself the option of spending a minute feeling panicky will help you to recover from your initial fears.

Finally, listen carefully to what an instructor says before the test is handed out. The instructor may tell you about a question that is optional or worth more points or inform you of a typographical error on the test. Whatever the instructor says just before the test, you can be sure it's information that you don't want to ignore.

Taking a Test Online or at a Testing Center

If you will be taking the test online, either because you are enrolled in a distance learning class or because your face-to-face course instructor has assigned an online quiz, there are several additional key factors to consider as you get ready to take the test:

- Have your computer ready and fully charged, and have reliable access to the Internet.
- Be sure to know exactly when the test will be available. You may be able to take the test only for a certain period. Miss that time, and you'll be out of luck.
- If an online test is being administered in a group setting such as a campus testing center, be sure to bring a photo ID. Even if the people running the testing center know you, they will almost certainly be required to verify your identity.
- Check the restrictions at online testing centers. If they say no cellphones, bluetooth devices, food, backpacks, or sunglasses, they are serious. Don't expect they will make an exception for you.

» LO 5-3 Taking the Test

The instructor hands you the test, and it's time to start. Here are some proven strategies that will help you maximize your success.

W Work Tackling the Test

Take a deep breath—literally.

There's no better way to start work on a test than by taking a deep breath, followed by several others. The deep breaths will help you overcome any initial panic and anxiety you may be experiencing. It's okay to give yourself over for a moment to panic and anxiety, but, to work at your best, use the relaxation techniques that we spoke about earlier to displace those initial feelings. Tell yourself, "It's okay. I am going to do my best." Even the most successful athletes, like Olympic swimmer Michael Phelps, use *positive self-talk,* brief phrases that can motivate or remind them of past successes, as well as *visualizations* of success, to help them focus on the task in a positive way.

Read the test instructions carefully. Even if instructors talk about what a test will be like beforehand, at the last minute, they may make changes. Consequently, it's critical to read the instructions for the test carefully. In fact, you should skim through the entire exam before you begin. Look at the kinds of questions and pay attention to the way they will be scored. If the point weighting of the various parts of the exam is not clear, ask your instructor to clarify it.

Knowing the point weighting is critical, because it will help you allocate your time. You don't want to spend 90 percent of your time on an essay that's worth only 10 percent of the points, and you want to be sure to leave time at the end of the test to check your answers.

Olympic gold-medalist Michael Phelps uses positive self-talk and visualizations to improve his performance.
©Leonard Zhukovsky/123RF

An initial read-through will also help you verify that you have every page of the exam and that each one is readable. It may also provide you with "intra-test knowledge," in which terms defined or mentioned in one part of a test trigger memories that can help answer questions in another part of the test.

If there are any lists, formulas, or other key facts that you're concerned you may forget, jot them down now on the back of a test page or on a piece of scrap paper. You may want to refer to this material later during the test.

Once this background work is out of the way, you'll be ready to proceed to actually answering the questions. These principles will help you do your best on the test:

- **Answer the easiest questions first.** By initially getting the questions that are easiest for you out of the way, you accomplish several important things. First, you'll be leaving yourself more time to think about the tougher questions. In addition, moving through a series of questions without a struggle will build your confidence. Finally, working through a number of questions will build up a base of points that may be enough to earn you at least a minimally acceptable grade.
- **Write legibly and on only one side of the paper.** If an instructor can't read what you've written, you're not going to get credit for it, no matter how brilliant your answer. So be sure to keep your handwriting legible. If your cursive writing is hard to read, then print your answers.

  It's also a good idea to write your answers to essay questions on only one side of a page. This will allow you to go back later and add or revise information.
- **Master computer-scored tests.** Tests will sometimes be scored, entirely or in part, by a computer scanner. In such cases, you'll usually have to indicate your answers by filling in—with a pencil—circles or squares on a computer answer sheet.

  Be careful! A stray mark or smudge can cause the computer scanner to misread your answer sheet, producing errors in grading. Be sure to bring a good eraser in addition to a pencil; the biggest source of mistakes in machine grading is incomplete erasing.

  It's best to write your answers not only on the answer sheet, but also on the test itself (if the test is not intended for future reuse). That way you can go back and check your answers easily—a step you should take frequently. It's also a good idea to match up your answers on the test with the spaces on the answer sheet every five or so items. This will help you make sure you haven't skipped a space or gotten off track in some other way. If you catch such problems early, they're easy to fix.

> "Computerized test-scoring isn't perfect. Smudges can kill you. If your grade seems incorrect, ask to see the answer sheet."
>
> **Graduate, physiology, Michigan State University, in Tyler, S. (1997).** ***Been There, Should've Done That.*** **Haslett, MI: Front Porch Press. P. 128.**

A variant of computer-scored testing is online testing. In such cases, you'll be taking an exam on a computer outside of class. Keep in mind that you shouldn't wait until just before the final deadline to start your test. Technical difficulties may prevent you from logging in or having enough time to finish. In addition, be sure to have paper and pencil available. Even though you use the computer to record your answers, you'll want to be able to jot down ideas and notes and do calculations the traditional way: using paper and pencil.

Use Strategies Targeted to Answering Specific Types of Test Questions

Every type of question requires a particular approach. Use the strategies below:

- **Essay questions.** Essay questions, with their emphasis on description and analysis, present a special challenge because they are relatively unstructured. Unless you're careful, it's easy to drift off track and begin to answer questions that were never asked. To prevent that problem, the first thing to do is read the question carefully, noting what specifically is being asked. If your essay will be lengthy, you might even want to write a short outline.

  Pay particular attention to keywords that indicate what, specifically, the instructor is looking for in an answer. Certain action words are commonly used in essays, and you should understand them fully. For instance, knowing the distinction between "compare" and "contrast" can spell the difference between success and failure. **Table 5.3** defines common action words.

  Use the right language in essays. Be brief and to the point in your essay. Avoid flowery introductory language. Compare the two sentences that follow:

  > *"In our study of world literature, it may be useful to ponder how The Canterbury Tales came to represent such an important milestone in the field, and it will be seen that there are several critical reasons why it did have such an impact."*
  >
  > *"The Canterbury Tales were groundbreaking for several reasons."*

  This second sentence says the same thing much more effectively and economically.

  Essays are improved when they include examples and point out differences. Your response should follow a logical sequence, moving from major points to minor ones, or following a time sequence. Above all, your answer should address every aspect of the question posed on the test. Because essays often contain several different, embedded questions, you have to be certain that you have answered every part to receive full credit. (After reviewing Table 5.3, complete **Try It! 4**.)

- **Short-answer and fill-in questions.** Short-answer and fill-in questions basically require you to generate and supply specific information in your own words. Unlike essays, which are more free-form and may have several possible answers, short-answer and fill-in questions are usually quite specific, requiring one particular answer.

  Use both the instructions for the questions and the questions themselves to determine the level of specificity that is needed in an answer. Try not to provide too much or too little information. Usually, brevity is best.

- **Multiple-choice questions.** If you've ever looked at a multiple-choice question and said to yourself, "But every choice seems right," you understand what can be tricky about this type of question. However, there are some simple strategies that can help you deal with multiple-choice questions.

table 5.3 Action Words for Essays
These words are commonly used in essay questions. Learning the distinctions among them will help you answer them effectively.
Analyze: Examine and break into component parts.
Clarify: Explain with significant detail.
Compare: Describe and explain similarities.
Compare and contrast: Describe and explain similarities and differences.
Contrast: Describe and explain differences.
Critique: Judge and analyze, explaining what is wrong—and right—about a concept.
Define: Provide the meaning.
Discuss: Explain, review, and consider.
Enumerate: Provide a listing of ideas, concepts, reasons, items, etc.
Evaluate: Provide pros and cons of something; provide an opinion and justify it.
Explain: Give reasons why or how; clarify, justify, and illustrate.
Illustrate: Provide examples; show instances.
Interpret: Explain the meaning of something.
Justify: Explain why a concept can be supported, typically by using examples and other types of support.
Outline: Provide an overarching framework or explanation—usually in narrative form—of a concept, idea, event, or phenomenon.
Prove: Using evidence and arguments, convince the reader of a particular point.
Relate: Show how things fit together; provide analogies.
Review: Describe or summarize, often with an evaluation.
State: Assert or explain.
Summarize: Provide a condensed, precise list or narrative.
Trace: Track or sketch out how events or circumstances have evolved; provide a history or timeline.

First, read the instructions carefully to determine whether only one response will be correct, or whether more than one of the choices may be correct. In most cases, only one choice will be right, but in some cases instructors may want you to check off more than one answer.

4 | **Try It!** POWER

Understand Action Verbs in Essay Questions

Answer the following questions about the Second Amendment to the United States Constitution by outlining your responses to them, paying attention to the different action verbs that introduce questions.

The Second Amendment states:

A well-regulated militia, being necessary to the security of a free State, the right of the people to keep and bear arms, shall not be infringed.[2]

1. Summarize the Second Amendment to the Constitution.

2. Analyze the Second Amendment to the Constitution.

3. Discuss the Second Amendment to the Constitution.

How do your answers differ for the each of the questions? Which of the questions provoked the lengthiest response? Which of the questions could you answer best?

Turn to the first question and read it carefully. *Before you look at the possible answers, try to answer the question in your head.* This can help you avoid confusion over inappropriate choices.

Next, *carefully read through every possible answer.* Even if you come to one that you think is right, read them all—there may be a subsequent answer that is better.

Look for absolute words like "every," "always," "only," "none," and "never." Choices that contain such absolute words, which suggest there are no exceptions to a statement or premise, are rarely correct. For example, an answer choice that says, "A U.S. president has never been elected without having received the majority of the popular vote" is incorrect due to the presence of the word "never." On the other hand, less-absolute words that allow for uncertainty, such as "generally," "usually," "often," "rarely," "seldom," and "typically," may indicate a correct response.

Be especially on guard for the word "not," which negates the sentence ("The one key concept that is not embodied in the U.S. Constitution is . . ."). It's easy to gloss over "not," and if you have the misfortune of doing so, it will be nearly impossible to answer the item correctly.

If you're having trouble understanding a question, underline key words or phrases, or try to break the question into different short sections. Sometimes it is helpful to work backwards, *Jeopardy* style, and look at the possible answers first to see if you can find one that is clearly accurate or clearly inaccurate.

Use an **educated guessing** *strategy*—which is very different from wild or random guessing. Unless your instructor penalizes you for wrong answers by deducting points for wrong answers from the points you have earned on other questions, it always pays to guess.

educated guessing The practice of eliminating obviously false multiple-choice answers and selecting the most likely answer from the remaining choices.

The first step in educated guessing is to eliminate any obviously false answers. The next step is to examine the remaining choices closely. Does one response choice include an absolute or qualifying adjective that makes it unlikely ("The probability of war *always* increases when a U.S. president is facing political difficulties")? Does one choice include a subtle factual error? For example, the answer to a multiple-choice question asking why Columbus took his journey to the New World that says, "The French monarchy was interested in expanding its colonial holdings" is wrong because it was not the French, but the Spanish, monarchy that funded his journey.

- **True-false questions.** Although most of the principles we've already discussed apply equally well to true-false questions, a few additional tricks of the trade may help you with this type of question.

  Begin a set of true-false questions by answering the ones you're sure you know. But don't rush; it's important to read every part of a true-false question, because key words such as "never," "always," and "sometimes" often determine the appropriate response.

  If you don't have a clue about whether a statement is true or false, here's a last-resort principle: Choose "true." In general, more statements on a true-false test are likely to be true than false. (The reason? Because it's easier for an instructor to think of true statements than to make up believable false statements.)

- **Matching questions.** Matching questions typically present you with two columns of related information, which you must link, item by item. For example, a list of terms or concepts may be presented in one column, along with a list of corresponding definitions or explanations in the second column. The best strategy is to reduce the size of both columns by matching the items you're most confident about first; this will leave a short list in each column, and the final matching may become apparent.

About Academic Honesty and Plagiarism

It's tempting: A glance at a classmate's test may provide the one piece of information that you just can't remember. But you owe it to yourself not to do it. Copying from a classmate's paper is no different from reaching over and stealing that classmate's cellphone or calculator. It is a violation of **academic honesty**, one of the foundations of civility in the classroom, as well as in society. Unless the work you turn in under your own name is your work, you are guilty of academic dishonesty.

academic honesty Completing and turning in only one's own work under one's own name.

Violations of academic honesty can take many forms. One form is *plagiarism,* copying another's work and passing it off as your own. (We'll talk more about plagiarism later in the book.) Academic dishonesty may also include using a calculator when it's not allowed, discussing the answer to a question, copying a computer file when it's unauthorized, taking an exam for another person, or stealing an exam. It can take the form of ripping a page out of a book in the library or lying to an instructor about the reason for a late paper. It includes using your textbook or conferring with a friend when taking a closed-book exam in an online, distance-learning course.

You may feel that "everyone does it," so cheating is not so bad. Wrong. Everyone doesn't do it, just as most people don't embezzle from their companies or steal from others. Although you may know of a few exceptionally dishonest classmates, most of your classmates try to be honest—you just don't notice their honesty.

Whatever form it takes, academic dishonesty is just plain wrong. It lowers the level of civility in the classroom, it makes the grading system unfair, and it ultimately reduces the meaning of your grade. It certainly hinders academic and personal growth. It can't help but reduce one's self-esteem, and it robs the cheater of self-respect.

Finally, academic dishonesty violates the regulations of every college (rules that you should familiarize yourself with), and instructors feel it is their obligation to uphold standards of academic honesty. Violations of honesty policies will lead to any number of potentially devastating scenarios: failing the exam on which the cheating has taken place, failing the entire course, being brought before a disciplinary board, having a description of the incident permanently placed on your grade transcript, being placed on academic probation, or even being thrown out of school. A single instance of cheating can permanently prevent you from embarking on the career of your choice. Cheating is simply not worth it.

E Evaluate

Taking Your Own Final Examination

The last few minutes of a test may feel like the final moments of a marathon. You need to focus your energy and push yourself even harder. It can be make-or-break time.

Save some time at the end of a test so you can check your work. You should have been keeping track of your time all along, so plan on stopping a few minutes before the end of the test period to review what you've done. It's a critical step, and it can make the difference between a terrific grade and a mediocre one. It's a rare person who can work for an uninterrupted period of time on a test and commit absolutely no errors—even if he or she knows the material backwards and forwards. Consequently, checking what you've done is crucial.

Start evaluating your test by looking for obvious mistakes. Make sure you've answered every question and haven't skipped any parts of questions. If there is a separate answer sheet, check to see that all your answers have been recorded on the answer sheet and in the right spot.

Academic honesty is the bedrock of college life. The risks of cheating—getting caught and causing damage to your academic future and sense of self-worth—far outweigh any momentary benefits.
©David Schaffer/Getty Images

If the test has included essay and short-answer questions, proofread your responses. Check for obvious errors—misspellings, missing words, and repetitions. Make sure you've responded to every part of each question and that each essay, as a whole, makes sense.

Check over your responses to multiple-choice, true-false, and matching questions. If there are some items that you haven't yet answered because you couldn't remember the necessary information, now is the time to take a stab at them. As we discussed earlier, it usually pays to guess, even randomly if you must. On most tests, no answer and a wrong answer are worth the same amount—nothing!

What about items that you initially guessed at? Unless you have a good reason to change your original answer—such as a new insight or a sudden recollection of some key information—your first guess is likely your best guess.

Career Connections

Tests for a Lifetime

If you think the last tests you'll ever have to take are the final exams just before you graduate from college, you're probably wrong.

For one thing, increasing numbers of professions require initial licensing exams, and some even require periodic exams to remain in good standing within the profession. For example, in some states, people who wish to become teachers must pass an exam, as in the case of Imani Brown described at the beginning of the chapter. Even experienced teachers are required to take periodic tests throughout their careers to remain in the teaching field.

In addition, you may have to take tests to continue your course of study for some professions. For example, if you are thinking about a career in medicine, law, or business, you'll need to take a national, standardized test (such as the MCAT or LSAT) to enroll in a postundergraduate program. How well you do on the test will determine whether you can go to graduate school and which graduate schools will accept you.

In short, good test-taking skills won't just bring you success in college. They're something that may benefit you for a lifetime as you pursue your career.

Know When to Stop

After evaluating and checking, and rechecking, your answers, you may reach a point when there is still some time left before the scheduled end of the test. What to do?

If you're totally satisfied with your responses, it may be time to simply tell yourself, "Let it go." Permit yourself the luxury of knowing that you've done your best, and hand the test in to your instructor. You don't have to review your work over and over just because there is time remaining and some of your classmates are still working on their tests. In fact, such behavior is often counterproductive, because you might start overinterpreting and reading things into questions that really aren't there.

Disaster! I'm running out of time! It's a nightmarish feeling: The clock is ticking relentlessly, and it's clear that you don't have enough time to finish the test. What should you do?

Stop working! Although this advice may sound foolish, in fact the most important thing you can do is to take a minute to calm yourself. Take some deep breaths to replace the feelings of panic that are likely welling up inside you. Collect your thoughts, and plan a strategy for the last moments of the test.

If there are essays that remain undone, consider how you'd answer them if you had more time. Then write an outline of each answer. If you don't have time even for that, write a few keywords. Writing anything is better than handing in a blank page, and you may get at least some credit for your response. The key principle here: Something is better than nothing, and even one point is worth more than zero points.

The same principle holds for other types of questions. Even wild guesses are almost always better than not responding at all to an item. So rather than telling yourself you've certainly failed and giving up, do as much as you can in the remaining moments of the exam.

R Rethink The Real Test of Learning

Your instructor is about to hand the graded exams back. All sorts of thoughts run through your head: How did I do? Did I do as well as my classmates? Will I be happy with my results? Will the results show how much I studied? Will I be embarrassed by my grade?

Most of us focus on the evaluative aspects of tests. We look at the grade we've received on a test as an end in itself. It's a natural reaction.

> "The test of any man lies in action."
>
> Pindar, in Pindar & Lattimore, R. (1947). *The Odes of Pindar.* Chicago, Ill: The University of Chicago Press.

But there's another way to look at test results: They can help guide us toward future success. By looking at what we've learned (and haven't learned) about a given subject, we'll be in a better position to know what to focus on when we take future exams. Furthermore, by examining the kinds of mistakes we make, we can learn to do better in the future.

When you get your test back, you have the opportunity to reflect on what you've learned and consider your performance. Begin by actively listening to what your instructor says as he or she hands back the test. You may learn about things that were generally misunderstood by the class, and you'll get a sense of how your performance compares to that of your classmates. You also may pick up some important clues about what questions will be on future exams.

Then examine your own mistakes. Chances are they'll jump out at you since they will be marked incorrect. Did you misunderstand or misapply some principle? Was there a certain aspect of the material covered on the test that you missed? Were there particular kinds of information that you didn't realize you needed to know? Or did you lose some points because of your test-taking skills? Did you make careless errors, such as forgetting to fill in a question or misreading the directions? Was your handwriting so sloppy that your instructor had trouble reading it?

Once you have a good idea of what material you didn't fully understand or remember, get the correct answers to the items you missed—from your instructor, fellow classmates, or your book. If it's a math exam, rework problems you've missed. Finally, summarize—in writing—the material you had trouble with. This will help you study for future exams that cover the same material.

If you're dissatisfied with your performance, talk to your instructor—not to complain, but to seek help. Instructors don't like to give bad grades, and they may be able to point out problems in your test that you can address readily so you can do better in the future.

If you do talk to your instructor, be polite! Don't say how unfair the test was, don't imply that the instructor is mean or uncaring, and don't talk about how you absolutely have to get a certain grade in order to go to graduate school or keep your scholarship or anything else that will make the instructor think you are asking for special privileges.

Instead, demonstrate to your instructor that you want to do better and are willing to put in the work to get there. Describe how you studied for the test, and see if the instructor has any advice on what you might do differently the next time you take a test.

The worst thing to do is crumple up the test, quickly leave the class in embarrassment, and try to put your performance out of your mind. Remember, you're not the first person to get a bad grade, and the power to improve your test-taking performance lies within you. (Now, take a deep breath and complete **Try It! 5**.)

5 Try It! POWER

Take a Test-Taking Test

Take the following test on test-taking skills, which illustrates every question type discussed in this chapter. Answers to all questions except short-answer and essay questions are provided at the end of the chapter. That section contains general approaches for those two question types as well.

Before taking the test, think of the test-taking strategies we've discussed in the chapter and try to employ as many of them as possible.

MULTIPLE-CHOICE SECTION

Choose one of the possible responses following each question.

1. Tests are useful tools for which of the following purposes?
   a. Determining people's likely level of future career success.
   b. Indicating strengths and gaps in people's knowledge.
   c. Defining people's fundamental abilities and potentials.
   d. Evaluating people's individual worth and contributions.
2. One of the main advantages of study groups is that
   a. Every individual must contribute equally to the group.
   b. Group members can help one another during the test.
   c. Each member has to memorize only a fraction of the material.
   d. Groups motivate their members to do good work.
3. Which of the following is a good way to deal with test anxiety?
   a. Visualizing success on the test.
   b. Drinking coffee or other stimulants.
   c. Telling yourself to stop worrying.
   d. Focusing on the importance of the test.

MATCHING SECTION

____ 1. Essay question	A. A question in which the student supplies brief missing information to complete a statement.
____ 2. Multiple-choice question	B. Hurried, last-minute studying.
____ 3. Matching question	C. A question in which the student must link information in two columns.
____ 4. Fill-in question	D. A question requiring a lengthy response in the student's own words.
____ 5. Guessing penalty	E. Deduction of points for incorrect responses.
____ 6. Cramming	F. Representing another's work as one's own.
____ 7. Academic dishonesty	G. A question that requires selection from several response options.

FILL-IN SECTION

1. Fear of testing that can interfere with test performance is called ______.
2. The primary source of error on machine-scored tests is incomplete ______.

(continued)

5 *continued*

Try It!

TRUE-FALSE SECTION

1. The best way to prepare for an essay test is to review detailed factual information about the topic.
   T ______ F ______
2. True–false questions require students to determine whether given statements are accurate or inaccurate.
   T ______ F ______
3. You should never permit yourself to feel panicky during a test. T ______ F ______
4. A good evaluation strategy toward the end of a test is to redo as many questions as time permits.
   T ______ F ______
5. In a multiple-choice question, the words "always" and "never" usually signal the correct response.
   T ______ F ______
6. If you run out of time at the end of a test, it is best to write brief notes and ideas down in response to essay questions rather than to leave them completely blank. T ______ F ______

SHORT-ANSWER SECTION

1. What are five things you should find out about a test before you take it?

2. What is academic honesty?

ESSAY SECTION

1. Discuss the advantages of using a study group to prepare for an examination.

2. Why is academic honesty important?

(Answers can be found at the end of the chapter.)

After you have completed the test, consider these questions: Did you learn anything from taking the test that you might not have learned if you hadn't been tested? How effective were the test-taking strategies you employed? Were any types of strategies easier for you to employ than others? Were any types of questions easier for you to answer than others?

WORKING IN A GROUP

Exchange your essay responses with a classmate, and critique the essay. How do the responses of your partner compare with your own?

Speaking *of* Success

Courtesy of Cammeron Dangerfield

NAME: **Camerron Dangerfield**

SCHOOL: **Alabama Agricultural & Mechanical University, Huntsville, Alabama**

To offset the cost of education, many students participate in work-study programs. And then there are students like Camerron Dangerfield, who not only works two jobs, but runs his own business as well, all while pursuing a college degree.

"Growing up in an impoverished neighborhood gave me a drive to want to better my life," said Dangerfield, a senior. "Seeing the daily struggles firsthand that my grandmother had to go through made my decision final. I wanted to become the first in my family to go to college."

Choosing Alabama A&M University because of its family-oriented atmosphere and scholarship opportunities, Dangerfield left his hometown of Chicago to pursue his college education, but a personal tragedy almost derailed him.

"The biggest adversity I faced as a student was not the work, but the loss of my grandmother. As my legal guardian I was so dependent on her to take care of so many of my needs, so her passing crippled me," he said. "My studies took a tremendous fall, due to the overwhelming grief I dealt with day to day. I felt as if I could not recover academically, but the faculty and staff at Alabama A&M worked with me to get me back on track. Her passing brought about a change in my life, and motivated me to start cooking for others."

That motivation, coupled with studying international business, led to starting his own business, "Cooking with Cam," that includes his own cooking show on YouTube.

"My grandmother was known for feeding anyone who was hungry. So I started my business, and I also had two other part-time jobs. It was very demanding at first but the driving force that keeps me going is knowing how much my grandmother invested in my future, so I plan on living up to my potential."

With a clear set of goals and a degree, Dangerfield is confident that he will reach his dream of opening a chain of restaurants.

"My advice to students in college would be to find your passion, and make your degree work for you, instead of working for your degree," he said. "My passion in life is cooking, and my major is international business. Partnering the two allows me to share my food with others while reaping all the financial benefits."

[RETHINK]

- What do you think Dangerfield means when he says, "Make your degree work for you, instead of working for your degree"?
- What are some principles of time management that are likely to have permitted Dangerfield to juggle two jobs, and run his own business?

Looking Back

LO 5-1 Identify the kinds of tests you will encounter in college.

- Although tests are an unpopular fact of college life, they can provide useful information about one's level of knowledge and understanding about a subject.
- There are several types of tests, including brief, informal quizzes; more substantial tests; and even more weighty exams, which tend to be administered at the midpoint and end of a course.

LO 5-2 Explain the best ways to prepare for and take various kinds of tests.

- Good test preparation begins with doing the course assignments, attending class regularly, and paying attention in class. It also helps to find out as much as possible about a test beforehand and to form a study group to review material.
- If cramming becomes necessary, focus on summarizing factual information broadly, identifying key concepts and ideas, and rehearsing information orally.
- When you first receive the test, skim it to see what kinds of questions are asked, figure out how the different questions and sections will be weighted, and jot down complex factual information that is likely to be needed for the test.

LO 5-3 Analyze the best strategies for answering specific kinds of test questions.

- Answer the easiest questions first, write legibly, use only one side of each sheet of paper, mark answer sheets carefully, and record answers in the test book as well as on the answer sheet.
- For essay questions, be sure to understand each question and each of its parts, interpret action words correctly, write concisely, organize the essay logically, and include examples.
- The best strategy for short-answer and fill-in questions is to be very sure what is being asked. Keep answers complete but brief.
- For multiple-choice questions, read the question very carefully and then read all response choices. Educated guessing based on eliminating incorrect response choices is usually a reasonable strategy.
- For true–false and matching questions, answer all the items that you are sure of quickly and then go back to the remaining items.

[KEY TERMS AND CONCEPTS]

Academic honesty (p. 137)
Cramming (p. 130)
Educated guessing (p. 137)
Study group (p. 128)
Test anxiety (p. 125)

[RESOURCES]

ON CAMPUS

Colleges provide a variety of resources for students having difficulties with test taking. Some offer general workshops for students, reviewing test-taking strategies. Furthermore, if you are planning to take a specific standardized test, such as the tests required for admission to business, law, or medical school, you may be able to sign up for a course offered through your college (or through such commercial organizations as Princeton Review or Kaplan).

If you are experiencing difficulties in a specific course, you may be able to find a tutor to help you out. Some colleges have tutoring centers or campus learning centers that can provide one-to-one assistance. You also can talk to your advisor, who may be able to point you in the right direction. It's also important to speak to your instructor, who more than likely has encountered many students with similar problems and may have some useful test-taking strategies.

If you find that you are experiencing significant test anxiety when taking a test or in the days leading up to it, talk to someone at your campus counseling center or health center. They can help you learn relaxation techniques and provide counseling to help make your anxiety manageable.

IN PRINT

Ace Any Test (Cengage Learning PTR, 2011, 6th ed.), by educator Ron Fry, offers easy-to-follow strategies that can be used for all types of tests, from quizzes to the SAT.

Doc Orman's *The Test Anxiety Cure* (Stress Management Group, 2014) offers what the author describes as 10 root causes of test anxiety and how to deal with them.

You can find test strategies for all types of questions in *Test Secrets,* by The Complete Test Preparation Team (CreateSpace Independent Publishing Platform, 2013).

ON THE WEB

- "Taking Multiple Choice Exams" is an online presentation from the University of Wisconsin–Eau Claire outlining a series of strategies and approaches for taking multiple-choice exams. **http://people.uwec.edu/ivogeler/multiple.htm**
- The University of Reading, England, "Answering Exam Questions" site is a comprehensive collection of information on how to prepare for a variety of tests, including open-book and oral exams. **https://www.reading.ac.uk/internal/studyadvice/StudyResources/Exams/sta-answering.aspx**
- "Test Taking Anxiety," prepared by undergraduates and scholars-in-residence at Penn State Learning, provides apt advice on preparing for tests and managing the physical tension and mental stress that can be associated with test taking. **https://pennstatelearning.psu.edu/test-taking-anxiety**

[ANSWERS TO TEST ITEMS IN TRY IT! 5]

Short Answer:

1. Possible answers include what the test is called, what it will cover, how many questions will be on it, how much time it will take, what kinds of questions will be on it, how it will be graded, whether sample questions will be provided, and whether tests from prior terms are available.
2. Academic honesty is completing and turning in only one's own work under one's own name.

Essay:

1. Strong essays would include a brief definition of a study group, followed by a discussion of the advantages of using study groups (including such things as helping to organize and structure material, providing different perspectives, and rethinking material). A mention of the disadvantages of study groups would also be reasonable.
2. After starting with a brief definition of academic honesty, the bulk of the answer should concentrate on the reasons academic honesty is important and what the drawbacks are of academic dishonesty.

Multiple-choice: 1b, 2d, 3a

Matching: 1D, 2G, 3C, 4A, 5E, 6B, 7F

Fill-in: test anxiety, erasing

True–False: 1F, 2T, 3F, 4F, 5F, 6T

The Case of . . .

Too Many Questions, Too Little Time

There was no reason to panic, said Mia Varela to herself at the start of the test. The exam, a midterm in her Greek civilization class, contained 50 multiple-choice questions (each worth 1 point) and two short-answer essays (worth a total of 50 points). And she had 75 minutes to complete the test.

"Let's see," she said to herself. "At one and a half minutes per multiple-choice question, that would take 75 minutes. Hmm . . . that's no good. How about a minute for each one? Fifty minutes for the multiple-choice questions, leaving 25 minutes for the essays. That ought to work. I'll get the multiple-choice questions out of the way first."

But things didn't work out the way she had planned. After an hour she had completed only 40 of the multiple-choice questions and hadn't even started on the essay questions. With only 15 minutes left, panic began to set in. She had trouble thinking. She began to be certain that she'd fail the test. She thought about how she hadn't studied enough. If only she'd worked harder. How could she explain this failure to her friends . . . to her parents . . . to herself? The thoughts kept coming, and time kept ticking away.

1. Is there evidence that Mia didn't study effectively for this type of test?

2. What was right about Mia's initial approach to the test?

3. What should Mia have done differently in calculating the amount of time to devote to each portion of the test? Why?

4. What should Mia have done to be aware of, and address, her timing problem sooner?

5. How should Mia have dealt with her panic? Were her thoughts productive or counterproductive? Why?

6. If you were in Mia's shoes, what would you do with only 15 minutes left in the test?

CHAPTER

6 Reading and Remembering

Learning Outcomes

By the time you finish this chapter you will be able to

» LO 6-1 Explain how reading style and attention span affect reading.

» LO 6-2 Identify how to improve concentration and read and remember more effectively.

» LO 6-3 Discuss how best to retain what you have read.

©Rachel Frank/Corbis/Glow Images

"Read the first two chapters in your text by next Thursday." "I've put three articles on e-reserve. You'll need to have them read by our next class." "Take a look at the first three Shakespeare sonnets in your book, and see if you can identify the major themes."

For Chris O'Hara, these reading assignments–handed down by different instructors on the same day in early October–felt like nails in his coffin. How was he supposed to finish all this reading in the next two days, in addition to studying for a Spanish test, writing a paper for history, and putting in eight hours at his part-time job?

Although the papers and tests were hard enough to deal with, it was the constant reading that was proving the most difficult challenge for Chris during his first term of college. He was a conscientious student who attempted to get everything done. But no matter how hard he tried, he just couldn't get everything read on time, let alone remember all that material. When he pushed himself to read quicker and absorb more, he actually read and retained less. Thoughts about falling behind crowded out the meaning of whatever he was reading. In order to remember what he read, he found that he had to go through the material all over again, slowing him down even more.

©Siede Preis/Photodisc/Getty Images

Looking Ahead

For students like Chris, reading assignments are the biggest challenge in college. The amount of required reading is often enormous. Even skilled readers may find themselves wishing they could read and remember the material more quickly and effectively.

Fortunately, there are ways to improve your reading and memory skills. In this chapter, we'll first go over a number of strategies for reading more effectively. You'll assess your reading style and your attention span, consider what you should do before you even start reading an assignment, and discover some ways of getting the most out of your reading.

Then we'll focus on memory and retaining what you've read. You'll learn how you can improve the memory skills you already have. We'll examine what memory is and why it sometimes fails us. Finally, you will become acquainted with specific ways to learn information so that you can recall it when you need to.

» LO 6-1 Sharpen Your Reading and Memory Skills

What kind of reader are you? Ask yourself first of all about your reading *preferences*: What do you *like* to read, and why? What makes you pick up a book and start reading–and what makes you put one down?

Second, what's your reading *style*? Do you read at a steady, comfortable pace and feel reasonably satisfied with how much you retain? Or do you plod through

Journal Reflections

My Reading Preferences

Think about what you like and don't like to read by answering these questions.

1. Do you read for pleasure? If so, what do you read (e.g., magazines, newspapers, novels, humor, short stories, nonfiction, illustrated books)?
2. What makes a book enjoyable? Have you ever read a book that you "couldn't put down"? If so, what made it so good?
3. What is the most difficult book you are reading this semester? Why is it difficult? Are you enjoying it?
4. Think about when you read for pleasure compared to when you read material for a class. How does the way you read differ between the two types of material?
5. Do you think there should be a difference between reading for pleasure and reading for a class? Why?

reading assignments, novels, and magazines and, like Chris, end up feeling that you're taking far too long? Perhaps you whip through chapters, devour books, and fly through the daily newspaper, but then find you can't recall the information as precisely as you'd like?

Before going any further, think about your own reading preferences by completing the **Journal Reflections**, and then consider your reading style–your characteristic way of approaching reading tasks–by completing **Try It! 1**.

Read for Retention, Not Speed

You may have come across advertisements on the web promoting reading "systems" that promise to teach you to read so quickly that you'll be reading entire books in an hour and whizzing through assigned readings in a few minutes.

Unfortunately, it's not going to happen. For one thing, certain biological facts relating to the eye movements involved in reading simply prevent people from reading (and comprehending) so rapidly. Research has shown that claims of speed reading are simply groundless; it is unlikely that any system will overcome the built-in limitations of the human eye.

1 PERSONAL STYLES

Try It! POWER

Discover Your Reading Style

Use the following questions to learn *how* you read—that is, your characteristic reading style. Rate how well each statement below describes you. Use this rating scale:

1 = Doesn't describe me at all

2 = Describes me only slightly

3 = Describes me fairly well

4 = Describes me very well

	1	2	3	4
1. I often reread passages in books that I particularly like.				
2. I often read good passages aloud to whoever is around.				
3. I often stop while reading to check that I understood what I just read.				
4. If I come across a long, unfamiliar name, I try to sound it out and pronounce it correctly.				
5. If there's a word I don't understand, I look it up in a dictionary right away or mark it so I can look it up later.				
6. Before I start reading a textbook or other serious book or article, I look for clues about how it is organized.				
7. I often question what I'm reading and "argue" with the author.				
8. I often try to guess what the chapter I'm about to read will cover.				
9. I often write comments or make notes in books that I own.				
10. I'm always finding typographical errors in books and articles I read.				

Reading styles range from a very holistic (i.e., broad-brushstroke, noncritical) style to a very analytic (i.e., detailed, critical) style. Add up the points you assigned yourself. Use this informal scale to find your reading style:

10–12 = Very holistic reading style

13–20 = Mostly holistic reading style

21–28 = Mostly analytic reading style

29–40 = Very analytic reading style

How do you think your reading style affects the way you learn material in textbooks? Is your style related to the kinds of subjects you prefer? Do you think your reading style affects your leisure reading?

But even if it were physically possible to read a book in an hour, it probably doesn't matter very much. If we read too fast, comprehension and retention plunge. Reading is not a race, and the fastest readers are not necessarily the best readers.

The act of reading is designed to increase our knowledge and open up new ways of thinking. It can help us achieve new levels of understanding and get us to think more broadly about the world and its inhabitants. Speed matters far less than what we take away from what we've read. That's not to say we shouldn't try to become more efficient readers who comprehend and recall more effectively. Ultimately, though, the key to good reading is understanding—not speed.

In describing how you can use the principles of P.O.W.E.R. Learning to become a better reader, we'll focus on the type of reading that is typically called for in academic pursuits—textbook chapters, articles, handouts, and the like. However, the same principles will help you get more benefit and enjoyment out of your recreational reading as well.

P Prepare Approaching the Written Word

Preparation to begin reading isn't hard, and it won't take very long, but it's a crucial first step in applying P.O.W.E.R. Learning (summarized in the P.O.W.E.R. Plan on this page). Your aim in preparation is to become familiar with advance organizers. **Advance organizers** are outlines, overviews, section objectives, or other clues to the meaning and organization of new information presented in what you are reading. Advance organizers pave the way to learning the material.

advance organizers Outlines, overviews, objectives, and other clues to the meaning and organization of new material in what you are reading, which pave the way for subsequent learning.

Most textbooks have advance organizers built in. For an example, look at the start of every chapter in this book, which includes a chapter outline, plus a set of questions at the end of the "Looking Ahead" section. You can also create your own advance organizers by skimming material to be read and sketching out the general outline of the material you'll be reading.

Advance organizers help us tie information that we already know to new material we're about to encounter. Ultimately, they can help us recall material better after we've read it.

In short, the more we're able to make use of advance organizers and our own prior knowledge and experiences, the better we can understand and retain new material.

P.O.W.E.R. Plan

What's the Point of the Reading Assignment?

Before you begin an assignment, think about what your goal is. Will you be reading a textbook on which you'll be thoroughly tested? Is your reading supposed to provide background information that will serve as a context for future learning but that won't itself be tested? Is the material going to be useful to you personally? Realistically, how much time can you devote to the reading assignment?

Your goal for reading will help you determine which reading strategy to adopt. You aren't expected to read everything with the same degree of intensity. Some material you may feel comfortable skimming; for other material you'll want to put in the maximum effort.

Understand the Point of View of the Material Itself

What are you reading—a textbook, an essay, an article? If it is an essay or article, why was it written? To prove a point? To give information? To express the author's personal feelings? Knowing the author's purpose (even if his or her specific point and message aren't yet clear) can help you a great deal as you read.

Start with the Frontmatter

If you'll be using a text or other book extensively throughout the term, start by reading the preface and/or introduction and scanning the table of contents—what publishers call the frontmatter. The **frontmatter** is the preface, introduction, and table of contents of a book.

frontmatter
The preface, introduction, and table of contents of a book.

Instructors often don't formally assign the frontmatter, but reading it can be a big help because it is there that the author has a chance to step forward and explain, often more personally than elsewhere in an academic book, what he or she considers important. Knowing this will give you a sense of what to expect as you read.

By reading the frontmatter, you can get inside the author's head, obtaining insight into the author's goals, values, and strategies in writing the book. You might also find information about the author's background, and perhaps even a photo. Use this material to "personalize" the author, to gain some insight into the kind of person he or she is. The information you obtain from the frontmatter will provide a mental "hook" on which you can hang the new ideas to which you'll be exposed.

Create Advance Organizers

To provide a context for your reading, create your own advance organizers in addition to any outlines, overviews, section objectives, or other clues to the meaning and organization that are already present. Skim through the table of contents, which provides the main headings of what you will be reading. Pay special attention to chapter outlines, which also provide a way of previewing the chapter content. As you read over the outline, you can begin to consider how the new material in the book may relate both to what you know and to what you expect to learn—from the reading assignment itself and from the course.

Textbooks often have end-of-chapter summaries, and many articles include a final section in which the author states his or her conclusions. Take a look at these ending sections as well. Even though you haven't read the material yet and the summary probably won't make complete sense to you, by reading the summary, you'll get an idea of what the author covers and what is important.

Your instructor may also provide an advance organizer for readings. Sometimes instructors will mention things to pay particular attention to or to look for, such as, "When you read Thomas Paine's *Common Sense*, notice how he lays out his argument and what his key points are." Sometimes they will say why they assigned a reading. Such information provides clues that can help you develop a mental list of the reading's key ideas.

However you construct advance organizers, be sure they provide a framework and context for what you'll be reading; this framework and context can spell the difference between fully comprehending what you read and misunderstanding it.

Now it's time to put all this practice to good use. Create an advance organizer for a textbook chapter in **Try It! 2**.

Identify What You Need to Remember

Memorize what you need to memorize. Forget about the rest.

The average textbook chapter has something like 20,000 words. If you had to recall every word of the chapter, it would be nearly impossible. Furthermore, it would be a waste of time. Being able to spew out paragraphs of material is quite

2 **Try It!** POWER

Create an Advance Organizer

Use any information you have available to create an advance organizer for a chapter in a text that you are using this term. Skim the section headings in the chapter, read the chapter summary, consult the book's frontmatter, and recall anything your instructor may have said about the chapter.

Complete the following statements to prepare your organizer:

1. The general topics that are covered in the chapter are . . .

2. The most critical topics and concepts in the chapter are . . .

3. The most difficult material in the chapter includes . . .

4. Words, phrases, and ideas that are unfamiliar to me include . . .

5. Ways that the material in this chapter relate to other material that I've previously read in the text include . . .

Use this Try It! as a starting point for advance organizers for future chapters in the book.

> "An education isn't how much you have committed to memory, or even how much you know. It's being able to differentiate between what you do know and what you don't."
>
> **Anatole France, French novelist (1844–1924). Quoted in *Telephony*, Vol. 150 (1956), p. 23.**

different from the more important ability to recall and deeply understand academic material in meaningful ways.

Within those 20,000 words, there may be only 20 different concepts that you need to learn. And perhaps there are only 10 keywords. *Those* are the pieces of information that should be the focus of your efforts to memorize.

How do you know what's so important that you need to recall it? One way is to use the guides built into most textbooks. Key concepts and terms are often highlighted or in boldface type. Chapters often have summaries that recap the most important information. Use such guideposts to understand what's most critical in a chapter.

Write down what you determine is important. Not only does putting critical information in writing help you manage what you need to remember, but the very act of writing it down makes it easier to memorize the information later.

In short, the first step in building a better memory is to determine just what it is that you wish to recall. By extracting what is important from what is less crucial, you'll be able to limit the amount and extent of the material that you need to recall. You'll be able to focus, laserlike, on what you need to remember.

Organize Gathering the Tools of the Trade

It's obvious that the primary item you'll need to complete a reading assignment is the material that you're reading. But there are other essential tools you should gather, potentially including the following:

- A copy of the assignment, so you'll be sure to read the right material.
- A pad of paper and/or index cards for notetaking if the material is particularly complex. If you use a computer to take notes, get it ready.
- Pencils or pens to write notes in the margin, if it's a traditional paper book, and highlighters to indicate key passages in the text.
- Access to a dictionary, either online or as a hard copy. You never know what new words you'll encounter while you're reading. If a dictionary isn't easily accessible, you'll be tempted to skip over unfamiliar words—a decision that may come back to haunt you. All word processing software includes a dictionary, and there are also many good dictionaries available online (e.g., Merriam-Webster's at **www.m-w.com**, where you will also find an online thesaurus).

Give Yourself Time

There's one more thing you need to prepare successfully for a reading assignment: enough time to complete it. The length of reading assignments is almost never ambiguous. You will typically be given a specific page range, so you will know just how much material you will need to cover.

Now get a watch and time yourself as you read the first three pages of your assignment, being sure to pay attention to the material, not the time! Timing how long it takes to read a representative chunk of material provides you with a rough measure of your reading speed for the material—though it will vary even within a single reading assignment, depending on the complexity of the material.

You'll also need to consider an aspect of your personal learning style: your reading attention span. **Attention span** is the length of time that a person usually is able to sustain attention. People with long attention spans can read for relatively lengthy periods without getting jumpy, while those with shorter ones can maintain attention for only a short while. You can get a general sense of this by using **Try It! 3**, "Discover Your Attention Span."

attention span
The length of time that attention is typically sustained.

Use the three pieces of information you now have—the length of the assignment, your per-page reading speed at full attention, and your typical attention span—to estimate roughly how long it will take you to complete the reading assignment. For example, if you are asked to read 12 pages, you have found that you need approximately 4 minutes to read a page, and your reading attention span is, on average, 25 minutes long, you can expect your reading to take at least 60 minutes, assuming you'll take a short break when your attention begins to fade after 25 minutes.

In addition, you may need to interrupt your reading to look up words in the dictionary, get a drink, stretch, or answer the phone. You may also decide to break your reading into several short sessions, in which case your total reading time may be greater since you will have to get reacquainted with the reading assignment each time you sit down again.

Try It! POWER

Discover Your Attention Span

You should be aware of your attention span, the length of time you usually are able to sustain attention to a task, as you prepare for reading assignments. To get an idea of the length of your current attention span for reading, perform this exercise over the next few days.

1. Choose one of the textbooks that you've been assigned to read this semester.
2. Start reading a chapter, without any preparation, noting in the chart below the time that you start reading.
3. As soon as your mind begins to wander and think about other subjects, stop reading and note the time on the chart below.
4. Using the same textbook, repeat this process four more times over the course of a few days, entering the data on the chart below.
5. To find your reading attention span, calculate the average number of minutes across the five trials.

Trial #1	Starting time: ______	Ending time: ______
	Number of minutes between start and end times: ______	
Trial #2	Starting time: ______	Ending time: ______
	Number of minutes between start and end times: ______	
Trial #3	Starting time: ______	Ending time: ______
	Number of minutes between start and end times: ______	
Trial #4	Starting time: ______	Ending time: ______
	Number of minutes between start and end times: ______	
Trial #5	Starting time: ______	Ending time: ______
	Number of minutes between start and end times: ______	

Reading attention span (the average of the number of minutes in the last column, found by adding up the five numbers and dividing by 5) = ______ minutes

Ask yourself these questions about your reading attention span:

1. Are you surprised by the length of your reading attention span? In what way?
2. Does any number in the set of trials stand out from the other numbers? For instance, is any number much higher or lower than the average? If so, can you account for this? For example, what time of day was it?
3. Do the numbers in your trials show any trend? For instance, did your attention span tend to increase slightly over the course of the trials, did it decrease, or did it stay about the same? Can you explain any trend you may have noted?
4. Do you think your attention span times would be very different if you had chosen a different textbook? Why or why not?
5. What things might you do to improve your attention span?

» LO **6-2**

W Work

Getting the Most Out of Your Reading and Using Proven Strategies to Memorize New Material

Once you've familiarized yourself with the material as a whole and gathered the necessary tools, it's time to get down to work and start reading. Here are several things that will help you get the most out of the reading process.

Stay Focused

The TV show you watched last night . . . your boyfriend forgetting to meet you at the bus stop . . . the replacement toothbrush you need to buy tomorrow . . . your grumbling stomach. There are a million and one possible distractions that can invade your thoughts as you read. Your job is to keep distracting thoughts at bay and focus on the material you are supposed to be reading. It's not easy, but there are things you can do to help yourself stay focused:

- **Read in small bites.** If you think it is going to take you 4 hours to read an entire chapter, break up the 4 hours into more manageable time periods. Promise yourself that you'll read for 1 hour in the afternoon, another hour in the evening, and the next 2 hours spaced out during the following day. One hour of reading is far more manageable than a 4-hour block.
- **Give yourself enough time.** Check out how long a book chapter is before you start studying. Some chapters are 24 pages in length; others are double that. Make sure you leave yourself enough time.
- **Take a break.** Actually, plan to take several short breaks to reward yourself while you're reading. During your break, do something enjoyable—eat a snack, watch a bit of a ball game on television, play a video game, or the like. Just try not to get drawn into your break activity to the point that it takes over your reading time.
- **Deal with mental distractions.** Sometimes problems have a way of popping into our minds and repeatedly distracting us. If a particular problem keeps interrupting your concentration—such as a difficulty you're having on the job—try to think of an action-oriented strategy to deal with it. You might even write your proposed solution down on a piece of paper. Putting it down in words can get the problem off your mind, potentially making it less intrusive.

If you are reading a long assignment, taking a break can be a reward and reinvigorate you.
©Minerva Studio/Alamy Stock Photo

- **Manage interruptions.** You can't stop your roommate from receiving a cell phone call or—if you are a student who is also a parent—you can't prevent your children from getting a cut and needing immediate attention. But there are some things you can do to reduce interruptions and their consequences. For instance, you can schedule reading to coincide with periods when you know you'll be alone. You can also plan to read less critical parts of assignments (such as the summaries or book frontmatter) when distractions are more likely, saving the heavier reading for later. Or, if you are a parent with small children, you can get your children involved in an activity that they can perform independently.

Write While You Read

Writing is one of the most important aspects of reading. If you haven't highlighted, underlined, jotted notes to yourself, placed check marks on the page, drawn arrows, constructed diagrams, and otherwise defaced and disfigured your book while you're reading, you're not doing your job as a P.O.W.E.R. reader.

"What is reading but silent conversation?"

Walter Savage Landor, "Aristoteles and Callisthenes," *Imaginary Conversations* (1824–1853).

The idea of writing on a book page may go against everything you've been taught in the past. (And of course you should never write on a library book or one that you've borrowed from a friend.)

However, once you've bought your book, *you own it and you should make it your own*. Don't keep your textbooks spotless on the off-chance they will fetch a higher price if you sell them later. Instead, think of textbooks as documents recording your active learning and engagement in a field of study. In addition, you should look at your textbooks as the foundation of your personal library, which will grow throughout your lifetime. In short, writing extensively in your book while you're reading is an important tactic for achieving success.

©Ariel Skelley/Blend Images LLC

One of the advantages of buying a new, rather than used, textbook is that you can add your own personal notes, underlining, and other annotations to a clean text while you're reading. Can you really trust the original owner's judgment over your own regarding what's important to underline? You can mark up new books in your own, personal style, without the distraction of competing voices.

If you have purchased access to an *electronic textbook*, or *e-book*, you'll be able to read it on a laptop computer, an iPad, or even a smartphone. E-books have several advantages over traditional books. You can easily follow links to visuals and interactive exercises, search for key terms, listen to music, watch embedded videos, and manipulate 3-D images. And, as with traditional textbooks, you can highlight and take notes as you are reading and save (and organize) your notes for future study.

Writing the Right Way

After all this preliminary work, it's time to get started actually reading your text. What should you be writing while you are reading? There are several things you should write down (or—if you are using an e-book—add to your electronic text):

- **Rephrase key points.** Make notes to yourself, in your own words, about what the author is trying to get across. Don't just copy what's been said. Think about the material, and rewrite it in words that are your own.

  Writing notes to yourself in your own words has several consequences, all good. First, you make the material yours; it becomes something you now understand and part of your own knowledge base.

  Second, trying to summarize a key point in your own words will make it very clear whether you truly understand it. It's easy to be fooled into thinking we understand something as we're reading along. But the true test is whether we can explain it to ourselves (or someone else) on our own, without referring to the book or article.

  Third, the very act of writing engages an additional type of perception—involving the physical sense of moving a pen or pressing a keyboard. This will help you learn the material in a more active way.

  Finally, writing notes and phrases will help you study the material later. Not only will the key points be highlighted, but your notes will also quickly bring you up to speed regarding your initial thoughts and impressions.
- **Highlight or underline key points.** Very often the first or last sentence in a paragraph, or the first or last paragraph in a section, will present a key point. (Remember those lessons about "topic sentences" you had in high school English classes? Writers really use them.)

  Before you highlight anything, though, read the whole paragraph through. Then you'll be sure that what you highlight is, in fact, the key information. Topic sentences do not always fall at the beginning of a paragraph.

  Be selective in your highlighting and underlining. A page covered in yellow highlighter may be artistically appealing, but it won't help you understand the material any better. Highlight only the key information. You might find yourself highlighting only one or two sentences or phrases per page. That's fine. *In highlighting and underlining, less is more.* One guideline: No more than 10 percent of the material should be highlighted or underlined.

  If you want to use different-colored highlighters, that's fine, but be consistent in their use. For instance, some people use one color for important material that they already understand, and another for particularly difficult information.
- **Use arrows, diagrams, outlines, tables, timelines, charts, and other visuals to help you understand and later recall what you are reading.** If there are three examples given for a particular point, number them. If a paragraph discusses a situation in which an earlier point does not hold, link the original point to the exception by an arrow. If a sequence of steps is presented, number each step.

  For example, after you have annotated *this* page of *P.O.W.E.R. Learning,* it might look something like what is shown in **Figure 6.1**.

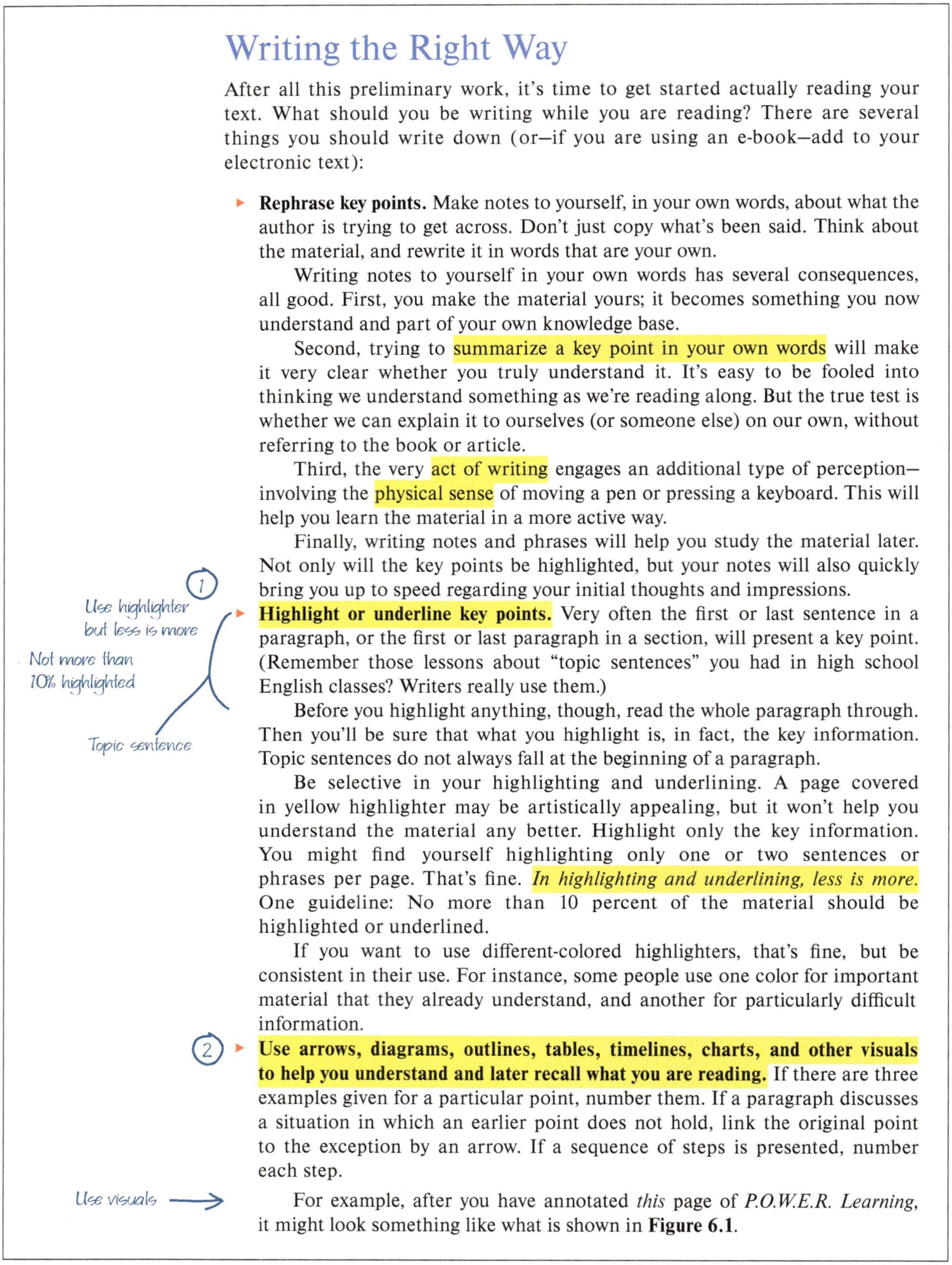

Writing the Right Way

After all this preliminary work, it's time to get started actually reading your text. What should you be writing while you are reading? There are several things you should write down (or—if you are using an e-book—add to your electronic text):

- **Rephrase key points.** Make notes to yourself, in your own words, about what the author is trying to get across. Don't just copy what's been said. Think about the material, and rewrite it in words that are your own.

  Writing notes to yourself in your own words has several consequences, all good. First, you make the material yours; it becomes something you now understand and part of your own knowledge base.

  Second, trying to summarize a key point in your own words will make it very clear whether you truly understand it. It's easy to be fooled into thinking we understand something as we're reading along. But the true test is whether we can explain it to ourselves (or someone else) on our own, without referring to the book or article.

  Third, the very act of writing engages an additional type of perception—involving the physical sense of moving a pen or pressing a keyboard. This will help you learn the material in a more active way.

  Finally, writing notes and phrases will help you study the material later. Not only will the key points be highlighted, but your notes will also quickly bring you up to speed regarding your initial thoughts and impressions.

- **Highlight or underline key points.** Very often the first or last sentence in a paragraph, or the first or last paragraph in a section, will present a key point. (Remember those lessons about "topic sentences" you had in high school English classes? Writers really use them.)

  Before you highlight anything, though, read the whole paragraph through. Then you'll be sure that what you highlight is, in fact, the key information. Topic sentences do not always fall at the beginning of a paragraph.

  Be selective in your highlighting and underlining. A page covered in yellow highlighter may be artistically appealing, but it won't help you understand the material any better. Highlight only the key information. You might find yourself highlighting only one or two sentences or phrases per page. That's fine. *In highlighting and underlining, less is more.* One guideline: No more than 10 percent of the material should be highlighted or underlined.

  If you want to use different-colored highlighters, that's fine, but be consistent in their use. For instance, some people use one color for important material that they already understand, and another for particularly difficult information.

- **Use arrows, diagrams, outlines, tables, timelines, charts, and other visuals to help you understand and later recall what you are reading.** If there are three examples given for a particular point, number them. If a paragraph discusses a situation in which an earlier point does not hold, link the original point to the exception by an arrow. If a sequence of steps is presented, number each step.

  For example, after you have annotated *this* page of *P.O.W.E.R. Learning*, it might look something like what is shown in **Figure 6.1**.

figure 6.1
Sample of Annotated Page

Course Connections

Using Specialized Reading Strategies for Special Subjects

Although the approaches to reading we've been discussing cut across different subject areas, certain disciplines warrant specialized strategies. Consider the following:

- **Reading mathematics texts.** With their many formulas, math books can be especially intimidating. Although it may be tempting to skip over the formulas, that's a big mistake. Look at them, think about them, annotate them, and make them concrete by substituting actual numbers for abstract letters. Above all, try practice problems and exercises to be sure that you fully grasp the formulas and concepts.
- **Reading in a foreign language.** Use of a dictionary may be a big help when reading in a foreign language. But don't rely on it too much: If you can't remember the meaning of a word, first try to figure out what is being said from the context, and only then look it up. Also keep in mind this fundamental rule of language study: The more you immerse yourself in a language, the easier it will become.
- **Reading in the sciences.** Science textbooks can be daunting. Not only are they dense with words, but they include equations, tables, and graphs. As you are reading, make sure you understand the variables and equations that support the written word. Even the photos can be important and need to be studied.

  Be aware that the scientific method is the basis for much writing about scientific topics. In particular, scientists conduct experiments to support hypotheses, specific predictions that are derived from a theory. When reading about scientific research, try to identify the hypothesis that is being tested and what alternative hypotheses might be used.
- **Reading history texts.** History textbooks often include long, complex chapters. Before reading a chapter, pay particular attention to the chapter headings to get an overview of what is covered. Look at any maps, which will help you orient yourself to the chapter content. As you read a chapter, don't think of it in terms of a collection of dates and facts. Instead, think of larger trends and themes. Then you can use those trends and themes to organize dates and facts.

Particularly if your learning style is a visual one, representing the material graphically will get you thinking about it—and the connections and points in it—in new and different ways. Rather than considering the material solely in verbal terms, you now add visual images. The act of creating visual annotations will not only help you understand the material better but also ease its later recall. Practice this technique on one of your textbook pages.

- **Look up unfamiliar words.** Even though you may be able to figure out the meaning of an unfamiliar word from its context, use a dictionary—either online or in a hard copy version—to determine if your guess is correct. An online dictionary will also tell you what the word sounds like, which may be important if your instructor uses the word in class.
- **Use your own reading system.** If you've already learned a reading system in the past and it works for you, use it. Many students have been taught the *SQ4R* method, which consists of six steps, designated by the initials ***S.Q.R.R.R.R.***
  - ***Survey.*** Create an overview of the major points of the material.
  - ***Question.*** Write or say aloud questions about the material prior to actually reading a section of text.

- ***R**ead.* Read the material carefully and, even more important, actively and critically. While you are reading, answer the questions you have asked yourself.
- ***R**ecite.* Describe and explain to yourself the material you have just read and answer the questions you have posed earlier.
- ***R**ecord.* Write in your textbook, make notes, or create flash cards.
- ***R**eview.* Review the material, looking it over, reading end-of-chapter summaries, and answering the in-text review questions.

In addition to *SQ4R*, you can also make up your own system. The truth is that it doesn't matter what system you use, as long as you use a system. What does matter is that you're systematic in the work of reading.

Memory Strategies

Many of the reading strategies discussed above will help fix key material in your mind. Rephrasing key points, highlighting or underlining essential material and then rereading it, and creating visuals will all help you recall the information you've read.

Sometimes, though, these strategies are not enough. You may need to memorize a great deal of information, more than you'll be able to recall just through the process of reading, underlining, and so forth. Many people find extensive memorization daunting. Happily, though, you have your choice of literally dozens of techniques specifically targeted to memorization.

As we sort through the various options, keep in mind that no one strategy invariably works. And some popular strategies don't seem to work at all. (Forget about food supplements and vitamins like ginkgo biloba–there's no clear scientific evidence that they are effective.) Instead, try the following proven strategies and find those that work best for you. Feel free to devise your own strategies or add those that have worked for you in the past.

Rehearsal

Think this word: *rehearsal*. Say it aloud: *rehearsal*. Think of it in terms of the three syllables that make up the word: *re-hear-sal*. OK, one more time–say the word *rehearsal*.

If you're scratching your head over the last paragraph, it's to illustrate the point of **rehearsal**: to transfer material that you encounter into memory. If you don't rehearse information in some way, it will end up like most of the information to which we're exposed: on the garbage heap of lost memory.

rehearsal
The process of practicing and learning material.

To test if you've succeeded in transferring the word "rehearsal" into your memory, walk away from this text and go off for a few minutes. Do something entirely unrelated to reading this book. Have a snack, catch up on the latest sports scores on ESPN, or read the front page of the newspaper.

Are you back? If the word "rehearsal" popped into your head when you picked up this book again, you've passed your first memory test. You can be assured that the word "rehearsal" has been transferred into your memory.

Rehearsal is the key strategy in remembering information. If you don't rehearse material, it will never make it into long-term memory. To help material get into long-term memory, repeat it, summarize it, associate it with other memories, and, above all, think about it when you first encounter it.

Mnemonics

This odd word (pronounced in an equally odd fashion, with the "m" silent—"neh MON ix") describes formal techniques used to make material more readily remembered. **Mnemonics** are the tricks of the trade that professional memory experts use, and you too can use them to nail down the sort of information you will often need to recall for tests.

Among the most common mnemonics are the following:

- **Acronyms.** You're already well acquainted with **acronyms**, words or phrases formed by the first letters of a series of terms. For instance, though you may not have known it, the word "laser" is actually an acronym for "light amplification by stimulated emissions of radiation," and "radar" is an acronym for "radio detection and ranging."

  Acronyms can be a big help in remembering things. If you took music lessons, you may know that FACE spells out the names of the notes that appear in the spaces on the treble clef music staff ("F," "A," "C," and "E," starting at the bottom of the staff). Roy G. Biv is a favorite of physics students who must remember the colors of the spectrum (red, orange, yellow, green, blue, indigo, and violet). And P.O.W.E.R. stands for—well, by this point in the book, you probably remember.

  The benefit of acronyms is that they help us recall a complete list of steps or items. The drawback, though, is that the acronym itself has to be remembered, and sometimes we may not recall it when we need it. For instance, Roy G. Biv is not exactly the sort of name that readily comes to mind. And even if we do remember Roy G. Biv, we might get stuck trying to recall what a particular letter stands for. (For example, we'd probably prefer not to spend a lot of time during a test trying to remember if the "B" stands for brown or beige or blue.)
- **Acrostics.** Many beginning musicians learn that the names of the lines on a music staff (E, G, B, D, and F) by using the acrostic, "Every Good Boy Deserves Fudge." **Acrostics** are sentences in which the first letters spell out something that needs to be recalled. The benefits—as well as the drawbacks—of acrostics are similar to those of acronyms. (You can explore acronyms and acrostics in **Try It! 4**.)
- **Rhymes and jingles.** "Thirty days hath September, April, June, and November. . . ." If you know the rest of the rhyme, you're familiar with one of the most commonly used mnemonic jingles in the English language. Similarly, some of us learned the main theme of Schubert's Unfinished Symphony by singing the words "This is the symphony that Schubert wrote and never finished" when the theme first appears. For those who learned to recognize the symphony by using this mnemonic, it is virtually impossible to hear the symphony without recalling the words.

Although mnemonics are helpful, keep in mind that they have a number of significant shortcomings. First, they don't focus on the *meaning* of the items being remembered. Information that is learned in terms of its surface characteristics—such as first letters that form a word—is harder to retain than information that is learned in terms of its meaning. Consequently, mnemonic devices are an imperfect route to memorization.

Second, sometimes it takes as much effort to create a mnemonic device as it would to memorize the material in the first place. Third, because a mnemonic has no meaning in and of itself, it can easily be forgotten.

mnemonics
Formal techniques used to make material more readily remembered.

acronym
A word or phrase formed by the first letters of a series of terms.

acrostic
A sentence in which the first letters of the words correspond to material that is to be remembered.

4  WORKING IN A GROUP

Try It!

Do-It-Yourself Acronyms and Acrostics

In the first part of this Try It!, work individually to create an acronym and an acrostic.

1. Figure out an acronym to remind you of the names of the five Great Lakes, using the first letters of their names (which are Erie, Huron, Michigan, Ontario, Superior).

2. Devise an acrostic for the nine planets in order of their average distance from the sun. Their names, in order, are Mercury, Venus, Earth, Mars, Jupiter, Saturn, Uranus, Neptune, Pluto. (Bonus question: Because many astronomers no longer believe Pluto is a planet, devise an acrostic that omits Pluto and just contains the first eight planets.)

After you've tried to create the acronym and acrostic, meet in a group and discuss these questions: How successful were you in devising effective acronyms and acrostics? Do some of the group members' creations seem more effective than others? Why? Is the act of creating them an important component of helping to remember what they represent, or would having them created by someone else be as helpful in recalling them? For your information, a common acronym for the Great Lakes is HOMES (**H**uron, **O**ntario, **M**ichigan, **E**rie, **S**uperior), and a traditional acrostic for the order of the planets is **M**y **V**ery **E**ducated **M**other **J**ust **S**erved **U**s **N**ine **P**izzas. (As for the bonus question that omits Pluto, future generations may use the acrostic My Very Educated Mother Just Served Us Noodles.)

Despite their drawbacks, mnemonics can be useful. They are particularly helpful when the material being memorized includes a list of items or a series of steps.

Chunk Material into Meaningful Groupings

When we learn new material, we face a physical limitation of our brains: We can hold only a limited amount of information in our heads at the same time. Although the specific amount varies, it's generally around five to nine individual bits of information.

But there's a way around that limitation, known as chunking. A *chunk* is a grouping of information that can be stored in working memory, the memory store where information is processed before it moves into long-term memory. For example, a chunk can be a group of seven individual letters or numbers, permitting us to hold a seven-digit phone number (such as 226-4610) in working memory.

But a chunk also may consist of larger categories, such as words or other meaningful units. For example, consider the following list of 21 letters:

P B S F O X C N N A B C C B S M T V N B C

Because the list of individual letters exceeds seven items, it is difficult to recall the letters after one exposure. But suppose they were presented as follows:

PBS FOX CNN ABC CBS MTV NBC

In this case, even though there are still 21 letters, you'd be able to store them in working memory since they represent only seven chunks.

The principle of chunking can help us store information more efficiently. Rather than considering individual bits of information, try to link them into meaningful groups. The larger the meaningful groupings, the more information you'll be able to recall.

Involve Multiple Senses

The more senses you can involve when you're trying to learn new material, the better you'll be able to remember. Here's why: Every time we encounter new information, all of our senses are potentially at work. For instance, if we witness a car crash, we receive sensory input from the sight of the two cars hitting each other, the sound of the impact, and perhaps the smell of burning rubber. Each piece of sensory information is stored in a separate location in the brain, and yet all the pieces are linked together in extraordinarily intricate ways.

What this means is that when we seek to remember the details of the crash, recalling a memory of one of the sensory experiences—such as what we heard—can trigger recall of the other types of memories. For example, thinking about the *sound* the two cars made when they hit can bring back memories of the way the scene looked.

You can make use of the fact that memories are stored in multiple ways by applying the following techniques:

- **When you learn something, use your body.** Don't sit passively at your desk or in a chair. Instead, move around. Stand up; sit down. Touch the page. Trace figures with your fingers. Talk to yourself. Think out loud. It may seem strange, but doing this increases the number of ways in which the information is stored. By involving every part of your body, you've increased the number of potential ways to trigger a relevant memory later, when you need to recall it. And when one memory is triggered, other related memories may come tumbling back.
- **Draw and diagram the material.** It's often useful to create a *concept map*, a method of structuring written material by graphically grouping and connecting key ideas and themes. A concept map is a visual summary that illustrates how related ideas fit together. When we create a concept map, one of the things we're doing is expanding the modalities in which information can be stored in our minds.

  Other types of drawing can be useful in aiding later recall. Creating drawings, sketches, and even cartoons can help us remember better. Your creations don't have to be great art or detailed, involved illustrations. Even rough sketches are effective, because creating them gets both the visual and the tactile senses involved.
- **Visualize. Visualization** is a technique by which images are formed to ensure that material is recalled. For instance, you now know that memory requires three basic steps: the initial recording of information, the storage of that information, and, ultimately, the retrieval of the stored information. As you read the three steps, you probably see them as logical and straightforward processes. But how do you remember them?

  You might visualize a computer, with its keyboard, disks, and monitor (see **Figure 6.2**). The keyboard represents the initial recording of information. The disk represents the storage of information, and the monitor represents the display of information that has been retrieved from memory. If you can put these images in your mind, it will help you remember the three basic memory steps later.

visualization
A memory technique by which images are formed to help recall material.

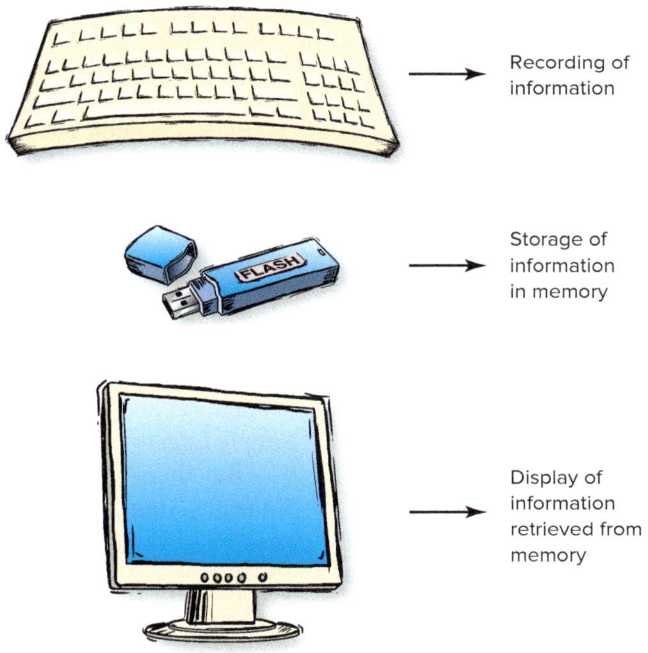

figure 6.2
Visualizing Memory

Don't stop at visualizing images just in your mind's eye. Actually drawing what you visualize will help you remember the material even better.

Visualization is effective because it serves several purposes. It helps make abstract ideas concrete; it engages multiple senses; it permits us to link different bits of information together; and it provides us with a context for storing information.

What kind of visualization works best? There's a simple rule: Weird is good. The more extreme, outlandish, and eccentric the image you create, the more notable it will be and so the easier it will be to remember. And if you can remember the image, you'll probably remember the information that's attached to it.

In fact, just as we have preferred learning styles, many of us have a favorite memory style—one that we use most often when trying to recall information. Take a moment to learn about your own memory style by completing **Try It! 5**.

Overlearning

Think back to when you were learning your basic multiplication facts ($1 \times 1 = 1$; $2 \times 2 = 4$; and so forth). Let's suppose you had put each multiplication problem on a flash card, and you decided to go through your entire set of cards, trying to get every problem right.

The first time you went through the set of cards and answered all the problems correctly, would you feel as if you'd memorized them perfectly and that you'd never again make an error? You shouldn't. You would need several instances of perfect performance to be sure you had learned the multiplication facts completely.

overlearning
Studying and rehearsing material past the point of initial mastery to the point at which recall becomes automatic.

Lasting learning doesn't come until you have overlearned the material. **Overlearning** consists of studying and rehearsing material past the point of initial mastery. Through overlearning, recall becomes automatic. Rather than searching for a fact and going through mental contortions until perhaps the information surfaces, overlearning permits us to recall the information automatically, without even thinking about it. The more facts and mental operations that you have memorized through overlearning, the quicker you can move through a test.

To put the principle of overlearning to work, don't stop studying at the point when you can say to yourself, "Well, I'll probably squeak by and pass this test." You may be right, but that's all you'll do—pass. Instead, spend extra time overlearning the material until it becomes as familiar as an old pair of jeans.

» LO 6-3

E Evaluate

What Does It Mean? What Do I Know?

Evaluation is a crucial step in reading. You need to be able to answer the seemingly simple question: "What does all this mean?"

But there's another aspect to evaluation. You need to evaluate, truthfully and honestly, your own level of understanding. What do you know as a result of your reading? Evaluation, then, consists of the following steps:

- **Identify the main ideas and themes and their value *to you personally.*** Try to determine the take-home message of the material you've read. For example, the take-home message of a chapter of an American history text might be, "Although Abraham Lincoln eventually called for the end of slavery, initially he was hesitant because of political considerations."

Determine Your Memory Style

What's your dominant memory style? Do you most easily remember sounds, sights, or the way things feel? Read the statements below and circle the response choice that most closely describes your habits.

To help recall lectures, I . . .

V. Read the notes I took during class.

A. Close my eyes and try to hear what the instructor said.

K. Try to place myself back in the lecture room and feel what was going on at the time.

To remember a complex procedure, I . . .

V. Write down the steps I have to follow.

A. Listen carefully and repeatedly to the instructions.

K. Do it over and over again.

To learn sentences in a foreign language, I do best if I . . .

V. Read them on paper to see how they're written.

A. Hear them in my head until I can say them aloud.

K. See someone speaking them and then practice moving my mouth and hands the way the speaker did.

If I have to learn a dance move, I like . . .

V. To see a diagram of the steps before trying it.

A. Someone to coach me through it while I try it.

K. To watch it once and then give it a try.

When I recall a very happy moment, I tend to . . .

V. Visualize it in my head.

A. Hear the sounds that I heard when experiencing it.

K. Feel with my hands and body what I felt at the time.

When I have to remember driving directions, I usually . . .

V. See a map of the route in my mind.

A. Repeat the directions aloud to myself.

K. Feel my hands steering and the car driving along the correct route.

ANSWER KEY:

If you chose mostly **V**s, your main memory style is visual; your preference is to remember things in terms of the way they appear. If you chose mostly **A**s, your main memory style is auditory; your preference is to recall material in terms of sound. If you chose mostly **K**s, your main memory style is kinesthetic; your preference is to remember using your sense of touch.

Keep in mind that this questionnaire only gives a rough idea of how we usually use our memories. Remember: All of us use all of the memory styles during the course of each day.

(continued)

5 continued

Try It! POWER

After completing the questionnaire, answer these questions:

1. How does your memory style affect the way you recall information?

2. How does your memory style affect the way you learn things initially?

3. How does your memory style relate to your preferred learning style?

4. How could you make greater use of your less-preferred memory style?

Sometimes the main ideas and themes are spelled out, and at other times you will have to deduce them for yourself. Evaluating the main ideas and themes in terms of how they relate to you personally will help you understand and remember them more easily.

- **Prioritize the ideas.** Of all the information that is presented, which is the most crucial to the main message and which is the least crucial? Make a list of the main topics covered and try to rank them in order of importance.
- **Think critically about the arguments presented in the reading.** Do they seem to make sense? Are the author's assertions reasonable? Are there any flaws in the arguments? Would authors with a different point of view dispute what is being said? How would they build their own arguments?
- **Pretend you are explaining the material (talking—out loud!—about the material) to a fellow classmate who missed the assignment.** This is one time when talking out loud when no one is around is not only normal, but beneficial. Summarize the material aloud, as if you were talking to another person.

  Talking out loud does two things. First, it helps you identify weak spots in your understanding. Talking to yourself will help you nail down concepts that are still not clear in your own mind. Second, and equally important, because you are transforming the written word into the spoken word, you are thinking about the information in another way, which will help you remember it better.
- **Be honest with yourself.** Most of us are able to read with our minds on cruise control. But the net result is not much different from not reading the passage at all. If you have drifted off while you've been reading, go back and reread the passage.

Testing Your Recall of New Information

The reading and memory strategies we've been discussing can bring you to a point where you probably feel comfortable in your ability to remember the material you've been learning. Once you've used one or more of them to help you, it's time to test

Course Connections

Special Memorization Strategies for Special Courses

Foreign language courses, as well as those in math and science, often pose particular memorization challenges. Here are some special strategies you can use to attack these subject areas:

For foreign language courses:

- When memorizing vocabulary, don't just read words silently—say them aloud and write them out.
- Using Post-It notes, write the names of objects around your living space in the foreign language.
- Practice speaking in the language lab.
- When others are called on in class, give answers silently to every question.
- Don't be afraid to make mistakes—you probably occasionally mispronounce words in your native language, without dire consequences.

For math and science courses:

- Memorize formulas by learning how to derive them.
- Practice formulating problems, not just solving them.
- Don't memorize problems—memorize concepts. Once you fully understand a concept and know how to apply it, there's often little left to memorize.
- Memorize in an organized way, starting with the most simple concepts and moving to more complex ones. Think about how the concepts build on one another.

yourself—to evaluate whether you'll be able to recall the material when you need it. There are several ways to evaluate your memory:

- **Use in-text review questions and tests.** Many textbook chapters end with a quiz or a set of review questions about the material. Some have questions scattered throughout the chapter. Don't ignore them! Not only do such questions indicate what the writer of the book thought was important for you to learn and memorize, but they can also provide an excellent opportunity for evaluating your memory.

  Even if you've answered the review questions earlier, while you were first reading the material (which is always a good idea), answer them again later as you study for the test and then the final.
- **Test yourself.** Temporarily transform yourself into your instructor, and prioritize what you're most likely to be tested on. Then create your own test, writing out some questions.

  Later, after as little as a few hours, take the test, and then grade it. How have you done? If you've achieved a grade that you're satisfied with, then, fine. If, on the other hand, you've missed some key pieces of information, then you'll want to return to work and spend more time on memorization.
- **Team up with a friend or use a study group.** When it comes to evaluating your memory, two heads (or more!) are often better than one. Working with a classmate or study group—especially others who may have a different preferred

learning style from your own—can help you test the limits of your memory and assess areas in which you need work.

For instance, you and a friend can take turns testing yourselves, switching back and forth between asking and answering questions. Turn it into a contest: One of you can be Alex Trebek of *Jeopardy*, and the other, a contestant. Or work with several people, forming a study group. The important thing is to switch who's asking and who's answering the questions. Even when you're directing questions to others—evaluating their memory—you're giving your own memory a workout.

Consolidating Memories

memory consolidation
The process by which the physical links between brain cells that represent memory become fixed and stable over time.

Like fine wines, memories need time to age. Psychologists talk about this as memory consolidation. **Memory consolidation** is the process by which the physical links between brain cells that represent memory become fixed and stable over time. Memory consolidation needs time to enter long-term memory, which explains why information is not suddenly and permanently established in memory the first time we're exposed to it. In fact, the process of consolidation may continue for days and even—in some cases—for years.

Obviously, you don't have years to wait. But it does pay to try to memorize material in advance of the time that you'll really need to use it. Then, when you go back to reconsider it, it will become even more well-established in your mind.

The phenomenon of memory consolidation explains why cramming is not a great idea. As we discussed in the chapter on taking tests, cramming is the process of spending the preceding evening or even the hours just before a test trying to memorize as much as possible. The memories that come from cramming simply don't last, because they aren't rehearsed and processed sufficiently. It's far more effective to distribute studying over many shorter sessions.

The best way to ensure good recall is to return to the material even after your personal evaluation tells you that you've got it down. Wait several days, if possible, and then review it again. You'll be able to identify the aspects of the material that you know well, as well as the things that just haven't jelled yet in memory. Rethinking the material, then, not only permits you to consolidate memory but also helps you identify where you need more work.

Players of games such as *Trivial Pursuit*® know the value of having a teammate to help dredge up obscure facts from memory. In the same way, studying with others can help you test and expand your own memory and uncover areas that need improvement.
©Anurat Imaree/Shutterstock

R Rethink — Getting It the Second Time

You're human, so—like the rest of us—when you finish a reading assignment you'd probably like nothing more than to heave a sigh of relief and put the book away.

By now you know that there's a crucial step you should take that will assist you in cementing what you've learned into memory: rethinking what you've read. If you do it within 24 hours of first reading the assignment, it can save you hours of work later.

Reading and Memory on the Job

Career Connections

- Military genius Julius Caesar could dictate as many as seven letters at a time to his secretaries.
- Conductor Arturo Toscanini memorized every note of 400 different musical pieces. When a musician told him, just before a concert, that his instrument had just broken and he was unable to play a particular note, Toscanini paused a moment, but then told him not to worry, because that note was not in the piece they were about to play.
- Warren Buffett, one of the world's most successful investors, could read and recall sales figures from companies in which he had invested dozens of years earlier.[1]

Improving your reading and memory is not only something that will help you do better in college. Whatever your future job—be it military general, musician, business tycoon, or anything else—good reading skills and memory will further your career success.

Not all professionals need the same kinds of memory skills, of course. A camera operator at a television network must remember lighting combinations; lawyers need to recall the details of witness testimony; elementary school teachers must remember what kinds of exercises work best for certain students; physicians need to keep track of a host of medical conditions and medicines. But in each of these professions, memory abilities are an important aspect of job performance.

Memory is also important in terms of keeping track of people's names and functions. Being able to recall the names of those with whom you work, professional colleagues from other companies, and clients is an important skill. People are flattered when you remember their names. It says you think they are important and worth noticing.

In short, remember this: The strategies that you learn in college to improve your reading and memory will pay big dividends in the world of work.

The best way to rethink an assignment is to reread it, along with any notes you've taken. "Yeah, right," you're probably thinking. "Like I have time for that." The goal, though, is not a literal rereading. In fact, it isn't necessary to reread word for word. You already know what's important and what's not important, so you can skim some of the less important material. But it is wise to reread the more difficult and important material carefully, making sure that you fully understand what is being discussed and why.

What's most critical, though, is that you think deeply about the material. Consider the take-home message of what you've read. You need to be sure that your understanding is complete and that you're able to answer any questions that you had earlier about the material.

> "Reading furnishes the mind only with materials of knowledge; it is thinking that makes what we read ours."
>
> **John Locke, *Conduct of the Understanding*, 1706.**

Rethinking should be the central activity as you reread a passage and your notes about it. It is a crucial step, because rethinking transfers material from your short-term memory to your long-term memory. It solidifies information so that it will be remembered far better over the long haul.

Dealing with Learning Disabilities

If you, like millions of people in the United States, have a learning disability of one sort or another, reading and remembering may prove to be particularly challenging. **Learning disabilities** are defined as difficulties in processing information when

learning disabilities
Difficulties in processing information when listening, speaking, reading, or writing, characterized by a discrepancy between learning potential and actual academic achievement.

John Irving, a well-known author who suffered from dyslexia.
©Tupungato/Shutterstock

listening, speaking, reading, or writing; in most cases, learning disabilities are diagnosed when there is a discrepancy between learning potential and actual academic achievement.

One of the most common kinds of learning disabilities is *dyslexia*, a reading disability that produces the misperception of letters during reading and writing, unusual difficulty in sounding out letters, spelling difficulties, and confusion between right and left. Although its causes are not yet completely understood, one likely explanation is a problem in the part of the brain responsible for breaking words into the sound elements that make up language.

Another common disability is *attention deficit hyperactivity disorder* (or *ADHD*), which is marked by an inability to concentrate, inattention, and a low tolerance for frustration. For the 1 to 3 percent of college students and other adults who have ADHD, planning, staying on task, and maintaining interest present unusual challenges. These challenges not only are present in college but also affect job performance.

People with learning disabilities are sometimes viewed as unintelligent. Nothing could be further from the truth: There is no relationship between learning disabilities and I.Q. For instance, dozens of well-known and highly accomplished individuals suffered from dyslexia, including physicist Albert Einstein, U.S. General George Patton, poet William Butler Yeats, and author John Irving.

By the time they reach college, most people with learning disabilities have already been diagnosed. If you do have a diagnosed learning disability and you need special services, it is important to disclose your situation to your instructors and other college officials.

In some cases, students with learning disabilities have not been appropriately evaluated prior to college. If you have difficulties such as mixing up and reversing letters frequently and suspect that you have a learning disability, there usually is an office on campus that can provide you with guidance. One place to start is your college counseling or health center.

Many sorts of treatments, ranging from learning specific study strategies to the use of medication, can be effective in dealing with learning disabilities. In addition, colleges that accept support from the federal government have a legal obligation to provide people with diagnosed learning disabilities with appropriate support. This obligation is spelled out in the Americans with Disabilities Act, and it provides important legal protections.

However, just because you are having trouble with reading assignments doesn't automatically mean that you have a learning disability. Not only is the kind of reading you do in college more difficult than what you did in high school, but there's also more of it. It's only when reading represents a persistent, long-term problem—one that won't go away no matter how much work you do—that a learning disability becomes a possible explanation.

Speaking *of* Success

Courtesy of Judy Jiang

NAME: **Judy Jiang**

SCHOOL: **Oregon State University, Corvallis, Oregon**

Some first-year college students have decided specifically what major they wish to pursue, and follow that with entering a profession that matches their academic pursuits.

Judy Jiang knew she wanted to pursue a degree in engineering, but being a person whose interests are varied and diverse, she realized that her initial choice was not necessarily the final one.

"I decided on engineering when entering college because I think that if a person is capable of succeeding in a field with rewarding, long-lasting, and important outcomes, he or she should pursue that work for the benefit of the rest of society," said Jiang, an Honors student.

Planning on working for a few years before entering graduate school, Jiang notes that it's important that students shouldn't always lock themselves into a specific path.

"I think one of the most important things is that you don't need to figure out your life right now. Your major is not going to box you in for the rest of your career, and your career does not have to define your life.

"I fully expect to have multiple careers, spanning different fields, and I am excited for that opportunity. It's fine if you don't know what you want to do in your first year, your second year, or even when you graduate," Jiang said.

"Additionally, grades aren't the most important thing in the world. Being happy with your daily routine is," Jiang notes. "Go to your professor's office hours–they aren't that scary–and ask your peers for help. And if you find yourself unhappy for what feels like a long period of time, know that you have the power to change things, even if you're afraid to do so."

[RETHINK]

- Why do you think Jiang says it is important not to tie yourself into a specific career path too early in college? What would be the benefits of postponing those decisions? What would be the drawbacks?
- Engineering is a discipline that covers many fields. How would this allow Jiang more freedom to pursue other career paths in the future?

Looking Back

LO 6-1 Explain how reading style and attention span affect reading.

- The most important aspect of reading is understanding, not speed. People have different reading styles that can be modified to improve their ability to read with understanding.
- One problem people have with reading is a limited attention span. However, attention spans can be increased with self-awareness and practice.

LO 6-2 Identify how to improve concentration and read and remember more effectively.

- Reading should be approached with a clear sense of purpose and goals, which will vary from assignment to assignment. Examining the frontmatter of a book and creating advance organizers is also useful.
- As you read, identify and focus on the key material you will need to remember later. Don't try to memorize everything you read.
- Maintain focus by breaking down the reading into small chunks, taking breaks as needed, dealing with distractions, and writing while reading.
- Many techniques are available to improve memorization. Rehearsal is a primary one, as is the use of mnemonics such as acronyms, acrostics, and rhymes.
- Overlearning is a basic principle of memorization.

LO 6-3 Discuss how best to retain what you have read.

- Understanding of reading assignments can be cemented in memory by identifying the main ideas, prioritizing them, thinking critically about the arguments, and explaining the writer's ideas to someone else.
- Quickly rereading assignments and notes taken on them can greatly help in solidifying memories of what has been read. Concept maps that structure and relate ideas can also help.

[KEY TERMS AND CONCEPTS]

Acronym (p. 163)
Acrostic (p. 163)
Advance organizers (p. 152)
Attention span (p. 155)
Frontmatter (p. 153)
Learning disabilities (p. 171)
Memory consolidation (p. 170)
Mnemonics (p. 163)
Overlearning (p. 166)
Rehearsal (p. 162)
Visualization (p. 165)

[RESOURCES]

ON CAMPUS

If you are experiencing unusual difficulties in reading and with memory, and the problem is one you encountered in high school, you may have a learning disability. If you suspect this is the case, take action. Many colleges have an office that deals specifically with learning disabilities. You can also talk to someone at your college's counseling center; he or she will arrange for you to be tested, which can determine whether you have a problem.

IN PRINT

The seventh edition of Joe Cortina and Janet Elder's book, *Opening Doors: Understanding College Reading* (McGraw-Hill, 2015), provides complete guidelines for reading textbooks and other kinds of writing that you will encounter during college. Another useful volume is *Breaking Through: College Reading* (Longman, 2015, 11th ed.), by Brenda Smith.

In *Improving Your Memory* (Johns Hopkins, 2014, 4th ed.), Janet Fogler and Lynn Stern provide an overview of practical tips on maximizing your memory. And, in *Unlimited Memory* (TCKPublishing, 2016), memory World Record holder, Kevin Horsley, provides tips to increase the capacity of your memory.

ON THE WEB

- "Editor Eric's Greatest Literature of All Time: The Works" (**http://editoreric.com/greatlit/indexB.html**): Check out this lengthy list of books. While it is one person's interpretation of what constitutes great books, it nevertheless contains a variety of great literature, with links to outlines of each work.
- SQ3R Improving Reading Comprehension is the title of this site offered by Virginia Tech University (**https://ucc.vt.edu/academic_support/online_study_skills_workshops/SQ3R_improving_reading_comprehension.html**). It offers a clear and detailed outline on how to use the SQ3R method, as well as links to other reading comprehension aids such as critical reading, proofreading, and selective reading.
- Need a mnemonic? Have one you'd like to share? Then just go to **www.mnemonic-device.com/**, a site devoted entirely to mnemonics. This fun and educational site covers a variety of subjects from astronomy to weather.
- Mind Tools, a bookstore specializing in works on memory, offers a number of free online articles (**www.mindtools.com/memory.html**) detailing methods for improving memory. It includes examples of how each technique can be applied to such topics as remembering lists and foreign languages.

The Case of . . .

Remember the Alamo

For Kyle Binder, history had always been a hard subject. Although he had no trouble learning general historical trends and concepts, he had difficulty keeping names, dates, and places sorted out.

Consequently, when his American history instructor, Ms. Teeler, announced that a major history exam was scheduled for the following week, Kyle panicked. He hadn't finished 100 pages of the assigned reading (300 pages altogether!), and here he was expected to learn what seemed to be virtually everything there was to know about the United States' western expansion during the 1800s. Ms. Teeler had said that the test would focus in particular on the Battle of the Alamo and its significance in U.S. history. When Kyle couldn't even recall where the Alamo was located, he knew he'd better get started memorizing. But where to begin?

1. How should Kyle prepare for the history exam? Should he simply get the history text and start reading? Why or why not?

2. How can Kyle prevent the facts of history from appearing to be a jumble of random words and numbers? How should he use his existing knowledge to structure historical information? Why might this become easier the more often Kyle does it?

3. Suppose Kyle is expected to remember the names of several officers in the two armies involved in the Battle of the Alamo, names that seem unusual to him and very hard to remember. Which memory technique is likely to be most effective? How would it work?

4. To remember lists of events in the western expansion movement, what technique would you recommend that Kyle use? How would it work?

5. How could Kyle use multiple senses while learning about the western expansion and the Battle of the Alamo?

CHAPTER 7

Writing and Speaking

Learning Outcomes

By the time you finish this chapter you will be able to

» LO 7-1 Explain the best technique for getting started and writing a first draft.

» LO 7-2 Identify the process of moving from first draft to final draft.

» LO 7-3 Discuss how to conquer fears of public speaking and make effective oral presentations.

Staring at the blank page on her computer screen, Maria Ramos felt another surge of anxiety wash over her. She was beginning to panic.

The paper she was trying to get started on was due in two days, and she had not yet put a word down on paper. The problem was . . . well, that was just it: She didn't know what the problem was. The topic was completely hazy; she had no idea what her instructor was looking for.

As the minutes turned into hours, Maria was becoming increasingly desperate. Finally, for lack of a better idea, she decided to start writing down whatever came to mind, producing a flurry of stream-of-consciousness thoughts, recollections, and ideas.

Although most of the things that found their way to her computer screen had nothing to do with the paper topic, she was surprised to come up with a few thoughts that were relevant. And suddenly, she had an idea about how she could approach the assigned topic. Things gradually began to fall into place.

Maria had found her writing voice.

Looking Ahead

Few activities raise so many concerns and anxieties as writing and public speaking. Yet few skills are as important to your success, not only in college but also in the world outside the classroom. Taking time now to learn how to write well and speak well will not only increase your chances of success, but also improve your peace of mind!

This chapter focuses on writing and speaking. We begin by considering how to write, with a focus on composing college-level papers. We'll talk about how to get started and how you can move from a rough first draft to a final draft of which you can be proud.

The second part of the chapter looks at oral presentations. We'll discuss ways of getting over stage fright and how to engage listeners from the very start of your talk. We consider the importance of practicing neither too little nor too much.

» LO 7-1 The Writing Process

What happens when you sit down to write? Does the sight of a blank page or blank screen leave your mind blank as well? Do your fingers, which move so quickly when you're playing a game on the computer, become sluggish when poised over a keyboard to write a paper?

Writing is not easy, and for many students, writing assignments raise more anxieties than any other academic task. There are many reasons for this anxiety. For one thing, papers often have a large impact on your final course grades. If you do all your writing at the last minute, with a deadline looming, writing is almost certainly a tense experience. Perhaps you've never really been taught how to write well. Or maybe you believe that there's some sort of special writing gene that you just weren't born with.

Stop! Erase from your memory any negative preconceptions you may have about writing. There is no mystery to writing; it's a skill that can be taught and a skill that, with practice, anybody can learn. Writing is a *process,* one that allows others to understand the thinking and reasoning behind the written word.

Journal Reflections

How I Feel about Writing

Reflect on the feelings you have about writing by answering the following questions:

1. Complete this sentence: When I receive a writing assignment, my initial reaction is. . . .
2. Do you ever write for pleasure? When? Under what circumstances?
3. Which writing experiences are particularly pleasant for you? Which are unpleasant?
4. Are you particularly good at finding ways to put off writing tasks? Do you do anything to prevent this?
5. Writing experts believe that the very act of writing can help one think better. Why would this be true about writing? Have you ever experienced this phenomenon?

Using strategies based on P.O.W.E.R. Learning (summarized in the P.O.W.E.R. Plan), you will be able to achieve the goal of writing clearly and competently. These strategies will help you build upon your strengths and maximize your abilities. They will permit you to translate what's inside your head into words that communicate your experience or thoughts directly.

P Prepare — Approach writing as a process

O Organize — Construct a scaffold by creating an outline and thesis statement

W Work — Get it down in the first draft; refine it in the second draft

E Evaluate — Be your own best critic: Fine-tune your work

R Rethink — Reflect on the writing process: what worked, what didn't

P.O.W.E.R. Plan

P Prepare — Confronting the Blank Page

There is nothing more intimidating than a blank piece of paper or computer screen. It is something that every writer faces, no matter how proficient. William Shakespeare, Jane Austen, Mark Twain, Anna Akhmatova, Ralph Ellison, and Sandra Cisneros all felt the challenge of having to fill that void with words.

Looked at another way, though, there is something liberating about a blank page. It offers a world of possibilities, and it gives you the freedom to say whatever you want to say. And that's one of the keys to good writing: deciding what it is you want to say.

Preparation will help you decide. Writing is a process, and preparation for it encompasses the following steps:

Decide What Your Goal Is

To write successfully, you need to think about the end product. Is it a long research paper, based on information you must gather? An essay arguing a particular point

Nothing is more intimidating than a blank piece of paper—or a blank computer screen. On the other hand, it can also be liberating, offering you the freedom and opportunity to say what *you* want to say.

of view? A fictional short story? A critique of someone else's work or argument? A book or movie review?

Most often, you'll be working to complete a class assignment that explicitly clarifies the goal and form of the writing (see **Table 7.1**). But sometimes the assignment will provide you with several choices; it may even be vague or imprecise. If this is the case, your first step will have to be to decide what your goal is.

If there is a choice among different types of writing, decide which will make you most comfortable. If one choice is to prepare an essay, and you are creative and enjoy expressing your opinions, choose that option. If you enjoy gathering information and drawing a conclusion from your findings, a research paper might well be the best choice.

Choose Your Topic

Once you've determined the specific type of writing you are going to do, the next step is to choose a topic. Although instructors often assign a particular topic, in some cases the choice will be left to you. However, the freedom to choose a topic does not come without a price. In fact, many students find that choosing what to write about is harder than actually writing the paper itself. Here are some things you can do that will help you pick an appropriate topic:

- **Use freewriting.** According to Peter Elbow, a writing expert who has revolutionized the teaching of writing, one of the reasons we find writing so hard is that we have a set of censors inside our heads.[1] Just as we set pen to paper, those censors are ready to spring up and whisper, "That's no good."

  However, there is a way to keep these internal voices at bay. You can use a technique called **freewriting**). In freewriting, you write continuously for a fixed period of time—say, 5 or 10 minutes. The only rule that governs freewriting is to write continuously, without stopping. It doesn't matter whether the

freewriting
A technique involving continuous, nonstop writing, without self-criticism, for a fixed period of time.

table 7.1 Major Types of College Writing

Research paper	A paper requiring abstract, critical thinking supported through the collection of existing information. Often requires analysis and synthesis of the material to develop a conclusion.
Essay	A paper written from an author's personal point of view and arguing a particular point. It may take the form of a review, criticism, or personal recollection, or it may argue a political viewpoint.
Critical review	Criticism of an argument, article, musical piece, or other work.
Journal	Personal reflections on class readings or assignments.

product is bad; it doesn't matter whether it's good. The only principle you must follow in freewriting is to get something—anything—down on paper.

Try it, and you'll see how liberating freewriting can be. Of course the product will not be perfect, but you'll most likely find that you've written something of value to you.

> "How can I know what I think till I see what I say?"
>
> **Graham Wallas, author, in** *The Art of Thought* **(New York: Harcourt, Brace and Company, 1926).**

Suppose, for example, you are stuck for a topic. Through freewriting you can explore your feelings about the course you are going to be writing for, what you like and don't like, and from there go on to get some rough ideas down on paper. What's more, you'll probably form an "attitude" toward one or more potential topics, which can be used to add a personal voice and authenticity to your writing.

Once the freewriting session is completed, you may want to write a single sentence that captures the main point of what you have written—the "center of gravity," Elbow calls it. You can then use this sentence as a springboard for further exploration of ideas the next time you write. (Test this method by completing **Try It! 1**.)

- **Use brainstorming.** The oral equivalent of freewriting is **brainstorming**). While freewriting is done alone, brainstorming is most often done with others. In brainstorming, you say out loud as many ideas as you can think of in a fixed period of time. Although brainstorming works best when you do it with a group of friends or classmates, you can also do it by yourself. (This is one of those times when talking to yourself has its benefits.) Initially, the goal is simply to produce as many ideas as possible, no matter how implausible, silly, or irrelevant. Jot down the ideas that intrigue you as they come up, so you don't forget them.

  As with freewriting, the point is to silence the censors in our heads that hinder us from coming up with ideas because we're afraid of how others might react. In brainstorming, the initial goal is to produce a high quantity of ideas, not necessarily high-quality ideas. You can revisit and evaluate the ideas you've come up with later (see **Try It! 2**).

brainstorming
A technique for generating ideas by saying out loud as many ideas as can be thought of in a fixed period of time.

Decide Who Your Audience Is

That's easy, you may be thinking: It's my instructor. Not so fast. Although the instructor is the most obvious reader for what you write, you should think of your audience in terms of the ultimate purpose of the writing assignment. For example, if you're writing a paper about the dangers of global warming, are you directing it to a layperson who knows little about the issue? Or are you writing it for someone with a good understanding of science, someone who already knows about atmospheric pressure, El Niño, and the ozone layer? Clearly, the answer to this question will make a difference in how and what you write.

In short, it's crucial to know—and to keep in mind—the persons to whom you are writing. What is their level of knowledge about the topic? Are they already predisposed to a particular position? What do you think they would like to take away with them after reading what you've written?

Keeping an audience in mind serves another purpose: It personalizes your writing. Rather than targeting your writing to a nondescript group of individuals ("all the people who might be worried about global warming"), you individualize your audience. Think of the reader as your sister, or a friend, or your next-door neighbor. Think of how that individual would feel after reading what you've written, and what you would say to convince him or her.

1 **Try It!** POWER

Set Yourself Free: Freewriting

Use this space (or a separate sheet of paper) to practice freewriting for a 5-minute period. Optional guidance is offered below, but if you want to go ahead and "just do it," simply start writing. Be sure to keep your hand moving; stop controlling yourself. Write only for yourself; forget about what others might think.

If you need a little more guidance, you are not alone; most people need help the first time they try to freewrite. There are actually two kinds of freewriting: plain vanilla freewriting (like that above) and *focused* freewriting. Focused freewriting gives you a starting point.

Here are some starting points for focused freewriting:

Today I feel . . .

I remember . . .

I don't like . . .

I really like . . .

I get sick when . . .

I know . . .

I am . . .

I am not . . .

Using one of these lead-in phrases as a starting point, return to the blank space and begin your freewriting.

What is the main point of what you wrote? Was freewriting effective in helping you get something down on paper? Was it easy or difficult for you? Can you think of how the process of freewriting might help you when it's time to write a paper?

2  WORKING IN A GROUP

Try It! POWER

Get Your Brain Storming: Using Brainstorming to Generate Ideas

Your American history professor has asked you to come up with 10 ideas for a five-page paper on some aspect of the 1960s. Brainstorm in a group and come up with a list of possible topics, assigning one member of the group to record ideas below.

As you brainstorm, keep the length of the paper assigned and the sort of topic suited to American history generally in mind. But remember, the idea is to produce as many possibilities as you can, without evaluating how realistic or feasible they may be. Don't react negatively to others' ideas, and don't self-censor yourself for fear that others will react negatively. Think quantity over quality.

After your group has concluded brainstorming, go back to your answers and circle each that you think is realistic for a paper topic. Did brainstorming work? Did you surprise yourself with the number of alternative possibilities you generated for each item?

Research the Topic

To write most papers, you must do research, either in the library or on the Web. To put the information you find in a useable form, consider using a file folder and note card system, a proven technique that involves three steps:

1. Assemble information folders, in either hard-copy or virtual form. Break down material you've found into subtopics by placing the raw information you've located (such as photocopies, computer printouts, and articles) into different multicolored file folders. Label each folder with a stick-on Post-It-type label, which will permit you to easily modify the topic of the folder if necessary in the future.

This system can work virtually, as well, with a computer. Using an app such as *Evernote,* or even a simple word-processing program, you can create a virtual file-folder structure into which you put your notes and related material.

Remember that your notes are going to be only as good as the quality of your source materials. Always think critically about what is the source of the information. Not only may you encounter inaccurate or biased information, you may find "fake news" that is intentionally meant to mislead you. So use your critical thinking skills to evaluate the information you find.

Whatever the sources of information you use, if you are working on a computer, save your work frequently, which is something that you should be doing at every stage of the writing process. Saving your work in multiple formats (on hard drives, memory sticks, and printouts) is insurance against experiencing major headaches later on.

2. Create note cards, in either hard-copy or virtual formats. Taking notes on index cards is the best way of making information easy to use. The note cards can be traditional hard-copy formats, or they can be virtual (using an app such as *Evernote*).

figure 7.1
Sample Note Cards

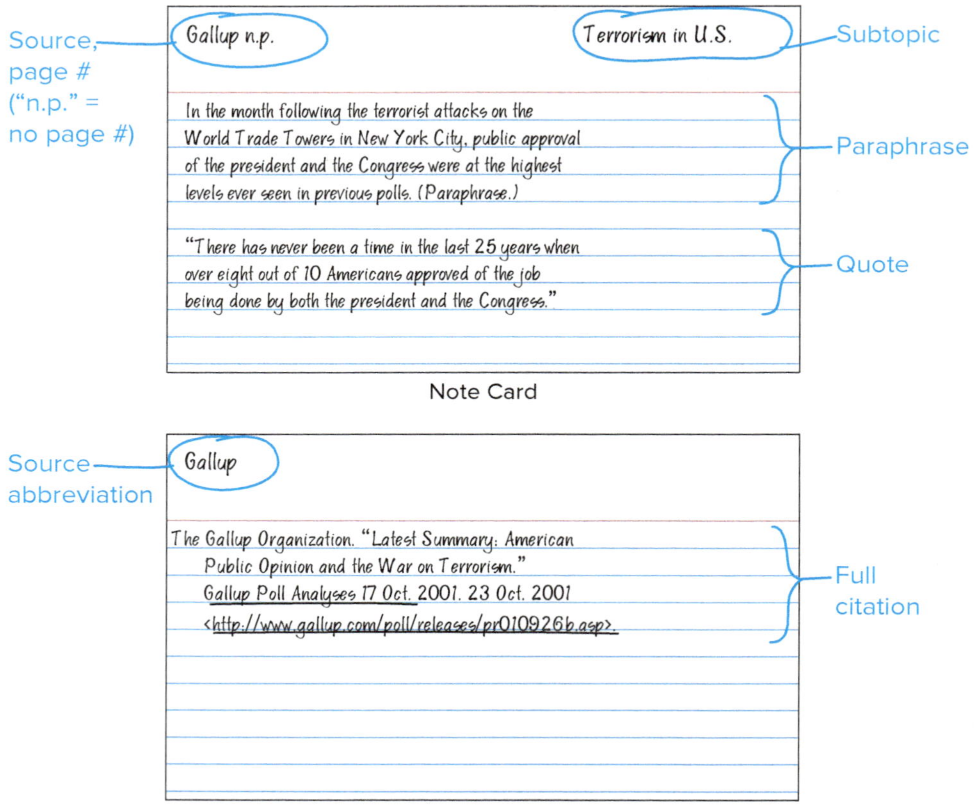

Bibliographic (Source) Card

paraphrase
A restatement of a passage using different words.

Be sure to write the ideas on the note card in your own words, unless you are directly quoting from a source—in which case you must remember to use quotation marks. It's also a good idea to mark a note card with the word "paraphrase" when you put someone else's unique idea in your own words, as in the sample note cards in **Figure 7.1**. (A **paraphrase**) is a restatement of a passage using different words.) Using your own words will prevent you from accidentally copying others' words and passing them off as your own—which, as we'll discuss, is the gravest of academic sins.

Keep in mind that even paraphrased material needs to be cited, unless it is what is called common knowledge. *Common knowledge* is information that is widely known and easily verified. For example, the September 11, 2001, terrorist attack on the United States is common knowledge and would not need to be cited if you mentioned it. In contrast, a specific political scientist's explanation of *why* the terrorist attack occurred would need to be cited.

The key is to place no more than one major idea on each card. If you stick to this rule, you will later find it easy to sort the cards and put them in logical order. It often helps to write the relevant subtopic (such as "Early Influences" or "Husband" or "Politics") at the top right-hand corner of the card for easy reference. (Once again, it is also possible to type notes directly into your computer and store them in a subfolder labeled "Early Influences," "Husband," "Politics," etc.)

3. Place source information on every note card. Make sure every note card contains information that clearly identifies its source. It is extremely important that you know where the idea on the note card came from so you can credit this source when you write your paper. You do not need to include complete bibliographical information on every note card, but you must keep a master list—either on a separate set of note cards or in a computer file—with the full citation.

Table 7.2 illustrates examples of citations for different types of sources. For each source, the table shows citations using style guidelines of the Modern Language

table 7.2 Sample Citations for Different Types of Sources

Book with one author	MLA	Nunez, Sigrid. *The Friend.* New York: Riverhead , 2018.
	APA	Nunez, S. (2018). *The Friend.* New York: Riverhead.
Book with more than one author	MLA	Butler, Isaac, and Dan Kois. *The World Only Spins Forward: The Ascent of Angels in America.* New York, Bloomsbury, 2018.
	APA	Butler, I., & Kois, D. (2018). *The World Only Spins Forward: The Ascent of Angels in America.* New York: Bloomsbury.
Magazine or newspaper article	MLA	Johnson, Steven, "Beyond the Bitcoin Bubble." *The New York Times Magazine* January 21, 2018: MM6
	APA	Johnson, S. (2018, January 21). Beyond the Bitcoin Bubble. *The New York Times Magazine.* p. MM6
Scholarly journal article	MLA	Rivera, Lauren A. "When Two Bodies Are (Not) a Problem: Gender and Relationship Status Discrimination in Academic Hiring." *American Sociological Review* 82 (2017): 1111–1138.
	APA	Rivera, L. A. (2017). When Two Bodies Are (Not) a Problem: Gender and Relationship Status Discrimination in Academic Hiring. *American Sociological Review , 82,* 1111–1138.
Article with no author listed	MLA	"7th Inning Stretch: Roberto Clemente Award." *Baseball Digest* 2006: 69.
	APA	7th inning stretch: Roberto Clemente award. (2006). *Baseball Digest,* 69.
Article reproduced on Internet	MLA	Chen Brian X. "Untethered, but Connected." *New York Times,* 21 Sept. 2017, (pp. B1-B7 in original publication). Available on Internet (http://www.nytimes.com/). Retrieved 24 January 2018.
	APA	Chen, B. X. (2017, September 21). Untethered, But Connected. *New York Times.* (pp. B1-B7 in original publication). Retrieved January 24, 2018, from World Wide Web (http://www.nytimes.com/).
Web document with author listed	MLA	Gregersen, Erik. "100 Years of Orson Welles." *Britannica* (Internet site at www.britannica.com/story/100-years-of-orson-welles). Retrieved 17 January 2018.
	APA	Gregersen, E. 100 years of Orson Welles. *Britannica.* Retrieved January 17, 2018 from World Wide Web (www.britannica.com/story/100-years-of-orson-welles).
Web document with no author listed	MLA	"Reporting Tip Income." *IRS* (Internet site at www.irs.gov). Retrieved 17 January 2018.
	APA	Reporting Tip Income. Retrieved January 17, 2018 from World Wide Web (www.irs.gov).
E-mail	MLA	Wymer, Maria, curator, Hallington Art Institute. "Pre-Columbia Art," E-mail to Deborah Markan. 5 August 2019.
	APA	Wymer, M., curator, Hallington Art Institute. (2019, August, 5). Pre-Columbia Art. E-mail to Deborah Markan.

(continued)

table 7.2 Sample Citations for Different Types of Sources *(concluded)*

Interview	MLA	Ahmed, Helen, M.D., pediatrician. Personal interview. 5 May 2018.
	APA	Ahmed, Helen, M.D., pediatrician. (2018, May 5). Personal interview.
TV program	MLA	Wertheim, Jon, reporter, "Japan's Babe Ruth." *60 Minutes*. CBS News. 24 December 2017.
	APA	Wertheim, J., reporter. (2017, December 24). Japan's Babe Ruth. *60 Minutes*. CBS News.
Twitter tweets	MLA	Yousafzai, Malala (Malala). 5 years ago, I was shot in an attempt to stop me from speaking out for girls' education. Today, I attend my first lectures at Oxford. 9 October 2017, 8:39 a.m. Tweet.
	APA	Yousafzai, M. [Malala]. (2017, October 9). 5 years ago, I was shot in an attempt to stop me from speaking out for girls' education. Today, I attend my first lectures at Oxford. [Tweet]. Retrieved from https://twitter.com/Malala/status/917414203186667520
Blog post	MLA	Spruch, Kirsten. "Grammy Spotlight: Robert Randolph and the Family Band." *Music Blog*. Baeble. 17 January 2018. http://www.baeblemusic.com/musicblog 17 January 2018
	APA	Spruch, K. (2018, January 17). Grammy Spotlight: Robert Randolph and the Family Band [Music Blog Home Page on Baeblemusic]. Retrieved from http://www.baeblemusic.com/musicblog
YouTube video	MLA	Last Week Tonight with John Oliver – Economic Development. 15 November 2017. YouTube. https://www.youtube.com/watch?v=8bl19RoR7lc. 5 November 2017.
	APA	Oliver, J. (2017, November 5). Last week tonight with John Oliver – Economic Development. [Video file]] Retrieved from https://www.youtube.com/watch?v=8bl19RoR7lc.
Facebook post	MLA	Haley, Nikki. "Hard to believe a year ago today was my confirmation in the Senate. What a year it has been! #BlessedToServe" Facebook. 18 January 2018. [https://www.facebook.com/NikkiHaley]
	APA	Haley, Nikki. (2018, January 18). Hard to believe a year ago today was my confirmation in the Senate. What a year it has been! #BlessedToServe [Facebook status update]. Retrieved from https://www.facebook.com/NikkiHaley.

Association (MLA) or the American Psychological Association (APA), which are the two most frequently used styles. Courses in the humanities and the arts usually use MLA style, while courses in the sciences typically use APA style (or, alternatively, the Council of Science Editors style). Your instructor will tell you which citation style he or she prefers.

O Organize Constructing a Scaffold

When builders begin construction on a building, initially they often create a scaffold, a wooden platform that is the physical framework allowing them to build the exterior of the building. When we're writing, we need to do something analogous: create an intellectual scaffold for presenting the framework for our arguments.

Construct an Outline (and Be Ready to Change It!)

The key to organizing an extended piece of writing is the outline. Outlines provide a roadmap to follow when we're writing, a set of sequential steps that show us where we are heading and how we are going to get there.

The secret of successful outlining is flexibility: It is essential to keep an open mind about sequencing and to avoid getting "locked in" too early to a pattern that might later prove unworkable. The best approach is to write possible subtopics, based on your research, on index cards–or simply to type all of them into your computer. Then try to place them in a logical order. (If you use the computer, the program's outlining feature will even renumber the outline as you make changes.) Ask yourself how the subtopics build into a complete and convincing presentation. In doing this, always remember your audience: Consider what a reader would have to know already to understand a given fact or argument. Then try out several sequences and determine which order works best.

Develop the Paper's Structure

Although instructors sometimes provide a structure for a paper, you will ordinarily have to construct one yourself. One way to do this is to follow the **ABBCC structure**). "ABBCC" stands for the five parts of a typical research paper: *a*rgument, *b*ackground, *b*ody, *c*ounterarguments, and *c*onclusion. Each of these plays a specific role:

- **Argument.** Just as we introduce ourselves when we meet someone for the first time, a writer needs to introduce a reader to the main argument being put forward in the paper. Every paper should have a main **argument** or **thesis**), a one- or two-sentence description of the main point of the paper. For instance, your thesis might make the argument that "Honesty does not matter in leaders; what matters is their effectiveness in accomplishing the goals for which they were elected."

  A thesis should be stated as an assertion ("People are their own worst enemies."). An effective thesis statement takes a position on some issue; many times this is signaled by use of an action verb ("The current technological revolution *requires* that people receive computer training") or the use of such keywords as "should" or "ought." For instance, "Smoking should be banned from restaurants and bars" presents a thesis statement. "This paper will discuss smoking in restaurants and bars," on the other hand, simply states the topic: We have no idea what stand the writer takes on smoking in restaurants and bars. **Try It! 3** will help you turn ideas into thesis statements.

  The thesis or argument need not be the first sentence of the paper. In fact, it is usually wise to start off with something that grabs readers' attention. Begin with a controversial quote, an illustrative story, or a personal encounter–anything that is likely to make a reader sit up and take notice.

  In addition to presenting the main thesis of the paper, the first section should lay out the areas that you will cover and the general scope of the paper. You should use this section to present the paper's overall perspective and point of view. For example, "Taxpayers have every right to expect . . ." signals the writer's perspective on campaign finance reform–he or she is thinking about it as a taxpayer, as opposed to a legislator or political candidate.

ABBCC structure
The structure of the typical research paper, consisting of argument, background, body, counterarguments, and conclusion.

argument
The main idea of a paper; what the writer is claiming.

thesis
The main point of a paper, typically stating the writer's opinion about the topic of the paper.

3 | **Try It!** POWER

Make Your Point: Write a Thesis Statement

Write a thesis statement for each of the topics below. Remember that the thesis should be an *assertion*.

restricting access to particular World Wide Web pages in school libraries

the death penalty

same-sex marriage

cloning

global warming and modern technology

campaign finance reform

prayer in schools

stem-cell research

Evaluate each of the thesis statements that you wrote. Do they all contain an assertion? Is there a relationship between how controversial a topic is and how easy it is to write a thesis statement?

WORKING IN A GROUP

Each group member should generate three potential topics for a paper and compose a thesis statement for each. Then, as a group, evaluate each of the thesis statements.

- **Background.** You'll need to provide readers with a context in which to place your paper's arguments, and the background section is the place to do it. The **background** provides a backdrop and context for your arguments. Provide a brief history of the topic, talking about different schools of thought on it. Introduce any unusual terms you might need to use. If the topic is highly controversial, discuss the reasons for the controversy. For example, if you are arguing that capital punishment should be abolished, you could briefly review the history of its use and of opposition to it.

background
The backdrop and context for one's arguments in a paper.

- **Body.** The body makes up the bulk of most papers. In the paper's body, you provide evidence as to why your thesis is correct.

  This evidence should be presented in a logical order. Exactly what this means depends upon your topic. You may need to work chronologically if you are discussing a historical event. In other cases, you will want to start with the least controversial arguments and gradually move into the ones that are most debatable.

  When deciding on the order, keep your audience firmly in mind. For instance, a paper on the dangers of electromagnetic radiation written for a community law class would be very different from one written for a physics class.

- **Counterarguments.** You will also need to touch on the counterarguments to your position: Acknowledge them and then go on to systematically refute each one. This section need not be long, but it is crucial. By doing this you help reinforce your own position and strengthen your argument, showing that you have arrived at your point of view fully aware of—and unconvinced by—opposing views.

- **Conclusion.** A good ending to a paper is as important as a good beginning. It's where you pull everything together. And it is your last chance to drive home your thesis.

  The conclusion should summarize the thesis and the arguments that you have made regarding it. Do not introduce new information: The conclusion is a recap. Do make an effort to close with a flourish. You might cite a quotation, present an anecdote that is linked to one you presented at the start of the paper, or pose a rhetorical question ("If the government turns its back on welfare recipients, how can we claim to have a just society?"). However you choose to conclude the paper, make sure that your conclusion ties the various pieces together.

» LO 7-2 W Work Writing the Work

Now comes the moment that so many dread: It's time to face that blank page or screen and actually start writing. However, if you've followed the steps above and carefully prepared and organized, this phase is likely to be easier than you expect.

In fact, you should be so well prepared that you know just how to proceed: Your outline offers a clear roadmap, and your research notes will help you explain your ideas along the way. Your outline, if carefully composed, will actually provide you with the major headings of your paper. The job of writing the paper then becomes a matter of matching up the research to the appropriate outline heading. Looked at in this way, that blank page isn't so blank after all.

Don't try to do too much at one sitting. Professional authors writing a 500-page book don't think about the 500 pages they need to write; such thoughts are at best mind-numbing and at worst unproductive and paralyzing. Instead, professionals break their task down into smaller, more manageable pieces. They might decide that they'll write a certain number of pages in a given period of time—perhaps four or five pages a day. Or maybe they plan on writing one chapter per month.

You won't have as much time to devote to your writing as a professional writer, so you should break your writing into shorter chunks. For instance, if you have to write a 10-page paper, don't think of it as 10 pages. Instead, break it down into chunks of 2 pages a day, spread out over 5 days. Or think of it in terms of the major sections: an introduction, a description of the background of an issue, arguments in favor of a position, arguments against a position, and a conclusion. You could then schedule writing each of those sections on a different day.

It's also helpful to divide the actual work of writing into two stages: writing the first draft and revising your draft.

Writing the First Draft

Starting a first draft is like diving into a cold lake. You know the initial plunge will be painful because the water is icy cold, but you also know that once you're in, it won't feel so bad.

It's the same thing with writing a first draft. Getting started is often the hardest part. However, once you've put even a few words on paper, it gets easier.

When you set pen to paper or fingers to keyboard to begin writing, don't feel that you are carving your words in stone. Permit yourself to be less than perfect. Don't worry about word choice, grammar, sentence structure, spelling, or punctuation. That can come later. The first draft is meant to give you something to go on. The important thing is to fill up that blank space with *something*.

There are several strategies you can use to make writing the first draft less painful:

- **Start where you like.** You need not follow the order of the outline when you write. For example, some writers start a paper by writing the conclusion first. By keeping the end in mind, they know just where they are headed, making the journey a little easier. Similarly, other writers save the beginning of the paper for last, reasoning that they'll be better able to tell their readers where the paper is going after it has actually gotten there.

  Write whatever part of the paper you feel most comfortable writing, because just having something on paper will encourage you to write the rest.
- **Turn off your inner critic.** If you're anything like most people, with every word you write, there's probably a voice somewhere in your head that's whispering, "Terrible sentence. Dumb idea. Forget it, you idiot, you'll never finish this paper." Your job is to turn off the voice of that inner critic, at least for now. (You'll want to use it later, when the nagging may come in handy as you revise your work.) While you're working on your first

If you've ever gone whitewater rafting, you know that following the water's rhythm permits you to remain afloat. In the same way, on those occasions when you achieve a steady rhythm while writing and the words are coming rapidly, stick with it and go with the flow. Revising can come later.

draft, you want to give yourself permission to be creative. As long as you write things down, you'll be able to go back later and make your paper better. But you can't revise what isn't there.

> "I spend a great deal of my time thinking about the power of language—the way it can evoke an emotion, a visual image, a complex idea, or a simple truth."
>
> **Amy Tan, author, in** *The Opposite of Fate: Memories of a Writing Life* **(New York: Penguin Books, 2004).**

- **Go with the flow.** When you're writing your first draft, try to write quickly. Writing often takes on a rhythm, and you should try to write in sync with that rhythm. If you're on a roll, go with it: Don't stop (yet) to edit your work.

  On the other hand, if you're having trouble getting into a rhythm, and each word is like pulling teeth, take a break. Do something entirely different for a few minutes and then return with a fresh mind.

  If you're really having trouble, try rearranging your note cards (or scrambling your outline). Placing them in a new or even a random order may provide a fresh way of looking at your topic, and this may in turn free you enough to get your writing started.

- **Don't be afraid to modify your outline.** When you start writing, it's easy to fall into the trap of viewing an outline as a rigid, unbending framework. Your outline is a living document, and you should feel free to rearrange headings and to deviate from it as you're creating your first draft.

  Many writers find that their outlines need to be revised, and so might you. That's fine; that's why you're writing a first draft and not pretending to start with a final one.

- **Use your own voice.** Just as you have a distinctive speaking voice, each of us has a distinct **writing voice)**. That voice represents our own unique style, a reflection of our outlook on life and of our past writing experiences. Novice writers sometimes get hung up trying to use a voice that isn't their own. For example, they may use words they would never normally use when speaking.

  Avoid the temptation to write as if you were someone else. Instead, use your own natural voice and vocabulary, and don't use big words in an effort to impress your audience. If you'd feel foolish saying "heretofore" in a conversation, you shouldn't use it when you're writing a paper. Don't scan the thesaurus in search of unusual words to use in place of simple ones.

  On the other hand, keep in mind that course papers use a more formal voice than you probably use in e-mails and instant messaging to close friends and family. You'll need to avoid the abbreviated and sometimes ungrammatical style of communicating you may be in the habit of using when you write electronic messages.

- **Forget about it.** The last step in creating a first draft is the easiest: When you have finished your sketch of the entire paper, from introduction through conclusion, put it aside and try to forget about it for a while.

  You need to let your mind idle in neutral for a while so that it will be at full strength when you move on to the next phase of writing: revision.

writing voice
The unique style of a writer, expressing the writer's outlook on life and past writing experiences.

Reading the first draft of a paper aloud can help you identify problems that need to be addressed in a revised draft.
©Erik Isakson/Getty Images

Revising Your Draft

Remember that inner critic–that voice in your head–that you tuned out while you were writing the first draft? It's time to tune it back in.

The fact is that most of writing is *re*writing. Sure, it's possible to hand in a first draft, and sometimes you'll even get a passable grade. But if you want to reach your own potential as a writer, you *must* revise.

Don't feel that revising is something that only students have to do. Professional writers may go through dozens of drafts and still not be completely satisfied. Virtually no one has the ability to write a first-draft paper that is so clear and convincing that it's ready to stand on its own.

Following several basic rules can make the revision process work smoothly for you:

- **Read the first draft out loud.** Read your paper out loud–to yourself, a friend, a pet, or your computer. It doesn't matter who's listening.

  Reading out loud does several things. You'll more easily discover missing words, verbs that don't match the subject of the sentence, shifts in tense, missing transitions, and other things that you might have to fix. This is partly because speaking takes longer than silent reading; the slowed pace of reading out loud can help you identify problems that you'd otherwise miss.

- **Take the long view.** Start off by taking the broadest perspective possible and asking yourself a series of questions:

  What is the purpose of my paper? Has that purpose been fulfilled?

  Have I addressed every part of the assignment?

  Does the paper tell its readers everything they need to know?

  Will readers be able to follow its logic?

  Does the paper make its points clearly?

  Are the transitions between sections clear?

- **Be ruthless.** Words that we've put on paper tend to take on a life of their own–a life that we have created and so are often reluctant to change or part with.

  It is natural to feel a bit parental toward our first draft, but it is important to fight this instinct. You need to be merciless and unforgiving with passages, paragraphs, phrases, and words that don't sound right or that do not ultimately add to your argument. Don't tear *yourself* down but, like a coach demanding the best from his or her players, be demanding of your performance.

  Start pruning at the paragraph level. Assess each paragraph to make sure that it adds to the final message, that it flows from the previous paragraph logically, and that it is consistent with what you are trying to accomplish.

  Then move to the level of sentences and words. Evaluate each sentence, and then each word, to make sure that it adds to the clarity of your message.

  By paring down your writing, you let your ideas shine through. If you are extremely fond of a phrase or a group of words that you suspect are unnecessary, write down or print out the sections and phrases, put them into an envelope, and toss the envelope into the top drawer of your dresser. You never know when you might need them. More important, knowing that you can save the cut material may make it easier to do the necessary cutting.

> "Wrestling with words gave me my moments of greatest meaning."
>
> Richard Wright, author

- **Check sequence and logic.** It's now time to reverse course. Whereas before the focus was on cutting unnecessary material, you now need to check for what's *missing* from your paper.

Writing in Class: Strategies for Getting It Right

Course Connections

Your instructor pauses halfway through her lecture and says that for the next 5 minutes you are to complete a short written assignment. Whether she calls it an in-class essay, a reaction paper, or a "pop paper," it calls for somewhat different strategies than an out-of-class writing assignment. Unlike traditional paper assignments—in which you have the luxury of time—an in-class writing assignment requires that you react immediately.

Here are some tips for completing in-class writing assignments:

- *Be prepared.* You should always come to class with pen and pencil, as well as knowing your student ID number (at least in big classes). Just as important, make sure you're up to date in the reading assignments.
- *Think first.* Before you start writing, spend a minute thinking about the assignment. What is its goal? How can you best approach it? What is it that you want to get across?
- *Make a quick outline.* Creating an outline—even a short one—will help you collect your thoughts and prepare for what you're going to say.
- *Timing is everything.* Assuming your instructor lets you know how much time you'll have (and ask how much, if he or she doesn't mention it), plan ahead appropriately. You don't want to run out of time before completing your assignment.
- *Be sure to answer every part of the question.* If your instructor asks for your opinion, be sure to give it, but if he or she also wants to know *why* you feel the way you do, don't forget that part.
- *Neatness counts.* Be sure your answer is legible. If your handwriting is terrible, then print. The most brilliant of responses does you no good if your instructor can't read it.

For example, earlier cuts might have made it necessary to add or modify transitions between sections and paragraphs. You might also need to improve logic by reordering your ideas, reordering sentences within paragraphs, and reordering paragraphs within sections.

- **Check punctuation and spelling.** Check for the obvious stuff: Sentences should start with capital letters and end with the appropriate punctuation, commas should set off dependent clauses, and the like. Use a handbook or style manual if you're unsure.

  Check your spelling carefully. This is one of the areas in which word processors earn their keep best. The spell-check feature will not only identify every misspelled word (that is, every word not in its dictionary), but it will also prompt you with alternative spellings.

  Be careful not to rely completely on the spell-checker, however. Such programs can find only misspellings that do not form recognized words; if what you typed is a word, the spell-checker will ignore it, even if it is not the word you wanted to use. *Foe instants, know spelt-cheek pogrom wood fined eras inn thus sent-tense.* And yet every word in the preceding "sent-tense" is spelled incorrectly in this context.
- **Check that all quotations are cited and referenced correctly.** As we'll discuss in detail later, it is critical that you give proper credit to others' ideas and words. Make sure that you haven't directly quoted or paraphrased a source without acknowledging it.
- **Make it pleasing to the eye.** Instructors are human. They can't help but react differently to a paper that is neatly typed compared with one that is handwritten in a difficult-to-read scrawl.

A neat paper conveys a message: I'm proud of this paper. I've put time and effort into it. This is my best work.

A sloppy paper says something different.

Take the time, then, to make sure your paper looks good. This doesn't mean that you need to invest in a fancy plastic cover, or worry about the alignment of the staples, or spend a lot of time deciding which font to use on your word processor. But it does mean that the quality of the paper's appearance should match the quality of the writing.

E Evaluate — Acting as Your Own Best Critic

Because you've already put so much work into your paper, you might be tempted to rush through the final stages of the P.O.W.E.R. process. Avoid the temptation. If you've carefully revised your paper, the last stages will not be time-consuming, and they may have a significant impact on your paper's ultimate quality–and your success.

Take these steps to *evaluate* what you've written:

- **Ask yourself if your paper accomplishes what you set out to do.** The beginning of your paper contains a thesis statement and the argument that you intended to make. Does your paper support the thesis? Is your argument upheld by the evidence you've reported? Would an impartial reader be convinced by what you've written?
- **Put yourself in your instructor's shoes.** Does the paper precisely fit the assignment requirements? Does it meet the instructor's underlying goals in giving the assignment?
- **Check the mechanical aspects of the paper.** The grammar and spelling must be correct; the paper should also look good. If your instructor requires that citations or references be reported in a certain style, make sure you've followed it. For example, your instructor might specify Modern Language Association style (used in the humanities), American Psychological Association style (used in the social sciences), or Council of Science Editors style (used in the sciences).
- **Have an objective reader take a look.** Many colleges have writing labs or centers that will help you with your writing. In many cases, their staff will take a look at a paper and provide feedback. You can also have a friend or family member read the paper, giving you comments.

If you've revised the paper with care, it will likely pass muster. If it doesn't, though, go back and work on it once again. By this point, it should require only minor tinkering to get it into shape.

R Rethink — Reflecting on Your Accomplishment

Rethinking is the homestretch of the writing process. It's a moment to savor, because it permits you to take a long view of what you've accomplished. You've gone from a blank page to words on paper that tell a story. You've turned nothing into something–an achievement in and of itself.

Rethinking occurs on several levels. Once a day or two has passed, rethink the message, rethink the mechanics of your writing, and and rethink the method you

Write Away

The first step in getting a job is putting pen to paper (or, probably more accurately, finger to keyboard). Whether you receive a lead for a job from a college career center, read an ad in the paper, or see a job listing on the Internet, you'll need to communicate in writing to the potential employer.

You are selling yourself in a letter of application. To be effective, keep these guidelines in mind:

- **Brief is better.** Employers are likely to get many letters, and long ones are least likely to be read.
- **State what you can do for the employer, not what the employer can do for you.** Don't tell a potential employer you really, really need a job to pay off your credit card bills. Instead, explain how your skills can help further the organization's goals.
- **Summarize your qualifications.** Respond specifically to the skills required for the job. List specific experiences you've had that are relevant to what the employer is looking for.
- **Enclose a résumé.** Your résumé should contain a detailed summary of your educational background and work experience, as well as other relevant qualifications.
- **Ask for an interview.** Close your letter with a request to meet and discuss the job. Provide your telephone number and e-mail address.
- **Proofread!** You must have zero tolerance for errors. Any mistake is likely to put you at the bottom of the pile of applications.

Career Connections

used to create the paper. Using your critical thinking skills, reflect on each of these parts of the rethinking process:

- **Rethink the message.** Be sure that the overall message your paper conveys is appropriate. A paper can be like an advertisement. In most papers, you are seeking to communicate information to convince someone of a particular opinion. Make sure that the message is what you wish to communicate and that ultimately the paper is successful in making the case.
- **Rethink the mechanics.** A television commercial filled with fuzzy images and annoyingly unsteady camera shots would not be very compelling, no matter how good the underlying product. In the same way, a paper with mechanical errors will not impress your readers or persuade them. Take another look at your writing style; look at grammar, punctuation, and word usage to make sure the choices you've made are appropriate.
- **Rethink the method.** Every time you finish a paper, you learn something—something about the topic of your writing and something about yourself. Ask yourself what you have learned to help you become a better writer in the future. What might you have done to improve the writing process? What could have gone better? What will you do differently the next time you write? Above all, remember what you've accomplished: You've transformed what's inside your head—your thoughts, your ideas, your values—into something that can potentially influence other people. You have exercised the ability to move others and get them to think in new ways. You've made a difference. That's the real power of writing.

Acknowledging Others' Ideas: Academic Honesty and Plagiarism

As you move through the process of writing a paper, there are many temptations to cut corners. A friend may have written a paper the previous year on the same topic and offer to "lend" it to you . . . you may find a paper on the web that addresses just what you intended to write . . . you and a friend may be enrolled in a very large class, and he may suggest that you each write part of the paper and "share" sections.

Don't yield to temptations such as these. Not only is honesty the best policy, but it's also the *only* policy in the world of academics. There's no greater academic sin than **plagiarism)**, taking credit for someone else's words, thoughts, or ideas. In the academic world, plagiarism is about the same as stealing a stranger's car. Even if you just mean to "borrow" a passage, passing another person's work off as your own is totally wrong.

plagiarism
Taking credit for someone else's words, thoughts, or ideas.

Furthermore, penalties for plagiarism are severe. In many colleges, plagiarism results in a comment on your transcript or can result in expulsion. You even could face legal charges, because almost all published material is copyrighted, which means that it is someone's *intellectual property*. If an author learns that you have used his or her writing as your own, the author has the right to take you to court and sue for damages. It's unlikely, but it's possible.

If the moral and intellectual arguments against plagiarism don't convince you, here's the hard reality: It is likely you are going to get caught. Increasing numbers of instructors and colleges routinely use web-based computer programs to check students' papers for plagiarism. The process is simple. Students turn in papers in electronic form, and they are passed through sophisticated software programs such as **Turnitin.com**. Turnitin checks papers against a database that includes more than 20 billion web pages and 200 million student papers. Alternatively, instructors may also type in passages that sound suspicious to them. Programs such as Turnitin work extraordinarily well.

The bottom line: Plagiarism is wrong. Instructors hate it, and they often go to great lengths to identify it. Because the odds are that if you plagiarize, you are likely to be caught, *just don't do it.*

Types of Plagiarism

Plagiarism comes in many varieties. Among them:

- Turning in someone else's work, word for word.
- Cutting and pasting large portions of text from a single source.
- Copying portions of several sources and weaving them together with little change from each of the original sources.
- Taking sentences from other sources but changing key words in various places.
- Rewording each sentence, putting them into one's own words, but keeping the same sequence as in an original source.
- Self-plagiarism, that is, using material from a previous paper that one has written and passing it off as new.

It's important to keep in mind that you will be considered guilty of plagiarism even if only a few sentences are directly copied from other sources. In other words, even if only 1 percent of a paper is copied directly from another source, you will be considered 100 percent guilty of plagiarism.

Avoiding Plagiarism

The best way to avoid plagiarism is to be very, very careful. Following these guidelines will help you:

- If you are writing a paper that requires the use of source materials from the library or the web, *always* note the source, and distinguish between your ideas, quotations, and your paraphrases of others' ideas. If you've recorded something in your notes without indicating the source, don't use it in your writing until you identify the source.
- Don't rely on a single source. It's too easy to make use of the same wording and terminology without being aware of it.
- When you quote directly from the work of another, use quotation marks, even in your notes.
- Be sure to keep accurate records as you are taking notes. When you paraphrase, be careful: It's not just a matter of rearranging the words and choosing synonyms for them. For instance, consider the following passage from the book *Nation of Nations:*[2]

  In the 1860s they had come in a trickle; in the 1870s they became a torrent. They were farmers from the East and Midwest, black freedmen from the rural South, and peasant-born immigrants from Europe. What bound them together was a craving for land.

  Here's one way of rephrasing the passage, but one that is so close to the original that it amounts to plagiarism:

  In the 1860s they had come in a drizzle; in the 1870s, they became a deluge. There were crop-growers from the East and Midwest, former black slaves from the rural South, and common people from Europe. Holding them together was a hunger for land.

  A more appropriate rewording of the original passage would be the following, which more clearly paraphrases the authors' ideas:

  There was a great deal of growth in the number of settlers from 1860 to 1879. The settlers represented several groups, including farmers from the eastern and midwestern United States, former Southern slaves, and poor Europeans who had come to the United States to better their lives. They all shared a dream of obtaining land.

- Even when paraphrasing, *it is necessary to cite the source* of the facts or ideas that you are using. In the example above, one way to cite would be to add a footnote or endnote reference similar to the one at the end of this book, in the Annotations section.

  Citation is necessary for two reasons: (1) to give credit where credit is due and (2) to allow your readers to follow up for more information on a subject. Facts and ideas that are unique to a source or even those that are infrequently heard should be cited. It is probably advisable to cite too much rather than risk plagiarizing, but it is *not* necessary to have a citation after every sentence.

Some facts are so basic ("Japan and Germany were the enemies of the United States in World War II") that no source is necessary.

- Keep in mind that you must cite material that you find on the web. It was produced by someone else and that someone must be given credit. The rules for how to cite material found on the web are still in flux, but you should at the very least include the site name, web address (URL), and author, as well as the date you accessed the site.
- Check your own paper with plagiarism-detection software. If your college has an arrangement with a plagiarism-detection software company such as **Turnitin.com**, you may be able to use it *before* you hand in an assignment. If it's available to you, run your paper through the program just to make sure you haven't unintentionally copied something and inserted it into your paper.

Finally, remember this: In your research on the web, you might come across sites that offer to sell you term papers. Don't even think about it. The academic and legal consequences would be severe. In addition, the papers are often of low quality, and the same paper may be sold to dozens of students—potentially even to other students in your own class, making it easy for an instructor to identify plagiarized papers.

Try It! 4 will give you some practice in the proper use of other people's information and ideas. Before we turn to the topic of public speaking, which we consider next, make sure the distinction between summarization and plagiarism is clear in your mind.

» LO 7-3 Speaking Your Mind

Surveys find that most people are more afraid of public speaking than of dying! In a way, it's not surprising. How often are we so totally exposed to others' scrutiny? Not only do we have to worry about the message we're communicating—just as with our writing—but each of us also has to be concerned about nonverbal behavior and the impression we are making: *Is my hair sticking out? . . . This sweater was a big mistake. . . . Are they bored? . . . I wish my hands would stop shaking.*

Although you may be self-conscious about public speaking (complete **Try It! 5** to see where you stand), it's important to keep several points in mind:

- Audiences are generally sympathetic. They've all been where you are and probably share your fears about public speaking. They're on your side and are rooting for you to succeed.
- Being nervous is normal. Even accomplished entertainers like Bono and Meryl Streep report high levels of anxiety before and during performances.
- Once you start speaking, it will become easier. Anxiety tends to be highest *before* you start talking. Most people find that after they start to talk, their nervousness declines.
- Practice helps. Practice and preparation for the talk will go a long way toward easing your tension.

Keep in mind, too, that in many fundamental ways, speaking is like writing. You need to consider who your audience is, muster your arguments, and decide how to sequence those arguments.

The P.O.W.E.R. writing framework that we presented earlier in the chapter applies to speaking as well:

- **Prepare** what you will say and how you will say it. Think about your audience and the occasion on which you will speak, and try to be sure your words match both audience and occasion.

4 **Try It!**

Summarize, Don't Plagiarize

Try to capture in your own words the meaning of the following quoted passages, without plagiarizing them in any way. Assume that you intend to reflect the main points of each author in a paper of your own, summarizing the arguments.

1. From Goodwin, D. K. (1995). *No Ordinary Time: Franklin And Eleanor Roosevelt : The Home Front in World War II.* New York: Simon & Schuster. pp. 628–629.

   It was said jokingly in Washington during the war years that Roosevelt had a nightly prayer: "Dear God, please make Eleanor a little tired." But in the end, he often came around to her way of thinking. Labor advisor Anna Rosenberg had been one of those who criticized Eleanor's unceasing pressure on the President, but years later she changed her mind. "I remember him saying. 'We're not going to do that now. Tell Eleanor to keep away; I don't want to hear about that anymore.' And then 2–3 weeks later he would say, 'Do you remember that thing Eleanor brought up? Better look into it, maybe there's something to it—I heard something to indicate that maybe she's right.' I'm not sure she would have had the opportunity to bring things to his attention unless she pressured him—I mean he was so involved and in retrospect it was never anything for herself. . . . He would never have become the kind of President he was without her."

2. From Gould, S. J. (1991). *Bully for Brontosaurus: Reflections in Natural History.* New York: Norton. pp. 466–467.

   Ed Purcell, Nobel laureate in physics but, for purposes of this subject, just another baseball fan, has done a comprehensive study of all baseball streak and slump records. His firm conclusion is easily and swiftly summarized. Nothing ever happened in baseball above and beyond the frequency predicted by coin-tossing models. The longest runs of wins or losses are as long as they should be, and occur about as often as they ought to. . . .

   But "treasure your exceptions," as the old motto goes. There is one major exception, and absolutely only one—one sequence so many standard deviations above the expected distribution that it should not have occurred at all. Joe DiMaggio's fifty-six–game hitting streak in 1941. . . . Purcell calculated that to make it likely (probability greater than 50 percent) that a run of even 50 games will occur once in the history of baseball up to now (and 56 is a lot more than 50 in this kind of league), baseball's rosters would have to include either four lifetime .400 batters or 52 lifetime .350 batters over careers of 1,000 games. In actuality, only three men have lifetime batting averages in excess of .350, and no one is anywhere near .400 (Ty Cobb at .367, Rogers Hornsby at .358, and Shoeless Joe Jackson at .356). DiMaggio's streak is the most extraordinary thing that ever happened in American sports.

3. From Marshall, I. N., Zohar, D., & Peat, F. D. (1997). *Who's Afraid of Schrödinger's Cat?: All the New Science Ideas You Need to Keep Up with the New Thinking.* New York: Morrow. pp. 170–171.

   In 1916, Albert Einstein proposed an interaction between mass-energy and the structure of space-time. Mass-energy produces "curvature" in space-time—i.e., it deviates from flat, Euclidean space. Curved space-time in turn changes the paths of mass-energy through it. . . .

   One test of the worth of any new scientific theory is whether it offers us additional predictions. How do the predictions of General Relativity differ from those of Newtonian gravity? One obvious one is that curved space will deflect not only matter but also light rays passing through it. Thus, light from a distant star should be deflected if it passes near the sun. Newtonian gravitation predicts a similar effect, but only half as much. During an eclipse of the sun in 1919, the measured deflection of light from a distant star won international acclaim for Einstein's theory. Given the technology of the time, one other experimental verification was possible, an explanation for an anomaly in the orbit of Mercury, and this, too, was achieved successfully.

WORKING IN A GROUP

After you summarize the passages on your own, compare your answers to those of other classmates in your group. What different approaches did others in your group take? Which passages did people find particularly hard to summarize? Why? Did your group arrive at one best way to capture the authors' main points?

5 PERSONAL STYLES **Try It!** POWER

Determine Your Level of Self-Consciousness

One of the main reasons people feel nervous when speaking in public is their self-consciousness. To explore your own level of self-consciousness, answer the following questions, choosing the phrase from the rating scale that is closest to your feelings.

0 = Extremely uncharacteristic

1 = Generally uncharacteristic

2 = Equally characteristic and uncharacteristic

3 = Generally characteristic

4 = Extremely characteristic

1. I think a lot about my style of doing things. ______
2. I worry about how I present myself to others. ______
3. My looks make me self-conscious. ______
4. I am concerned about making a good impression. ______
5. I usually look in the mirror before I leave my home. ______
6. I'm concerned about what other people think of me. ______
7. I really care about my appearance. ______

Scoring: Add up the numbers to get a total score. If you score below 16, you are unusually low in self-consciousness, and public speaking should be less of a burden than it is for most other people. If you score between 16 and 22, you have a medium level of self-consciousness. Public speaking is not necessarily easy for you, but it does not provoke too many fears. If you score above 22, your level of self-consciousness is relatively high. Public speaking is likely to be particularly challenging for you.

- **Organize** your thoughts, using notes to cue you to the main parts of your presentation and making logical connections for your audience to follow.
- **Work** carefully during your presentation by speaking clearly and calmly to your audience and avoiding distracting mannerisms or body language.
- **Evaluate** your performance after you finish your presentation and ask others to evaluate it, too. Take notes on the feedback.
- **Rethink** your entire approach when preparing for and delivering presentations each time you make one. Make the changes you feel you should make to improve your performance over time.

Meeting the Challenge of Public Speaking

Although speaking and writing share many features, speaking presents several unique challenges. Among the factors that you need to take into account when you are speaking are these:

- **The first minute counts—a lot.** Get your audience's attention, arouse their interest, and engage them in the first few minutes of your talk. If you can do that, you're on your way to a successful speech. On the other hand, let them drift off early on and you've lost them—potentially for good.

6 Try It! POWER

Let's Talk

Devise a 1-minute opening to a talk about the thing you know most about in this world: you. The topic can be one of your experiences or anything that concerns you or reveals a little bit about your past, your feelings, or your opinions. Use any of the opening strategies that we've considered, and write it below:

After writing your opening, try it out on a friend or classmate. When you're finished, ask yourself how well you think your strategy worked. Why? Would another strategy have worked as well or better? What did your audience think of your opening? Why do you think it had the effect it did? Did your opening make your audience want to hear more? Did your opening make you want to *write* more?

How do you get them interested? There are several ways:

Begin with an anecdote. *"It was a scientist's dream, experienced as he dozed off in front of a fire, that led to one of the most important biological discoveries of all time."*

Start with a quotation. *"'I have seen the enemy, and he is us.' But are we really the enemy? I believe . . ."*

Arouse their curiosity. *"I have a secret, one that I've kept hidden for many years—until now."*

Talk about the significance of the topic. *"If you think that global warming is not a problem, take a look at what's happening to the beachfront up and down the Atlantic coast this year."*

Ask a question. *"Have you ever wondered how you could save enough money to buy a new car?"*

Use humor. *"My introduction to gardening was not promising: Seeking to surprise my mother, I 'weeded' her garden so enthusiastically that I pulled up all her flower seedlings."*

Try It! 6 will help get you started.

- **Provide oral transition points.** When we're reading a textbook selection, we usually have the luxury of knowing exactly when a transition point occurs. It's marked by a title, section heading, or new paragraph. These markers help us construct a mental map that permits us to understand the overall structure of the piece we're reading.

  Listeners don't have the same advantage. Unless the speaker orally signals that he or she is moving to a new part of a talk, listeners might get lost.

  However, there are several ways to erect verbal signposts throughout a speech. By using phrases such as the following, you can alert listeners that a twist in the journey lies ahead:

"To understand the problem, we need to consider . . ."

"The problems are clearly daunting. But there are solutions. Let's consider some of them . . ."

"Now that we've considered the solutions, we need to take a look at their costs . . ."

"Let's go back for a moment to an earlier point I made . . ."

"To sum up, the situation offers some unexpected advantages . . ."

- **Make your notes work for you, not against you.** A speaker is giving a talk, and suddenly she loses her place in her notes. She fumbles around, desperately trying to find her place and figure out what comes next.

  It's a painful situation to watch—and even worse for the person experiencing the problem. How do you avoid finding yourself in such a predicament?

  One way is by being thoroughly acquainted both with what you are going to say *and* with your notes. Once again, practice is your best friend.

  But the type of notes you have also makes a big difference. Some speakers write out their entire talk in advance; others use no notes at all, counting on memorizing their talk. Avoid either extreme. If you write out your complete speech in advance, you'll experience an overwhelming urge to read it to your audience. Nothing could be more deadly. On the other hand, if you memorize your talk and have no notes at all, you'll be susceptible to a memory lapse that can make you feel completely foolish. Even if you can remember your talk successfully, you may end up sounding mechanical, like an amusement park guide who has given the same speech about the "jungle cruise" a thousand times.

  Choose a middle ground. Develop an outline that includes the major points you wish to cover and have this outline in front of you when you speak. It might be written or typed on a sheet of paper, or you might use index cards (number them!). In addition, write out and memorize your opening and closing statements.

  By memorizing the opening and closing statements, you'll have the opportunity to look your audience in the eye and engage them nonverbally at two of the most crucial junctures in your talk—the beginning and the end. Using an outline for most of your talk permits you to sound natural as you speak. You'll probably use slightly different words every time you give your talk, which is fine.

- **A picture can save you a thousand words.** Maps, charts, photos, drawings, figures, and other illustrations add another dimension to a presentation, helping engage listeners. Computer programs, such as PowerPoint, permit you to create graphics relatively painlessly (as we'll discuss further in **Chapter 9**). Just be sure to give full credit to the source of anything you use that someone else created—the rules of plagiarism hold for talks you give, as much as for your writing.

  You can even use props. For example, if you are talking about a series of Supreme Court rulings, you might incorporate a gavel into your talk. Effective visual aids make abstract concepts more concrete and immediate.

- **Use the right amount and kind of practice.** After you've written your opening and closing statements, constructed an outline, and decided what visual aids to use, it's time to practice. It's not just the amount of practice that is critical: How you practice is as important as how much you practice.

When used in a talk, visual aids help to keep an audience interested in what you are saying. They also take the focus away from you, making public speaking less nerve-wracking.
©Purestock/Superstock

Running through your speech mentally will help you familiarize yourself with your presentation, but you really need to give the speech out loud. Only by hearing yourself speak can you actually get a sense of how the presentation works as an oral presentation.

Use your "speaking voice" when you practice. When you practice, speak more loudly than your usual conversational voice, using the volume level that you'll want to use when you actually give the speech. Because your voice sounds different to you when you speak loudly, this tactic will help you get used to the sound of your voice at a louder-than-usual level.

Try to eliminate repeated, unnecessary phrases. We all have verbal "tics," such as the use of "umm," "ah," "you know," and "kind of." As you practice, avoid using them. In fact, it's a good idea to eliminate them from everyday speech as well. So each time you hear yourself using them, in any context, pause and remind yourself that you're trying to purge them from your speech.

Practice in front of a friend or classmate. It is only by actually trying your talk out in front of a warm body that you'll be able to approximate the experience of actually speaking in public, and your audience can provide you with feedback regarding what is working and what is not.

How much practice is enough practice? You've probably done enough when you do a good job giving a talk two or three times in a row. If you practice your talk too many times, you'll become so bored with it that the actual talk will sound canned and unconvincing.

- **Fight stage fright.** As you know, for many people, the mere thought of speaking in front of others causes a knot of fear to form deep in their gut. Even those who routinely speak in front of others experience some degree of anxiety. (Ask one or two of your course instructors if they ever feel nervous when teaching a class. Their answers may surprise you.)

  Although you won't be able to alleviate your stage fright completely, several techniques can reduce the anxiety that public speaking produces. First, make sure you're wearing clothes that are comfortable and that make you feel pleased with your appearance. If you feel good about your appearance, you'll be more relaxed.

  Five minutes before you get up to speak, take three slow, deep breaths. Concentrate on the feeling of the air going in and out of your body. If a particular part of your body feels tense, tighten it up even more and then relax it. Do it several times. Finally, visualize yourself giving the speech successfully and the relief that you'll feel afterward.

- **Monitor your nonverbal behavior.** Anxiety about public speaking can do strange things to people's bodies. Their hands may shake or feel icy cold. They may pace back and forth like a caged lion. They may sweat profusely. They may stand rigidly while speaking, looking like stiff toy soldiers. Or they may slump over a podium as if they wished they could dissolve into thin air.

  To avoid appearing as if you were scared to death—even if you are—stand up straight and tall. Look directly at different members of your audience, shifting your gaze from one person to the next. Eye contact engages audience members, making them feel that your words are directed straight toward them.

  If the thought of eye contact scares you, try a trick that some speakers use. Look directly at the *hairline* of different audience members; to your listeners, this is generally indistinguishable from eye contact.

Speaking Off-the-Cuff: Impromptu Speaking

impromptu talks
Unprepared presentations that require speaking on a moment's notice.

What do you do when an instructor calls on you in class and asks, "What do you think the point of this poem is?" Just as anxiety-producing as giving a prepared talk (and probably a lot more common) is public speaking that is impromptu. **Impromptu talks** are unprepared presentations that require you to speak on a moment's notice.

Impromptu speaking happens far more frequently than you may think: Your professor asks you to explain why some historians consider Reconstruction a failed enterprise; a co-worker or classmate asks you to explain how a software program works; you visit your landlord to complain about the water heater that keeps breaking, and the landlord asks you for details. The response you give in each of these situations (and many others) is an exercise in impromptu speaking.

"PREPing" to Give an Impromptu Talk

Just because speaking impromptu is, by definition, unplanned, it does not have to be totally off the top of your head. There is a simple process that you can use when you're put on the spot. Known as the PREP formula, it consists of breaking down an answer into four parts:

- **Point of view.** Initially provide your point of view or your stand on the issue.
- **Reasons.** Provide the chief reasons you believe your position is correct.
- **Evidence or examples.** Give specific evidence to support your point of view.
- **Point of view, restated.** Restate your point of view.

Here's an example:

Professor Fiske:

Who can tell me if racism is a uniquely American problem? Stephanie, why don't you take a stab at the question?

Stephanie:

I don't believe racism is uniquely American at all. ***[point of view]*** *If we look at other times in history or other parts of the world today, we find all sorts of racial problems.* ***[reasons]*** *For example, consider Iraq and the Middle East. Or look at the difficulties that South Africa had. Or look at Nazi Germany.* ***[evidence or examples]*** *So it's hard for me to understand how anyone could contend that racism is uniquely American. Racism, unfortunately, is a universal fact of life.* ***[point of view, restated]***

Although using the PREP system may seem awkward at first, you'll find it easy to learn. And with sufficient practice, it will become automatic, saving you lots of mental scrambling the next time you're called on in class (see **Try It! 7**).

Remember: You're Already an Accomplished Public Speaker

Speaking in front of others is something you've done all your life. It might have been a heart-to-heart with a friend. It might have been with a group of friends deciding on what kind of pizza to order, with you arguing against anchovies and your friends arguing in favor. It might have been as a sports team member, with you shouting encouragement to your fellow athletes. The point is that you've already spoken in front of others—lots of times.

When you are faced with giving a formal presentation, give yourself credit for the times you've already spoken publicly. Let go of your fears and enjoy your moment in the spotlight. You may well find the experience satisfying and rewarding.

Try It! POWER

Put Yourself on the Spot

Each member of a class group should write two questions on separate note cards. Some examples: "Are basketball players paid too much?" "What's the best way to wash dishes?" "How can you get people to exercise more?"

Place the cards, face down, on a table. Have the first group member choose one of the cards at random, and immediately answer the question using the PREP system. Every person should take a turn answering a question.

After each person gives his or her extemporaneous speech, evaluate the responses by answering the following questions as a group:

Generally, how effective was the person's response to the question?

What were its greatest strengths?

What could have been done better?

Speaking *of* Success

©Tinselltown/Shutterstock

NAME: **Tom Hanks**

SCHOOL: **Chabot College, Hayward, California**

Tom Hanks is considered one of the biggest and most successful figures to ever come out of Hollywood. To what does he attribute his success? You might be surprised to learn that much of what makes Tom Hanks so successful was the education he received at Chabot College in Hayward, California.

Self-admittedly not the best student out of high school, Hanks noted that Chabot offered exactly what he needed.

"I graduated from high school as an underachieving student with lousy SAT scores, and knowing I couldn't afford tuition for college anyway, I sent my final set of stats to Chabot because it accepted everyone and was free," he said.

The classes Hanks took at Chabot are reflected in his professional successes. For example, he produced an HBO mini-series on John Adams with material he learned from his history class, and he learned about performing Shakespeare from a class on the playwright. Even his speaking abilities were honed by a public-speaking class he took at Chabot.

As a result of his own personal experience, Hanks feels that his choice was an excellent path to not only getting an education, but pursuing a profession.

"That place made me what I am today," he said.

[RETHINK]

- **What do you think Hanks means when he says, "That place made me what I am today"?**
- **Which of the courses in which you are enrolled might lead to a future profession? How?**

Looking Back

LO 7-1 Explain the best technique for getting started and writing a first draft.

- Freewriting and brainstorming can help you choose a topic.
- Identifying the audience for writing is essential.
- Breaking down large writing tasks into smaller, more manageable pieces helps pave the way to completing a writing assignment.
- Good organization, which is essential to both writer and reader, often follows the ABBCC structure: *a*rgument, *b*ackground, *b*ody, *c*ounterarguments, and *c*onclusion.

LO 7-2 Identify the process of moving from first draft to final draft.

- Use your outline as your roadmap.
- The best way to begin writing the first draft is to plunge in, starting anywhere in the paper.
- Revision is an essential part of writing: Most writing is rewriting.

LO 7-3 Discuss how to conquer fears of public speaking and make effective oral presentations.

- Although public speaking can be intimidating, audiences are generally sympathetic, speaking becomes easier once it is under way, and practice leads to success.
- The first minute of the presentation, oral transition points, visual aids, and having enough practice are important.
- Use the PREP system for giving impromptu (unrehearsed) talks.

[KEY TERMS AND CONCEPTS]

ABBCC structure (p. 187)
Argument (p. 187)
Background (p. 189)
Brainstorming (p. 181)
Freewriting (p. 180)
Impromptu talks (p. 204)
Paraphrase (p. 184)
Plagiarism (p. 196)
Thesis (p. 187)
Writing voice (p. 191)

[RESOURCES]

ON CAMPUS

If you are having difficulties with writing, the first place to turn to is a cooperative classmate. Ask someone to read a draft of a writing assignment. He or she may be able to make enough constructive comments to allow subsequent drafts to come more easily. In addition, some colleges have writing clinics where you can bring a draft of your paper and work with a counselor. Finally, your instructors may be willing to read preliminary drafts of your work.

IN PRINT

John Langan's book *College Writing Skills* (McGraw-Hill, 2013, 9th ed.) presents a fine introduction to the art and practice of writing, with specific suggestions for how to get started and for editing and polishing first drafts.

Another excellent guide to writing is William Zinsser's classic, *On Writing Well: The Classic Guide to Writing Nonfiction* (HarperResource, 2013). A widely used guide to writing, Zinsser's book is helpful both for beginners and for more experienced writers.

Finally, Stephen Lucas's book *The Art of Public Speaking* (McGraw-Hill, 2015, 12th ed.) provides an excellent introduction to public speaking. It is filled with tips for planning and delivering a talk. Carmine Gallo's *Five Stars: The Communication Secrets to Get from Good to Great* (St. Martin's Press, 2018) instructs readers how to both gain confidence in their speaking and become more persuasive in their arguments.

ON THE WEB

- Sponsored by the Capital Community College Foundation, this "Guide to Grammar and Writing" offers an abundance of links covering all aspects of good writing (**http://grammar.ccc.commnet.edu/grammar/**).
- An easy-to-use, 10-step approach to preparing a speech, with extensive links to each step, is offered by the University of Hawaii (**www.hawaii.edu/mauispeech/html/preparing_speeches.html**).
- **Bartleby.com** offers William Strunk, Jr., and E. B. White's *The Elements of Style* (**www.bartleby.com/141/**), the first edition of the classic text recommended by writing instructors for many years. This text is filled with helpful hints on word usage, punctuation, and avoiding common mistakes. It's a must for writers serious about improving their writing.
- "Plagiarism: What It Is and How to Recognize and Avoid It" at **wts.indiana.edu/writing-guides/plagiarism.html** provides excellent advice and practice in avoiding plagiarism.

The Case of . . .

The Reluctant Speaker

"No one," thought Erik Phillips, "could hate public speaking more than I do."

Erik was horrified at the thought of giving a presentation. Not only did he not like standing up in front of others, exposing himself to their scrutiny, but he was also embarrassed by his thick Louisiana accent, which his friends at the northern college he attended teased him about constantly.

He was sure he'd never be able to do it. Erik made up his mind to ask his instructor if he could write a paper instead of making the oral presentation. But before he could, one of his friends in the class told him that he had already asked for an alternative assignment and that the instructor had flatly refused, saying that it would be a "good experience" to give the talk.

Erik was stuck.

1. How would you advise Erik to prepare for and organize his talk?

2. Erik expressed a willingness to write a paper instead of giving a talk. Should he prepare the paper and read it for his presentation? Why or why not? How might he use the research for his paper to help with his talk?

3. Erik is especially nervous about speaking because he believes that his accent interferes with understanding. How might he deal with this particular anxiety? How could friends or classmates help him?

4. Do you think props would be helpful for Erik? What purpose might they serve?

5. What advice would you give Erik to reduce his anxiety?

CHAPTER

8 Choosing Your Courses and Major

Learning Outcomes

By the time you finish this chapter you will be able to

» LO 8-1 Create a plan to prepare for the academic choices that college demands.

» LO 8-2 Outline a strategy for choosing courses that ensures you are getting the most out of your studies.

» LO 8-3 Explain the criteria for choosing a major.

"Physics for Poets." The course title jumped out at Gwen Izell. She had never liked science much, but she was intrigued by this title. Here was a class that seemed designed with her in mind. "Physics for Poets," the description began, "is designed for nonscience majors. It presents the links between physics and the arts." Gwen decided to take a chance and enroll in the class.

It turned out to be one of the best decisions she ever made. She loved the course. The instructor was terrific, making physics fascinating. Not only did she begin to like the subject matter, but she was also good at it.

Gwen was hooked. She took several other science courses over the next semesters. And during her senior year she found herself in an interview with a middle school principal, telling him—a bit to her surprise—that she'd be glad to teach seventh-grade physical science.

Looking Ahead

Our academic and professional careers are propelled by many forces, not the least of which is chance. Gwen Izell, like many other students, found a new direction while leafing through her course list. Although she never would have predicted at the start of college that she would end up taking a variety of science courses and teaching physics, her willingness to take a chance in selecting a course led to a new passion and to a career opportunity.

In this chapter we focus on choosing an academic course of study, one of the central challenges of college life. Not only do the choices we make color our entire college experience, but they also may determine the path we follow once we graduate.

This chapter begins by considering the many choices that you'll have to make as a routine part of attending college, including the choice of courses, instructors, and especially majors—each of which has long-term implications. You'll learn ways to select courses each term that meet your personal needs and maximize your chances of getting the courses you want.

Ultimately, the degree to which your college education benefits you is in your hands. By learning various strategies, you can act decisively to get the most out of your college experience.

» LO 8-1 Making Academic Choices

It's a moment filled with promise.

A list of courses for the upcoming term pops up on the computer screen in front of you. Many of the courses sound interesting. Each offers the possibilities of new knowledge and therefore has the potential to change your life in significant ways.

As you scroll through the listing of courses and begin to make your decisions, you may be feeling a range of emotions: anticipation over what you'll learn; hope that the course can bring you closer to your dreams; fear that you won't be able to do well; and excitement that you're proceeding with your college career, taking another of the many small steps that will eventually add up to a complete journey through college.

Choosing what courses to take can be intimidating. But if you approach the problem thoughtfully, your final choices will make the best of the possibilities offered. Let's consider how to proceed, using the P.O.W.E.R. Plan as a guide.

P Prepare Becoming Familiar with Your Options and Requirements

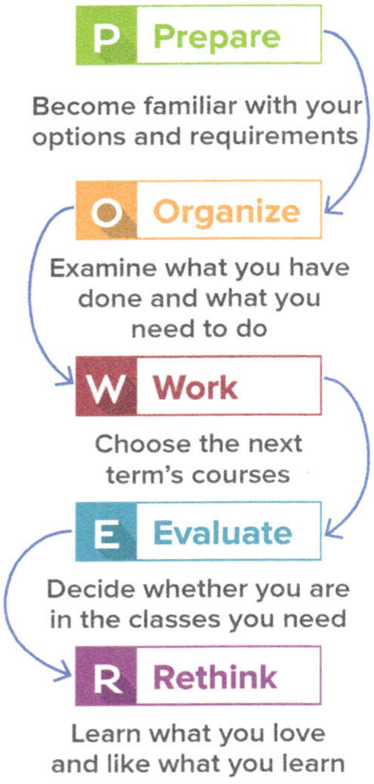

P.O.W.E.R. Plan

Choosing which courses to take requires that you take several significant preparatory steps before you jump in. These include the following:

Familiarize Yourself with Your College Requirements

Every college has a *catalog of courses and requirements*—which may be in a document located entirely online, published as a hard-copy booklet, or both. The catalog provides you with information about your education: what's offered, its cost, and the steps you need to take in obtaining a college degree.

The catalog of college requirements is actually a legally binding document that offers you a contract. If you are admitted to the college and you fulfill certain requirements (such as taking a particular set of courses, maintaining a certain level of grades, and—let us not forget—paying your tuition bills on time), you'll get something in return. That something is a college degree.

Because they outline contractual obligations, catalogs containing college requirements are important. They provide a summary of what your institution expects and offers in a number of areas:

1. **Academic regulations.** Every college has strict rules, requirements, and policies; these are all spelled out either online or in a written document. For example, to graduate you need to take a certain number of courses or course credits. Similarly, if you wish to add or drop a course, you must do so by a certain date.

   In addition, colleges often require that you maintain a certain grade point average. A **grade point average** (or **GPA**; also known as a *quality point average*) is a numeric average in which letter grades are transformed into numbers. Most colleges use a four-point scale in which A = 4, B = 3, C = 2, D = 1, and F = 0. In such a system, a 3.0 GPA is equivalent to a B average, while a 3.5 would be halfway between an A and a B.

   For example, if your five grades for a term were A, A, B, B, and C, and all the courses had the same number of credits, you would translate your grades into 4, 4, 3, 3, and 2. Next, you would sum the numbers and divide by the number of courses to find the average. That works out to $[(4 + 4 + 3 + 3 + 2) \div 5]$, or a 3.2 GPA. In addition, if you have access to your transcript online, your college may calculate your GPA for you each semester.

2. **Academic programs.** Most listings of college requirements contain a description of the school's academic departments and its majors. A **major** is a specialization in a particular subject area, each requiring a set course of study.

   Requirements for majors generally fall into two or three categories:

   - *College-wide or university-wide requirements* that every student enrolled in the college or university must fulfill.
   - *Major requirements.* These are specific requirements for each particular major. To major in an area, you must take a specified number of courses or credits in that area. Furthermore, there also may be specific courses you must take.

grade point average (GPA)
Also known as quality point average. A numeric average in which letter grades are transformed into numbers.

major
A specialization in a particular subject area, requiring a set course of study.

- *Academic unit requirements.* Finally, if the major falls within a broader academic unit (such as a school of education or school of business), that broader entity may have its own requirements for a degree. For example, an accounting major might have to complete not only the requirements for an accounting major, but the requirements for the school of management, and the requirements for the university or college.

For instance, a psychology major might be required to fulfill college-wide requirements that apply to all students enrolled in the college, such as a specified number of English, writing, math, and science courses. The Department of Psychology will have its own separate requirements for its majors to complete, such as taking no fewer than six psychology courses. Finally, because the Department of Psychology may be housed in a more general division of Social Sciences, there may be divisional requirements to fulfill (perhaps a course in social science methodology or a foreign language requirement).

The college requirements also provide information for students who have transferred from another college. For instance, transfer students may receive credit for only a certain number of courses or credits earned at their first institution. Or they may be required to take particular courses even if they already took them at their previous school.

If you attend a two-year community college, your college may also provide information on transferring to a four-year school. Many two-year colleges often have articulation agreements. *Articulation agreements* are formal agreements between a two-year and a four-year college in which the four-year college automatically accepts certain courses or credits taken at your current institution.

Articulation agreements may even spell out what groups or blocks of courses will be accepted, as a set, by a four-year college. Knowing what courses will automatically be counted at other colleges is crucial if you are thinking about transferring later.

3. **Course listings.** The list of requirements usually includes all the courses the school offers, even though not all of them may be offered every term. Courses are listed by department, and the descriptions typically include the course name, the number of credits the course provides, and a short description.

   Sometimes course descriptions also name the instructors who teach the course and the time and place the class meets. However, this information may also be published separately.

4. Some courses have **prerequisites**—requirements that must be fulfilled before one can enroll. If the course has a prerequisite, this will be stated. Take these prerequisites seriously, because you will not be permitted to enroll in a course if you haven't completed the prerequisite for it. In addition, the prerequisite course may not be offered every term, so you may have to wait a year (or more!) before getting into the course you want.

prerequisites
Requirements that must be fulfilled before a student may enroll in a course or discipline.

Make an Appointment with Your College Advisor

The job of a **college advisor** (sometimes called a *college counselor*) is to give you good, clear-headed advice. Your advisor will be someone who knows the ins and outs of the college's regulations, and whose experience working with other students provides a good deal of knowledge in other areas as well. Advisors can help you figure out what classes to take, how to overcome academic bureaucracies, whom to go to about a problem, and generally how to prepare yourself for graduation and beyond. They can even provide information on extracurricular activities, volunteer opportunities, and part-time jobs.

college advisor
An individual who provides students with advice about their academic careers.

College advisors can play an important role in your academic career, providing valuable advice, helping you overcome problems, and making sure that you meet all the requirements needed to graduate.
©Monkey Business Images/Shutterstock

Advisors are particularly busy at the beginning of each term (as well as when the course schedule comes out). Consequently, find out their office hours, schedule an appointment early, and be sure to keep your scheduled appointment. Don't go unprepared when you do go. **Figure 8.1** provides a checklist you should go through before your appointment.

Advisors can be tremendously valuable resources. Take some time to get to know your advisor as a person—and to let him or her get to know you. To get a better sense of who your own advisor is, complete **Try It! 1**, "Get to Know Your College Advisor."

If you find that you and your advisor aren't a good match and you know of another advisor who is willing and qualified to advise you, you might consider making a switch. Just be sure you have given your original advisor a chance. It is not your advisor's fault, for example, that you missed your only chance this year to take astronomy. Similarly, even though you may not like your advisor's message ("You still need to take a science course"), this doesn't mean that he or she doesn't have your best interests at heart. If you feel you can trust and speak with your advisor frankly, you and your college career will have gained a valuable ally.

> "It can be no dishonor to learn from others when they speak good sense."
>
> **Sophocles, author,** ***The Antigone of Sophocles: With Short English Notes for the Use of Schools*** **(Oxford: J. Parker and Co, 1867).**

No matter how helpful your advisor is (or how unsupportive, for that matter), remember that ultimately *you* are responsible for your academic career. Advisors

figure 8.1
Advisor Visit Checklist

- ______ Check the college catalog for information about the advisor, noting any potential links or conversational topics that might be used to open the meeting.
- ______ Be on time, be aware of how much time is scheduled for your appointment, and check the time frequently during the appointment.
- ______ Summarize who you are (e.g., hometown, high school, grades in high school, interests, high school or community college activities, etc.) to begin the more formal part of the meeting.
- ______ List some or all of the courses you plan to take in the next term.
- ______ Prepare some questions about your course choices (e.g., difficulty of the courses, whether they match your interests, whether they will fulfill your requirements, what future courses or career choices they might lead to, personality of the instructors, etc.).
- ______ List the extracurricular activities you're considering.
- ______ Prepare some questions about these activities (e.g., how time-consuming, how interesting, what sorts of students participate in them, etc.).
- ______ Be prepared to ask about the advisor's impressions of the college.
- ______ Be prepared to ask the advisor to recommend activities, events, and the like, on campus or off, and which to avoid.
- ______ List any other issues you would like to raise (e.g., impressions of the college so far, roommate issues, personal issues, etc.).
- ______ Be prepared to ask about the availability of the advisor during the future (e.g., office hours, calling outside office hours, etc.).
- ______ Remember to thank the advisor before leaving.

1 | **Try It!** POWER

Get to Know Your College Advisor

It is helpful to get a feel for who your advisor is, so schedule a 15- to 30-minute appointment with him or her. Before you meet with your advisor, do some background research by looking at your college requirements. You can also usually find information on the background of faculty and staff, listing their titles, where they went to college and graduate school, what departments they teach in, and what their areas of academic interest are. In addition, many instructors have their own home pages that describe their background.

To learn more about your advisor, cover some of these topics when you meet:

- Philosophy of college advising
- Words of advice
- Things to try at the college
- Things to avoid at the college

After you have met with your advisor, answer the following questions:

1. How would you describe your advisor as a person?
2. What things did you learn that can help you?
3. How can you use your advisor's responses to take better advantage of what your college has to offer?

are human like the rest of us, they can't know everything, and they can make mistakes. You should double-check what your advisor tells you. Remember that in the end you need to take charge of your own college experience.

O Organize

Examining What You Have Done and What You Need to Do

Where Are You?

If you've prepared well, you have a basic understanding of how the courses you are taking now or have already taken fulfill your college requirements. To figure out what you still need to do, you should organize a complete list of the requirements you need to fulfill to graduate.

Try It! 2, "Create a List of Required Courses," provides a form that you can complete. (Sometimes colleges will offer such a list–known as a *degree audit*–online.

2

Try It! POWER

Create a List of Required Courses

Use the form below to list all of your required courses. The form covers both prerequisite courses (i.e., courses you must take before you can take other courses) and requirements imposed by your college, the division of which your department is a part, and your department. In addition, the form allows you to indicate both credit requirements and grade requirements.

List of Required Courses							
Type of Course	Credits Required	Credits Completed	Grade Required	Grade Achieved	Whose Requirement?		
					College	Division	Department
I. Prerequisite Courses							
Total Prerequisite Courses							
II. Required Courses							
Total Required Courses							

What does the information in the chart tell you? How can you use it to plan your future course selections? What courses do you wish to take that are not requirements? How much leeway do you have to take nonrequired courses?

If yours does, you should check it frequently to make sure you are moving ahead in the right direction.)

Even if you have yet to decide on a major, you might now be taking courses to satisfy requirements for a major you are considering. Noting this on your list will help you make decisions and plan for the future.

If this is just the start of your college career, you'll probably have completed only a few of the requirements. Don't let the blank spaces on the form overwhelm you; the credits have a way of adding up quickly.

> "Choosing courses can make or break you in college. The better you are at it, the better your grades and the less your aggravation."
>
> **Student, University of Colorado, in Tyler, S. *Been There, Should've Done That.* (Haslett, MI: Front Porch Press, 1997).**

If you are farther along in your college career and have trouble remembering what courses you've taken, get a copy of your transcript from the registrar, or–if you have online access–print out a copy. The **registrar** is the college official who oversees the scheduling of courses, the maintenance of transcripts, and the creation and retention of other official documents. (A **transcript** is the official record of the courses you've taken and the grades you received in them.)

It's also a good idea to check your transcript periodically to make sure it's accurate and to keep a record of course descriptions from your college course listings. You might need the course descriptions if you apply for graduate school or must be certified for a particular occupation.

registrar
The college official designated to oversee the scheduling of courses, the maintenance of grades and transcripts, and the creation and retention of other official documents.

transcript
A college's official record of courses taken and grades received by students.

As you're recording the courses you've taken, remember that meeting graduation requirements may not be the same as meeting your major's requirements. For instance, some schools require not only that you take and pass certain courses, but sometimes also that you achieve a certain minimum grade in your courses as a whole. Or you may have to get a grade of C or better in a course for it to be counted toward your major. In this case, if you received a C– in the course, you'd still get credit toward graduation, but the course wouldn't count toward the number of credits you needed in your major.

Confusing? You bet. That's why it's important to keep track of where you stand from the very start of your college career. (It's a good idea to keep all relevant information together on your computer or in a file folder.) There's no worse surprise than finding out a month before you thought you'd be graduating that you lack some critical requirement. Don't count on others to keep track of this information for you. No one knows more about what you've done than you do.

Where Are You Going?

You should also use the information you have recorded to help determine which courses you should take in the upcoming term. Once you have declared a major, you can add those requirements to your record.

Now that you know where you are and where you are going, you are ready to start selecting courses to take you there.

» LO 8-2

W Work

Choosing the Next Term's Courses

The course listings for the next term are published online or in print in a *course schedule.* It is typically organized by department, with each course in the department having a number, such as "History 204: The French Revolution." Generally, the higher the number, the more advanced the course. The course schedule will tell you when and where the class meets and whether there are any prerequisites for the course.

Go with What You Know

Chances are, you already know of at least one or two courses you need to take in a given term. Perhaps this is the term you plan to fulfill your natural science or your foreign language requirement. There may be some courses you have been waiting to take, since some courses are taught only once a year. A good place to begin is to find out when these courses are given and where.

Draft a Personal Schedule for the Term

First, make a list of when the courses you absolutely have to take are scheduled. If you have a choice of days of the week and times when a course meets, choose one you prefer. Take into consideration whether you are a "morning person," at your best first thing in the morning, or whether you usually drag yourself out of bed in the morning and don't fully function until noon. This will be the beginning of your time management for the upcoming term.

electives
Courses that are not required.

Next, choose **electives**—courses that are not required. Keep in mind broad considerations about the kinds of courses you need to take for your major and for graduation. But also explore courses that simply sound interesting to you. College offers the opportunity to discover who you are and what you like and do best, but the only way that can happen is by your taking intellectual risks.

Try to balance easier and more difficult courses for a particular term. You don't want to load up on all highly challenging courses. In addition, signing up for too many courses in a single term—beyond the norm for you—can be self-defeating. (For more on choosing courses, see the **Course Connections**.)

To get started in deciding which courses to take for the upcoming term, complete **Try It! 3**, "Choose Your Courses."

register
Formally enroll in courses.

When registering online, make sure to check that your course information is correct.
©James Woodson/Photodisc/Getty Images

Register for Courses

The rest of the work of choosing courses consists of registering. When you **register**, you formally enroll in your chosen classes.

Meeting with your advisor is an essential preliminary step. Sometimes it's mandatory, and you won't be allowed to register without your advisor's approval of the choices you've made. But even if it's not required, it's important to review your proposed course of studies with an advisor. You may have overlooked something, or your advisor may be able to suggest some alternative courses that will work better for you.

Remember, though, that the ultimate responsibility for taking the right courses rests with you. Advisors sometimes make mistakes and overlook a requirement; ultimately, you know best what's right for you.

Course **Connections**

What Are Courses *Really* Like? The Covert College Catalog

Although the official college catalog is the place to start to identify courses that you need to take, there's a wealth of other sorts of unofficial information about courses that you can make use of. Tapping into this often-hidden body of knowledge can help you make informed judgments about which courses are best for you.

Among the sources of information about courses you're considering:

- **Current instructors.** Your current instructors know their colleagues and their reputations and may be willing to provide you with off-the-record suggestions.
- **Your classmates.** Ask your classmates for experiences and advice in particular classes, knowing this is colored by their own performance in the class. In addition, students have their own biases, and they are not always objective in their evaluations of instructors. For some, "easy course" equals "good course." That's why you should be extremely wary of material on such online evaluation sites as "Rate My Professor." Sometimes the students who provide comments have a dispute with the instructor, and the students who bother to provide comments often do not represent a fair sampling of views.
- **Instructor evaluations.** Sometimes schools permit access to instructor evaluations from previous terms. If these are available, they can be used to get an idea of how other students have reacted to a class you're considering taking. (Although you might be tempted to consider social media public online ratings of instructors, be extremely suspicious of the information you find. Online ratings suffer from a variety of problems. You will have no idea how representative the online ratings are, because there's no way of knowing what percentage of a class is represented in the ratings. Furthermore, online rating systems often attract students with an ax to grind or students who care only about how easy a class is.)
- **Previous course syllabus.** An instructor may post a class syllabus online or may keep it on file in a departmental office. By examining the syllabus, you'll see exactly what a course covers (and how it compares to the official course description in the catalog).
- **Course instructors themselves.** Sit in on a class that you're thinking about taking, or talk with instructors during their office hours. There's nothing more direct than what you'll learn from the person who will be teaching the course in the upcoming term.

After meeting with your advisor, your next step will be to formally register. Course registration varies significantly from one school to another. In some cases, it's a matter of listing course numbers on a form, along with some alternatives.

In most schools, you register for your courses using an automated system, online or using your cell phone. If your college uses web-based registration, you will be prompted to enter course information on a web form, and your registration will be accomplished completely online (see **Figure 8.2**).

E Evaluate

Deciding Whether You Are in the Classes You Need

Picture this horror story:

You receive your grade report from the previous term. You're excited because you know you've done well. You're especially looking forward to seeing your Spanish grade because you know you were on the borderline between an A− and a B+.

3

Try It! POWER

Choose Your Courses

Use the form below to make your course selections for the coming term. The form will allow you to verify that you are meeting course requirements, avoiding schedule conflicts, and signing up for instructors you want.

Course Selections

Term: ______________________________

Course Name and Number	Credits	Required Course or Just for Fun?	Prerequisites Met?	Grade Required	Days Class Meets	Times Class Meets	Instructor Name	Instructor Permission Required?

After completing the chart, answer these questions: How does the next semester seem to be shaping up? Will you be able to take courses you *want* to take, as opposed to those you *need* to take? Have you encountered any conflicts and considered ways to deal with them? Have you made any choices that open you to new intellectual possibilities?

Instead you're astounded to see that there is no grade listed for the Spanish class, but you've received an F in a French class that you didn't even take. That F pulls down your grade point average, and at the bottom of your grade report is an announcement that you are on academic probation.

Here's the explanation: Because of an error during registration, you were never formally enrolled in the Spanish course, even though you actually spent the entire term attending classes in the course. To compound the mistake, your instructor never noticed that you weren't on her class roster. At the end of the term, when she was filling out her grade report, she didn't notice that your name wasn't listed. So no grade was reported for Spanish.

At the same time, the instructor of the French class in which you were erroneously enrolled had to give you a grade at the end of the semester. Because you never completed any assignments or took any tests, your average for the semester was 0—warranting an F for the term. That F is what appeared on your grade report.

Before you go online, fill in this entire worksheet, listing all courses you wish to add, drop, or change including laboratory and discussion sections, and the appropriate "action codes" you will enter. Be sure to fill in all boxed areas properly.

1. Call the system at (555) 444-3214 (From On-Campus, call 4-3214)
2. Enter your student ID number 1 2 6 - 0 4 - 9 8 1 1
3. Enter your branch code 1 (Undergraduate = 1, Graduate = 2)
4. Enter your personal ID number (PIN) 6 7 7 5
5. If the Schedule Confirmation you receive in the mail instructs you to get from your advisor a Registration Approval Code before add/drop, enter that code ☐ ☐ ☐ ☐
6. For each add, drop, or change you want to make, enter the appropriate action code from the list below and the schedule number for the course you want affected by that action.

Action Code*	Schedule Number of Course Requested	Dept	Course #	Section #	Crd	Day/Time
10	782840	Psych	102	1	3	T-T 11:15-12:30
10	672947	Engl	231	1	3	M-W-F 9:05-9:55
10	260463	Phed	102	2	1	M 4:00-4:50
10	120309	Latn	124	1	3	T-T 9:00-10:15
10	880181	Hist	102	1	3	M-W-F 10:10-11:05
10	724962	Phys	101	3	3	T-T 2:30-3:45

7. After completing the form, enter the online registration system at www.umass.edu/virtual-registrar and enter your username and password.

*Action Code	Action
10	**ADD** a course or Swap between sections of a course (To **SWAP**, simply add the new section; the old section will automatically be dropped from your schedule.)
30	**ADD** a course with **Pass/Fail** option or **CHANGE** existing course to **Pass/Fail**
90	**DROP** a course
80	**REMOVE Pass/Fail** or **Audit** option from existing course
50	**CHANGE** variable credit for an existing variable credit course
40	**ADD** a course with **AUDIT** grading option or **CHANGE** existing course to **AUDIT** grading
60	**LIST** your course schedule

Note: Action Codes 30 and 80 are not available to graduate students. 40 is not available to undergraduates.

figure 8.2
A Sample Telephone/Web Course Registration Worksheet

The situation—which is far more likely to occur at a large university than at a small college—might be seen as a comedy of errors if it weren't so painful. Fortunately, if this were actually your story, it would most likely have a happy ending—eventually. You would go to your college registrar, who would be able to tell you what to do to get the F erased and the appropriate grade added. Still, undoing the cascade of errors would take time and a considerable amount of effort.

Difficulties such as these are encountered by a surprising number of students every term. Many problems, however, can be avoided with a bit of "due diligence" on the part of the student. One key is to evaluate your success in registering.

First, be sure you actually are registered formally for the courses you think you are. In most schools, you can verify on the web whether you have successfully enrolled in the courses you want. If your college doesn't use an online registration system, you should receive an acknowledgement, in writing, of the courses in which you are enrolled for the upcoming term. Make absolutely sure you are enrolled in the courses you intended to enroll in.

Second, whether you have online access or a hard copy, carefully look over the courses in which you are enrolled. Use the following checklist to determine how successful your efforts to register have been:

- Are the courses in which you are enrolled the ones you wanted?
- Are the times accurate? Are there any conflicts?
- Have any substitutions been made?
- Are you registered for the number of credits that you wanted to be registered for?

Third, if there are any problems, try to correct the situation immediately. If there has been a clerical or computer error, you should pay a visit to the registrar's office. Sometimes, though, you'll find that there was no mistake. Class sizes are almost always limited, and not every student who wants to enroll can do so, either because of physical limitations (the room can hold only a certain number of students) or because of educational considerations (learning may be maximized when only a small number of students are in the class).

When a course is overbooked, you have several alternatives. One is to sign up for another section of the course that is not overbooked. Another is to attempt to register for an entirely different course.

Finally, you may appeal directly to the course instructor. Instructors sometimes will permit particularly interested or motivated students to enroll in the class, even if the official capacity has been reached. You may find that approaching an instructor with a polite request may yield you a slot in the course after all.

If none of these alternatives works, you will have to add a course to the ones you have already registered for. How do you add courses after the registration period has ended? Often, you'll need to complete a special form. Depending on the timing of your request, the form may require the signature of the instructor whose course you are adding. In other cases, you may be able to add and drop courses online, depending on the course registration system your college uses.

Also keep in mind that if you drop a class during a term, you must do it officially, through the registrar and course registration system. Simply ceasing to attend doesn't mean you'll be dropped from the class list. Instead, you'll probably end up with a failing grade in the course unless you complete the necessary paperwork to officially drop the course.

"Help—I Can't Get into the Courses That I Need to Graduate!"

For some students, their efforts to register result in utter disaster. Sometimes most or all of their first choices are unavailable, and they end up enrolled in only a few of the courses they had requested. Or perhaps they cannot get into the one crucial course required for graduation.

Whatever the problem, there are several steps you can take to improve the situation:

- **Don't despair–act!** There is virtually no academic problem that can't be solved in some way. Focus your energies on finding a creative solution to the problem.
- **Identify classes that are still available and enroll in them.** There are probably many classes offered at your college that are still available. Registrars or departments often maintain lists of classes that have many openings.
- **Talk with your advisor.** Perhaps what you think of as an absolute requirement can be waived or appealed. Or maybe some other course can substitute for a particular required course.
- **Speak with individual course instructors.** It may be that the instructor of the course you need will make an exception and permit you to enroll; it can't hurt to ask.
- **Take necessary courses through another division at your college.** Some schools have Continuing Education divisions that offer courses in the evenings, on weekends, during the summer, or online. It may be the same course you would take as part of your normal curriculum, but in this case it is offered through a separate division of your college. The big drawback: You'll have to pay extra for the course, above and beyond normal tuition and fees.
- **Consider taking a must-have, required course at another college.** If you live in an area where there are other schools in the vicinity, it may be possible to enroll in a course that you simply must take at another school. It also may be possible to take the course using distance learning. **Distance learning** courses (also known as online learning courses) are taught by many institutions, and students participate via the web.

distance learning
The teaching of courses at another institution, with student participation via video technology or the web.

Before you take a course offered by a college other than your own, make sure that you'll receive credit for the course at your school. Also keep in mind that you'll probably have to pay for courses offered by other schools over and above what you've already spent for your own school's tuition.

R Rethink

Learning What You Love and Loving What You Learn

Take one step back. No, make that two steps back.

Stepping back and taking stock of where you are in your course of studies and where you're headed are essential tasks. In fact, they are among the most important things you can do during your college career. In one extreme, you can plod through your courses, focused only on day-to-day deadlines and tribulations, and blindly move forward with only the goal of getting your requirements out of the way. Or, alternatively, you can gain a sense of satisfaction as you progress toward your own goals and see yourself grow as a person.

Taking stock of your course of studies is not something you need to do every day, or once a week, or even once a month. But you should do it, without fail, at least once every term. Circle a date on your calendar so you'll be sure to do it, and treat it no differently from any other deadline you simply can't miss.

When you do take stock, answer the questions in **Try It! 4**. If you're satisfied with your answers, feel affirmed in the choices you've made. You're on the right

4  WORKING IN A GROUP

Try It! P O W E R

Reflect on Your College Experience

As you proceed in college, take a few moments at regular intervals (e.g., once a semester, once a year) to rethink your entire college experience. With a small group of classmates, discuss your reactions to the following topics and questions:

COURSEWORK

- Are my courses moving me toward my educational, career, and personal goals?
- Are the classes I'm taking helping me meet my short- and long-term goals?
- Are the classes I'm taking meeting my expectations?

PERSONAL COMMITMENT

- Am I working hard to get the most out of the classes I'm taking?
- Am I doing my best in every class?
- Am I keeping the goal of learning—apart from doing well in classes—in mind as I progress through my classes?

PERSONAL GROWTH

- What personal growth am I experiencing?
- Am I becoming closer to the person I want to be?
- Are my critical thinking abilities growing?

COLLEGE

- Is my school providing me with the best educational experience possible?
- Am I learning not only in the classroom but also outside the classroom?
- Am I learning from my fellow students as well as my instructors?

CHANGES

- Is there anything (my course selections, my major, or my college) that I should consider changing?
- Have I made the best choices in the past? How can I remedy mistakes that I have made?

track, and you should feel secure in the knowledge that you're getting from college what you want to.

On the other hand, if you're less than satisfied with the answers you come up with, take action. Choose courses in the future that better match your goals. Consider changing your major to one that more closely reflects what you want to get out of college. And, if you're truly unhappy with the way your college career is proceeding, consider changing colleges.

Whichever option you choose, don't simply accept dissatisfaction with your college career. There are few times in our lives when we have the opportunity to partake of an experience that has the potential to raise us to new intellectual and emotional heights. College should be intellectually enlightening and exciting. We should be able to see how our education is preparing us for the rest of our lives. The worst thing we can do is let the time slip away without being confident that our college experience is the best experience possible.

Service Learning: Helping Yourself by Helping Others

As you make decisions about what courses to take, you should be sure to consider those that involve service learning. In courses with **service learning** components, you engage in community service activities–while getting course credit for the experience.

service learning
Courses that allow a student to engage in community service activities while getting course credit for the experience.

Service learning is a win-win activity. It links classroom education to real-world community needs. As a student, you are able to gain valuable experience and knowledge that can give you greater insight into a subject area. You can build on the material that you are learning in class and apply that information outside the classroom to real-world situations. Students in a class can share their service learning experiences, thereby expanding their understanding of the subject matter.

In addition, you can learn useful skills that can be helpful in your future career. Working outside the classroom can give you experience that will make you a more desirable job candidate. Finally, service learning can help you learn more about yourself and what your strengths and weaknesses are.

Your community is a winner, too. It receives critical support that immediately can improve the quality of life for its citizens. In fact, your efforts can have an impact that echoes for years.

Community service activities span a vast range. For instance, you might tutor an elementary school child in an after-school program as part of a course in elementary education. You'll learn firsthand about the reading process, while the skills (and perhaps motivation) of the child being tutored improve.

Or you might enroll in an abnormal psychology class and volunteer at a halfway house for patients with severe psychological disorders. You'll gain a firsthand understanding of disorders that would be impossible to gain simply from reading a textbook, while the patient may benefit from the social interaction you provide. Other examples of service learning activities are shown in **Table 8.1**.

table 8.1 Service Learning Possibilities
Here are just a few possibilities for service learning activities:
• Develop a website for a social service agency.
• Participate in a "Big Brother" or "Big Sister" program.
• Raise funds for a local food bank.
• Register voters for the next election.
• Volunteer at a local government office.
• Help organize a Special Olympics for people with developmental disabilities.
• Participate in an educational program to protect the environment.
• Help staff a shelter for battered women.
• Volunteer to feed the homeless.
• Organize a blood drive.
To learn of more service learning opportunities, go to the website of the National Clearinghouse for Service Learning Organizations, Networks, and Resources at **www.gsn.nylc.org/clearinghouse.**

Whatever service learning activity you do, there are several basic principles to keep in mind:

- **Ask questions.** Don't feel shy about asking for clarification of your responsibilities. It's the best way to maximize your learning. Remember, though, that the staff may be overworked and may not have time to immediately respond.
- **Maintain a positive outlook.** You may face challenges unlike those you've encountered before. You may see things that are upsetting and depressing. Keep your own good fortune in mind, and be grateful for the opportunity for growth that the experience is providing you.
- **Go with the flow.** You may not agree with everything that is being done at your placement site, but don't think that your ideas are necessarily better than those of the professionals who work there. Voice your concerns, but remember that you're at the site to help, not to make the rules.
- **Keep your commitments.** The staff depends on you. If you don't complete a task or fail to show up, you are leaving someone in the lurch and shirking your responsibilities.
- **If you have concerns, discuss them with your supervisor and faculty sponsor.** Don't let your concerns fester. If you're asked to do things that you believe are inappropriate, discuss them with the appropriate person.
- **Keep a journal.** You'll probably be required to keep a journal of your experiences for the academic class attached to your service learning experience. Even if you're not, keep a journal anyway. Writing in a journal offers a way of reflecting on the meaning of your experiences, as well as providing an enduring record of what you've accomplished.

Many students point to service learning as the high point of their college career. And for most, it's not because of what they have gained personally—even though that's a significant part of it—but because of the difference they made in improving the lives of others. To consider service learning further, complete **Try It! 5**.

If you're having trouble choosing a major, one strategy is to consider the kinds of activities you most like doing outside the academic arena. For example, if you've enjoyed coaching a youth baseball team, you might want to consider an education major.
©BananaStock/Alamy

» LO 8-3 Choosing Your Major

You attend a family gathering and encounter relatives you haven't seen for a while. What's the first question they ask when you say you're attending college? You can bet on it: "What's your major?"

Although one could argue that there are lots of other important questions that you could be asked—"What interesting things have you learned?" comes to mind—having a central focus of study is an important part of college. A major is important because it focuses what we study, leading us to become experts in a specific area.

Some students know what they want to major in when they begin college; some don't have a clue. That's fine. No one says you should know right away.

Try It! POWER

Explore Service Learning Opportunities

To find out about the service learning opportunities available to you, complete the following activities:

A. Examine the courses offered at your college and identify three that contain service learning components.

1. Course number and name ______________________
   What is the service learning activity?

2. Course number and name ______________________
   What is the service learning activity?

3. Course number and name ______________________
   What is the service learning activity?

B. Identify three potential service learning activities in your community by contacting social service agencies, food banks, the Red Cross, or religious organizations. You can also do research on the web.

1. Organization name ______________________
   What is the service learning activity you might conduct?

2. Organization name ______________________
   What is the service learning activity you might conduct?

3. Organization name ______________________
   What is the service learning activity you might conduct?

WORKING IN A GROUP

Compare your findings with those of other students in your class. What opportunities did you find? What service learning opportunities might you seek out in the future? Discuss what you see as the advantages and disadvantages of service learning.

In fact, some educators feel that it's better to delay choosing a major. Waiting gives you the opportunity to explore a range of possibilities and gain a more rounded education. Exposure to subjects such as history, art, and literature provides people with a common background and critical thinking skills that are useful, no matter what they eventually study and choose as a career.

Furthermore, taking a variety of classes in a broad range of courses can lead to quite practical outcomes. Look at **Table 8.2**, which shows areas that employers

table 8.2 Employer Priorities and Consensus on College Learning Outcomes

Knowledge of Human Cultures and the Physical and Natural World	
• Broad knowledge in the liberal arts and sciences	80%■
• Knowledge of global issues and about societies and cultures outside the US	78%■
• Knowledge about science and technology	56%❖
Intellectual and Practical Skills	
• Critical thinking and analytic reasoning	82%❖
• Complex problem solving	81%❖
• Written and oral communication	80%❖
• Information literacy	72%❖
• Innovation and creativity	71%❖
• Teamwork skills in diverse groups	67%❖
• Quantitative reasoning	55%❖
Personal and Social Responsibility	
• Problem solving in diverse settings	91%■
• Ethical issues/public debates important in their field	87%■
• Civic knowledge, skills, and judgment essential for contributing to the community and to our democratic society	82%■
• Ethical decision making	64%❖
Integrative and Applied Learning	
• Direct experiences with community problem solving	86%■
• Applied knowledge in real-world settings	78%❖

Notes:

■ indicates percentage of employers who "strongly agree" or "somewhat agree" that, "regardless of a student's chosen field of study," every student should attain this area of knowledge or skill.

❖ indicates percentage of employers who say they want colleges/universities to "place more emphasis" on this area of knowledge/skill.

Source: *Hart Research Associates. It Makes More than a Major: Employer Priorities for College Learning and Student Success* (Washington, DC: AAC&U, 2013), **www.aacu.org/leap/public_opinion_research.cfm**.

want emphasized in colleges. The skill areas in which employers are interested can be attained only by taking a broad array of courses.

In addition, taking a variety of classes in a broad range of subjects can help you identify a major that you're really interested in. You might find after taking a civics course that you have a passion for legal studies. Or a physics class may lead you to consider a major in engineering. College is meant to be a time of exploration, and leaving yourself open to the future—and the unknown—is a completely reasonable thing to do. (To begin your own exploration of majors, complete **Try It! 6**, "Identify Major Attractions.")

But what if you don't have any idea which major you wish to pursue? If you are still in your first year of college, you have plenty of time to make up your mind. Here are some approaches that should help:

1. **Celebrate your indecision.** If you don't have to make a decision for some time, take advantage of the situation. Enjoy the fact that you're uncommitted and that you have an uncommon degree of freedom. In addition, remember that there are a lot of others in the position of not knowing what to major in. Many students struggle to identify a major, and some change majors a number of times, just as most people change careers several times.
2. **Focus on your interests.** Take a long look inward, paying attention to what your interests are. What do you most like to do in life? What are your strengths and weaknesses? What do you want to get out of life? The more you know about yourself, the easier it will become to narrow down the choices for a major. Completing the **Journal Reflections**, "Focusing on Your Interests," is a good place to start.
3. **Seek the help of others.** College campuses provide many resources to help their students choose a major (and also to help narrow the choices for potential careers). Talk to other students majoring in areas that interest you. Find out what they like and don't like about the field and its requirements. You will probably find your interest in the major grows or diminishes depending on how you feel about the issues they mention.

   Speak with your advisor. If you've gotten to know your advisor, he or she can often provide reasonable, helpful information. For instance, you may be able to find out about the strengths and weaknesses of various departments.

   You can also turn to your college counseling or career center. Most colleges have offices that can provide information about the different majors, including information about career opportunities typically available to graduates with the various majors. Sometimes it's possible to take tests that will help focus your choices, pinpointing how your interests, values, and personality type fit with particular careers.
4. **Consider double-majoring—or inventing your own major.** Although it's not easy, there are paths you can take if you know clearly what you want to do, but find it doesn't fit a single existing major. A **double major** is a course of study that fulfills all the requirements for each of two majors. If you can't decide between two majors, or if you are interested in a career that overlaps two majors, this is a reasonable solution. The downside: It can be an awful lot of work. Because both majors usually carry a number of their own requirements, you may have

"I sat back thinking that the right major would just pop into my head. It didn't."

Senior, University of Connecticut, in Tyler, S., *Been There, Should've Done That* (Haslett, MI: Front Porch Press, 1997).

"He who hesitates is sometimes saved."

James Thurber, author, "The Glass in the Field," *The New Yorker* (31 October 1939).

double major
A course of study that fulfills all the requirements for two majors.

Journal Reflections

Focusing on Your Interests

The following questions are intended to lead you to explore areas of personal preference and interest that should inform your choice of a major. These questions are informal and designed to be answered briefly; more extended and formal "interest inventories" are available in your college's counseling office.

1. Do you think you would enjoy being told precisely what to do and how to do it, or would you rather work things out by yourself, without extensive instructions or supervision? What implications might your answer have for a choice of majors?

2. Are you ambitious and success-oriented and not ashamed to admit that you'd like to earn a lot of money, or are success and money of secondary importance to you? What implications might your answer have for a choice of majors?

3. Are you the artistic type, and do you enjoy performing, creating, and viewing/listening to artistic works, or is art of relatively little interest to you? What implications might your answer have for a choice of majors?

4. Do you enjoy working with others, or do you prefer to work on your own? What implications might your answer have for a choice of majors?

very little freedom to pick courses other than those directly relating to one of the two majors.

Another option that some, though not all, colleges permit is the creation of a **unique major** geared to your own needs. Again, this is not an easy road to take because you must put together a unified set of courses that centers upon a discipline not normally offered through a major. Furthermore, you must also get the support of a faculty member or a committee of faculty members to oversee the process. One more drawback: If your unique major is too specialized, future employers may not be able to make sense of it when it appears on your transcript or résumé.

unique major
Specialization in a particular subject area that is geared to the student's own needs. Not offered by all colleges, and generally requiring the support of faculty to oversee the process.

If double-majoring or inventing a major seems too daunting, there's another option that may resolve the difficulty of choosing between two majors: majoring in one field and minoring in another. A **minor** is a secondary specialization in a discipline different from one's major. Typically students must take at least four courses in a discipline for their study to qualify as a minor.

minor
A secondary specialization in a discipline different from one's major.

Try It! POWER

Identify Major Attractions

To complete this assessment, check off each of the characteristics that applies to you. Then use the pattern of results to determine how closely your interests and personality style match with the characteristics of others who are already in a particular field of study.

Characteristic	Is This Me?	Possible Field of Study
• High interest in creative expression • Appreciation of nonverbal communication • Understanding of aesthetics • Commitment to perfection • Ability to manipulate form and shape	______ ______ ______ ______ ______	Arts (e.g., dance, drama, music, art, creative writing)
• Interest in organization and order • Ability to lead and manage people • Interest in practical problem solving • Ambition and interest in financial incentives • Can-do attitude • Ability to simplify complexity	______ ______ ______ ______ ______ ______	Business
• Intense interest in solving real problems • "Tinkerer" mentality a plus • Extreme ability to focus on minute details • Commitment to exactness and perfection • Strong logical ability • Ability to work alone for long stretches	______ ______ ______ ______ ______ ______	Engineering sciences (e.g., engineering, computer science)
• Interest in people • Desire to solve real human problems • Commitment to people more than money • Tolerance of "messy" situations with multiple, partial solutions • Insight and creativity • Ability to work with people	______ ______ ______ ______ ______ ______	Helping professions (e.g., nursing, counseling, teaching, many areas of medicine)
• Interest in human emotions and motivations • Interest in cultural phenomena • Ability to integrate broad areas of study and inquiry • Good skills of human observation • Interest in the panorama of human life	______ ______ ______ ______ ______	Humanities (e.g., English literature, history, theater, film)

(continued)

6 *continued*

Try It! POWER

Characteristic	Is This Me?	Possible Field of Study
• Interest in words, word origins, and speech • View of language as a science • View of literature as human expression • Appreciation of cultural differences as scientific phenomena	______ ______ ______ ______	Languages and linguistics
• Interest in physical performance • Enjoyment of sports and athletics • Commitment to helping others appreciate physicality • Patience and perseverance • Commitment to perfection through practice	______ ______ ______ ______ ______	Physical education
• Enjoyment of research questions; high level of curiosity about natural phenomena • Quantitative thinking a requirement; high comfort level with mathematics and statistics • Minute problem-solving skills; attention at great level of detail • Strong logical ability • Ability to work with others	______ ______ ______ ______	Physical, biological, and natural sciences (e.g., physics, astronomy, chemistry, biology, some areas of medicine)
• Interest in people as individuals or groups • Ability to think quantitatively and qualitatively • High comfort level with mathematics and statistics • High level of creativity and curiosity • Ability to work with others • Interest in theory as much as problem solving	______ ______ ______ ______ ______ ______	Social sciences (e.g., psychology, communication, sociology, education, political science, economics)
• Interest in the inner life • Interest in highly theoretical questions • Ability to think rigorously about abstract matters • Appreciation of the human search for meaning	______ ______ ______ ______	Spiritual and philosophical studies

Use the results to focus on the kinds of courses and educational experiences that are involved in potential fields of study. Examining your responses may lead you toward some unexplored territory.

After you complete the chart, consider how you can use the information. Did you learn anything new about yourself or about various courses of study? Do your responses direct you toward a particular major? Do they direct you away from any major?

Choosing a Job That's Right for You

Career Connections

It's a question no family member can resist asking, and one that you've probably asked yourself: What kind of work are you going to do when you graduate?

Happily, it's a question you don't have to answer, at least not yet. Although some students know from their first day in college what they want to do (and actually choose their college on that basis), many—perhaps most—don't decide on a career path until late in their academic career.

And that's fine. After all, one of the reasons you are in college is to expose yourself to the universe of knowledge. In one sense, keeping your options open is a wise course. You don't want to prematurely narrow your options and discard possibilities too early. And even if you're quite sure in your choice of careers, it doesn't hurt to explore new possibilities.

In the Career Connections features in previous chapters, we've discussed various strategies for exploring future professions. Here, in summary, are some steps to take to identify a career:

1. **Clarify the goal of your search.** There's no single perfect career choice. Some people search for the ideal career, assuming that they need to identify the one, and only one, career for which they have been destined. The reality is, though, that there are many careers they could choose that would make them equally happy and satisfied.

   Start with what you already know about yourself. You've already done a lot of mental work toward narrowing down a profession. Do you hate the sight of blood? Then you're probably well aware you're not cut out to be a surgeon or a veterinarian. Does the sight of a column of numbers bring an immediate yawn? Count out accounting and statistics.

   Awareness of your likes and dislikes already puts you on the road to identifying a future career. Knowing what you don't want to do helps identify what you do want to do and narrow down the kinds of occupations for which you're more suited.

2. **Gather information.** The more you know about potential careers, the better. Examine career-planning materials, read industry profiles, and visit relevant websites (such as the excellent Department of Labor site at **www.bls.gov/oco/**). Talk with career counselors. Discuss your options with people who work in professions in which you're interested. Find out how they chose their career, how they got their current job, and what advice they have for you.

   In addition, consider participating in an internship in a profession that you think might be attractive. *Internships* are off-campus, temporary work situations that permit you to obtain experience in a particular field. They are not always paid, but in many cases can substitute for a course. For example, you might be able to receive three college credits for spending 10 hours a week at a work site during the course of a term.

   Internships are an excellent way to learn about a profession, up close and personal. Working as an intern will let you know the kinds of things employees do on a day-to-day basis and the responsibilities and duties of the profession you're interested in. You can gain experiences that you would not be able to get on campus.

3. **Narrow down your choices.** Once you've gathered enough information to give yourself a reasonable comfort level, narrow down the choices. If it's early in your college career, you don't need to make up your mind. If it's late and you feel the pressure to choose, then make the decision. Just do it. Remember, there's no single, absolutely correct decision; there are many right decisions.

   Whatever it is you ultimately choose as a career, think of it only as a first step. As the average life span continues to lengthen due to advances in medical technology, most people will pass through several careers during the course of their life. By periodically taking stock of where you are and considering your goals, you'll be in a position to make career changes that bring you closer to your ideal.

College counseling and career centers are excellent sources of information on potential majors and occupations.
©sturti/Getty Images

5. **Be career oriented, but not too career oriented.** If you have a good idea about what career you wish to embark upon once you graduate, you can easily find out which skills are required to be successful in that field. Knowing what you'll need to gain entry into a field can help you determine a good major that will set you on the road toward your desired profession.

   Don't narrow your options too much, however. Students sometimes fear signing up for classes that don't seem to lead directly toward a career. Or they may avoid courses that seem to point them in the direction of a career that would be "unacceptable" to their parents or friends. One of the greatest sources of indecision in choosing a major stems from the mistaken notion that when you choose your major, you're also choosing a career.

   Don't fall into that trap. Follow your heart–not always your head–and pursue courses without regard to how they may broaden or narrow your future job opportunities. You may discover a passion, and an aptitude, that you never knew you had. Even if you are oriented toward a specific profession, remember that employers often prefer well-rounded employees over ones who are narrowly focused on a particular subject area.

6. **Don't follow the money.** Yes, studies show that graduates with certain majors (like business) make more money, on average, than those with degrees in other fields (like English). But it turns out that those differences are not great, and there are large variations within fields. For example, a typical business major graduate makes $2.86 million over a lifetime; an English major in the 60th percentile of salaries makes $2.76 million in a lifetime. And don't assume it will be incredibly difficult to get a job if you're a liberal arts major. The reality is that the skills that you learn in liberal arts majors–critical thinking, writing expertise, problem-solving abilities–are skills that are highly valued by employers.

> "Far and away the best prize that life offers is the chance to work hard at work worth doing."
>
> **President Theodore Roosevelt (in a 1903 Labor Day speech).**

7. **Always keep in mind that education is a lifelong activity.** Educational opportunities will continue to present themselves not just through the undergraduate years, but for the rest of your life.

   Consequently, no matter what your choice of major, you're not ruling out the possibility of taking courses in other areas in the future. You may eventually end up in a graduate school pursuing a master's degree, a doctorate, or a medical or law degree. You also may take courses periodically at local colleges even after you graduate, enrolling in them because they will help you advance in your career or simply because they interest you.

   In addition, choosing a major is not an irreversible choice. Many students change their major to a new one at some point during college–just as most people change their careers several times over the course of their lifetimes.

   In short, choosing a major is not a decision that places your life on a set, unchangeable course. Instead, it's one step in what can be a lifetime of learning.

Accepting Responsibility for Your Academic Performance

You received the highest test grade in your class . . . your grade point average went way up . . . you received an A on a paper . . . your instructor tells you your class participation was the best of anyone's in the course.

Take pride in your success, and reflect on what you did to achieve it. If you're doing well academically, it's not an accident. It's because you've worked hard and put your intellectual capacities to full use.

On the other hand, each of us has moments of academic disappointment. When you get a poor grade in a course, it hurts. But even if you feel tempted to shrug it off publicly, don't make that mistake privately. It's just as important to take responsibility for and reflect on your academic disappointments as it is to accept your successes.

There is, of course, a great difference between reflecting on what has happened and blaming ourselves. When things go wrong, it's reasonable to reflect in order to understand what went wrong. It is not useful, however, to spend time and energy blaming ourselves.

Learn from your mistakes. Consider why something went wrong, analyze what you could have done—or avoided doing—to prevent it, and seek ways of preventing a similar outcome in the future.

Remember, success occurs because we want it to and because we've worked hard to make it happen. It can happen every day if we allow it. And success is not just reaching an end point, such as when we're handed our diploma. Success is a process. Any achievement that brings us closer to fulfilling our goals and dreams is a success.

Speaking *of* Success

Courtesy of Brittany Harder

NAME: **Brittany Harder**

SCHOOL: **University of Tampa**

It took Brittany M. Harder three weeks to realize she had chosen the wrong major. She moved from marine biology to accounting, and then added a second major, sociology. She never regretted her decision to change majors, especially because sociology became her life's passion. "I love sociology," she says, "because it brought together my passion for research, diversity and community engagement."

For Harder, realizing your passion is a key part of the educational experience. She tells current students not to worry about "practicality" in a major, "since the most practical thing you can do is find something you are interested in and a field that you would show up every day excited to be in."

Finding something that excites and motivates you isn't always easy, though, especially when you're balancing a more-than-full-time schedule. "I was waiting for something to hit me that would show me what I was supposed to be doing," she recalls. "However, it wasn't until I started taking classes outside of my major at the time, talking to people, meeting other students, becoming involved on campus and in the community, and participating in a second sociology course that led to a world of difference for me."

If you're trying to carve out time to get involved on campus, Harder suggests learning how to say "no": "You have to pick and choose between things others ask you to do," she says. "Students have to be their own schedule masters."

One thing that has helped her manage her own time is making a to-do list every day and then prioritizing that list. "Crossing off one thing at a time will limit the days one feels like a hamster on a wheel," she says. And feeling like you're still moving forward can be the key to staying motivated and eventually succeeding.

[RETHINK]

- How do Harder's experiences in college illustrate the importance of flexibility in determining one's major?
- What do you think Harder meant when she said not to worry about practicality when choosing a major?

Looking Back

LO 8-1 Create a plan to prepare for the academic choices that college demands.

- Making course choices involves finding out as much as possible about what your college has to offer. Your college's listing and description of courses, usually found online, is the best initial source of this information.
- An important source of information and personal guidance in college is your college advisor, who has training and experience in advising students on courses, instructors, requirements, and regulations.

LO 8-2 Outline a strategy for choosing courses that ensures you are getting the most out of your studies.

- In choosing courses, check out your selections with your academic advisor and then register for the courses. You should be prepared to choose different courses or course sections if your initial selections are unavailable.
- Verify that you have received your chosen courses, that the schedule of courses makes sense, and that your course schedule will help provide the number of credits needed to graduate.
- Be prepared to deal with errors during registration or cope with the unavailability of courses that you need to take.
- Reflect on your college experience regularly, verifying that course choices, academic performance, personal growth, choice of major, and your overall educational experience are satisfactory.
- In service learning courses, students engage in community service activities while receiving course credit.

LO 8-3 Explain the criteria for choosing a major.

- Choosing a major first involves accepting a period of indecision, finding out more about yourself, seeking the help and advice of others, considering going beyond the traditional structure of your college major, trying out unusual courses, and taking career plans into account.

[KEY TERMS AND CONCEPTS]

[RESOURCES]

ON CAMPUS

The obvious choice for information about courses is your advisor. Sometimes your advisor will be associated with a general program, such as liberal arts; sometimes with a particular department, such as English or sociology; or sometimes with a collegewide academic advising center. Your course instructors also can often give good advice about what future courses to sign up for. Finally, don't forget about your fellow students; they can be an excellent source of information about the most interesting and exciting courses. If you'd like advice about future careers, visit your college career center. Not only will it have pamphlets and books on different jobs, but also the staff can often provide tests that can help you see how your personal strengths fit with potential majors and careers.

IN PRINT

The *Book of Majors 2018* (College Board, 2017) provides a good overview of college majors, as does *Guide to College Majors,* published by the Princeton Review (2010).

Probably the most popular guide to careers is *What Color Is Your Parachute? 2018* (Ten Speed Press, 2017). In it you'll find ways to make decisions about choosing (and changing) professions, as well as ways to obtain a job.

ON THE WEB

- Rutgers University provides a four-step plan that that can help with choosing a major, as well a four-year action plan on using your major to pursue a career. **https://cc.camden.rutgers.edu/guide-choosing-major**
- Major Resource Kits are listed at the University of Delaware's Career Services Center **(www.udel.edu/CSC/students/major_resource_kits.html).** Dozens of majors are listed, ranging from Apparel Design to Women's Studies. Each major has a sample of job titles, types of employers, and resources for finding employment. This is a great site for getting ideas for future careers.

Design Elements: *Pencil/Notebook: ©Squared Studios/Photodisc/Getty Images; Group/Laptop: ©Jacob Lund/Shutterstock; Apples: ©I. Rozenbaum/PhotoAlto; People/Silhouette: ©Ingram Publishing; Colorful Notebooks: ©Dragan Nikolic/Alamy; Group/Occupations: ©Rawpixel.com/Shutterstock; Woman/Laptop: ©JGI/Jamie Grill/Getty Images; Man/Laptop: ©Westend61/Getty Images.*

The Case of . . .

Major Problems

As Chen Lee began his junior year, he still was unsure which major to choose. He had come to college as an "undeclared major" and that was still his official designation—though he thought "clueless major" would be a more accurate label.

Chen had thought seriously about several possibilities, including communications and marketing, but none seemed to offer just what he was looking for. Part of the trouble was, of course, that he really didn't know what he was looking for. In fact, he was a lot clearer about what he didn't want to major in than what he did want to major in.

The clock was ticking away, and he felt lost. His parents offered many suggestions, but that just seemed to increase the pressure. And now he was getting warnings from the school that he had to make a decision.

1. What seems to be Chen's main problem in coming to grips with the choice of a major?

2. How can Chen's prior consideration of majors such as communications and marketing help him move closer to a decision?

3. How would you advise Chen to make use of his understanding of what he doesn't want to major in?

4. How can Chen find out more about himself? Why is this important in choosing a major?

5. Do you think Chen is taking this decision too seriously or not seriously enough? What advice would you give him about the importance of the choice of a major?

CHAPTER

9 Technology and Information Competency

Learning Outcomes

By the time you finish this chapter you will be able to

» LO 9-1 Explain how technology impacts you and your education.

» LO 9-2 Describe strategies for effective distance learning.

» LO 9-3 Discuss approaches for developing information competency.

©Wavebreak Media Ltd/Shutterstock

Brian Sullivan didn't remember much about the auto accident that left him with two badly broken legs. But the aftermath of the accident, which occurred in August just before his second year of college, was all too clear. He was in terrible pain, and his physicians said there was no way he could return to college in the fall.

At first, Brian was dejected, because he didn't want to lose a term of study. But after a series of e-mail conversations with his campus advisor, he learned he did have an option: enroll in distance learning classes taught entirely online. He could participate fully and receive course credit for the classes without ever stepping foot on campus. He decided to give it a shot and signed up for three online courses.

The beginning of the term was tough, as Brian acclimated himself to the online course environment. But he soon got the hang of it. Within a few weeks he became adept at participating in online discussions, sending in assignments, and chatting with his fellow classmates and his instructor. He also found he could stay in touch with his friends on campus, who texted him frequently and whose lives he could follow on Facebook, Snapchat, and Instagram.

What Brian feared would be a lost term turned into something quite different: a term that brought him both academic success and contact with his friends—all thanks to technology.

Looking Ahead

The technology that permitted Brian to keep up with his classes and friends didn't even exist a few decades ago. Education is changing, especially as it takes increasing advantage of virtual resources—the web, e-mail, and other evolving technologies. In fact, you might already be taking a distance learning course entirely on the web, never setting foot in the same room as your instructor or your classmates.

Technology also is making a profound difference in how we are taught, the ways we study and carry out our work, and how we communicate with our professors and other students. It is changing the way you can access the vast quantities of information published each year—tens of thousands of books, journals, and other print materials, and literally billions of web pages. But successfully wading through all that information requires significant new skills in information competence that weren't necessary in the past.

In this chapter we discuss how technological advances increase your opportunities to achieve success in college.

We'll first consider the basic educational uses of technology. We'll also talk about distance learning, an approach to education that involves studying with an instructor who may be thousands of miles away. Finally, we'll consider how you can use technology to develop information competency—locating and using both the information traditionally held in libraries *and* information created for and in the virtual world of cyberspace.

» LO 9-1 You and Technology

It's a great tool that can help you achieve success in your classes. It can save you hours of time. At the same time, it can be extremely frustrating, annoying, and maddening. And sometimes instead of saving time, it can eat up hours.

"It," of course, is technology. Today, it is as much a necessity to use technology as it was for you to learn to write using pen and paper earlier in your schooling. No one facing the job market in the twenty-first century will want to leave college without a strong working knowledge of a variety of technologies and what they can do for you.

If you are not yet at ease with technology, relax. No one is born with technology skills. With practice, however, using a broad range of technologies will become second nature.

And if using technology is as familiar to you as brushing your teeth in the morning, be patient with those who are less at ease with it. An increasing number of

Journal Reflections

Could I Live Without Technology?

1. What do you use technology for most? Texting? E-mail? Surfing the web? Classwork?

2. How much time do you spend using technology? How does it affect your social relationships?

3. What technological devices could you live without? What devices could you not live without?

4. How much and what kinds of technology do you like to have in your courses? Why?

students can be called *digital natives*—those who have used technology virtually their entire lives—and their experiences lead them to be considerably more tech savvy.

In fact, a *digital divide* separates students, on the one hand, who have considerable and easy access to computers and technology, from those, on the other hand, for whom access to computers is difficult. The digital divide is especially pronounced for older or less affluent students, who may have little experience with technology or access to the Internet, and their younger and more affluent classmates. (To explore your feelings about the role technology plays in your life, complete the **Journal Reflections**.)

Technology and Your Academic Life

Even if you don't feel particularly proficient with technology in general, it already plays a big role in your life. Computers run your car's engine, make your digital camera work, allow you to record iPod tunes, and make sure the bus you're waiting for runs on time.

Technology also has revolutionized academic life. Here are some of the ways you may encounter technology in your classes:

- **Course websites.** Most college courses have a specific website associated with them. The website, which may require a username and password for access, will probably contain basic information about the course, such as a copy of the class syllabus. Or it may provide important emergency updates, such as class cancellations or changes in paper due dates.

In other classes, the website may be much more elaborate and play a central role in the class. For instance, class websites may contain exercises and quizzes to be completed (and scored) online. All your grades for the class may be stored on the website, accessible to you at any time of the day or night.

In some classes, you may electronically deposit papers and essays onto the class website. Later, your instructor can read them online, post comments on your submissions, and return them to you on the website. You may carry out group projects on the website, or hold virtual discussions on the site. You may even be required to take your major tests and final exams on the website.

- **Textbook Companion Websites.** Most textbooks have a website that is tied to the book. At a minimum, the website will include chapter summaries, interactive reviews, flash cards, and practice tests. In other courses, the website includes the entire textbook online, sometimes in an *adaptive learning* format that offers a means of learning the material online in a highly structured—and effective—way. These resources can be extremely valuable study tools.

- **Podcasts.** In some classes, instructors produce **podcasts**, video or audio recordings of instructional material relevant to the class. They might be mini-lectures or other material that supplements what is presented in class. You can either access them on the web or download them to a mobile device that permits you to listen to and view them outside of class whenever you want.

podcast
A video or audio recording that can be accessed on the web and viewed on a computer or downloaded to a mobile device.

- **Blogs.** Some instructors maintain blogs of their own. A **blog** is a kind of web-based public diary in which a writer offers ideas, thoughts, short essays, and commentary. If your instructor has a blog and tells you to read it, get in the habit of checking it routinely. Not only will it contain information relevant to the course that you'll need to know, but it also may reveal personal insights that can help you know your instructor better.

  Some instructors ask students to create their own blogs and share them with other students in the class. For instance, a political science instructor might ask students to keep a record of their reactions to an ongoing election campaign.

  If you are asked to create your own blog, your instructor will provide you with directions regarding what to write and how to post your blog on the web. Remember to follow the guidelines carefully. And never forget: Once you post your blog on the web, it becomes a public document.

blog
A web-based public diary in which a writer provides thoughts, essays, and commentary.

- **Classroom presentation programs.** Many instructors use technology during class itself. For example, most instructors present material electronically using PowerPoint slides or some other presentation program, such as Apple's Keynote. Presentation programs help instructors create professional-looking slides that contain not only text but also graphics, such as photos, charts, maps, and animations.

  If you are lucky, your instructor might later place the slides projected in class onto the class website, where they can be reviewed after class. Sometimes instructors even put the slides on websites before class. That gives you the chance to print them out and bring them to class, writing class notes on them. (For tips on making best use of instructors' presentation programs in class, see the **Course Connections**.)

- **Individual response technology. Individual response technology (IRT)** is a method used to involve students more actively during class. If you are in a class using IRT, you will be asked to download an app to your smartphone such as Poll Everywhere or Turning Point. (Older technology involves a dedicated wireless handset, similar to a television remote control, usually referred to as

Individual response technology:
Method using a smartphone app or wireless handset to transmit students' answers to the instructor's computer, resulting in more classroom interactivity.

Course **Connections**

Getting the Most Out of Instructors' PowerPoint Presentations

Traditional "chalk-and-talk" lectures are a thing of the past in many classes. Instead, increasing numbers of instructors are using presentation programs such as PowerPoint to project material in their classes.

This newer technology calls for fresh strategies for taking notes and absorbing the information. Here are some tips:

- **Listening is more important than seeing.** The information that your instructor projects on screen, while important, ultimately is less critical than what he or she is saying. Pay primary attention to the spoken word and secondary attention to the screen.
- **Don't copy everything that is on every slide.** Instructors can present far more information on their slides than they would if they were writing on a blackboard. Oftentimes there is so much information that it's impossible to copy it all down. Don't even try. Instead, concentrate on taking down the key points.
- **Remember that key points on slides are . . . key points.** The key points (often indicated by bullets) often relate to central concepts. Use these points to help organize your studying for tests, and don't be surprised if test questions directly assess the bulleted items on slides.
- **Check if the presentation slides are available online.** Some instructors make their class presentations available on the web to their students, either before or after class time. If they do this before class, print them out and bring them to class. Then you can make notes on your copy, clarifying important points. If they are not available until after a class is over, you can still make good use of them when it comes time to study the material for tests.
- **Remember that presentation slides are not the same as good notes for a class.** If you miss a class, don't assume that getting a copy of the slides is sufficient. Studying the notes of a classmate who is a good notetaker will be far more beneficial than studying only the slides.

a clicker.) Students' answers to multiple-choice or true–false questions posed by the instructor are combined and displayed to the class, providing an opportunity to discuss the class responses.

One of the best things about individual response technology is that it gives you immediate insight into how well you understand the material being discussed in class. It also allows you to see how your own personal results compare with those of your classmates.

lecture capture technology
Technology in which instructors upload in-class lectures, slides, and videos to a website, which students can later access to review the material presented in class.

- **Lecture capture technology.** In classes with **lecture capture technology**, instructors upload an audio or video recording of everything they say and do in the classroom, along with a feed of the PowerPoint slides or other material that is being presented. If you're in a class with lecture capture, you'll receive a link to the material and can review any or all of it later.

  Lecture capture offers several advantages. For one thing, if you miss a class, you'll be able to review exactly what you missed. When studying for a test, you can review material with which you may be having trouble. And because the lecture capture is indexed to words on the PowerPoint slides, you can review key concepts, skipping to the material that is most important or the hardest for you to understand and learn.

One of the key advantages of lecture capture is that it frees you up in class to focus on the big picture when taking notes. It relieves you of the sense that you need to write down everything on the PowerPoint slides and every detail the instructor discusses. Instead, you can be more engaged in class.

It's important not to use the availability of lecture capture technology as an excuse not to attend class. The classroom experience can't be recreated later, and you'll miss the opportunity to ask questions and engage in class discussions and other in-class work.

Using the Web

The web has revolutionized communication. And we haven't seen anything yet: Visionaries say it won't be too long before our refrigerators will order milk when supplies are running low and health providers will constantly monitor our vital organs.

The **web** (or, as it was originally called, the *World Wide Web*) provides a graphical means of locating and accessing information on the Internet. Using the web has become the standard way to find and use such information. The web provides a way to transmit typewritten text, visual material, and auditory information—graphics, photos, music, soundbites, video clips, and much more.

The Internet provides the backbone of virtual communication. Among its most common uses are the following:

- **E-mail. E-mail**, short for "electronic mail," offers a way for people to send and receive messages with incredible speed. On most college campuses, e-mail is the most common form of communication between students and faculty.
- **Text messaging (or texting). Text messaging** (or **texting**) permits you to send short messages from mobile phones to other phones or e-mail accounts. They are typically limited to 160 characters or less. Using text messaging, you can communicate with others in real time. You can also sign up to receive automatic text messages, such as receiving information whenever there are breaking news events. Most student-to-student communication uses text messaging.
- **Video messaging. Video message services** such as Skype or FaceTime allow users to communicate using video, voice, and instant messaging over the web. Skype alone has almost 300 million users. Video messaging is generally free, and it can be used on desktop computers, laptops, and smartphones.

web ("the web")
A highly graphical interface between users and the Internet that permits users to transmit and receive not only text but also pictorial, video, and audio information.

e-mail
Electronic mail, a system of communication that permits users to send and receive messages via the Internet.

text messaging (texting)
Short messages sent from mobile phones to other phones or e-mail accounts.

video messaging services
Video messages that are sent between smartphones.

Using E-Mail Effectively

Although e-mail (illustrated in **Figure 9.1**) has become a major means of written communication for many of us, you may be unaware of some of the basics of how it works. For example, every e-mail address contains three basic elements:

- **Mailbox name.** The mailbox name—the name assigned to your account on an e-mail system—is often some variant of your own name (e.g., conan_obrien), though it may also be totally fictitious (e.g., hepcat9).

©Hero Images/Getty Images

figure 9.1
E-Mail
E-mail sent via Google's Gmail.
©Ian Dagnall/Alamy Stock Photo

- **@.** The "at" sign.
- **Domain name.** The domain name is the name of the organization that hosts the e-mail "post office" to which the user subscribes—often an institution (e.g., umass.edu, mcgraw-hill.com) or an Internet service provider (e.g., gmail.com). *Host computers* are connected directly to the Internet. You can usually tell what kind of an organization hosts an e-mail account by the last part of the address (the *extension*); for example, *.edu* is an educational organization, *.com* is a commercial organization, *.org* is a nonprofit or charitable organization, *.mil* is the military, and *.gov* is a governmental organization (see **Table 9.1**).

Many e-mail providers (e.g., Gmail, Yahoo! Mail) have their own, unique e-mail systems on which e-mail can be retrieved anywhere you have access to the web. Others use particular software programs such as Microsoft's Outlook to send and receive mail; you must have that software installed on your computer to retrieve your e-mail. Sometimes colleges have their own unique e-mail system that you can access through your college website.

Many colleges require that you establish a college e-mail account to which they can send official communications. In such cases, even if you already have an e-mail account, you'll need to check mail coming to your official college address. One way to simplify matters is to have mail automatically forwarded from your college e-mail account to your original account.

table 9.1 Domain Extensions

E-Mail Address	Extension	Type of Organization
jasper.johns@asu.edu	.EDU	Arizona State University—Educational
dowd@nytimes.com	.COM	The New York Times—Commercial
send.help@redcross.org	.ORG	American Red Cross—Charitable or nonprofit
general@army.mil	.MIL	United States Army—Military
head.counter@census.gov	.GOV	U.S. Census Bureau—Government

Even better, start using your college e-mail account routinely, and have your messages forwarded to it from your original account. Not only will you be sure to receive essential college e-mails, you will avoid having to write your instructors using a return e-mail address that, while amusing to your friends ("stoned_mindless @gmail.com"), may be less appropriate for instructor e-mails.

Writing Effective E-Mail Messages

Although you may communicate more frequently with your peers via texting, most instructors are reluctant to give out their phone numbers, meaning that you are more likely to be communicating with them via e-mail. Even if you are an experienced e-mail user, there are several things you can do to improve the effectiveness of the messages you send. Among the most important to keep in mind when writing formal e-mail messages:

- **Use an informative subject line.** Don't say "IMPORTANT" or "meeting" or "question." None of those help recipients sort out your message from the dozens of others that may be clogging their inboxes. Instead, something like "Reminder: resident advisor applications due 5:00 P.M. 10/11" is considerably more useful. In addition, *always* use a subject line: Some recipients routinely delete messages without a subject line, fearing they contain viruses.
- **Make sure the recipient knows who you are.** If you are writing someone you know only casually, jog their memory with a bit of information about yourself. If you don't know them at all, identify yourself early in the message ("I am a college student who is interested in an internship. . . .").
- **Keep messages short and focused.** E-mail messages are most effective when they are short and direct. No one likes to receive long emails, so if at all possible, keep your message short enough that it fits on one screen without scrolling down to see the rest. In fact, recipients sometimes don't read beyond the beginning of a message. If you do need to include a good deal of material, number each point or set them off by bullets so recipients will know to read down. (And don't add a P.S. below your signature; almost no one will scroll beyond the signature line.)
- **Always check spelling and grammar before sending an e-mail.**

- **Try to include only one major topic per e-mail.** It's often better to write separate e-mails rather than including a hodgepodge of unrelated points in an e-mail. This is especially true if you want a response to each of the different points.
- **Put requests near the beginning of the e-mail.** If you want the recipient to do something in response to your message, respectfully put the request at the very beginning of your message. Be explicit, while being polite.
- **Keep attachments to a minimum.** If possible, include all relevant information in the body of your e-mail, unless requested to do otherwise. Large attachments clog people's e-mail accounts and may be slow to download. In addition, recipients who don't know you personally may fear your attachment contains a virus and not open it.
- **Avoid abbreviations and emojis in formal e-mails.** When writing texts and e-mails to friends, abbreviations such as AFAIK ("as far as I know"), BTW ("by the way"), OIC ("oh, I see"), and WTG ("way to go") are fine. So are **emojis**, which signal the emotion that you are trying to convey. However, they should be avoided in formal e-mails. Recipients may not be familiar with them, and they may make your e-mail seem overly casual.
- **Above all, always be respectful and courteous.** It always pays to be polite. In fact, as we discuss next, there are certain guiding principles that govern civility on the web and that you should always keep in mind when writing e-mails.

emojis
Symbols used in e-mail messages that provide information on the emotion that the writer is trying to convey. Emojis usually look like faces on their side, with facial expressions related to the intended emotion or tone.

Netiquette: Showing Online Civility

Although an e-mail or a text is usually less formal than a letter, it is essential to maintain civility and demonstrate good etiquette, which in the online world is known as *netiquette.* This is especially true when communicating with your instructors. Here are some rules:

- **Don't write anything in an e-mail or text message that you'll regret seeing on the front page of your local newspaper.** Yes, e-mails and texts are usually private, but the private message you write can easily be forwarded by the recipient to another person or even scores of other people. Worse yet, it's fairly easy to hit "reply all" in an e-mail when you mean simply to "reply": In this case, you might think that you are responding to an individual when in fact the e-mail will go to everyone who received the message along with you.
- **Be careful of the tone you convey.** It is harder in e-mails and texts to express the same kind of personality, and often the same degree of subtlety, that our voice, our handwriting, or even our stationery can add to other forms of communication. This limitation means that attempts at humor can backfire. And avoid sarcasm altogether; it is nearly impossible for an e-mail or text recipient to appreciate sarcastic communications.

If you're using humor, consider adding an emoji to clarify the intent of your message if you are writing to someone you know well. Avoid emojis in e-mails to people you don't know well. Better to err on the side of formality.

- **Never write anything in an e-mail or text that you wouldn't say in person.** If you wouldn't say something in a face-to-face conversation, don't say it electronically.
- **Don't use all capital letters.** Using all caps MAKES IT LOOK AS IF YOU'RE SHOUTING.

- **Never send an e-mail or text when you are angry.** No matter how annoyed you are about something someone has written in a message, don't respond in kind—or at least wait until you've cooled down. Take a deep breath, and wait for your anger to pass.
- **Be especially polite and professional when writing to instructors.** Instructors often get scores, and sometimes hundreds, of e-mails and texts from students each week, and they are especially sensitive to messages that are inappropriate. Follow these guidelines to be sure your e-mail will receive maximum attention:
  - Always use the subject line in e-mail messages, identifying the class you are in and describing the general topic of the e-mail (e.g., "Psych 100, Lec 3, exam query").
  - Address instructors politely (as in "Dear Professor xx," rather than, say, "Yo, Prof!" or "Hey!"). Unless your instructor has specifically told you otherwise, never use his or her first name.
  - Avoid the high-priority flag.
  - Be concise. Make your point quickly, and try not to write more than a few paragraphs. Make one point per e-mail.
  - Avoid emojis, non-standard abbreviations, and slang; you're writing an instructor, not a friend.
  - Don't tell your instructor that you need to hear from him or her immediately. It's fine to convey that your concerns are urgent, but don't make demands. If there is a deadline involved—for instance, if you are facing a registration deadline—respectfully ask for a response before that date.
  - At the end of every message, thank the instructor and be sure to sign your complete name.
  - Finally, proofread what you've written and make sure your spell-check tool is on.

  To consider e-mail and text message netiquette more, complete **Try It! 1**.

Classroom Netiquette: Using Technology Appropriately

Many instructors have guidelines about the appropriate use of technology while in their classrooms. Even if they don't explicitly provide rules, you can be sure they would want you to follow these guidelines:

- **Turn off your cell phone.** Most instructors ask that you keep your cell phones off (or set on "vibrate" mode) while in class. Cell phones ringing at random times are distracting and annoying, to both your fellow students and your instructor.
- **Don't send texts or make calls while in class.** It's obvious that you should be paying attention to what's going on in class.
- **If you use your laptop to take notes, stay on task.** No matter how tempting it is to check your e-mail messages, text with a friend, check Facebook, or surf the web, avoid the temptation. Use your laptop to take notes, and nothing else.
- **Don't use headphones connected to your computer.**
- **Never use your cell phone to text answers to problems in class.** Cheating is cheating, whether done using high-tech or low-tech methods. Don't do it.

1

Try It! POWER

Using E-Mail Netiquette

Read the e-mail below, written by a student to his instructor, and respond to the questions that follow.

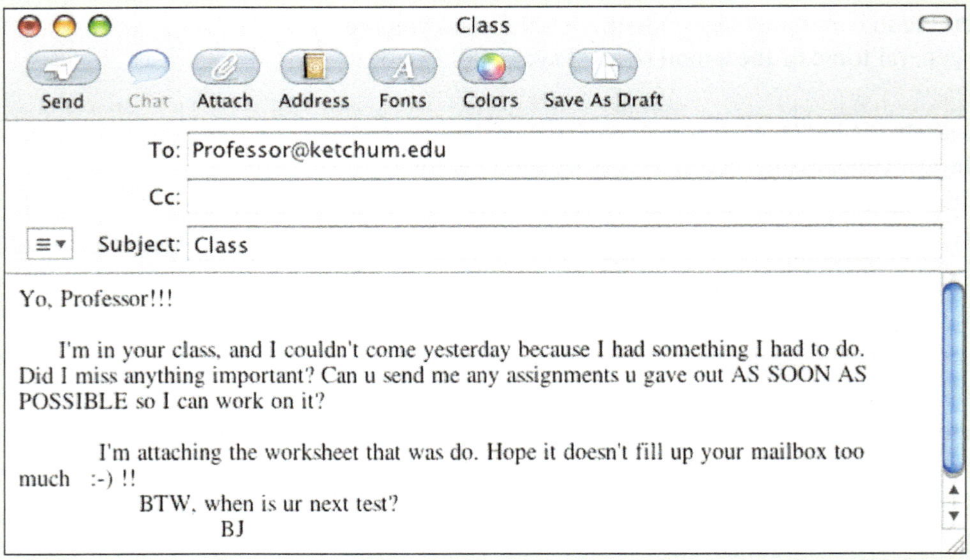
Class

Send Chat Attach Address Fonts Colors Save As Draft

To: Professor@ketchum.edu

Cc:

Subject: Class

Yo, Professor!!!

I'm in your class, and I couldn't come yesterday because I had something I had to do. Did I miss anything important? Can u send me any assignments u gave out AS SOON AS POSSIBLE so I can work on it?

I'm attaching the worksheet that was do. Hope it doesn't fill up your mailbox too much :-) !!

BTW, when is ur next test?

BJ

1. What rules of "netiquette" does the e-mail violate?

2. If you were the instructor to whom the e-mail message was sent, how do you think you would react to receiving it? What questions would you have about the message?

3. Based on the e-mail, what opinion might you have of the student who wrote it?

4. Rewrite the e-mail so that it is consistent with good netiquette.

Protecting Yourself: Spam, Cybersecurity, and Online Safety

The downside of e-mail is *spam*, the virtual equivalent of junk mail. Spam may range from get-rich-quick schemes to advertisements for body enhancements or pornography. Spam is more than a nuisance; it takes up valuable transmission resources (*bandwidth*), disk space, and computer time.

Some e-mail systems apply a filter that uses a few simple rules to separate e-mail you actually want to read from spam. Unfortunately, these systems are not perfect: They sometimes let junk through and can even at times dispose of messages you want. The only absolutely reliable way to deal with spam is to delete it yourself as quickly as possible.

Spam filters are one aspect of broader efforts to maintain security on computers. **Cybersecurity** refers to measures taken to protect computers and computer systems against unauthorized access or attack. Every computer connected to the web is subject to multiple attacks from *hackers*, criminals (and sometimes foreign governments) who illegally attempt to gain access to and tamper with information on your computer. In fact, the average computer connected to the web is attacked by hackers every 39 seconds, 24 hours a day.

cybersecurity
Measures taken to protect computers and computer systems against unauthorized access or attack.

Here are a few tips for dealing with spam and maintaining cybersecurity:

- Consider using two e-mail addresses—one for personal messages and one for college and professional messages.
- When you choose a password, make it long (8 or more characters) and complex (include letters, numbers, punctuation, and symbols).
- Don't use the same password on every program.
- *Never* give anyone your password, and change your password frequently.
- Install anti-virus programs on your personal computer. It is essential to protect yourself from hackers by installing an anti-virus program such as McAfee or Norton Security.
- *Never* respond to e-mails that ask for personal or financial information, even if they appear to be legitimate. Such requests may originate from efforts to steal personal financial information. For instance, in a practice called *phishing*, spam or pop-up messages are used to trick you into disclosing bank account or credit card numbers, passwords, or other personal information.

  In a phishing scam, the e-mail appears to be from a legitimate source and asks you to update or validate information by providing account information. It may even appear to be from your college, asking you to, say, verify your login information.

  In reality, such messages are from con artists seeking to steal your identity. E-mails that contain promises of riches for little effort, offer deals that seem too good to be true, or threaten that accounts will be closed unless you provide information immediately are likely bogus.
- *Do not* click on any link in the e-mail message until you're sure it's real. Not only can such links lead to the disclosure of personal information about you, but they may lead to the secret installation of software that can spy on you.
- *Never* open an attachment from someone you don't know. Computer viruses, which can ruin everything on your hard drive, are often spread through e-mail attachments.

- Finally, if your e-mail program has a spam filter, periodically check your spam folder to make sure no legitimate e-mails may have been directed there by mistake.

Keeping Safe

There's an even darker side to the web than financial criminals looking to steal from you. Specifically, you need to be wary of sexual predators who use the web to identify potential victims. To help protect yourself, use these guidelines:

1. Don't give out personal information to strangers, such as your name, phone number, address, hometown, or future schedule–anything that can be used to identify you.
2. Don't post personal information on social media that could allow others to track you down. Be especially wary about posting where you live, your phone number, and other identifying information unless you are sure you are using a social media site's privacy settings correctly.
3. Never send photos of yourself or your friends or family to someone you don't know.
4. Don't reply to e-mails or texts that are offensive, weird, or distressing in any way.
5. If you plan to meet someone you've known only from the web, for example, from a dating site, be cautious. Meet them in a visible, public location. Even then, meet someone only in a visible, public location in which many people will be present. *Don't* have someone you don't know pick you up at your home. Tell a friend or family member whom you are meeting and where you are going, and stay sober.
6. If you do have problems with someone over e-mail or through texting, immediately contact your college or local police.

Social Media Websites

Most college students use social media websites, such as Facebook, Twitter, Instagram, and Snapchat, to stay in touch with their friends, acquaintances, and even total strangers. The number of users is huge: Facebook has more than 2 billion active users and Twitter 330 million.

Facebook provides users with the ability to post information to share with friends who have access to their online profiles. Users can post updates and photos, exchange messages, list their personal interests, and share other information. Because it can be accessed on any computer or mobile device connected to the web, Facebook allows users to stay in constant touch with others.

Twitter instead provides users with the ability to send and receive short messages of up to 280 characters, called *tweets.* People can send short updates about what they are doing, offer opinions about events, or tell people where they are at a given moment. The tweets are sent to followers who have signed up to receive that person's tweets.

Although social networking websites offer many possibilities for interacting with friends, making new acquaintances, and sharing information, they need to be used appropriately. Remember that *what's posted on the web stays on the web*–potentially forever. Even if you delete information from a social networking site, it may still reside on someone else's computer.

Consequently, don't post information about yourself or photos that you wouldn't want your instructors, parents, or future employers seeing. For instance, faculty at colleges can–and sometimes do–read students' postings.

Furthermore, employers increasingly are using information posted on social networking sites in their hiring decisions. You might also want to consider maintaining two social media accounts: one for public consumption (that employers may read) and a personal account for close friends and family.

In short, be thoughtful of what you post about yourself. And be sure the privacy settings on your social network accounts are set in a way that protects your privacy.

At the same time, be an informed consumer of material you encounter about others on social networking websites. Some of the profiles contain bogus material or are entirely false. Individuals sometimes disguise their identities or make up false ones. It's important to verify whom you are communicating with before exchanging personal information.

» LO 9-2 Distance Learning: Classes Without Walls

Do you find that your schedule changes so much from one day to the next that it's hard to fit in a course that meets at a regularly scheduled time? Are you interested in an unusual course topic that your own college doesn't offer? Do you want to take a class during the summer but live too far from your college's campus?

The solution to your problem may be to enroll in a **distance learning** course. Distance learning is a form of education in which students participate via the web or other kinds of technology. Although most distance learning courses are taught via the web, some also use teleconferencing or other forms of communication.

distance learning The teaching of courses at another institution, with student participation via video technology or the web.

The key feature of distance learning courses is the nature of interaction between instructor and students. Rather than meeting in a traditional classroom, where the instructor, you, and the other students are physically present, distance learning classes are most often virtual.

Although some schools use webcasts of lectures with virtual discussion rooms, most students in distance learning courses will never sit through a lecture or even participate in a real-time conversation with students in the class. They may never even know what their instructor or classmates look like or hear their voices.

blended (hybrid) courses Courses in which instruction is a combination of traditional, face-to-face and online methods.

Most distance learning courses involve multiple students and an instructor assigned to the course. If you are taking a distance learning course, you may read lecture notes posted on the web, search and browse websites, write papers, and post replies, along with other students, to discussion topics posted by your instructor on a *message board.* You will see your instructor's and classmates' responses through comments they post on the web. You may be expected to read a textbook entirely on your own, and you may take online quizzes and exams.

In distance learning, you can take classes at another institution without physically having to be on that campus. Although taking courses online can help you fulfill graduation requirements, make sure before you register that your own college will accept the course credits. What do you think the future of distance learning will be?
©Onoky Photography/SuperStock

You may already be familiar with the kinds of technologies used in distance learning courses, because many traditional, face-to-face courses already contain elements of distance learning. In **blended (or hybrid) courses**, instruction is a combination of the traditional, face-to-face classroom interaction and a significant amount of online learning. Students in blended courses may spend less time in face-to-face classroom settings and more time working independently online. They also may collaborate with fellow students outside of class on the web.

In contrast to blended courses, *all* instruction takes place online in distance learning classes that are fully online. If you take a distance learning class that is fully online, you will probably never meet your instructor and fellow students in person. However, you will get to know them through virtual interactions online.

On the other hand, in *self-paced distance learning courses*, students move ahead at their own pace. There is no "live" instructor or other students with whom to interact; all instruction occurs in pre-recorded formats. Grading is entirely computer-scored. Because your progress is entirely self-paced, you need to manage your time carefully. It's a lot easier to stay caught up on assignments than to try to catch up on them.

Distance learning is not for everyone. Whether you're a good candidate for it or not depends on your preferred style of course taking. Complete **Try It! 2** to see whether you are suited to learn at a distance.

2 PERSONAL STYLES **Try It!** P O W E R

Assess Your Course-Taking Style

Your preferred course-taking style—how you participate in classes, work with your classmates, interact with your teachers, and complete your assignments—may make you more or less suitable for distance learning. Read the following statements and indicate whether you agree or disagree with them to see if you have what it takes to be a distance learner.

	Agree	Disagree
1. I need the stimulation of other students to learn well.		
2. I need to see my teacher's face, expressions, and body language to interpret what is being said.		
3. I participate a lot in class discussions.		
4. I prefer to hear information presented orally rather than reading it in a book or article.		
5. I'm not very good at keeping up with reading assignments.		
6. I'm easily distracted.		
7. I'm not very well organized.		
8. Keeping track of time and holding to schedules is NOT a strength of mine.		
9. I need a lot of "hand-holding" while I work on long assignments.		
10. I need a close social network to share my feelings, ideas, and complaints.		
11. I'm not very good at writing.		
12. Basically, I'm not very patient.		

The more you disagree with these statements, the more your course-taking style is suited to distance learning. Interpret your style according to this informal scale:

Disagreed with 10–12 statements = Excellent candidate for distance learning

Disagreed with 7–9 statements = Good candidate for distance learning

Agreed with 6–9 statements = Probably better taking classes on campus

Agreed with 10–12 statements = Avoid distance learning

Distance learning classes have both advantages and disadvantages. On the plus side, distance learning courses offer the following:

- **You can take a web-based distance learning course anywhere that you have access to the web.** You can be at home, at the college library, or on vacation at the beach and still participate.
- **Distance learning classes are often more flexible than traditional classes.** You can participate in a course any time of the day or night, and you typically don't have to be in class at a specific time.
- **Distance learning classes are often self-paced.** You may be able to spread out your work over the course of a week, or you may do the work in a concentrated manner on one day.
- **You may have more contact with your instructor than you do with a traditional class.** Even though you may not have face-to-face contact, you may have greater access to your instructor, via e-mail and the web, than in traditional classes. You can leave messages for your instructor any time of the night or day; most instructors of distance learning classes respond in a timely manner.
- **Shy students may find it easier to "speak up" in a distance learning class.** You can think through your responses to make sure you are communicating just what you wish to say. You don't have to worry about speaking in front of other people. For many people, distance learning is liberating.
- **You can become a better writer.** Because distance learning usually involves more writing than traditional courses, you receive more practice writing—and more feedback for it—than in traditional classes.
- **You can become skilled in an area for free.** There are several organizations, such as Coursera or edX, that offer a vast array of free online courses. Many of the courses are taught by master teachers, and some offer the opportunity to earn college credit or a badge for completing the course (although that may involve a fee).

On the other hand, distance learning has disadvantages that you should keep in mind:

- **You are a prisoner of technology.** If you lose access to a computer and the web, you won't be able to participate in the class until the problem is fixed.
- **You won't have direct, face-to-face contact with your instructor or other students.** Distance learning can be isolating, and students sometimes feel alone and lost in cyberspace.
- **You won't get immediate feedback.** In a distance learning class, it may be hours, or sometimes days, before you receive feedback on what you have posted to a message board, depending on how well the pace of other students matches your own.
- **Distance learning classes require significant discipline, personal responsibility, and time management skills.** You won't have a set time to attend class as you do in traditional courses. Instead, you must carve out the time yourself. Although instructors provide a schedule of when things are due, you have to work out the timing of getting them done.

Consequently, many students believe that distance learning courses are more difficult than traditional classes. You must be focused and committed to keeping up with the course. You need to be prepared to work hard on your own for a substantial number of hours each week.

Despite these potential challenges to distance learning courses, they are becoming increasingly popular. In fact, increasing numbers of colleges are offering *MOOCs*, or *Massive Open Online Courses*, which are free and in some cases attract tens of thousands of students. And many businesses encourage employees with crowded schedules to take distance learning as a way of providing continuing education.

If you are considering taking a distance learning course, follow these steps, which are summarized in the P.O.W.E.R. Plan on this page.

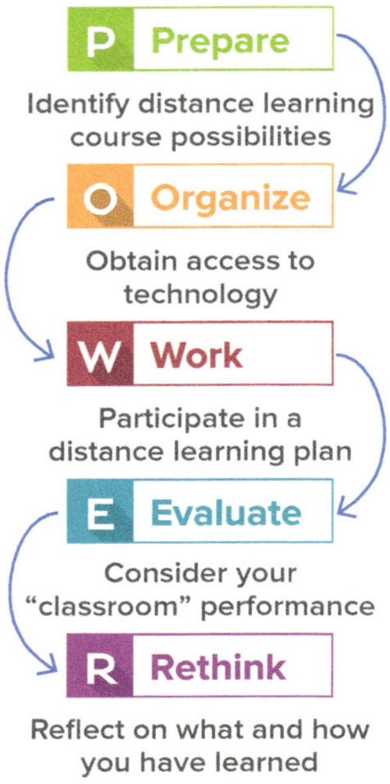

P.O.W.E.R. Plan

P Prepare — Identifying Distance Learning Course Possibilities

How do you find a distance learning course? In some cases, your own college may offer courses on the web and list them in your course catalog. In other cases, you'll have to find courses on your own.

The best place to look is on the web itself. By searching the web, you can find distance learning courses ranging from automotive engineering to zoology. Don't be deterred by the physical location of the institution that offers the course. It doesn't matter where the college is located, because for most distance learning classes, you'll never have to go to the campus itself.

But before you sign up for a potential course that you would like to have count toward your degree, *make sure that your own college will give you credit for it.* Check with your advisor and the registrar's office to be certain.

You should also find out what the requirements of a course are before you actually sign up for it. Check the syllabus carefully and see how it meshes with your schedule. If it is a summer course and you are going to be away from your computer for a week, you may not be able to make up the work you miss.

Finally, try to talk with someone who has taken the course before. Was the instructor responsive, providing feedback rapidly? If necessary, could you speak with the instructor by phone or via video technology such as Skype? Was the course load reasonable? (**Try It! 3** will help you work through the process.)

O Organize — Obtaining Access to Technology

Although you don't need to be a computer expert, you will need some minimal e-mail and web skills to take a distance learning course. If you don't have sufficient technological expertise, make the investment of time to beef up your computer skills by taking a computer workshop or course *before* you sign up for the course.

You'll also need regular access to a computer connected to the Internet. It doesn't have to be your own computer, but you will certainly need regular and convenient access to one. Make sure that the computer you plan to use is powerful enough and that you have access to a speedy Internet connection. Very slow Internet service will be extremely frustrating.

Be sure to make all your arrangements for computer access prior to the start of a course. It can take several weeks to set up Internet service on a home computer if you don't have it already.

learning management system (LMS)
The software that delivers a distance learning course and typically provides the course content, calendars, and tests, and tracks grades.

In addition, you should familiarize yourself with the course learning management system before the course starts. The **learning management system (LMS)** is the software that delivers the distance learning course to your computer. It typically provides the course content such as online lectures or material to read, as well as a course syllabus, calendar, tests, and a way to track your grades.

The most common LMS's are Blackboard, Canvas, Moodle, Desire2Learn, and Angel. In some cases, a college will brand its LMS with its own name.

3  WORKING IN A GROUP

Try It! POWER

Get Some Distance on the Problem

Working by yourself initially, see if you can find distance learning courses of interest to you. Start by checking your school's listing of courses to see what might be offered there. If you're already comfortable online, you might also try the following:

- *The Chronicle of Higher Education*'s Distance Education: Daily Updates (**chronicle.com**).
- Harvard Extension School's Distance Learning website offers a number of links and information on pursuing courses at Harvard (**www.extension.harvard.edu/distance-education**).

Try to find five courses you would be interested in and list them below. After you have completed your list, share your list with others in a group.

1. How diverse were the courses you were able to find?

2. Were particular subject areas better represented than others?

3. Why?

Although all LMS's are designed to work well with a variety of browsers, there are certain browsers that may work better with them than others. The common browsers are Mozilla Firefox, Google Chrome, and Apple Safari. Be sure to use the browser that is recommended to be best for the LMS you will be using.

W Work

Participating in a Distance Learning Class

Successfully participating in a distance learning course involves several skills that are distinct from those needed for traditional classes. To get the most out of a distance learning course, you'll need to do the following:

- **Manage your time carefully.** You won't have the luxury of a regular schedule of class lectures, so you'll have to manage your time carefully. No one is going to remind you that you need to sit down at a computer and work. You will need every bit of self-discipline to be successful in a distance learning course.

- **Check in frequently.** Instructors may make crucial changes in the course requirements. Make sure to check for any changes in due dates or class expectations.
- **Find a cyberbuddy.** At the start of the semester, try to make personal contact with at least one other student in the class. You can do this by e-mailing, phoning, or actually meeting the student if he or she is geographically nearby. You can share study strategies, form a study group, and share notes. Connecting with another student can help you avoid feelings of isolation that may interfere with your success.
- **Make copies of everything.** Don't assume everything will go well in cyberspace. Make a printed copy of everything you submit, or alternatively, have a backup stored on another computer.
- **Ask for help if you need it.** If you are having difficulties, whether with the course content or technology issues, ask for help. Working online can be isolating, and your instructor won't be able to use your nonverbal behavior to see that you may be flailing. It's important for you to ask for aid as soon as you realize you're in trouble.
- **Have a technology backup plan.** Computers crash, your connection to the Internet may go down, or an e-mailed assignment may be mysteriously delayed or sent back to you. Don't wait until the last minute to work on and submit assignments, and have a plan in place if your primary computer is unavailable.

  You might consider using a cloud storage system such as Dropbox or Google Drive. Even if your own computer crashes, you'll be able to access your computer files from any computer.

E Evaluate

Considering Your "Classroom" Performance

As with any class, you'll be receiving feedback from your instructor. Make the most of it to make any necessary course corrections.

But unlike many courses, in which almost all the feedback comes from the instructor, much of the feedback in a distance learning course may come from your fellow students. For example, students may respond to your comments on online discussion boards with their own feedback. Consider what you can you learn from their comments.

At the same time you'll be receiving feedback, you will likely be providing feedback to your classmates. Consider the nature of feedback you provide, and be sure that you use the basic principles of classroom civility.

R Rethink

Reflecting on What and How You Have Learned

Distance learning is not for everyone. If your preferred learning style involves extensive, face-to-face interaction with others, you may find that your experience is less than satisfying. On the other hand, if you are at ease with computers and enjoy working on your own, you may find distance learning highly effective.

As you reflect on your distance learning experience, go beyond the technology and think about what, and how much, you have learned. Ask yourself whether you learned as much as you would have in a traditional class.

Also think about how your distance learning experience could have been more effective for you. And think about whether you were so absorbed by the technology that you lost sight of the real goal of the course: learning new material.

Most educational experts believe that distance learning will play an increasingly important role in higher education. Furthermore, because it offers an efficient way of educating people in far-flung locales, it is a natural means of promoting lifelong learning experiences. In short, the first distance learning class you take is not likely to be your last.

» LO 9-3 Finding Facts: Developing Information Competency

One of the greatest advances brought about by technology involves the area of research. More than ever, people require **information competency**, the ability to determine what information is necessary, and then to locate, evaluate, and effectively use that information. The sheer abundance of material available today makes information competency a critical skill.

information competency
The ability to determine what information is necessary, and then to locate, evaluate, and effectively use that information.

We'll consider the ways in which you can use the two primary storehouses of information available today to boost your own level of information competency. One you can walk or drive to—the library. The other—the web—doesn't have a physical location. Both are indispensable in anyone's quest for information.

Libraries

No matter how imposing or humble their physical appearance, whether they contain only a few hundred volumes or hundreds of thousands of them, libraries are a good place to focus your efforts as you seek out and gather information. Although every library is different, all share two key elements: the material they hold—their basic collections—and tools to help you locate the material you need.

What Can Be Found in a Library's Basic Collection?

Libraries obviously contain books, but they typically have a lot more than that, including some or all of the following:

> "Knowledge is of two kinds: we know a subject ourselves, or we know where we can find information upon it."
>
> Samuel Johnson, author

- **Periodicals.** *Periodicals* include specialized journals for professionals in a field, magazines, and newspapers. Many, if not most, periodicals can now be found online.
- **Indexes and online databases.** An index provides a listing of periodical articles by title, author, and subject. Some indexes also provide a short summary, or *abstract*, of the contents of each article.

  Most indexes come in electronic form known as an online database. An **online database** is an organized body of information on a particular topic or subject area. For example, the National Center for Biotechnology Information (NCBI) maintains *Medline*, an online public database that provides information on medical research. The advantage of online databases over traditional, print-based indexes is that the database sometimes provides the full text of material it identifies in a search.

online database
An index in electronic form composed of an organized body of information on a particular topic or subject area.

- **Encyclopedias and handbooks.** Encyclopedias and handbooks provide overviews of information. Some encyclopedias, such as the *Encyclopedia Britannica* or *World Book Encyclopedia*, attempt to cover the entire range of knowledge, although they lack depth. Handbooks are more specialized, such as the *Handbook of Poultry Science* or the *Handbook of Nonverbal Behavior.* Use them at the earliest stage of your hunt for information for an overview of key issues, and move from there to more specific and current sources.

- **Government documents.** Census records, laws, and tax codes are some of the millions of government documents that are stored in libraries.
- **Musical scores.** The music to *A Chorus Line*, the Brahms *Alto Rhapsody*, and the Beatles' greatest hits are among the musical scores you can find in libraries.
- **Reserve collections.** Reserve collections hold items that instructors assign for a specific class. Although they are typically found, and accessed, online, sometimes they are in the form of physical material that may be borrowed from the library for a limited period of time. Reserve collections may contain not only books and articles, but also videos, CDs, laptops, and multimedia equipment.

Locating Information in a Library

The place to begin searching for information in a library is the library catalog. Catalogs list all materials that are held in the library and provide their physical location. Most library catalogs are computerized, though a few still use name cards filed in drawers or microform (microfiche or microfilm). You are usually able to access computerized catalogs from home or residence hall rooms, as well as from computers housed in the library itself.

Library catalogs allow searches by title, author name, and topical keywords. Individual catalog entries generally include additional information about the material, such as the publisher, date of publication, number of pages, and similar information.

Say, for example, you're writing a paper on Ernest Hemingway. To find books he *wrote* in an electronic catalog, you would enter his name in the "author" field. You may be presented with the listing shown in **Figure 9.2**.

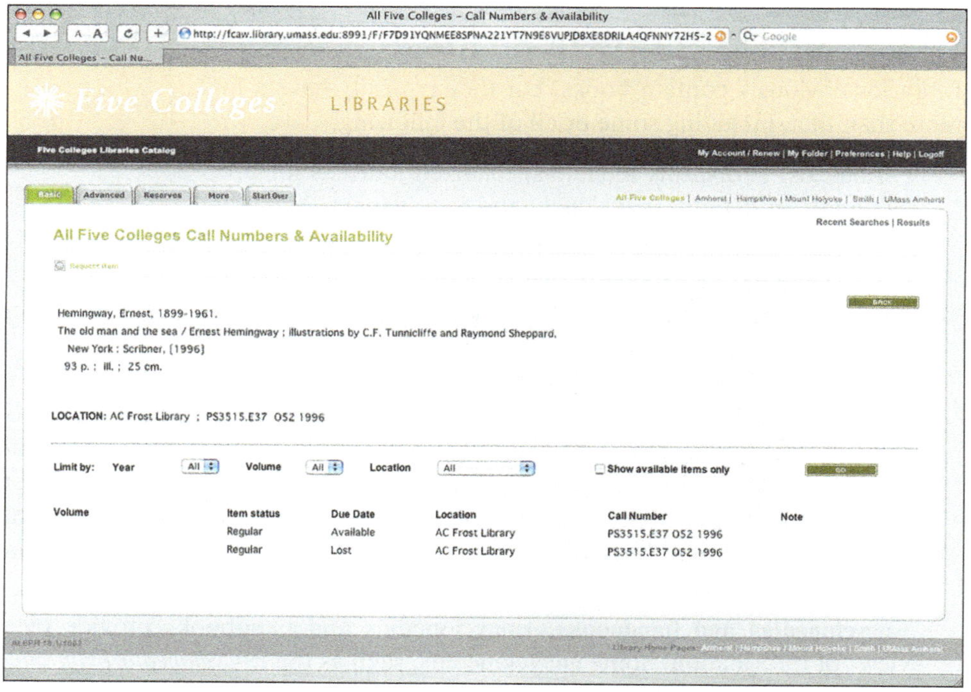

figure 9.2
Online Catalog Entry
Online catalog entry for a book called *The Old Man and the Sea.* Note especially the call number and due date, because these pieces of information tell you where the book is to be found and whether it is on the shelves or is checked out.

Of course, you could also search for "Hemingway" as the subject, which would yield a list of books *about* him and his work; if you entered his name in a "keyword" search, the catalog would return a more comprehensive list of books both by *and* about him.

The key piece of information in a catalog entry is the book's **call number**, a code that tells you exactly where to find it. Most college libraries use the Library of Congress classification system, which assigns a unique combination of letters and numbers to each book.

call number
A unique classification number assigned to every book (or other resource) in a library. Call numbers are used for ease of location.

Because the record illustrated in **Figure 9.2** is from an electronic search, it contains further helpful information. The word "Available" under "Due Date" tells you that one copy of the book has not been checked out by another patron and should be sitting on the shelf. You'll need to familiarize yourself with your library's particular system to know precisely how you can make most efficient use of the catalog. Chances are there's a handout or posted set of instructions nearby.

Once you have identified the material you need and where it is located, you'll need to go find it. In all but the biggest libraries, you can simply go into the **stacks**, the place containing shelves where the books and other materials are kept, and—using the call number—hunt for it. In libraries with closed stacks, you must fill out a form with the call numbers of the books you want. A library aide will find the material and deliver it to a central location.

stacks
The shelves on which books and other materials are stored in a library.

What if you go to the location in the stacks where the material is supposed to be and you can't find it? The material may be checked out, in use by someone else at that time, incorrectly shelved, or simply lost. Whatever the reason, *don't give up.* If the material is checked out to another user, ask a librarian if you can **recall** the material, a process by which the library contacts the person who has the book and asks him or her to return it.

recall
A way to request library materials from another person who has them.

If you need a particular book, journal article, or other material that the library does not have in its own collection, you may be able to get it through interlibrary loan. **Interlibrary loan** is a system by which libraries share resources. Another library may be able to provide what you're looking for, either electronically or in a physical copy.

interlibrary loan
A system by which libraries share resources, making them available to patrons of different libraries.

Finally, even if you do find exactly what you were looking for, take a moment to scan the shelves. Because books and other materials are generally grouped by topic, you may find other useful titles in the same place. One of the pleasures of libraries is the possibility of finding an unexpected treasure—material that your catalog search did not initially identify but that may provide you with exactly what you need.

Finding Information on the Web

The web is vast—sometimes frustratingly so. In fact, no one knows how much material exists on the web. Not only is more information added to the web every day, but the information also resides on thousands of individual computers. Anyone with minimal web savvy and access to a *server* (a computer with a permanent Internet connection) can set up a personal website.

The fact that anyone can put information on the web is both the biggest asset and the greatest disadvantage of using the web as an information source. Because minimal computer skill is the only expertise a person needs to set up a web page, there may be as much misinformation on the web

Searching for materials in the library stacks can be frustrating if they are not on the shelves. However, you may unexpectedly find relevant and interesting material while browsing.

as there is information. Consequently, keep the usual consumer rule in mind: Buyer beware. Unless the website has been established and is maintained by a reliable organization, the information it contains may not be accurate.

There are a number of key factors involved in each web search. They include a browser, web pages, links, and search engines.

browser
A program that provides a way of navigating around the information on the web.

- **Browsers.** To use the web, your computer has to have a browser. A **browser**, as its name implies, is a program that provides a way of looking at the information on the web. Among the major browsers are Microsoft's Internet Explorer, Google Chrome, and Firefox's Mozilla.

  Using a browser is a bit like taking a taxi: Once you get in, you get to where you want to go by providing an address. The address, also known as a URL (Uniform Resource Locator), identifies a unique location on the web, a *website* or a *web page* (one of the parts of a site).

  Web addresses are combinations of letters and symbols. They typically start off with "**www.[domain_name].[xxx]**"—the address of the hosting website (e.g., **www.iastate.edu** is the home page for Iowa State University). If you're looking for a subsite or a particular page on the site, the address becomes increasingly specific: **www.iastate.edu/visitors/** will take you to a "visitors" site—a collection of pages—hosted by **iastate.edu**. A *page* on that site—for example, **http://www.museums.iastate.edu/BAM.html**, which connects you with the Iowa State Museums—ends with a specific name, usually followed by ".htm," ".html," or ".shtml." Because most addresses begin with "http://," this part of the address is sometimes dropped in references to a site.

  You can often get a decent idea of what kind of site you're going to by taking a careful look at the web address: You can tell that **www.connect.mheducation.com/**, for example, is a site that is hosted by a commercial entity (which you might recognize as McGraw-Hill Higher Education).

web page
A location (or site) on the web that houses information from a single source and that (typically) links to other pages.

- **Web pages.** Web pages are the heart of the web. A **web page** is a document that presents you with information. The information may appear as text on the screen, to be read like a book (or more accurately, like an ancient scroll). It might include a video clip, an audio clip, a photo, a portrait, a graph, or a figure. It might offer a news service photo of the president of the United States or a backyard snapshot of someone's family reunion.

link
A means of "jumping" automatically from one web page to another.

search engine
A computerized index to information on the web.

- **Links.** Websites typically provide you with **links**—embedded addresses to other sites or documents that, at a click, cause your browser automatically to "jump" there. Just as an encyclopedia article on forests might say at the end, "*See also* Trees," web pages often refer to other sites on the web—only it's easier than with a book. You just have to click on the link with your mouse and—*poof!*—you're there.
- **Search engines.** A **search engine** is simply a computerized index to information on the web. When you know what information you want to find but don't have an address for it, a search engine can often steer you toward relevant sites.

It is becoming increasingly easy for anyone to put material on the web, and many students are creating their own personal web pages containing information and photos about their lives.
©Tim Robbins/Mint Images/Getty Images

The various parts of the web are similar to the components of traditional libraries, as illustrated in **Figure 9.3**. A web browser is equivalent to a library card; it gives you access to vast quantities of material. Websites are like the books of a library; web pages are the book pages, where the content resides. Links are analogous to "*see also*" portions of books that suggest related information. And search engines are like a library's card catalog, directing you to specific locations.

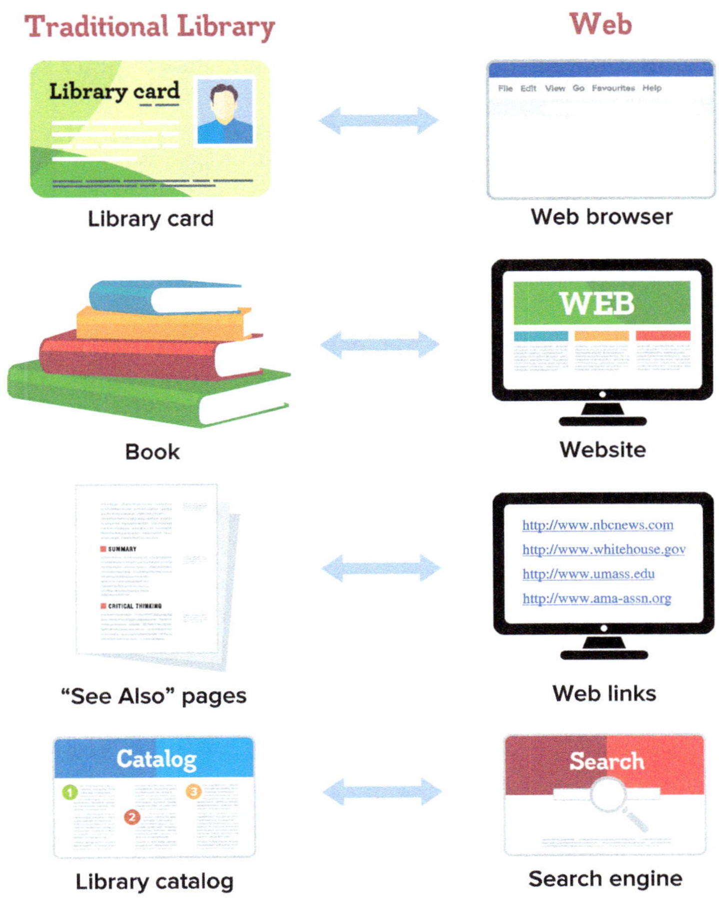

figure 9.3

Comparison of Library and Web

The various parts of the web are similar to the components of a traditional library.

Locating Information on the Web

There is no central catalog of the contents of the web; instead, there are a number of different search engines. Furthermore, depending on the search engine you use and the type of search you do, you'll identify different information.

Search engines themselves are located on the web, so you have to know their addresses. After you reach the "home" address of a search engine, you enter your search terms. The search engine then provides a list of websites that may contain information relevant to your search.

Although most people are familiar with the most popular search engine, Google, there are actually many search engines. Others include Bing, Yahoo!, Ask, and AOL. Although they all are useful for searches on the web, they do so using somewhat different strategies.

> "Don't let that little glowing screen become an adversary. If you plan correctly, the computer can become your most useful tool at college—next to your brain."
>
> **Greg Gottesman, author**

Some search engines, such as Yahoo!, specialize in organizing information by subject, making it easy to search for information on, say, different dog breeds, the Islamic religion, or car repair. Using Yahoo! for its subject directories is like searching for information using the subject entries in a library catalog.

Other search engines, such as Google, catalog many more pages than Yahoo! but don't group them by subject. Due to the breadth of their coverage, they might be more useful when you are looking for obscure pieces of information or for numerous sources for different perspectives on a topic. Using Google is like performing a keyword search in a library catalog.

Finally, a third type of search engine is exemplified by Ask. Known as metasearch tools, these sites send your search commands to other search engines, compiling the results into a single, unified list.

There's no single search engine that works best. Most people develop their own preferences based on their experience. The best advice: Try out several of them and see which works best for you. To get started, work through **Try It! 4**, "Work the Web: Information, Please!".

Becoming a Savvy Surfer

The process you use to search the web couldn't be easier–or more difficult. The vast amounts of material online and the relative ease of navigation afforded by the web make finding information quite simple: What is hard is finding appropriate information.

Consider a search in which you enter the question, "How do I use the web?" into the home page of Google. That search will identify over 2.6 *billion* websites related to the topic.

Using the list of sites generated by the search is simple. With the mouse, click on the site address of the relevant document, and the home page of the site will

4 **Try It!** POWER

Work the Web: Information, Please!

Try to find the answer to the first question below on Google **(www.google.com)**, Yahoo **(www.yahoo.com)**, and Bing **(www.bing.com)**. Then use whichever search engine you prefer to find answers to the remaining questions.

1. What was the French Revolution and when did it occur?
2. Who is Keyser Soze?
3. What are the words to Dr. Martin Luther King Jr.'s "I Have a Dream" speech?
4. Are diesel engines more efficient than gasoline engines?
5. What is the ecu?

How easy was it for you to find the answers to the questions? Which search engine(s) did you prefer, and why?

(eventually) appear on your computer screen. You can then take notes on the material, in the same way you'd take notes on material in a book.

Most of the million sites Google returns, however, are likely to be of little use. It's easy for a search to end up in a virtual dead end, in which the information you have found is only minimally related to the topic you're researching. If you do find yourself at a site that's of no use to you, simply hit the "back" button on your browser until you return to where you started.

How can you limit your search in the first place, so that you find sites more directly relevant? The following tips can help you to get the most from a search:[1]

1. **Before you even begin to type anything into your computer, ask yourself the question you want answered.** Then identify the two or three important words in that question.
2. **Go to your favorite search engine.** Google is the most popular today, but preferences vary.
3. **Type in three or four words into the search engine,** making sure they are spelled correctly. Then search. Note: You can do a few things here to limit the number of results returned, thus making your search more efficient. Most search engines allow you to use the following:
   - *Quotation marks*, to denote a phrase–words that should appear together, in a specific order (e.g., "animal rights").
   - *Plus signs*, used before terms that must appear in all results returned (+ "animal rights" + experimentation).
   - *Minus signs*, before terms you do not want to appear in results (+ "animal rights" + experimentation – fur).
   - *Boolean operators*–words like AND, OR, AND NOT, and NEAR (e.g., "animal rights" AND experimentation NOT fur).
   Check the "Help" section of your preferred search engine for more precise information on limiting your searches.
4. **Open a new window,** type in a different set of search terms, and search again.
5. **Identify the common links between the two searches.** Read the very brief summaries provided.
6. **Open a word processing window.** Copy and paste the site's address into that window and follow it with an annotation of your own.
7. **See if you have found the answer you were looking for.** If not, reformulate your question to come up with new key words. If you have found the answer, you're done!
8. **Avoid the temptation to rely on Wikipedia pages.** Very often, a search will yield a Wikipedia entry. *Wikipedia* is a free online encyclopedia created through the joint efforts of dozens, hundreds, or even thousands of people. Anyone can create or edit an article, and it is assumed that the power of multiple contributors can ensure the accuracy of the article.

   The reality is that Wikipedia entries vary considerably in accuracy. Although some involve the collective knowledge of so many people that they are largely accurate, in some cases the material is suspect. Consequently, use information in Wikipedia entries as a starting place, not an endpoint. In some cases, in fact, instructors will not allow the use of material obtained solely from Wikipedia in their students' papers.
9. **Beware of fake news sites.** As we know from efforts to influence the 2016 presidential election, hackers may set up a websites that provide false information

and propaganda. They may look authentic and mimic other, more legitimate websites. Try to verify the accuracy of the information you find on websites to avoid using fabricated disinformation.

10. **Resist the temptation to simply cut and paste the material you've found into a new document.** It's too easy to succumb to plagiarism if you simply copy material. Instead, take notes on the material using the critical thinking and notetaking skills you've developed.

    Then save your notes. You can save your notes on a computer's hard drive, on a flash drive, or in the cloud (if you use Dropbox or Google Docs). You can also print out hard copies of what you create virtually.

However you do it, *make sure you save material frequently and make backup copies.* Nothing is more frustrating than laboring over a document for hours and having it disappear into cyberspace.

Evaluating the Information You Find on the Web

In most instances, you'll find more information than you need, and you'll have to evaluate the information you have found. Some of the important questions you must address before you can feel confident about what you've found include the following:

- **How authoritative is the information?** It is absolutely essential to consider the source of the material. Approach every piece of information with a critical eye, trying to determine what the author's biases might be. The best approach is to use multiple sources of information. If one source diverges radically from the others, you may reasonably question the reliability of that source.

  Another approach is to consider the publisher of the material or the sponsoring institution. For instance, sites established by well-known publishers and organizations are more likely to contain accurate information than those created by unknown (and sometimes anonymous) authors. Remember, the web is completely unregulated: *Anyone* can put *anything* on the web. One way of evaluating web information is to consider a site's host. Commercial web pages (whose address includes the letters *.com*, short for commercial) often tend to include the least objective material. On the other hand, addresses including the letters *.gov* (government), *.org* (nonprofit organization), *.mil* (military), and *.edu* (educational and research institutions) generally include more objective information.

  But not always. For example, some instructors place student papers on the web, giving them an *.edu* address. Such papers vary considerably in their authoritativeness. Similarly, some nonprofit organizations with a *.org* address hold extreme positions. Furthermore, **blogs**, those personal websites that contain personal diaries, are pervasive on the web. Because they are not subject to any editorial scrutiny before they are published, they are of questionable authoritativeness. In short, any web content must be evaluated on its merits.

Being familiar with a variety of search engines is a useful skill.

- **How current is the information?** No matter what the discipline, information is changing at a rapid rate. Even a field like Chaucerian English, which concentrates on poetry written in the fourteenth century, advances significantly year by year as scholars make new discoveries, come to new insights, and reach new conclusions.

  Consequently, don't assume that because you're researching a historical topic, old sources will suffice.

Exploring Careers on the Web

The web is one of the newest ways to explore careers that may interest you. You can begin to gather information by going to a website devoted to jobs, such as **monster.com**, **glassdoor.com**, **salary.com**, or **indeed.com**. These sites present a variety of career-related information. You can also find other sites using the various search engines we've been discussing.

In addition, you can find postings for many jobs on the web. In fact, it is possible to apply for jobs using the web. Some firms advertise their job needs on their company sites, and you can e-mail a cover letter and a résumé listing your education and experience. An increasing number of jobs are obtained in this way.

Keep this in mind, too: The technological expertise you develop during college will later help you in your professional life. Already, more and more jobs require computer skills, and every projection of the future suggests that technology will become a central facet of the workplace.

Career Connections

Consider whether what you've found is the most recent and up-to-date approach. Compare older sources to newer ones to identify changes in the ways in which the topic is considered.

- **How well are claims documented?** Are there references and citations to support the information? Are specific studies identified?
- **Is anything missing?** One of the hardest questions to answer is whether your research is complete. Have you found all the relevant sources? Have you missed anything that is important?

Although there is no way to answer these questions definitively, you can do a couple of things. One way to ensure that you haven't missed anything important is to check out the sources that you have found. Many will have bibliographies and lists of suggested additional readings. By carefully considering this information, you'll be able to get a good sense of the important work in your topic area and verify that you haven't overlooked some critical source.

You can also talk to your course instructor, describing generally what you've found. Probably the best person to turn to, however, is a reference librarian.

The stereotype of a librarian as someone whose main job is to stop people from talking in the library is dead. Librarians today are masters at information management and technology. They are people who can help you find your way through a huge range of data sources—both in the library and on the web—and steer you to the right material.

Make use of librarians—but do it properly. If your library offers regular orientation sessions, sign up for one. Then try looking for material yourself. If you're having trouble sorting through what you've found (or can't find material in the first place), ask for help.

The better the question, the better the answer. Don't ask vague, unfocused questions (e.g., "Where are the books about nuclear power?"). Instead, sharpen your question, being as precise as possible ("I'm writing a paper on the environmental effects of using nuclear power to generate electricity. I've found two books and several websites, but they're not quite right. I wonder if you have any ideas about where I might find additional material?").

Don't be afraid to ask. Think of librarians as highly trained guides who can save you hours of aimless wandering in an increasingly dense forest of information.

A Final Word

The Information Age presents us with great promise and opportunity. Through the use of media such as e-mail and the web, we have at our fingertips the ability to communicate with others around the world. We can break the bounds of our physical location and reach across geography to learn about others. The computer keyboard truly can be said to contain keys to the entire earth and its peoples.

Speaking *of* Success

Courtesy of Joseph Kerlin-Smith

NAME: **Joseph Kerlin-Smith**

SCHOOL: **University of Massachusetts Amherst, Massachusetts**

Just seven months after returning from Afghanistan with the U.S. Marine Corps, Joseph Kerlin-Smith enrolled in college. Jumping in so quickly was a challenge: "My life experience differed drastically from the rest of the students who went to college right out of high school," he recalls. For instance, his most difficult semester included not only challenging coursework, but coping with the death of a friend who took his life because of PTSD.

As a non-traditional student, Kerlin-Smith was balancing a campus job, a full course load, and family life. As a Marine, he also had regular required trainings that pulled him out of school. "I was away a lot, and I was unable to do any kind of schoolwork while training, so my coursework added up quickly." He was grateful for understanding professors who would grant him extra time to catch up after he returned, but staying ahead of his assignments still required great discipline.

To keep himself from falling too far behind, he would use school breaks like Thanksgiving or spring break as benchmarks. "I wouldn't go home until I was all caught up," he says. Not only did that keep him on track for successful semesters, but it allowed him to be fully present with his family and enjoy his time off from school, something that was critical to keeping himself centered.

Besides familial and community support, especially from fellow veterans, Kerlin-Smith says something seemingly simple was central to his success: sleep. "I've pulled many all-nighters in the library hoping to catch up or get a little extra study time," he says. "But one of the best pieces of advice that I got from a professor and I would give is to others is to SLEEP! I accomplished more with a full night of sleep than spending all night in the library and being a zombie all day."

[RETHINK]

- What special challenges did Kerlin-Smith face as a military veteran and as an older student?
- How do you think the discipline that Kerlin-Smith encountered in the military helped him adjust to college life?

Looking Back

LO 9-1 Explain how technology impacts you and your education.

- Course websites, textbook websites, podcasts, blogs, wikis, classroom presentation programs, individual response technology (IRT), and lecture capture technology are among the major educational uses of technology.
- The web includes e-mail, text messaging, video messaging, and search engines.
- E-mail and text messaging permit instant communication with others. Although college students tend to communicate more using text messaging, most student–instructor communication is conducted via e-mail.

LO 9-2 Describe strategies for effective distance learning

- Distance learning is a form of education that does not require the physical presence of a student in a classroom. It is usually conducted over the web.
- Distance learning requires some adjustments for students, but it is increasingly popular.

LO 9-3 Discuss approaches for developing information competency

- There are two main sources of information today: libraries and the web.
- Information in libraries is available in print form, electronic form, and microform.
- Library resources can be found through the use of the library catalog, which may be print-based but is increasingly likely to be computerized.
- The web is another major source of information. Web users access web pages (or sites) by using a browser, locate information by using search engines, and move from site to site by following links on each web page.
- Using the web effectively to find information can be tricky. It has many dead ends, false trails, and distractions, and the accuracy of the information presented as fact can be difficult to assess.
- Information on the web must be carefully evaluated by considering how reliable the source is, how current the information is, how well the source's claims are documented, and how complete the information is.

[KEY TERMS AND CONCEPTS]

Blended (hybrid) courses (p. 253)
Blog (p. 243, 266)
Browser (p. 262)
Call number (p. 261)
Cybersecurity (p. 251)
Distance learning (p. 253)
E-mail (p. 245)
Emojis (p. 248)
Individual response technology (IRT) (p. 243)
Information competency (p. 259)
Interlibrary loan (p. 261)
Learning management system (LMS) (p. 256)
Lecture capture technology (p. 244)
Link (p. 262)
Online database (p. 259)
Podcast (p. 243)
Recall (p. 261)
Search engine (p. 262)
Stacks (p. 261)
Text messaging (texting) (p. 245)
Video messaging services (p. 245)
Web ("the web") (p. 245)
Web page (p. 262)

[RESOURCES]

ON CAMPUS

If you are having difficulty connecting to or surfing the web, the first place to turn is your college's computer center. Most campuses have consultants who can help you with the technical aspects of computer usage.

If you need access to computers, most colleges have computer labs. Typically, these labs provide computers with web access, as well as printers. It's important to check their hours, as they usually are not open 24/7. In addition, you may have to wait in line for a computer, so it is a good idea to bring some other work to the lab so you have something to do while waiting. You may also need to provide printer paper if you want to print something out.

The librarians at your college library are the people to whom you should turn first if you need help in locating information. In recent years, librarians—most of whom hold advanced degrees—have undergone a significant change in what they do, and most are equally at home using traditional print material and searching electronic information storehouses.

IN PRINT

A good introductory guide to computers and technology is is *"Is This Thing On?": A Friendly Guide to Everything Digital for Newbies, Technophobes, and the Kicking & Screaming* by Abby Stokes (Workman, 2015). As you begin to use online resources, or those "in the cloud," Jason Rich's *Working in the Cloud: Using Web-Based Applications and Tools to Collaborate Online* (Que, 2017) offers useful advice on how to best use some of the most popular programs.

A comprehensive and in-depth look at online research can be found in *Librarian's Guide to Online Searching* (Libraries Unlimited, 2015, 4th ed.), by Suzanne S. Bell.

Finally, Kevin J. Fandl and Jamie D. Smith's *Success as an Online Student: Strategies for Effective Learning* (Routledge, 2016) offers clear instruction on becoming an effective online learner.

ON THE WEB

- If you're interested in learning a new subject, be sure to look through **mooc.org** or **www.khanacademy.org**. Both sites offer free online courses in topics ranging from Centripetal Force and Gravitation to Accounting and Financial Statements.
- Pretty much anything you want to know about high tech, from the definition of a smartphone to an explanation of Utopic Unicorn, can be found at Webopedia (**www.webopedia.com/**). It also includes a list of the latest terms.
- Google (**www.google.com**) and Yahoo! **(www.yahoo.com)** are two of the more popular Internet search engines. They serve as useful starting points to identify more resources—from scholarly journal articles to photos and videos—related to whatever topic you are interested in researching.
- Microsoft offers free tutorials on the basic Office programs you are likely to use at some point in your college career, including Word, PowerPoint, and Excel (**support.office.com/en-us/office-training-center**). On the Mac side, Apple offers an introduction to its computer systems and software—from MacBooks to iPads—here: **support.apple.com/**

Design Elements: *Pencil/Notebook: ©Squared Studios/Photodisc/Getty Images; Group/Laptop: ©Jacob Lund/Shutterstock; Apples: ©I. Rozenbaum/PhotoAlto; People/Silhouette: ©Ingram Publishing; Colorful Notebooks: ©Dragan Nikolic/Alamy; Group/Occupations: ©Rawpixel.com/Shutterstock; Woman/Laptop: ©JGI/Jamie Grill/Getty Images; Man/Laptop: ©Westend61/Getty Images.*

The Case of . . .

The Missing File

Katrisha was almost done with her paper. She'd been working in a marathon session, sitting in front of her computer screen with only a couple of breaks over the course of an afternoon.

She'd begun work just after noon, when the sky was bright and clear. By now, some four hours later, it was dark and gray, and she heard thunder in the distance. But who cared about the weather? The main thing was that she was almost done.

She didn't usually put things off, but this time she'd gotten behind and was forced to do the work at the last minute. She was writing a report on software that blocks "adult" sites from home computers. Luckily she'd been able to find what she needed using various search engines and had incorporated the information into her paper.

The assignment was due by 5:00 P.M., but the professor accepted papers submitted via e-mail. As long as the message was sent before 5:00, she would be OK. She still had an hour to put the final touches on the paper and send it off.

Suddenly, there was a bright flash of lightning, followed by a clap of thunder. At the same moment, her computer screen went black as the electricity was cut.

Much to Katrisha's relief, the outage lasted only a few seconds. Her computer began to reboot, and the screen powered up again. In a few moments, she figured, she could continue her work.

But when the computer had fully restarted, the file with the paper that she'd been working on all day was nowhere to be found. She searched frantically through the various files on the computer, but to no avail. Her heart sinking, she realized that everything she had done over the afternoon was lost.

1. How well did Katrisha use her time to work on her paper? What advice would you give her about the preparation stage of working on a paper?

2. Did Katrisha organize her work well? What would you tell her to do next time?

3. Clearly, Katrisha should have saved her work frequently while she was working. What else should she have done while working on her paper to help her recover from such a catastrophe?

4. What should Katrisha do first to start solving her immediate problem with her professor?

5. What should she do next to begin reconstructing her paper and recovering as much of her work as possible?

Making Good Decisions

CHAPTER **10**

Learning Outcomes

By the time you finish this chapter you will be able to

» LO **10-1** Identify strategies for improving the quality of your decisions.

» LO **10-2** Implement plans to use for problem solving.

» LO **10-3** Recognize and avoid problems that affect critical thinking.

For Rich Rinkowski, the moment of truth was fast approaching. He had to make up his mind and decide what he was going to do when he graduated. Throughout his college career, he had intended to go to law school, and he had majored in criminal justice. He'd already been accepted to law school by the middle of his senior year, and it seemed that his future was well in hand.

Except for one thing: He was no longer sure he wanted to be a lawyer.

The reason for his indecision was an internship he had held working for a film director during the summer between his junior and senior years. Although Rich spent a good deal of his time photocopying and making coffee, he learned a lot about the film industry. In fact, after talking several times at length with the director, Rich began to wonder seriously if he might build a career in the movie industry.

Rich's girlfriend and family were dead set against it: They argued that law was a far safer choice. As his final term went by, Rich knew he had to make up his mind. But how?

Looking Ahead

Like Rich, all of us face important decisions in our lives at one time or another. How can we make the right decisions? The best way is to employ some basic techniques that can help improve the quality of our decision making.

This chapter will give you a sense of what decision making is and is not, and it discusses a structured process that can help make your decisions the right ones. We'll also consider the related issue of problem solving. You'll confront a variety of problems as you proceed through college. We'll look at a number of proven techniques that will help you solve them.

Neither making decisions nor solving problems is easy. Sometimes the best decision or solution to a problem is one that we don't see at first; we all have mental blind spots. The best problem solvers and decision makers have learned how to use critical thinking to see around these blind spots. To help you improve your critical thinking skills, we'll examine some common problems that can affect our thinking and discuss several biases that can make us jump too quickly to conclusions.

» LO 10-1 Making Good Decisions: A Framework

decision making
The process of deciding among various alternatives.

Decision making is the process of deciding among various alternatives. Whether you are trying to decide between a Ford and a Honda; between an apartment that is close to your job and one that is close to campus; or simply between a hamburger and pizza–every one of these choices requires a decision. Some decisions are easily made and have few consequences, but others, such as whether to major in music composition or follow a pre-med course of study, can involve the deepest examination of our beliefs and values.

Whatever you're deciding, you need to think critically to make a reasoned decision. You need to apply your past knowledge, synthesize and evaluate alternatives, and reason and reflect on a course of action. The greater your depth of thinking about the components of the decision, the more likely it is that you'll come up with the best choice.

How do we know a decision reflects critical thinking? It involves a number of basic characteristics, according to Gregory Bassham and colleagues, who wrote the book *Critical Thinking.* Among the most important:

- **Clarity.** Critical thinking reflects clear communication and thought.
- **Precision.** It's not only thinking involving the sciences that requires preciseness. Even the most everyday, common tasks can benefit from precision in thinking.
- **Accuracy.** To make decisions that reflect critical thinking, you need to base them on information that is accurate. No matter how good the logic you use to make a decision, if that logic is based on false information, it's bound to be a poor decision.
- **Consistency.** Good decisions need to be based on consistent reasoning, in which beliefs logically fit together and behavior is consistent with what we believe to be true.
- **Impartiality and Fairness.** The critical thinking behind decisions needs to be open minded, impartial, and fair. We need to try to avoid biases that may hinder the process of drawing appropriate conclusions.

With these considerations in mind, let's map out a strategy for making decisions that are best for you. Every decision can benefit from your effort to systematically think through the options involved, based on the P.O.W.E.R. Plan illustrated below.

P Prepare — Identifying Your Goals

Every decision starts with the end you have in mind: the goals you wish to accomplish by making the decision.

For example, suppose you are trying to decide between enrolling in one of two classes next term, neither of which is required: swimming or psychology. To decide, you need to consider both your short- and your long-term goals. For instance, the swimming class may raise your level of fitness, and you'll end up with a certificate that will allow you to be a lifeguard during the summer. The psychology class may provide you with some useful information—perhaps information you can use in other classes, perhaps techniques that will help you learn and remember better—but this is by no means certain. In terms of short-term goals, then, the swimming class may be the better choice. On the other hand, while the psychology class may not provide as clear-cut an immediate payoff, it may help you meet your longer-term goal of graduating with honors and becoming a successful teacher.

> "Nothing is more difficult, and therefore more precious, than to be able to decide."
>
> French Emperor Napoleon Bonaparte, 1804–1815

In short, every decision should start with a consideration of what our short- and long-term goals are. Identifying the goals that underlie decisions ensures that we make decisions in the context of our entire lives and not just to provide short-term answers to immediate problems.

O Organize — Considering and Assessing the Alternatives

Every decision is based on weighing various alternatives. Determining what those alternatives are, and their possible consequences, is often the most difficult part of decision making.

P Prepare

Identify your goals to help make decisions

O Organize

Consider and assess the alternatives

W Work

Make and carry out the decision

E Evaluate

Consider the outcomes

R Rethink

Reconsider your goals and options

P.O.W.E.R. Plan

Develop a List of Flexible Alternatives

It's important not only to think thoroughly about the obvious alternatives but also to consider those that are less obvious. For instance, if you are trying to obtain additional funds to support your college theater group, you might consider raising ticket prices for productions, holding a raffle to raise funds, or asking for sponsorship from a local business. After additional thought, though, you might reframe the issue, considering how best to place pressure on the college administration to increase funding for your group.

In short, the way you develop and frame alternatives is critical to the solution that you ultimately reach. The more alternatives you have, the better able you will be to come to a good solution.

How can you be sure that you've considered all the alternatives? You can't. But using the freewriting technique described below can help you maximize your efforts.

In *freewriting,* one writes continuously for a fixed period of time, perhaps 5 or 10 minutes. During this period, the idea is to write as many different ideas as possible, without stopping. It makes no difference whether the alternatives are good or bad or even whether they make sense. All that matters is that you let yourself brainstorm about the topic for a while and get it down on paper.

With freewriting, evaluating the worth of the ideas you've generated comes later. After you have produced as many possibilities as you can, then you go back and sift out the reasonable ones from those that are truly unlikely or just plain wacky. It's OK if you have to delete quite a few alternatives from your list; the process is likely to have liberated some truly reasonable alternatives that you might not otherwise have come up with. (Try the technique in the "Use Freewriting" exercise–see **Try It! 1**.)

Assess Alternatives

Once you have generated as extensive a list of alternatives as possible, assess them, weighing their pros and cons. You need to follow three key steps when judging each alternative:

1. *Determine the possible outcomes for each alternative.* Some outcomes are positive, some negative. Consider as many as you can think of. If you are considering ways of solving transportation problems, one alternative might be to purchase a car. That alternative produces several potential outcomes. You know that it will be easier to get wherever you want to go, and you might even have a better social life–clearly positive outcomes. But it is also true that buying and owning a car will be expensive, or it may be difficult to find convenient parking–both significant negative outcomes.
2. *Determine the likelihood that those outcomes will take place.* Some outcomes are far more likely than others. To take this into account, make a rough estimate of the likelihood that an outcome will come to pass, ranging from 100 percent (it is certain that it will occur) to 0 percent (it is certain that it will never occur). For instance, consider the possible outcomes of buying a car illustrated in **Figure 10.1**.

Obviously, the probabilities are just guesses, but going through the exercise of estimating them will make

We've all been there: facing a mind-boggling array of similar choices. However, by systematically assessing the alternatives, we can make informed decisions that will satisfy us.
©Kathleen Finlay/Getty Images

1 | Try It! POWER

Use Freewriting

Use freewriting to think of as many answers as you can to each of the following questions. The ground rules are that you should spend three minutes on each question, generating as many ideas as possible—regardless of whether they are feasible. To give yourself maximum freedom, write each answer on a separate page.

1. How can you make room in your schedule to take one more course next term than you're taking this term?
2. How can someone get from the 3rd floor to the 20th floor of a building?
3. What should you do if you suspect that one of your instructors is a space alien?
4. What would happen if humans' average life span were extended to 125 years?

After generating ideas, go back and evaluate them. How many were actually feasible or realistic? Do you think freewriting led to the production of more or fewer ideas than you would have come up with if you hadn't used the process? Did the quality of ideas change?

WORKING IN A GROUP

After you have answered the questions above, form a group of classmates and compare your answers against those of others. As a group, try to identify the best answers to each question.

the outcomes more real and will permit you to compare the various alternatives against one another more easily.

3. *Compare the alternatives, taking into account the potential outcomes of each.* Systematically compare each of the alternatives as illustrated in **Figure 10.1**. Then ask yourself the key question: Which alternative, on balance, provides the most positive (and most likely) outcomes?

   Obviously, not every decision requires such an elaborate process. In fact, most won't. But when it comes to major decisions, those that could have a large impact upon you and your life, it's worthwhile to follow a systematic process.

Take a look at **Career Connections** for another process that you can follow to help you make a career decision.

Alternatives	Probability
Outcomes in favor of purchasing a car	
Easier transportation	100%
Greater opportunities for part-time job	75%
Improvement in social life	30%
Outcomes against purchasing a car	
Increase in expenses for gas and maintenance	100%
Difficulty/time spent looking for parking	40%

figure 10.1
Outcomes of Buying a Car
Making a rough estimate of the positive and negative outcomes of buying a car, and how likely each of those outcomes will be, can help illuminate the consequences of a decision.

If all else fails, toss a coin to decide what alternative to follow. Tossing a coin at least brings you to a decision. Then, if you find you're unhappy with the result, you'll have gained important information about how you really feel regarding a particular choice.
©Evgeniy Mitroshkin/123RF

W Work

Making and Carrying Out the Decision

Working through the previous three steps of assessing the alternatives will lead you to the point of decision: choosing one of the alternatives you've identified.

Choose among Alternatives

The reason that important decisions are difficult is that the alternatives you have to choose from carry both benefits and costs. Choosing one alternative means that you have to accept the costs of that choice and give up the benefits of the other alternatives.

What if, after going through the steps of the process laid out here, you still can't make up your mind? Try these strategies:

- **Give the decision time.** Sometimes waiting helps. Time can give you a chance to think of additional alternatives. Sometimes the situation will change, or you'll have a change in viewpoint.
- **Make a mental movie, acting out the various alternatives.** Many of us have difficulty seeing ourselves in the future and envisioning how various options would play out. One way to get around this difficulty is to cast yourself into a series of "mental movies" that have different endings depending on the decision you make. Working through the different scripts in your head makes potential outcomes far more real and less abstract than they would be if you simply left them as items on a list of various options.
- **Toss a coin.** Tossing a coin isn't as crazy as it sounds. If each alternative seems equally positive or negative to you, then toss a coin—after first deciding that option A is "heads" and B is "tails." Then flip it.

  The real power of the coin-toss strategy is that it might help you discover your true feelings. It may happen while the coin is in the air, or it may be that when you see the result of the coin toss, you won't like the outcome and will say to yourself, "No way." In such a case, you've just found out how you really feel.
- **Ask for advice.** Although Western society teaches the virtues of rugged individualism, asking others for their advice is often an excellent strategy. A friend, instructor, parent, or counselor can provide helpful recommendations—sometimes because they've had to make similar decisions themselves. You don't have to take their advice, but it can help to listen to what they have to say.
- **Learn to view indecision as a decision.** Sometimes we spend so much time thinking about a decision that our indecision becomes a decision. It works like this: Suppose a friend asks you to help her work on a student government task force that is studying the use of alcohol on campus. You'd like to participate, but because you'll have to commit to a term-long series of meetings, you're worried about the amount of time it will take up.

Career Connections

Weighing Career Possibilities

One of the most important decisions you'll ever make is choosing a career. Here's one method that can help you:

- Generate a selection of choices to consider after graduation. Make a list of possibilities—including work (e.g., computer programming, banking, teaching, law, business, insurance, computer software development, etc.), further study (e.g., graduate school, business school, law school, etc.), and even some pie-in-the-sky possibilities (e.g., jazz musician, circus performer).
- Determine life-satisfaction considerations that are important to you. Generate a list of criteria to use in weighing these postgraduation possibilities. For instance, you might want to consider the following:

  Benefit to society
  Income
  Parents' opinions
  Friends' opinions
  Interest in the activity
  Prestige
  Job security/job openings
  Benefits (vacation, health insurance, etc.)
  Time off
  Practicality/attainability
  Geographic location
  Everyday working conditions

- Determine how well a particular option fulfills each of the life-satisfaction factors you consider important. By systematically considering how a potential postgraduation path fulfills each of the criteria you use, you'll be able to compare different options. One easy way to do this is to create a chart like the one in **Table 10.1** (which shows an example of how computer programming might fulfill the various criteria).
- Compare different choices. Using the chart, evaluate your possibilities. Keep in mind that this is just a rough guide and that it's only as accurate as (a) the effort you put into completing it and (b) your understanding of a given choice. Use the results in conjunction with other things you find out about careers—and yourself.

table 10.1 Making Career Decisions

Life-Satisfaction Considerations	Possible Choice #1 *Computer programming*	Possible Choice #2	Possible Choice #3	Possible Choice #4
Benefit society	√			
Income	√			
Parents' opinions	√			
Friends' opinions				
Interest in the activity	√			
Prestige				
Job security/job openings	√			
Benefits	√			
Time off				
Practicality/attainability	√			
Everyday working conditions				
Other				
Other				
Other				
Other				
Other				

Journal Reflections

My Decision Crossroads

Have you ever made a decision that proved to be of great importance in terms of the direction your life would take? For example, perhaps you broke off a romantic relationship, or decided to quit a sports team because practice took up so much time, or participated in an act of civil disobedience during a protest rally. Reflect on that decision by answering these questions.

1. What was an important decision you made that had significant effects on your life?
2. What have been the main benefits and disadvantages that you've derived from the decision?
3. Every decision to do something is also a decision not to do other things. What did your decision keep you from doing?
4. Considering both the benefits and the disadvantages of the decision, would you say that you made a good decision?
5. Thinking critically about the approach you used to make the decision, what alternative approaches might you have used to make it? Could these alternatives have produced a different decision? How?

Because the first meeting isn't going to occur for a few weeks, you have some time to make up your mind. But you just can't seem to decide. Finally, it's the day of the meeting, and you still don't know what to do.

The truth is, you've made the decision: You don't really want to be on the committee. Your indecision is telling you that—bottom line—you don't have sufficient interest to make the commitment.

- **Avoid over-analysis and over-thinking decisions.** Life is full of ambiguous problems. If you wait until you are absolutely, 100 percent certain you have made the right decision, you may never act. Remember that almost all decisions can be reversed.
- **Go with your gut feeling.** Call it what you like—gut feeling, intuition, hunch, a feeling in your bones—but sometimes we need to go with our hearts and not our minds. If you've thought rationally about a decision and have been unable to determine the best course of action but have a gut feeling that one choice is better than another, follow your feelings.

> "In any moment of decision, the best thing you can do is the right thing, the next best thing is the wrong thing, and the worst thing you can do is nothing."
>
> President Theodore Roosevelt

Following a gut feeling does not mean that you don't need to consider the pros and cons of a decision rationally and carefully. In fact, generally our "intuitions" are best when informed by the thoughtfulness of a more rational process.

Carry Out the Decision

Ultimately, decisions must move from thought to action–they have to be carried out. Consequently, the final stage in making a decision is to act upon it. You need to turn your decision into behavior.

E Evaluate Considering the Outcomes

Did you make the right decision?

Even if you've spent time and mental effort in thinking through a decision, you still need to consider the results. Even well-considered decisions can end up being wrong, either because you neglected to consider something or because something has changed: either you or the situation.

For instance, suppose you are trying to decide between a major in management and one in biology. If you decide to go into management, it means that you'll be taking more courses related to finance and economics. As you take these courses, you will find out whether you're enjoying them. If you find you are consistently unhappy with them, you should allow yourself to reevaluate your decision to major in management and reconsider the alternatives. It won't be too late to change your mind.

In fact, even major life decisions are often reversible. That's why it's so important to evaluate your choices. If you've chosen the wrong alternative, reverse course and reconsider your options.

Remember: It's not a bad thing to change your mind. In fact, admitting that a decision was a mistake is often the wisest and most courageous course of action. You don't want to be so rigidly committed to a decision that you're unable to evaluate the consequences objectively. Give yourself permission to be wrong.

R Rethink Reconsidering Your Goals and Options

We can get to most places by multiple routes. There's the fastest and most direct route, which will get us to our destination in the least amount of time. Then there's the longer, more scenic route, where the trip itself provides pleasure. You can "take the long way home," as the song goes.

Is one route better than the other? Often not. Both take us to our destination. However, the experience of reaching our goal will have been very different.

Decisions about how to achieve a goal are similar to traveling down different routes. There's often no single decision that is best, just as there's often no single road to a particular place. Consequently, it's important to periodically reconsider the major decisions that we've made about our lives.

Ask yourself these questions:

- Are my decisions still producing the desired consequences?
- Are my decisions still appropriate, given my circumstances and changes in my life?

- Are my decisions consistent with what I want to get out of life?
- Do my decisions fit with my mission statement (a written, guiding philosophy of life)?

Periodically taking stock like this is the best way to make sure that your decisions are taking you where you want to go. Taking stock also helps you be more effective in making future decisions.

Deciding to Change Colleges

transferring
Changing colleges.

One of the biggest decisions you'll potentially face involves changing colleges, or **transferring**. You may be changing from a two-year to a four-year school. Or you may find that your current school doesn't offer the course of study you want or meet some other important need. Whatever the reason, there are several questions to keep in mind when making such an important decision:

- **Do I meet the minimum requirements for admission?** Every college has its own requirements for admission. For example, you'll probably be required to have a minimum grade point average for admission.
- **What new requirements will I have to meet at another school?** Because every school has its own particular set of requirements, you'll want to know the courses you'll have to take to graduate.
- **What courses have I taken that the other school will accept as meeting its requirements?** You'll need to determine the degree of *course equivalency,* in which courses you've already taken substitute for courses at another college.
- **Is there an articulation agreement between my current school and the school I'm considering transferring to?** *Articulation agreements* are official pacts between schools that set out course equivalency.
- **Do I have a good reason for transferring?** Be sure you know exactly why you are considering transferring. Make certain that you've investigated all the options available at your current school.

Keep in mind that although your current school may smooth the way for a transfer, it's the school to which you are transferring that determines how successful the transfer process will be. (You'll find additional information on transferring to another college at the P.O.W.E.R. Learning Connect Library.)

» LO 10-2 Problem Solving: Applying Critical Thinking to Find Solutions

Two trains are approaching one another, each moving at 60 miles an hour. If the trains continue moving at the same speed, how long will it be before . . .

problem solving
The process of generating alternatives to work on.

If this is what comes to mind when you think of problem solving, think again. **Problem solving** encompasses more than the abstract, often unrealistic situations portrayed in math texts. It involves everyday, commonplace situations: How do we divide the grocery bill so that each person pays a fair share? How do I keep my

1-year-old from tumbling down the stairs when there seems to be no way to fasten a gate at the top? How can I stop a faucet from dripping? How do I manage to study for a test and complete a paper the same evening?

The central task of problem solving is *generating* appropriate alternatives. In problem solving, we need to define the problem and devise as many reasonable solutions as we can.

What's the Problem?

The first step in solving any problem is to define what the problem is, as clearly as possible. This may sound easy, but often it isn't. In fact, it may take some time to figure out just what problem you're solving.

The reason for the difficulty in defining problems is that while some problems are clear and precise, others are big and hard to define. For example, it's clear what the problem is when you're solving a mathematical equation or finding the solution to a jigsaw puzzle. In contrast, defining big, ill-defined problems such as stopping terrorism or finding peace in the Middle East is much more difficult. Simply determining what information is required to solve such problems can be a major undertaking.

To determine what the problem is and set yourself on a course for finding a solution, ask yourself these questions:

- What is the initial set of facts?
- What is it that you need to solve?
- Which parts of the problem appear to be most critical to finding a solution?
- Is there some information that can be ignored?

The more systematically you approach a problem, the better. For instance, you can apply the five P.O.W.E.R. steps to problems, in a way similar to how they can be used to make decisions. By considering a problem systematically and thinking through your options, your choices will become clearer to you.

As you clarify what the problem is, you may find that you have encountered similar problems before. Your experience with them may suggest the means to the solution of the current problem. For example, consider the problem of the trains rushing toward each other. If you have worked on this kind of problem before, you might know a fairly simple equation to determine how long it will take before they meet. If a mother asks you about a problem she has keeping her toddler from tumbling down the stairs, you might offer your experience in keeping your puppy from visiting an off-limits area of your house.

> "Problems are only opportunities in work clothes."
>
> Henry J. Kaiser (1882–1967), entrepreneur

In contrast, to solve many of the complex problems that we face in our daily lives, we need to go beyond strategies that we've used in the past. Instead, we need to devise novel approaches. How do you do this? There are several strategies you might use.

Strategies for Solving Life's Messier Problems

- **Break the problem down into smaller, more manageable pieces.** Break a problem down into a series of subgoals. As you reach each subgoal, you get closer to your overall goal of solving the problem. For example, if your goal is to spend your junior year in your school's program in St. Petersburg, a subgoal would probably be to learn some basic Russian. By reaching this subgoal, you move closer to reaching your ultimate goal: a year abroad in a country that interests you.

- **Work backward.** Sometimes you know the answer to the problem, but not how to get there. Then it's best to work backward. A **working backward** strategy starts at the desired solution or goal and works backward, moving away from the goal. For example, consider this problem:

working backward
The strategy of starting at the desired solution or goal and working toward the starting point of the problem.

> *Water lilies on a certain lake double in area every 24 hours. From the time the first water lily appears until the lake is completely covered takes 60 days. On what day is the lake half covered?*

Most people solve this problem readily if they work backward. Here's how: If the pond is fully covered on day 60, how much is it covered the day before? Because the water lilies double each day, there had to be half as many the day before day 60. The answer, then, is that half the lake is covered on day 59. Only by moving backward could one see the solution clearly.

Some kinds of academic problems can be solved using the same strategy. For example, if you know what courses you must have completed to graduate, it's sometimes easiest to work backward from that point, determining the courses you need to take each year.

- **Use a graph, chart, or drawing to redefine the problem.** Transforming words into pictures often can help us to devise solutions that otherwise would elude us. One good example is this problem:

> *A hiker climbs a mountain on Saturday, leaving at sunrise and arriving at the top near sunset. He spends the night at the top. The next day, Sunday, he leaves at daybreak and heads down the mountain, following the same path that he climbed the day before. The question is this: Will there be any time during the second day when the hiker will pass exactly the same point on the mountain that he passed at exactly that time on the first day?*

analogy
A comparison between concepts or objects that are alike in some respects, but dissimilar in most others.

Trying to solve the problem through the use of math or words is quite difficult. However, there's a simpler way: drawing the two paths. As you can see from **Figure 10.2**, the drawing helps provide a solution.

- **Consider the opposite.** Problems can sometimes be solved by considering the opposite of the problem you're seeking to solve. For example, to define "good mental health" you might try to define "bad mental health."
- **Use analogies.** Some problems can be solved through the use of **analogies**, comparisons between concepts or objects that are alike in some respects but dissimilar in most others. For instance, if you liken a disastrous experience attending summer camp to a voyage on the *Titanic,* you're using an analogy.

Analogies may help us gain additional insight into the problem at hand, and they may provide an alternative framework for interpreting the information that is provided. For instance, the manufacturers of Pringles potato chips found that they could cut packaging costs if they slightly moistened the chips before packaging them—an idea that came when researchers noticed that tree leaves, which normally crumble easily when dry, could be packed together tightly when they were wet.

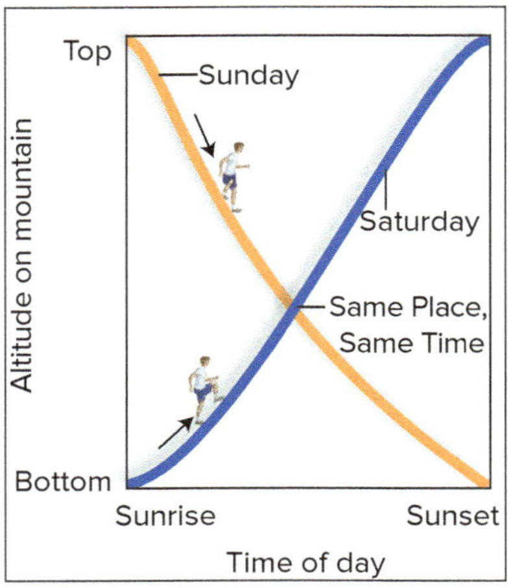

figure 10.2
Up and Down the Mountain: The Paths to a Solution

2  WORKING IN A GROUP

Try It! P O W E R

Exercise Your Problem-Solving Skills

Working in a group, try to solve these problems. To help you devise solutions, a hint regarding the best strategy to use is included after each problem.

1. One cold, dark, and rainy night, a college student has a flat tire on a deserted stretch of country road. He pulls onto the shoulder to change it. After removing the four lug nuts and placing them into the hubcap, he removes the flat tire and takes his spare out of the trunk. As he is moving the spare tire into position, his hand slips and he upsets the hubcap with the lug nuts, which tumble off into the night where he can't find them. What should he do? (*Hint:* Instead of asking how he might find the lug nuts, reframe the problem and ask where else he might find lug nuts.)
2. Cheryl, who is a construction worker, is paving a walk, and she needs to add water quickly to the concrete she has just poured. She reaches for her pail to get water from a spigot in the front of the house, but suddenly realizes the pail has a large rust hole in it and cannot be used. As the concrete dries prematurely, she fumbles through her toolbox for tools and materials with which to repair the pail. She finds many tools, but nothing that would serve to patch the pail. The house is locked and no one is home. What should she do? (*Hint:* When is a pail not a pail?)
3. What day follows the day before yesterday if two days from now will be Sunday? (*Hint:* Break it up or draw a diagram.)
4. A caterpillar has to climb up the muddy wall of a well that is 12 feet deep. Each day the caterpillar advances 4 feet, but each night as he sleeps, he slips back 2 feet. How many days will it take him to get out? (*Hint:* Draw it.)
5. Carrie has four chains, each three links long. She wants to join the four chains into a single, closed chain. Having a link opened costs 2 cents and having a link closed costs 3 cents. How can Carrie have the chains joined for 15 cents? (*Hint:* Can only end links be opened?)
6. What is two-thirds of one-half? (*Hint:* Reverse course.)
7. Juan has three separate large boxes. Inside each large box are two separate medium-sized boxes, and inside each of the medium boxes are four small boxes. How many boxes does Juan have altogether? (*Hint:* Draw it.)

After working to solve these problems, consider these questions: Which problems were the easiest to solve, and which were more difficult? Why? Were the hints helpful? Do you think there was more than one solution to any of the problems? Did your initial assumptions about a problem help or hinder your efforts to solve it? (*Note:* Answers to the problems are found at the end of the chapter.)

Sources: D. F. Halpern, *Thought and Knowledge: An Introduction to Critical Thinking,* 3rd ed. (Mahwah, NJ: Erlbaum, 1996); and J. D. Bransford and B. S. Stein, *The Ideal Problem Solver,* 2nd ed. (New York: W. H. Freeman, 1993).

- **Take another's perspective.** By viewing a problem from another person's point of view, it is often possible to obtain a new perspective on the problem that will make the problem easier to solve.
- **Forget about it.** Just as with decision making, sometimes it's a good strategy to simply temporarily walk away from a problem, giving our mind a break. Only a few hours or days away from a problem may give us enough of a mental break to jar some hidden solutions from the recesses of our minds. The idea of "sleeping on it" also can work; we may wake up refreshed and filled with new ideas.

Test these problem-solving strategies in **Try It! 2**.

Assess Your Potential Solutions

If a problem (such as a math problem) has only one answer, assessment of the solution you've come up with is relatively straightforward. You should be able to work on the problem and figure out whether you've been successful.

Course **Connections**

Using Critical Thinking in Your Classes

Nowhere is critical thinking more important to use—and demonstrate to your instructors—than when you're in your classes. Here are some strategies to foster your skills as a critical thinker when you are in class:

- **Ask questions.** Most instructors welcome questions. Even if an instructor doesn't have time to provide a full response, the very act of formulating a question will help you think more critically about the course material.
- **Accept that some questions have no right or wrong answers.** Understanding that some questions have no simple answer is a sign of cognitive sophistication. Sometimes the best an instructor can do is present competing theories. Although you may want to know which theory is right, accept that sometimes no one knows the answer to that question—that's why they're theories, not facts!
- **Keep an open mind.** Your instructor and classmates have their own perspectives and opinions. Even if you disagree with them, try to figure out why they hold their views. It will help you see the multiple sides of different issues.
- **Don't deny your emotional reactions—manage them.** There may be times that an instructor or classmate says something that is bothersome or even makes you angry. That's OK. But be sure to manage your emotions so that they don't overwhelm your rational self. And use your emotional reactions to gain self-understanding into what's important to you.

- **Try to think like a professional in the discipline you're studying.** If you're in a biology class, try to think like a biologist. If you're taking an art history course, put yourself in the shoes of an art historian. Professionals in various disciplines have different perspectives regarding what's important and what's not, and you should try to temporarily adopt those perspectives when you're in a particular class.
- **Don't be afraid of looking unintelligent.** No one wants to look foolish, especially in front of a roomful of classmates. But don't let self-defeating feelings prevent you from expressing your concerns. Take intellectual risks!

In contrast, messier problems have several possible solutions, some of which may be more involved and complicated than others. In these cases, it's necessary to compare alternative solutions and choose the best one. For example, suppose you want to surprise your best friend on her birthday. She is working in Omaha, about 90 miles from you, and you need to find a way to get there. Perhaps you could rent a car, take a Lyft or Uber, or find some other way. Money is an issue. You will want to figure out how much each alternative costs before choosing one as your solution to the problem. Since every penny you spend getting there is a penny less that you will have to celebrate, you will want to weigh the options carefully.

Finally, spend a bit of time seeing whether there is a way to refine the solution. Is the solution you've devised adequate? Does it address all aspects of the problem? Are there alternative approaches that might be superior? Answering these questions, and refining your solution to address them, can give you confidence that the solution you've come up with is the best. For example, if you're trying to get to Omaha, you might check online at your school's ride-sharing website to try to find a ride with someone going to Omaha that day. Maybe your friend's family is going to be driving in and could pick you up or could even lend you a car for the trip.

Remember that not every problem has a clear-cut solution. Sometimes we need to be satisfied with a degree of uncertainty and ambiguity. For some of us, such a lack of clarity is difficult, making us uneasy, and it may push us to choose a solution—any solution—that seems to solve the problem. Others of us feel more comfortable with ambiguity, but this may lead us to let problems ride, without resolving the situation.

3 PERSONAL STYLES **Try It!** POWER

Find Your Problem-Solving Style

To get a sense of how much you prefer ambiguity versus clarity in the problems you face, rate how much you agree with each of the statements in the questionnaire below. Use this rating scale:

1 = Strongly disagree
2 = Disagree
3 = Not sure, but probably disagree
4 = Not sure, but probably agree
5 = Agree
6 = Strongly agree

1. If you're an expert and can't come up with a good answer, then you're probably not much of an expert. ________
2. All problems can be solved eventually. ________
3. Good jobs have a lot of clarity in terms of what needs to be done. ________
4. You'll probably get more done by focusing on small, easy problems than on complicated problems. ________
5. It's better to focus on the familiar, rather than the unfamiliar. ________
6. You've got to be grateful for having a routine life, rather than one with a lot of unanticipated events. ________
7. The best kind of party is one where I know most of the people instead of one with a lot of strangers. ________
8. The world would be better if people shared similar beliefs and values. ________
9. I don't want to live in a foreign country; I like it better to live in my own country. ________
10. Keeping to a routine in life makes people happier. ________
11. It's better to solve an easy problem correctly than to try one that's hard and fail at it. ________
12. I don't like people who try to be different; it's better to try to fit in. ________
13. Most questions have a yes or no answer. ________
14. There's never a situation in which you have too much information. ________
15. Bosses who give ambiguous tasks to their employees make life harder for them. ________
16. Good teachers provide clear, definite answers to questions. ________

To score this questionnaire, add up your total score.

If you scored above 60, you have a low tolerance for ambiguity in problem solving. You prefer problems to be clear-cut and dislike uncertainty.

If you scored between 30 and 60, you have an average tolerance for ambiguity. Most of the time problems that are vague don't present you with any particular difficulty, although you generally prefer things to be fairly concrete.

If you scored below 30, you have a high tolerance for ambiguous problems. You don't mind—and in fact prefer—problems that are unclear.

Source: Based on Budner, 1962.

Either way, it's important to consider what your own problem-solving style is when you seek to identify solutions. And keep in mind that often there is no perfect solution to a problem—only some solutions that are better than others. (To find out whether you have a high need for clarity in problem solving or whether you tolerate ambiguity more easily, complete **Try It! 3**.)

Reflect on the Process of Problem Solving

It's natural to step back and bask in the satisfaction of solving a tough problem. That's fine—but take a moment to consider your success. Each time we solve a problem we end up a couple steps ahead, but only if we've thought about the process we went through to solve it.

Go back and consider what it took to solve the problem. Can the means you used to come up with your solution be applied to more complex kinds of problems? If you arrived at a solution by drawing a chart, would this work on similar problems in the future? Taking a moment to rethink your solution can provide you with an opportunity to become an expert problem solver and, more generally, to improve your critical thinking skills. Don't let the opportunity slip away.

» LO 10-3 Don't Fool Yourself: Avoiding Everyday Problems in Critical Thinking

cognitive bias
A limitation, blind spot, or mistake in thinking that leads to illogical or erroneous decisions.

Critical thinking requires thinking that is clear and unbiased. The quality of the thinking that you use in problem solving and decision making plays a crucial role in determining how successful you are in coming to solutions.

However, it is sometimes the alternative you *didn't* think of that can end up being the most satisfactory decision or solution. This is true in part because we are susceptible to **cognitive biases**, limitations, blind spots, and outright mistakes in our thinking that lead us to illogical or erroneous decisions. Cognitive biases occur because we apply habitual patterns of thought that may not be applicable to a problem at hand, due to failures of memory, or to outright miscalculations.

The good news is that we learn to think critically and avoid blind spots that hinder us in our decision making and problem solving. We can start by considering the common obstacles to critical thinking.

Here are some of the decision-making and problem-solving pitfalls to look out for. Avoiding them will improve your critical thinking greatly.

- **Don't assume that giving something a name explains it.** The mere fact that we can label an idea or problem with a name doesn't mean we are explaining it. Yet we often confuse *naming* something with *explaining* something. For instance, consider the following sequences of questions and answers:

  Q. *Why do I have so much trouble falling asleep?*

  A. *Because you have insomnia.*

  Q. *Why is he so unsociable?*

  A. *Because he's an introvert.*

  Q. *Why did the defendant shoot those people?*

  A. *Because he's a killer who is insane.*

  Q. *How do you know he's insane?*

  A. *Because only someone who was insane would kill people in that way.*[1]

  None of these answers is satisfactory. All use circular reasoning, in which the alleged explanation for the behavior is simply the use of a label.

- **Don't accept vague generalities that appear to be definitive statements.** Read the following personality analysis and think about how well it applies to you:

  You have a need for other people to like and admire you and a tendency to be critical of yourself. You also have a great deal of unused potential that you have not turned to your advantage, and although you have some personality weaknesses, you are generally able to compensate for them. Nonetheless, relating to members of the opposite sex has presented problems to you, and while you appear to be disciplined and self-controlled to others, you tend to be anxious and insecure inside.

If you believe that these statements provide an surprisingly accurate description of what you're like, you're not alone: Most college students believe that the descriptions are tailored specifically to them.[2] But how is that possible? It isn't. The reality is that the statements are so vague that they are virtually meaningless. The acceptance of vague but seemingly useful and significant statements about oneself and others has been called the *Barnum Effect,* after showman and circus master P. T. Barnum, who coined the phrase "There's a sucker born every minute."

One impediment to critical thinking is difficulty in distinguishing fact from opinion. For example, although many people are of the opinion that older people have a hard time learning new material, age need not be a deterrent to learning.
©Mike Watson/West Coast Surfer/Glow Images

- **Don't confuse opinion with fact.** Opinions are not fact. Although we may be aware of this simple formula, almost all of us can be fooled into thinking that someone's opinion is the same as a fact.

A fact is information that is proven to be true. In contrast, an opinion represents judgments, reasoning, beliefs, inferences, or conclusions. If we accept some bit of information as a fact, we can use it to build our opinions. But if we are presented with an opinion, we need to determine the facts on which it is built to judge its reliability.

The difference between fact and opinion can sometimes be subtle. For instance, compare these two statements:

1. Every college student needs to take a writing course during the first term of college.
2. Many college students need to take a writing course during the first term of college.

The first statement is most likely an opinion, because it is so absolute and unqualified. Words such as "every," "all," and "always" are often evidence of opinion. On the other hand, the second statement is more likely a fact, since it contains the qualifier "many." In general, statements that are qualified in some way are more likely to be facts.

Complete **Try It! 4** to see the difficulties sometimes involved in distinguishing between fact and opinion.

- **Avoid jumping to conclusions.**

When Ellen Philips, an African-American student at a small, largely white college in Alabama, stopped by a fraternity house to visit a friend, the student who answered the door asked if she was there to apply for the position of cook.

People jump to conclusions, sometimes based on racial bias, sometimes because they are misinformed, or sometimes because they make the wrong assumptions.

4

Try It! POWER

Distinguish Fact from Opinion

Read the following statements and try to determine which are facts and which are opinions.

1. College students should get at least 7 hours of sleep every night. ________
2. The average college student sleeps less than 7 hours a night. ________
3. Nike offers better styling and comfort than any other brand of shoe. ________
4. Two out of five sports figures surveyed preferred Nike over Converse shoes.
5. The U.S. government spends too much money on guns and missiles and not enough money on education. ________
6. Government figures show spending is much higher for guns and missiles than for education. ________
7. In general, U.S. high school students receive less classroom instruction in foreign languages than their counterparts in Europe and Asia. ________
8. No student in the United States should graduate without having studied a language other than English for at least 4 years. ________
9. Michael Jordan is the most outstanding, most exciting, and certainly most successful basketball player who ever stepped onto a court. ________

Items 1, 3, 5, 8, and 9 are opinions; the rest are facts. What are the main differences between opinion and fact?

Why is it so easy to jump to conclusions? One reason is that we sometimes aren't aware of the assumptions that underlie our thinking. Another is our reliance on "common sense."

- **Be skeptical of "common sense."** Common sense, judgement that is derived from experience, rather than scientific study, should not be considered a guide to what is fact. The reality is that much of what we call common sense is wrong and in fact contradictory with other statements of common sense. For example, if you believe in the notion "Absence makes the heart grow fonder," you may assume that your high school girlfriend, now in college across the country from you, will arrive home at Christmas even more in love with you than before. But what about "Out of sight, out of mind," another bit of common sense that suggests a less positive outcome? Common sense often presents us with contradictory advice, making it a less than useful guide to decision making and problem solving.
- **Avoid the confirmation bias.** The *confirmation bias* occurs when we favor the first conclusion we come to and then ignore contradictory information that supports alternative solutions. Even when we find evidence that contradicts a solution we have chosen, we are apt to stick with our original conclusion.

The confirmation bias occurs for several reasons. For one thing, because rethinking a problem that appears to be solved already takes extra effort, we are apt to stick with our first solution. For another, we give greater weight to subsequent information that supports our initial position than to information that is not supportive of it.

5

Try It! POWER

What's the Real Explanation?

Even though two events are related to each other, it doesn't mean that one causes the other. Instead, there is often some other factor that is the actual cause of the relationship.

To see this for yourself, consider each of the following (actual!) findings. What might be a plausible explanation for each one?

1. Ice cream sales and the timing of shark attacks are highly related. Why?

2. The number of cavities children have and the size of their vocabulary are closely related. Why?

3. Skirt hemlines tend to rise as stock prices rise. Why?

4. Women with breast implants have a higher rate of suicide than those without breast implants. Why?

5. People who own washing machines are more likely to die in car accidents than those who don't. Why?

6. Men who carry their cell phones in their front pants pockets have a lower sperm count than those who don't carry them in their front pants pockets. Why?

Once you've completed this **Try It!**, look at the possible explanations listed below. Keep in mind that these are simply suggested explanations; we don't know for sure if they're correct.

1. The actual cause is probably an increase in temperatures during summertime, which causes both sales of ice cream and ocean swimming to increase.
2. Both the number of cavities children have and the size of their vocabularies are related to their age.
3. Skirt hemlines go up, as does the stock market, when people are feeling less conservative and more optimistic.
4. Having breast implants and committing suicide both may be a result of unhappiness or a poor self-image.
5. People who own washing machines are more likely to own cars, and therefore, they stand a higher risk of dying in a car crash.
6. Men with high-stress jobs may be more likely to have cell phones, and it is the stress that produces the low sperm count—not the placement of a phone in their pocket.

- **Don't assume that just because two events occur together, one causes the other.** Just because two events appear to be associated with each other—or, in the language of social science, are *correlated* with each other—we cannot conclude that one event has caused the other to occur. It's a basic rule: *Correlation does not prove causation.*

  For example, suppose you read that a study showed that 89 percent of juvenile delinquents use marijuana. Does this mean that smoking marijuana *causes* juvenile delinquency?

  No, it doesn't. It is pretty safe to say that 100 percent of juvenile delinquents grew up drinking milk. Would you feel comfortable saying that milk causes delinquency? With correlations such as marijuana use and delinquent behavior, it is very likely that there's some third factor—such as influence of peers—that causes people to both (a) try drugs and (b) engage in delinquent behavior. The bottom line: We do not know the cause of the correlation.

  In short, we need to be careful in assuming causality. Even if two events or other kinds of variables occur together, it does not mean that one causes the other. To see this for yourself, take a look at the statements in **Try It! 5**, "What's the Real Explanation?"

Speaking *of* Success

Courtesy Alexa Irene Canady

NAME: **Dr. Alexa Irene Canady**

SCHOOL: **Michigan State University; University of Michigan Medical School**

As a young girl growing up just outside of Lansing, Michigan, Alexa Canady showed signs of a strong intellect and curiosity, but never realized it until her grandmother, taking a course in psychological testing, gave her an exam.

"I became a guinea pig for testing conducted by her class. After I scored exceptionally well on an exam, my grandmother's professor asked for further testing," Canady said. "A week later, the professor called our house during dinner. My mom came back to the table looking puzzled. 'He wants to know if Alexa is in any special programs–he says her intelligence testing is off the charts.' She looked at my father. 'That's odd,' my father said. 'Her scores at school are just average.'"

Along with her brother, being the only black kids in their elementary school during the 1950s, it came as little surprise to her when she later found out that her teacher had lied to the school about her test results, attributing them to a white girl in her class.

Through perseverance, determination, and hard work, she became a National Achievement Scholar in 1967 and enrolled in Michigan State University, planning to pursue a career in mathematics. But things changed.

"I had trouble because I didn't know what I wanted to do," Canady said, noting she no longer felt a passion for math. "I had a crisis of confidence, and had lost mathematics as a dream."

Uncertain at this point, she took a suggestion from her brother to apply for a minority medical scholarship at Michigan. The move ignited her true passion, medicine, that propelled her on to become the first African-American female neurosurgeon in the United States.

But there were still challenges as Canady pursued medical school, confronting a world dominated by men.

"It quickly became apparent that we were in a man's world. Professors frequently overlooked the women's raised hands, and most of the prestigious clubs and societies were all-male," she noted. "The white women in my class were shocked and outraged that they weren't being taken seriously. It was the first time they had felt pushed aside. But I just put my head down and worked harder. I was used to being disregarded," she said.

Never one to let adversity block her path, Dr. Canady strongly believes that hard work can overcome the biggest obstacles.

"Challenge yourself with the hardest courses and material you can find," said said. "At a certain point in your schooling, everyone is smart and the one who does the best works the hardest."

Sources:

1. https://www.nlm.nih.gov/changingthefaceofmedicine/physicians/biography_53.html.
2. http://www.nywici.org/features/blogs/aloud/first-woman-and-first-african-american-neurosurgeon-alexa-irene-canady-md.
3. National Women's Law Center. (2012). Faces of Title IX. Accessed online, 4-22-15, http://www.nwlc.org/title-ix/alexa-canady.

[RETHINK]

- **Dr. Canady faced a number of challenges in pursuing her medical career, but says that through hard work she was able to overcome them. Describe a challenge in your own life that was overcome through hard work.**
- **How do you think Dr. Canady's experience regarding being lied to about her test scores helped form her determination to succeed?**

Looking Back

LO 10-1 Identify strategies for improving the quality of your decisions.

- A structured process of decision making can clarify the issues involved, expand our options, and improve the quality of our choices.
- Good decision making begins with understanding your short- and long-term goals.
- Decision making is improved if you have a large number of alternatives.
- For difficult decisions, strategies include giving the decision time, acting out alternatives, tossing a coin to test your feelings, understanding that indecision is often a decision itself, and acting on gut feelings.

LO 10-2 Implement plans to use for problem solving.

- Problem solving entails the generation of alternatives to consider.
- We need to first understand and define the problem and to determine the important elements in coming to a solution to a problem.
- Approaches to generating solutions include breaking problems into pieces, working backward, using pictures, considering the opposite, using analogies, taking another's perspective, and "forgetting" the problem.
- Problem solving ultimately requires the evaluation and refinement of the solutions that have been generated.

LO 10-3 Recognize and avoid problems that affect critical thinking.

- Labeling, using vague generalities, accepting opinion as fact, jumping to conclusions, mistaking common sense, the confirmation bias, and assuming causation all pose threats to critical thinking.
- Awareness of the biases that may affect our thinking can help us avoid them.

[KEY TERMS AND CONCEPTS]

Analogy (p. 284)
Cognitive bias (p. 288)
Decision making (p. 274)
Problem solving (p. 282)
Transferring (p. 282)
Working backward (p. 284)

[RESOURCES]

ON CAMPUS

Some colleges offer courses in critical thinking, and they are a good bet to help increase decision-making and problem-solving skills. In addition, courses in logic and philosophy will help improve critical thinking skills.

If you are having a personal problem that is difficult to solve, don't hesitate to turn to staff at a campus counseling center, mental health center, or residential life office. Trained counselors and therapists can help you sort through the different options in an objective manner. They may identify possibilities for solutions that you didn't even know existed.

Even if the person with whom you speak initially is not the right one, he or she can direct you to someone who can help.

IN PRINT

Steve Padget's *Creativity and Critical Thinking* (Routledge, 2012) provides an overview of how to use critical thinking in an educational context, while Tina Seeling's *Creativity Rules: Get Ideas Out of Your Head and into the World* (HarperOne, 2017) offers advice on putting your creative ideas into action.

Critical Thinking, by Brooke Moore and Richard Parker (McGraw-Hill, 2016, 12th ed.), teaches readers how to effectively consider alternate points of view while making personal choices.

For a general overview of critical thinking skills, read Richard Paul and Linda Elder's *Critical Thinking: Tools for Taking Charge of Your Learning and Your Life* (Pearson, 2013, 2nd ed.)

ON THE WEB

- Santa Clara University's site on ethical decision making covers topics such as fairness, common good, and rights. It also includes numerous links and a smartphone app. (**www.scu.edu/ethics/practicing/decision/**)
- "Basic Guidelines to Problem Solving and Decision Making" (**www.managementhelp.org/prsn_prd/prob_slv.htm**) by Carter McNamara provides basic guidelines to problem solving and decision making in seven steps. This site is rich in links to comprehensive approaches to decision making, critical and creative thinking, time management, and organization.
- Cuesta College offers a concise approach to critical thinking and problem solving at this site: **http://www.cuesta.edu/student/servs_classes/ssc/study_guides/critical_thinking/index.html**

[ANSWERS TO TEST ITEMS IN TRY IT! 2]

1. Remove one lug nut from each of the other three tires on the car and use these three to attach the spare tire. This will hold until four more lug nuts can be purchased.
2. Dump the tools out of the toolbox and use it as a pail.
3. Thursday.
4. Five days; on the fifth day the caterpillar will reach the top and will not have to slide down again.
5. Open all three links on one chain (cost = 6 cents) and use them to fasten the other three chains together (cost = 9 cents; total cost = 15 cents).
6. It is the same as one-half of two-thirds, or one-third.
7. 33 boxes (3 large, 6 medium, 24 small).

The Case of . . .

Left Holding the Lease

Erica has a problem.

In the spring of her first year of college, she and her friend Shira found a two-bedroom apartment to share for the upcoming school year. The apartment was on the expensive side, but they decided that it was worth it because it was so close to campus. She and Shira jointly paid the security deposit on the apartment. However, because Shira wasn't around when it came time to sign the lease, only Erica signed it. Consequently, Erica is legally responsible for fulfilling the terms of the lease.

Now, only two weeks before the start of the fall term, Shira has told Erica that she has realized she can't afford the rent and that she has decided she has to live with her parents. Erica is simultaneously furious with Shira and panicky at the thought of having to pay the rent by herself.

How is she going to deal with the problem?

1. Is the problem a purely financial and legal one, or are there personal and social considerations that should be taken into account in solving the problem?

2. Is the problem solely Erica's problem, or should Shira take responsibility for solving it as well?

3. What alternatives does Erica have for dealing with the situation?

4. How should Erica go about evaluating the outcomes for each alternative?

5. Based on your analysis of the problem, what advice would you give Erica for dealing with the situation?

CHAPTER 11

Diversity and Your Relationships with Others

©Pamela Moore/Getty Images

Learning Outcomes

By the time you finish this chapter you will be able to

» LO 11-1 Discuss why the increasing diversity of society is important to you.

» LO 11-2 Utilize strategies to become more at ease with differences and diversity.

» LO 11-3 Build lasting relationships and learn to deal with conflict.

He was born in the Kapi'olani Maternity and Gynecological Hospital in Honolulu, Hawaii. His mother was an American of primarily English descent from Wichita, Kansas. His father was born in Africa, in Nyang'oma Kogelo, Nyanza Province, Kenya. His parents met while taking a Russian language class. He spent most of his childhood in Hawaii, except for a few years in Indonesia.

In describing his childhood, he later said, "The opportunity that Hawaii offered–to experience a variety of cultures in a climate of mutual respect–became an integral part of my world view, and a basis for the values that I hold most dear."

He is Barack Obama, who grew up to be president of the United States.

Looking Ahead

Whether you have skin that is black or white or brown, are Jewish or Protestant or Muslim or Greek Orthodox, were born in Cuba or Vietnam or Boise, are able-bodied or physically challenged, college presents a world of new opportunities. Because almost every college draws students from a wider sphere than the average high school, college permits you to encounter people with very different backgrounds from your own. If you take the opportunity to form relationships with a variety of individuals, you will increase your understanding of the human experience and enrich your life.

In this chapter, we consider how social diversity and relationships affect your college experience. We examine the increasing diversity of college campuses, which reflects that of society at large, and consider the meanings and social effects of race, ethnicity, and culture. We look at practical strategies for acknowledging—and shedding—prejudice and stereotypes and being receptive to others on their own merits.

We next discuss relationships from a broader perspective, exploring ways that you can build lasting friendships with others. Finally, the chapter discusses the conflicts that can arise between people and what you can do to resolve them.

» LO 11-1 Living in a World of Diversity

No matter where we live, our contacts with others who are racially, ethnically, and culturally different from us are increasing. The web is bringing people from across the globe into our homes, as close to us as the computer sitting on our desk. Businesses now operate globally, so co-workers are likely to come from many different countries and cultures. Being comfortable with people whose backgrounds and beliefs may differ from our own is not only a social necessity, but virtually a requirement for career success.

By the mid-twenty-first century, the percentage of people in the United States of African, Latin American, Asian, and Arabic ancestry will be greater than the percentage of those of Western European ancestry–a profound statistical, and social, shift. College enrollments will mirror these changes, as populations that were in the minority become the majority.

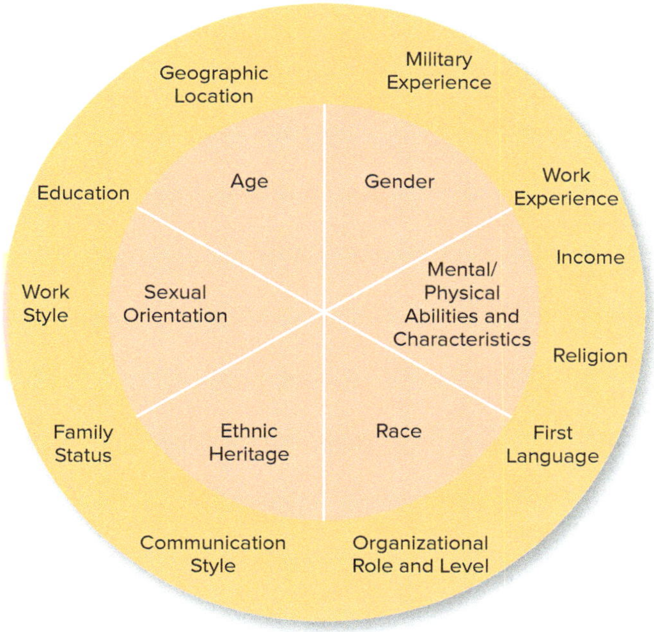

figure 11.1
Diversity Wheel
Diversity comprises many different characteristics as exemplified by the Diversity Wheel.
Source: © Nolan, M. F. (1997, April 26). Tiger's racial multiplicity. The Boston Globe, p. A11. Loden: Implementing Diversity, Best Practices for Making Diversity Work in Your Organization.

In addition, the number of college students from countries outside the United States has increased substantially in the last several decades. These students can hold dramatically different perspectives and cultural attitudes.

Furthermore, it's not just racial, ethnic, and cultural characteristics that constitute diversity. As you can see in the Diversity Wheel in Figure 11.1, diversity comprises characteristics such as gender, sexual orientation, age, and mental and physical characteristics. Layer on top of that factors such as education, religion, and income level, and the complexity of others–and ourselves–becomes apparent. In addition, people often have multiple diversities, known as intersectionality: One can be, for instance, a hearing-impaired lesbian African American woman, evoking responses from others that reflect any, all, or none of these identities. (You can examine the diversity of your own campus by completing **Try It! 1**.)

Our cultural heritage plays an important role in shaping who we are.
©Idealink Photography/Alamy

1 **Try It!** POWER

Determine the Diversity of Your College Community

Assess the degree of diversity that exists at your college, and the overall attitude toward diversity on your campus, by answering these questions. When thinking of diversity, remember to include the many different ways in which people can be different from one another, including race, ethnicity, culture, sexual orientation, physical challenges, and so on.

1. Overall, what is your sense of how diverse your campus is?

2. What is the nature of your college's *student* diversity in terms of statistics for membership in different racial, ethnic, or cultural groups? (You may be able to find these statistics on your college's website.)

3. What is the nature of your college's *faculty* diversity in terms of statistics for membership in different racial, ethnic, or cultural groups?

4. What courses are available that directly address diversity as an issue? (A good place to check is your college catalog listing of courses in the social sciences and humanities.)

The Language of Diversity

Are you African American or Black? Caucasian or white or Euro-American? Hispanic or Latino? American Indian or Native American? Gay or lesbian or straight? Transgender or male or female? Physically challenged? A combination of various identities?

The language we use to describe our own ethnic, racial, and cultural group membership, and those of other people, is in constant flux. And what we call people matters. The subtleties of language affect how people think about members of particular groups, and how they think about themselves.

One of the difficulties in understanding diversity is that many of the terms we use are ill-defined and often overlapping. The term **race** is generally used to refer to obvious physical differences that set one group apart from others. But depending on how race is defined, there are between 3 and 300 races, with no race genetically distinct. And the reality is that 99.9 percent of our genetic makeup is similar across all human beings. So today race is generally thought of as a *social construction,* something that is defined by people's attitudes and beliefs.

race
Traditionally, biologically determined physical characteristics that set one group apart from others.

ethnicity
Shared national origins or cultural patterns.

Ethnicity refers to shared national origins or cultural patterns. In the United States, for example, Puerto Rican, Irish, and Italian Americans are categorized as ethnic groups. However, ethnicity—like race—is very much in the eye of the beholder. For instance, a Cuban American who is a third-generation citizen of the United States may feel few ties or associations to Cuba. Yet whites may view her as "Hispanic," and Blacks may view her as "white."

Journal Reflections

Thinking about Race, Ethnicity, Gender, and Culture

1. Were race, ethnicity, or gender identity discussed in your family as you were growing up? In what ways?

2. Do you demonstrate—through your behavior, attitudes, and/or beliefs—your own ethnic background? How?

3. Are there cultural differences between you and members of other races or ethnicities? What are they?

4. Are you proud of your ethnicity? Why?

5. Think what it would be like to be a member of a racial group or ethnicity other than your own. In what ways would your childhood and adolescence have been different? How would you view the world differently?

Finally, **culture** comprises the learned behaviors, beliefs, and attitudes that are characteristic of an individual society or population. But it's more than that: Culture also encompasses the products that people create, such as architecture, music, art, and literature. Culture is created and shaped by people, but at the same time it creates and shapes people's behavior.

culture
The learned behaviors, beliefs, and attitudes that are characteristic of an individual society or population, and the products that people create.

Race, ethnicity, and culture shape each of us to an enormous degree. They profoundly influence our view of others, as well as who we are. They affect how others treat us and how we treat them in turn. They determine whether we look people in the eye when we meet them, how early we arrive when we're invited to dinner at a friend's house, and even, sometimes, how well we do in school.

Even the words we use to describe others reflect our beliefs and values. For instance, the term *African American* is a label that has geographical and sociological implications. On the other hand, *Black* focuses on race and skin color.

Similarly, there is no common language for the varieties of gender identities and sexualities that individuals may hold. For example, *transgender* refers to individuals whose sense of whether they are male or female (their *gender identity*) does not match the sex that they were assigned at birth. Transgender people may refer to themselves as trans or transsexual, and they may prefer the use of pronouns different from those traditionally used.

Furthermore, gender identity is not the same thing as *sexual orientation,* which describes a person's physical and emotional attraction to another person. For example, people may be straight, lesbian, gay, or bisexual, depending on whom they are attracted to sexually.

Because you may have grown up in neighborhoods that are homogeneous or in environments in which gender identity and sexual orientation were kept hidden, you may have little or even no experience interacting with people who are different from you. At some time, though, that will change. As the United States becomes increasingly diverse, it's not a matter of "if" but of "when" you will be exposed to people who have profoundly different backgrounds from your own. Whether in the workplace or in the neighborhood in which you reside, living in a diverse environment will be part of your life.

Building Cultural Competence

cultural competence
Knowledge and understanding about other races, ethnic groups, cultures, and minority groups.

We're not born knowing how to drive a car or cook. We have to learn how to do these things. The same is true of developing a basic awareness of other races, ethnic groups, and cultures–what is referred to as cultural competence. **Cultural competence**, the knowledge and understanding of others' customs, perspectives, background, and history, can teach us a great deal about others, as well as ourselves. Cultural competence also provides a basis for civic engagement, permitting us to act with civility toward others and to make the most of our contributions to society.

Building cultural competence proceeds in several steps, outlined in the P.O.W.E.R. Plan that follows.

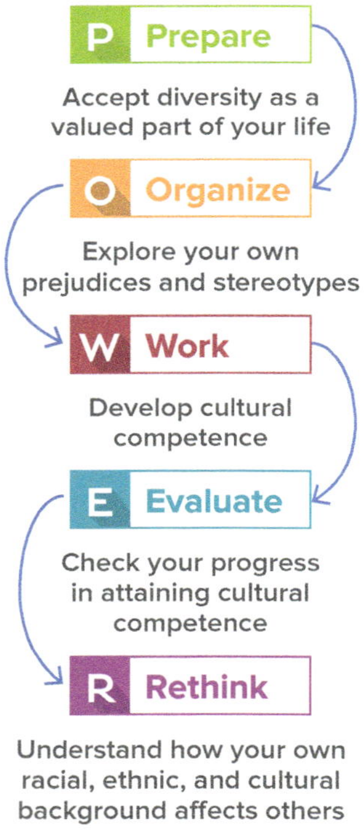

P.O.W.E.R. Plan

P Prepare

Accepting Diversity as a Valued Part of Your Life

In the title of her book on social diversity, psychologist Beverly Tatum asks, *Why Are All the Black Kids Sitting Together in the Cafeteria?*[1] She might just as well have asked a similar question about the white kids, the Asian American kids, and so forth. It often appears as if the world comes already divided into separate racial, ethnic, and cultural groups.

It's more than appearances: We form relationships more easily with others who are similar to us than with those who are different from us. It's easier to interact with others who look the same as we do, who come from similar backgrounds, and who share our race, ethnicity, and culture, because we can take for granted certain shared cultural assumptions and views of the world.

But that doesn't mean that "easy" and "comfortable" translate into "good" or "right." We can learn a great deal more, and grow and be challenged, if we seek out people who are different from us. If you look beyond surface differences and find out what motivates other people, you can become aware of new ways of thinking about family, relationships, earning a living, and the value of education. It can be liberating to realize that others may hold very different perspectives from your own and that there are many ways to lead your life.

Letting diversity into your own life also has very practical implications: As we discuss in **Career Connections**, learning to accept and work with people who are different from you is a crucial skill that will help you in whatever job you hold.

Organize

Exploring Your Own Prejudices and Stereotypes

Arab. Gay. African American. Hispanic. Female. Disabled. Overweight.

Quick: What comes into your mind when you think about each of these labels? If you're like most people, you don't draw a blank. Instead, a collection of images and feelings comes into your mind, based on what you know, have been told, or assume about the group.

The fact that we don't draw a blank when thinking about each of these terms means that we already have a set of attitudes and beliefs about them and the groups they represent. Acknowledging and then examining these preexisting assumptions is a first step toward developing cultural competence: We need to explore our own prejudices and stereotypes.

Prejudice refers to evaluations or judgments of members of a group based on their membership in the group and not on their particular characteristics as individuals. Prejudice is demonstrated when we judge others not in terms of who they are but in terms of what group they belong to.

prejudice
Evaluations or judgments of members of a group that are based on their membership in the group and not on their particular characteristics as individuals.

For example, the auto mechanic who doesn't expect a woman to understand auto repair or the job supervisor who finds it unthinkable that a father might want to take a leave for child care are engaging in gender prejudice. *Gender prejudice* is evaluating individuals on the basis of their being male, female, or transgender and not on their own specific characteristics or abilities. Similarly, prejudice can be directed toward individuals because of their race, ethnic origin, gender or sexual orientation, age, physical disability, or even physical attractiveness.

Prejudice leads to discrimination. **Discrimination** is behavior directed toward individuals on the basis of their membership in a particular group. Discrimination can result in exclusion from jobs and educational opportunities. It also may result in members of particular groups receiving lower salaries and benefits.

discrimination
Behavior directed toward individuals on the basis of their membership in a particular group.

Prejudice and discrimination are maintained by stereotypes. **Stereotypes** are beliefs and expectations about members of a group. For example, do you think that women don't do as well as men in math? Do you agree that "white men can't jump"? Do you think that people on welfare are lazy?

stereotypes
Beliefs and expectations about members of a group that are held simply because of their membership in the group.

If you answered yes to any of these questions, you hold stereotypes about the group being referred to. It is the degree of generalization involved that makes stereotypes inaccurate. Some women don't do well in math. But the fact is, many women do perfectly fine in math, and many men don't. Stereotypes ignore this diversity.

To develop cultural competence, it's important to identify our prejudices and stereotypes and to fight them. Sometimes they are quite subtle and difficult to detect. For instance, a wealth of data taken from observation of elementary school classrooms shows that teachers are often more responsive to boys than to girls. The teachers don't know they're doing it; it's a subtle, but very real, bias.

> "Prejudice is the child of ignorance."
> William Hazlitt, 18th-century English essayist

Why does this happen? In part it's because we're exposed to stereotypes from a very young age. Parents and relatives teach them to us, sometimes unwittingly, sometimes deliberately. The media illustrate them constantly and often in very subtle ways. For instance, African Americans and Latinos are often portrayed

Career Connections

Diversity in the Workplace

Diversity, and issues relating to it, are a part of today's workplace. For example, in one California computer assembly company with several thousand employees, 40 different languages and dialects are spoken among people representing 30 nationalities.[2] Furthermore, employers must deal with issues ranging from whether time off for religious holidays should count as vacation time to whether the partner of a gay or lesbian worker should be covered by the worker's medical insurance.

The gulf in the workplace between people with different cultural backgrounds may be wide. For instance, an immigrant from Japan might consider it the height of immodesty to outline his or her accomplishments in a job interview. The explanation? In Japan, the general cultural expectation is that people should stress their incompetence; to do otherwise would be considered highly immodest.

The increasing diversity of the workplace means that increasing your cultural competence will serve you well. It will help you perform on work teams that are composed of people of different races and ethnic backgrounds. It will allow you to supervise people whose native language and customs may be different from yours. And it will help you develop the skills to work for a boss from another country and cultural background. Equally important, gaining cultural competence will help you respond to the legal issues that surround diversity. It is illegal for employers to discriminate on the basis of race, ethnic background, age, gender, or physical disability. Cultural competence will help you not only to deal with the letter of the law but also to understand why embracing diversity is so essential to getting along with others in the workplace.

as unemployed or as criminals, women are less likely than men to be shown as employed, and gay men are frequently depicted as effeminate.

But it's not only stereotypes that lead us to view members of other groups differently from those of our own. For many people, their own membership in a cultural or racial or ethnic group is a source of pride and self-worth. There's nothing wrong with this. However, these feelings can lead to a less desirable outcome: the belief that their own group is superior to others. As a result, people inflate the positive aspects of their own group and belittle groups to which they do not belong. The bottom line is continuing prejudice.

To overcome stereotypes and to develop cultural competence, we must first explore our stereotypes. To this end, we've provided **Try It! 2**, "Check Your Stereotype Quotient."

» LO **11-2**

W Work

Developing Cultural Competence

Although it's neither easy nor simple to increase your understanding of and sensitivity to other cultures, it can be done. Several strategies are effective:

- **Study other cultures and customs.** Take an anthropology course, study religion, or learn history. If you understand the purposes behind different cultural customs, attitudes, and beliefs, you will be able to understand the richness and meaning of other people's cultural heritage.

  Many colleges offer workshops on diversity and prejudice reduction. These can help too. The important point is that understanding comes from knowledge, and you won't be able to fully appreciate others without learning about their background.

2 | **Try It!** POWER

Check Your Stereotype Quotient

Do you hold stereotypes about other people? How pervasive do you think they are? Respond to the following informal questionnaire to get a sense of your susceptibility to stereotyping.

1. When you see five African American students sitting together in a cafeteria, do you think that they are exhibiting racism? Do you think the same thing when you see five white students sitting together in a cafeteria?

2. When you are speaking with a person who has a speech-related disorder such as stuttering, are you likely to conclude that the person is less intelligent than a fluent speaker?

3. When an elderly woman can't remember something, do you assume her forgetfulness is because she is old or perhaps has Alzheimer's disease?

4. When an attractive blonde female student states an opinion in class, are you surprised if the opinion is intelligent and well expressed?

5. If a person with a mobility disorder turns down your offer for assistance, are you offended and resentful?

6. If you found out that a star professional football player is gay, would you be surprised?

What do you think your answers tell you about yourself and your views of others?

WORKING IN A GROUP

Compare your answers with those of your classmates. What do you think causes the similarities and differences in responses?

- **Travel.** There is no better way to learn about people from other cultures than to see those cultures firsthand. College vacations offer you the time to travel, and relatively inexpensive charter flights can take you to Europe, Asia, and other places around the globe. Sometimes, in fact, it's cheaper to take a transoceanic flight than to travel to closer locations in the United States.

  If you can't afford airfare, take a car or bus ride to Mexico or Canada. In many parts of Canada, French is spoken and the culture is decidedly different from that in the United States (or the rest of Canada, for that matter).

  Travel needn't be international, however. If you are from the northern states, head south. If you are from California, consider heading east. If you live in a large metropolitan area, travel to a different area from ones you're familiar with. No matter where you go, simply finding yourself in a new context can aid your efforts to learn about other cultures.
- **Participate in service learning.** Sometimes you can learn about people who are different from you in your own backyard—or, more precisely, the backyard of your college. By becoming involved in community service, such as tutoring middle school students, volunteering to work with the homeless, or working on an environmental cleanup, you get the opportunity to interact with people who may be very different from those you're accustomed to.
- **Don't ignore people's backgrounds.** None of us is color blind. Or blind to ethnicity. Or to culture. It's impossible to be completely unaffected by people's racial, ethnic, and cultural backgrounds. So why pretend to be? Cultural heritage is an important part of other people's identity, and to pretend that their background doesn't exist and has no impact on them is unrealistic at best, and insulting at worst. It's important, though, to distinguish between accepting the fact that other people's backgrounds affect them and pigeonholing people and expecting them to behave in particular ways.
- **Don't make assumptions about who people are.** Don't assume that someone is heterosexual because most people are heterosexual. Don't assume that someone with an Italian-sounding last name is Italian. Don't assume that a Black person has two Black parents. Although such guesses might be right statistically in terms of assumptions when considering people as a group, they may be wrong in terms of individual cases. (To get a sense of how our assumptions color our thinking, think about the questions in **Try It! 3**.)
- **Accept differences.** Different does not mean better. Different does not mean worse. Different just means not looking, acting, or believing exactly the same as you. We shouldn't attach any kind of value to being different; it's neither better nor worse than being similar.

Travel provides us with an opportunity to become immersed in very different cultures and to see the world—and ourselves—through different eyes.
©Roberto Westbrook/Getty Images

In fact, even people who seem obviously different on the surface probably have many similarities with you. Like you, they are students; they have fears and anxieties like yours; and they have aspirations and dreams, just as you do.

The important point about differences is that we need to accept and embrace them. Think about some differences you may have from people who are similar to you. Perhaps you really can't stand classical music, yet one of your childhood friends has taken piano lessons since he was five and loves it. Chances are you both accept that you have different tastes and see this difference as part of who each of you is.

3

Try It! POWER

Contemplate a Questionnaire

Read and consider each of the following questions:[3]

1. What do you think caused your heterosexuality?
2. When and how did you decide you were heterosexual?
3. Is it possible that heterosexuality is just a phase you may grow out of?
4. Is it possible your heterosexuality stems from a neurotic fear of others of the same sex?
5. To whom have you disclosed your heterosexual tendencies?
6. Why do you insist on showing off your heterosexuality?
7. Why do heterosexuals place so much emphasis on sex?
8. There seem to be many unhappy heterosexuals. Techniques have been developed that might enable you to change your sexual orientation. Have you considered changing?
9. Considering the menace of hunger and overpopulation, could the human race survive if everyone were heterosexual like yourself?

What are your reactions to this questionnaire?

What do your reactions tell you about the assumptions you hold about what others are like?

Substitute the label "homosexual" for each occurrence of "heterosexual" in the questionnaire and read through it again. How have your reactions changed?

Source: Adapted from Martin Rochlin, Ph.D., *The Heterosexual Questionnaire,* 1972.

E Evaluate

Checking Your Progress in Attaining Cultural Competence

Because cultural groups are constantly changing, developing cultural competence is an ongoing process. To evaluate where you stand, ask yourself the following questions. Be honest!

- Do I make judgments about others based on external features, such as skin color, ethnic background, cultural customs, gender, weight, or physical appearance?
- Who are my friends? Do they represent diversity or are they generally similar to me?

- Do I openly express positive values relating to diversity? Do I sit back passively when others express stereotypes and prejudices, or do I actively question their remarks?
- Am I educating myself about the history and varying experiences of different racial, ethnic, and cultural groups?
- Do I give special treatment to members of particular groups, or am I even-handed in my relationships?
- Do I recognize that, despite surface differences, all people have the same basic needs?
- Do I feel so much pride in my own racial, ethnic, and cultural heritage that it leads me to look less favorably upon members of other groups?
- Do I seek to understand events and situations through the perspectives of others and not just my own?

R Rethink

Understanding How Your Own Racial, Ethnic, and Cultural Background Affects Others

If you are a member of a group that traditionally has been the target of prejudice and discrimination, you probably don't need to be told that your race, ethnicity, and cultural background affect the way that others treat you. But even if you are a member of a traditionally dominant group in society, the way in which others respond to you is, in part, a result of others' assumptions about the groups of which you are a part.

In short, how others view us is affected by the groups to which we belong. And how we view others is affected by the groups to which they belong.

But keep this in mind: No matter how different other students are from you in terms of their race, ethnicity, and cultural background, they undoubtedly share many of the same concerns you have. Like all of us, they question themselves, wonder whether they will be successful, and fret about what they will do for the rest of their lives. Bridging the surface difference between you and others can result in the development of close, lasting social ties, a topic we consider next.

Building Lasting Relationships

Few of us lead our lives in isolation. There's a reason for this: Relationships with others are a critical aspect of our sense of well-being. The support of friends and relatives helps us feel good about ourselves. In fact, studies have found that our physical and psychological health may suffer without friendships. The social support of others acts as a guard against stress and illness. And if we do get sick, we recover more quickly if we have a supportive network of friends.

Our relationships with others also help us understand who we are. To understand our own abilities and achievements, we compare them with those of others who are similar to ourselves. Our attitudes, beliefs, and values are influenced—and shaped—by others. We are who we are largely because of the people with whom we come in contact.

> "I have met the most amazing individuals and made the most incredible friends in such a short amount of time."
>
> **Student, Wittenberg University, in Sponholz, M., & Sponholz, J., *The Princeton Review College Companion* (New York: Random House. 1996), p. 24.**

Course Connections

Diversity in the Classroom

The increasing diversity of classrooms presents both opportunity and challenge. The opportunity comes from the possibility of learning on a firsthand basis about others and their experiences. The challenge comes when people who may be very different from us call into question some of our most fundamental beliefs and convictions.

Here are some ways that you can be better equipped to deal with the classroom challenges involved in diversity:

- **Present your opinions in a respectful manner.** Don't get annoyed or angry when others disagree with your point of view. Be tolerant of others' perspectives and their thinking.
- **Don't assume you can understand what it's like to be a member of another race, ethnicity, cultural group, or gender.** Talk about your own experiences, and don't assume you know what others have experienced.
- **Don't treat people as representatives of the groups to which they belong.** Don't ask someone how members of his or her racial, ethnic, or cultural group think, feel, or behave with respect to a particular issue. No single individual can speak for an entire group. Furthermore, group members are likely to display little uniformity on most issues and in most behaviors. Consequently, this type of question is ultimately impossible to answer.
- **Seek out students who are different from you.** If you are assigned a group project, volunteer to work with others who are different from you. You may learn more working with others who are not similar to you than working with those who are like you.
- **Don't be afraid to offer your opinion out of concerns for "political correctness."** If you offer an opinion in a respectful, thoughtful, and tolerant manner, you should feel free to voice your opinion. Even if your views are minority opinions, they deserve to be considered.

Making Friends

Although some of us naturally make friends with ease, for others making friends is more difficult. But building relationships is not a mystery. Here are several ways to go about it:

- **Invest time in others.** There's no better way to demonstrate that you are interested in being friends than investing time. Relationships need to be nourished by the commitment of time. You can't expect friendships to flourish unless you spend time with people.
- **Reveal yourself.** Good friends understand each other. The best way to make that happen is to let others get to know you. Be open and honest about the things you like and dislike. Talk about where you come from, what your family is like. Find out about the other person. Having a deeper understanding of where someone comes from not only helps build bridges between people of different racial and ethnic backgrounds, but also helps build friendships. By honestly communicating your beliefs and attitudes, you give others the chance to learn those things you have in common.
- **Let others know you like them.** It may seem scary, but don't be coy and try to pretend you are uninterested in the friendships of others. Take the risk of being rebuffed. You don't have to announce outright that you like someone. Instead, reveal your interest in a friendship by inviting the person to do something with you or simply by engaging in conversation, sharing something about your life. Your actions will speak louder than words.

- **Accept others as they are, not as you would like them to be.** One mark of friendship is acceptance of people the way they are, warts and all, and not the way you would like them to be. Do not impose conditions on accepting others. Keep in mind that no one is perfect and that everyone has both good and bad qualities.
- **Show concern and caring.** This is really the substance of friendship and the basis for the trust that develops between friends. Don't be afraid to show your interest in the fortunes of others and to share the sadness when they suffer some setback or loss.
- **Be open to friendships with people who are very different from you.** Don't assume that the only "appropriate" friends are your peers who are similar to you, such as other college students. Open yourself to friends who are older, who are younger, who work at your school, and who are different from you in fundamental ways.
- **Recognize that not everyone makes a good friend.** People who put you down, consistently make you feel bad, or behave in ways that violate your own personal standards are not friends. Choose your friends based on the good feelings you have when you are with them and the concern and care they show for you. Friendship is a two-way street.

The R-Word: Relationships

Relationships move beyond friendship. They occur when two people feel emotionally attached, fulfill each other's needs, and generally feel interdependent. When a true relationship exists, several components are present:

- **Trust.** Relationships must be built on a foundation of trust. We need to be able to count on others and feel that they will be open with us.
- **Honesty.** No relationship can survive if the partners are not honest with each other. Each partner must share a commitment to the truth. Your life does not have to be a completely open book–it's the rare individual who has no secrets whatsoever–but it is important to be honest about your fundamental beliefs, values, and attitudes. Those in good relationships accept each other, blemishes and all. A relationship based on untruths or even half-truths lacks depth and meaning.
- **Mutual support.** Healthy relationships are characterized by mutual support. A partner's well-being should have an impact on you, and your well-being should affect your partner. In good relationships, the partners seek out what is best for both, and they act as advocates for and defend each other.
- **Loyalty.** The mark of a good relationship is loyalty. Loyalty implies that relationship partners are supportive of each other, even in times of adversity and difficulty.
- **Acceptance.** Your best friend develops a love for the Dave Matthews Band and listens to the CDs seemingly without interruption. You can't stand to listen to them. Do you decide that you can no longer be friends? Of course not.

  In good relationships, small annoyances don't get in the way of the deeper connection between you and another person. We don't have to like everything others

What you *don't* say matters. Close, lasting relationships are often built on good listening skills.
©Daniel Thislethwai/Image Source

do to maintain relationships with them. We don't even have to appreciate or approve of every aspect of their personality. What is crucial is the willingness to accept others as they are, without constantly yearning for changes. All of us wish to be accepted by others as we are, not as they'd like us to be; we should offer the same approval to those with whom we maintain relationships.

- **Willingness to embrace change.** Change is part of everyone's life. As people grow and develop, they change. So do relationships.

  We need to accept change as a fundamental part of relationships and build upon that change. In fact, we need to welcome change. Although change brings challenges with it, it also helps us understand ourselves and our own place in the world more accurately.

  It is only natural that some relationships will fade over time. People do outgrow one another. That's inevitable. What's important is not to live in fear that your relationship is so fragile that you have to avoid or ignore changes in who you and a partner are. Instead, both partners in a relationship should do their best to accept transformations in the relationship as a part of life. (To learn more about your views of close relationships, complete **Try It! 4**.)

Loneliness

loneliness
A subjective state in which people do not experience the level of connection with others that they desire.

Loneliness is a subjective state: We can be totally alone and not feel lonely, or we can be in the midst of a crowd and feel lonely. Loneliness occurs when we don't experience the level of connection with others that we desire. There are also different types of loneliness. Some of us feel lonely if we lack a deep emotional attachment to a single person, which can occur even if we have many friends. Others feel loneliness because they believe they don't have enough friends.

The reality is that there is no standard that indicates the "right" number of relationships. There's no standard against which to measure yourself and the number, and kind, of relationships that you have. It's something you need to decide. It is clear, though, that first-year college students almost always report higher degrees of loneliness than students in subsequent years of study.

On the other hand, loneliness is not inevitable. Several strategies for dealing with loneliness follow:

- **Become involved in campus activities.** Join a club. Volunteer to help some social organization. Try out for a play. You'll soon get to know others who have similar interests.
- **Find a study partner.** Ask one of your classmates to study with you. You can review your class notes, work together on a project, or study for tests together. Working together will not only help you master the class material, but also help you make what can become an important social connection.
- **Know that you're not alone in your loneliness.** If you're feeling lonely, you may find yourself looking at your classmates and noticing groups of people engaged in social activities. This can make you feel even more isolated. Don't be fooled by such social illusions into believing that you are the only one experiencing loneliness. Remember that for every person you notice who is socializing, there are others who are not doing so.

Participating in campus activities is a good way to meet people with similar interests and to avoid the loneliness that is sometimes a part of college life.

4 PERSONAL STYLES **Try It!** P O W E R

Understand Your Relationship Style

Each of us has a general manner in which we approach close relationships with others. Read the three statements below, and determine which best describes you:

1. I find it relatively easy to get close to others and am comfortable depending on them and having them depend on me. I don't often worry about being abandoned or about someone getting too close to me.
2. I am somewhat uncomfortable being close to others; I find it difficult to trust them completely and to allow myself to depend on them. I am nervous when anyone gets too close, and often love partners want me to be more intimate than I feel comfortable being.
3. I find that others are reluctant to get as close as I would like. I often worry that my partner doesn't really love me or won't want to stay with me. I want to merge completely with another person, and this desire sometimes scares people away.

The choice you make suggests the general style of emotional bonds that you develop with others.

If you thought the first statement described you best, it is probably easy for you to develop close ties with others. Around 55 percent of people describe themselves in this way.

If statement 2 describes you best, you probably have a more difficult time getting close to others, and you may have to work harder to develop close ties with other people. About 25 percent of people place themselves in this category.

Finally, if statement 3 describes you best, you, along with the 20 percent of people who describe themselves in this way, aggressively seek out close relationships. However, they probably present a source of concern to you.

Keep in mind that this is an inexact assessment and presents only a very rough estimate of your general approach to close relationships. But your response can be helpful in answering these questions: Are you generally satisfied with your relationships? Would you like to change them in some way?

Source: Adapted from Hazan, C., & Shaver, P. (1987). Romantic love conceptualized as an attachment process. *Journal of Personality and Social Psychology*, 52, pp. 511–524.

- **Take advantage of orientation and first-year student social events.** Even if you don't consider yourself particularly good at socializing, it's important to make the effort. If you're shy—and even if you're not—consider it a social success if you meet just one new person at such an event.
- **Take a job on campus.** Campus jobs provide not only income but social connections as well. Through work you can meet members of the college staff and make connections with other students.
- **Remember that loneliness is a subjective—and typically temporary—state.** If you interpret your feelings of isolation as due to your personal failings ("I'm alone because I'm not a very likable or interesting person"), you'll experience loneliness. On the other hand, if you view your isolation as a consequence of temporary, short-term factors ("Everyone has a lot of work this semester and there are few opportunities to socialize"), you're less likely to feel loneliness. In short, don't blame yourself for your sense of loneliness.

  What if your feelings of loneliness are extreme and you experience a sense of complete isolation and alienation from your classmates? If the feeling persists, it's wise to talk to someone at a health service or college counseling center, or to your advisor. Although everyone feels isolated at times, such feelings shouldn't be extreme. Counselors can help you deal with them.

Lonely in a Crowd: Dealing with Too Many People

For some students, it's not a lack of social companionship that is difficult. Instead, juggling too many obligations leads to social overload and, in fact, a kind of loneliness. This is particularly true for nontraditional, older students who may be managing classes, jobs, and families.

If you are one of those students who feel they never have a moment to themselves, it is important to carve out time for solitude. Write in breaks in your weekly schedule every once in while, where you can get away from it all. Just taking a lunch break, eating by yourself on a park bench, can be rejuvenating if you're not interrupted. That means turning off your cell phone and not telling others where you'll be. Just 30 minutes of quality "alone time" can make a difference.

» LO 11-3 Communicating in Relationships

Communicating well in personal relationships is a blend of talking and listening. Not only does it help to do both well, but it is also important to know when it's time to listen and when it's time to speak up. Listening is an often overlooked skill in personal relationships. We may be so busy trying to communicate our feelings and interests that we overlook the need of the other person to be heard. As friendships develop into personal relationships, simply talking isn't enough. How you express yourself, especially in moments of difficulty, can be very important in getting your message across.

Being a Good Listener: The Power of Supportive Silence

When it comes to building relationships, how you listen is sometimes more important than what you say. The silence involved in listening is a powerful force, one that can bind us more closely to others.

You may already have discussed the art and science of listening as it applies to academic success. The same principles that promote learning about lecture topics also promote learning about our friends. You can't call yourself a good friend without knowing what others are like and what they are thinking. Good listening is one of the ways to enhance your understanding of others.

> "The reason why we have two ears and only one mouth is that we may listen the more and talk the less."
>
> Zeno of Citium, philosopher

When we are heard, we appreciate it because we get the message that our listeners care about us, not just about themselves. Similarly, when we listen, we show that we have respect for those who are speaking, are interested in their ideas and beliefs, and are willing to take the time to pay attention to them.

There are several ways you can improve your ability to listen:

1. **Stop talking!** Are you the kind of person who revels in telling stories about what happened to you? Do you wait eagerly for others to finish what they are saying so that you can jump in with a response? Do you accidentally cut other people off or finish their sentences while they are speaking?

   No one likes to be interrupted, even in casual conversation. In more personal relationships, it is a sign of not respecting what the other person has to say and is hurtful.

2. **Demonstrate that you are listening.** Linguists call them "conversational markers"—those nonverbal indications that we're listening. They consist of head nods, uh-huhs, OKs, and other signs that we're keeping up with the conversation. Eye contact is important too. Listening this way shows that we're paying attention and are interested in what the other person is saying.

   In addition, don't multitask. If you're having a serious conversation, turn off your cell phone. If it does ring, don't look at caller ID. Even glancing at your phone for a moment shows you're not paying full attention.

3. **Use reflective feedback.** Carl Rogers, a respected therapist, developed a very useful way to lend support to someone and draw him or her out. In **reflective feedback**, a listener rephrases what a speaker has said, trying to echo the speaker's meaning. For example, a listener might say, "as I understand what you're saying . . ." or "you seem to feel that . . ." or "in other words, you believe that . . ."

   In each case, the summary statement doesn't just "play back" the speaker's statements literally. Instead, it is a rephrasing that captures the essence of the message in different words.

   Reflective feedback has two big benefits. First, it provides speakers with a clear indication that you are listening and taking what they're saying seriously. Second, and equally important, it helps ensure that you have an accurate understanding of what the speaker is saying.

reflective feedback
A technique of verbal listening in which a listener rephrases what a speaker has said, trying to echo the speaker's meaning.

4. **Ask questions.** Asking questions shows that you are paying attention to a speaker's comments. Questions permit you to clarify what the speaker has said, and they can move the conversation forward. Further, people feel valued when others ask them about themselves.

5. **Admit when you're distracted.** We've all had those moments: Something is bothering you and you can't get it out of your mind, or you've simply got to finish something and don't really have time to chat. If at the same time someone wants to engage you in conversation, your distraction will undoubtedly show, making the other person feel you are not interested in her or him.

   The way to deal with this situation is to admit that you're distracted. Simply saying, "I'd love to talk, but I've got to finish reading a chapter," is enough to explain the situation to a classmate who wants to talk about his date.

It's Not Just Talk: Avoiding and Handling Conflicts in Relationships

Listening communicates a great deal in personal relationships, but as discussed previously, it is also important to put yourself forward. Generally, close relationships are built on good communication, so day to day there may be no problem in this regard. But when misunderstandings or conflicts occur—as they definitely will from time to time—communication can fall apart. In these situations your ability to communicate in words is tested, and more sensitive listening and more careful ways of saying what you think and feel are needed.

The Subject Is "I" and Not "You"

Suppose a close friend says something with which you disagree: "All you guys are the same—you expect to get everything your way!" You might respond by directing anger at the other person, directly or indirectly accusing the person of some imperfection: "You're always looking for something to complain about!" Such responses (and, as you will notice, the initial statement) typically include the word *you.*

For instance, consider these possible responses to indicate disagreement: "*You* really don't understand"; "*You're* being stubborn"; and "How can *you* say that?"

These types of statements cast blame, make accusations, express criticism, and make assumptions about what's inside the other person's head. And they lead to defensive replies that will probably do little to move the conversation forward: "I do so understand"; "I'm not being stubborn"; and "I can say that because that's the way I feel."

A far more reasonable tactic is to use "I" statements. **"I" statements** cast responses in terms of yourself and your individual interpretation. Instead of saying, for example, "You really don't understand," a more appropriate response would be, "I think we're misunderstanding each other." "You're not listening to me" could be rephrased as "I feel like I may not be getting my point across." And "Why don't you call when you're going to be late?" becomes "I worry that something has happened to you when you don't call if you are going to be late." In each case, "I" statements permit you to state your reaction in terms of your perception or understanding, rather than as a critical judgment about the other person. (Practice using "I" statements in **Try It! 5**.)

"I" statements
Statements that cast responses in terms of oneself and one's individual interpretation.

Resolving Conflict: A Win-Win Proposition

Even with careful attention to putting our own feelings forward instead of making accusations, whenever two people share their thoughts, concerns, fears, and honest reactions with each other, the chances are that sooner or later some sort of conflict will arise.

Conflict is not necessarily bad.

Often, people are upset simply by the fact that they are having a conflict. It is as though they believe conflicts don't occur in "good" relationships. In fact, however, conflict is helpful in some very important ways. It can force us to say what is really on our minds. It can allow us to clear up misconceptions and miscommunications before they begin to undermine the relationship. It can even give us practice at resolving conflicts with others with whom we might not share such good relations.

Outside the context of close relationships, conflict is not necessarily a bad thing, either. In the working world, conflict is often inevitable. Yet as in relationships, conflicts on the job can be beneficial. Misconceptions can be cleared up and new processes devised when co-workers engage in productive discussions.

Like anything else, though, there are good ways to resolve conflict, and there are bad ways. Good ways of resolving conflict move people and situations forward, identifying the problem and promoting creative problem solving. Bad ways of resolving conflict make the situation worse, driving people apart rather than bringing them together.

Here are the fundamental principles of conflict resolution that you can use when conflict occurs in personal and professional relationships:

- **Stop, listen, and think.** In the heat of an argument, all sorts of things get said. If you find yourself making rash or hurtful statements, stop, listen to what you and the other person are saying, and think about what is being said.

  Stopping works like a circuit breaker that prevents a short circuit from causing a deadly fire. You've probably heard about counting to 10 to cool off when you're angry. Do it. Take a break and count to 10 . . . or 20 . . . or more. Whether you count to 10 or 100, stopping gives you time to think and not react rashly.

5  WORKING IN A GROUP

Try It! POWER

Switch "You" to "I"

Working in a group or in pairs, turn the following "you" statements into less aggressive "I" statements. For example, a possible "I" statement alternative to "You just don't get it, do you?" would be "I don't feel I'm making my feelings clear."

1. You just don't get it, do you?
2. You never listen to what I say.
3. You don't see where I'm coming from.
4. You don't really believe that, do you?
5. You never try to see my point of view.
6. Please stop interrupting me and listen to what I'm saying for a change.
7. Stop changing the subject!
8. You're not making sense.
9. You keep distorting what I say until I don't even know what point I'm trying to make.
10. You use too many "you" statements. Use more "I" statements when you're talking to others.

- **Defuse the argument.** Anger is not an emotion that encourages rational discourse. When you're angry and annoyed with someone, you're not in the best position to evaluate logically the merits of various arguments others may offer. It may feel exhilarating to get our fury off our chests in the heat of an argument, but you can bet it isn't taking anyone any closer to resolving the problem.

  Don't assume that you are 100 percent right and the other person is 100 percent wrong. Make your goal *solving the problem* rather than winning the argument.

- **Get personal.** Perhaps you've heard others suggest that you shouldn't get personal in an argument. In one sense that's true: Accusing people you're arguing with of having character flaws does nothing to resolve real issues.

  At the same time, you should be willing to admit personal *responsibility* for at least part of the conflict. The conflict would not exist without you, so you need to accept that the argument has two sides and that you are not automatically blameless. This creates some solid ground from which you and the other person can begin to work on the problem.

- **Listen to the real message.** When people argue, what they say is often not the real message. There's typically an underlying communication—a subtext—that is the source of the conflict.

  It's important, then, to dig beneath what you're hearing. If someone accuses you of being selfish, the real meaning hidden in the accusation may be that you don't give anyone else a chance to make decisions. Remember, arguments are usually about behavior, not underlying character and personality. What people *do* is not necessarily synonymous with what they *are.*

  If you rephrase the person's statement in your own mind, it moves from an insult ("You're a bad person") to a request for a change of behavior ("Let me participate in decision making"). You're much more likely to respond reasonably when you don't feel that the essence of your being is under attack.

- **Show that you're listening.** It's not enough only to listen to the underlying message that someone is conveying. You also need to acknowledge the *explicit* message. For example, saying something like, "OK. I can tell you are concerned about sharing the burden on our group project, and I think we should talk about it" acknowledges that you see the issue and admit that it is worthy of discussion. This is a far more successful strategy than firing back a countercharge each time your partner makes a complaint.

- **If you are angry, acknowledge it.** Don't pretend that everything is fine if it isn't. Ultimately, relationships in which the partners bottle up their anger may suffer more than those in which the partners express their true feelings. If you're angry, say so.

- **Ask for clarification.** As you're listening to another person's arguments, check out your understanding of what is being said. Don't assume that you know what's intended. Saying something like "Are you saying . . ." or "Do you mean that . . ." is a way of verifying that what you *think* someone means is really what is meant.

- **Make your requests explicit.** If you're upset that your roommate leaves clothes lying around your apartment or dorm room, remarking that he or she is a "pig" shows more than that you are angry. It also shows that your intent is to hurt rather than to solve the problem.

It's far better to be explicit in your concerns. Say something like "It would make me feel better if you would pick up your clothes from the floor." Couching your concern in this way changes the focus of the message from your roommate's personality to a specific behavior that can be changed.

- **Always remember that life is not a zero-sum game.** Many of us act as if life were a *zero-sum game*, a situation in which when one person wins, the other person automatically loses. It's what happens when you make a bet: If one person wins the bet, the other person loses.

  Life is not like that. If one person wins an argument, it doesn't mean that others automatically have to lose it. And if someone loses an argument, it doesn't mean that others have automatically won. In fact, all too often conflict escalates so much that the argument turns into a lose-lose situation, where everyone ends up a loser.

  However, life can be a win-win situation. The best resolution of conflict occurs when both parties walk away with something they want. Each may not have achieved *every* goal but will at least have enough to feel satisfied.
- **Finally, if a relationship involves emotional or physical abuse, you must seek help or decide to end the relationship immediately.** If a partner is emotionally or physically abusive to you, seek assistance from trained counselors. Don't wait. It is virtually impossible to deal with abuse on your own. Your college counseling center, mental health center, or medical center can offer you help. If you are physically threatened or injured, call 911.

When Relationships Are Over: Dealing with Endings

Not all relationships last a lifetime. Sometimes they just wind down, as the two people involved slowly lose interest in maintaining their partnership. At other times, they break apart, as disagreements build and there is not a strong enough bond to hold the two parties together. Or there may be an abrupt rupture if some event occurs that destroys one partner's feeling of trust.

Caring for others is rewarding, but risky. When relationships don't work out, their endings can be painful, even devastating, for a time. Even when relationships evolve naturally and change is expected, the transformation in a relationship may not be easy. Parents die. Children grow up and move away from home. Siblings get new jobs on the other side of the country.

There is one sure cure for the heartache of a lost relationship: time. There are some other things you can do, however, as you wait for time to pass and for the pain to ease:

1. **Accept that you feel bad.** If you're not experiencing unhappiness over the end of a relationship, it means that the relationship wasn't terribly meaningful in the first place. Understand that unhappiness normally accompanies the end of a relationship, and allow yourself some satisfaction over the fact that you'd been able to maintain a relationship that, at least at one point, was meaningful.
2. **Do something—anything.** Mow the lawn, clean out the closets, go for a run, see a movie. It won't completely get your mind off your loss, but it beats languishing on your bed, thinking about what you might have done differently or what could have been.

3. **Block the other person from your social media.** You don't need to be reminded about what they're doing; it will just stir up negative feelings.
4. **Treat yourself to something special.** Go away for the weekend. Buy yourself a new pair of designer jeans. Purchase a box of candy. The idea is to do something special for yourself.
5. **Talk to a friend or relative.** Talking about your sadness will help you to deal with it better. Other people can help you feel better about yourself, offer different perspectives, and simply support you by listening. Make use of your network of existing relationships to get you through a difficult period.
6. **Write about the relationship.** If you have a journal, writing about the relationship and its aftermath can be therapeutic. You can say whatever you want without fear of being contradicted.
7. **Talk to a professional.** If your sadness over a relationship feels totally overwhelming or continues for what you perceive to be too long a time, talk to a counselor or other professional. He or she can help you gain a better understanding of the situation and perhaps help you understand why you are taking it so hard. And remember that, ultimately, the pain will disappear: Time does heal virtually all wounds.

Speaking *of* Success

Courtesy of Dr. Nicole Evans

NAME: **Dr. Nicole Edwards Evans**

SCHOOL: **B.A., Jackson State University; M.A and Ph.D., University of Southern Mississippi, Hattiesburg, Mississippi; Lane College, Jackson, Tennessee**

Nicole Edwards Evans, currently vice president for Enrollment Management and Institutional Research at Jackson State University, used to teach incoming first-year students at Lane College how to adjust to college life. Her inspiration for her teaching: her own personal life experience. Her academic career started off like any other student's, until her daughter Jalysa Monique was born during her sophomore year. Being a single parent was hard enough. But coupled with her daughter's numerous medical problems, Evans faced a tough academic road.

"Previously I had only been responsible for myself," she noted. "I wasn't sure if I could work, go to school, and take care of a sick baby. It was overwhelming but I knew there wasn't another option."

Determined and committed, Evans cited an undergraduate course on the introduction to university life at Jackson State University as providing her with the key to not only complete her undergraduate program, but go on to earn a doctoral degree at the age of 27.

"The portion of the course geared toward time management was by far the most beneficial," she said. "I took full advantage of my day planner. I used it to account for every waking moment during the day. I scheduled activities from the time I got up in the morning to the time I went to bed at night. This included work, school, time set aside for studying, as well as time designated for personal and social activities. This taught me self-discipline. I learned to stick with my schedule and I still practice this today in my professional career."

In addition to time management, it is also very important to stay on top of required academic work, and avoid waiting until the last minute. "I see so many students who wait until the last minute to work on projects and papers that may count for a significant share of their grade in a course," Evans said.

"As a student, I would see upcoming projects and begin to work on them immediately. I would submit them early and ask my instructor for feedback. This allowed me sufficient time to make necessary modifications to my work and still meet the deadline. I found this to increase the quality of my work and decrease my level of stress. This is also a tactic that has stayed with me over the years."

[RETHINK]

- What benefits do you think submitting your work early to an instructor provide beyond getting early feedback?
- What principles of time management suggested by Evans might you incorporate into your own life?

Looking Back

LO 11-1 Discuss why the increasing diversity of society is important to you.

- The diversity of the United States—and of U.S. college campuses—is increasing rapidly, and the world is becoming smaller as television, radio, the web, and international commerce bring people and cultures closer together.
- Being aware of diversity can allow you to accept the challenge and opportunity of living and working with others who are very different from you.

LO 11-2 Utilize strategies to become more at ease with differences and diversity.

- Cultural competence begins with accepting diversity by seeking out others who are different from you, as well as exploring your own prejudices and stereotypes.
- You can learn about other cultures by traveling to other countries and geographic areas. It also helps to accept differences simply as differences.
- Relationships not only provide social support and companionship, but also help people understand themselves.
- The central components of good relationships are trust, honesty, mutual support, loyalty, acceptance, and a willingness to embrace change.

LO 11-3 Build lasting relationships and learn to deal with conflict.

- Listening is an important skill for relationship building, demonstrating that the listener really cares about the other person.
- Conflict is inevitable in relationships, and sometimes it is useful because it permits us to clear up misconceptions and miscommunications before they escalate.
- Although the end of a relationship can be very painful, the pain does subside over time.

[KEY TERMS AND CONCEPTS]

Cultural competence (p. 302)
Culture (p. 301)
Discrimination (p. 303)
Ethnicity (p. 300)
"I" statements (p. 315)
Loneliness (p. 311)
Prejudice (p. 303)
Race (p. 300)
Reflective feedback (p. 314)
Stereotypes (p. 303)

[RESOURCES]

ON CAMPUS

For first-year students who reside on campus, one of the most frequent sources of difficulties involves roommates. If you and your roommate are having problems getting along, begin by speaking with your resident advisor or residence hall director. If the problem persists, talk with a member of the residential life office. You can also speak with a counselor at the college counseling office.

Anyone who feels he or she is facing discrimination based on race, gender, ethnic status, sexual orientation, or national origin should contact a university official *immediately.* Often there is a specific office that handles such complaints. If you don't know which campus official to contact, speak to your academic advisor or someone in the dean's office, and you'll be directed to the appropriate person. The important thing is to act and not suffer in silence. Discrimination is not only immoral, but also against the law.

IN PRINT

Beverly Tatum's *Why Are All the Black Kids Sitting Together in the Cafeteria? And Other Conversations about Race* (Basic Books, 2017 anniversary ed.) explores race, racism, and the everyday impact of prejudice.

In *Readings for Diversity and Social Justice* (Routledge, 2018, 4th ed.), editors Maurianne Adams, et al. compile a comprehensive collection of essays covering a wide variety of social issues.

Finally, Joseph Folger, Marshall Poole, and Randall Stutman's *Working through Conflict: Strategies for Relationships, Groups, and Organizations* (Allyn & Bacon, 2012, 4th ed.) suggests a variety of practical approaches to resolving conflict.

ON THE WEB

- "Beyond Intractability" (**https://www.beyondintractability.org/**) is a resource created by the Conflict Information Consortium at the University of Colorado Boulder. It includes interviews, essays, case studies, and more related to dealing with and responding to conflict.
- This site provides a comprehensive look at language and culture covering all aspects of communication, from speech to body language, as used by cultures around the world. (**http://anthro.palomar.edu/language/default.htm**).
- "Race Relations" (**https://www.thoughtco.com/race-relations-4132982**), a comprehensive site on ThoughtCo.com, discusses topics ranging from affirmative action to white privilege. Hundreds of links are provided for more in-depth discussions and background on a variety of subjects, including race relations, hate crimes, gay/lesbian issues, and many other topics.

Design Elements: *Pencil/Notebook: ©Squared Studios/Photodisc/Getty Images; Group/Laptop: ©Jacob Lund/Shutterstock; Apples: ©I. Rozenbaum/PhotoAlto; People/Silhouette: ©Ingram Publishing; Colorful Notebooks: ©Dragan Nikolic/Alamy; Group/Occupations: ©Rawpixel.com/Shutterstock; Woman/Laptop: ©JGI/Jamie Grill/Getty Images; Man/Laptop: ©Westend61/Getty Images.*

The Case of . . .

Answering for All

Jace Kinkaid stood out in any crowd. With his six-foot-eight-inch height, he towered above most of his classmates. Even when he was seated at a desk, he looked huge. And since he was an African American, his skin color set him apart from his classmates, almost all of whom were white.

Although, by and large, people were polite and nice enough to him, Jace felt isolated from most of his peers and instructors. While he had one or two good friends from high school with whom he kept in touch, he was not close to many people on campus. His isolation came to a head, however, in the most public of places: his English literature class. It happened when his instructor, a white man, was leading a discussion on *The Fire Next Time,* a novel by noted black writer James Baldwin. The instructor turned to Jace and asked him to comment on a passage from the novel.

"Does it ring true to you, Jace, as an African American?" asked his instructor, who then went on to inquire, "What do African Americans think about the perspective that Baldwin is taking?"

Jace was taken aback. What was he supposed to say? He hardly felt like a representative of every black person. He barely knew how he felt, let alone everyone else who was African American. What an absurd situation to be placed in—his instructor asking him to answer for millions of other people. He felt awful—embarrassed, upset, and angry at his instructor for putting him on the spot.

1. Why was the instructor's question so troubling to Jace? If the instructor really wanted Jace's opinion about the passage, what should he have said?

2. Would the question have had a different effect if the instructor had also been African American? Why or why not?

3. What are some cultural assumptions that the instructor is making about Jace? About African Americans? About white people?

4. What response might Jace make in this situation to make his feelings clear without causing excessive conflict?

CHAPTER

12 Money Matters

©Brand X Pictures/PunchStock

Learning Outcomes

By the time you finish this chapter you will be able to

- **LO 12-1** Explain how to develop a financial philosophy and its value.
- **LO 12-2** Discuss strategies for managing your money.
- **LO 12-3** Describe approaches to paying for your college education.

Leah Flores's college career depended on the contents of the envelope she held in her hands.

The letter inside from the financial aid office spelled out her school's offer of aid for the upcoming term. As she tore open the envelope, Leah wondered whether it would be enough. She knew that without a substantial amount of support, she would have to drop out. She couldn't stand the thought, particularly because she had been doing so well.

As she looked at the numbers on the form, Leah's heart soared. Not only had she been given a loan, but also most of her aid was in the form of a direct scholarship.

Things would still be tight, but she could manage. Her financial worries were over—at least for one more term.

Looking Ahead

Money problems aren't always solved as happily as they were for Leah Flores. Even under the best of circumstances, our finances present us with many challenges. Money often plays a large role in where we go to college, where we live, and what jobs we take. It is the source of many of our problems and stress, forcing us to find a balance between what we need and what we want.

This chapter will show you how to manage your money. It begins by discussing the process of preparing a budget and identifying your financial goals—the basis for money management. The chapter goes on to examine ways you can keep track of your spending and estimate your financial needs and resources, and it discusses ways to control your spending habits and save money.

Education is one of the largest financial expenditures anyone encounters in life. Knowing the best ways to meet the costs of a college education—finding loans, grants, and scholarships—can give your finances a big boost and help you avoid graduating with thousands of dollars of debt. You will also learn what to do if your personal finances get out of control and discover how to stop the downward spiral of unpaid bills, defaulted loans, and unfavorable credit ratings. The chapter ends by considering the true value of college, which extends well beyond financial considerations.

» LO 12-1 Building a Financial Philosophy

Do you know where your money goes? Do you spend more than you think you should? Do you never have quite enough cash to buy the things you want?

Answering these questions and understanding the role money plays in your life is the first step of wise money management. To begin getting a grip on your finances, answer the questions in the **Journal Reflections** exercise.

Exploring your views of money is the first step in developing a meaningful financial philosophy, a way of viewing the role that money plays in one's life. For example, there's a famous line from *Jerry Maguire,* a Tom Cruise movie about a sports agent, in which an athlete claims his family motto is "Show me the money." That blunt statement might be used to illustrate one financial philosophy—that life revolves around money.

Journal Reflections

My Sense of Cents

Answer the following questions about your financial sense.

1. How much money do you now have in your pockets and wallet? (Guess first, then look.) How close did you come?

2. Do you know how much money you typically spend in a month, including money spent on food, lodging, and other items?

3. How good a sense of your finances do you think you have? How secure do you feel in your understanding of where your money goes?

4. How important is money to you? Why?

5. Research shows that although winning the lottery or other large sums of money brings an initial surge in happiness, a year later the winners' level of happiness returns to what it was before.[1] Why do you think this is true in general, and would it be true for you?

Others would disagree. For instance, some take the opposite viewpoint, arguing that money controls too many people and is a major source of stress. To combat an obsession with money, living a frugal existence in which money plays virtually no role is seen as the key to happiness.

Whether you choose to follow the path of Jerry Maguire or a more frugal existence, the important thing is to develop your own personal financial philosophy. Consider the role that money plays in your life. How much does money motivate what you do? Are you interested in becoming rich, or do you tend to think more in terms of simply having enough to have a comfortable life, without lots of luxuries? What activities bring you the greatest satisfaction in life? Do those activities require a certain level of income? Explore these questions further in **Try It! 1**.

Developing a financial philosophy is the first step to gaining control over the role money plays in your life. The next step is to build a budget, a way of determining how you already use money and a plan for the future.

1 **Try It!** P O W E R

Discover Your Personal Financial Philosophy

Begin to create a personal financial philosophy by completing this exercise. Start by completing this Attitudes Toward Money questionnaire.

	Strongly Disagree	Disagree	Neutral	Agree	Strongly Agree
1. Money is essential for happiness.					
2. Having money guarantees happiness.					
3. Money makes no difference to one's happiness.					
4. More money equals more happiness.					
5. Having enough to live modestly on, money doesn't make much of a difference.					
6. I frequently worry about money.					
7. I frequently daydream about having a lot of money.					
8. If I suddenly had to live on very little money, I could adjust easily.					
9. If I suddenly won a lot of money, I would go on a spending spree.					
10. If I suddenly won a lot of money, I would share it with my relatives.					
11. If I suddenly won a lot of money, I would give a large percentage to charity.					
12. If I found a substantial amount of cash in a bag, I would try hard to find its rightful owner.					
13. If I could carry out of a burning building only a briefcase full of $100 bills or my pet dog, I would take the dog.					
14. I plan to make a lot of money in my career.					
15. I plan to make only enough money to live in reasonable comfort.					
16. It's great to have money.					
17. Money is a necessary evil.					
18. Money is the root of all evil.					

(continued)

1 *continued*

Try It! POWER

After completing the questionnaire, answer these questions about your sources of satisfaction.

1. Which activities that you engaged in over the last 5 years have given you the greatest satisfaction?

2. How much money did those activities cost?

3. How would you spend your time if you could do anything you chose?

4. How much money would this cost each year?

PERSONAL FINANCIAL PHILOSOPHY

Based on the results of your Attitudes Toward Money questionnaire and the sources of your satisfaction, sum up your personal financial philosophy here in a short paragraph:

Budgeting on the Job

If you've ever held a job, the salary you received was determined, in part, by your employer's budget.

Although they may not always be accessible to every employee, budgets are part of the world of work. Regardless of who the employer is—be it a small dry cleaning business or the massive federal government—there is a budget outlining anticipated income and expenditures. Managers are expected to keep to the budget, and if their expenditures exceed what is budgeted, they are held accountable.

For this reason, the ability to create and live within a budget is an important skill to acquire. Not only will it help keep your own finances under control, but it will also prepare you to be financially responsible and savvy on the job—qualities that are highly valued by employers.

Career Connections

» LO 12-2 Managing Your Money

If you have money problems—and there's virtually no one who doesn't have some concerns about finances—the solution is to develop a budget. A **budget** is a formal plan that accounts and plans for expenditures and income. Taking your goals into account, a budget helps determine how much money you should be spending each month, based on your income and your other financial resources. Budgets also help prepare for the unexpected, such as the loss of a job or an illness that would reduce your income, or for sudden, unanticipated expenses, such as a major car repair.

budget
A formal plan that accounts for expenditures and income.

All budgets are based on an uncomplicated premise: that expenditures should not exceed income. But that doesn't mean that budgeting is not simple, particularly when you are a student.

There are several times during the year that require especially large expenditures, such as the start of a term, when you must pay your tuition and purchase books. Furthermore, your income may be erratic. For example, it may be lower during the school year and higher during the summer. But a budget will help you deal with the ups and downs in your finances. Learning budgeting skills also helps prepare you for the world of work, as discussed in this chapter's **Career Connections**.

Most of all, a budget provides security. It will let you take control of your money, permitting you to spend it as you need to without guilt, because you have planned for the expenditure. It also makes it easier to put money aside because you know that your current financial sacrifice will be rewarded later, when you can make a purchase that you've been planning for.

Budgeting is very personal: What is appropriate for one person doesn't work for another. For a few people, keeping track of their spending comes naturally; they enjoy accounting for every dollar that passes through their hands. For most people, though, developing a budget—and sticking to it—does not come easily.

> "There was a time when a fool and his money were soon parted, but now it happens to everybody."
>
> Adlai Stevenson, politician

P Prepare

Identify financial goals

O Organize

Determine expenditures and income

W Work

Make a budget that adds up

E Evaluate

Review the budget

R Rethink

Rethink financial options

P.O.W.E.R. Plan

P Prepare — Identifying Your Financial Goals

Your first reaction when asked to identify your financial goals may be that the question is a no-brainer: You want to have more money to spend. But it's not that simple. You need to ask yourself *why* you want more money. What would you spend it on? What would bring you the most satisfaction? Purchasing an iPad? Paying off your debt? Saving money for a vacation? Starting a business? Paying for college rather than taking out loans?

You won't be able to develop an effective budget until you identify your short- and long-term financial goals. To determine them, use **Try It! 2**, "Identify Your Financial Goals."

O Organize — Determining Your Expenditures and Income

Determine Your Expenditures

Do you open your wallet for the $10 that was there yesterday and find only a dollar? Spending money without realizing it is a common affliction.

There's only one way to get a handle on where your money is going: Keep track of it. To get an overview of your expenditures, go through any records you've kept to identify where you've spent money for the last year—online records of the checks you've written, bills that have been paid online, physical receipts for expenditures, and copies of college bills can help you.

In addition, keep track of everything you spend for a week. *Everything.* When you spend $1.00 for a candy bar from a vending machine, write it down. When you buy a grande half-caff vanilla latte for $4.50 at Starbucks, write it down. When you buy lunch for $8.36 at the student union, add it to the list.

Record your expenditures in a small notebook or on your smartphone. It may be tedious, but you're doing it for only a week. And it will be eye-opening: People are usually surprised at how much they spend on little items without thinking about it.

Make a list of everything you think you'll need to spend over the next year. Some items are easy to think of, such as rent and tuition payments, because they occur regularly and the amount you pay is fixed. Others are harder to budget for because they can vary substantially. For example, the price of gasoline changes frequently. If you have a long commute, the changing price of gasoline can cause substantial variation in what you pay each month. Similarly, the cost of books varies considerably from one term to another. (Use **Table 12.1** to estimate your expenditures for the coming year. You can also prepare a monthly budget online using Connect.).

Keeping to a budget is a constant balancing act. For example, even though you know you'll need to purchase books at the start of each semester, you can't predict exactly how much they'll cost.

2  WORKING IN A GROUP

Try It! POWER

Identify Your Financial Goals

Determining your financial goals will help set you on the path to securing your financial future. Use this Try It! to get started.
Use the planning tool below to identify and organize your financial goals.

SHORT-TERM GOALS

What would you like to have money for in the short term (over the next 3 months)? Consider these categories:

Personal necessities (such as food, shelter, clothes, household supplies, transportation, loan and credit card payments, medical or child care expenses):

Educational necessities (such as tuition, fees, books, school supplies, computer expenses):

Social needs (e.g., getting together with family, friends, and others; charitable contributions; clubs and teams):

Entertainment (e.g., movies and shows, trips, recreation, and sports):

Other:

MID-RANGE GOALS

What would you like to have money for soon (3 months from now to a year from now), but not immediately? Use the same categories:

Personal necessities:

Educational necessities:

Social needs:

Entertainment:

Other:

(continued)

2 *continued* **Try It!**

LONG-RANGE GOALS

What would you like to have money for 1 to 3 years from now? Use the same categories:

Personal necessities:

Educational necessities:

Social needs:

Entertainment:

Other:

Step 2. Now put each of your lists in **priority** order.

Short-Term Priorities:

Mid-Range Priorities:

Long-Range Priorities:

What does the list tell you about what is important to you? Did you find any surprises? Would you classify yourself as a financial risk taker or someone who values financial security?

WORKING IN A GROUP

Consider these questions: Compare your priorities with those of your classmates. What similarities and differences do you find, and what can you learn from others' priorities?

table 12.1 Estimated Expenditures, Next 12 Months

Category	Now to 3 Months from Now	3–6 Months from Now	6–9 Months from Now	9–12 Months from Now
Personal Necessities				
Food				
Shelter (rent, utilities, etc.)				
Clothing				
Household supplies				
Transportation (car payments, gas, repairs, bus tickets, etc.)				
Loan and credit card payments				
Medical expenses				
Child care expenses				
Other				
Educational Necessities				
Tuition and fees				
Books				
School supplies				
Computer expenses				
Other				
Social Needs				
Relationships				
Clubs and teams				
Charitable contributions				
Other				
Entertainment				
Movies and shows				
Trips				
Recreation and sports				
Other				
TOTAL				

table 12.2 Estimated Income, Next 12 Months

Category	Now to 3 Months from Now	3–6 Months from Now	6–9 Months from Now	9–12 Months from Now
Wages				
Family support				
Financial aid				
Tuition reductions				
Loan income				
Scholarship payments				
Other				
Interest and dividends				
Gifts				
Other				
TOTAL				

When you are listing your upcoming expenditures, be sure to include an amount that you will routinely put aside into a savings account that pays you interest. It's important to get into the habit of saving money. Even if you start off small—putting aside just a few dollars a week—the practice of regularly putting aside some amount of your income is central to good financial management.

Determine Your Income Sources

You probably have a pretty good idea of how much money you have each month. But it's as important to list each source of income as it is to account for everything you spend.

Add up what you make from any jobs you hold. Also list any support you receive from family members, including occasional gifts you might get from relatives. Finally, include any financial aid (such as tuition reductions, loan payments, or scholarships) you receive from your college. Use **Table 12.2** to record this information. When you do, be sure to list the amounts you receive in terms of after-tax income.

W Work

Making a Budget That Adds Up

If you've prepared and organized your budget, actually constructing your budget is as easy as adding 2 + 2. Well, not exactly; the numbers will be larger. But all you need to do is add up your list of expenses, and then add up your sources of income. In a perfect world, the two numbers would be equal.

But most of the time, the world is not perfect: Most of us find that expenditures are larger than our income. After all, if we had plenty of excess cash, we probably wouldn't be bothering to make a budget in the first place.

If you find you spend more than you make, there are only two things to do: decrease your spending or increase your income. It's often easiest to decrease expenditures, because your expenses tend to be more under your control. For instance, there are many things you can do to save money, including the following:

Bag it! One way to cut down on expenditures is to reduce everyday expenses, such as by making your own lunch, rather than grabbing a bite at a campus snack bar. Even small savings like this can add up fast.
©Steve Mason/Getty Images

- **Control impulse buying.** If you shop for your groceries, always take a list with you, and don't shop when you're hungry.
- **Make and take your own lunch.** Brown-bag lunches can save you a substantial amount of money over purchasing your lunches, even if you go to a fast-food restaurant or snack bar.
- **Read the daily newspaper and magazines at the library or online.** Not only do college libraries subscribe to many daily newspapers and magazines, but major newspapers and magazines are also online.
- **Check bills for errors.** Computers make mistakes, and so do the people who enter the data into them. So make sure that your charges on any bill are accurate.
- **Cut up your credit cards and pay cash.** Using a credit card is seductive; when you take out your plastic, it's easy to feel as if you're not really spending money. If you use cash for purchases instead, you'll see the money going out.
- **Make major purchases only during sales.** Plan major purchases so they coincide with sales.
- **Share and trade.** Pool your resources with friends. Carpool, share resources such as computers, and trade CDs.
- **Live more simply.** Is cable TV an absolute necessity? Is it really necessary to eat out once a week? Do you buy clothes because you need them or because you want them? If you don't have an unlimited service plan, do you really need to send so many text messages? Could you move to a less expensive cell phone plan?

There are as many ways to save money as there are people looking to save it. But keep in mind that saving money should not necessarily be an end in itself. Don't spend hours thinking of ways to save a dime, and don't get upset about situations where you are forced to spend money. The goal is to bring your budget into balance, not to become a tightwad who keeps track of every penny and feels that spending money is a personal failure. To help you get started, get a sense of your current style of saving money in **Try It! 3.**

Finally, it's important to remember that budgets may be brought into balance not only by decreasing expenditures but also by increasing income. The most direct way to increase income is to get a part-time job that will accommodate your academic schedule, or to work a few more hours at a job if you already have one.

The majority of all students enrolled in college work at some point during college. Although working adds to the time management challenges you will face, it does not necessarily mean that your grades will suffer. In fact, some students who

Try It! POWER

Determine Your Saving Style

Read each of the following statements and rate how well it describes you, using this scale:

1 = That's me

2 = Sometimes

3 = That's not me

	1	2	3
1. I count the change I'm given by cashiers in stores and restaurants.			
2. I always pick up all the change I receive from a transaction in a store, even if it's only a few cents.			
3. I don't buy something right away if I'm pretty sure it will go on sale soon.			
4. I feel a real sense of accomplishment if I buy something on sale.			
5. I always remember how much I paid for something.			
6. If something goes on sale soon after I've bought it, I feel cheated.			
7. I have money in at least one interest-bearing bank account.			
8. I rarely lend people money.			
9. If I lend money to someone repeatedly without getting it back, I stop lending it to that person.			
10. I share resources (e.g., CDs, books, magazines) with other people to save money.			
11. I'm good at putting money away for big items that I really want.			
12. I believe most generic or off-brand items are just as good as name brands.			

Add up your ratings. Interpret your total score according to this informal guide:

12–15: Very aggressive saving style

16–20: Careful saving style

21–27: Fairly loose saving style

28–32: Loose saving style

33–36: Nonexistent saving style

What are the advantages and disadvantages of your saving style? How do you think your saving style would affect your ability to keep to a budget? If you are dissatisfied with your saving style, how might you be able to change it?

work do better in school than those who don't work, because those with jobs need to be more disciplined and focused. In addition, a part-time job in an area related to your future career may prove to be helpful in getting a job after you graduate.

On the other hand, working too much can be harmful. Jobs take their toll not only in hours away from your studies but also in added stress. Consequently, it's sometimes better to take out a student loan to cover college costs than to work excessive amounts. Obviously you don't want to thoughtlessly get into debt, because you don't want to burden your future with loan payments. But the well-thought-out use of loans, if they allow you to focus on your studies, may be a good investment in your future.

E Evaluate Reviewing Your Budget

Budgets are not meant to be set in stone. You should review where you stand financially each month. Only by monitoring how closely actual expenditures and income match your budget projections will you be able to maintain control of your finances.

You don't need to continually keep track of every penny you spend to evaluate your success in budgeting. As you gain more experience with your budget, you'll begin to get a better sense of your finances. You'll know when it may be possible to consider splurging on a gift for a friend, and when you need to operate in penny-pinching mode.

The important thing is to keep your expenditures under control. Review, and if necessary revise, your budget to fit any changes in circumstances. Maybe you receive a raise in a part-time job. Maybe the financial aid office gives you more support than you expected. Or maybe you face a reduction in income. Whatever the change in circumstances, evaluate how it affects your budget, and revise the budget accordingly.

R Rethink Reconsidering Your Financial Options

If all goes well, the process of budgeting will put you in control of your financial life. Your expenditures will match your income, and you won't face major money worries.

In the real world, of course, events have a way of inflicting disaster on even the best-laid plans:

- You lose your job and can't afford to pay next term's tuition.
- Your roommate moves out and leaves you with a $300 cable bill. You don't have $300.
- Your parents, who have promised to pay for your education, run into financial difficulties and say they can't afford to pay your college costs any longer.
- Your car breaks down, and repairing it will cost $1,500. If you don't have a car, you can't get to campus. But if you pay for repairs, you can't afford a tuition payment.

All of us face financial difficulties at one time or another. Sometimes it happens suddenly and without warning. Other times people sink more gradually into financial problems, each month accumulating more debt until they reach a point at which they can't pay their bills.

table 12.3 Steps in Dealing with Financial Difficulties

Assess the Problem	Make a list of what you owe and to whom. Figure out a reasonable amount you can put toward each debt. Work out a specific plan.
Contact Each of Your Creditors	Start with your bank, credit card companies, and landlord. Explain the situation. Show them your plan to pay off debt.
See a Credit Counselor	If you cannot work out a repayment plan on your own, visit a credit counseling service.
Stick to the Plan	Once you have a plan, make a commitment to stick to it. Your bank or creditor can help you identify a credit counselor.

No matter what the reason, finding yourself with too little money to pay your bills requires action. You need to be proactive and take steps to solve the problem. The worst thing to do is nothing. If a creditor, whether it's a bank, credit card company, or an individual, doesn't hear from you, they will assume that you don't care, and they'll be spurred on to take harsher actions.

These are the steps to take if you do find yourself with financial difficulties (also see **Table 12.3**).

- **Assess the problem.** Make a list of what you owe and to whom. Look at the bottom line and figure out a reasonable amount you can put toward each debt. Work out a specific plan that can lead you out of the situation.

  If you have multiple loans, there are two main approaches to paying off what you owe. The *avalanche model of debt reduction* suggests paying off loans with the highest interest rate first. That helps reduce the accumulation of interest charges. In contrast, the *snowball model of debt reduction* emphasizes paying off loans with the lowest balance first. By paying off the smaller debts, you'll have more money to pay off other loans. In addition, it gives you a psychological boost to rid yourself of at least some debt.

  Both methods work. What's important is making a choice, and having a plan.

- **Contact each of your creditors.** Start with your bank, credit card companies, and landlord, and continue through each creditor. It's best to visit personally, but a phone call will do.

  When you speak with them, explain the situation. If the problem is due to illness or unemployment, let them know. If it's due to overspending, let them know that. Tell them what you plan to do to pay off your debt, and show them your plan. The fact that you have a plan demonstrates not only what you intend to do but also that you are serious about your situation and capable of financial planning.

  If you've had a clean financial record in the past, your creditors may be willing to agree to your plan. Ultimately, it is cheaper for them to accept smaller payments over a longer time than to hire a collection agency.

- **See a credit counselor.** If you can't work out a repayment plan on your own, visit a credit counseling service. These are nonprofit organizations that help people who find themselves in financial trouble. (Make sure the individuals you seek out are legitimate; there are scams in which individuals pose as credit counselors. Your bank or a creditor can help you identify a reputable one, or call the National Foundation for Credit Counseling at 1-800-388-2227, or visit its website at **www.nfcc.org.**)

- **Stick to the plan.** Once you have a plan to get yourself out of debt, follow it. Unless you diligently make the payments you commit to, you'll find your debt spiraling out of control once again. It's essential, then, to regard your plan as a firm commitment and stick to it.

Credit Cards

"Congratulations! You've been preapproved for a Gold card! Just send us your signature on the enclosed authorization form, and we'll rush you your card."

Have you ever gotten such a letter in the mail? If so, you're far from the only one: Millions of people in the United States are regularly enticed to receive credit cards in just such a manner, and college students are especially attractive targets. In many cases, it doesn't even matter if you have income; the mere fact that you're a college student is sufficient to win you approval to receive a card.

> "It is difficult to learn the meaning of fiscal responsibility, especially when you've got a new VISA and there's a great-looking sweater in the shop window. It's even harder when the sweater is on sale."
>
> **Lauren Pass, student, Grossmont Community College, in G. Gottesman, *College survival* (New York: Macmillan, 1994), p. 206.**

Credit cards are not necessarily bad. In fact, used appropriately, they can help get you through brief periods when you must make a purchase–such as replacing a tire for your car–but temporarily don't have enough money to do so. But it's easy to fall into debt. That's why the average credit card debt owed by college students is over $2,700. And about 10 percent of college students owe more than $7,000.

You don't want to be years past your college graduation and still paying for a slice of pizza you purchased in your first month on campus. That's why it's important to consider the use of credit cards very carefully.

There are several questions you should ask when deciding whether to get and use a credit card:

1. **Is there an annual fee?** Many cards charge an annual fee, ranging from $20 a year to $100 a year. You need to determine whether the advantages of the card are worth the cost of an annual fee.
2. **What is the interest rate?** Interest rates–the percentage of the unpaid balance you are charged on credit cards–vary substantially. Some interest rates are as low as 12 percent per year, while some are as high as 25 percent per year. If the rate is 25 percent, you will be charged an additional $250 each year if you owe an average of $1,000.

   Furthermore, interest rates may vary depending on whether they are fixed or variable. *Fixed interest rates* do not change; they don't vary from month to month. In contrast, *variable interest rates* can move up or down each month because they are tied to a financial index, such as the rate of inflation. To get a better sense of how interest rates add up, try "Maintain Your Interest" (**Try It! 4**).
3. **Do I need a credit card?** There are good reasons for getting a credit card, and bad ones. The next sections discuss each of these.

It's easy for most college students to get credit cards, and even easier to use them once they have them. The hard part comes later—paying the bills.
©johan2011/123RF

4

Try It! POWER

Maintain Your Interest

Suppose you saw a $275 television set on sale "for a limited time" for $240. The $35 discount tempts you. The trouble is you don't have $240 to spare. But you *do* have a credit card—and you decide to buy the TV with the card and pay it off over time.

The advantages of this strategy are that you get the discount and have immediate use of the television set. The main disadvantage is that you will end up paying more than the $240 figure that you have in mind as the bargain price for the TV. In fact, depending on how high your credit card's interest rate is, how long you take to pay your bill in full, and how large each monthly payment is, you may wipe out most or all of the $35 savings that caused you to make the purchase in the first place. The more slowly you pay off the loan, the more money you pay for the television set.

For example, suppose you use a card with an annual interest rate of 12 percent, compounded monthly, meaning that the interest charge is applied each month, rather than at the end of the year—making the true annual rate 12.68 percent. (Some cards even compound on a *daily* basis, resulting in a real interest rate that is even higher.) At the end of a year, assuming you pay $10 per month toward the $240 purchase, you will have paid $120 and still have $143.61 to pay. At the end of 2 years, you would end up paying $35 in interest on top of the $240 purchase price.

The 12-month calculation is illustrated in the first table below. To see how much of a factor the interest rate is, complete the second table, which shows the same purchase on a credit card with a 20 percent annual (approximately 1.67 percent monthly) interest rate, compounded monthly. (These calculations can also be figured automatically on several websites, including **www.bankrate.com** and **www.quicken.com**.)

Credit Card Payments: 12% Interest, Compounded Monthly (1% per month)

	Month 1	2	3	4	5	6	7	8	9	10	11	12
Unpaid Balance	$240.00	$232.40	$224.72	$216.97	$209.14	$201.23	$193.24	$185.18	$177.03	$168.80	$160.49	$152.09
Plus Interest of	2.40	2.32	2.25	2.17	2.09	2.01	1.93	1.85	1.77	1.69	1.60	1.52
Minus Payment of	10.00	10.00	10.00	10.00	10.00	10.00	10.00	10.00	10.00	10.00	10.00	10.00
Balance Due	$232.40	$224.72	$216.97	$209.14	$201.23	$193.24	$185.18	$177.03	$168.80	$160.49	$152.09	$143.61

Credit Card Payments: 20% Interest, Compounded Monthly (approx. 1.67% per month)

	Month 1	2	3	4	5	6	7	8	9	10	11	12
Unpaid Balance	$240.00	$234.01	$227.92	$221.72	$215.42							
Plus Interest of	4.01	3.91	3.81	3.70								
Minus Payment of	10.00	10.00	10.00	10.00	10.00	10.00	10.00	10.00	10.00	10.00	10.00	10.00
Balance Due	$234.01	$227.92	$221.72	$215.42								

How much would the $240 TV set cost if you bought it with this higher-rate card, paying $10 per month for 12 months and then paying the remaining balance by check? How does this compare with the nondiscounted purchase price of $275?

5 **Try It!** POWER

Learn What Your Credit History Shows

Big Brother is alive and well, at least in terms of your credit history. If you've ever had a credit card in your own name, taken out a student loan, or simply received an unsolicited offer for credit in the mail, there's probably a computer file describing who you are, where you live, and your financial history. It shows how high your credit lines are on every credit card you have, if you've ever been late on a payment, and a considerable amount of additional information.

Even worse: Many people's credit histories are riddled with errors. That's why it's important to check the record periodically. To get a complimentary copy of your credit report, go to the website maintained by the three major credit companies (Transunion, Experian, and Equifax): **www.annualcreditreport.com**.

Be prepared: You will be asked for a variety of information, including your name, address, Social Security number, birthdate, prior addresses for the past 5 years, and other names (like a maiden name) you may have been known by. In addition, you may be asked to sign up for future reports for a fee; if you don't want them, say "no." Eventually, you will receive an online copy of your credit report.

Once you get your credit report, check it carefully. If you find any mistakes, contact the credit bureau and explain the error. They are legally responsible for investigating the report and correcting the file. It's a good idea to check your file once a year.

The Pluses of Credit Cards

- **Using a credit card responsibly establishes a good credit history.** If you've ever owed money to a bank or your college, there is a record describing your payment history. If you have never missed a payment and always pay on time, you have a good credit history. If you haven't paid on time, or have missed payments, your history will reflect this—for the next seven years.

  Your credit history is summarized in a *credit score,* a number assigned to a person that summarizes for lenders the likelihood that a loan will be repaid. Credit scores can range from 300 to 850. Almost any time you apply for a credit card or loan, lenders will want to know your credit history and credit score.

  Because negative information can stay in a file for 7 years, it can keep you from getting credit cards or loans for a long while. So it's important to establish and keep a clear credit history. (To get a copy of your credit report, complete **Try It! 5**, "Learn What Your Credit History Shows.")
- **Emergency needs.** Few of us carry around enough cash to deal with emergencies. A credit card can be a life saver if we're on a trip and the car breaks down and needs emergency repairs.
- **Convenience.** Sometimes it's easier to make purchases using a credit card. For instance, we can make purchases online or over the phone if we have a credit card. Furthermore, credit cards not only provide a record of purchases, but also give us a degree of consumer protection should a product prove to be defective.

The Minuses of Credit Cards

On the other hand, there can be significant drawbacks to the use of credit cards. Potential problems include the following:

- **Interest costs can be high.** As you saw in **Try It! 4**, the interest rate on credit card purchases can be significant. Unless you pay off your entire balance each month, your account will be charged interest, which can add up rapidly.
- **It's too easy to spend money.** Credit cards are so convenient to use that you may not realize how much you're spending in a given period. Furthermore, spending can become addictive. Unless you're careful, you can end up exceeding your budget by a significant amount.
- **If you're late in making your payments or exceed your credit limit, your credit rating will be damaged.** Credit card companies have long memories, and any mistakes you make will be reflected in your credit record for close to a decade. That may prevent you from buying a car or house in the future and jeopardize your ability to take out student loans.
- **You become susceptible to identity theft.** *Identity theft* occurs when your credit card number (or Social Security number) and name are used by someone fraudulently. Identity thieves may use your credit card number to make purchases, open new credit card accounts in your name, open new phone accounts, or even rent a house in your name. They can change the address on existing accounts so you don't even know that they are running up bills in your name. Detecting identity theft is one of the reasons you should examine your credit card statements—in fact, all your financial statements, such as bank account statements—very carefully every month.

» LO 12-3 Paying for College

Tuition costs vary greatly from one school to another, but they are substantial everywhere. The average public community college costs $3,570 per year in tuition and fees; the average four-year public college costs $9,970 for in-state students and $25,620 for out-of-state students; and the average private four-year college costs $34,740 per year.[2] If you live on campus, count on another eight to ten thousand dollars for room and board.

Nothing about college is cheap. It takes enormous expenditures of three often scarce commodities: energy, time, and money. Perhaps surprisingly, many students find money the easiest of them to find. While it's not simple to get financial aid and no one is going to walk up to you and offer you an all-expenses-paid scholarship, you can find many sources of funding for your education if you are persistent.

To find this money, however, you will need to spend ample amounts of the other two scarce commodities: time and energy. The entire process of securing financial aid takes a considerable amount of preparation, because you need to identify potential sources of funds and then apply for them. You should assume the process will take somewhere between several weeks and several months, depending on the type of aid you're applying for.

Identifying the Different Types of Funding Available

Funding for college comes in three basic categories: loans, grants, and scholarships. Although each supplies you with funds for college, they do so in very different ways.

Course **Connections**

Getting the Most Out of Your Classes: How Cutting Classes Costs

Think about how much college costs you each term. Go ahead and add it up: tuition, books, transportation, housing, food, supplies, etc., etc. It's a pretty hefty sum.

Now count the number of hours you're in class during the term. If you divide the number of hours into the amount you spend on college, you'll come up with a dollar value that shows how much every hour of the courses in which you're enrolled is worth.

What you'll immediately see is that every class is worth a great deal. For most students, missing a day's worth of classes is the equivalent of giving up $50 at the very minimum. Students attending expensive private colleges may be losing hundreds of dollars.

If all the other reasons for not missing a class aren't convincing enough, then think in these economic terms. Giving away something you've paid for is irrational. It's really no different from buying thousands of dollars' worth of clothing and then throwing them away, one by one, over the course of the semester. Only in the case of your college courses, what you're giving is far more precious—your education.

Consequently, resolve to get your money's worth out of your courses by attending them faithfully. Not only will you benefit economically, but you'll maximize your chances for learning the material and ultimately being successful in your college career and beyond.

Loans

When you receive a **loan**, a bank, credit union, or other agency provides funds that must be repaid after a specified period of time. A loan carries a particular interest rate, which is stated as an annual percentage rate. Banks and other lending agencies make money through the interest they charge on loans, just as they do with credit cards.

loan
Funds provided by a bank, credit union, or other agency that must be repaid after a specified period of time.

Think of a loan as renting money: As long as you have the use of someone else's money, you have to pay them "rent" for the privilege.

For example, suppose a bank gives you a $5,000 loan that has an interest rate of 8 percent per year. Not only must you pay back the $5,000 over a specified period, but you must pay the bank interest of 8 percent on the balance that you owe on the loan. Obviously, the higher the interest rate, the more you are paying for the privilege of borrowing the bank's money.

Three factors must be considered when you receive a loan: the principal, interest rate, and term of the loan. The **principal** is the amount of the loan. If you borrow $5,000, the $5,000 is known as the principal.

principal
The stated amount of a loan.

The interest rate (stated as a percentage) is the cost of the loan, and the **term** is the length of the loan. For example, the interest rate may be 6.5% a year, and the term of the loan may be 10 years, meaning that you pay back the loan over 10 years, while being charged an additional 6.5% per year on the amount of the loan.

term
The length of time for which money is lent.

All three factors–principal, interest rate, and term of the loan–are important, because they determine how much your payments will be when you pay the loan back. Remember, too, that initial interest rates don't always last the life of a loan. *Variable interest rate loans* have interest rates that rise and fall according to some index. So a low initial interest may increase over time, forcing you to pay more.

Many loans for college have an enormous advantage over loans you'll take out for other purchases, such as a car or house, because payments on college loans are *deferred* until you graduate and (presumably!) begin to earn an income–that is, it is often not necessary to start paying back the loan until you graduate. Depending on the type of loan you take out, interest on the loan is either paid for by the

"If you would be wealthy, think of saving as well as getting."
Benjamin Franklin

government while you are enrolled in college or deferred until you graduate.

There are several national loan programs, sponsored by the federal government, that lend money to students. The major ones include the following:

- **Stafford loans.** *Stafford loans* (also referred to more simply as subsidized and unsubsidized federal loans) are available to any student who is registered at least half-time and is a U.S. citizen or permanent resident. They provide from $5,500 to as much as $12,500 a year.

  Stafford loans come in two types, subsidized and unsubsidized:

  - *Subsidized Stafford loans* are awarded by colleges on the basis of student financial need. For subsidized loans, the federal government takes care of paying the interest until repayment begins, typically after the student graduates.
  - *Unsubsidized Stafford loans* do not require demonstration of financial need. Interest is not paid by the government; instead, it accumulates while the student is in college. However, the student doesn't have to make any payments until after graduation, when both principal and accumulated interest must be repaid over a specified period, which is up to 10 years.

- **PLUS loans (for parents).** If your parents support you and claim you as a deduction on their income tax return, they may take out a PLUS loan. PLUS loans can cover up to the full amount of a student's cost of college attendance and can be paid back over a 10- to 25-year period. In some cases, the loan does not need to be fully repaid if a student is employed in a public service profession such as teaching after graduation.

- **Perkins loans.** Perkins loans have a low interest rate, subsidized by the federal government. They are awarded on the basis of exceptional financial need, as determined by a student's college. The loans are made by a school's financial aid office. You can borrow up to $5,500 per year.

  College loans like these are relatively simple to get. It is also essential to remember that someday you'll need to pay them back. And many students are paying back a great deal. For instance, the average indebtedness is more than $10,000 for community college students and $34,000 for four-year college students when they graduate. The total amount of student debt is staggering: Students and their parents in the United States owe $1.3 *trillion* in debt, which is more than what is owed on credit cards.[3]

  Because college graduates often start off earning less than they thought they would after graduation, high levels of debt can lead to difficulties. More than half of graduates feel burdened by their debt, and a quarter report having significant problems paying back their loans. Consequently, think hard when taking out a loan and consider how much you'll have to pay back each month after you graduate.

Grants

grant
An award of money that does not have to be repaid.

A **grant** is money that does not have to be repaid. Obviously, it's more advantageous to receive a grant than to acquire a loan. And not surprisingly, it's harder to qualify for grants than for loans–harder, but not impossible. Several grant programs exist that can help reduce the amount you'll need to pay for college. They include the following:

- **Pell grants.** Based on need, Pell grants are provided to undergraduate students who have earned no previous degrees. They are awarded by college financial aid offices, which follow a formula provided by the federal government. Every student who meets certain need criteria is eligible for a Pell grant, ensuring that the neediest students receive some support. The maximum Pell Grant is almost $6,000 a year.

- **Federal Supplemental Educational Opportunity Grants (FSEOG).** The government supplies a limited number of FSEOGs to every college, which can provide these grants to needy students. Unlike Pell grants, which are guaranteed to every eligible student, FSEOGs are in limited supply. Once a college awards its allotment for a given year, no other awards are possible. You can receive from $100 to $4,000 a year, depending on financial aid.
- **Work-study grants.** Work-study grants provide jobs for undergraduates with financial needs. The jobs are typically related to a student's course of study or involve community service work, and part of the salary is paid by the government. Because a work-study position is often part of a student's total package of financial aid, it is generally considered a grant, even though work is required.

Scholarships

Scholarships are support awarded by colleges, organizations, and companies. Like a grant, a scholarship is money that does not have to be repaid. Most scholarships are based primarily on a student's financial need, although some are based on merit. For instance, students with exceptional academic or athletic abilities may receive a scholarship even though they wouldn't necessarily qualify under typical need-based measures.

scholarship
An award of money to a student based on need or merit.

The most frequent source of scholarships is one's own college, which may give money to reduce tuition and fees. But there are literally thousands of organizations that provide scholarships, ranging from companies such as Microsoft to nonprofit groups, such as the Boy Scouts and Girl Scouts.

The federal government also provides some scholarships to students whose family income does not rise above certain levels. These include the following:

- **American Opportunity Tax Credit (AOTC).** The AOTC scholarship is a federal income tax credit that helps free up funds for college. There is an annual maximum credit of $2,500.
- **Lifetime Learning Credit (LLC).** This tax credit is targeted to older students who are going back to school, changing careers, or taking courses to upgrade their skills, as well as to juniors and seniors in four-year colleges. Families can receive a 20 percent tax credit for the first $10,000 of tuition and fees.

Researching Possible Sources of Financial Aid

As you can see, there are many sources of financial aid. The biggest problem often is finding them.

Your first stop on your search for sources of financial aid should be your college's financial aid office. Every college has one, and it tends to be one of the busiest places on campus.

Most student aid offices contain a great deal of information about possible sources of aid. But that's only a starting point. The library and the web also contain many types of information that can direct you to specific possibilities. One place to get started is the Federal Student Aid Information Center in Washington, which can be reached at 1-800-4-FED-AID (1-800-433-3243) or at **studentaid.ed.gov/students/publications/student_guide/index.html**. The center will send you the

"Guide to Federal Student Aid," which describes programs that account for almost three-fourths of all financial aid awarded to students.

Keep in mind, however, that where money is involved, there are scams. Do not pay money to someone who offers to identify obscure scholarships that will yield you thousands of dollars. It's unlikely that anyone could find sources that you couldn't find yourself through careful research. Be especially wary of websites that ask for a credit card number to provide you with online information. The results are likely to be disappointing. (The websites we provide at the end of the chapter are completely reputable.)

Whatever the potential source of financial aid, you'll be asked to bare your financial soul. There will also be forms galore. Before actually completing the forms, it will be important to gather the information you will need. If you are being supported by your parents, they will have to complete some of the forms.

Keep track of deadlines! If you miss a deadline for applying for financial aid, you'll be out of luck; no exceptions are made. You'll just have to wait for another aid cycle.

Regardless of the origin of your financial aid, you almost always will have to maintain minimum standards of academic success and progress through your program of study to be eligible for continued aid. The federal government, in particular, requires that you be making what is officially called satisfactory academic progress, as defined by your particular college.

Finally, make sure you know what your needs are. The typical costs of college include not only tuition but also fees, books, and supplies, as well as associated costs, such as transportation, housing, food, and child care.

Applying for Financial Aid

It may seem that for every dollar in aid you get, there is a different line to complete on a complicated form. Prepare yourself for a blizzard of paperwork.

Here are the steps you should follow to apply for financial aid:

- **Speak with a financial aid counselor at your school.** Because the best source of financial aid is your own college, make an appointment to discuss your needs with a campus financial aid counselor or officer. In addition to giving you the most up-to-date information about possible sources of aid, the college financial aid officer can provide you with the forms you need to fill out and a list of the deadlines you need to meet.
- **Decide how much aid you need.** It's important to ask for just the right amount of aid, neither too little nor too much. If you ask for too little aid, you may be strapped for funds during the school term. It's much more difficult to get aid in the middle of a term than during the normal application period.

  At the same time, don't apply for more financial aid than you actually need. First, there is an issue of equity: What you get in aid may reduce the pool for others, and if you receive surplus aid you may be preventing other students from getting their fair share. Second, you don't want to load yourself up with unnecessary debt. The average graduate with loans pays around $250 a month to pay off student loans; you don't want to end up with so much debt that your loan payments are even higher than this.
- **Fill out your college's application for financial aid.** Colleges have their own forms to apply for financial aid. Carefully fill the form out, making sure you file it before the required deadline. In fact, the earlier you get the form in, the better: Most schools have a limited pool of funds, and the earlier you get your

application in, the higher your chances of getting an appropriate share of the financial aid pie.

- **Write a personal letter to explain any special circumstances.** If you think there are factors that affect your ability to pay for college which are not adequately reflected in the application, write an explanatory letter. It might be a recent layoff, job loss, or a costly illness of a family member that has drained financial resources. Talk about the the circumstances and ask for special consideration of your application.
- **Complete a Free Application for Federal Student Aid (FAFSA) and CSS Profile.** The FAFSA and the CSS Profile are standard forms used to assess a student's financial capabilities and determine how much the student and family can be expected to contribute toward college expenses. Nearly every college requires the FAFSA, while more than 400 colleges and scholarship programs use the CSS Profile. They require a great deal of information, including past, present, and expected income from all sources. Copies of several tax returns from prior years are also required.

  Be scrupulously honest when you complete the forms, which you can do online at **www.fafsa.ed.gov** (for the FAFSA) and **cssprofile.collegeboard.org** (for the CSS Profile). If you fail to include a source of income that is later discovered by a financial aid provider, you may be required to repay immediately any aid that you have received. In addition, you may face disciplinary measures that put your education in jeopardy; in the worst case, you may even face legal charges.
- **Wait.** It takes time for loan applications to be processed and financial aid decisions to be made. Be prepared to wait, and consider contingency plans for various possibilities.

Your Financial Aid Package

Sometime later, when the college has had time to consider your application for aid, you will receive an official response. This is most likely to be in the form of a "package"–a combination of loans, grants, scholarships, and, perhaps, an offer of an on-campus job. This is the time for a thorough evaluation of the offer. Consider the various elements of the package carefully to determine whether, taken together, they will fully meet your financial needs.

Keep in mind that you may not have to accept every element of the package that is offered to you. For instance, you may decide to accept a scholarship but turn down a loan. That decision may mean that you'll have less debt after you graduate, but also that you'll have to work more hours at a part-time job–a trade-off that you may or may not wish to make.

What if the package doesn't seem sufficient? The most important thing is not to give up. A polite visit or call to the financial aid office is in order.

When you speak to someone from financial aid, lay out your difficulty with the package. If the aid is so low that you won't be able to attend college, let the financial aid office know. If you had noted special circumstances in a letter, ask if they were taken into account. (Sometimes letters and other vital pieces of information get overlooked.) Ask if there is a formal appeal process and, if there is, ask how to begin it.

Your main goal is to get the financial aid office to take a second look at your application. By being polite and to the point in your dealings with the office staff, you stand a better chance of having them reevaluate your application.

Having good grades will help your chances of getting the financial aid office to take a second look, and poor grades will hurt: If you are not doing well in your classes, you have less bargaining power.

What if the school is unable to come up with a greater level of support? The first step is to ask the staff of the financial aid office for advice. They may be able to suggest an approach that you initially overlooked. The second step is to redouble your research efforts. You may be able to take out a loan to make up the deficit. Finally, consider alternatives to full-time college attendance. It may be a better option to attend school part-time while working than to give up college altogether or to get so much into debt that it will be hard to pay off your loans.

Above all, don't give up! If it's important enough to you, you will be able to find some way to afford an education.

Keeping in Mind the Value of a College Education

Our present focus on paying for college has led us, of necessity, to focus on the dollars and cents of education. Without a doubt, college is expensive. On the other side of the equation, there's no question that having a college education has vast financial value: People who are college graduates earn nearly twice as much money each year as those with only a high school degree.

But the money we spend on education buys us far more than a better salary. It gives us a better understanding of the world and its people, insight into who we are, better job opportunities, and a chance to befriend people who share the common goal of becoming well-educated citizens of a global society.

It would be terribly shortsighted to put a price tag on education, deciding, in effect, that if you must pay a lot you won't bother with an education. You may need to choose your school according to the tuition it charges and the financial aid package it offers you, but that's not the same as choosing to skip college altogether because it is going to be financially stressful. An experience that will permit us to reach our potential is worth *everything.*

Speaking *of* Success

Source: Steven Petteway, Collection of the Supreme Court of the United States

NAME: **Sonia Sotomayor**

SCHOOL: **Princeton University, B.A., 1976; Yale Law School, J.D., 1979**

U.S. Supreme Court Justice Sonia Sotomayor's educational journey was not an easy one, but hard work, determination, and a supportive family helped her become the first Latina and the third woman to serve in the Supreme Court's 220-year history.

Sotomayor's parents moved from Puerto Rico to New York City in the 1950s, and she grew up in a working-class Bronx neighborhood where both of her parents worked. At the age of 9 her father's death was an emotional blow, but she immersed herself in books–particularly the Nancy Drew series, which started her thinking about crime solving. That, and doing her homework in front of the TV while watching lawyer Perry Mason, ignited her goal of pursuing law.

She went on to graduate from Cardinal Spellman High School in New York City and was able to earn a scholarship to college. Although her undergraduate years were challenging, she was ultimately successful, graduating with honors. After graduation, she went on to law school.

"Although I grew up in very modest and challenging circumstances, I consider my life to be immeasurably rich," Sotomayor said.

"My mother taught us that the key to success in America is a good education," Sotomayor said at her Senate confirmation hearing. "And she set the example, studying alongside my brother and me at our kitchen table so that she could become a registered nurse."

Close to her family, the Supreme Court Justice notes that her mother, who worked six days a week as a nurse to support her and her brother, is her greatest inspiration. And while her achievements have been attained through hard work, she points to an appreciation for the opportunities she has had.

"It is our nation's faith in a more perfect union that allows a Puerto Rican girl from the Bronx to stand here now," she said during her swearing-in ceremony. "I am struck again by the wonder of my own life and the life we in America are so privileged to lead."

[RETHINK]

- Why do you think Sotomayor's closeness to her family was important in helping her be academically successful?
- What do you think it was about the Nancy Drew books that proved inspirational to Sotomayor? (Look up "Nancy Drew" on the web if you are unfamiliar with the books.)

Looking Back

LO 12-1 Explain how to develop a financial philosophy and its value.

- Exploring your views of money is the first step in developing a meaningful financial philosophy.
- It is important to understand how you view the role of money in your life.

LO 12-2 Discuss strategies for managing your money.

- Concerns about money can be significantly reduced through the creation of a budget by which spending and income can be planned, accounted for, and aligned with your goals.
- Budgets provide security by helping you control your finances and avoid surprises.
- The process of budgeting involves identifying your financial goals, keeping track of current expenses and estimating future expenses, and making the necessary adjustments to keep income and spending in balance.

LO 12-3 Describe approaches to paying for your college education.

- Loans for education are available with reasonable interest rates and conditions, especially the ability to defer paying the loans back until after graduation. Several federal programs offer loan guarantees, interest subsidies, and lower interest rates.
- Grants offer money without requiring repayment. They are harder to receive than loans because they are typically reserved for people with exceptional financial need.
- Scholarships are usually awarded by colleges and other institutions based on either financial need or academic, athletic, or other abilities.
- Ultimately, it is important to consider the value of college beyond its costs. A college degree leads to a significantly higher salary (college graduates earn nearly twice as much as those with only a high school degree). In addition, a college education offers a better understanding of the world and insight into ourselves.

[KEY TERMS AND CONCEPTS]

Budget (p. 329)
Grant (p. 344)
Loan (p. 343)
Principal (p. 343)
Scholarship (p. 345)
Term (p. 343)

[RESOURCES]

ON CAMPUS

The bursar's or treasurer's office handles money affairs. Not only does it collect money owed for tuition, but it also may perform other services such as cashing checks.

If you are receiving financial aid, there is usually a financial aid office devoted to the complexities of scholarships, loan processing, and other forms of aid. The personnel in the office can be very helpful in maximizing your financial aid package as well as in solving financial problems related to your schooling. If you have a problem with your finances, see them sooner rather than later.

IN PRINT

Paying for College without Going Broke 2018, by Kalman Chany (Princeton Review, 2017), includes many practical tips for finding ways to finance a college education. *The Ultimate Scholarship Book 2018,* by Gen and Kelly Tanabe (Supercollege, 2017), offers a variety of ways to identify scholarships to pay for college.

Emily Sawtelle's *How to Make a Simple Budget and a Winning Financial Plan* (Saverie Books, 2012) offers helpful guidance on financial management. In addition, Michelle Higgins's *College Poor No More* (New Year Publishing, 2015) offers dozens of easy tips on how to be frugal without the sacrifice, and Andrew O. Smith's *Financial Literacy for Millennials: A Practical Guide to Managing Your Financial Life for Teens, College Students, and Young Adults* (Praeger, 2016) introduces a generation to financial concepts and plans necessary for financial security.

ON THE WEB

- "Finaid: The SmartStudent Guide to College Financial Aid" (**www.finaid.org**) provides a free, comprehensive, independent, and objective guide to student financial aid. It was created by Mark Kantrowitz, author of *The Prentice Hall Guide to Scholarships and Fellowships for Math and Science Students*. The site's "calculators" page (**www.finaid.org/calculators/**) offers loads of online calculators, including College Cost Projector, Savings Plan Designer, Expected Family Contribution and Financial Aid Calculator, Loan Payment Calculator, and Student Loan Advisor (undergraduate).
- "Money Management" (**http://www.ndm.edu/admissions-aid/financial-aid/money-management**), sponsored by Notre Dame of Maryland University, offers a variety of links covering everything from debt management to loan forgiveness programs.
- *Federal Student Aid* is a comprehensive resource on the types of student financial aid from the U.S. Department of Education. It provides information on how to apply for grants, loans, and work-study through the Federal Student Aid office. This publication is available in pdf form on the U.S. Department of Education's website at **https://studentaid.ed.gov/sa/resources**

Design Elements: *Pencil/Notebook: ©Squared Studios/Photodisc/Getty Images; Group/Laptop: ©Jacob Lund/Shutterstock; Apples: ©I. Rozenbaum/PhotoAlto; People/Silhouette: ©Ingram Publishing; Colorful Notebooks: ©Dragan Nikolic/Alamy; Group/Occupations: ©Rawpixel.com/Shutterstock; Woman/Laptop: ©JGI/Jamie Grill/Getty Images; Man/Laptop: ©Westend61/Getty Images.*

The Case of . . .

Overdrawn, Overwrought, and Over Her Head

Her life was a house of cards, and someone had just pulled one out from the bottom.

At least that's what it felt like to Tara Kenko. The month had started out badly when Tara found that she had made a mistake in her checking account balance and had only $439, instead of the $939 she thought she had. After paying her share of the rent– $210–she didn't have enough money left to make her car payment. So she just put the bill aside, figuring that she'd take care of it later in the month when she got paid.

Things went from bad to worse 2 days later when her car refused to start. She had to have it towed to a mechanic, who told her that it would cost about $350 to get it fixed. She didn't have that either, but she figured she could put it on her credit card. But later, when she went to pick up her car and pay for the repair, which turned out to be closer to $400 than $350, her card was rejected. She called the credit card company from the repair shop and was told that she had exceeded her authorized credit limit. The mechanic wouldn't let her take her car until she paid for the repairs, so she was forced to leave it and catch a bus to campus.

The final straw came in her chemistry class. The instructor announced that students in the class would have to buy yet another textbook to help them with a particular set of experiments. Having already spent $150 for books in that class alone, Tara was both angry and dismayed. She had no idea how she was going to find the money to pay for the book, let alone her regular car payment and the car repairs. She was in deep financial trouble, and she didn't know what to do.

1. What should Tara do now to start addressing her problem? What steps should she take immediately?

2. Can you suggest some approaches Tara can take to deal with the problem of the new book for her chemistry class?

3. How do you think the mistake may have occurred in Tara's checking account? What advice would you give her to avoid a similar mistake in the future?

4. Given that Tara does not have a lot of leeway in her finances for multiple disasters such as the ones that befell her this month, what general course would you advise her to take as a way to plan her expenditures more effectively?

5. What steps might Tara take to decrease her expenses? What might she do to increase her income?

CHAPTER 13

Stress, Health, and Wellness

Learning Outcomes

By the time you finish this chapter you will be able to

» LO 13-1 Explain what stress is and how to control it.

» LO 13-2 Discuss what is involved in keeping well.

» LO 13-3 Identify approaches to making safer choices about health and wellness.

Louisa Denby's day began badly: She slept through her alarm and had to skip breakfast to catch the bus to campus. Then, when she went to the library to catch up on the reading she had to do before taking a test the next day, the one article she needed was missing. The librarian told her that replacing it would take 24 hours. Feeling frustrated, she walked to the computer lab to print out the paper she had completed at home the night before.

The computer wouldn't read her flash drive. She searched for someone to help her, but she was unable to find anyone who knew any more about computers than she did.

It was only 9:42 a.m., and Louisa had a wracking headache. Apart from that pain, she was conscious of only one feeling: stress.

Looking Ahead

Have you had days like Louisa's? Are most of your days like hers? Then you're no stranger to stress. It's something that all college students experience to varying degrees throughout their college careers. In fact, almost one-third of first-year college students report feeling frequently overwhelmed with all they need to do.[1]

Coping with stress is one of the challenges that college students face. The many demands on your time can make you feel that you'll never finish what needs to get done. This pressure produces wear and tear on your body and mind, and it's easy to fall prey to ill health as a result.

However, stress and poor health are not inevitable outcomes of college. In fact, by following simple guidelines and deciding to make health a conscious priority, you can maintain good physical and mental health.

This chapter covers the ways you can keep fit and healthy during—and beyond—college. It offers suggestions on how you can cope with stress, improve your diet, get enough exercise, and sleep better. It also will help you consider particular threats to mental and physical health that you're likely to face while you are in college, including alcohol and drugs, pregnancy, sexually transmitted infections, and rape.

» LO 13-1 Living with Stress

Stressed out? Tests, papers, reading assignments, job demands, roommate problems, volunteer activities, committee work. . . . It's no surprise that these can produce stress. But it may be a surprise to know that so can graduating from college, starting your dream job, falling in love, getting married, and even winning the lottery.

Virtually *anything*—good or bad—is capable of producing stress if it presents us with a challenge. **Stress** is the physical and emotional response we have to events that threaten or challenge us. It is rooted in the primitive "fight or flight" response wired into all animals—human and nonhuman. You see it in cats, for instance, when confronted by a dog or other threat: Their backs go up, their fur stands on end, their eyes widen, and, ultimately, they either take off or attack. The challenge stimulating this revved-up response is called a *stressor.* For humans, stressors can range from a first date to losing our biology notes to experiencing a tornado or hurricane.

stress
The physical and emotional response to events that threaten or challenge us.

Because our everyday lives are filled with events that can be interpreted as threatening or challenging, stress is commonplace in most people's lives. There are three main types of stressors:

cataclysmic events
Sudden, powerful events that occur quickly and affect many people simultaneously.

1. **Cataclysmic events** are events that occur suddenly and affect many people simultaneously. Tornadoes, hurricanes, and plane crashes are examples of cataclysmic events. Although they may produce powerful immediate consequences,

ironically they produce less stress than other types of stressors. The reason? Cataclysmic events have a clear end point, which can make them more manageable. Furthermore, because they affect many people simultaneously, their consequences are shared with others, and no individual feels singled out.

2. **Personal stressors** are major life events that produce a negative physical and psychological reaction. Failing a course, losing a job, and ending a relationship are all examples of personal stressors. Sometimes positive events—such as getting married or starting a new job—can act as personal stressors. Although the short-term impact of a personal stressor can be difficult, the long-term consequences may decline as people learn to adapt to the situation.

personal stressors
Major life events that produce stress.

3. **Daily hassles** are the minor irritants of life that singly produce relatively little stress. Waiting in a traffic jam, receiving a bill riddled with mistakes, and being interrupted by noises of major construction while trying to study are examples of such minor irritants. However, daily hassles add up, and cumulatively they can produce even more stress than a single larger-scale event. (**Figure 13.1** indicates the most common daily hassles in people's lives.)

daily hassles
The minor irritants of life that, by themselves, produce little stress, but which can add up and produce more stress than a single larger-scale event.

What Is Happening When We Experience Stress?

Stress does more than make us feel anxious, upset, and fearful. Beneath responses that we're aware of, we are experiencing many different physical reactions. Our hearts beat faster, our breathing becomes more rapid and shallow, and we produce more sweat. Our internal organs churn out a variety of hormones. Each of these physical responses places a high demand on our body's resources.

In the long run, extended physical responses to stress can wear down our *immune system,* our body's natural defense against disease. That makes us more susceptible to a variety of diseases, ranging from the common cold and headaches to strokes and heart disease. In fact, surveys have found that the greater the number of stressful events a person experiences over the course of a year, the more likely it is that he or she will have a major illness (see **Try It! 1**, "Assess Your Susceptibility to Stress-Related Illness").

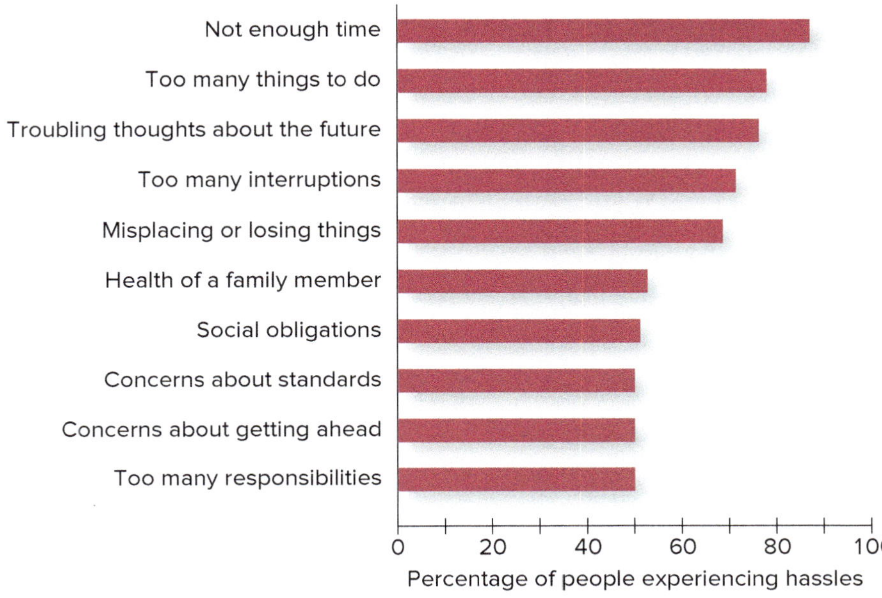

figure 13.1
Daily Hassles
Source: Chamberlain, K., & Zika, S. (1990). The minor events approach to stress: Support for use of daily hassles. *British Journal of Psychology,* 81, pp. 469–481.

1 **Try It!** P O W E R

Assess Your Susceptibility to Stress-Related Illness

Are you susceptible to a stress-related illness? The more stress in your life, the more likely it is that you will experience a major illness.

To determine the stress in your life, take the stressor value given beside each event you have experienced and multiply it by the number of occurrences over the past year (up to a maximum of four), and then add up these scores.

87 Spouse dies
77 Married
77 Close family member dies
76 Divorced
74 Marriage separation
68 Close friend dies
68 Was pregnant or was father to a pregnant woman
65 Major illness or injury
62 Got fired
60 Terminated a marriage or close relationship
58 Experienced sexual problems
58 Marriage was reconciled
57 Major shift in self-concept
56 Witnessed a major change in the health or behavior of a family member
54 Became engaged
53 Suffered a major change in finances
52 Took out a large mortgage or loan
52 Change in drug use
50 Experienced a major change in values
50 Change in number of arguments with your spouse
50 New family member joins
50 Started college
50 Started at a new school
50 Began a new type of work
49 Large change in independence and responsibility
47 Large change in work responsibilities
46 Major change in alcohol use
45 Changed personal habits
44 Difficulty with school administration
43 Attended school while working
43 A major change in social activities
42 In-law difficulties
42 Changes in working hours or conditions
42 Moved to a new house
41 Spouse starts or stops working outside the home

1 | *continued* **Try It!** P O W E R

41 Changed majors

41 Change in dating life

40 Significant personal achievement

38 Boss problems

38 Changed amount of school activities

37 Changed amount or type of recreation

36 Major change in religious activities

34 Major change in sleeping habits

33 Took a trip or vacation

30 Major change in eating habits

26 Major change in the number of family events

22 Guilty of minor law violations

Scoring: If your total score is above 1,435, you are in a high-stress category and therefore more at risk for experiencing a stress-related illness.

But keep in mind the limitations of this questionnaire. There may be factors in your life that produce high stress that are not listed. In addition, a high score does not mean that you are sure to get sick. Many other factors determine ill health, and high stress is only one cause. Other positive factors in your life, such as getting enough sleep and exercise, may prevent illness.

Still, having an unusually high amount of stress in your life is a cause for concern. If you do score high, you may want to take steps to reduce it.

Handling Stress

Stress is an inevitable part of life. In fact, a life with no stress at all would be so boring, so uneventful, that you'd quickly miss the stress that had been removed.

That doesn't mean, though, that we have to sit back and accept stress when it does arise. **Coping** is the effort to control, reduce, or tolerate the threats that lead to stress. Using the P.O.W.E.R. principles (illustrated in the P.O.W.E.R. Plan) can help you ward off stress and actively deal with it.

coping
The effort to control, reduce, or learn to tolerate the threats that lead to stress.

P Prepare — Readying Yourself Physically

Being in good physical condition is the primary way to prepare for future stress. Stress takes its toll on your body, so it makes sense that the stronger and fitter you are, the less negative impact stress will have on you. For example, a regular exercise program reduces heart rate, respiration rate, and blood pressure at times when the body is at rest—making us better able to withstand the negative consequences of stress. Furthermore, vigorous exercise produces endorphins, natural painkilling chemicals in the brain. Endorphins produce feelings of happiness—even euphoria—and may be responsible for the "runner's high," the positive feelings often reported by long-distance runners following long runs. Through the production of endorphins, then, exercise can help our bodies produce a natural coping response to stress.

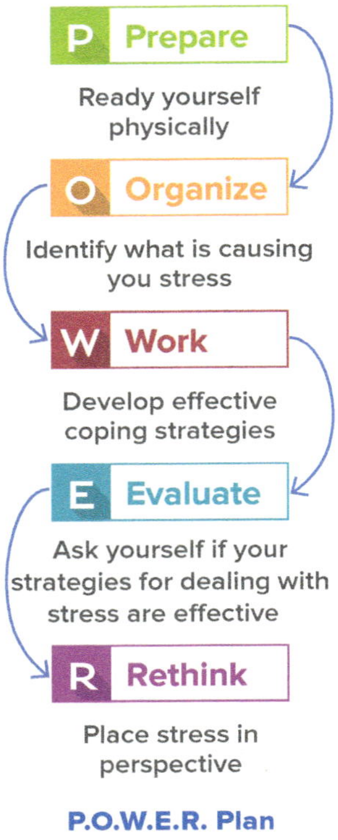

If you drink a lot of coffee or soda, a change in your diet may be enough to bring about a reduction in stress. Coffee, soda, chocolate, and a surprising number of other foods contain caffeine, which can make you feel jittery and anxious even without stress; add a stressor, and the reaction can be very intense and unpleasant.

Eating right can alleviate another problem: obesity. Around one-third of people in the United States are obese, defined as having body weight more than 20 percent above the average weight for a person of a given height. In addition, students often gain weight during the first year of college, averaging an increase of 5 to 7 pounds. One in six students gains 10 pounds or more.

Being overweight can bring on stress for several reasons. For one thing, the extra pounds drag down the functioning of the body. This can lead to fatigue and a reduced ability to bounce back when we encounter challenges to our well-being. In addition, feeling heavy in a society that acclaims the virtues of slimness can be stressful in and of itself.

O Organize

Identifying What Is Causing You Stress

You can't cope effectively with stress until you know what's causing it. In some cases, it's obvious—a series of bad test grades in a course, a roommate problem that keeps getting worse, a job supervisor who seems to delight in making things difficult. In other cases, however, the causes of stress may be more subtle. Perhaps your relationship with your significant other is rocky, and you have a nagging feeling that something is wrong.

Whatever the source of stress, you can't deal with it unless you know what it is. To organize your assault on stress, take a piece of paper and list the major circumstances that are causing you stress. Just listing them will help put you in control, and you'll be better able to figure out strategies for coping with them.

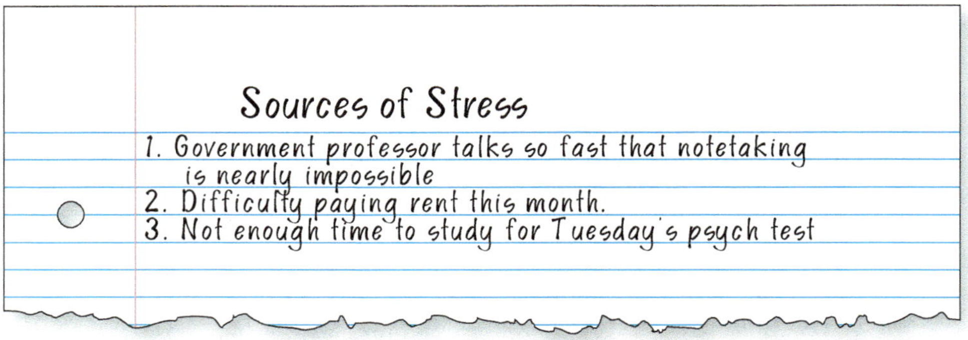
Sources of Stress
1. Government professor talks so fast that notetaking is nearly impossible
2. Difficulty paying rent this month.
3. Not enough time to study for Tuesday's psych test

W Work

Developing Effective Coping Strategies

A wide variety of tactics can help you deal with stress. Among the most effective approaches to coping are these:

- **Take charge of the situation.** Stress is most apt to arise when we are faced with situations over which we have little or no control. If you take charge of the situation, you'll reduce the experience of stress. For example, if several assignments are all due on the same day, you might try negotiating with one of your instructors for a later due date.

- **Don't waste energy trying to change the unchangeable.** There are some situations that you simply can't control. You can't change the fact that you have come down with a case of mono, and you can't change your performance on a test you took last week. Don't hit your head against a brick wall and try to modify things that can't be changed. Use your energy to improve the situation, not to rewrite history.

> "There is more to life than increasing its speed."
> **Mahatma Gandhi**

- **Look for the silver lining.** Stress arises when we perceive a situation as threatening. If we can change how we perceive that situation, we can change our reactions to it. For instance, if your information technology instructor requires you to create a difficult computer program in a very short time, the saving grace is that you may be able to use the skill to your advantage in getting a high-paying job down the road. (You can practice finding the silver lining in **Try It! 2**.)
- **Talk to friends and family. Social support**, assistance and comfort supplied by others, can help us through stressful periods. Turning to our friends and family and simply talking about the stress we're under can help us tolerate it more effectively. Even anonymous telephone hotlines can provide us with social support. (The U.S. Department of Health and Human Services maintains a master toll-free number that can provide telephone numbers and addresses of many national helplines and support groups. You can reach it by calling 1-800-336-4797 or going to their website at **https://health.gov/nhic/pubs/tollfreenumbers/#S**.)

social support
Assistance and comfort supplied by others in times of stress.

- **Relax.** Because stress produces constant wear and tear on the body, practices that relax the body lead to a reduction in stress. In fact, there are several techniques for producing physical relaxation. Among the best relaxation techniques:

  Meditation. Though often associated with its roots in the ancient Eastern religion of Zen Buddhism, meditation, a technique for refocusing attention and producing bodily relaxation, is practiced in some form by members of virtually every major religion. Meditation reduces blood pressure, slows respiration, and in general reduces bodily tension.

  How do you meditate? The process is actually rather simple. As summarized in **Table 13.1**, it includes sitting in a quiet room with eyes closed or focused on a point about 6 feet away from you and paying attention to your breathing. Though the specifics of what you do may vary, meditation works by helping you concentrate on breathing deeply and rhythmically, sometimes murmuring a word or sound repeatedly.

  Progressive relaxation. Progressive relaxation does some of the same things that meditation does, but in a more direct way. To use progressive relaxation, you systematically tense and then relax different groups of muscles. For example, you might start with your lower arm, tensing it for 5 seconds and then relaxing it for a similar amount of time. By doing the same thing throughout the parts of your body, you'll be able to learn the "feel" of bodily relaxation. You can use the technique when you feel that stress is getting the better of you. (Use **Try It! 3** to experience progressive relaxation for yourself.)

2

Try It!

POWER

Look for the Silver Lining

Consider the following list of potentially stressful situations. Try to find something positive—a silver lining—in each of them. The first two are completed to get you started.

Situation	Silver Lining
1. Your car just broke down and repairing it is more than you can afford right now.	1. This is the perfect time to begin exercising by walking and using your bicycle.
2. Your boss just yelled at you and threatened to fire you.	2. Either this is a good time to open an honest discussion with your boss about your job situation, OR this is a good time to get a more fulfilling job.
3. You have two papers due on Monday and there's a great concert you wanted to go to on Saturday night.	3.
4. You just failed an important test.	4.
5. You're flat broke, you have a date to go to a play on Saturday night, and you can't afford the tickets.	5.
6. Your last date went poorly and you think your girlfriend/boyfriend was hinting that it was time to break up.	6.
7. You just found out you missed the due date for your student loan application.	7.
8. You just got cut from a sports team you loved.	8.
9. Your best friend is starting to act coldly and seems not to enjoy being with you as much as before.	9.
10. You just realized you don't really like your academic major, and you're not even sure you like your college much anymore.	10.

WORKING IN A GROUP

After you have considered each of these situations individually, discuss each of them in a group. What similarities and differences in others' responses did you find? Evaluate the different responses, and consider whether—and why—some ways of reframing the situations were better than others.

- **Keep your commitments.** Suppose you've promised a friend that you'll help him move, and you've promised yourself that you'll spend more time with your children. You've also been elected to the student body governing board, and you've made a commitment to bring more speakers to campus. Now you are facing all the demands connected to these commitments and feeling stressed.

table 13.1 Methods of Meditation

Step 1. Pick a focus word or short phrase that's firmly rooted in your personal belief system. For example, a nonreligious individual might choose a neutral word like *one* or *peace* or *love.* A Christian person desiring to use a prayer could pick the opening words of Psalm 23, *The Lord is my shepherd;* a Jewish person could choose *Shalom.*
Step 2. Sit quietly in a comfortable position.
Step 3. Close your eyes.
Step 4. Relax your muscles.
Step 5. Breathe slowly and naturally, repeating your focus word or phrase silently as you exhale.
Step 6. Throughout, assume a passive attitude. Don't worry about how well you're doing. When other thoughts come to mind, simply say to yourself. "Oh, well," and gently return to the repetition.
Step 7. Continue for 10 to 20 minutes. You may open your eyes to check the time, but do not use an alarm. When you finish, sit quietly for a minute or so, at first with your eyes closed and later with your eyes open. Then do not stand for one or two minutes.
Step 8. Practice the technique once or twice a day.

It may be tempting to cope with the feeling of stress by breaking your commitments, thinking, "I just need to chill and watch a show on Netflix!" This is not coping. It is escaping, and it doesn't reduce stress. Ducking out of commitments probably will make you feel guilty and anxious. So rather than dealing with the stress, you've made yourself feel even more stressed. The moral: Do not run away from your commitments.

E Evaluate

Asking If Your Strategies for Dealing with Stress Are Effective

Just as the experience of stress depends on how we interpret circumstances, the strategies for dealing with stress also vary in effectiveness depending on who we are. So if your efforts at coping aren't working, it's time to reconsider your approach. If talking to friends hasn't helped ease your stress response, maybe you need a different approach. Maybe you need to see the silver lining or cut back on some of your commitments.

If one coping strategy doesn't work for you, try another. What's critical is that you not become paralyzed, unable to deal with a situation. Instead, try something different until you find the right combination of strategies to improve the situation.

3

Try It! P O W E R

Try Progressive Relaxation

You can undertake progressive relaxation almost anywhere, including the library, a sports field, or a classroom, because tensing and relaxing muscles is quiet and unobtrusive. Although the following exercise suggests you lie down, you can use parts of it no matter where you are.

1. Lie flat on your back, get comfortable, and focus on your toes.
2. Become aware of your left toes. Bunch them up into a tight ball, then let them go. Then let them relax even further.
3. Now work on your left foot, from the toes to the heel. Without tensing your toes, tighten up the rest of your foot and then let it relax. Then relax it more.
4. Work your way up your left leg, first tensing and then relaxing each part. You may move up as slowly or as quickly as you wish, using big leaps (e.g., the entire lower leg) or small steps (e.g., the ankle, the calf, the front of the lower leg, the knee).
5. Repeat the process for the right leg.
6. Now tense and relax progressively your groin, buttocks, abdomen, lower back, ribs, upper back, and shoulders.
7. Work your way down each arm, one at a time, until you reach the fingers.
8. Return to the neck, then the jaw, cheeks, nose, eyes, ears, forehead, and skull.

By now you should be completely relaxed. In fact, you may even be sleepy or even asleep—this technique works well as a sleep-induction strategy.

Now answer the following questions:

1. How effective were these techniques for reducing feelings of stress?
2. Can you think of additional ways of reducing stress by directly altering your physical feelings?
3. Why do you think producing physical relaxation might change your psychological interpretations of stress in your life?

R Rethink Placing Stress in Perspective

It's easy to think of stress as an enemy. In fact, the coping steps outlined in the P.O.W.E.R. Plan are geared to overcoming its negative consequences. But consider the following two principles, which in the end may help you more than any others in dealing with stress:

- **Don't sweat the small stuff . . . and it's all small stuff.** Stress expert Richard Carlson[2] emphasizes the importance of putting the circumstances we encounter into the proper perspective. He argues that we frequently let ourselves get upset about situations that are actually minor.

  So what if someone cuts us off in traffic, or does less than his or her share on a group project, or unfairly criticizes us? It's hardly the end of the world. If an unpleasant event has no long-term consequences, it's often best to let it go. One of the best ways to reduce stress, consequently, is to maintain an appropriate perspective on the events of your life.
- **Make peace with stress.** Think of what it would be like to have no stress—none at all—in your life. Would you really be happier, better adjusted, and more

Anticipating Job Stress

Career Connections

Students are not the only ones who have to cope with stress. It's also one of the prime hazards of the world of work. Illnesses related to job stress result in costs of $150 billion each year.

Consequently, taking potential stress into account should be an important consideration when choosing a profession. Asking yourself the following questions can help you identify the factors that may induce stress on the job:

- How much control over working conditions will I have? (The more control an employee has in day-to-day decision making, the lower the level of stress.)
- What are the demands of the job? Will I face constant demands to do more work and to work more quickly? (Higher work demands create a more stressful work environment.)
- What is the tolerance for error? (Some occupations, such as air traffic controller, have no margin for error, while others, such as many white-collar professions, give workers a second chance if they make a mistake.)
- How closely do my abilities and strengths match the requirements of the job? (A good match between one's abilities and the demands of a job is the best insurance against an unduly stressful work environment.)
- How well do I cope with stress?

If your coping skills are good, you may be suited for entering a high-stress occupation. But if you have difficulty dealing with stress, choosing a career in a field that produces less stress makes more sense.

successful? The answer is "probably not." A life that presented no challenges would probably be, in a word, boring. So think about stress as an exciting, although admittedly sometimes difficult, friend. Welcome it, at least in moderation, because its presence indicates that your life is stimulating, challenging, and exciting—and who would want it any other way?

» LO 13-2 Keeping Well

It's hard to be successful in college if we don't maintain our physical and mental health. Let's start with ways in which we can help develop habits that promote physical health.

Physical Health

Eat right. Exercise. Get plenty of sleep.

Pretty simple, isn't it? We learn the fundamentals of fitness and health in the first years of elementary school.

Yet for millions of us, wellness is an elusive goal. We eat on the fly, stopping for a bite at the drive-in window of a fast-food restaurant. Most of us don't exercise enough, either because we feel we don't have enough time or because it's not much fun for us. And as for sleep, we're a nation in which getting by with as little sleep as possible is seen as a badge of honor.

> "The first wealth is health."
> Ralph Waldo Emerson, author and poet

You can buck the trends, however; you can begin to eat more properly, exercise effectively, and sleep better by following several basic rules. They include the following:

Eating Right

- **Eat a variety of "whole" foods, including fruits, vegetables, and grain products.** Strive to eat a range of different foods. If you make variety your goal, you will end up eating the right foods. You can learn more about maintaining variety in your diet by visiting the government website **(www.choosemyplate.gov)** that describes the food guide "plate" and allows you to construct a personalized eating plan.
- **Avoid processed foods.** Make an effort to choose "whole" foods, or foods in a state as close as possible to their natural state: Brown rice is better than white rice, and both are better than a preservative-filled, packaged "rice casserole" mix.
- **Avoid foods that are high in sugar and salt content.** Read labels on product packages carefully and beware of hidden sugars and salts. Many ingredients that end in -ose (such as dextrose, sucrose, maltose, and fructose) are actually sugars; salt can lurk within any number of compounds beginning with the word *sodium.*

The lure of fast food is difficult to resist, and eating a balanced, nutritious diet is a challenge for most college students.
©YinYang/Getty Images

- **Seek a diet low in fat and cholesterol.** The fat that is to be especially avoided is saturated fat—the most difficult for your body to rid itself of.
- **Remember: Less is more.** You don't need to walk away stuffed from every meal. Moderation is the key. To be sure you don't eat more than your body is telling you to eat, pay attention to internal hunger cues.
- **Schedule three regular meals a day.** Eating should be a priority—a definite part of your daily schedule. Avoid skipping any meals. Breakfast is particularly important; get up early enough to eat a full meal.
- **Be sensitive to the hidden contents of various foods.** Soda and chocolate can contain substantial quantities of caffeine, which can disrupt your sleep and, along with coffee, become addictive. Many cereals—even those labeled "low fat"—contain a considerable amount of sugar or salt. Pay attention to labels. And watch out for fast foods: Research finds that eating fast foods just a few times a week leads to significant weight gains over the long run.[3]
- **If you want to lose weight, follow a sensible diet.** There's really only one proven way to lose weight: Control your food portions, eat a well-balanced diet, and increase the amount of exercise you get. Fad, quick-fix diets are ineffective. (And, of course, consult a physician before making any major changes in your diet.)
- **Beware of eating disorders.** Between 1 and 4 percent of college-age women, and a smaller percentage of men, suffer from an eating disorder. Those with *anorexia nervosa* may refuse to eat, while denying that there is anything unusual in their behavior and appearance—which can become skeletal. Some 15 to 20 percent of those with anorexia literally starve themselves to death. *Bulimia* is a disorder in which individuals binge on incredibly large quantities of food, such as a gallon of ice cream and a whole pie, but later feel so much guilt and depression that they induce vomiting or take laxatives to rid themselves of the food. Eating disorders represent serious threats to health and require aggressive medical intervention. (If you need advice or help with an eating problem, contact the National Eating Disorders Association at **www.nationaleatingdisorders.org** or call 800-931-2237.)

Making Exercise a Part of Your Life

Exercise produces a variety of benefits. Your body will run more efficiently, you'll have more energy, your heart and circulatory system will run more smoothly, and you'll be able to bounce back from stress and illness more quickly.

- **Choose a type of exercise that you like.** Exercising will be a chore that you end up avoiding if you don't enjoy what you're doing.
- **Incorporate exercise into your life.** Take the stairs instead of elevators. When you're on campus, take the longer way to reach your destination. Leave your car at home and walk to campus or work. If you drive, take the farthest parking space from the building to which you are heading.
- **Make exercise a group activity.** Exercising with others brings you social support and turns exercise into a social activity. You'll be more likely to stick to a program if you have a regular "exercise date" with a friend.
- **Vary your routine.** You don't need to do the same kind of exercise day after day. Choose different sorts of activities that will involve different parts of your body and keep you from getting bored. For example, for cardiovascular fitness, you might alternate among running, swimming, biking, and using a cardio training machine.

One note of caution: Before you begin an exercise program, it is a good idea to have a physical checkup, even if you feel you're in the peak of health. This is especially true if you're starting an exercise program after years of inactivity. You also might consult a personal trainer at the gym to set up a program that gradually builds you up to more vigorous exercise.

To maintain the habit of exercising, you need to choose an activity you enjoy doing. In addition, working out with others turns exercise into a social activity and gives you social support, increasing the chances you'll stick with an exercise regimen.
©Vesna Andjic/E+/Getty Images

Getting a Good Night's Sleep

Do you feel as if you don't get enough sleep? You probably don't. Most college students are sleep-deprived, a condition that causes them to feel fatigued, short-tempered, and tense. Sleep deprivation makes staying alert in class nearly impossible (see the **Course Connections** feature).

Ultimately, insufficient sleep leads to declines in academic and physical performance. You can't do your best at anything if you're exhausted—or even tired.

Often the solution to the problem is simply to allow yourself more time to sleep. Most people need around 8 hours of sleep each night, though there are wide individual differences. In addition to sleeping more, there are also some relatively simple changes you can make in your behavior that will help you to sleep better. They include the following:

- **Exercise more.** Regular exercise will help you sleep more soundly at night, as well as help you cope with stress that might otherwise keep you awake.
- **Have a regular bedtime.** By going to bed at pretty much the same time each night, you give your body a regular rhythm and make sleep a habit.
- **Use your bed for sleeping and not as an all-purpose area.** Don't use your bed as a place to study, read, eat, or watch TV. Let your bed be a trigger for sleep.

Course **Connections**

Staying Alert in Class

If you're having trouble staying alert and—even worse—staying awake in class, the best solution is to get more sleep. Short of that, there are several strategies you can try to help you stay awake:

- Throw yourself into the class. Pay close attention, take notes, ask questions, and generally be fully engaged in the class. You should do this anyway, but making a special effort when you're exhausted can get you through a period of fatigue.
- Sit up straight. Pinch yourself. Stretch your muscles in different parts of your body. Fidget. Any activity will help you thwart fatigue and feel more alert.
- Eat or drink something cold in class (if your school and instructor permit it). The mere activity of eating a snack or drinking can help you stay awake.
- Avoid heavy meals before class. Your body's natural reaction to a full stomach is to call for a nap, the opposite of what you want to achieve.
- Stay cool. Take off your coat or jacket and sit by an open window. If it's warm, ask your instructor if there's a way to make the classroom cooler.
- Take off *one* shoe. This creates a temperature difference, which can be helpful in keeping you awake.

- **Avoid caffeine after lunch.** The stimulant effects of caffeine (found in coffee, tea, and some soft drinks) may last as long as 8 to 12 hours after it's consumed.
- **Drink a glass of milk at bedtime.** Your mom was right: Drinking a glass of milk before you go to bed will help you get to sleep. The reason: Milk contains a natural chemical that makes you drowsy.
- **Avoid sleeping pills.** Steer clear of sleeping pills. Although they may be temporarily effective, in the long run they impair your ability to sleep because they disrupt your natural sleep cycles.
- **Don't try to force sleep on yourself.** Although this advice sounds odd, it turns out that one of the reasons that we have trouble sleeping is that we try too hard. Consequently, when you go to bed, just relax, and don't even attempt to go to sleep. If you're awake after 10 minutes or so, get up and do something else. Go back to bed only when you feel tired. Do this as often as necessary. If you follow this regimen for several weeks—and don't take naps or rest during the day—eventually getting into your bed will trigger sleep.

Mental Health

Our physical well-being is one piece of the puzzle that leads to overall well-being. The other aspect of wellness is mental health. Let's next consider some of the threats to well-being related to mental health.

Depression and Suicide

Almost no student passes through college without at least occasionally feeling depressed. The stress of college life can lead to feeling sadness, unhappiness, and even hopelessness on occasion.

Most of the time, depression is a normal reaction to distressing circumstances. It may occur in response to the death of a loved one, the end of a relationship, failure at an important task, or any number of events. Usually, the depression is temporary, and people return to their normal emotional state.

For some students, however, depression is more than fleeting. Around 3 percent of people suffer from *major depression,* a psychological disorder in which depression is severe and lasts more than two weeks. Major depression can occur without any obvious cause, and students who suffer from it feel extremely sad, hopeless, tired, and worthless.

Major depression ultimately can lead to suicide. But suicide occurs for other reasons. For instance, some—but not all—people who commit suicide are perfectionists, are socially inhibited, or suffer from extreme anxiety when they face any social or academic challenge. In other cases, though, none of those characteristics are present.

Several warning signs indicate when a student's problems may be severe enough to justify concern about the possibility of a suicide attempt. They include

- Academic problems, such as a pattern of missing classes and a sudden change in grades.
- Frequent incidents of self-destructive behavior, such as careless accidents.
- Loss of appetite or excessive eating.
- Withdrawal from friends and peers.
- Sleeping problems.
- Signs of depression, tearfulness, or overt indications of psychological difficulties, such as hallucinations.
- A preoccupation with death, an afterlife, or what would happen "if I died."
- Putting affairs in order, such as giving away prized possessions or making arrangements for the care of a pet.
- An explicit announcement of suicidal thoughts.

If you know someone who shows signs that he or she may be considering suicide, urge that person to seek professional help. You may need to take assertive action, such as enlisting the assistance of family members, counselors, or instructors. The need to take action is especially true if someone explicitly says they feel the urge to harm themselves or others. If someone says they are thinking about hurting themselves, it is a serious signal for help, and you should act. You should not feel that you are betraying a confidence by alerting someone who can help about the situation.

For immediate help with a suicide-related problem or emotional support generally, call (800) 273-8255, a national hotline that is staffed with trained counselors. The counselors provide immediate, nonjudgmental emotional support. If you wish to use online chat to contact them, go to **https://suicidepreventionlifeline.org/chat/**. Or if you prefer to text, text HOME to 741741; someone will respond immediately, 24/7.

Posttraumatic Stress Disorders (PTSD)

Some students who have been exposed to severe personal stressors experience **posttraumatic stress disorder (PTSD)**, in which a highly stressful event has long-lasting consequences that may include re-experiencing the event in vivid flashbacks or dreams. An episode of PTSD may be triggered by an otherwise innocent stimulus, such as the sound of a textbook dropping to the floor, that leads a person to re-experience a past event that produced considerable stress.

posttraumatic stress disorder (PTSD)
A psychological disorder in which a highly stressful event has long-lasting consequences that may include re-experiencing the event in vivid flashbacks or dreams.

An estimated 20 percent of veterans returning from Afghanistan and Iraq show symptoms of PTSD. Furthermore, people who have experienced child abuse or rape, rescue workers facing overwhelming situations, and victims of sudden natural disasters or accidents that produce feelings of helplessness and shock may suffer from the same disorder.[4]

Symptoms of posttraumatic stress disorder may include emotional numbing, sleep difficulties, interpersonal problems, alcohol and drug abuse, and, in some cases, suicide. The suicide rate for military veterans, many of whom participated in the Iraq and Afghanistan wars, is twice as high as that for nonveterans.

Responding to Death and Grief

One of the most stressful experiences that one can endure is the death of a loved one. Even if the death is not unexpected, as with an elderly grandparent, the finality and sense of loss can be immense. When it is a surprise—as when a friend commits suicide, a family member is killed in war, or a parent unexpectedly succumbs to a heart attack—the pain can be overwhelming.

Although everyone's grief is different, people's reactions usually follow a pattern. Initially, people feel shock and numbness, and they may even deny the death. Reality soon sets in, however, and people experience the pain of the death. They typically feel enormous sadness, depression, and yearning for the dead individual.

In time, however, people accept the death and move on with their lives. Although intense feelings of grief may occur, people usually are able to pick up their lives, and their happiness returns to its previous level.

If you experience the death of a loved one, there are several things you can do to maintain your mental health and your academic standing:

- Expect that your grief will be intense and painful—but understand that it will not always be so painful. With time, feelings of sadness begin to subside.
- Talk to others about your feelings. Family and friends, some of whom may also be experiencing the grief, can help you sort out your reactions and bring you comfort.
- Don't hesitate to voice your recollections of the person who has died. Talking about the person who has died can be therapeutic.
- Be sure to let your college officials know about your situation. If you have to leave campus to attend a funeral, tell someone in your Dean's Office, and they can contact your instructors. When you return to campus, get in touch with each of your instructors to catch up on the work you missed.

» LO 13-3 Making Safer Choices

College is about making choices, and some of those choices involve decisions that can have important implications for our health and well-being. We'll consider several of the major decisions you'll make, including those concerning drug and alcohol use and sexual health.

Drug Use and Abuse

For better or worse, drugs—ranging from legal drugs such as vitamins, cold-relief medicine, and the nicotine in cigarettes to illegal drugs such as marijuana and methamphetamines—are common in contemporary society. Because patterns of drug use or avoidance are often established in college, it is a good idea to learn what you can do now, before negative patterns of use, and in some cases, abuse, take hold.

Nicotine

Despite the clear evidence of its dangers, smoking remains a significant health problem. Smoking causes lung damage and increases the risks of developing cancer, emphysema, and a host of other diseases.

Why do people smoke, when the evidence is so clear about its risks? They start to smoke for a variety of reasons. Smoking is sometimes viewed as a kind of initiation into adulthood, a sign of growing up. In other cases, teenagers see smoking as "cool," a view promoted by movies and television.

The problem is that, no matter what reason persuades a person to try out a few cigarettes, smoking can quickly become a habit, because a major ingredient of tobacco–nicotine–is an addictive drug. An addictive drug produces a biological or psychological dependence. The absence of the drug leads to a craving for it that may be nearly irresistible.

Smoking is one of the hardest addictions to break. Among the suggestions for quitting are the following:

- **Remain smoke-free one day at a time.** Don't think about not smoking tomorrow, or next week, or for the rest of your life. Instead, think of not smoking for the rest of the day. You can worry about tomorrow . . . tomorrow.
- **Visualize the consequences of smoking.** Visualize blackened, rotting lungs filled with smoke. Then think about the fresh, pink lungs that you'll have after you've stopped smoking.
- **Exercise.** The all-purpose antidote, exercise, will make you feel better physically and take your mind off smoking.
- **Use nicotine patches or nicotine gum.** "The Patch" and nicotine gum can provide enough nicotine to satisfy your craving for the drug, while permitting you to stop smoking. Physicians can also prescribe drugs that help reduce the craving for nicotine.
- **Avoid people when they're smoking.** It's nearly impossible to avoid the urge to smoke when others are lighting up. If you're trying to quit, stay away from people who are smoking.
- **Enlist the social support of family and friends.** Tell others that you're trying to quit, and accept their encouragement and praise.
- **Reward yourself.** Every few days, give yourself some kind of reinforcement for spending a period of time smoke-free. Go to a movie; download an album. Think about how you can afford these more easily since you aren't buying cigarettes anymore.
- **Join a quit-smoking program.** Many college health services hold periodic programs to help students who want to stop smoking. By enrolling in one, you'll receive the support of others who are in the same boat as you.
- **Keep trying.** If after quitting you start smoking again, just consider lapsing as part of the process of quitting. Many people quit several times before they manage to quit for good.

What about the use of *electronic cigarettes,* or *e-cigarettes*? E-cigarettes are battery-powered cigarette-shaped devices that deliver nicotine that is vaporized to form a mist. They simulate the experience of smoking tobacco. Although less harmful than traditional cigarettes, their health effects are unclear. Still, their use is growing.

The jury is out on whether e-cigarettes will provide a safer alternative to traditional cigarettes, or their increasing use will ultimately give rise to a new health threat. In fact, there is increasing evidence that e-cigarette use increases the risk of using traditional tobacco products among youths and young adults.

Alcohol

The drug most likely to be found on college campuses is alcohol. It may surprise you to know that though it initially seems to raise your spirits, alcohol is actually a depressant. As the amount of alcohol one consumes increases, its depressive effects become more obvious. You've probably seen its other negative effects: Drinkers show poor judgment and less impulse control. As judgment is impaired, drinkers may engage in casual or risky sexual behavior or act aggressively. Memory is impaired, and speech becomes slurred and eventually incoherent. As they drink more, people become less coordinated and their reaction time slows. If you drink enough, you'll pass out. And as some well-publicized cases in the news illustrate, if you consume enough alcohol in a short period, you can die. It's that simple.

The potential negative consequences of drinking have done little to prevent the use of alcohol on college campuses. Although a not insignificant number of students drink little or no alcohol, more than 75 percent of college students say they've had a drink within the last 30 days. Some drink a great deal: Almost a third of students report having consumed five or more drinks in a sitting at least once within the previous two weeks.

Some students drink even more, and the extent of alcohol consumption can reach astonishing levels. Half of all male college students and 40 percent of all female college students have engaged in **binge drinking**, defined as having at least four (for females) or five (for males) drinks in a single sitting. Such heavy drinking doesn't affect just the drinker. Most college students report having had their studying or sleep disturbed by drunk students. Further, around one-third of students have been insulted or humiliated by a drunk student, and 25 percent of women have been the target of an unwanted sexual advance by a drunk classmate.

binge drinking
Having at least four (for females) or five (for males) drinks in a single sitting.

One out of 12 people in the United States (close to 20 million people) are alcoholics, and college students make up their fair share of the total. **Alcoholics**, individuals with serious alcohol-abuse problems, become dependent on alcohol, experiencing a physical craving for it. They continue to drink despite serious consequences. Furthermore, they develop a tolerance for alcohol and must drink increasing amounts to experience the initially positive effects that alcohol brings about.

alcoholics
Individuals with serious alcohol-abuse problems who become dependent on alcohol and continue to drink despite serious consequences.

The long-term consequences of high levels of alcohol consumption are severe. Heavy drinking damages the liver and digestive system and can even affect brain cells. In fact, virtually every part of the body is eventually affected by heavy alcohol use.

To examine your own use of alcohol, complete **Try It! 4**.

Illegal Drugs

"Just say 'no.'"

If it were only so easy. Decisions about drugs are quite a bit more complicated than simplistic antidrug slogans would have you believe. Using or not using drugs involves, at a minimum, the changes in mood they may produce, your body's craving for them, peer pressure, your values, and your self-image.

Several things are clear, however. Despite the prevalence of illicit drug use among college students—surveys show that around one-third of college students report having used an illegal drug at least once in the previous year—the benefits of drug use are difficult to enumerate. Apart from a temporary high, the advantages of using drugs are minimal, and the use of illegal drugs is among the riskiest activities in which people can engage. Not only does illegal drug use make you vulnerable to arrest, but it also poses short- and long-term health risks. The escape from one's responsibilities that drugs provide is likely to make it even harder to later deal with those responsibilities—which aren't going to go away.

Journal Reflections

College Drinking Experiences

Examine your own feelings about alcohol use by answering these questions.

1. Why do you think people use alcohol?
2. What do you think the minimum age to legally drink alcohol should be, and why?
3. Do you know people who drink only to get drunk?
4. Have you ever suspected any of your friends or acquaintances of being alcoholics? Why? Did you do anything about it?
5. Efforts to alter one's states of consciousness through the use of alcohol or other drugs are found in almost every culture. Why do you think this is the case?

Not all illegal drugs are the same, and they produce widely varying effects and consequences (see **Table 13.2**). But they all share a common result: a reduction in awareness of and engagement with what is happening around you.

People often fall into drug use without much thought. But doing so is still a choice. Preaching and slogans are not going to help you to make a sensible decision. You need to employ every critical thinking skill you can to determine exactly what you wish—and don't wish—to introduce into your body. Give some thought to why escape is attractive and consider seeking counseling instead. Allow yourself to consider the long- and short-term effects of drug use—both the physical effects and the potential effects on your own aspirations and dreams. Think about the legal consequences of drug use: A drug conviction can lead to expulsion from college and refusal by many employers to hire you. Furthermore, random drug tests are increasingly a part of corporate life, and your ability to qualify for and keep a job may be placed at risk if you use drugs—even only occasionally.

Drugs that produce addiction, such as cocaine and heroin, present a further set of problems. The lives of people with drug addictions become centered on the drug. They enter into a pattern of alternating highs—when on the drug—and lows. During their lows, much of their thinking is centered on obtaining the drug and looking forward to their next high.

4 PERSONAL STYLES

Try It! POWER

Consider Your Drinking Style

If you drink alcohol, do you have a style of use that is safe and responsible? Read the statements below and rate the extent to which you agree with them, using the following scale:

1 = Strongly disagree

2 = Disagree

3 = Neutral

4 = Agree

5 = Strongly agree

	1	2	3	4	5
1. I usually drink alcohol a few times a week.					
2. I sometimes go to class after I've been drinking alcohol.					
3. I frequently drink when I'm alone.					
4. I have driven while under the influence of alcohol.					
5. I've used a fake ID card to purchase alcohol.					
6. I'm a totally different person when I'm drinking alcohol.					
7. I often drink so much that I feel drunk.					
8. I wouldn't want to go to a party where alcohol wasn't being served.					
9. I avoid people who don't like to drink alcohol.					
10. I sometimes urge others to drink more alcohol.					

The lower your score (i.e., the more 1s and 2s), the better able you are to control your alcohol consumption and the more likely it is that your alcohol use is responsible. The higher your score (i.e., the more 4s and 5s), the greater is your use and reliance on alcohol, and the more likely it is that your alcohol consumption may be reckless. If your score is over 40, you may have an alcohol problem and should seek professional help to control your alcohol usage.

The use of some addictive drugs has reached epidemic proportions, with opiate and opioid use skyrocketing. For example, heroin use more than doubled among young adults 18 to 25 years old from 2002–2004 to 2011–2013. Furthermore, the rate of overdose deaths related to heroin increased 500% between 2000 and 2016.

Although it's not totally clear why use of opioids has increased so rapidly, one reason is that the cost of the drugs has plummeted at the same time that the supply has increased substantially. Furthermore, some of the newest opioids are 100 times as potent as natural heroin. And that means drugs bought on the street, which could contain virtually anything, are particularly dangerous and can easily lead to overdoses.

Drug addiction and abuse are not confined to illegal drugs. An increasing number of people use over-the-counter drugs for the high they produce. For example, cold and cough medications containing dextromethorphan (DXM) are among the

table 13.2 Common Illegal Drugs

Drugs	Street Name	Effects	Withdrawal Symptoms	Adverse/ Overdose Reactions
Stimulants				
Amphetamines	Speed	Increased confidence, mood elevation, sense of energy and alertness, decreased appetite, anxiety, irritability, insomnia, transient drowsiness, delayed orgasm	Apathy, general fatigue, prolonged sleep, depression, disorientation, suicidal thoughts, agitated motor activity, irritability, bizarre dreams	Elevated blood pressure, increase in body temperature, face picking, suspiciousness, bizarre and repetitious behavior, vivid hallucinations, convulsions, possible death
Benzedrine	Speed			
Dexedrine				
Cocaine	Coke, blow, snow, lady, crack			
Cathinone	Bath salts			
Depressants				
Alcohol	Booze	Anxiety reduction, impulsiveness, dramatic mood swings, bizarre thoughts, suicidal behavior, slurred speech, disorientation, slowed mental and physical functioning, limited attention span	Weakness, restlessness, nausea and vomiting, headaches, nightmares, irritability, depression, acute anxiety, hallucinations, seizures, possible death	Confusion, decreased response to pain, shallow respiration, dilated pupils, weak and rapid pulse, coma, possible death
Barbiturates	Yellowjackets			
Nembutal	Reds			
Seconal				
Phenobarbital				
Rohypnol	Roofies, rope, "date-rape drug"	Muscle relaxation, amnesia, sleep	Seizures	Seizures, coma, incapacitation, inability to resist sexual assault
Narcotics				
Heroin	H, Hombre, junk, smack	Reduction of anxiety and pain, difficulty in concentration, slowed speech, decreased physical activity, euphoria	Anxiety, vomiting, sneezing, diarrhea, lower back pain, watery eyes, runny nose, yawning, irritability, tremors, panic, chills and sweating, cramps	Depressed levels of consciousness, low blood pressure, rapid heart rate, shallow breathing, convulsions, coma, possible death
Morphine	Drugstore dope, cube, first line, mud			
Opioids (synthetic drugs such as Vicodin, Percocet, fentanyl, OxyContin)	Oxy, OC, Percs	Pain reduction, shallow breathing, slow heartbeat, seizure (convulsions); cold, clammy skin; confusion	Sweating, chills, abdominal cramps, insomnia, vomiting, diarrhea	Extreme drowsiness, muscle weakness, confusion, cold and clammy skin, pinpoint pupils, shallow breathing, slow heart rate, fainting, or coma
Hallucinogens				
Cannabis	Bhang, kif, ganja, dope, grass, pot, hemp, joint, weed, bone, Mary Jane, reefer	Euphoria, relaxed inhibitions, increased appetite, disoriented behavior	Hyperactivity, insomnia, decreased appetite, anxiety	Severe reactions rare but include panic, paranoia, fatigue, bizarre and dangerous behavior, decreased testosterone over long term; immune system effects
Marijuana				
Hashish				
Hash oil				

(continued)

table 13.2 Continued

MDMA	Ecstasy, Molly	Heightened sense of oneself and insight, feelings of peace, empathy, energy	Depression, anxiety, sleeplessness	Increase in body temperature, memory difficulties
LSD	Acid, quasey, microdot, white lightning	Heightened aesthetic responses; vision and depth distortion; heightened sensitivity to faces and gestures; magnified feelings; paranoia, panic, euphoria	Not reported	Nausea and chills; increased pulse, temperature, and blood pressure; slow, deep breathing; loss of appetite; insomnia; bizarre, dangerous behavior
Steroids	Rhoids, juice	Aggression, depression, acne, mood swings, masculine traits in women and feminine traits in men	Symptoms can mimic other medical problems and include weakness, fatigue, decreased appetite, weight loss; women may note menstrual changes	Long-term, high-dose effects of steroid use are largely unknown but can include swelling and weight gain

most commonly abused over-the-counter drugs. Taken in the large quantities that produce a high, they put users at risk for vomiting, hallucinations, seizures, brain damage, and even death.

Addiction's Warning Signs

Addictions to drugs—including alcohol—can begin subtly, and you may not be aware of the extent of the problem. Here are some signs that indicate when use becomes abuse:

- Feeling you need to be high to have a good time.
- Being high more often than not.
- Getting high to "get yourself going."
- Going to class or work high.
- Missing class or work because you are high.
- Being unprepared for class because you were high.
- Feeling regret over something you did while you were high.
- Driving while high.
- Having a legal problem due to being high.
- Behaving, while high, in a way you wouldn't otherwise.
- Being high in nonsocial, solitary situations.
- Thinking about drugs or alcohol much of the time.
- Avoiding family or friends while using alcohol or drugs.
- Hiding drug or alcohol use from others.

Any one of these symptoms may indicate that you have a drug or alcohol problem. If you do have a problem, *seek professional help.* Addictions to illegal drugs or alcohol are virtually impossible to deal with on your own. Almost no one can overcome the cravings brought about by an addiction to a particular substance without help.

Here are some places to which you can turn for help:

1. **College health services, counseling centers, and mental health centers.** Most colleges provide services to help you overcome an addiction. They can evaluate the extent of the problem and refer you to the proper place for further help. (To learn about your own campus resources, complete **Try It! 5**.)
2. **Drug treatment centers and clinics.** Sometimes located in hospitals and sometimes independently run, drug treatment centers or clinics can provide help. You can also check your telephone book for a local listing of Alcoholics Anonymous or Narcotics Anonymous.
3. **Government hotlines.** The federal government provides extensive information about drug and alcohol use. For starters, call the National Clearinghouse on Alcohol and Drug Information at 1-800-729-6686. For alcohol difficulties in particular, call the National Council on Alcoholism and Drug Dependence at 1-800-622-2255. For drug problems, you can call the National Institute on Drug Abuse at 1-800-662-4357. Finally, you can visit the National Council on Alcoholism and Drug Dependence website at **www.ncadd.org** for help with alcohol and drug problems.

Sexual Health and Decision Making

Relationships. Contraception. HIV-AIDS. Rape.

Sexual health includes a host of issues, involving not just your body, but your heart and mind as well. In fact, it is often said that our most important sexual organ is our brain. It determines what we view as sexually arousing, and it's what we use to make decisions and choices about our sexuality.

Although the focus of the brief discussion of sexual health here is on strategies for protecting yourself (from sexually transmitted infections, pregnancy, and rape), sexual decisions are also a reflection of your basic values. You can't make responsible decisions about sex without knowing what is important to you and how you view yourself. So you don't want to wait until a sexual encounter begins before thinking through your views of sexuality and what is and is not right for you. Deciding to have—or not to have—sex should be a conscious decision between two individuals that must be made with great responsibility and thoughtfulness.

Relationships and sexuality raise substantial issues, involving your attitudes, beliefs, values, and emotions, as well as your body, in a complex intermix. Making responsible decisions requires that you know who you are and what's important to you.
©Digital Vision/Getty Images

Avoiding Sexually Transmitted Infections

Right now, 20 percent of people in the United States are infected with one or more sexually transmitted infections. **Sexually transmitted infections (STIs)** (also known as sexually transmitted diseases, or STDs) are infections acquired through sexual contact.

sexually transmitted infections (STIs)
Infections acquired through sexual contact.

There are many varieties of STIs, although all share a similar origin: sexual contact. Depending on the type of infection, symptoms may include warts in the genital area, pelvic infection, painful urination, infertility, blindness, and even death.

These are the major STIs:

- *Human papilloma virus (HPV).* HPV is the most common sexually transmitted infection, with more than 14 million new cases each year. Spread through vaginal, anal, or oral sex, it is usually not harmful, although it can lead to serious health

5 | **Try It!** POWER

Tap into Campus Resources

Complete the following chart to identify the campus office locations and their services that deal with alcohol and drug problems.

Campus Resource	Where Is It?	What Service Does It Provide?	How Do You Get in Touch?
Health Center			
Mental Health Center			
Campus Chaplain			
Drug and Alcohol Education Center(s)			
Counseling Center			
Residential Life Office			
Ombudsman			
Campus Security Services			
(add other offices here)			
(add other offices here)			
(add other offices here)			
(add other offices here)			

problems such as genital warts and cervical cancer. HPV vaccines are now available that protect against some of the most harmful types of HPV.

- *Chlamydia.* Another widespread STI is *chlamydia,* a disease that in women initially produces no symptoms and in men causes a burning sensation during urination and a discharge from the penis. If it is left untreated, chlamydia can lead to pelvic inflammation, urethral damage, arthritis, and even sterility. There are almost 3 million new cases each year in the United States. Because it usually produces no symptoms in females, the Centers for Disease Control and Prevention recommends that sexually active women under age 26 should be tested for the disease every year. Once diagnosed, chlamydia can be cured with antibiotics.
- *Genital herpes. Genital herpes* is a virus related to the cold sores that sometimes appear around the mouth. Herpes first appears as small blisters or sores around the genitals that later break open, causing severe pain. These sores heal after a few weeks, but the disease usually reappears typically four or five times in the year following infection. Later outbreaks are less frequent, but the infection, which cannot be cured, often causes psychological distress for those who know they are infected. During the active phases of the disease, it can be transmitted to sexual partners. Genital herpes is common among college-age students: About 17% of 20- to 29-year-olds have the infection.
- *Trichomoniasis. Trichomoniasis* is an infection in the vagina or penis. Caused by a parasite, it is often without symptoms, especially in men. Eventually, it can cause painful

urination and intercourse, a discharge from the vagina, itching, and an unpleasant odor. The 5 million cases reported each year can be treated with antibiotics.

- *Gonorrhea. Gonorrhea* often has no symptoms but can produce a burning sensation during urination or a discharge from the penis or vagina. The infection can lead to fertility problems and, in women, pelvic inflammatory disease. Although antibiotics usually can cure gonorrhea, the number of drug-resistant strains of the disease is growing, making treatment more difficult.
- *Syphilis.* If untreated, *syphilis* may affect the brain and heart. It can even be fatal. Syphilis first reveals itself through a small sore at the point of sexual contact. In its secondary stage, it may include a rash. Syphilis can be treated successfully with antibiotics if it is diagnosed early enough.
- *HIV-AIDS.* In the near past, no sexually transmitted infection has had a greater impact on sexual behavior–and society as a whole–than *HIV-AIDS (Human Immunodeficiency Virus-Acquired Immune Deficiency).* In the United States, HIV-AIDS is the seventh leading cause of death among men 25–44 years of age, and 1.8 million people are living with the disease. The worldwide figures are even more daunting: Already, 39 million people have died from HIV-AIDS, and people living with the disease number 37 million worldwide.

The only completely effective way to avoid sexual transmission of these infections is through avoiding sexual activity. However, many people are unwilling to make such a choice. Several alternative approaches, called "smart sex" or "safe sex" practices, reduce the risk of contracting STIs. They include the following:

- **Know your sexual partner–well.** You should not have sexual contact with a person who is only a casual acquaintance. You want to know the person well enough to have a discussion with him or her in which you both talk about your sexual histories.
- **Prevent the exchange of bodily fluids during all sex acts.** Avoid unprotected intercourse (vaginal or anal) and oral sex.
- **Use condoms.** Condoms not only prevent the spread of HIV-AIDS and other STIs, but they also prevent pregnancy.
- **Be faithful to a single partner.** People in long-term relationships with only one other individual are less likely to contract HIV-AIDS and other STIs than those with multiple sexual partners.

Preventing Unwanted Pregnancy

There is one and only one totally effective means of preventing pregnancy: not having sexual intercourse. **Abstinence**, refraining from intercourse, however, works only if you practice it with absolute consistency–something that many people find difficult. But it certainly is possible. Despite the folklore that insists "everybody's doing it," they're not. In fact, if you think critically about what others say about their sexual activity, you'll probably conclude that what they say is more boasting (and outright lying) than straight talk.

abstinence
The avoidance of sexual contact.

Those who do want to have a sexual relationship can still avoid pregnancy. Methods of contraception include the following:

- **Birth control pills.** Composed of artificial hormones, birth control pills are among the most effective ways of preventing pregnancy–as long as they are taken as prescribed. Except for women with certain medical conditions, the side effects are minimal.
- **Implants.** One of the newest forms of birth control, implants work through a simple surgical procedure in which a small capsule is inserted into a woman's arm.

Implants last for 5 years, preventing pregnancy for the entire period. With few side effects, implants are highly effective, but they are practical only for women who wish to avoid pregnancy for extended periods.

- **Intrauterine device, or IUD.** IUDs are small pieces of plastic or copper inserted by a medical practitioner into a woman's uterus. Although highly effective, some have been found to produce unacceptable side effects, including infections and scarring that can make it impossible for a woman to get pregnant when she wants to.
- **Diaphragms and cervical caps.** Diaphragms and cervical caps are circular, dome-shaped pieces of thin rubber that a woman inserts into her vagina to cover the cervix. A sperm-killing (spermicidal) cream or jelly must be used simultaneously, and the diaphragm or cervical cap must be removed after sexual intercourse. Although side effects are few, the risk of pregnancy is somewhat higher than with the other forms of birth control we've discussed; some 18 percent of women using them become pregnant.
- **Condoms.** Condoms are thin sheaths that fit over the penis and prevent sperm from entering the vagina. When used with a contraceptive jelly that kills sperm and positioned properly, condoms are highly effective, with 2 pregnancies per 100 users per year. But with condoms used as they typically are, there are 15 pregnancies per 100 users per year.
- **Injections.** Progestin, administered as an injection every three months, provides excellent protection, but it cannot be used for more than two years.
- **Ring.** A polymer ring with hormones is worn in the vagina for three weeks, and then removed for one week. It provides excellent protection when used properly.
- **Contraceptive sponge.** The sponge, shaped like a large mushroom cap, is inserted into the vagina. It can be left in place for 24 hours, during which time it can be used for multiple acts of intercourse. Although it has few side effects, it has a failure rate of between 17 and 25 percent.
- **Periodic abstinence.** The only form of birth control that involves no chemical or mechanical intervention, periodic abstinence (also known as the rhythm method or fertility awareness method) consists of refraining from intercourse during times in a woman's menstrual cycle when pregnancy is possible. With a failure rate approaching 24 percent, periodic abstinence requires close scrutiny of calendars, body temperature, and cervical mucus—all of which can be indicators of the time of the month to avoid intercourse.
- **Sterilization.** Sterilization is a surgical procedure that causes a person (either a man or a woman) to become permanently incapable of having children.
- **Emergency contraception.** Several forms of birth control can prevent pregnancy after unprotected intercourse. These involve taking a dose of certain oral contraceptive pills within 3–5 days. Certain kinds of pills, such as Plan B, do not require a prescription. Most effective is insertion of a copper intrauterine device (IUD) within 5 days following unprotected sex.
- **Withdrawal and douching (*ineffective* birth control).** Withdrawal, in which a man removes his penis from a woman's vagina before ejaculating, and douching, flushing the vagina with a liquid *after* the man has ejaculated, just don't work. *They should not be used for birth control* because they are so ineffective.

Date Rape

We usually think of rape as a rare crime, committed by strangers. Unfortunately, rape is surprisingly common, and rapists usually know their victims. In a national survey conducted on college campuses, one out of eight women reported having been raped. In about half the reported cases, the rape involved situations categorized as **date rape**, rapes involving first dates, casual dates, or romantic acquaintances.

date rape
Forced sex in which the rapist is a date or romantic acquaintance.

Overall, women are far more likely to be raped by someone they know than by a stranger. Although the statistics are hard to verify and controversial, the most accepted figure is that there is a 14 to 25 percent chance that a woman will be the victim of rape during her lifetime.[5] Although date rape is the more common type on campus, it is different from any other form of rape only in that the victim is acquainted with the rapist.

What leads to rape? Most often, rape has less to do with sex than with power and anger. Rapists use forced sex to demonstrate their power and control over the victim. The rapist's pleasure comes not so much from sex as from forcing someone to submit. Sometimes sexual behavior is a demonstration of the rapist's rage at women in general.

In addition, rapes sometimes are brought about by the common—but untrue—belief that when women offer resistance to sex, they don't really mean it. If a man holds the view that when a woman says no to sex, she really means yes, he is likely to ignore a woman's protests, and the encounter may end in rape. Some men may even believe that it is unmasculine to accept no for an answer.

Some rapists employ the illegal drug rohypnol, which has come to be known as the "date rape drug." When it is mixed with alcohol, it can prevent victims from resisting sexual assault. People who are unknowingly given the drug don't even remember the rape, so it's important to keep a careful eye on anything one drinks at a party.

Whatever the cause, rape is devastating to the victim. Victims experience extreme anxiety, disbelief, fear, and shock. These reactions may linger for years, and rape victims may experience a long-lasting fear of entering into relationships. (Victims of rape and other sexual assaults can call a 24-hour hotline at 1-800-656-HOPE or visit the Rape, Abuse, and Incest National Network website at **www.rainn.org**.)

Both men and women must be sensitive to the issue of date rape. Among the suggestions for reducing its incidence are the following:

- **Set limits.** You have the right to set firm limits, and these should be communicated clearly, firmly, and early on.
- **Understand that no means no.** When a partner says no, it means no—nothing else.
- **Be assertive.** You should never passively accept being pressured into an activity in which you don't want to engage. Remember that passivity may be interpreted as consent.
- **Communicate.** Women and men should talk about their views of sexual behavior and what is and is not permissible.
- **Be vigilant.** Women should keep close tabs on what they are given to drink in social situations; victims of date rape have sometimes been given mind-altering drugs.
- **Avoid assumptions.** Don't assume that certain kinds of dress or flirtatious behavior are an invitation to sex.
- **Keep in mind that alcohol and drugs cloud judgment.** Nothing hinders communication more than alcohol and drugs.

Speaking *of* Success

Courtesy of Mandi Barringer

NAME: **Mandi Barringer**

SCHOOL: **University of Central Florida**

Time is a precious commodity for Mandi N. Barringer, and effective time management is one of the critical keys to her success.

"Adequate time management is something many students (and humans in general) struggle with in college," she says. "I think students are sold this idea of having it all—success in college, maintaining a job, social life—but in actuality, this ideal is quite difficult to obtain." Mandi recalls having to decline social events with family and friends and sacrificing weekends when she needed to focus on her studies.

As Mandi worked hard to ensure school was her number one priority, she also became more thoughtful about her schoolwork. Studying became more than just memorizing facts to regurgitate on an exam, and interactions with faculty became central to her success. "I had to create a system that worked best for me," she says. "I realized that studying and absorbing knowledge served a purpose beyond performing well on an exam. For me, taking proper notes in class, conversing with faculty outside of the classroom, and keeping up with the required readings, as well as trial and error in applying my new knowledge to assignments and papers, were all part of the studying process."

Focusing so intently on school, however, can make it especially difficult to get past academic setbacks. Mandi understands this internal pressure. "The voice in our head that whispers—well, it sometimes screams—negative and disparaging remarks can be hard to ignore," she acknowledges. "But if you messed up on a test or the paper you submitted was not your best, accept the poor grade and move on. Do not let those things define you, and do not give up when you are feeling defeated." The path may be difficult, she says, but it is rewarding and can lead you to discover your true drive and motivations.

[RETHINK]

- What challenges do you think Barringer faced in juggling college, job, and a social life? How do you cope with such challenges?
- How do you deal with the "negative voices" that Barringer talks about?

Looking Back

LO 13-1 Explain what stress is and how to control it.

- Stress is a common experience, appearing in three main forms: cataclysmic events, personal stressors, and daily hassles. Not only is excessive stress unpleasant and upsetting, but it also has negative effects on the body and mind.
- Coping with stress involves becoming prepared for future stress through proper diet and exercise, identifying the causes of stress in one's life, taking control of stress, seeking social support, practicing relaxation techniques, training oneself to redefine and reinterpret stressful situations, and keeping one's promises.

LO 13-2 Discuss what is involved in keeping well.

- For all people, keeping fit and healthy is both essential and challenging. It is vital to learn to eat properly, especially by eating a variety of foods on a regular schedule and by restricting your intake of fat, cholesterol, and salt.
- Exercise is valuable because it improves health and well-being. Choosing exercises that we like, making everyday activities a part of exercise, and exercising with others can help form the habit of exercise.
- The third key element of good health is sleeping properly. Good exercise and eating habits can contribute to sound sleep, as can the development of regular sleeping habits and the use of sleep-assisting practices
- In extreme cases, stress can lead to posttraumatic stress disorder and suicide.

LO 13-3 Identify approaches to making safer choices about health and wellness.

- One of the major threats that college students (and others) face is the improper use of drugs. The most commonly abused drug is alcohol, which is a depressant (despite an initial reduction of inhibitions and feeling of euphoria) and can lead to a physical or psychological dependence. Nicotine is the second most commonly abused drug.
- The use of illegal drugs presents not only potential dangers related to law-breaking and prosecution but short- and long-term health risks as well. Drugs cause a reduction in awareness and involvement in life, and some drugs can be dangerously addictive.
- Sexual health is as important as other forms of health. People must make their own individual decisions about their sexuality and how they will express it.
- The incidence of sexually transmitted infections (STIs) is high in the United States, with about 25 percent of the population contracting an STI at some point in life.
- Rape is a surprisingly common crime, with most victims knowing the rapist—often in a circumstance known as date rape.

[KEY TERMS AND CONCEPTS]

Abstinence (p. 377)
Alcoholics (p. 370)
Binge drinking (p. 370)
Cataclysmic events (p. 354)
Coping (p. 357)
Daily hassles (p. 355)
Date rape (p. 379)
Personal stressors (p. 355)
Posttraumatic stress disorder (PTSD) (p. 367)
Sexually transmitted infections (STIs) (p. 375)
Social support (p. 359)
Stress (p. 354)

[RESOURCES]

ON CAMPUS

Your college health service/medical provider is the first line of defense if you become ill. The staff can provide you with advice and often medical care and can give help if you are the victim of rape or in other emergencies. Furthermore, colleges often have health education offices that help educate students on safer sex practices, how to eat in healthier ways, and generally how to increase wellness. Colleges sometimes offer stress reduction workshops to help students cope more effectively.

Finally, many colleges have mental health counselors that can help you deal with emotional problems. If you are depressed, have trouble sleeping, or face other problems coping with the problems of life, speaking with a counselor can be extremely helpful. Check with your school's counseling center or health center to identify someone appropriate with whom to speak.

IN PRINT

Kelci Lucier's *College Stress Solutions: Stress Management Techniques to *Beat Anxiety *Make the Grade *Enjoy the Full College Experience* (Adams Media, 2014) offers an array of information to ease the stress. *A Mindfulness-Based Stress Reduction Workbook for Anxiety* by Bob Stahl and Florence Meleo-Meyer (New Harbinger Publications, 2014) offers insights and practical exercises.

Mindfulness: The New Science of Health and Happiness (*Time,* 2016), from the editors of *Time* magazine, is a practical owner's manual for maintaining a healthy mind, body, and lifestyle.

A good source for information on the causes and symptoms of the most common STDs, as well as real-life examples of students who contracted them, can be found in *Seductive Delusions: How Everyday People Catch STIs* (Johns Hopkins, 2016, 2nd ed.), by Jill Grimes. Lisa Wade also addresses sex on college campuses in *American Hookup: The New Culture of Sex on Campus* (W. W. Norton & Company, 2017).

ON THE WEB

- The Academy of Nutrition and Dietetics's website not only provides information for its professional members but also includes updated consumer tips and articles **(www.eatright.org).** Features include strategies for smart grocery shopping, discussion of the latest fad diets, and guidelines for healthy eating.
- The Partnership for a Healthier America runs a Healthier Campus Initiative, a program that partners with colleges and universities to support better fitness and nutrition choices for college students: **www.ahealthieramerica.org/articles/healthier-campus-initiative-146**
- "What Coping Strategies Are Effective?" **(https://www.verywell.com/what-coping-strategies-are-effective-3144562),** on **www.verywell.com** offers in-depth and comprehensive information on coping with stress. Dozens of links cover teens through the elderly, self-assessment, psychotherapy, and relaxation techniques.
- "Eating Disorders: Mirror, Mirror" **(www.mirror-mirror.org/eatdis.htm)** is a guide to eating disorders offering definitions, coping strategies, links to related organizations, and personal messages from survivors.
- "Healthy Women" **(www.healthywomen.org),** from the National Women's Health Resource Center, offers a number of good articles on health issues, including a concise presentation and discussion of various methods of contraception.

- The Personal Health and Counseling Center at California State University, Monterey Bay offers definitions, resources, and coping strategies for students of color and their allies who experience race-related stress on college campuses (**csumb.edu/pgcc/coping-racism-discrimination**)
- Medline Plus, from the U.S. National Library of Medicine in the National Institutes of Health, offers a wide array of information regarding STDs, including a variety of links on causes and treatments. **(www.nlm.nih.gov/medlineplus/sexuallytransmitteddiseases.html)**

Design Elements: Pencil/Notebook: ©Squared Studios/Photodisc/Getty Images; Group/Laptop: ©Jacob Lund/Shutterstock; Apples: ©I. Rozenbaum/PhotoAlto; People/Silhouette: ©Ingram Publishing; Colorful Notebooks: ©Dragan Nikolic/Alamy; Group/Occupations: ©Rawpixel.com/Shutterstock; Woman/Laptop: ©JGI/Jamie Grill/Getty Images; Man/Laptop: ©Westend61/Getty Images.

The Case of . . .

The Opposing Perspectives

It started out innocently, as a date to study for an exam. And then it turned wrong.

Here's what Bob had to say:

Patty and I were in the same statistics class. She usually sat near me and was always very friendly. I liked her and thought maybe she liked me, too.

Last Thursday after class I suggested that she come to my place so we could study for midterms together. She agreed immediately.

That night everything seemed to go perfectly. We studied for awhile and then took a break. I could tell that she liked me, and I was attracted to her. I started kissing her. I could tell that she really liked it.

We started touching each other and it felt really good. All of a sudden she pulled away and said "stop." I figured she didn't want me to think that she was "easy" or "loose." . . .

I just ignored her protests and eventually she stopped struggling. I think she liked it but afterwards she acted bummed out and cold.

Patty, on the other hand, had a very different view of their encounter:

I knew Bob from my statistics class. He's cute and we are both good at statistics, so when a tough midterm was scheduled, I was glad that he suggested we study together. It never occurred to me that it was anything except a study date.

That night everything went fine at first. We got a lot of studying done in a short amount of time, so when he suggested we take a break, I thought we deserved it.

Well, all of a sudden he started acting really romantic and started kissing me. I liked the kissing, but then he started touching me below the waist. I pulled away and tried to stop him but he didn't listen. After a while I stopped struggling; he was hurting me and I was scared. He was so much bigger and stronger than me. I couldn't believe it was happening to me. I didn't know what to do.

He actually forced me to have sex with him. I guess looking back on it I should have screamed or done something besides trying to reason with him, but it was so unexpected. I couldn't believe it was happening.

1. Was Bob being dishonest in setting up the study date? Was he dishonest during the sexual encounter?

2. What could Patty have done when Bob began acting "romantic"?

3. Was Bob right to interpret Patty's initial responsiveness to his advances as acceptance of a sexual relationship? Was Patty "leading him on"?

4. Did Patty's initial responsiveness justify Bob's pursuing sex beyond the point at which she said "stop"?

A Final Word

Throughout this book, you've seen how the principles of P.O.W.E.R. Learning can be applied to a variety of situations, ranging from reading and writing to coping with stress. You can use the framework in any situation where you need to organize your thinking and behavior in a systematic way. It's a tool you can call on throughout your lifetime.

College is the beginning of a journey that leads to your future. This book has been designed to help you with the demands and challenges of college, but at the same time to prepare you for life after school. It has tried to show you that it is *you* who must make things happen to fulfill your goals and aspirations.

Ultimately, however, there are some key ingredients to success that no book can teach you and that only you can provide: integrity and honesty, intellectual curiosity, and love. I hope this book will help you as you consider what your contribution to the world will be and as you work to make that contribution.

Glossary

ABBCC structure: The structure of the typical research paper, consisting of argument, background, body, counterarguments, and conclusion.

Abstinence: The avoidance of sexual contact.

Academic honesty: Completing and turning in only one's own work under one's own name.

Acronym: A word or phrase formed by the first letters of a series of terms.

Acrostic: A sentence in which the first letters of the words correspond to material that is to be remembered.

Active listening: The voluntary act of focusing on what is being said, making sense of it, and thinking about it in a way that permits it to be recalled accurately.

Advance organizers: Outlines, overviews, objectives, and other clues to the meaning and organization of new material in what you are reading, which pave the way for subsequent learning.

Alcoholics: Individuals with serious alcohol-abuse problems who become dependent on alcohol and continue to drink despite serious consequences.

Analogy: A comparison between concepts or objects that are alike in some respects, but dissimilar in most others.

Argument: The main idea of a paper; what the writer is claiming.

Attention span: The length of time that attention is typically sustained.

Auditory/verbal learning style: A style that favors listening as the best approach to learning.

Background: The backdrop and context for one's arguments in a paper.

Binge drinking: Having at least four (for females) or five (for males) drinks in a single sitting.

Blended (hybrid) courses: Courses in which instruction is a combination of traditional, face-to-face and online methods.

Blog: A web-based public diary in which a writer provides thoughts, essays, and commentary.

Brainstorming: A technique for generating ideas by saying out loud as many ideas as can be thought of in a fixed period of time.

Browser: A program that provides a way of navigating around the information on the web.

Budget: A formal plan that accounts for expenditures and income.

Burnout: A condition in which an athlete feels dissatisfaction, physical or emotional exhaustion, disillusionment, and frustration.

Call number: A unique classification number assigned to every book (or other resource) in a library. Call numbers are used for ease of location.

Cataclysmic events: Sudden, powerful events that occur quickly and affect many people simultaneously.

Classical conditioning: A type of learning in which a neutral stimulus elicits a response after being paired with a natural stimulus.

Cognitive bias: A limitation, blind spot, or mistake in thinking that leads to illogical or erroneous decisions.

College advisor: An individual who provides students with advice about their academic careers.

Community service: Making contributions to the society and community in which you live.

Concept map: A graphical representation that structures written material by grouping and connecting key ideas and themes.

Coping: The effort to control, reduce, or learn to tolerate the threats that lead to stress.

Cramming: Hurried, last-minute studying.

Critical thinking: A process involving reanalysis, questioning, and challenge of underlying assumptions.

Cultural competence: Knowledge and understanding about other races, ethnic groups, cultures, and minority groups.

Culture: The learned behaviors, beliefs, and attitudes that are characteristic of an individual society or population, and the products that people create.

Cybersecurity: Measures taken to protect computers and computer systems against unauthorized access or attack.

Daily hassles: The minor irritants of life that, by themselves, produce little stress, but which can add up and produce more stress than a single larger-scale event.

Daily to-do list: A schedule showing the tasks, activities, and appointments due to occur during the day.

Date rape: Forced sex in which the rapist is a date or romantic acquaintance.

Decision making: The process of deciding among various alternatives.

Discrimination: Behavior directed toward individuals on the basis of their membership in a particular group.

Distance learning: The teaching of courses at another institution, with student participation via video technology or the web.

Double major: A course of study that fulfills all the requirements for two majors.

Educated guessing: The practice of eliminating obviously false multiple-choice answers and selecting the most likely answer from the remaining choices.

Electives: Courses that are not required.

E-mail: Electronic mail, a system of communication that permits users to send and receive messages via the Internet.

Emoticons (smileys): Symbols used in e-mail messages that provide information on the emotion that the writer is trying to convey. Emoticons usually look like faces on their side, with facial expressions related to the intended emotion or tone.

Ethnicity: Shared national origins or cultural patterns.

Evaluation: An assessment of the match between a product or activity and the goals it was intended to meet.

Fixed mindset: The erroneous belief that individual characteristics, such as intelligence, talent, and motivation, are set at birth and vary little throughout the life span.

Flash cards: Index cards that contain key pieces of information to be remembered.

Freewriting: A technique involving continuous, nonstop writing, without self-criticism, for a fixed period of time.

Frontmatter: The preface, introduction, and table of contents of a book.

Grade point average (GPA): Also known as quality point average. A numeric average in which letter grades are transformed into numbers.

Grant: An award of money that does not have to be repaid.

Grit Perseverance and passion for long-term goals.

Growth mindset: The belief that individual characteristics, such as intelligence, talent, and motivation, can improve through hard work.

Hazing: An activity that humiliates or degrades a person joining a team or other group.

Hearing: The involuntary act of sensing sounds.

Impromptu talks: Unprepared presentations that require speaking on a moment's notice.

Individual response technology: Method using a smartphone app or wireless handset to transmit students' answers to the instructor's computer, resulting in more classroom interactivity.

Information competency: The ability to determine what information is necessary, and then to locate, evaluate, and effectively use that information.

Interlibrary loan: A system by which libraries share resources, making them available to patrons of different libraries.

"I" statements Statements that cast responses in terms of oneself and one's individual interpretation.

Learning disabilities: Difficulties in processing information when listening, speaking, reading, or writing, characterized by a discrepancy between learning potential and actual academic achievement.

Learning Management System (LMS): The software that delivers a distance learning course and typically provides the course content, calendars, and tests, and tracks grades.

Learning style: One's preferred manner of acquiring, using, and thinking about knowledge.

Learning theory: A broad explanation about how one learns.

Lecture capture technology: Technology in which instructors upload in-class lectures, slides, and videos to a website, which students can later access to review the material presented in class.

Left-brain processing: Information processing primarily performed by the left hemisphere of the brain, focusing on tasks requiring verbal competence, such as speaking, reading, thinking, and reasoning; information is processed sequentially, one bit at a time.

Link: A means of "jumping" automatically from one web page to another.

Loan: Funds provided by a bank, credit union, or other agency that must be repaid after a specified period of time.

Loneliness: A subjective state in which people do not experience the level of connection with others that they desire.

Long-term goals: Aims relating to major accomplishments that take some time to achieve.

Major: A specialization in a particular subject area, requiring a set course of study.

Master calendar: A schedule showing the weeks of a longer time period, such as a college term, with all assignments and important activities noted on it.

Memory consolidation: The process by which the physical links between brain cells that represent memory become fixed and stable over time.

Meta-message: The underlying main ideas that a speaker is seeking to convey; the meaning behind the overt message.

Minor: A secondary specialization in a discipline different from one's major.

Mnemonics: Formal techniques used to make material more readily remembered.

Motivation: The inner power and psychological energy that directs and fuels behavior.

Online database: An index in electronic form composed of an organized body of information on a particular topic or subject area.

Operant conditioning: Learning in which a behavior is modified by the presence of a reinforcer.

Overlearning: Studying and rehearsing material past the point of initial mastery to the point at which recall becomes automatic.

Paraphrase: A restatement of a passage using different words.

Personal Mission Statement: A formal statement regarding what a person hopes to achieve during his or her lifetime.

Personal stressors: Major life events that produce stress.

Plagiarism: Taking credit for someone else's words, thoughts, or ideas.

Podcast: A video or audio recording that can be accessed on the web and viewed on a computer or downloaded to a mobile device.

Posttraumatic stress disorder (PTSD): A psychological disorder in which a highly stressful event has long-lasting consequences that may include re-experiencing the event in vivid flashbacks or dreams.

P.O.W.E.R. Learning: A system designed to help people achieve their goals, based on five steps: Prepare, Organize, Work, Evaluate, and Rethink.

Prejudice: Evaluations or judgments of members of a group that are based on their membership in the group and not on their particular characteristics as individuals.

Prerequisites: Requirements that must be fulfilled before a student may enroll in a course or discipline.

Principal: The stated amount of a loan.

Priorities: The tasks and activities that one needs and wants to do, rank-ordered from most important to least important.

Problem solving: The process of generating alternatives to work on.

Procrastination: The habit of putting off and delaying tasks that need to be accomplished.

Race: Traditionally, biologically determined physical characteristics that set one group apart from others.

Read/write learning style: A style that involves a preference for written material, favoring reading over hearing and touching.

Recall: A way to request library materials from another person who has them.

Receptive learning style: Learning style related to the way in which we initially receive information from our sense organs.

Reflective feedback: A technique of verbal listening in which a listener rephrases what a speaker has said, trying to echo the speaker's meaning.

Register: Formally enroll in courses.

Registrar: The college official designated to oversee the scheduling of courses, the maintenance of grades and transcripts, and the creation and retention of other official documents.

Rehearsal: The process of practicing and learning material.

Reinforcer: Action or consequence that increases the probability that a behavior will occur again.

Right-brain processing: Information processing primarily performed by the right hemisphere of the brain, focusing on information in nonverbal domains, such as the understanding of spatial relationships and recognition of patterns and drawings, music, and emotional expression.

Scholarship: An award of money to a student based on need or merit.

Search engine: A computerized index to information on the web.

Self-actualization: A state of self-fulfillment in which people realize their highest potential in their own unique way.

Self-concept: One's view of oneself that forms over time, comprising three components: the physical self, the social self, and the personal self.

Self-efficacy: The expectation that one is capable of achieving one's goals in many different kinds of situations.

Self-esteem: The overall evaluation we give ourselves as individuals.

Self-fulfilling prophecy: A phenomenon that occurs when we hold a belief or expectation that affects our behavior, thereby increasing the likelihood that our beliefs or expectations will come true.

Service learning: Courses that allow a student to engage in community service activities while getting course credit for the experience.

Sexually transmitted infections (STIs): Infections acquired through sexual contact.

Short-term goals: Relatively limited steps toward the accomplishment of long-term goals.

Social support: Assistance and comfort supplied by others in times of stress.

Stacks: The shelves on which books and other materials are stored in a library.

Stereotypes: Beliefs and expectations about members of a group that are held simply because of their membership in the group.

Stress: The physical and emotional response to events that threaten or challenge us.

Study group: A small, informal group of students whose purpose is to help members work together and study for a test.

Study notes: Notes taken for the purpose of reviewing material.

Tactile/kinesthetic learning style: A style that involves learning by touching, manipulating objects, and doing things.

Term: The length of time for which money is lent.

Test anxiety: A temporary condition characterized by fears and concerns about test taking.

Text messaging (texting): Short messages sent from mobile phones to other phones or e-mail accounts.

Thesis: The main point of a paper, typically stating the writer's opinion about the topic of the paper.

Time log: A record of how one spends one's time.

Transcript: A college's official record of courses taken and grades received by students.

Transferring: Changing colleges.

Unique major: Specialization in a particular subject area that is geared to the student's own needs. Not offered by all colleges, and generally requiring the support of faculty to oversee the process.

Values: The qualities we see as desirable and most important.

Video messaging services: Video messages that are sent between smartphones.

Visual/graphic learning style: A style that favors material presented visually in a diagram or picture.

Visualization: A memory technique by which images are formed to help recall material.

Web ("the web"): A highly graphical interface between users and the Internet that permits users to transmit and receive not only text but also pictorial, video, and audio information.

Web page: A location (or site) on the web that houses information from a single source and that (typically) links to other pages.

Weekly timetable: A schedule showing all regular, prescheduled activities due to occur in the week, together with one-time events and commitments.

Working backward: The strategy of starting at the desired solution or goal and working toward the starting point of the problem.

Writing voice: The unique style of a writer, expressing the writer's outlook on life and past writing experiences.

Endnotes

Chapter 1

1. G. Gottesman. *College Survival.* NY: Macmillan, 1994, p. 70.
2. Adapted from "How Is College Different from High School?" *Southern Methodist University Altshuler Learning Enhancement Center,* **www.smu.edu/alec/transition.html**.
3. Quoted in Karen W. Arenson, "In a First, 2 CUNY Students Win Rhodes Scholarships," *The New York Times,* November 22, 2004.

Chapter 3

1. **www.benjerry.com/activism/mission-statement**.
2. C. L. Powell. *A Soldier's Way: An Autobiography.* Random House (2011).
3. S. V. Roberts, B. B. Auster, and M. Barone, "Colin Powell, Superstar: Will America's Top General Trade His Uniform for a Future in Politics?", *U.S. News & World Report,* September 20, 1993.

Chapter 4

1. W. Pauk, W., *How to Study in College,* 8th ed. Boston: Houghton Mifflin, 2004.

Chapter 5

1. S. Tobias, *Overcoming Math Anxiety.* New York: W.W. Norton & Company, 1995.
2. Second Amendment to the United States Constitution.

Chapter 6

1. J. Greenberg and R. A. Baron. *Behavior in Organizations,* 6th ed. Upper Saddle River, NJ: Prentice Hall, 1997.

Chapter 7

1. P. Elbow, *A Community of Writers.* New York: McGraw-Hill, 2001.
2. Davidson, J. W., Gienapp, W. E., Heyrman, C. L., Lytle, M. H., & Stoff, M. B. (1996). *Nation of Nations: A Concise Narrative of the American Republic.* NewYork: McGraw-Hill, p. 540.

Chapter 9

1. L. Liebovich ,"Choosing Quick Hits over the Card Catalog," *The New York Times* (2000, August 10), pp. 1, 6. Based on material from Eliot Soloway, University of Michigan, School of Education.

Chapter 10

1. B. Forer, (1949). "The fallacy of personal validation: A classroom demonstration of gullibility." *Journal of Abnormal and Social Psychology,* 44 (1949), pp. 118-123.
2. D. Byrne and L. Kelley. *An Introduction to Personality,* 3rd ed. Englewood Cliffs, NJ: Prentice Hall, 1981, p. 304.

Chapter 11

1. B. D. Tatum, *"Why Are All the Black Kids Sitting Together in the Cafeteria?" And Other Conversations about Race.* New York: Basic Books, 1997.
2. M. S. Malone, "Translating Diversity into High-Tech Gains," *The New York Times,* July 18, 1993, p. B2.
3. Adapted from Martin Rochlin, "Working it out: The newsletter for gay and lesbian employment issues."

Chapter 12

1. E. Diener and R. Biswas-Diener, "Will Money Increase Subjective Well-Being?" *Social Indicators Research* 57 (2002), pp. 119-169.
2. The College Board, "Annual Survey of Colleges, 2018."
3. Federal Reserve Bank of New York. (2017). Household borrowing, student debt trends and homeownership. Retrieved from **https://www.newyorkfed.org/press/pressbriefings/household-borrowing-student-loans-homeownership**. January 29, 2018.

Chapter 13

1. L. J. Sax, A. W. Astin, W. S. Korn, and K. Mahoney, *The American Freshman: National Norms for Fall 1999.* Los Angeles: Higher Education Research Institute, UCLA, 1999.
2. R. Carlson, *Don't Sweat the Small Stuff . . . And It's All Small Stuff* (New York: Hyperion, 1997).
3. M. Pereira, A. I. Kartashov, C. B. Ebbeling, L. Van Horn, M. L. Slattery, D. R. Jacobs, Jr., and D. S. Ludwig, "Fast-Food Habits, Weight Gain, and Insulin Resistance (The CARDIA Study): 15-Year Prospective Analysis," *The Lancet* 365 (2005, January 1), pp. 36-42.
4. M. J. Friedman, "Posttraumatic Stress Disorder among Military Returnees from Afghanistan and Iraq," *American Journal of Psychiatry* 163 (2006), pp. 586-593; C. Marmar, "Mental Health Impact of Afghanistan and Iraq Deployment: Meeting the Challenge of a New Generation of Veterans," *Depression and Anxiety* 26 (2009), pp. 493-497; Horesh et al., "Delayed-Onset PTSD among War Veterans: The Role of Life Events Throughout the Life Cycle," *Social Psychiatry and Psychiatric Epidemiology* 46, no. 9 (2011), pp. 863-870.
5. M. P. Koss, "Rape: Scope, Impact, Interventions, and Public Policy Responses," *American Psychologist* 48 (1993), pp. 1062-1069.

Appendix

1. J. O'Hara, "The Hell of Hazing," *Maclean's,* March 6, 2000, p. 50.
2. N. C. Hoover, *National Survey: Initiation Rites and Athletics for NCAA Sports Teams* (Alfred University, August 30, 1999).
3. Quoted in L. Quitmeir, "Olympic Trial and Error," *Columbia Missourian,* November 16, 2000, pp. B1, B3.
4. Paige quotes from T. Fields-Meyer and L. Kramer, "Class Act," People Magazine. November 19, 2001, pp. 151-155, **https://people.com/archive/class-act-vol-56-no-21/**; R. Winters, "Teacher in Chief," February 5, 2001, **http://www.cnn.com/ALLPOLITICS/time/2001/02/12/teacher.html**; and K. Chappell, "Rod Paige America's Education Chief," Ebony, October 2001. 56(12) 170-174.

Index

Note: Page numbers followed by *n* indicate material in source notes

A

D

E

H

I

J

K

L

M

N

O

P

Q

R

S

T

Y

Z